APPRECIATIVE INQUIRY

AN EMERGING DIRECTION FOR ORGANIZATION DEVELOPMENT

Edited by
David L. Cooperrider
Professor of Organizational Behavior
Case Western Reserve University

Peter F. Sorensen, Jr.
Director, Ph.D. Program of Organization Development
Professor and Chair of Management and Organizational Behavior
Benedictine University

Therese F. Yaeger
Associate Director, Ph.D. Program of Organization Development
Benedictine University

Diana Whitney
President of Corporation for Positive Change

ISBN 1-58874-121-4

Published by

Stipes Publishing L.L.C.
Champaign, Illinois

ii

CONTENTS

PART II

PREFACE

This book is intended as a source book for our students, as a way of introducing them to and assisting them in their shared—our shared—mission for the creation of better, more fulfilling and more productive work places, places where the potential for OD and OD values are most fully realized.

Consistent with our intent to provide our students the opportunity to share in learning about appreciative inquiry, we have waived all royalties in an effort to provide the book at the lowest possible cost.

DEDICATION

To our families and students

INTRODUCTION

Appreciative Inquiry: An Emerging Direction for Organization Development: An Award-Winning Approach to OD

This book is an extension and further development of ideas and applications presented in the initial book of readings on Appreciative Inquiry, *Appreciative Inquiry: Rethinking Human Organization Toward a Positive Theory of Change.* This book retains the articles included in the original reader but extends the materials by two-thirds with the inclusion of twelve additional articles. This book retains much of the original three-part structure.

Appreciative Inquiry (AI) is an approach, which in its brief lifetime has made considerable impact on the field of Organization Development. It provides a critical new way of thinking about organizational change and improvement, yet at the same time is deeply rooted in the historical values of OD. Appreciative Inquiry draws on the best of "what is" and envisioning, and consequently creates what is at the heart of OD, which is perhaps best expressed by Marvin Weisbord as *the creation of productive workplaces with dignity, meaning, and community.* As the title of this introduction indicates it is very much an award-winning approach to OD. AI has been recognized by many of the OD professional associations, including an Award for Best Organizations Change Program from the American Society for Training and Development, and a Best Paper Award from the Academy of Management. It was part of the change effort that won the Outstanding OD Project of the Year Worldwide from the OD Institute, and was the topic of one of the articles selected and published as "The Best of the OD Journal in the 20th Century," and two special issues of the *OD Practitioner* published by the OD Network.

The book is clearly about a significant new approach to Organization Development. Throughout the book several major themes emerge:

1. Appreciative Inquiry is defined as a social construction based on a sociorationalist paradigm as opposed to the paradigm of logical positivism. Nevertheless it appears that AI is capable of drawing on the best of what exists from logical positivism and does not suffer, but in fact, is strengthened by evaluation which draws from the logical positivist tradition.

2. Appreciative Inquiry contributes to the refinements and extension of established interventions at the core of OD such as action research, team building and survey feedback, and at the same time incorporates into the AI process more recently developed approaches such as large group interventions and Search Conference methods.

3. Appreciative Inquiry addresses the large issues, which again reflects its rootedness in the fundamental values of OD. It deals with diversity, with global social change, and with conflict — conflict in the most meaningful way possible illustrated by the United Religions work and the drive, the hope and the vision of World Peace.

This book is divided into three sections. Part I, *Rethinking Human Organization toward a Positive Theory of Change*, is comprised of an introduction and overview of Appreciative Inquiry, including classic articles and a contemporary review.

The second section describes various applications of AI and how it deals with the experiences. Illustrations, applications and assessment of its impact as a way of changing groups and organizations are discussed.

In a sense the final section, *New Horizons*, moves the reader and AI to a grander scale. Here questions are raised about the nature and possibility of AI's universal application, with illustrations of large-scale change and global applications. The book concludes, we feel, appropriately with a discussion of Appreciation and Hope, "that the very act of appreciation will itself contribute to transforming our organizations into places of genuine human hopefulness" (Ludema), and with additional resources for continued learning and exploration of Appreciative Inquiry.

But rather than elaborate further we feel it best to let the contributors and their articles speak for themselves.

AWARDS AND RECOGNITION

Award	Recipient
Best Paper Award, International Management Association, 1999, entitled "Appreciative Inquiry as a Team Development Intervention for Newly Formed Heterogeneous Groups."	Robert Head
Best Organization Change Project Award from the American Society of Training and Development, 1997.	GTE
Best Paper Award, OD Institute 1998, entitled "Changing organizational culture through leadership development: A case in leadership transformation," *OD Journal*, Fall 1999.	Linda Sharkey
O.D. Institute's Outstanding OD Project World-wide 1998 entitled "Changing Management Culture to Achieve Success," 1998.	Dale Spartz
Best Paper Award, OD Institute, entitled "A Field Experiment in Appreciative Inquiry," 1998.	David A. Jones
Finalist, Outstanding OD Project of the Year Award Worldwide, 1997.	Akinyinka O. Akinyele, Peter F. Sorensen, Jr. and Therese Yaeger
The Best of *OD Journal* in the 20 the Century "Advances in Appreciative Inquiry as an Organization Development Intervention," Fall, 1995.	Gervase Bushe

Best Paper Award, Academy of Management, Organization Development and Change Division, "Using Generative Metaphor to Intervene in a System Divided by Turfism and Competition: Building Common Visions," 1998.	Frank Barrett and David Cooperrider
Catalyst Award for "Best Place to Work in the Country for Women 1997."	Avon — Mexico
"Award for Educational Achievement, 1998."	Scandinavian School System

ABOUT THE EDITORS

David L. Cooperrider, Ph.D.
Case Western Reserve University

David L. Cooperrider is Chairman of the SIGMA Program for Human Cooperation and Global Action and Associate Professor of Organizational Behavior, at Case Western Reserve University's Weatherhead School of Management.

David is past Chair at the National Academy of Management—the Division of Organization Development—and he is a co-founder of The Taos Institute. He has taught at Stanford University, Katholieke University in Belgium, Benedictine University, Pepperdine University, and others. Currently he serves as the PI of a multi-million dollar grant working with international organizations dealing with global issues of human health, environment, peace, and sustainable economic development.

Dr. Cooperrider has served as researcher and consultant to a wide variety of organizations including: Motorola, GTE, BP America, World Vision, Seattle Group Health, Teledesic, Imagine Chicago, Technoserve, the Mountain Forum, and United Way of America. Currently, as part of the above mentioned grant, David and his colleagues have organizational learning projects active in 57 organizations working in over 100 countries in Africa, Asia, Europe, and North and South America. Most of these projects are inspired by the Appreciative Inquiry methodologies for which David is best known.

His ideas have been published in such journals as *Administrative Science Quarterly, Human Relations, Journal of Applied Behavioral Science, The OD Practitioner*, and in research series such as *Advances In Strategic Management*. More popularly, his work has been covered by *The New York Times, Crain's Business, Cleveland's Plain Dealer, San Francisco Chronicle* and others. He has been the recipient of Innovation and Best Paper of the Year Awards at the Academy of Management, and numerous clients have received awards for their work with Appreciative Inquiry—GTE, for example, has just been recognized as 1998 Best Organization Change Program in the country by ASTD. David's most recent books include *Organizational Courage and Executive Wisdom*; and *Appreciative Leadership and Management* (both with Suresh Srivastva); *International and Global OD* (with Peter Sorensen); and *The Organization Dimensions of Global Change: No Limits to Cooperation* (with Jane Dutton). David has just been named editor of a new Sage Publication Book Series on the Human Dimensions of Global Change.

Peter F. Sorensen, Jr., Ph.D.
Benedictine University

Peter F. Sorensen, Jr., Ph.D., is Professor and Director of the Ph.D. program in Organization Development and the M.S. program in Management and Organizational Behavior at Benedictine University. He was instrumental in developing one of the first Masters Level programs in OD in 1967, and one of the first Ph.D. programs in OD in 1996.

He has authored more than 200 articles, papers and books, including several best paper selections. His work has appeared in the *Academy of Management Journal, Group and Organization Studies, Leadership and Organization Development Journal, Journal of Management Studies*, and *Organization and Administrative Sciences*, among others. In 1996, he was Guest Editor of a double issue of the *O.D. Practitioner* on Appreciative Inquiry. He was the invited Guest Editor for the first New Millennium issues for both the *OD Journal* and the *OD Practitioner.*

Sorensen's recent publications are *Perspectives on Organization Behavior* and *Global and International OD* with Cooperrider, Head, Mathys and Preston. He has worked with over 100 organizations including the U.S. Food and Drug Agency, U. S. Steel, DuPage County Health Department, Commonwealth Edison, and CNA.

He is Chair of the Organization Development and Change Division of the Academy of Management, and serves on the Editorial Boards for the *OD Journal*, the *OD Practitioner*, CCASTD's *Training Today*, and is a board member of the Midwest Academy of Management Journal.

Peter was an invited, distinguished scholar to the first Academy of Management Conference on Global Change. In 1993, he received the "Outstanding OD Consultant of the Year Award" from the OD Institute. He holds a Ph.D. in Management from the Stuart School of Management, Illinois Institute of Technology.

Therese F. Yaeger, Ph.D.
Benedictine University

Dr. Therese Yaeger is the Associate Director of the Ph.D. in Organization Development program at Benedictine University, where she also teaches Organization Development and Management and Organizational Behavior courses to various audiences in graduate, undergraduate and corporate settings. She is instrumental in developing the Benedictine University Distance Learning Executive Program for the U.S. Postal Service, and Off-Site Executive Development Programs for some of the largest Chicago-area corporations including John Deere, Motorola, McDonald's Corporation, and The University of Chicago Academy. She is also a Registered OD Consultant through the OD Institute.

Yaeger has more than twenty years management experience, particularly in start-up operations and small business management. She has authored more than

50 papers and articles including two books on Appreciative Inquiry, a third book on *Global and International Organization Development* with Sorensen, Head and Cooperrider (2001), and a forthcoming book on Global Organization Development with Pfeiffer-Jossey-Bass. She is an Editorial Associate of the *OD Journal*, and Chicago's ASTD *Training Today*, has been a guest editor for Vol. 32, No.1 of the *OD Practitioner*, as well as guest editor of Vol. 18, No. 2, of the *OD Journal, Summer 2000*.

She frequently presents at national and international conferences such as the Academy of Management, the O. D. Institute, and the American Psychological Association, and is the recipient of awards such as the Best Paper Presentation at the OD Institute's Annual Conference 2001, and a team member of three Outstanding ODI Project Awards. Since 1999, she has been the co-chair the Organization Development Track for the Midwest Academy of Management. She is an active member of the Academy of Management, Midwest Academy of Management, the OD Network, OD Institute, and the American Society for Training and Development. Her research interests include international organization development, organizational change, and appreciative inquiry.

Diana Whitney

President of Corporation for Positive Change

Diana Whitney, Ph.D., President of Corporation for Positive Change, is internationally recognized for her consulting, teaching and writing on innovative, large-scale processes for positive social and organizational change and has been instrumental in integrating appreciatieve inquriy in corporate change and leadership practices. Her work focuses on organization transformation, strategic culture change, communication and leadership development. Dr. Whitney applies social constructionist theory to mergers and acquisitions, organization development and strategic planning. She works collaboratively and creatively with executives, managers, and organization members, building teams and supporting them in the construction of the organization's future. She consults with corporate, non-profit and government organizations including: Hunter Douglas, GTE, SmithKline Beecham, Johnson & Johnson, United Religions and Price Waterhouse. Her recent publications and presentations include: "Partnership at Work," "The Appreciative Inquiry Summit: Overview and Applications," "Postmodern Principles and Practices for Large Scale Organization Change," and "Spirituality as a Global Organizing Potential." Diana is a cofounder of the Taos Institute, where appreciative inquiry is taught to consultants and leaders of change. She can be contacted through email at whitneydi@aol.com.

PART I

Rethinking Human Organization Toward a Positive Theory of Change

The first section, *Rethinking Human Organization toward a Positive Theory of Change,* is comprised of six articles. These articles present the theoretical underpinnings for Appreciative Inquiry. The articles range from what might be considered "classics", articles that present the initial development and articulation by David Cooperrider and Suresh Srivastva to a recent review of the literature on themes identified in work with Appreciative Inquiry.

The first article by Cooperrider and Whitney provides an overview of the AI process. It provides a definition of AI, and a description of the most frequently cited application model – the 4-D cycle consisting of Discovery, Dream, Design and Destiny. The article also sets forth the basic principles of AI: the Constructionist Principle, the Principle of Simultaneity, the Poetic Principle, the Anticipatory Principle, and the Positive Principle. The article also provides examples and illustrations from some of the best-known AI projects: GTE, LeadShare, Imagine Chicago, and others.

The second article, "Positive Image, Positive Action: The Affirmative Basis of Organizing" by David Cooperrider stands as one of the most important classics. This is one of the early articles which sets forth one of the most central and critical elements of AI. In this article, David reviews and draws on the literature of medicine and sports in developing the importance of the positive image. In the article he presents seven statements pertaining to the "emerging theory of affirmation" which serves as an important if not the most important foundation principle for Appreciative Inquiry.

The next article "Appreciative Inquiry in Organizational Life" is the first public statement of AI. In this article, Cooperrider and Srivastva present their generative theory of Action Research based on their discussion of socio-rationalist conceptions of the social sciences. Next Ken Murrell discusses the international and intellectual roots of AI in the form of the work by Sir Geoffrey Vickers and the work of the Coverdale Group of the U.K., work over 20 years ago in the Middle-East and Africa.

Gervase Bushe extends the theoretical discussion of AI with a review of the social construction of reality, the heliotropic hypothesis, and the introduction of the concepts of an organization's inner dialogue's paradoxical dilemmas and the implementation of Appreciative Inquiry.

Concluding this first section, the final chapter by Yaeger and Sorensen, "What Matters Most in Appreciative Inquiry: Review and Thematic Assessment" the authors present a review of 50 articles relating to Appreciative Inquiry resulting in the identification of ten themes appearing in the AI literature. The most frequently identified theme is the power of the positive question – a theme which appeared in the over 70% of the articles reviewed.

Chapter 1

A Positive Revolution in Change: Appreciative Inquiry

David L. Cooperrider
Case Western Reserve University
Diana Whitney
The Taos Institute

Introduction

Appreciative Inquiry (AI) begins an adventure. The urge and call to adventure has been sounded by many people and many organizations, and it will take many more to fully explore the vast vistas that are now appearing on the horizon. But even in the first steps, what is being sensed is an exciting direction in our language and theories of change—an invitation, as some have declared, to "a positive revolution".

The words just quoted are strong and, unfortunately, they are not ours. But the more we replay, for example, the high-wire moments of our several years of work at GTE, the more we find ourselves asking the very same kinds of questions the people of GTE asked their senior executives: "Are you really ready for the momentum that is being generated? This is igniting a grassroots movement . . . it is creating an organization in full voice, a center stage for the positive revolutionaries!"

Tom White, President of what was then called GTE Telops (making up 80% of GTE's 67,000 employees) responds, with no hesitation: "Yes, and what I see in this meeting are zealots, people with a mission and passion for creating the new GTE. Count me in, I'm your number one recruit, number one zealot." People cheer.

Enthusiasms continue, and they echo over subsequent months as a lot of hard work pays off. Fourteen months later—based on significant and measurable changes in stock prices, morale survey measures, quality/customer relations, union-management relations, etc.—GTE's whole system change initiative is given professional recognition by the American Society for Training and Development. It wins the 1997 ASTD award for best organization change program in the country. Appreciative inquiry is cited as the "backbone".

How Did They Do It?

This paper provides a broad update and overview of AI. The GTE story mentioned at the outset is, in many ways, just beginning but it is scarcely alone. In the ten years since the theory and vision for "Appreciative Inquiry Into Organizational Life" (Cooperrider and Srivastva, 1987; Cooperrider, 1986) was published, there have been literally hundreds of people involved in co-creating new practices for doing AI and in bringing its spirit and methodology into organizations all over the world. We believe the velocity and largely informal spread of the ideas suggest a growing sense of disenchantment with exhausted theories of change, especially those wedded to vocabularies of human deficit. This also suggests a corresponding urge to work with people, groups, and organizations in more constructive, positive, life-affirming, even spiritual ways.

In this paper we hope to serve as conduit to this impulse as we touch on exciting examples and concepts and provide references for future study. And while the outcomes and illustrations we have selected are often dramatic, we do want to emphasize, throughout, that AI is clearly only in its infancy. Questions are many, and we believe they will be a source of learning for many years.

Could it be, for example, that we as a field have reached "the end of problem solving" as a mode of inquiry capable of inspiring, mobilizing and sustaining significant human system change? What would happen to our change practices if we began all of our work with the positive presumption—that organizations, as centers of human relatedness, are "alive" with infinite constructive capacity? If so, how would we know? What do we mean by infinite capacity? What would happen to us, let's say, as leaders or catalysts of change if we approached the question of change only long after we have connected with people and organizations through systematic study of their already "perfect" form? How would we talk about "it"—this account of the ideal-in-the-real? Would we, in our work, have to go any further once we and others were connected to this positive core? How can we better inquire into organization existence in ways that are economically, humanly, and ecologically significant, that is, in ways that increasingly help people discover, dream, design and transform toward the greatest good?

What is Appreciative Inquiry?

Ap-pre'ci-ate, v., 1. valuing; the act of recognizing the best in people or the world around us; affirming past and present strengths, successes, and potentials; to perceive those things that give life (health, vitality, excellence) to living systems. 2. to increase in value, e.g., the economy has appreciated in value. Synonyms: VALUING, PRIZING, ESTEEMING, and HONORING.

In-quire' (kwir), v., 1. the act of exploration and discovery. 2. To ask questions; to be open to seeing new potentials and possibilities. Synonyms: DISCOVERY, SEARCH, and SYSTEMATIC EXPLORATION, STUDY.

AI has been described by observers in a myriad of ways: as a paradigm of conscious evolution geared for the realities of the new century (Hubbard, 1998); as a methodology that takes the idea of the social construction of reality to its positive extreme—especially with its emphasis on metaphor and narrative, relational ways of knowing, on language, and on its potential as a source of generative theory (Gergen, 1994); as the most important advance in action research in the past decade (Bushe, 1995); as offspring and "heir" to Maslow's vision of a positive social science (Chin, 1998; Curran, 1991); as a powerful second generation OD practice (French and Bell, 1995; Porras, 1991; Mirvis, 1988/89); as model of a much needed participatory science, a "new yoga of inquiry" (Harman, 1990); as a radically affirmative approach to change which completely lets go of problem-based management and in so doing vitally transforms strategic planning, survey methods, culture change, merger integration methods, approaches to TQM, measurement systems, sociotechnical systems, etc. (White, 1996); and lastly, as OD's philosopher's stone (Head and Sorensen, et al., 1996). Indeed it is difficult to sum up the whole of AI— as a philosophy of knowing, a normative stance, a methodology for managing change, and as an approach to leadership and human development. However, for purposes here, it might be most useful to begin with a practice-oriented definition of AI, one that is more descriptive than theoretical and one that provides a compass for the examples to follow:

Appreciative Inquiry is about the co-evolutionary search for the best in people, their organizations, and the relevant world around them. In its broadest focus, it involves systematic discovery of what gives "life" to a living system when it is most alive, most effective, and most constructively capable in economic, ecological, and human terms. AI involves, in a central way, the art and practice of asking questions that strengthen a system's capacity to apprehend, anticipate, and heighten positive potential. It centrally involves the mobilization of inquiry through the crafting of the "unconditional positive question," often involving hundreds or sometimes thousands of people. In AI, the arduous task of intervention gives way to the speed of imagination and innovation; instead of negation, criticism, and spiraling diagnosis, there is discovery, dream, and design. AI seeks, fundamentally, to build a constructive union between a whole people and the massive entirety of what people talk about as past and present capacities: achievements, assets, unexplored potentials, innovations, strengths, elevated thoughts, opportunities, benchmarks, high point moments, lived values, traditions, strategic competencies, stories, expressions of wisdom, insights into the deeper corporate spirit or soul, and visions of valued and possible futures. Taking all of these together as a gestalt, AI deliberately, in everything it does, seeks to work from accounts of this "positive change core"—and it assumes that every living system has many untapped and rich and inspiring accounts of the positive. Link the energy of this core directly to any change agenda and changes never thought possible are suddenly and democratically mobilized.

The positive core of organizational life, we submit, is one of the greatest and largely unrecognized resources in the field of change management today. As said earlier, we are clearly in our infancy when it comes to tools for working with it, talking about it, and designing our systems in synergistic alignment with it. But one thing is evident and clear as we reflect on the most important things we have learned with AI: human systems grow in the direction of what they persistently ask questions about and this propensity is strongest and most sustainable when the means and ends of inquiry are positively correlated. The single most prolific thing a group can do if its aims are to liberate the human spirit and consciously construct a better future is to make the positive change core the common and explicit property of all.

Let's Illustrate: The Appreciative Inquiry "4-D" Cycle

You have just received the following unsettling phone call:

My name is Rita Simmel. I am President of a New York consulting partnership. Our firm specializes in dealing with difficult conflict in organizations: labor-management issues, gender conflict, issues of diversity. We have been retained by a Fortune 500 corporation for the past several years. The contract is around sexual harassment, an issue that is deeper and more severe than virtually any corporation realizes. The issues are about power, the glass ceiling, and many things. As you know, millions of dollars are being expended on the issues. Our firm has specialized in this area for some years and now I'm beginning to ask myself the Hippocratic oath. Are we really helping? Here is the bottom line with our client. We have been working on the issues for two years, and by every measure—numbers of complaints, lawsuits, evaluations from sexual harassment training programs, word of mouth—the problem continues in its growth. Furthermore people are now voting with their feet. They are not coming to the workshops. Those that do seem to leave with doubts: our post-workshop interviews show people feel less able to communicate with those of the opposite gender, they report feeling more distance and less trust, and the glass ceiling remains. So here is my question. How would you take an appreciative inquiry approach to sexual harassment?

This was a tough one. We requested time to think about it, asking if we could talk again in a day or two. We can do the same for you right now (give you a bit of time) as we invite you to think about things you might seriously propose in the callback.

Before going further with the story let's pause and look at a typical flow for AI, a cycle that can be as rapid and informal as in a conversation with a friend or colleague, or as formal as an organization-wide analysis involving every stakeholder, including customers, suppliers, partners, and the like.

Figure 1.1 shows four key stages in AI: *Discovery*—mobilizing a whole system inquiry into the positive change core; *Dream*—creating a clear results-oriented vision in relation to discovered potential and in relation to questions of higher purpose, i.e., "What is the world calling us to become?"; *Design*—creating possibility propositions of the ideal organization, an organization design which people feel is

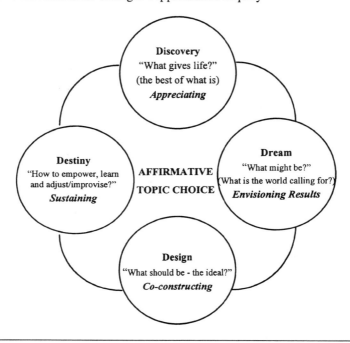

Figure 1.1. Appreciative Inquiry 4-D Cycle.

capable of magnifying or eclipsing the positive core and realizing the articulated new dream; and *Destiny*—strengthening the affirmative capability of the whole system enabling it to build hope and momentum around a deep purpose and creating processes for learning, adjustment, and improvisation, like a jazz group over time (Barrett, 1998).

At the core of the cycle, is Affirmative Topic Choice. It is the most important part of any AI. If, in fact, knowledge and organizational destiny are as intricately interwoven as we think, then isn't it possible that the seeds of change are implicit in the very first questions we ask? AI theory says yes and takes the idea quite seriously: It says that the way we know people, groups, and organizations is fateful. It further asserts the time is overdue to recognize that symbols and conversations, emerging from all our analytic modes, are among the world's paramount resources.

Topic Choice

Back to our phone call. If inquiry and change are a simultaneous moment, if the questions we ask set the stage for what we "find", and if what we "discover" (the data) creates the material out of which the future is conceived, conversed about, and constructed—then how shall we proceed with an appreciative approach to sexual harassment? Here is an excerpt from the response:

D.C.: Hello, Rita. Before we get into our proposal we have an important question. What is it that you want to learn about and achieve with this whole intervention, and by when?

Rita: We want to dramatically cut the incidence of sexual harassment. We want to solve this huge problem, or at least make a significant dent in it.

D.C.: O.K. Rita... But is that all?

Rita: You mean what do I really want to see? (Long pause . . . then she blurts out her response.) What we really want to see is the development of the new century organization—a model of high quality cross-gender relationships in the workplace!

DC: Great topic. What would happen if we put an invitation in the company newsletter, asking people to step forward in pairs to nominate themselves as candidates to study and share their stories of what it means to create and sustain high quality cross-gender relationships in the workplace? It might be interesting to do a large conference, and really put a magnifying lens to the stages of development, contextual factors, tough questions of adult attraction, breakthroughs in terms of power relations, and so on. What do you think?

To fastforward, a relatively small pilot project was created which surpassed everyone's expectations. Hundreds, not dozens, of pairs nominated themselves. That was surprise number one. Then other organizations got word of the pilot and a truly major effort, moving through the 4-D framework, was conceptualized by another consulting firm, Marge Schiller and Associates. The pioneering organization she worked with, which now can happily be named, was the Avon Corporation in Mexico. Again there were similar issues—including the glass ceiling at senior management levels—but again there was interest in framing the whole thing in terms of an inquiry.

To begin, a hundred people were trained in the basics of AI interviewing. They in turn went out into every part of the organization and over the next several weeks completed many more interviews, about 300 in all. At the end of each interview, the interviewers asked the person interviewed if they too could help do some interviewing. A waterfall was experienced. Stories poured in—stories of achievement, trust building, authentic joint leadership, practices of effective conflict management, ways of dealing with sex stereotypes, stages of development and methods of career advancement.

The second two Ds—articulating the new century dream and creating designs for an organization that maximally supported the development of high quality cross-gender relationships—came next. These were combined in a large group format much like a future search. Using stories from the interviews as a basis for imagining the future, expansive and practical propositions were created, for example, "Every task force or committee at Avon, whenever possible, is co-chaired by a cross-gender pairing." The significance of even this simple proposal proved to be big. Likewise, propositions in other areas of organization design were also carefully crafted. Soon, literally everything in the organization was opened to discussion:

corporate structures, systems, work processes, communications, career opportunities, governance, compensation practices, leadership patterns, learning opportunities, customer connections, and more.

In the end, some 30 visionary propositions were created. Subsequent changes in system structures and behaviors were reported to be dramatic (Schiller, 1998). As it turns out, this story, like GTE's, gets even better. Avon Mexico was recently singled out, several years later, by the Catalyst organization. They received the 1997 Catalyst Award for best place in the country for women to work.

It is a classic example of the power of topic choice. Affirmative topics, always homegrown, can be on anything the people of an organization feel gives life to the system. As a rule of thumb most projects have between three and five topics. Words like empowerment, innovation, sense of ownership, commitment, integrity, ecological consciousness, and pride are often articulated as worthy of study. Topics can be on anything an organization feels to be strategically and humanly important. AI topics can be on technical processes, financial efficiencies, human issues, market opportunities, social responsibilities, or anything else. In each case of topic choice, the same premise is firmly posited: Human systems grow in the direction of their deepest and most frequent inquiries.

Discovery

The inquiry we are talking about is anything but wishful. If we were to underline one of the two words—appreciative or inquiry—our pen would immediately move to the latter. In "Vital Speeches of the Day" (1996), Tom White, President of what was then called GTE Telephone Operations, puts his interpretation of AI in executive language, months before GTE's change effort was recognized by ASTD:

Appreciative Inquiry can get you much better results than seeking out and solving problems. That's an interesting concept for me—and I imagine most of you—because telephone companies are among the best problem solvers in the world. We troubleshoot everything. We concentrate enormous resources on correcting problems that have relatively minor impact on our overall service and performance (and which)...when used continually and over a long period of time, this approach can lead to a negative culture. If you combine a negative culture with all the challenges we face today, it could be easy to convince ourselves that we have too many problems to overcome—to slip into a paralyzing sense of hopelessness. ... Don't get me wrong. I'm not advocating mindless happy talk. Appreciative Inquiry is a complex science designed to make things better. We can't ignore problems—we just need to approach them from the other side.

What Tom White calls "the other side", we are describing as the positive change core. AI, most simply, is a tool for connecting to the transformational power of this core. Willis Harman (1990) talks about AI as a participatory science, a yoga of inquiry, where the term yoga comes from the Sanskrit root *yug* which means link or bond. In that sense, if we remember something or someone, it can be said that there is a form of yoga happening. AI helps make the memory link by concentrating systematic inquiry into all aspects of the appreciable world, into an organization's infinite and surplus capacity—past, present and future. By concentrating on the atom, human beings have unleashed its power. AI says we can do the same in every living system once we open this ever emergent positive core—every strength, innovation, achievement, resource, living value, imaginative story, benchmark, hope, positive tradition, passion, high point experience, internal genius, dream—to systematic inquiry.

The core task of the discovery phase is to discover and disclose positive capacity, at least until an organization's understanding of this "surplus" is exhausted (which has never happened in our experience). AI provides a practical way to ignite this "spirit of inquiry" on an organization-wide basis. Consider this example:

At LeadShare in Canada, AI was used to help this big eight accounting firm make the tough transition in the executive succession of a "legendary" managing partner. The managing partner seized the moment as an incredible leadership development opportunity for all 400 partners. Everyone was interviewed with AI. An extensive interview protocol was designed (ultimately taking about 2 hours per interview) focusing on affirmative topics like innovation, equality, partnership, speed to market, and valuing diversity (in Canada between francophone and anglophone). Not one outside consultant did the interviews. All were done internally, by 30 junior partners as part of a leadership development program. A powerful and instant intergenerational connection was made, and organizational history came alive in face-to-face stories. Instead of amnesia, or a problem-to-be-solved, people began to relate to their history in a whole new way. Like a good piece of poetry filled with endless interpretive meaning, people at Leadshare ascended into their history as a reservoir of positive possibility. At the next annual partners meeting, with over 400 people in the conference hall, the material was showcased and coupled to the future, as the strategic planning became one of the "best" the partners could ever remember (Rainey, 1996).

Perhaps it is obvious, but the process of doing the interviews is as important as the data collected. When managers ask us how many people should be interviewed or, who should do the interviews, we increasingly find ourselves saying "everyone." It is not uncommon in AI work to talk about doing thousands of interviews. A hospital in Seattle recently did three thousand interviews in preparation for an organization-wide Appreciative Inquiry Summit (Whitney and Cooperrider, 1998). People themselves, not consultants, generate the system-wide organization analysis using questions like this: "Obviously you have had ups and downs in your career here at XYZ. But for the moment I would like you to focus on a high point, a time in your work experience here where you felt most alive, most engaged, or most successful. Can you tell me the story? How did it unfold? What was it organizationally that made it stand out? What was it about you that made it a high point? What key insights do you have for all of us at XYZ?"

In Chicago, in one of the most exciting AI's we have seen, there is talk of over a million interviews. And guess whose interviews have produced the best data—the most inspiring, vision-generating stories? It is the children's. It is happening through inter-generational inquiry where the elders are valued and share hopes in settings with the young. One of our favorite papers is about the Imagine Chicago story and the leadership of Bliss Browne. It is titled "The Child as the Agent of Inquiry" (Cooperrider, 1996). It argues that the spirit of inquiry is something all of us in change work need to reclaim and aspire to: openness, availability, epistemological humility, the ability to admire, to be surprised, to be inspired, to inquire into our valued and possible worlds.

What distinguishes AI, especially in this phase of work, is that every carefully crafted question is positive. Knowing and changing are a simultaneous moment. The thrill of discovery becomes the thrill of creating. As people throughout a system connect in serious study into qualities, examples, and analysis of the positive core—each appreciating and everyone being appreciated—hope grows and community expands.

Dream

When an artist sits in front of a landscape the imagination is kindled not by searching for "what is wrong with this landscape," but by a special ability to be inspired by those things worth valuing. Appreciation, it appears, draws our eye toward life, stirs our feelings, sets in motion our curiosity, and provides inspiration to the envisioning mind. In his analysis of esthetics and the origins of creative images, Nietzsche once asked of the power of appreciation: "Does it not praise? Does it not glorify? Does it not select? Does it not bring [that which is appreciated] to prominence?" (Rader, 1973, p. 12) Then in the same passage he takes a next step, linking valuing (discovery) and imagination (dream). He elaborates: "Valuing is creating: hear it, ye creating ones! Valuation is itself the treasure and jewel of valued things."

During the dream phase, the interview stories and insights are put to constructive use. As people are brought together to listen carefully to the innovations and moments of organizational "life," sometimes in storytelling modes and sometimes in interpretive and analytic modes, a convergence zone is created where the future begins to be discerned in the form of visible patterns interwoven into the texture of the actual. The amplified interaction among innovators and innovations makes something important happen: very rapidly we start seeing outlines of the New World. Some organizations turn the data into a special commemorative report celebrating the successes and exceptional moments in the life of the organization (Liebler, 1997). Others have created a thematic analysis—careful to document rich stories and not succumb to "narrative thin" one line quotes (Ludema, 1996). In all cases the data onto the positive change core serves as an essential resource for the visioning stages of the appreciative inquiry 4-D model.

Before their strategic planning session in 1997, Nutrimental Foods of Brazil closed down the plant for a full day to bring all 700 employees together for a day of Discovery into the factors and forces that have given life to the system when it had been most effective, most alive, and most successful as a producer of high quality health foods. With cheers and good wishes a "smaller" group of 150 stakeholders—employees from all levels, suppliers, distributors, community leaders, financiers, and customers—then went into a four day strategy session to articulate a new and bold corporate dream. The stories from the day before were used just as an artist uses a palette of colors—before painting a picture the artist assembles the red paints, blue, green, yellow and so on. With these "materials" in hand people were asked to dream: "What is the world calling us to become? What are those things about us that no matter how much we change, we want to continue into our new and different future? Let's assume that tonight while we were all asleep a miracle occurred where Nutrimental became exactly as we would like it to be—all of its best qualities are magnified, extended, multiplied the way we would like to see…in fact we wake up and it is now 2000 . . . as you come into Nutrimental today what do you see that is different, and how do you know?" After four days of appreciative analysis, planning, and articulation of three new strategic business directions, the organization launches into the future with focus, solidarity, and confidence. Six months later, record bottom line figures of millions of dollars are recorded—profits are up 300%. The co-CEOs, Rodrigo Loures and Arthur Lemme Netto, attribute the dramatic results to two things: bringing the whole system into the planning proces; and realizing that organizations are, in fact, "centers of human relatedness"(Loures and Lemme Netto, 1998) which thrive when there is an appreciative eye—when people see the best in one another, when they can dialogue their dreams and ultimate concerns in affirming ways, and when they are connected in full voice to create not just new worlds but better worlds.

Design

Once the strategic focus or dream is articulated (usually consisting of three things in our model—a vision of a better world, a powerful purpose, and a compelling statement of strategic intent) attention turns to the creation of the ideal organization, the social architecture or actual design of the system in relation to the world of which it is part. What we have found is that the sequencing is crucial, moving first through in-depth work on Dream before Design, followed with back and forth iterations. In Zimbabwe we recently worked with a partner organization of Save the Children. It was fascinating to observe how easy it was to re-design the organization in terms of structures and systems once broad agreement was reached on a powerful Dream. The articulation of the image of the future was simple: "Every person in Zimbabwe shall have access to clean water within five years." The critical design shift, demanded by the large dream, was to a new form of organization based on a network of alliances or partnerships, not bureaucracy's self-sufficient hierarchy.

One aspect that differentiates Appreciative Inquiry from other visioning or planning methodologies is that images of the future emerge out of grounded examples from an organization's positive past. Sometimes this "data" is complemented with benchmark studies of other organizations creating a "generative metaphor" for circumventing common resistances to change (Barrett and Cooperrider, 1990). In both cases, the good news stories are used to craft possibility propositions that bridge the best of "what is" with collective speculation or aspiration of "what might be". In the working of the material, people are invited to challenge the status quo as well as common assumptions underlying the design of the organization. People are encouraged to "wander beyond" the data with the essential question being: "What would our organization look like if it were designed in every way possible to maximize the qualities of the positive core and enable the accelerated realization of our dreams?"

When inspired by a great dream we have yet to find an organization that did not feel compelled to design something very new and very necessary. Here is an example of a possibility proposition, one of about twenty organization design visions that were created at DIA Corporation, a rapidly growing distributor of consumer products. Today this proposition is modus operandi at the corporation:

DIA has become a learning organization that fosters the cross fertilization of ideas, minimizes the building of empires, harnesses the synergy of group cooperation, and cultivates the pride of being a valued member of one outstanding corporation. DIA accelerates its learning through an annual strategic planning conference that involves all five hundred people in the firm as well as key partners and stakeholders. As a setting for "strategic learning," teams present their benchmarking studies of the best five other organizations, deemed leaders in their class. Other teams present an annual appreciative analysis of DIA, and together these databases of success stories (internal and external) help set the stage for DIA's strategic, future search planning.

Recently we have had the opportunity to team up with Dee Hock, one of the greatest visionary CEOs with whom we have ever worked. Dee was the founder of VISA, a breakthrough organization that has over 20,000 offices, a   since 1970 has grown something like 10,000%; this year annual sales expected to pass $1 trillion. The whole Visa system, from Calcutta to Chicago, in over 200 countries is completely unmanageable from the perspective of using centralized, command-and-control design principles.

If General Motors once defined the shape of the old model, perhaps Dee's "chaordic organization"—combining chaos and order in ways which interweave (like nature's designs) infinite variety and self-organizing order—is a foreshadowing of an emerging prototype. What we have learned by working with Dee is how to move pragmatically and substantively from appreciative Discovery and Dream to truly post-bureaucratic Design that distributes power and liberates human energy in a way we have never seen. Most recently we have collaborated on a re-constitution of the United Way of America as well as an initiative to design something akin to a United Nations among the world's great religions and spiritual traditions. (It is called United Religions.) In each case helping people agree on a set of design principles is crucial. That is "principles" as in, "We hold these truths to be self evident: that all people are created equal." Again, this is not a set of platitudes, but a manifesto, what people believe in and care about in their gut.

Destiny

William James said in 1902 that of all the creatures of earth, only human beings can change their pattern: "Man alone is the architect of his destiny."

In our early years of AI work, the fourth D was called Delivery. We emphasized planning for continuous learning, adjustment, and improvisation in the service of shared ideals. It was a time for action planning, developing implementation strategies, and dealing with conventional challenges of sustainability. But the word delivery simply did not go far enough. It did not convey the sense of liberation we were seeing—like the well documented hotel case, where the system tranformed itself from a one-star to four-star hotel by using AI and literally putting a moratorium on all the traditional problem solving efforts that it had going (Barrett and Cooperrider, 1990).

Executives like Jane Watkins (former Chair of the Board at NTL) and Jane Pratt (executive at the World Bank and now CEO of the Mountain Institute) argued that AI engenders a repatterning of our relationships, not only with each other, but also our relationship to reality itself. Reminiscent of Paulo Friere's concept of pedagogy of the oppressed—where people move in their relationship to reality from "submergence" to "reflexive awareness" to "co-participation"—these leaders insisted that AI's gift is at the paradigmatic level. AI is not so much about new knowledge but new knowing. Indeed people frequently talk, as they move through the pedagogy of life-giving Discovery, Dream, and Design, that something suddenly hits home: that interpretation matters—that the manner in which they/we read the world filters to the level of our imaginations, our relationships, and ultimately to the direction and meaning of our actions. We create the organizational worlds in which we live.

What we discovered, quite honestly, was that momentum for change and long-term sustainability increased the more we abandoned "delivery" ideas of action planning, monitoring progress, and building implementation strategies. What was done instead, in several of the most exciting cases, was to focus only on giving AI away to everyone, and then stepping back. The GTE story, still unfolding but already attracting national recognition, is suggestive. It is a story that says organizational change needs to look a lot more like an inspired movement than a neatly packaged or engineered product. Dan Young, the head of OD at GTE, and his colleagues Maureen Garrison and Jean Moore, call it "organizing for change from the grassroots to the frontline." Call it the path of positive protest, or a strategy for positive subversion—whatever it is called it is virtually unstoppable once "it" is up and running. Its structure is called the Positive Change Network (PCN). One especially dramatic moment gives the sense:

The headline article in GTE Together described what was spreading as a grassroots movement to build the new GTE. Initiated as a pilot training to see what would happen if the tools and theories of appreciative inquiry were made available to frontline employees, things started taking off. Suddenly, without permission having been granted, frontline employees are launching interview studies into positive topics like innovation, inspired leadership, revolutionary customer responsiveness, labor-management partnerships, and "fun". Fresh out of a training session on AI, one employee, for example, did 200 interviews into the positive core of a major call center. Who is going to say no to a complementary request like, "Would you help me out? . . . I'm really trying to find out more about the best innovations developing in your area and I see you as someone who could really give me new insight into creating settings where innovation can happen. . . . It is part of my leadership development. Do you have time for an interview? . . . would be glad to share my learnings with you later!" Soon the topics are finding their way into meetings, corridor conversations, and senior planning sessions—in other words the questions, enthusiastically received, are changing corporate attention, language, agendas, and learnings. Many start brainstorming applications for AI. Lists are endless. Have we ever done focus groups with the 100% satisfied customer? How about changing call center measures? What would happen if we replaced the entire deficit measures with equally powerful measures of the positive? How can we revitalize the TQM groups, demoralized by one fishbone analysis after another? What would happen if we augmented variance analysis with depth studies that help people to dream and define the very visions of quality standards? How about a star stories program to generate a narrative rich environment—where customers are asked to share stories of encounters with exceptional employees? How about a gathering with senior executives so we can celebrate our learnings with them, share with them how seeing the positive has changed our work and family lives, and even recruit them to join the PCN?

The pilot program now had a momentum all its own. The immediate response— an avalanche of requests for participation—confirmed that there were large numbers at GTE ready to be called to the task of positive change. To grow the network by the hundreds, even thousands, it was decided to do a ten region training session, all linked and downloaded by satellite conferencing. A successful pilot of three sites—Seattle, Indianapolis, and Dallas—confirmed the same kind of energy and response could happen through distance technologies. Quite suddenly the power of a 1000 person network caught people's attention. Just imagine the 1000 "students" of organization life coming together in a year at an AI Summit to share learning from 10,000 innovations discovered at GTE. Very rapidly, by connecting and consistently noticing breakthroughs, new patterns of organizing would become commonplace knowledge. Changes would happen not by organized confrontation, diagnosis, burning platforms, or piecemeal reform but through irresistibly vibrant and real visions. And when everyone's awareness grows at the same time— that basic change is taking place in this area and that area, it is easier to coalesce a new consensus that fundamental change is possible. PCN was becoming a lightning rod for energy and enthusiasm we all greatly underestimated. Then the unions raised questions. There were serious concerns, including the fact that they were not consulted in the early stages. We were told the initiative was over. There was to be a meeting of the unions and GTE at the Federal Mediation Offices in Washington, D.C. to put the whole thing to rest.

But at the meeting with the IBEW and the CWA, leaders from both groups said they saw something fresh and unique about AI. They agreed to bring 200 union leaders together for a two-day introduction. Their purpose: "to evaluate AI . . . to see if it should have any place in the future at GTE." A month later, the session took place. It looked as if it was going pretty well and then the moment of decision. Tables of eight were instructed to evaluate the ideas and cast a vote as a group: "Yes, we endorse moving forward with AI" or "No, we withhold endorsement." For thirty minutes the 30 groups deliberated. Dan Young calls the vote. Tensions were felt. "Table one, how do you vote?" The response was ready: "We vote 100% for moving forward with AI and feel this is an historic opportunity for the whole system." Then the next table: "We vote 100% with a caveat—that every person at GTE have the opportunity to get the AI training, and that all projects going forward be done in partnership, the unions and the company." On and on the vote goes. Thirty tables spoke. Thirty tables voted. Every single one voted to move forward. It was stunning. Eight months later AI was combined with the "conflictive partnership" model of John Calhoun Wells of the Federal Mediation Services at the kickoff session and announcement of a new era of partnership. The historic statement of Partnership states: "The company and the Unions realize that traditional adversarial labor-management relations must change in order to adapt to the new global telecommunications marketplace. It is difficult to move to cooperation in one quantum leap. However the company and the Unions have agreed to move in a new direction. This new direction emphasizes partnership."

AI accelerates the nonlinear interaction of organization breakthroughs, putting them together with historic, positive traditions and strengths to create a "convergence zone" facilitating the collective repatterning of human systems. At some point, apparently minor positive discoveries connect in accelerating manner and quantum change, a jump from one state to the next that cannot be achieved through incremental change alone, becomes possible. What is needed, as the Destiny Phase of AI suggests, are the network-like structures that liberate not only the daily search into qualities and elements of an organization's positive core but the establishment of a convergence zone for people to empower one another—to connect, cooperate, and co-create. Changes never thought possible are suddenly and democratically mobilized when people constructively appropriate the power of the positive core and simply... let go of accounts of the negative. But then the question is always voiced: "What do we do with the real problems?"

Basic Principles of Appreciative Inquiry

To address this question in anything other than Pollyannaish terms, we need to at least comment on the generative-theoretical work that has inspired and given strength to much of AI in practice. Here are five principles and scholarly streams we consider as central to AI's theory-base of change.

The Constructionist Principle: Simply stated—human knowledge and organizational destiny are interwoven. To be effective as executives, leaders, change agents, etc., we must be adept in the art of understanding, reading, and analyzing organizations as living, human constructions. Knowing (organizations) stands at the center of any and virtually every attempt at change. Thus, the way we know is fateful.

At first blush this statement appears simple and obvious enough. We are, as leaders and change agents, constantly involved in knowing/inquiring/reading the people and world around us—doing strategic planning analysis, environmental scans, needs analysis, assessments and audits, surveys, focus groups, performance appraisals, and so on. Certainly success hinges on such modes of knowing. And this is precisely where things get more interesting because throughout the academy a revolution is afoot, alive with tremendous ferment and implication, in regard to modernist views of knowledge. In particular, what is confronted is the Western conception of objective, individualistic, historic knowledge—"a conception that has insinuated itself into virtually all aspects of modern institutional life" (Gergen, 1985; p. 272). At stake are questions that pertain to the deepest dimensions of our being and humanity: how we know what we know, whose voices and interpretations matter, whether the world is governed by external laws independent of human choices and consciousness, and where is knowledge to be located (in the individual "mind", or out there "externally" in nature or impersonal structures)? At stake are issues that are profoundly fundamental, not just for the future of social science but for the trajectory of all our lives.

In our view, the finest work in this area, indeed a huge extension of the most radical ideas in Lewinian thought, can be found in Ken Gergen's Toward Transformation in Social Knowledge (1982) and Realities and Relationships: Soundings In Social Construction (1994). What Gergen does, in both of these, is synthesize the essential whole of the post modern ferment and crucially takes it beyond disenchantment with the old and offers alternative conceptions of knowledge, fresh discourses on human functioning, new vistas for human science, and exciting directions for approaching change. Constuctionism is an approach to human science and practice which replaces the individual with the relationship as the locus of knowledge, and thus is built around a keen appreciation of the power of language and discourse of all types (from words to metaphors to narrative forms, etc.) to create our sense of reality—our sense of the true, the good, the possible.

Philosophically it involves a decisive shift in western intellectual tradition from *cogito ergo sum*, to *communicamus ergo sum* and in practice constructionism replaces absolutist claims or the final word with the never ending collaborative quest to understand and construct options for better living. The purpose of inquiry, which is talked about as totally inseparable and intertwined with action, is the creation of "generative theory," not so much mappings or explanations of yesterday's world, but anticipatory articulations of tomorrow's possibilities. Constructionism, because of its emphasis on the communal basis of knowledge and its radical questioning of everything that is taken-for-granted as "objective" or seemingly immutable, invites us to find ways to increase the generative capacity of knowledge. However there are warnings: "Few are prepared," says Gergen (1985, p. 271) "for such a wrenching, conceptual dislocation. However, for the innovative, adventurous and resilient, the horizons are exciting indeed." This is precisely the call to which AI has responded. Principle number two takes it deeper.

The Principle of Simultaneity: Here it is recognized that inquiry and change are not truly separate moments, but are simultaneous. Inquiry is intervention. The seeds of change—that is, the things people think and talk about, the things people discover and learn, and the things that inform dialogue and inspire images of the future—are implicit in the very first questions we ask. The questions we ask set the stage for what we "find," and what we "discover" (the data) becomes the linguistic material, the stories, out of which the future is conceived, conversed about, and constructed.

One of the most impactful things a change agent or practitioner does is to articulate questions. Instinctively, intuitively and tacitly we all know that research of any kind can, in a flash, profoundly alter the way we see ourselves, view reality, and conduct our lives. Consider the economic poll, or the questions that led to the discovery of the atom bomb, or the surveys that, once leaked, created a riot at a unionized automobile plant in London. (See Cooperrider and Srivastva, 1987.) If we accept the proposition that patterns of social-organizational action are not fixed by nature in any direct biological or physical way, that human systems are made and imagined in relational settings by human beings (socially constructed), then attention turns to the source of our ideas, our discourses, our researches—that is, our questions. Alterations in linguistic practices—including the linguistic practice of crafting questions—hold profound implications for changes in social practice.

One great myth that continues to dampen the potential here is the understanding that first we do an analysis, and then we decide on change. Not so, says the constructionist view. Even the most innocent question evokes change—even if reactions are simply changes in awareness, dialogue, feelings of boredom, or even laughter. When we consider the possibilities in these terms, that inquiry and change are a simultaneous moment, we begin reflecting anew. It is not so much "Is my question leading to right or wrong answers?" but rather "What impact is my question having on our lives together...is it helping to generate conversations about the good, the better, the possible . . . is it strengthening our relationships?"

The Poetic Principle: A metaphor here is that human organizations are a lot more like an open book than, say, a machine. An organization's story is constantly being co-authored. Moreover, pasts, presents, or futures are endless sources of learning, inspiration, or interpretation—precisely like, for example, the endless interpretive possibilities in a good piece of poetry or a biblical text. The important implication is that we can study virtually any topic related to human experience in any human system or organization. We can inquire into the nature of alienation or joy, enthusiasm or low morale, efficiency or excess, in any human organization. There is not a single topic related to organizational life that we could not study in any organization.

What constuctionism does is remind us that it is not the "world out there" dictating or driving our topics of inquiry but again the topics are themselves social artifacts, products of social processes (cultural habits, typifying discourses, rhetoric, professional ways, power relations). It is in this vein that AI says: Let us make sure we are not just reproducing the same worlds over and over again because of the simple and boring repetition of our questions (not "one more" morale survey which everybody can predict the results ahead of time). AI also says, with a sense of excitement and potential, that there can be great gains made in a better linking of the means and ends of inquiry. Options begin to multiply. For example, informally, in many talks with great leaders in the NGO world (Save the Children, World Vision), we have begun to appreciate the profound joy that CEO's feel as "servant leaders"—and the role this positive affect potentially plays in creating healthy organizations. But then one questions: Is there a book on the Harvard Business book-list, or anywhere for that matter, titled Executive Joy? And even if there isn't, does this mean that joy has nothing to do with good leadership, or healthy human systems? Why aren't we including this topic in our change efforts? What might happen if we did?

What the poetic principle invites is re-consideration of aims and focus of any inquiry in the domain of change management. It is becoming clearer that our topics, like windsocks, continue to blow steadily onward in the direction of our conventional gaze. As we shall soon explore, seeing the world as a problem has become "very much a way of organizational life."

The Anticipatory Principle: The infinite human resource we have for generating constructive organizational change is our collective imagination and discourse about the future. One of the basic theorems of the anticipatory view of organizational life is that it is the image of the future, which in fact guides what might be called the current behavior of any organism or organization. Much like a movie projector on a screen, human systems are forever projecting ahead of themselves a horizon of expectation (in their talk in the hallways, in the metaphors and language they use) that brings the future powerfully into the present as a mobilizing agent. To inquire in ways that serve to refashion anticipatory reality—especially the artful creation of positive imagery on a collective basis—may be the most prolific thing any inquiry can do.

Our positive images of the future lead our positive actions—this is the increasingly energizing basis and presupposition of Appreciative Inquiry.

Whether we are talking about placebo studies in medicine (Ornstein and Sobel, 1987); reviews of a myriad of studies of the Pygmalion dynamic in the classroom

(Jussim, 1986); studies of the rise and fall of cultures (Boulding, 1966; Polak, 1973); research into the relationships between optimism and health (Seligman, 1990); studies of positive self-monitoring and ways for accelerating learning (Kirschenbaum, 1984); analysis of the importance of imbalance, positive inner dialogue to personal and relational well-being (Schwartz, 1986); research on positive mood states and effective decision making (Isen, 1983); studies from the domain of "conscious evolution" (Hubbard, 1998); or theories on how positive noticing of even "small wins" can reverberate throughout a system and change the world (Weick, 1984)—the conclusions are converging on something Aristotle said many years ago. "A vivid imagination," he said "compels the whole body to obey it." In the context of more popular writing, Dan Goleman (1987), in a well-written New York Times headline-article declares "Research Affirms the Power of Positive Thinking."

The Positive Principle: This last principle is not so abstract. It grows out of years of experience with appreciative inquiry. Put most simply, it has been our experience that building and sustaining momentum for change requires large amounts of positive affect and social bonding—things like hope, excitement, inspiration, caring, camaraderie, sense of urgent purpose, and sheer joy in creating something meaningful together. What we have found is that the more positive the question we ask in our work the more long lasting and successful the change effort. It does not help, we have found, to begin our inquiries from the standpoint of the world as a problem to be solved. We are more effective the longer we can retain the spirit of inquiry of the everlasting beginner. The major thing we do that makes the difference is to craft and seed, in better and more catalytic ways, the unconditional positive question.
    Although the positive has not been paraded as a central concept in most approaches to organization analysis and change, it is clear we need no longer be shy about bringing this language more carefully and prominently into our work. And personally speaking, it is so much healthier. We love letting go of "fixing" the world. We love doing interviews, hundreds of them, into moments of organizational life. And we are, quite frankly, more effective the more we are able to learn, to admire, to be surprised, to be inspired alongside the people with whom we are working. Perhaps it is not just organizations—we too become what we study. So suggested, over and over again, is the life-promoting impact of inquiry into the good, the better, and the possible. A theory of affirmative basis of human action and organizing is emerging from many quarters—social contructionism, image theory, conscious evolution and the like. And the whole thing is beginning, we believe, to make a number of our change-management traditions look obsolete.

Appreciative Inquiry and Power in Organizations

We could have easily called this section "Eulogy for Problem Solving". In our view, the problem solving paradigm, while once perhaps quite effective, is simply out of sync with the realities of today's virtual worlds (Cooperrider, 1996). Problem solving approaches to change are painfully slow (always asking people to look backward to yesterday's causes); they rarely result in new vision (by definition we can describe something as a problem because we already, perhaps implicitly, assume an ideal, so we are not searching to expansive new knowledge of better ideals but searching how to close "gaps"); and in human terms problem approaches are notorious for generating defensiveness (it is not my problem but yours). But our real concern, from a social constructionist perspective, has to do with relations of power and control. It is the most speculative part of this chapter; and hopefully, it better illuminates the potentials advocated by AI. In particular is the more conscious linking of language, including the language of our own profession, to change. Words do create worlds—even in unintended ways.

There was an unforgettable moment in a conference in Chicago on AI for inner city change agents, mostly community mobilizers from the Saul Alinsky school of thought, Rules for Radicals. After two days a participant challenges: "This is naïve . . . Have you ever worked in the depths of the inner city, like the Cabrini Green public housing projects? You're asking me to go in and 'appreciate' it . . . Just yesterday I'm there and the impoverished children are playing soccer, not with a ball, no money for that, but with a dead rat. Tell me about appreciative inquiry in the housing projects!"

It was a powerful question. It was one that made us go deeper theoretically. At one level we were arguing typical approaches to problem diagnosis, including the Alinsky confrontation methods, would work, but at about half the speed of AI. But then as we explored the subject of the cultural consequences of deficit discourse we began seeing a disconcerting relationship between the society-wide escalation of deficit-based change methods and the erosion of people power. The analysis, from here, could proceed from virtually any professional discipline—the diagnostic vocabularies of social work, medicine, organization development, management, law, accounting, community development, editing—but let's begin with psychology and the social sciences (ample linkage will be made to our own field). Ken Gergen's (1994) work is at the forefront for anyone wanting something more than a suggestive summary.

Consider the following characterizations of the self: impulsive personality, narcissism, anti-social personality, reactive depressive, codependent, self-alienated, type-A, paranoid, stressed, repressed, authoritarian, midlife crisis. These are all terms commonly used by the mental-health professions and are now common among people in the culture itself. But importantly, these terms, and several thousand others (Gergen, 1994), have come into conventional usage only within the present century, many in only the last decade. But something else is noteworthy: the terminology's discredit, draws attention to problems, shortcomings, and incapacities. Interestingly, the trajectory of the "professional" development of vocabularies of human deficit is rising at geometric rates, correlated as might be expected with the sheer growth in numbers of the profession. In 1892 when the American Psychological Association was founded there were thirty-one members. By 1906 there were 181. The next thirty-one years witnessed an expansion of almost a hundredfold, to over 3,000. In the next twenty-two years the figure grew again by twenty times, over 63,000. Add to this similar growth figures in social work, psychiatry, community development, and organization development and one realizes that the spiraling production of languages of deficit have become quite a growth industry. By 1980 mental illness was the third most expensive category of health disorder in the United States at more than $20 billion annually. By 1983, the costs for mental illness, exclusive of alcoholism and drug abuse, were estimated to be almost $73 billion. We have no figures for the consulting industry, but we can guess. While intentions are good, argues Gergen, some of the unintended consequences may not be.

From a constructionist perspective one realizes that words do not so much innocently "mirror" a world out there as they become vehicles for coordinating our actions with one another. Words in any profession function a bit like tools of the trade. When I used to give my son Matt a hammer, inevitably everything in the house soon became a nail. What happens when the "scientifically" legitimated vocabularies of human deficit become the common and explicit tool kit of all? Gergen suggests not everything about it is healthy. Such deficit discourse, when chronically used, "generates a network of increasing entanglements for the culture at large. Such entanglements are not only self serving for the professions, they also add exponentially to the sense of human misery." (1994, p. 142)

In particular, deficit based change approaches have an unfortunate propensity to reinforce hierarchy, wherein "less than ideal" individuals, who learn to accept what sometimes becomes a lifelong label, are encouraged to enter "treatment programs" under expert supervision; to erode community, wherein the mental health professions appropriate the process of interpersonal realignment that might otherwise (in other eras) have happened in nonprofessional contexts like the family or community; to instill a sense of self-enfeeblement, wherein deficit terms essentialize the person and like a birthmark or fingerprint, the deficit is expected to inevitably manifest itself into many aspects of their lives (it is a "thing"); to stimulate endless vocabulary expansion wherein people increasingly construct their problems in the professional languages (diagnosing each other) and seek more help which in turn increased the numbers in the profession who are rewarded when they expand the vocabulary—"to explore a new disorder within the mental health sciences is not unlike discovering a new star in astronomy." (Gergen, p. 159) Gergen sums up: "As I am proposing, when the culture is furnished with a professionally rationalized language of mental deficit and people are increasingly understood according to this language, the population of 'patients' expands. This population, in turn, forces the profession to extend its vocabulary, and thus the array of mental deficit terms available for cultural use." (Gergen, p. 161) Is there no exit from such progressive infirmity?

After talking this over with the people in the inner city Chicago conference—and tracing the vocabularies of human deficit not only to the rise of the professions but also to the rise of bureaucracy, skeptical science, original sin theological accounts, the cynical media—the Alinsky-trained activist sat down with a gasp. He said: "In the name of entertainment, my people are being fed negative views of human violence—and they are surrounded by endless description of their negative 'needs' their 'problem lives'. Even in my methods, the same. And what do I see? I see people asleep in front of their TVs. Unable to move, like sleeping dogs. Yes, they have voice in the housing project assessments. But it is a certain kind of voice . . . it is visionless voice. They get to confirm the deficit analysis; all the reports are the same. 'Yes,' they say, 'the reports are true.' What is hitting me right now is how radical the AI message might be. Marx could have said it better: Perhaps the vocabularies of human deficit are the opiates of the masses. People have voice in the analyses—this involvement is what we fought for. But people are not mobilized by it anymore. No, they are asleep. Visionless voice is probably worse than no voice."

Elsewhere we have cautioned, in our own discipline, that it is not so much the problem solving methodologies per se that are of central concern, but the growing sense that we all, throughout the culture, have taken the tools a step further. It is not so much that organizations have problems, they are problems. (See Figure 1.2.) Somewhere a shift of this kind has taken place. Once accepted as fundamental truth about organizations, virtually everything in change-management becomes infused with a deficit consciousness. For example, as French and Bell (1995) define it, "Action-research is both an approach to problem solving—a model or paradigm, and a problem solving process—a series of activities and events" (p. 88). Levinson, in the classic on Organizational Diagnosis (1972, p. 37) likens it to therapy—"Like a therapeutic or teaching relationship it should be an alliance of both parties to

PROBLEM SOLVING	APPRECIATIVE INQUIRY
"Felt Need" Analysis of Causes	Appreciating Valuing the Best of "What Is"
⬇	⬇
Analysis of Causes	Envisioning "What Might Be"
⬇	⬇
Analysis of Possible Solutions	Dialoguing "What Will Be"
⬇	⬇
Action Planning (Treatment)	Envisioning "What Will Be"

Figure 1.2. Problem Solving through Appreciative Inquiry.

discover and resolve these problems...looking for experiences which appear stressful to people. What kinds of occurrences disrupt or disorganize people?" Chris
Argyris, in another classic, asserts: One condition that seems so basic as to be
defined as axiomatic is the generation of valid information...Valid information is
that which describes the factors, plus their interrelationships, that create the problem (1970, pp. 16–17).

Tough questions remain about power and deficit discourse. And of course
there are an array of new innovations in the field, many in this volume, that are
signaling significant departures. So at this point all we want to do is make a call for
reflection and caution, taking a lesson from the wisdom of anthropology — beware
of the solid truths of one's own culture.

Conclusion

To be sure, Appreciative Inquiry (AI) begins an adventure. The urge for and call to
adventure have been sounded by many people and many organizations, and it will
take many more to fully explore the vast vistas that are now appearing on the
horizon.

As said at the outset, we believe we are infants when it comes to our understanding of appreciative processes of knowing and social construction. Yet we are
increasingly clear the world is ready to leap beyond methodologies of deficit based
changes and enter a domain that is life-centric. Organizations, says AI theory, are
centers of human relatedness, first and foremost. And relationships thrive where
there is an appreciative eye—when people see the best in one another, when they
share their dreams and ultimate concerns in affirming ways, and when they are
connected in full voice to create not just new worlds, but better worlds. The velocity and largely informal spread of the appreciative learnings suggests, we believe, a
growing sense of disenchantment with exhausted theories of change, especially
those wedded to vocabularies of human deficit; and a corresponding urge to work
with people, groups, and organizations in more constructive, positive, life-affirming, even spiritual ways. AI, we hope it is being said, is more than a simple 4-D cycle
of discovery, dream, design, and destiny. What is being introduced is something
deeper at the core.

Perhaps our inquiry must become the positive revolution we want to see in the
world. Albert Einstein's words clearly compel: "There are only two ways to live
your life. One is as though nothing is a miracle. The other is as though everything
is a miracle."

Bibliography

Argyris, C. (1970). *Intervention Theory and Methods.* Reading, MA: Addison-Wesley.

Barrett, F. J. (1998). Creativity and Improvisation in Jazz and Organizations: Implications for Organizational Learning. *Organization Science,* 9 (5) 605–622.

Barrett, F. J., and Cooperrider, D. L. (1990). Generative Metaphor Intervention: A New Approach to Intergroup Conflict. *Journal of Applied Behavioral Science,* 26(2), 223–244.

Boulding, K. (1966). *The Image.* Ann Arbor: University of Michigan Press.

Bushe, G. R. (1995). Advances in Appreciative Inquiry as an Organization Development Intervention. *Organization Development Journal,* 13(3), 14–22.

Chin, A.L. (1998). Future Visions. *Journal of Organization and Change Management,* Spring.

Cooperrider, D. L. (1986). Appreciative Inquiry: Toward a methodology for understanding and enhancing organizational innovation. Unpublished Ph.D., Case Western Reserve University, Cleveland.

Cooperrider, D. L. (1996). The "Child" As Agent of Inquiry. *Organization Development Practitioner,* 28(1 and 2), 5–11.

Cooperrider, D. L. (1996). Resources for Getting Appreciative Inquiry Started: An Example OD Proposal. *Organization Development Practitioner,* 28(1 and 2), 23–33.

Cooperrider, D. L., and Srivastva, S. (1987). Appreciative Inquiry in Organizational Life. *Research in Organizational Change and Development,* 1, 129–169.

Curran, M. (1991). Appreciative Inquiry: A Third Wave Approach to OD. *Vision/ Action, December,* 12–14.

French, W., and Bell, C. (1994). *Organization Development: Behavioral Science Interventions for Organization Improvement. (5th ed.).* Englewood Cliffs, NJ: Prentice Hall.

Gergen, K. (1982). *Toward Transformation in Social Knowledge.* New York: Springer-Verlag.

Gergen, K. (1985). The Social Constructionist Movement in Modern Psychology. *American Psychologist,* 40, 266–275.

Gergen, K. (1994). *Realities and Relationships: Soundings in Social Construction.* Cambridge, MA: Harvard University Press.

Goleman, D. (1987, Feb. 3). Research Affirms Power of Positive Thinking. New York Times, pp. 15–19.

Harman, W. W. (1990). Shifting Context for Executive Behavior: Signs of Change and Revaluation. In S. Srivastva, D. L. Cooperrider, and Associates (Eds.), Appreciative Management and Leadership: The Power of Positive Thought and Action in Organizations (1st ed., pp. 37–54). San Francisco, CA: Jossey-Bass Inc.

Head, T. and Sorensen, P., et.al. (1997) Is Appreciative Inquiry the Philosopher's Stone? An unpublished paper, Doctoral Program in Organizational Behavior. Naperville, IL. Benedictine University.

Hubbard, B. M. (1998). Conscious Evolution: Awakening the Power of Our Social Potential. Novato, CA: New World Library (See Chp. 11 on AI).

Isen, A., and Means, B. (1983). The Influence of Positive Affect on Decision Making Strategy. Social Cognition, 2, 18–31.

Jussim, C. (1986). Self-Fulfilling Prophecies: A Theoretical and Integrative Review. Psychological Review, 93(4), 429–445.

Kirschenbaum, D. (1984). Self-Regulation and Sport Psychology: Nurturing and Emerging Symbiosis. Journal of Sport Psychology, 8, 26–34.

Levinson, H. (1972). Organizational Diagnosis. Cambridge, MA: Harvard University Press.

Liebler, C. J. (1997 Summer). Getting Comfortable With Appreciative Inquiry: Questions and Answers. Global Social Innovations, Journal of the GEM Initiative, Case Western Reserve University, 1(2), 30–40.

Ludema, J. (1996). Narrative Inquiry. Unpublished Doctoral Dissertation, Case Western Reserve University, Cleveland, Ohio.

Mirvis, P. H. (1988/89). Organization Development: Part 1-An Evolutionary Perspective. In W. Pasmore and R. Woodman (Eds.), Research in Organizational Change and Development (Vol. 2 and 3). Greenwich, CT: JAI Press, Inc.

Netto, L., and Netto, L. (1998). Journal of the Nutrimental Foods, 1(January), 2.

Ornstein, R., and Sobel, D. (1987). The Healing Brain. New York: Simon and Schuster.

Polak, F. (1973). The Image of the Future. New York: Elsevier.

Porras, J., I. (1991). Organization Development and Transformation. Annual Review of Psychology, 42, 51–78.

Rader, M. (1973). A Modern Book of Esthetics: An Anthology. New York: Holt.

Rainey, M. A. (1996). An Appreciative Inquiry Into the Factors of Culture Continuity During Leadership Transition. Organization Development Practitioner, 28(1 and 2), 34–41.

Schwartz, R. (1986). The Internal Dialogue: On the Assymmetry Between Positive and Negative Coping Thoughts. Cognitive Therapy and Research, 10, 591–605.

Seligman, M. (1990). Learned Optimism. New York: Pocket Books.

Weick, K. (1984). Small Wins: Redefining the Scale of Social Problems. *American Psychologist*, 39(1), 40–49.

White, T. W. (1996). Working In Interesting Times. Vital Speeches Of The Day, LXII(15), 472–474.

Whitney, D., and Cooperrider, D. (1998). The Appreciative Inquiry Summit: Overview and Applications. *Employment Relations Today*, Summer, 17–28.

Whitney, D., and Schau, C. (1998). Appreciative Inquiry: An Innovative Process for Organization Change. Employment Relations Today,(Spring)11–21.

Chapter 2

POSITIVE IMAGE, POSITIVE ACTION: THE AFFIRMATIVE BASIS OF ORGANIZING

David L. Cooperrider
Case Western Reserve University

> Be not afraid of life. Believe that life is worth living, and your belief will
> help you create the fact. —William James.

> We can easily forgive a child who is afraid of the dark.
> The real tragedy of life is when men are afraid of the light. —Plato.

Modern management thought was born proclaiming that organizations are the triumph of the human imagination. As made and imaged, organizations are products of human imagination. As made and imagined, organizations are products of human interaction and mind rather than some blind expression of an underlying natural order (McGregor, 1960; Berger and Luckmann, 1967; Pfeffer, 1981; Gergen, 1982; Srivastva and Associates, 1983; Schein, 1985; Unger, 1987). Deceptively simple yet so entirely radical in implication, this insight is still shattering many beliefs—one of which is the longstanding conviction that bureaucracy, oligarchy, and other forms of hierarchical domination are inevitable. Today we know that this simply is not true.

Recognizing the symbolic and socially constructed nature of the human universe, we now find new legitimacy for the mounting wave of sociocognitive and sociocultural research, all of which is converging around one essential and empowering thesis: that there is little about collective action or organization development that is preprogrammed, unilaterally determined, or stimulus bound in any direct physical or material way. Seemingly immutable ideas about people and organizations are being directly challenged and transformed on an unprecedented scale. Indeed, as we move into a postmodern global society we are breaking out of our parochial perspectives and are recognizing that organizations in all societies exist in a wide array of types and species and function within a dynamic spectrum of beliefs and lifestyles. And according to the social constructionist viewpoint, the possibilities are infinite.

S. Srivastva and D. L. Cooperrider and Associates (Eds.) (1990) *Executive Appreciation and Leadership: 91–125*. San Francisco: Jossey-Bass.

Interestingly, there is an important parallel to this whole area of thought that has grown out of the neurosciences and studies of cognition and mind–brain interaction. The "consciousness revolution" of the 1970s is well documented and represents, argues Nobel Laureate Roger Sperry (1988), more than a mere Zeitgeist phenomenon; it represents a profound conceptual shift to a different form of causal determinism. According to the mentalist paradigm, mind can no longer be considered the opposite of matter. Mental phenomena, this paradigm contends, must be recognized as being at the top of the brain's "causal control hierarchy" whereby, after millenniums of evolution, the mind has been given primacy over bioevolutionary (Darwinian) controls that determine what human systems are and can become. In direct contradiction to materialist and behaviorist doctrine, where everything is supposed to be governed from below upward through microdeterminist stimuli and physiochemical forces, the new mentalist view gives subjective mental phenomena a causal role in brain processing and thereby a new legitimacy in science as an autonomous explanatory construct. Future reality, in this view, is permeable, emergent, and open to the mind's causal influence; that is, reality is conditioned, reconstructed, and often profoundly created through our anticipatory images, values, plans, intentions, beliefs, and the like. Macrodeterminisim or the theory of downward causation is a scheme, asserts Sperry, that idealizes ideas and ideals over chemical interactions, nerve impulse traffic and DNA. It is a brain model in which conscious, mental, and psychic forces are recognized as the crowing achievement of some 500 million years or more of evolution.

The impetus for the present contribution grows from the exciting challenge that is implicitly if not explicitly posed by the social constructionist and mentalist paradigms: that to a far greater extent than is normally acknowledged, we human beings create our own realities through symbolic and mental processes and that because of this, consciousness evolution of the future is a human option. Taking this challenge—that of a future-creating mental activism—one step further, the thesis explored in this paper is that the artful creation of positive imagery on a collective basis may well be the most prolific activity that individuals and organizations can engage in if their aim is to help bring to fruition a positive and humanly significant future. Stated more boldly a *New York Times* headline recently apprised the public that "Research Affirms Power of Positive Thinking" (Goleman, 1987, p. 15). Implied in the popular news release and the scholarly research that we will soon sample is the intriguing suggestion that human systems are largely *heliotropic* in character, meaning that they exhibit an observable and largely automatic tendency to evolve in the direction of positive anticipatory images of the future. What I will argue is that just as plants of many varieties exhibit a tendency to grow in the direction of sunlight (symbolized by the Greek god Helios), there is an analogous process going on in all human systems.

As a whole this essay is intended to serve as an invitation to broadly consider a number of questions: What is the relationship between positive imagery and positive action? More specifically, what are the common processes, pathways, or global patterns whereby mental phenomena attract or even cause those actions that bring about movement toward an ideal? Where do positive images of some unknown and neutral future come from in the first place? Could it be that organizations are in fact affirmative systems, governed and maintained by positive projections about what the organization is, how it will function, and what it might become? If so, what are the implications for management? Is it true that the central executive task in a postbureaucratic society is to nourish the *appreciative* soil from which affirmative projections grow, branch off, evolve, and become collective projections?

To set the stage for our discourse, the first section will begin with a general introduction to the concept of imagery. The second will look specifically at the relationship between positive imagery and positive action by reviewing recent works from diverse areas of study—medicine, cognitive psychology, cultural sociology, and athletics. While I am careful not to suggest that the studies sampled make anything close to an exhaustive case, I do submit, nevertheless, that the convergence of insight, across disciples, represent an exciting step forward in our understandings of the intricate pathways that link mind and practice. Finally, in the third section, I will discuss how such knowledge from diverse quarters holds a thread of continuity that has broad relevance for understanding organizations. In particular, I will offer a set of eight propositions about the *affirmative basis of organizing*. These propositions are provided for discussion, elaboration, and active experimentation and converge around three basic conclusions: (1) Organizations are products of the affirmative mind; (2) when beset with repetitive difficulties or problems, organizations need less fixing, less problem solving, and more reaffirmation—or more precisely, more *appreciation*; (3) the primary executive vocation in a postbureaucratic era is to nourish the appreciative soil from which new and better guiding images grow on a collective and dynamic basis.

Imagery: An Introduction

Throughout the ages and from a diversity of perspectives, the image has been considered a powerful agent in the guidance and determination of action:

A vivid imagination compels the whole body to obey it.
—Aristotle (in Sheikh, 1984, p. 5).

One of the basic theorems of the theory of image is that it is the image which in fact determines what might be called the current behavior of any organism or organization. The image acts as a field. The behavior consists in gravitating toward the most highly valued part of the world.
—Kenneth Boulding (1966, p. 155).

Mental anticipation now pulls the future into the present and reverses the direction of causality.   —Erich Jantsch (1980, p. 14).

Man is a being who, being in the world, is ever ahead of himself, caught up in bringing things alive with his projection. . . . Whatever comes to light owes its presence to the fact that man has provided the overall imaginative sunlight for viewing.   —Edward Murray (1986, p. 64).

To the empowering principle that people can withhold legitimacy, and thus change the world, we now add another. By deliberately changing the internal image of reality, people can change the world.
                                                         —Willis Harman (1988, p. 1).

Imagination is more important than knowledge.
                                         —Albert Einstein (in Sheikh, 1984, p. 5).

It is clear that images are operative virtually everywhere: Soviet and U.S. diplomats create strategies on the basis of images; Theory X managers construct management structures that reflect the pictures they hold of subordinates; days or minutes before a public speech we all feel the tension or anxiety that accompanies our anticipatory viewing of the audience; we all hold self-images, images of our race, profession, nation, and cultural belief systems; and we have images of our own potential as well as the potential of others. Fundamentally, too, it can be argued that every organization, product, or innovative service first started as a wild but not idle dream and that *anticipatory realities* are what make collectivities click. (This is why we still experience King, Jr's "I Have a Dream" and sometimes find ourselves enlivened through the images associated with the mere mention of such figures as John F. Kennedy, Gandhi, Winston Churchill, Buddha, or Christ.)

Given the central and pervasive role of the image in relation to action, it is not surprising that research on the workings of the image has risen to be "one of the hottest topics in cognitive science" (Block, 1981, p. 1). Theorists disagree over definitions and argue whether images are direct encoding of perceptual experience (Pavid, 1971), are an artifact of the propositional structuring of reality (Pylyshyn, 1973), represent the sensory system par excellence that undergirds and constitutes virtually every area of cognitive processing, are primarily eidetic or visual (Ashen, 1977), or represent constructive or reconstructive process (Kosslyn, 1980). But in spite of the largely technical differences, Richardson (1969, pp. 2–3) seems to have provided adequate synthesis of a number of competing views in his often-quoted definition of the image as quasi-sensory, stimulus-independent representative experience: "Mental imagery refers to (1) all those quasi-sensory or quasi-perceptual experiences of which (2) we are self consciously aware and which (3) exist for us in the absence of those stimulus conditions that are know to reproduce their sensory or perceptual counterparts, and which (4) may be expected to have different consequences."

In subsequent work, Richardson (1983) retracts the fourth criterion; between 1969 and 1983 there was simply too much new evidence showing that self-initiated imagery can and often does have consequences, many of them physiological, that are indistinguishable from their genuine sensory counterparts. Merely an anticipatory image, for example, of a hostile encounter can raise one's blood pressure as much as the encounter itself. Similarly, numerous new studies now show that consciously constructed images can lead directly to such things as blood glucose increases, increased gastric acid secretion, blister formation, and changes in skin temperature and pupillary size. In an example closer to home, Richardson (1983, p. 15) suggests that "it suffices to remind the reader of what every schoolboy (or girl) knows. Clear and unmistakable physiological consequences follow from absorption in a favorite sexual fantasy." Mind and body are indeed a unified interdependent system.

Perhaps most important, as the above begins to make clear, it is the time dimension of the future—what Harry Stack Sullivan (1947) referred to as "anticipatory reality"—that acts as a prepotent force in the dynamic of all images (for a decision theory counterpart to this view, see Mitchell, Rediker, and Beach, 1986; Polak, 1973). The recognition that every social action somehow involves anticipation of the future, in the sense that it involves a reflexive look-forward-to and backward-from, has been analyzed by Alfred Schultz (1967) and Karl Weick (1976). Similarly, in Heidegger's brilliant formulation it is our nature not only to be thrown into existence (*Geworfenheil*) but to always be ahead of ourselves in the world, to be engaged in the unfolding of projected realities; all action, according to Heidegger, has the nature of a project (Heidegger refers to this as *Entwurf*, the continuous projecting ahead of a design or a blueprint). Much like a movie projection on a screen, human systems are forever projecting ahead of themselves a horizon of expectation that brings the future powerfully into the present as a causal agent.

Recent Works on the Positive Image–Positive Action Relationship

What all this suggests, of course, is that the power of positive imagery is not just some popular illusion or wish but is arguably a key factor in every action. To illustrate the heliotropic propensity in human systems at several levels of functioning I will now turn to six areas of research as example—placebo, Pygmalion, positive emotion, internal dialogue, cultural vitality, and metacognitive competence.

Positive Imagery, Medicine, and the Placebo

The placebo response is a fascinating and complex process in which projected images, as reflected in positive belief in the efficacy of a remedy, ignite a healing response that can be every bit as powerful as conventional therapy. Though the placebo phenomenon has been controversial for some twenty years, most of the medical profession now accepts as genuine, the fact that anywhere from one-third to two-thirds of all patients will show marked physiological and emotional improvement in symptoms simply by believing they are given an effective treatment, even when that treatment is just a sugar pill or some other inert substance (Beecher, 1955; White, Tursky, and Schwartz, 1985).

Numerous carefully controlled studies indicate that the placebo can provide relief of symptoms in postoperative-wound pain, seasickness, headaches, angina, asthma, obesity, blood pressure, ulcers, and many other problems. In fact, researchers are now convinced that no system of the body is exempt from the placebo effect and that it is operative in virtually every healing encounter. Even more intriguing, the placebo is sometimes even more potent than typically expected drug effects: "Consider a series of experiments with a woman suffering from severe nausea and vomiting. Nothing the doctors gave her seemed to help. Objective measurement of her gastric contractions showed a disrupted pattern consistent with the severe nausea she reported. The doctors then offered her a 'new extremely powerful wonder drug' which would, they said, unquestionably cure her nausea. Within twenty minutes of taking this new drug, her nausea disappeared, and the same objective gastric tests now read normal. The drug which was given was not, of course, a new drug designed to relieve nausea. It was syrup of ipecac, which is generally used to induce vomiting, In this case, the placebo effect associated with the suggestion that the drug would relieve vomiting was powerful enough to counteract and direct an opposite pharmacological action of the drug itself" (Ornstein and Sobel, 1987, p. 79).

According to Norman Cousins, now a faculty member at the UCLA School of Medicine, and understanding of the way the placebo works may be one of the most significant developments in medicine in the twentieth century. Writing in *Human Options* (1981), Cousins suggests that beyond the central nervous system, the hormonal system, and the immune system, there are two other systems that have conventionally been overlooked but that need to be recognized as essential to the proper functioning of the human being: the healing and the belief system. Cousins (1983, p. 203) argues that the two work together: "The healing system is the way the body mobilizes all its resources to combat disease. The belief system is often the activator of the healing system."

Using himself as a living laboratory, Cousins (1983, p. 44) has movingly described how the management of his own anticipatory reality allowed him to overcome a life-threatening illness that specialists did not believe to be reversible and then, some years later, to again apply the same mental processes in his recovery from an acute heart attack: "What were the basic ideas involved in that recovery? The newspaper accounts had made it appear that I had laughed my way out of a serious illness. Careful readers of my book, however, knew that laughter was just a metaphor. . . . Hope, faith, love, will to live, cheerfulness, humor, creativity, playfulness, confidence, *great expectations*—all these, I believed, had therapeutic value."

In the end, argues Cousins, the greatest value of the placebo is that it tells us that indeed positive imagery can and often does awaken the body to its own self-healing powers. Research in many areas now confirms this view and shows that the placebo responses are neither mystical nor inconsequential and that ultimately mental and psychophysiological responses may be mediated through more than fifty different neuropeptide molecular messengers linking the endocrine, autonomic, and central nervous systems (White, Tursky, and Schwartz, 1985). While the complex mind-body pathways are far from being resolved, there is one area of clear agreement: Positive changes in anticipatory reality through suggestion and belief play a central role in all placebo responses. As Jaffe and Bresler (1980, pp. 260–261) note, the placebo "Illustrates another important therapeutic use of imagery, namely, the use of positive future images to activate positive physical changes. Imagining a positive future outcome is an important technique for countering initial negative images, beliefs, and expectations a patient may have. In essence it transforms a negative placebo effect into a positive one. . . . The power of positive suggestion plants a seed which redirects the mind—and through the mind, the body—toward a positive goal."

Before moving on, there is one other perhaps surprising factor that adds significantly to the patient's placebo response—the expectancy or anticipatory reality of the physician. Placebo effects are strongest, it appears, when belief in the efficacy of the treatment is shared among a group (O'Regan, 1983). This then raises a whole new set of questions concerning not only the individual but the interpersonal nature of the positive image-positive action relationship.

Pygmalion and the Positive Construction of the Other

In effect, the positive image may well be the sine qua non of human development, as we now explore in the Pygmalion dynamic. As a special case of the self-fulfilling prophesy, Pygmalion reminds us that from the moment of birth we each exist within a complex and dynamic field of images and expectations, a vast share of which are projected onto us through an omnipresent environment of others.

In the classic Pygmalion study, teachers are led to believe on the basis of "credible" information that some of their students possess exceptionally high potential while others do not. In other words, the teachers are led, on the basis of some expert opinion, to hold a positive image (PI) or expectancy of some students and a negative image (NI) or expectancy of others. Unknown to the teachers, however, is the fact that the so-called high-potential students were selected at random; in objective terms, all student groupings were equivalent in potential and are merely dubbed as high, regular, or low potential. Then, as the experiment unfolds, differences quickly emerge, not on the basis of any innate intelligence factor or some other predisposition but solely on the basis of the manipulated expectancy of the teacher. Over time, subtle changes among students evolve into clear differences as the high-PI students begin to significantly overshadow all others in actual achievement. Over the last twenty years there have been literally hundreds of empirical studies conducted on this phenomenon, attesting both to its continuing theoretical and to its practical importance (Jussim, 1986; see Rosenthal and Rubin, 1978, for an analysis of over 300 studies).

One of the remarkable things about Pygmalion is that it shows us how essentially modifiable the human self is in relation to the mental projections of others. Indeed, not only do performance levels change, but so do more deeply rooted "stable" self-conceptions (Parsons and others, 1982). Furthermore, significant Pygmalion effects have been experimentally generated in as little time as fifteen minutes (King, 1971) and have the apparent capacity to transform the course of a lifetime (Cooper and Good, 1983). (I wonder how many researchers on this subject would volunteer their own children to be part of a negatively induced expectancy grouping?) Specific to the classroom, the correlation between teacher expectation and student achievement is higher than almost any predictive IQ or achievement measure, ranging in numerous studies from correlations of .5 all the way to an almost perfect (Brophy and Good, 1974; Crano and Mellon, 1978; Hymphreys and Stubbs, 1977). Likewise, in one of the earliest organizational examinations of this phenomenon, Eden and Shani (1982) reported that some 75 percent of the variance in achievement among military trainees could be explained completely on the basis of induced positive expectation on the part of those in positions of authority.

Obviously the promise of Pygmalion as a source of human development depends more on the enactment of positive rather than negative interpersonal expectancy. But how does the positive dynamic work and why?

A summary of the three stages of the positive Pygmalion dynamic is presented in Figure 2.1. In the first phase of the model, positive images of the other are formed through any number of means—for example, stereotypes, reputation, hearsay, objective measures, early performances, and naive prediction processes. As interactions occur over time, positive images begin to take shape and consist not only of *prophesies* but also tend to become elaborated by one's sense of its other *possibilities* as well as one's sense of "what should be," or *normative valuations*. Taken together the prophesies, possibilities, and normative valuations combine to create a broad brushstroke picture of interpersonal expectancy that has its pervasive effect through two primary mediators—expectancy-consistent cognition and expectancy-consistent treatment.

Considerable evidence, for example, indicates that a positive image of another serves as a powerful cognitive tuning device that appears to trigger in the perceiver an increased capacity to (1) perceive the successes of another (Deaux and Ernswiller, 1974), (2) access from memory the positive rather than negative aspects of the other (Hastie and Kumar, 1979), and (3) perceive ambiguous situations for their positive rather than negative possibilities (Darley and Gross, 1983).

While often spoken about in pejorative ways as cognitive bias or distortion ("vital lies," to use Goleman's popular term), it is quite possible that this affirmative capacity to cognitively tune into the most positive aspects of another human being is in fact a remarkable human gift; it is not merely an aberration distorting some "given" reality but is a creative agent in the construction of reality. We see what our images make us capable of seeing. And affirmative cognition, as we will later highlight in our discussion of positive self-monitoring, is a unique and powerful competency that owes its existence to the dynamic workings of the positive image.

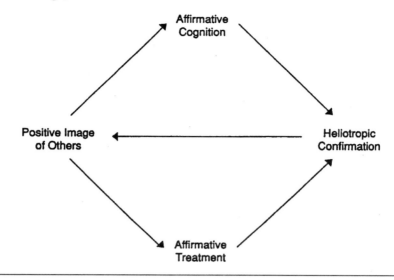

Figure 2.1. The Positive Pygmalion Dynamic (adapted from Jussim, 1986).

The key point is that all of our cognitive capacities—perception, memory, learning—are cued and shaped by the images projected through our expectancies. We see what our imaginative horizon allows us to see. And because "seeing is believing," our acts often take on a whole new tone and character depending on the strength, vitality, and force of a given image. The second consequence of the positive image of the other, therefore, is that it supports differential behavioral treatment in a number of systematic ways.

For example, it has been shown, both in the field and the laboratory, that teachers who hold extremely positive images of their students tend to provide those students with (1) increased emotional support in comparison to others (Rist, 1970; Rubovitz and Maeher, 1973); (2) clearer, more immediate, and more positive feedback around effect and performance (Weinstein, 1976; Cooper, 1979); and (3) better opportunities to perform and learn more challenging materials (Brophy and Good, 1974; Swann and Snyder, 1980).

Finally, in the third stage of the model, people begin to respond to the positive images that others have of them. When mediated by cognitive, affective, and motivational factors, according to Jussim (1986), heliotropic acts are initiated on the basis of increased effort, persistence, attention, participation, and cooperation, so that ultimately, high PIs often perform at levels superior to those projected with low-expectancy images. Research also shows that such effects tend to be long lasting, especially when the Pygmalion dynamic becomes institutionalized. High-PI students, for example, when assigned to the higher academic tracks, are virtually never moved to a lower track (the same is also true for negative-expectancy students, according to Brophy and Good's 1974 review of the "near permanence" of tracking).

The greatest value of the Pygmalion research is that it begins to provide empirical understanding of the relational pathways of the positive image-positive action dynamic and of the transactional basis of the human self. To understand the self as a symbolic social creation is to recognize—as George Herbert Mead, John Dewey, George Simmel, Lev Vygotsky, Martin Buber, and many others have argued—that human beings are essentially modifiable, are open to new development, and are products of the human imagination and mind. We are each made and imagined in the eyes of one another. There is an utter inseparability of the individual from the social context and history of the projective process. And positive interpersonal imagery, the research now shows, accomplishes its work very concretely. Like the placebo response discussed earlier, it appears that the positive image plants a seed that redirects the mind of the perceiver to think about and see the other with affirmative eyes.

Positive Affect and Learned Helpfulness

While often talked about in cognitive terms, one of the core features of imagery is that it integrates cognition and affect becomes a catalytic force through its sentiment-evoking quality. In many therapies, for example, it is well established that focusing on images often elicits strong emotional reactions; whereas verbal mental processes are linear, the image provides simultaneous representation, making it possible to vicariously experience that which is held in the imagination (Sheikh and Panagiotou, 1975).

So what about the relation between positive emotion—delight, compassion, joy, love, happiness, passion, and so on—and positive action? To what extent is it the affective side of the positive image that generates and sustains heliotropic movement so often seen in human systems? While still in the formative stages, early results on this issue are making clear that there is indeed a unique psychophysiology of positive emotion (as Norman Cousins has argued) and that individually as well as collectively, positive emotion may well be the pivotal factor determining the heliotropic potential of images of the future.

This line of research is partly predicated on knowledge growing out of studies of negative affectivity. In one of the most hotly pursued lines of research of the last decade, investigators are now convinced of the reciprocal connections between high negative affectivity and (1) experiences of life stress; (2) deficiency cognition; (3) the phenomenon of "learned helplessness"; (4) the development of depression; (5) the breakdown of social bonds; and (6) the triggering of possible physiological responses like the depletion of brain catecholamine, the release of corticosteroids, the suppression of immune functioning, and ultimately the development of disease (Watson and Clark, 1984; Seligman, 1975; Brewin, 1985; Peterson and Seligman, 1984; Beck, 1967; Schultz, 1984; Ley and Freeman, 1984). Table 2.1, for example, illustrates the linkage between negative affect and disease. In spite of diversity of subjects, methods, and measures, a salient pattern emerges: A host of diseases, especially various forms of cancer, are associated with chronic and persistent nega-

TABLE 2.1. The Relationship Between Negative Affect and Disease: Conclusions from 28 Papers on Affect and Disease (adapted from Ley and Freeman, 1984, p. 57).

Disease	Affective State
Cancer	Depression
Cancer	Loss of hope
Leukemia	Depression, anxiety
Leukemia	Loss of significant other
Neoplasm	Hopelessness, despair
Cancer	Self-directed aggression
Cancer	Depression
Cancer	Hopelessness
Cancer	Depression, hostility
Lung cancer	Rigidity, repression, hostility, despair
Cancer	Decreased depression
Cancer	Lethargy, depression
Cancer	Affective disorder
Cancer	Affective disorder
Cancer	Affective disorder
Cancer	Repression of anger
'Physical illness'	Depression
Pernicious anemia	Depression
Hay fever	Helplessness
Asthma	Helplessness
Tuberculosis	Poor coping with stress
Coronary heart disease	High and frustrated aspiration
Coronary bypass, mortality	Hopelessness, depression
Psychosomatic illness	Hostility, depression, frustration, anxiety, helplessness
Various illnesses	Helplessness, hopelessness

tive images, expressed and embodied in feelings of helplessness and hopelessness. As one physician from Yale concludes, "cancer is despair experienced at the cellular level" (Siegel, 1986).

Probably the one finding that emerges most conclusively on the other side of the ledger is that while negative affectivity is notably linked to the phenomenon of learned helplessness, positive affect is intimately connected with *social helpfulness*. Somehow positive affect draws us out of ourselves, pulls us away from self-oriented preoccupation, enlarges our focus on the potential good in the world, increases feelings of solidarity with others, and propels us to act in more altruistic and prosocial ways (see Brief and Motowildo, 1986, for a review of altruism and its implications for management).

According to the work of Alice Isen and her colleagues, mood, cognition, and action form an inseparable triad and tend to create feedback loops of amplifying intensity. Positive affect, the evidence indicates, generates superior recall or access to pleasant memories (Isen, Shalker, Clark, and Karp, 1978); helps create a heightened sense of optimism toward the future (Isen and Shalker, 1982); cues a person to think about positive things (Rosenhan, Salovey, and Hargis, 1981); and, as a result, predisposes people toward acts that would likely support continued positive affect, like the prosocial action of helping others (Cunningham, Steinberg, and Grev, 1980; Isen and Levin, 1972; Isen, Shalker, Clark and Karp, 1978). In addition, positive affect has been associated with (1) increased capacity for creative problems solving (Isen, 1984); (2) more effective decision making and judgment (Isen and Means, 1983); (3) optimism and increased learning capacity—in particular, a sharpened capacity for perceiving and understanding mood-congruent or positive things (Bower, 1981; Clark and Isen, 1982).

In perhaps the most intriguing extension of this line of thought, Harvard's David McClelland has hypothesized a reinforcing set of dynamics between positive imagery, positive affect, prosocial action, and improved immune functioning. McClelland has even gone so far as to argue that merely watching an altruistic act would be good for the observer. He may be right.

For example, in one of McClelland's experiments, students were shown a film of Mother Theresa, a Nobel Peace Prize recipient, attending to the sick and dying poor in Calcutta. During the film, measures were taken of the student's immune functioning as defined by increases in salivary immunogobulin A (IgA—a measure of defense against respiratory infection and viral disease). In all cases, it was found that IgA concentrations immediately increased during the film and for some observers remained elevated for a period of up to one hour afterward.

It should be emphasized that these findings are controversial and that we are clearly in our infancy when it comes to really understanding the role of positive emotion as it relates to individual and collective well-being. The most important fact, however, is that studies like these are even being done at all. They represent a vital shift in research attention across a whole series of disciplines and reflect a change in the mood and spirit of our times. For example, as Brendan O'Regan (1983, p. 3) observes in relation to the field of psychoneuroimmunology, "We will no longer be focused on only the reduction of symptoms or the removal of something negative, and instead begin to understand health and well-being as the presence of something positive. It [the focus on the psychophysiology of positive emotion] may well be the first step in the development of what might be called an affirmative science . . . a science for humankind."

The Off-Balance Internal Dialogue

One of the more fascinating refinements of the notion of positive imagery comes from Robert Schwart's development of a cognitive ethology: the study within human systems of the content, function, and structure of the internal dialogue. Here the image is conceptualized as self-talk. Traced back to Plato and Socrates, cognition is seen as discourse that the mind carries on with itself. As in James's stream of consciousness, it is argued that all human systems exhibit a continuing "cinematographic-show of visual imagery" (Ryle, 1949) or an ongoing "inner newsreel" (Becker, 1971) that is best understood in the notion of inner dialogue.

The inner dialogue of any system—individual, group, organization, society—can be understood, argues Schwartz (1986), by categorizing its contents at the highest level of abstraction with respect to its functional role in achieving a specified aim. It is illustrated, for example, from a study of stressful medical procedure, that people may have thoughts that either impede the aim of the clinical intervention ("the catheter might break and stick in my heart"—negative image) or conversely may facilitate the goals of the care ("this procedure may save my life"—positive image). Hence, the inner dialogue functions as an inner dialectic between positive and negative adaptive statements, and one's guiding imagery is presumably an outcome of such an inner dialectic.

A whole series of recent studies have looked at this process, and results suggest a clear and definitive pattern of difference in the cognitive ecology of "functional" (healthy) versus "dysfunctional" (unhealthy) groups.

Table 2.2 presents data showing the ratios of positive to negative image statements for functional and dysfunctional groups across a series of seven independent studies. In all cases, there is a definite *imbalance* in the direction of positive imagery for those identified as more psychologically or socially functional. As can be seen, the functional groups are characterized by approximately a 1.7 : 1 ratio of positive to negative images. Mildly dysfunctional groups ("high" dysfunction was not studied) demonstrate equal frequencies, a balanced 1 : 1 internal dialogue.

Obviously, the sheer quantification of cognition has certain weaknesses. For one thing, it is clear that just one idea or image can transform the entire gestalt of a thousand others. But the findings do have meaning, especially when linked to other studies showing that images of hope or hopelessness can affect the body's innate healing system, its immune functioning, and other neurochemical processes. Especially disturbing are reports indicating that many of our children today are growing up in family settings where as much as 90 percent of the home's internal dialogue is negative, that is, what not to do, how bad things are, what was done wrong, who is to blame (Fritz, 1984).

But it is not just our children. In his powerful *Critique of Cynical Reason*, Peter Sloterdijk (1987) observes that the whole of postmodern society is living within an internal dialogue or cognitive environment of a universal, diffuse cynicism. As a predominant mindset of the post-1960s era, Sloterdijk takes the cynic not as an exception but rather as the average social character. It is argued that at both the personal and institutional levels, throughout our society there is a widespread disturbance of vitality, a bleakening of the life feeling, a farewell to defeated idealisms, and a sense of paralyzing resentment. Sociologically, Sloterdijk contends, today's cynicism is bureaucratic and it has become the predominant way of seeing things; psychologically, the modernist character is said to be a borderline melancholic, one who is able to keep the symptoms of depression under control and keep up appearances at both home and work. Our internal dialogue, as a society, Sloterdijk laments, has become more and more morose, and nowhere, he argues (1987, p. 12), is this better exemplified than in the halls of academia: "The scenery of the critical intelligensia is . . . populated by aggressive and depressive moralists, problematists, 'problemholics,' and soft rigorists whose existential stimulus is no."

TABLE 2.2. Ratios of Positive and Negative Thoughts for Functional and Dysfunctional Groups Across Seven Independent Studies (reported in Schwartz, 1986).

Focus of Study	Cognitive assessment	Functional M			Dysfunctional M		
		Positive	Negative	Ratio	Positive	Negative	Ratio
Assertiveness							
1. High vs. low assertive	Inventory/ASST[a]	57.0	33.0	1.7:1	48.0	51.0	1:1.1
2. High vs. low assertive	Inventory/ASST	59.0	35.0	1.7:1	48.0	51.0	1:1.1
3. High vs. low assertive	Inventory/ASST-R[b]	41.8	35.8	1.8:1	38.0	33.2	1.1:1
Social anxiety							
4. High vs. low socially anxious	Inventory/SISST[c]	54.9	33.0	1.7:1	42.7	47.3	1:1.1
Sample 2: Females and males combined							
5. High vs. low socially anxious	Production/thought listening[d]	1.6	1.2	1.3:1	1.5	2.0	1:1.3
Test anxiety							
6. High vs. low test-anxious	Production/talking aloud	67.3	32.0	2.1:1	45.0	61.3	1:1.4
Self-seteem							
7. High vs. low self-esteem	Production/though sampling	2.4	1.5	1.6:1	2.3	2.0	1.2:1
Mean ratio			1.70:1			1:1.14	

[a]Assertiveness Self-Statement Test.
[b]ASST-Revised generalizes to a broader range of assertive situations.
[c]Social Interaction Self-Statement Test.
[d]Scores averaged across high and low anonymity conditions.

Whether one agrees with Sloterdijk or not, it is important to recognize that all human systems are conditioned by their internal dialogue. Our minds are bathed within any number of cognitive environments—family, school, church, play, and even the environments created by our research methods and problem-solving technologies—that provide cues to the ways we perceive, experience, and imagine reality.

So the question must therefore be asked, What kinds of cognitive environments maximize the "human possible"? What kinds of cognitive ecologies are we generating, and why? Can cognitive ecologies be developed, transformed, or enhanced? And what kinds of cognitive ecologies do we want?

The Positive Image as a Dynamic Force in Culture

As various scholars (for instance, Markley, 1976; Morgan, 1987) have noted, the underlying images held by a civilization or culture have an enormous influence on its fate. Ethical values such as "good" or "bad" have little force, except on an abstract level, but if those values emerge in the form of an image (for example, good = St. George, or bad = the Dragon), they suddenly become a power shaping the consciousness of masses of people (Broms and Gahmberg, 1983). Behind every culture there is a nucleus of images—the "Golden Age," "child of God," "Enlightenment," "Thousand-Year Reign of Christ," or "New Zion"—and this nucleus is able to produce countless variations around the same theme.

In his sweeping study of Western civilization, the Dutch sociologist Fred Polak (1973) argues essentially the same point concerning the heliotropic propensity of the positive image. For him (1973, p. 19), the positive image of the future is the single most important dynamic and explanatory variable for understanding cultural evolution: "Any student of the rise and fall of cultures cannot fail to be impressed by the role played in this historical succession of the future. *The rise and fall of images of the future precedes or accompanies the rise and fall of cultures.* As long as a society's image is positive and flourishing, the flower of culture is in full bloom. Once the image begins to decay and lose its vitality, however, the culture does not long survive."

For Polak, the primary question then is not how to explain the growth and decay of cultures, but how to explain the successful emergence or decay of positive images. Furthermore, he asks, how do the successive waves of optimism and pessimism or cynicism and trust regarding the images fit into the cultural framework and its accompanying dynamics? His conclusions, among others, include:

1. Positive images emerge in contexts of "influence-optimism" (belief in an open and influenceable future) and an atmosphere that values creative imagination mixed with philosophical questioning, a rich emotional life, and freedom of speech and fantasy.

2. The force that drives the image is only part cognitive or intellectual; a much greater part is emotional, esthetic, and spiritual.

3. The potential strength of a culture could actually be measured by the intensity, energy, and belief in its images of the future.

4. The image of the future not only acts as a barometer but actively promotes cognition and choice and in effect becomes self-fulfilling because it is self-propelling.

5. When a culture's utopian aspirations die out, the culture dies: "where there is no vision, the people perish" (Proverbs 29:18). Of special note here, anthropologists have shown that certain tribes have actually given up and allowed themselves to die when their images of the future have become too bleak. Ernest Becker (1971) notes the depopulation of Melanasia earlier in this century as well as the loss of interest by the Marquesan Islanders in having children. In the second case it appears that the islanders simply gave up when, in the face of inroads from white traders and missionaries, everything that gave them hope and a sense of value was eroded.

On this final point, Polak was intrigued with the following conclusion: Almost without exception, everything society has considered a social advance has been prefigured first in some utopian writing. For example Plato's *Politeia* opened the way, shows Polak, for a series of projections that then, via Thomas More's *Utopia*, had an impact on England's domestic and foreign policy. Similarly, Harrington's *Oceana* had immediate impact on France through the work of Abbé Sieyès, who used Harrington's model as a framework for his *Constitution de l'An VII* (about 1789). Later, these themes were "eagerly absorbed" by John Adams and Thomas Jefferson and emerged in a variety of American political institutions, not to mention the Declaration of Independence. While the word *utopia* has, in our society, often been a derogatory term, the historical analysis shows utopia to be, in Polak's words (1973, p. 138) "a powerhouse": "Scientific management, full employment, and social security were all once figments of a utopia-writer's imagination. So were parliamentary democracy, universal suffrage, planning, and the trade union movement. The tremendous concern for child-rearing and universal education, for eugenics, and for garden cities all emanated from the utopia. The utopia stood for the emancipation of women long before the existence of the feminist movement. All the concepts concerning labor, from the length of the work week to profit sharing (and sociotechnical systems design and QWL), are found in utopia. Thanks to the utopists, the twentieth century did not catch humanity totally unprepared."

Metacognition and Conscious Evolution of Positive Images

To the extent that the heliotropic hypothesis has some validity—that human systems have an observable tendency to macrodeterministically evolve in the direction of those "positive" images that are the brightest and boldest, most illuminating and promising—questions of volition and free agency come to the fore. Is it possible to create our own future-determining imagery? Is it possible to develop our metacognitive capacity and thereby choose between positive and negative ways of construing the world? If so, with what result? Is the quest for affirmative competence—the capacity to project and affirm an ideal image as if it is already so—a realistic aim or merely a romantic distraction? More important, is it possible to develop the affirmative competence of a large collectives, that is, of groups, organizations, or whole societies affirming a positive future together?

With the exception of the last question (there just has not been enough research here), most of the available evidence suggests quite clearly that affirmative competence can be learned, developed, and honed through experience, disciplined practice, and formal training.

Reviews on this topic, for example, are available in the areas of athletics and imagery, psychotherapy and imagery, imagery and healing, hypnosis and imagery, imagery and sexual functioning, and others related to overall metacognitive capacity (see Sheikh, 1983, for ten excellent reviews on these subjects).

In the case of athletics, as just one example, imagery techniques are fast becoming an important part of all successful training. In *Superlearning*, Ostrander (1979) discusses the mental methods used by Soviet and Eastern European athletes who have had such success in the Olympics in recent decades. Similarly, Jack Nicklaus's book *Golf My Way* (1974) offers a compendium of mental exercises to sharpen the affirmative function. For Nicklaus there is an important distinction to be made between a negative affirmation (for example, an image that says "don't hit it into the trees") and a positive affirmation (for instance, "I'm going to hit it right down the middle of the fairway"). Here again we find that the whole body, just like a whole culture, responds to what the mind imagines as possible. The important lesson, according to Nicklaus, is that affirmative competence can be acquired through discipline and practice and that such competence may be every bit as important to one's game as sheer physical capability.

Recent experimental evidence confirms this view and suggests something more: It is quite possible that the best athletes are as successful as they are because of a highly developed metacognitive capacity of differential self-monitoring. In brief, this involves being able to systematically observe and analyze successful performances (positive self-monitoring) or unsuccessful performances (negative self-monitoring) and to be able to choose between the two cognitive processes when desired. Paradoxically, while most in our culture seem to operate on the assumption that elimination of failures (negative self-monitoring) will improve performance, exactly the opposite appears to hold true, at least when it comes to learning new tasks. In one experiment, for example, Kirschenbaum (1984) compared a set of bowlers who received lessons on the components of effective bowling to those who did not receive the lessons (controls) and to groups who followed the lessons with several weeks of positive self-monitoring or negative self-monitoring (that is, they videotaped performances, edited out the positive or negative, and then selectively reviewed the corresponding tapes with the appropriate groups). As predicted, the positive self-monitors improved significantly more than all the others, and the unskilled bowlers (average of 125 pins) who practiced positive self-monitoring improved substantially (more than 100 percent) more than all other groups. Since then, these results have been replicated with other athletic activities such as golf, and evidence repeatedly indicates that positive self-monitoring significantly enhances learning on any task and is especially potent in the context of novel or poorly mastered tasks.

Some Implications for Management: Toward a Theory of the Affirmative Organization

> We are some time truly going to see our life as positive, not negative, as made up of continuous willing, not of constraints and prohibition.
> —Mary Parker Follett.

That was a judgment of one of the great management prophets of the early 1940s who, in moving out of step with her time, prefigured virtually every new development in organizational thought and practice. Today, her ideas do not seem quite as strange as they once must have been. As we have seen in our overview of the placebo effect, Pygmalion dynamic, positive emotion, imbalanced inner dialogue, and positive self-monitoring, as well as the role of utopian imagery in the rise and fall of cultures, scholars are recognizing that the power of positive imagery is not just some popular illusion or wish but an expression of the mind's capacity for shaping reality. A theory of affirmation is emerging from many quarters. Admittedly its findings are still limited; unifying frameworks are lacking, and generalization across levels of analysis and disciplines makes for unintelligible and often confusing logic. Nevertheless that knowledge–limited though it is—has important practical implications for organizations and management. In the rest of this discussion, I hope to push the current perspective onward by offering an exploratory set of propositions concerning what might be called the affirmative basis of organizing. When translated from the various disciplines into organizationally relevant terms, the emerging "theory of affirmation" looks something like this:

1. *Organizations as made and imagined are artifacts of the affirmative mind. As understanding of organizational life requires an understanding of the dynamic of the positive image as well as the process through which isolated images become interlocked images and of how nascent affirmations become guiding affirmations.* The starting point for a theory of affirmation is simply this: When it comes to understanding organizational existence from the perspective of human action, there is no better clue to a system's overall well-being than its guiding image of the future. In the last analysis, organizations exist because stakeholders who govern and maintain them carry in their minds some sort of shared positive projection

about what the organization is, how it will function, and what it might become. Although positive imagery (in the form of positive thinking, utopian visions, affirmation, and the like) has not been paraded as a central concept in organizational and management thought, it can be usefully argued that virtually every organizational act is based on some positive projection on the part of the individual or group. Organizational birth itself, to take just one example, is impossible in the absence of some affirmative projection. But positive or negative, enabling or limiting, conscious or unconscious — all action is conditioned by the fact that we live in an anticipatory world of images. These guiding images are not detailed objectives but are paintings created with a larger brush stroke. They encompass many aspects of organizational life that mission statements, corporate strategies, or plans alone do not reveal. Just as it has been observed that the rise and fall of images of the future precede or accompany the rise and fall of societies, it can be argued that as long as an organization's image is positive and flourishing, the flower of organizational life will be in full bloom.

2.   *No matter what its previous history is, virtually any pattern of organizational action is open to alteration and reconfiguration. Patterns of organizational action are not automatically fixed by nature in any blind microdeterminist way—whether biological, behavioral, technological, or environmental.* There is no such thing as an inevitable form of organization. There are no "iron laws." While affected by microdeterminist factors, existing regularities that are perceived are controlled by mentalist or "macro" factors exerting downward control. Just as in the Pygmalion dynamic reviewed earlier, organizations are genetically constituted socially in and through the images born in transaction among all participants. In this sense, existing regularities that are observed depend not on some dictate of nature but on the historically and contextually embedded continuities in what we might call (1) the prophetic image—expectancies and beliefs about the future; (2) the poetic image—imagined possibilities or alternatives of what might be; (3) the normative image—ideological or value-based images of what should be. When organizations continue to hold the same expectations and beliefs; when they continue to envision the same possibilities or alternatives; or when they continue to project the same conventional values, norms, or ideologies—it is under these macrodeterminist conditions that continuities in structures and practices will in fact be found.

3.   *To the extent that organizations' imaginative projections are the key to their current conduct, organizations are free to seek transformations in conventional practice by replacing conventional images with images of a new and better future.* To a far greater extent than is normally assumed, organizational evolution is isomorphic with the mental evolution of images. In many respects, it can usefully be argued that organizations are limited primarily or even only by (1) their affirmative capacities of mind, imagination, and reason, and (2) their collective or *coaffirmative capacity* for developing a commanding set of shared projections among a critical segment of stakeholders.

In regard to the latter point, it can be argued further that the guiding image of the future exists deep within the internal dialogue of the organization. The image is not, therefore, either a person-centered or a position-centered phenomenon; it is a situational and interactional tapestry that is a public "property" of the whole rather than of any single element or part. While such things as executive vision and charismatic leadership may be understood as parallels to what I am talking about, their emphasis on the "Great Man" leads them to seriously understate and miscast the complex cooperative aspect of an organization's guiding image of the future. When it comes to collective entities like groups, organizations, or even whole societies, we must emphatically argue that the guiding image of the future does not, even metaphorically, exist within some individual or collective mass of brain. It exists in a very observable and tangible way in the living dialogue that flows through every institution, expressing itself anew at every moment.

4. *Organizations are heliotropic in character in the sense that organizational actions have an observable and largely automatic tendency to evolve in the direction of positive imagery. Positive imagery and hence heliotropic movement is endemic to organizational life, which means that organizations create their own realities to a far greater extent than is normally assumed.* As we have seen in the placebo, Pygmalion, and self-monitoring studies, the positive image carries out its heliotropic task by generating and provoking image-consistent affirmative cognition, image-consistent emotion, and self-validating action. Hence, it can be argued that positive images of the future generate in organizations (1) an affirmative cognitive ecology that strengthens peoples' readiness and capacity to recall the positive aspects of the past, to selectively see the positive in the present, and to envision new potentials in the future; (2) it catalyzes an affirmative emotional climate, for example, of heightened optimism, hope, care, joy, altruism, and passion; and (3) it provokes confident and energized action (see Weick, 1983, on this third point).

Another aspect of the heliotropic hypothesis is that it predicts the following: When presented with the option, organizations will move more rapidly and effectively in the direction of affirmative imagery (moving toward the light) than in the opposite direction of negative imagery (moving against the light or toward "overpowering darkness"). Existing in a dynamic field of images, it can be argued that organizations move along the path of least resistance (Fritz, 1984) toward those images that are judged to represent the organization's highest possibilities — those images that are the brightest, most purposeful, or most highly valued. Positive images whose prophetic, poetic, and normative aspects are congruent will show the greatest self-fulfilling potential.

5. *Conscious evolution of positive imagery is a viable option for organized systems as large as global society or as small as the dyad or group. Also, the more an organization experiments with the conscious evolution of positive imagery the better it will become; there is an observable self-reinforcing, educative effect of*

affirmation. Affirmative competence is the key to the self-organizing system. Through both formal and informal learning processes, organizations, like individuals, can develop their metacognitive competence—the capacity to rise above the present and assess their own imaginative processes as they are operating. This enhances their ability to distinguish between the affirmative and negative ways of construing the world. The healthiest organizations will exhibit a 2 : 1 or better ratio of positive-to-negative imagery (as measured through inner dialogue), while less healthy systems will tend toward a 1 : 1 balanced ratio. Similarly, it can usefully be argued that positively biased organizational monitoring (with selective monitoring and feedback of the positive) will contribute more to heliotropic movement than either neutral (characterized by inattention) or negative organizational monitoring (with a focus on problems or deficiencies). This effect, we would expect based on studies in athletics, will be more pronounced in situations where the affirmative projection is of a novel or complex future and where the tasks or actions required to enact the images are not yet fully tested or mastered.

The more an organization experiments with the affirmative mode, the more its affirmative and heliotropic competence will grow. This is why, in many organizations that have experimented with it, people have come to believe that organizationwide affirmation of the positive future is the single most important act that a system can engage in if its real aim is to bring to fruitation a new and better future. An image that asserts that the future is worth living for will, as William James ([1895] 1956) argued, provoke those actions that help create the fact. While not every future can be created as locally envisioned, there is always a margin within which the future can be affected by positive affirmation. The size of this margin can never be known a priori. Put another way, an organization will rarely rise above the dominant images of its members and stakeholders; or as Willis Harman (1988, p. 1) hypothesizes, "perhaps the only limits to the human mind are those we believe in."

6. *To understand organizations in affirmative terms is also to understand that the greatest obstacle in the way of group and organizational well-being is the positive image, the affirmative projection that guides the group or the organization.* Theorist Henry Wieman (1926, p. 286) gave a clear description of the seeming paradox involved here many years ago in his comparative analysis of *Religious Experience and Scientific Method*: "We are very sure that the greatest obstacle in the way of individual growth and social progress is the ideal [affirmative projection] which dominates the individual or group. The greatest instrument of achievement and improvement is the ideal, and therefore our constant failures, miseries, and wickedness are precisely due to the inadequacy of our highest ideals. Our ideals have in them all the error, all the impracticability, all the perversity and confusion that human beings that themselves erring, impractical, perverse and confused, can put into them. Our ideals are no doubt the best we have in the way of our constructions. But the best we have is pitifully inadequate. Our hope and full assurance . . . [are] that we can improve our ideals. If we could not be saved from our ideals, we would be lost indeed."

One of the ironies of affirmation is that it partially cripples itself in order to function. By definition, to affirm means to "hold firm." As we have seen, it is precisely the strength of affirmation, the degree of belief or faith invested, that allows the image to carry out its heliotropic task. So when our institutions are confronted with repetitive failure and amplifying cycles of distress; when time and energies are expended on such issues as compliance, discipline, obedience, motivation, and the like; or when almost every "new" surefire problem-solving technique does little but add a plethora of new problems—in every one of these cases the system is being given a clear signal of the inadequacy of its "firm" affirmative projections. To repeat, our positive images are no doubt the best we have, but the best is often not responsive to changing needs and opportunities. The real challenge, therefore, is to discover the processes through which a system's best affirmations can be left behind and better ones developed. For if we could not be saved from our best affirmative projections, "we would be lost indeed."

7. *Organizations do not need to be fixed. They need constant reaffirmation. More precisely, organizations as heliotropic systems need to be appreciated. Every new affirmative projection of the future is a consequence of an appreciative understanding of the past or the present.* Up to this point we have examined the nature of the positive image-positive action relationship but have said nothing about the mental artistry by which guiding images—prophesies, possibilities, and normative values—are in fact generated. We seem to have become preoccupied with the question of "how to translate intention into reality and sustain it" (see for example Bennis and Nanus, 1985) and have ignored what is perhaps the more essential question.

An earlier set of writings (Cooperrider and Srivastva, 1987; Cooperrider, 1986) described a process of knowing that was preeminently suited to the task of providing both the data and mental inspiration through which human systems can fashion new affirmative projections on a dynamic and continuous basis. It was argued that appreciative inquiry is based on a "reverence for life" and is essentially biocentric in character: It is an inquiry process that tries to apprehend the factors that give life to a living system and seeks to articulate those possibilities that can lead to a better future. More than a method or technique, the appreciative mode of inquiry was described as a means of living with, being with, and directly participating in the life of a human system in a way that compels one to inquire into the deeper life-generating essentials and potentials of organizational existence.

As this concept relates specifically to leadership, an important clue to the meaning of executive appreciation is found in Isaiah Berlin's (1980, pp. 14–15) account of Winston Churchill's leadership during England's darkest hour:

> In 1940 he [Churchill] assumed an indomitable stoutness, an unsurrendering quality on the part of his people. . . . He idealized them with such intensity that in the end they approached his ideal and began to see themselves as he saw them: "the buoyant and inperturbable temper of Britain which I had the honour to express"—it was indeed, but he had the

lion's share in creating it. So hypnotic was the force of his words, so strong his faith, that by the sheer intensity of his eloquence he bound his spell upon them until it seemed to them that he was indeed speaking what was in their hearts and minds. Doubtless it was there; but largely dormant until he had awoken it within them.

After he had spoken to them in the summer of 1940 as no one else has ever before or since, they conceived a new idea of themselves. . . . They went forward into battle transformed by his words. . . . He created a heroic mood and turned the fortunes of the Battle of Britain not by catching the [life-diminishing] mood of his surroundings but by being impervious to it, as he had been to so many of the passing shades and tones of which the life around him had been composed.

Churchill's impact and the guiding images he helped create were the result of his towering ability to cognitively dissociate all seeming impossibilities, deficiencies, and imperfections from a given situation and to see in his people and country that which had fundamental value and strength. His optimism, even in Britain's darkest moment, came not from a Pollyanna-like sense that "everything is just fine" but from a conviction that was born from what he, like few others, could actually see in his country: "Doubtless it was there; but largely dormant until he had awoken it."

In almost every respect the cognitive and perceptual process employed by Churchill, like many great executives, was that of the artist. The appreciative eye we are beginning to understand apprehends "what is" rather than "what is not" and in this represents a rigorous cognitive ability to bracket out all seeming imperfections from that which has fundamental value. For as the poet Shelly suggests, appreciation "makes immortal all that is best and most beautiful in the world. . . . It exalts the beauty of that which is most beautiful. . . . It strips the veil of familiarity from the world, and lays bare and naked sleeping beauty, which is in the spirit of its forms" (in Cooperrider and Srivastva, 1987, p. 164).

But this is only part of the story: Appreciation not only draws our eye toward life, but stirs our feelings, excites our curiosity, and provides inspiration to the envisioning mind. In this sense, the ultimate generative power for the construction of new values and images is the apprehension of that which has value. Nietzsche once asked of appreciation, "Does it not praise? Does it not glorify? Does it not select? Does it not bring 'that which is appreciated' to prominence? In all this, does it not strengthen or weaken certain valuations?" (in Rader, 1973, p. 12).

No one has expressed this more effectively than the artist Vincent van Gogh, who, in a letter to his brother (in Rader, 1973, p. 10), spelled out what could actually be an entire leadership course on the relationship between appreciation and the emergence of new values:

I should like to paint a portrait of an artist friend, a man who dreams great dreams, who works as the nightingale sings, because it is in his nature. He'll be a fine man. I want to put into my picture of appreciation, the love I have for him. So I paint him as he is, as faithfully as I can. But the picture is not finished yet. To finish it, I am now the arbitrary colorist. I exaggerate the fairness of the hair; I come even to use orange tones, chromes, and pale lemon-yellow. Behind the head, instead of painting the ordinary wall of the mean room, I paint infinity, a plain background of the richest, intensest blue that I can contrive—and by this simple combination of the bright head against the rich blue background, I get a mysterious effect, like a star in the depths of an azure sky.

Like Churchill, van Gogh began with a stance of appreciative cognition. He viewed his friend through a loving and caring lense and focused on those qualities that "excited his preference" and kindled his imagination. The key point is that van Gogh did not merely articulate admiration for his friend: He created new values and new ways of seeing the world through the very act of valuing. And again, as Nietzsche (in Rader, 1973, p. 12) has elaborated: "valuing is creating: hear it, ye creating ones! Valuation is itself the treasure and jewel of valuating things."

In contrast to the affirmative projection that seeks certainty and control over events, the appreciative eye actually seeks uncertainty as it is thrown into the elusive and emergent nature of organizational life itself. Appreciation is creative rather than conservative precisely because it allows itself to be energized and inspired by the voice of mystery. As an active process of valuing the factors that give rise to the life-enhancing organization, appreciation has room for the vital uncertainty, the indeterminancy that is the trademark of something alive. In this sense, too, it differs from affirmation in that it is not instrumental. It does not have the capability of shaping the world closer to preexisting wants because it tends, in the end, to transform those wants into something very different from that which was originally affirmed. Executive appreciation, then, represents the capacity to rediscover in organizations what Bruner refers to as the "immensity of the common-place" or what James Joyce terms the "epiphanies of the ordinary" (see Bruner, 1986, p. 198). Appreciation, as Churchill must have understood, is the mental strength that allows a leader to consciously peer into the life-giving present, only to find the future brilliantly interwoven into the texture of the actual.

   8.   *The executive vocation in a postbureaucratic society is to nourish the appreciation soil from which affirmative projections grow, branch off, evolve, and become collective projections. Creating the conditions for organizationwide appreciation is the single most important measure that can be taken to ensure the conscious evolution of a valued and positive future.* The "how" of appreciative inquiry is beyond the scope of this discussion. But a number of final thoughts can be offered on the organizational prerequisites of appreciation. These comments stem from the experiences with a number of systems that have actually experimented with appreciative inquiry on a collective and organizationwide basis.

First, it is clear that the appreciative process has been most spontaneous and genuine in relatively egalitarian systems—organizations committed to an ideology of inclusion, consent, and coevolution (Srivastva and Cooperrider, 1986). Put more strongly, experience suggests that the creative power of appreciation will never be realized in a world that continues to place arbitrary restrictions or constraints on speech and action. It is the realm of action, not mind, that is the preeminent basis of those creative images that have the power to guide us into a positive future.

Second, experience indicates that if pursued deeply enough, appreciative inquiry arrives at a dynamic interpersonal ideal. It arrives at knowledge that enlarges our sense of solidarity with other human beings and provides an ever-expanding universe of examples and images concerning the possibilities for a more egalitarian future.

We are infants when it comes to our understanding of appreciative processes of knowing and social construction. Yet we are beginning to see that the power of appreciation rests with its self-reinforcing and self-generative capacity. Through appreciation of organizational life, members of an organization learn to value not only the life-enhancing organization but also learn to affirm themselves. As new potentials for inquiry are revealed and experienced within the "student," new insights are made available and shared with others in the organization. As sharing occurs, the inquiry becomes a joint process of knowing—others are invited to explore and question their own ideals or affirmative projections. Through dialogue, new knowledge and new images of possibility are constantly being made available. And while such knowledge is always felt as an interruption in the status quo, it is valued and turned into a heliotropic project because it represents a joint creation of a world that corresponds to the jointly imagined projection of human and social possibility.

Chapter 3

Appreciative Inquiry in Organizational Life

David L. Cooperrider and Suresh Srivastva
Case Western Reserve University

Abstract

This chapter presents a conceptual refiguration of action-research based on a "sociorationalist" view of science. The position that is developed can be summarized as follows: For action-research to reach its potential as a vehicle for social innovation it needs to begin advancing theoretical knowledge of consequence; that good theory may be one of the best means human beings have for affecting change in a postindustrial world; that the discipline's steadfast commitment to a problem solving view of the world acts as a primary constraint on its imagination and contribution to knowledge; that *appreciative inquiry* represents a viable complement to conventional forms of action-research; and finally, that through our assumptions and choice of method we largely create the world we later discover.

We are sometime truly to see our life as positive, not negative, as made up of continuous willing, not of constraints and prohibition.
—Mary Parker Follett.

We are steadily forgetting how to dream; in historical terms, the mathematicist and technicist dimensions of Platonism have conquered the poetical, mythical, and rhetorical context of analysis. We are forgetting how to be reasonable in nonmathematical dialects.
—Stanley Rosen.

W. A. Pasmore & R. W. Woodman (eds.), *Research in organizational change and development (Vol. I)*, pp. 129-169. Greenwich, CT: JAI Press, 1987.

Introduction

This chapter presents a conceptual reconfiguration of action research.[1] In it we shall argue for a multidimensional view of action-research which seeks to both generate theory and develop organizations. The chapter begins with the observation that action-research has become increasingly rationalized and enculturated to the point where it risks becoming little more than a crude empiricism imprisoned in a deficiency mode of thought. In its conventional *unidimensional* form action research has largely failed as an instrument for advancing social knowledge of consequence and has not, therefore, achieved its potential as a vehicle for human development and social-organizational transformation. While the literature consistently signals the worth of action-research as a managerial tool for problem solving ("first-order" incremental change), it is conspicuously quiet concerning reports of discontinuous change of the "second order" where organizational paradigms, norms, ideologies, or values are transformed in fundamental ways (Watzlawick, et al., 1974).

In the course of this chapter we shall touch broadly upon a number of interrelated concerns—scientific, metaphysical, normative, and pragmatic. Linking these streams is an underlying conviction that action-research has the potential to be to the postindustrial era what "scientific management" was to the industrial. Just as scientific management provided the philosophical and methodological legitimacy required to support the bureaucratic organizational form (Clegg and Dunkerly, 1980; Braverman, 1974), action-research may yet provide the intellectual rationale and reflexive methodology required to support the emergence of a more egalitarian "postbureaucratic" form of organization. Unlike scientific management however, which provided the means for a technorational science of administration, action-research holds unique and essential promise in the sociorational realm of human affairs. It has the potential to become the paradigmatic basis of a truly significant—a humanly significant—generative science of administration.

In the first part of the essay it is suggested that the primary barrier limiting the potential of action-research has been its romance with "action" at the expense of "theory." This tendency has led many in the discipline to seriously underestimate the power of theory as a means for social-organizational reconstruction. Drawing largely on the work of Kenneth Gergen (1978, 1982), we re-examine the character of theoretical knowledge and its role in social transformation, and then appeal for a redefinition of the scientific aims of action-research that will dynamically reunite theory and practice. The aim of science is not the detached discovery and verification of social laws allowing for prediction and control. Highlighted here instead, is

---

[1] While we draw most of our examples from the Organization Development (OD) school of action-research, the argument presented here should be relevant to other applications as well. As noted by Peters and Robinson (1984), the discipline of action-research has been prevalent in the literature of community action, education and educational system change, and organization change, as well as discussions of the social sciences in general.

an alternative understanding that defines social and behavioral science in terms of its "generative capacity," that is, its "capacity to challenge the guiding assumptions of the culture, to raise fundamental questions regarding contemporary social life, to foster reconsideration of that which is 'taken for granted' and thereby furnish new alternatives for social actions" (Gergen, 1978, p. 1346).

Assuming that generative theory is a legitimate product of scientific work and is, in fact, capable of provoking debate, stimulating normative dialogue, and furnishing conceptual alternatives needed for social transformation, then why has action-research till now so largely downplayed creative theorizing in its work with organizations? Here we will move to the heart of the chapter and argue that the generative incapacity of contemporary action-research derives from the discipline's unquestioned commitment to a secularized problem-oriented view of the world and thus to the subsequent loss of our capacity as researchers and participants to marvel, and in marveling to embrace, the miracle and mystery of social organization. If we acknowledge Abraham Maslow's (1968) admonition that true science begins and ends in wonder, then we immediately shed light on why action-research has failed to produce innovative theory capable of inspiring the imagination, commitment, and passionate dialogue required for the consensual re-ordering of social conduct.

Appreciative inquiry is presented here as a mode of action-research that meets the criteria of science as spelled out in generative-theoretical terms. Going beyond questions of epistemology, appreciative inquiry has as its basis a metaphysical concern: it posits that social existence as such is a miracle that can never be fully comprehended (Quinney, 1982; Marcel, 1963). Proceeding from this level of understanding we begin to explore the uniqueness of the appreciative mode. More than a method or technique, the appreciative mode of inquiry is a way of living with, being with, and directly participating in the varieties of social organization we are compelled to study. Serious consideration and reflection on the ultimate mystery of being engenders a reverence for life that draws the researcher to inquire beyond superficial appearances to deeper levels of the life generating essentials and potentials of social existence. That is, the action researcher is drawn to affirm, and thereby illuminate, the factors and forces involved in organizing that serve to nourish the human spirit. Thus, this chapter seeks to enrich our conception of administrative behavior by introducing a "second dimension" of action-research that goes beyond merely a secularized problem-solving frame.

The proposal that appreciative inquiry represents a distinctive complement to traditional action-research will be unfolded in the following way: First, the role of theory as an enabling agent of social transformation will be considered; such consideration can help to eliminate the artificial dualism separating theory from practice. Second, we will challenge the problem-oriented view of organizing inherent in traditional definitions of action-research, and describe an affirmative form of inquiry uniquely suited for discovering generative theory. Finally, these insights will be brought together in a general model of the conceptual underpinnings of appreciative inquiry.

Toward Generative Theory in Action-Research

The current decade has witnessed a confluence of thinking concerning the paradigmatic refiguration of social thought. As Geertz (1980) notes, there is now even a "blurring of genres" as many social scientists have abandoned—without apology—the misdirected quest to mimic the "more mature" physical sciences. Turning away from a Newtonian laws-and-instances-type explanation rooted in logical empiricist philosophy, many social theorists have instead opted for an interpretive form of inquiry that connects organized action to its contextually embedded set of meanings, "looking less for the sorts of things that connect planets and pendulums and more for the sorts that connect chrysanthemums and swords" (Geertz, 1980, p. 165).

In the administrative sciences, in particular, this recent development has been translated into observable movement away from mechanistic research designs intended objectively to establish universal causal linkages between variables, such as organizational size and level of centralization, or between technology, environment, and organizational structure. Indeed, prominent researchers in the field have publicly given up the logical positivist idea of "certainty through science" and are now embarking on approaches to research that grant preeminence to the historically situated and ever-changing "interpretive schemes" used by members of a given group to give life and meaning to their actions and decisions (Bartunek, 1984). Indicative of the shift away from the logical positivist frame, researchers are converging around what has been termed the "sociorationalist" metatheory of science (Gergen, 1982). Recognizing the symbolic nature of the human universe, we now find a flurry of innovative work supporting the thesis that there is little about human development or organizational behavior that is "preprogrammed" or stimulus-bound in any direct physical or biological way. In this sense, the social universe is open to indefinite revision, change, and self-propelled development. And, this recognition is crucial because to the extent to which social existence is situated in a symbolic realm, beyond deterministic forces, then to that extent the logical positivist foundation of social science is negated and its concept of knowledge rendered illusionary.

Nowhere is this better evidenced than in the variety of works concerned with such topics as organizational paradigms (Brown, 1978; McHugh, 1970); beliefs and master scripts (Sproull, 1981; Beyer, 1981); idea management and the executive mind (Srivastva, 1983; 1985); theories of action and presumptions of logic (Argyris and Schon, 1980; Weick, 1983); consciousness and awareness (Harrison, 1982; Lukes, 1974); and, of course, an array of work associated with the concept of organizational or corporate culture (Ouchi and Johnson, 1978; Schein, 1983; Van Maanen, 1982; Deal and Kennedy, 1982; Sathe, 1983; Hofstede, 1980). As Ellwood prophetically suggested almost half a century ago, "This is the cultural view of human society that is [or will be] revolutionizing the social sciences" (Ellwood, 1938, p. 561).

This developing consensus on the importance of the symbolic realm—on the power of ideas—by such independent sources embracing such diverse objectives reflects the reality of organized life in the modern world. However reluctantly, even the most traditional social thinkers are now recognizing the distinctiveness of the postindustrial world for what truly is—an unfolding drama of human interaction whose potential seems limited or enhanced primarily by our symbolic capacities for constructing meaningful agreements that allow for the committed enactment of collective life.

Never before in history have ideas, information, and beliefs—or theory—been so central in the formulation of reality itself. Social existence, of course, has always depended on some kind of idea system for its meaningful sustenance. The difference now, however, is that what was once background has become foreground. Today, the very fact that society continues to exist at all is experienced not so much mechanistically (an extension of machines) or even naturalistically (a by-product of fateful nature) but more and more humanistically as a social construction of interacting minds—"a game between persons" (Bell, 1973). And under these conditions—as a part of the change from an agrarian society to a goods-producing society at first and then to an information society—ideas and meaning systems take on a whole new life and character. Ideas are thrust center stage as the prime unit of relational exchange governing the creation or obliteration of social existence.

This line of argument applies no less potently to current conceptions of social science. To the extent that the primary product of science is systematically refined idea systems—or theory—science too must be recognized as a powerful agent in the enhancement or destruction of human life. And while this presents an unresolvable dilemma for a logical empiricist conception of science, it spells real opportunity (and responsibility) for a social science that wishes to be of creative significance to society. Put most simply, the theoretical contributions of science may be among the most powerful resources human beings have for contributing to change and development in the groups and organizations in which they live. This is precisely the meaning of Kurt Lewin's early view of action-science when he proposed: "There is nothing so practical as good theory" (1951, p. 169).

Ironically, the discipline of action-research continues to insist on a sharp separation of theory and practice, and to underrate the role of theory in social reconstruction. The irony is that it does so precisely at a time when the cultural view of organizing is reaching toward paradigmatic status. The sad and perhaps tragic commentary on action-research is that it is becoming increasingly inconsequential just as its opportunity to contribute is on the rise (Argyris, 1983).

Observers such as Rappaport (1970) and Bartunek (1983) have lamented the fact that action-researchers have come to subordinate research aims to action interests. Levinson (1972) has gone even further by branding the discipline "atheoretical." And, Friedlander and Brown (1974) have noted that the definition of action-research in classic texts give virtually no mention to theory-building as an integral and necessary component of the research/diagnostic process, or the process of organizational change. Whenever theory is mentioned, it is almost always referred to as a springboard for research or diagnosis, not the other way around. Bartunek (1983, pp. 3–4) concludes that "even the most recent papers that describe action-research strategies tend to focus primarily on the process of action-research and only secondarily on the specific theoretical contributions of the outcomes of such research" (e.g., Frohman, Sashkin, and Kavanaugh, 1976; Shani and Pasmore, 1982; Susman and Evered, 1978; see Pasmore and Friedlander, 1982, for an exception). For those of us trained in the field this conclusion is not surprising. Indeed, few educational programs in organizational behavior even consider theory-building as a formal part of their curriculum, and even fewer place a real premium on the development of the theoretical mind and imagination of their students.

According to Argyris (1983), this lack of useful theorizing is attributable to two major factors. On the one hand practice-oriented scholars have tended to become so client-centered that they fail to question their clients' own definition of a problem and thereby to build testable propositions and theories that are embedded in everyday life. Academics, on the other hand, who are trained to be more scientific in their bent, also undercut the development of useful theory by their very insistence on the criteria of "normal" science and research—detachment, rigor, unilateral control, and operational precision. In a word, creative theorizing has literally been assaulted on all fronts by practitioners and academic scientists alike. It must also be noted that implicit in this critique by Argyris (1983), and others (e.g., Friedlander and Brown, 1974), is an underlying assumption that action-research has built into it certain natural conflicts that are likely to lead either to "action" (consulting) or "research" (diagnosis or the development of organizational theory), but not to both.

The situation is summed up by Friedlander and Brown (1974) in their comprehensive review of the field:

> We believe that research will either play a far more crucial role in the advancement of this field, or become an increasingly irrelevant appendage to it. . . . We have generally failed to produce a theory of change, which emerges from the change process itself. We need a way of enriching our understanding and action synergistically rather than at one or the other's expense—to become a science in which knowledge-getting and knowledge-giving are an integrated process, and one that is valuable to all parties involved (p. 319).

Friedlander and Brown concluded with a plea for a metatheoretical revision of science that will integrate theory and practice. But in another review over a decade later, Friedlander (1984) observed little progress coming from top scholars in the discipline. He then put words to a mounting frustration over what appears as a recurring problem:

> They pointed to the shortcomings of traditional research and called for emancipation from it, but they did not indicate a destination. There is as yet no new paradigm that integrates research and practice, or even optimizes useful

knowledge for organizations. . . . I'm impatient. Let's get on with it. Let's not talk it, write it, analyze it, conceptualize it, or research it. Instead let's actively engage and experiment with new designs for producing knowledge that is, in fact, used by organizations (p. 647).

This recurrent problem is the price we pay for continuing to talk about theory and practice in dualistic terms. In a later section in this chapter another hypothesis will be advanced on why there is this lack of creative theorizing, specifically as it relates to action-research. But first we need to look more closely at the claim that social theory and social practice are, indeed, part of a synthetic whole. We need to elaborate on the idea that scientific theory is a means for both understanding *and* improving social practice. We need to examine exactly what it means to merge the idea and the act, the symbolic and the sociobehavioral, into a powerful and integral unity.

The Sociorationalist Alternative

As the end of the twentieth century nears, thinkers in organizational behavior are beginning to see, without hesitation, why an administrative science based on a physical science model is simply not adequate as a means for understanding or contributing in relevant ways to the workings of complex, organized human systems (see, for example, Susman and Evered, 1978; Beyer and Trice, 1982). Kurt Lewin had understood this almost half a century earlier but his progressive vision of an action science fell short of offering a clear metatheoretical alternative to conventional conceptions of science (Peters and Robinson, 1984). Indeed, the epistemological ambiguity inherent in Lewin's writing has been cited as perhaps the critical shortcoming of all his work. And yet, in hindsight, it can be argued that the ambiguity was intentional and perhaps part of Lewin's social sensitivity and genius. As Gergen (1982) suggests, the metatheoretical ambiguity in Lewin's work might well have been a protective measure, an attempt to shield his fresh vision of an action science from the fully dominant logical positivist temper of his time. In any event, whether planned or not, Lewin walked a tightrope between two fundamentally opposed views of science and never did make clear how theory could be used as both an interpretive and a creative element. This achievement, as we might guess, would have to wait for a change in the intellectual ethos of social science.

That change, as we earlier indicated, is now taking place. Increasingly the literature signals a disenchantment with theories of science that grants priority to the external world in the generation of human knowledge. Instead there is growing movement toward granting preeminence to the cognitive processes of mind and the symbolic processes of social construction. In *Toward Transformation in Social Knowledge* (1982), Kenneth Gergen synthesizes the essential whole of this movement and takes it one crucial step beyond disenchantment to a bold, yet workable conception of science that firmly unites theory with practice—and thereby elevates the status of theoretical-scientific work. From a historical perspective there is no question that this is a major achievement; it brings to completion the work abruptly halted by Lewin's untimely death. But more than that, what Gergen offers, albeit indirectly, is a desperately needed clue to how we can revitalize an action-research discipline that has never reached its potential. While a complete statement of the emerging sociorationalist metatheory is beyond the scope of this chapter, it is important at least to outline the general logic of the perspective, including its basic assumptions.

At the heart of sociorationalism is the assumption of impermanence—the fundamental instability of social order. No matter what the durability to date, virtually any pattern of social action is open to infinite revision. Accepting for a moment the argument of the social constructionists that social reality, at any given point, is a product of broad social agreement (shared meanings), and further granting a linkage between the conceptual schemes of a culture and its other patterns of action, we must seriously consider the idea that alterations in conceptual practices, in ways of symbolizing the world, hold tremendous potential for guiding changes in the social order. To understand the importance of these assumptions and their meaning for social science, let us quote Gergen (1982) at length:

> Is not the range of cognitive heuristics that may be employed in solving problems of adaptation limited only by the human imagination?
>
> One must finally consider the possibility that human biology not only presents to the scientist an organism whose actions may vary in an infinity of ways, but it may ensure as well that novel patterns are continuously emerging . . . variations in human activity may importantly be traced to the capacities of the organism for symbolic restructuring. As it is commonly said, one's actions appear to be vitally linked to the manner in which one understands or construes the world of experience. The stimulus world does not elicit behavior in an automatic, reflex-like fashion. Rather, the symbolic translation of one's experiences virtually transforms their implications and thereby alters the range of one's potential reactions. Interestingly, while formulations of this variety are widely shared within the scientific community, very little attention has been paid to their ramifications for a theory of science. As is clear, without such regularities the prediction of behavior is largely obviated . . . to the extent that the individual is capable of transforming the meaning of stimulus conditions in an indeterminate number of ways, existing regularities must be considered historically contingent—dependent on the prevailing meaning systems of conceptual structure of the times. In effect, from this perspective the scientist's capacity to locate predictable patterns of interaction depends importantly on the extent to which the population is both homogeneous and stable in its conceptual constructions (pp. 16–17).

While this type of reasoning is consistent with the thinking of many social scientists, the ramifications are rarely taken to their logical conclusion: "Virtually unexamined by the field is the potential of science to shape the meaning systems of the society and thus the common activities of the culture" (Gergen, 1978, p. 1349). Virtually unexamined is the important role that science can—and does—play in the scientific construction of social reality.

One implication of this line of thought is that to the extent the social science conceives its role in the logical positivist sense, with its goals being prediction and control, it not only serves the interests of the status quo (you can't have "good science" without stable replication and verification of hypotheses) but it also seriously underestimates the power and usefulness of its most important product, namely theory; it underestimates the constructive role science can have in the *development* of the groups and organizations that make up our cultural world. According to Gergen, realization of this fact furnishes the opportunity to refashion a social science of vital significance to society. To do this, we need a bold shift in attention whereby theoretical accounts are no longer judged in terms of their predictive capacity, but instead are judged in terms of their generative capacity—their ability to foster dialogue about that which is taken for granted and their capacity for generating fresh alternatives for social action. Instead of asking, "Does this theory correspond with the observable facts?" the emphasis for evaluating good theory becomes, "To what extent does this theory present provocative new possibilities for social action, and to what extent does it stimulate normative dialogue about how we can and should organize ourselves?" The complete logic for such a proposal may be summarized in the following ten points:

1. The social order at any given point is viewed as the product of broad social agreement, whether tacit or explicit.

2. Patterns of social-organizational action are not fixed by nature in any direct biological or physical way; the vast share of social conduct is potentially stimulus-free, capable of infinite conceptual variation.

3. From an observational point of view, all social action is open to multiple interpretations, no one of which is superior in any objective sense. The interpretations (for example, "whites are superior to blacks") favored in one historical setting may be replaced in the next.

4. Historically embedded conventions govern what is taken to be true or valid, and to a large extent govern what we, as scientists and lay persons, are able to see. All observation, therefore, is theory-laden and filtered through conventional belief systems and theoretical lenses.[2]

5. To the extent that action is predicated on ideas, beliefs, meanings, intentions, or theory, people are free to seek transformations in conventional conduct by changing conventional codes (idea systems).

---

[2]As physicist Jeremy Hayward (1984) has put it, "I'll see it when I believe it," or oppositely, "I won't see it because I don't believe it." The point is that all observation is filtered through belief systems which act as our personal theories of the world. Thus, what *counts* as "fact" depends largely on beliefs associated with theory and therefore, on the community of scientists espousing this belief system.

6. The most powerful vehicle communities have for transforming their conventions—their agreements on norms, values, policies, purposes, and ideologies—is through the act of dialogue made possible by language. Alterations in linguistic practices, therefore, hold profound implications for changes in social practice.

7. Social theory can be viewed as a highly refined language with a specialized grammar all its own. As a powerful linguistic tool created by trained linguistic experts (scientists), theory may enter the conceptual meaning system of culture and in doing so alter patterns of social action.

8. Whether intended or not, all theory is normative and has the potential to influence the social order—even if reactions to it are simply boredom, rebellion, laughter, or full acceptance.

9. Because of this, all social theory is morally relevant; it has the potential to affect the way people live their ordinary lives in relation to one another. This point is a critical one because there is no such thing as a detached/technical/scientific mode for judging the ultimate worth of value claims.

10. Valid knowledge or social theory is therefore a communal creation. Social knowledge is not "out there" in nature to be discovered through detached, value-free, observational methods (logical empiricism); nor can it be relegated to the subjective minds of isolated individuals (solipsism). Social knowledge resides in the interactive collectivity; it is created, maintained, and put to use by the human group. Dialogue, free from constraint or distortion, is necessary to determine the "nature of things" (sociorationalism).

In Table 3.1 the metatheory of sociorationalism is both summarized and contrasted to the commonly held assumptions of the logical empiricist view of science. Especially important to note is the transformed role of the scientist when social inquiry is viewed from the perspective of sociorationalism. Instead of attempting to present oneself as an impartial bystander or dispassionate spectator of the inevitable, the social scientist conceives of himself or herself as an active agent, an invested participant whose work might well become a powerful source of change in the way people see and enact their worlds. Driven by a desire to "break the hammerlock" of what appears as given in human nature, the scientist attempts to build theories that can expand the realm of what is conventionally understood as possible. In this sense the core impact of sociorationalist metatheory is that it invites, encourages, and requires that students of social life rigorously exercise their theoretical imagination in the service of their vision of the good. Instead of denial it is an invitation to fully accept and exercise those qualities of mind and action that make us uniquely human.

Now we turn to a question raised earlier: How does theory achieve its capacity to affect social practice, and what are some of the specific characteristics of generative theory?

TABLE 3.1. Comparison of Logical Empiricist and Socio-Rationalist Conceptions of Social Science

Dimension for Comparison	Logical Empiricism	Socio-Rationalism
1. Primary Function of Science	Enhance goals of understanding, prediction, and control by discerning general laws or principles governing the relationship among units of observable phenomena.	Enhance understanding in the sense of assigning meaning to something, thus creating its status through the use of concepts. Science is a means for expanding flexibility and choice in cultural evolution.
2. Theory of Knowledge and Mind	Exogenic—grants priority to the external world in the generation of human knowledge (i.e., the preeminence of objective fact). Mind is a mirror.	Endogenic—holds the processes of mind and symbolic interaction as preeminent source of human knowledge. Mind is both a mirror and a lamp.
3. Perspective on Time	Assumption of temporal irrelevance: searches for transhistorical principles.	Assumption of hstorically and contextually relevant meanings; existing regularities in social order are contingent on prevailing meaning systems.
4. Assuming Stability of Social Patterns	Social phenomena are sufficiently stable, enduring, reliable and replicable to allow for lawful principles.	Social order is fundamentally unstable. Social phenomena are guided by cognitive heuristics, limited only by the human imagination: the social order is a subject matter capable of infinite variation through the linkage ofideas and action.
5. Value Stance	Separation of fact and values. Possibility of objective knowledge through behavioral observation.	Social sciences are fundamentally nonobjective. Any behavioral event is open to virtually any interpretative explanation. All interpretation is filtered through prevailing values of a culture. "There is no description without prescription."

(continued)

TABLE 3.1. Comparison of Logical Empiricist and Socio-Rationalist Conceptions of Social Science *(continued)*

Dimension for Comparison	Logical Empiricism	Socio-Rationalism
6. Features of "Good" Theory	Discovery of transhistorically valid principles; a theory's correspondence with face.	Degree to which theory furnishes alternatives for social innovation and thereby opens vistas for action; expansion of "the realm of the possible."
7. Criteria for Confirmation or Verification (Life of a Theory)	Logical consistency and empirical prediction; subject to falsification.	Persuasive appeal, impace, and overall generative capacity; subject to community agreement; truth is a product of a community of truth makers.
8. Role of Scientist	Impartial bystander and dispassionate spectator of the inevitable; content to accept that which seems given.	Active agent and coparticipant who is primarily a source of linguistic activity (theoretical language) which serves as input into common meaning systems. Interested in "breaking the hammerlock" of what appears as given in human nature.
9. Chief Product of Research	Cumulation of objective knowledge through the production of empirically disconfirmable hypothesis.	Continued improvement in theory building capacity; improvement in the capacity to create generative-theoretical language.
10. Emphasis in the Education of Future Social Science Professionals	Rigorous experimental methods and statistical analysis; a premium is placed on method (training in theory construction is a rarity).	Hermenuetic interpretation and catalytic theorizing; a premium is placed on theoretical imagination. Sociorationalism invites the student toward intellectual expression in the service of his or her vision of the good.

The Power of Theory in Understanding Organizational Life

The sociorationalist vision of science is of such far-reaching importance that no student, organizational scientist, manager, educator, or action-researcher can afford to ignore it. Good theory, as we have suggested, is one of the most powerful means we have for helping social systems evolve, adapt, and creatively alter their patterns over time. Building further on this metatheoretical perspective we can talk about five ways by which theory achieves its exceptional potency:

1. Establishing a conceptual and contextual frame;
2. Providing presumptions of logic;
3. Transmitting a system of values;
4. Creating a group-building language;
5. Extending visions of possibility or constraint.

Establishing a Perceptual and Contextual Frame

To the extent that theory is the conceptual imposition of order upon an otherwise "booming, bustling, confusion that is the realm of experience" (Dubin, 1978), the theorist's first order of business is to specify what is there to be seen, to provide an "ontological education" (Gergen, 1982). The very act of theoretical articulation, therefore, highlights not only the parameters of the topic or subject matter, but becomes an active agent as a cueing device, a device that subtly focuses attention on particular phenomena or meanings while obscuring others. In the manner of a telescope or lens, a new theory allows one to see the world in a way perhaps never before imagined.

For example, when American eugenicists used the lens of biological determinism to attribute diseases of poverty to the inferior genetic construction of poor people, they literally could see no systematic remedy other than sterilization of the poor. In contrast, when Joseph Goldberg theorized that pellagra was not genetically determined but culturally caused (as a result of vitamin deficiency and the eating habits of the poor), he could discover a way to cure it (Gould, 1981). Similarly, theories about the "survival of the fittest" might well help executives locate "predators," "hostile environments," and a world where self interest reigns, where it is a case of "eat or be eaten." Likewise, theories of leadership have been known quickly to facilitate the discovery of Theory X and Theory Y interaction. Whatever the theory, it provides a potential means for members of a culture to navigate in an otherwise neutral, meaningless, or chaotic sea of people, interactions and events. By providing an "ontological education" with respect to what is there, a theory furnishes an important cultural input that affects people's cognitive set. In this sense "the world is not so constituted until the lens is employed. With each new distinction the groundwork is laid for alterations in existing patterns of conduct" (Gergen, 1982, p. 23).

As the reader may already surmise, an important moral issue begins to emerge here. Part of the reason that theory is, in fact, powerful is that it shapes perceptions, cognition's, and preferences often at a preconscious level, much like subliminal communications or even hypnosis. Haley (1973) talks about how Milton Erickson has made this a central feature of this psychotherapeutic work. But Lukes (1974) cautions that such thought control may be "the supreme and most insidious exercise of power," especially when it prevents people from challenging their role in the existing order of things and when it operates contrary to their real interests.

Providing Presumptions of Logic

Theories are also powerful to the extent to which they help shape common expectations of causality, sequence, and relational importance of phenomena within a theoretical equation. Consider, for example, the simple logic underlying almost every formal performance-appraisal system. Stripped to essentials, the theoretical underpinnings run something like this: "If you want to evaluate performance (P), then you must evaluate the individual employee (E); in other words, 'P = E'." Armed with this theory, many managers have entered the performance-appraisal meeting shaking with the thought of having to pass godlike judgment on some employee. Similarly, the employee arrives at the meeting with an arsenal of defenses, designed to protect his or her hard-won self-esteem. Little genuine communication occurs during the meeting and virtually no problem-solving takes place. The paperwork is mechanically completed, then filed away in the personnel office until the next year. So powerful is this subtle P = E equation that any alternative goes virtually unnoticed, for example the Lewinian theory that behavior (performance) is a function of the person and the environment (in this case the organizational situation, the "OS" in which the employee works). Following this Lewinian line, the theory underlying performance appraisal would now have to be expanded to read P = E × OS. That is, P ≠ E. To adequately assess performance there must be an assessment of the individual *in relation* to the organizational setting in which he or she works and vice-versa. What would happen to the performance-appraisal process if this more complete theory were used as a basis for re-designing appraisal systems in organizations throughout the corporate world? Isn't it possible that such a theory could help shift the attribution process away from the person-blame to systems analysis?[3] By attributing causality, theories have the potential to create the very phenomena they propose to explain. Karl Weick, in a recent article examining managerial thought in the context of action, contends that thought and action are part and parcel of one another; thinking is best viewed as a kind of activity, and activity as the ground of thought. For him,

---

[3]A group of colleagues and we are engaged in a two-year study of a major industrial plant where introduction of this simple theory has led to changes in job design, work relations, training programs, motivational climate, and hierarchical ideology. For an introduction to this work see Pasmore, Cooperrider, Kaplan and Morris, 1983.

managerial theories gain their power by helping people overlook disorder and presume orderliness. Theory *energizes* action by providing a *presumption of logic* that enables people to act with certainty, attention, care, and control. Even where it is originally inadequate as a description of current reality, a forceful theory may provoke action that brings into the world a new reality that then confirms the original theory. Weick (1983) explains:

> Once the action is linked with an explanation, it becomes more forceful, and the situation is thereby transformed into something that supports the presumed underlying pattern. Presumptions [theories] enable actions to be tied to specific explanations that consolidate those actions into deterministic events. . . .
>
> The underlying explanation need *not* be objectively "correct." In a crude sense any old explanation will do. This is so because explanation serves mostly to organize and focus the action. The focused action then modifies the situation in ways that confirm the explanation, whatever it is.
>
> Thus, the adequacy of any explanation is determined by the intensity and structure it adds to potentially self-validating actions. More forcefulness leads to more validation and more perceived adequacy. Accuracy is subordinate to intensity. Since situations can support a variety of meanings, their actual content and meaning are dependent on the degree to which they are arranged in sensible, coherent configurations. More forcefulness imposes more coherence. Thus, those explanations that induce greater forcefulness become more valid, not because they are more accurate, but because they have a higher potential for self-validation. . . . the underlying explanations they unfold (for example, "This is war") have great potential to intensify whatever action is underway (1983, pp. 230–232).

Thus, theories are generative to the extent that they are forceful (e.g., Marx), logically coherent (e.g., Piaget), and bold in their assertions and consistency (e.g., Freud, Weber). By providing a basis for focused action, a logic for attributing causality, and a sequence specification that grounds expectations for action and reaction, a theory goes a long way toward forming the common expectations for the future. "And with the alteration of expectation, the stage is set for modification of action" (Gergen, 1982, p. 24).

Transmitting a System of Values

Beyond abstract logic, it is often the affective core of social theory that provides its true force and appeal, allowing it to direct perception and guide behavior. From the tradition of logical positivism, good "objective" theory is to be value-free, yet upon closer inspection we find that social theory is infused with values and domain assumptions throughout. As Gouldner (1970) so aptly put it, "Every social theory facilitates the pursuit of some, but not all, courses of action and thus, encourages us to change or accept the world as it is, to say yea or nay to it. In a way, every theory is a discrete obituary or celebration of some social system."

Nowhere is this better exemplified—negatively—than in the role scientific theory played in the arguments for slavery, colonialism, and belief in the genetic superiority of certain races. The scientific theory in this case was, again, the theory of biological determinism, the belief that social and economic differences between human beings and groups—differences in rank, status, political privilege, education privilege—arise from inherited natural endowments, and that existing social arrangements accurately reflect biological limits. So powerful was this theory during the 1800s that it led a number of America's highest-ranking scientific researchers unconsciously to miscalculate "objective" data in what has been brilliantly described by naturalist Steven Jay Gould (1981, p. 54) as a "patchwork of fudging and finagling in the clear interest of controlling a priori convictions". Before dismissing this harsh judgment as simple rhetoric, we need to look closely at how it was determined. One example will suffice.

When Samuel Morton, a scientist with two medical degrees, died in 1851, the *New York Tribune* paid tribute saying, "Probably no scientific man in America enjoyed a higher reputation among scholars throughout the world than Dr. Morton" (in Gould, 1981, p. 51). Morton gained this reputation as a scientist who set out to rank racial groups by "objectively" measuring the size of the cranial cavity of the human skull, which he regarded as a measure of brain size. He had a beautiful collection of skulls from races throughout the world, probably the largest such collection in existence. His hypothesis was a simple one: The mental and moral worth of human races can be arrived at objectively by measuring physical characteristics of the brain; by filling skull cavities with mustard seed or lead shot, accurate measurement of brain size is possible. Morton published three major works, which were reprinted repeatedly as providing objective, "hard" data on the mental worth of races. Gould comments:

> Needless to say, they matched every good Yankee's prejudices—whites on top, Indians in the middle, and blacks on the bottom; and among whites, Teutons and Anglo-Saxons on top, Jews in the middle, and Hindus on the bottom. . . . Status and access to power in Morton's America faithfully reflected biological merit (p. 54).

Morton's work was undoubtedly influential. When he died, the South's leading medical journal proclaimed: "We of the South should consider him as our benefactor, for aiding most materially in giving the Negro his true position as an inferior race" (in Gould, 1981, p. 69). Indeed Morton did much more than only give "the Negro his true position," as the following remarks by Morton himself convey:

> Negroes were numerous in Egypt, but their social position in ancient time, was the same as it is now, that of servants and slaves. The benevolent mind may regret the inaptitude of the Indian civilization . . . [but values

must not yield to fact]. The structure of his mind appears to be different from that of the white man, or can the two harmonize in social relations except on the most limited scale. [Indians] are not only averse to restraints of education, but for the most part are incapable of a continued process of reasoning on abstract subjects (in Gould, 1981, p. 53).

The problem with these conclusions—as well as the numerical data, which supported them—was that they were based not on "fact" but purely and simply on cultural fiction, on Morton's belief in biological determinism. As Gould meticulously shows, all of Morton's data was wrong. Having reworked it completely, Gould concludes:

Morton's summaries are a patchwork of fudging and finagling in the clear interest of controlling a priori convictions. Yet—and this is the most intriguing aspect of the case—I find no evidence of conscious fraud; indeed, had Morton been a conscious fudger, he would not have published his data so openly.

Conscious fraud is probably rare in science. . . . The prevalence of unconscious finagling, on the other hand, suggests the general conclusion about the social context of science. . . . prior prejudice may be found anywhere, even in the basics of measuring bones and totaling sums (pp. 55–56).

Morton represents a telling example of the power of theory. Theory is not only a shaper of expectations and perceptions. Under the guise of "dispassionate inquiry" it can also be a peddler of values, typecasting arbitrary value as scientific "fact." Along with Gould, we believe that we would be better off to abandon the myth of "value-free" science and that theoretical work "must be understood as a social phenomenon, a gutsy, human enterprise, not the work of robots programmed to collect pure information" (Gould, 1981, p. 21). Even if Morton's data were correct, his work still could not be counted as value-free. His data and theories were not only shaped by the setting in which he worked; they were also used to support broad social policy. This is akin to making nature the source of cultural values, which of course it never can be ("What is" does not equal "what should be").

Creating a Group-Building Language

The sociorationalist perspective is more than a pessimistic epitaph for a strictly logical positivist philosophy. It is an invitation to inquiry that raises the status of theory from mere appendage of scientific method to an actual shaper of society. Once we acknowledge that a primary product of science—theory—is a key resource for the creation of groups, the stage is set for theory-building activity intended for the use and development of human society, for the creation of human options.

Students of human behavior have been aware of the group as the foundation of society since the earliest periods of classical thought. Aristotle, for example, discussed the importance of bands and families. But it was not until the middle of the present century that scientific interest in the subject exploded in a flurry of general inquiry and systematic interdisciplinary research (for a sample review of this literature see Hare, 1976). Among the conclusions of this recent work is the crucial insight that:

The face-to-face group working on a problem is the meeting ground of individual personality and society. It is in the group that personality is modified and socialized and it is through the workings of groups that society is changed and adapted to its times (Thelen, 1954, p. vi).

Similarly, in the field of organization development, Srivastva, Obert, and Neilsen (1977) have shown that the historical development of the discipline has paralleled advances in group theory. And this, they contend, is no accident because:

Emphasis on the small group is responsive to the realities of social change in large complex organizations. It is through group life that individuals learn, practice, develop, and modify their roles in the larger organization. To enter programmatically at the group level is both to confront and po-tentially co-opt an important natural source of change and development in these systems (p. 83).

It is well established that groups are formed around common ideas that are expressed in and through some kind of shared language which makes communica-tive interaction possible. What is less clear, though, is the exact role that science plays in shaping group life through the medium of language. However, the fact that science frequently does have an impact is rarely questioned. Andre Gorz (1973) offers an explosive example of this point.

In the early 1960s a British professor of sociology by the name of Goldthorpe was brought in from a nearby university to make a study of the Vauxhall automobile workers in Luton, England. At the time, management at the factory was worried because workers in other organizations throughout the United Kingdom were show-ing great unrest over working conditions, pay, and management. Many strikes were being waged; most of them wildcat strikes called by the factory stewards, not by the unions themselves. Goldthorpe was called in to study the situation at Vauxhall, to find out for management if there was anything to worry about at their factory. At the time of the study there were at Vauxhall no strikes, no disruptions, and no challenges by workers. Management wanted to know why. What were the chances that acute conflict would break out in the "well-managed" and "advanced" big factory?

After two full years of research, the professor drew his conclusions. Manage-ment, he said, had little to worry about. According to the study, the workers were completely socialized into the system, they were satisfied with their wages and neither liked or disliked their work—in fact, they were indifferent to it, viewing it as boring but inevitable. Because their job was not intrinsically rewarding, most people did it just to be done with it—so they could go home and work on other more worthwhile projects and be with their family. Work was marginal and instrumental. It was a means to support other interests outside the factory, where "real life" began. Based then on his observations, Goldthorpe theorized that management had nothing to worry about: Workers were passively apathetic and well integrated into the system. They behaved according to middle-class patterns and showed no signs of strength as a group (no class-consciousness). Furthermore, most conflict with management belonged to the past.

The sociologist's report was still at the printer's when some employees got hold of a summary of his findings. They had the conclusions copied and distributed reports to hundreds of co-workers. Also at around this time, a report of Vauxhall's profits was being circulated, profits that were not shared with the employees. The next day something happened. It was reported by the *London Times* in detail:

> Wild rioting has broken out at the Vauxhall car factories in Luton. Thousands of workers streamed out of the shops and gathered in the factory yard. They besieged the management offices, calling for managers to come out, singing the 'Red Flag,' and shouting. 'String them up!' Groups attempted to storm the offices and battled police which had been called to protect them (quoted in Gorz, 1973).

The rioting lasted for two days. All of this happened, then, in an advanced factory where systematic research showed workers to be apathetic, weak as a group, and resigned to accept the system. What does it all mean? Had the researchers simply misread the data?

To the contrary. Goldthorpe knew his data well. He articulated the conclusions accurately, concisely, and with force. In fact, what happened was that the report gave the workers a *language* with which to begin talking to one another about their plight. It brought them into interaction and, as they discussed things, they discovered that Goldthorpe was right. They felt alike, apathetic but frustrated; and they were apathetic because they felt as individuals working in isolated jobs, that no one could do anything to change things. But the report gave them a way to discuss the situation. As they talked, things changed. People were no longer alone in their feelings, and they did not want things to continue as they were. As an emergent group, they now had a means to convert apathy into action, noninvolvement into involvement, and individual powerlessness into collective strength. "In other words," analyzes Gorz, "the very investigation of Mr. Goldthorpe about the lack of class-consciousness helped tear down the barriers of silence and isolation that rendered the workers apathetic" (p. 334).

The Vauxhall case is an important one for a number of reasons. At a general level it demonstrates that knowledge in the social sciences differs in quality and kind from knowledge generated in the physical sciences. For instance, our knowledge of the periodic chart does not change the elements, and our knowledge of the moon's orbit does not change its path. But our knowledge of a social system is different. It can be used by the system to change itself, thus invalidating or disconfirming the findings immediately or at some later time. Thus the human group differs from objects in an important way: Human beings have the capacity for symbolic interaction and, through language, they have the ability to collaborate in the investigation of their own world. Because of our human capacity for symbolic interaction, the introduction of new knowledge concerning aspects of our world carries with it the strong likelihood of changing that world itself.

Gergen (1982) refers to this as the "enlightenment effect" of scientific work, meaning that once the formulations of scientific work are made public, human beings may act autonomously either to disconfirm or to validate the propositions. According to logical positivist philosophy, potential enlightenment effects must be reduced or—ideally—eliminated through experimental controls. In social psychology, for example, deception plays a crucial role in doing research; enlightenment effects are viewed as contaminants to good scientific work. Yet there is an alternative way to look at the reactive nature of social research: it is precisely because of the enlightenment effect that theory can and does play an important role in the positive construction of society. In this sense, the enlightenment effect—which is made possible through language—is an essential ingredient making scientific work worthwhile, meaningful, and applicable. It constitutes an invitation to each and every theorist to actively participate in the creation of his or her world by generating compelling theories of what is good, and just, and desirable in social existence.

Extending Visions of Possibility

The position taken by the sociorationalist philosophy of science is that the conduct of inquiry cannot be separated from the everyday negotiation of reality. Social-organizational research is, therefore, a continuing moral concern, a concern of social reconstruction and direction. The choice of what to study, how to study it, and what to report each implies some degree of responsibility. Science, therefore, instead of being considered an endpoint, is viewed as one means of helping humanity create itself. Science in this sense exists for one singular overarching purpose. As Albion Small (1905) proposed almost a century ago, a generative science must aim at "the most thorough, intense, persistent, and systematic effort to make human life all that it is capable of becoming" (pp. 36–37).

Theories gain their generative capacity by extending visions that expand to the realm of the possible. As a general proposition it might be said that theories designed to empower organized social systems will tend to have a greater enlightenment effect than theories of human constraint. This proposition is grounded in a simple but important consideration which we should like to raise as it relates to the unity of theory and practice: Is it not possible that scientific theory gains its capacity to affect cultural practices in very much the same way that powerful leaders inspire people to new heights? Recent research on the functioning of the executive mind (Srivastva, 1983; 1985) raises a set of intriguing parallels between the possibilities of a generative science and the workings of the executive mind.

The essential parallel is seen in the primary role that ideas or ideals play in the mobilization of diverse groups in the common construction of a desired future. Three major themes from the research stand out in this regard:

1. **Vision:** The executive mind works largely from the present and extends itself out to the longer-term future. It is powerful to the extent that it is able to envision a desired future state which challenges perceptions of what is possible and what can be realized. The executive mind operates beyond the frontier of conventional practice without losing sight of either necessity or possibility.

2. **Passion:** The executive mind is simultaneously rational and intuitive, which allows it to tap into the sentiments, values, and dreams of the social collectivity. Executive vision becomes "common vision" to the extent that it ignites the imaginations, hopes, and passions of others-and it does so through the articulation of self-transcending ideals which lend meaning and significance to everyday life.

3. **Integrity:** The executive mind is the mental muscle that moves a system from the present state to a new and different future. As such, this muscle gains strength to the extent that it is founded upon an integrity able to withstand contrary pressures. There are three dimensions to executive integrity. The first, system integrity, refers to the fact that the executive mind perceives the world (the organization, group, or society) as a unified whole, not as a collection of individual parts. The second type of integrity is *moral integrity*. Common-vision leadership is largely an act of caring. It follows the "path of the heart," which is the source of moral and ethical standards. Finally, integrity of vision refers to consistency, coherence, and focus. Executive vision—to the extent to which it is compelling—is focused and unwavering, even in the midst of obstacles, critics, and conflicting alternatives.

Interestingly, these thematic dimensions of the executive mind have their counterparts in recent observations concerning the utilization of organizational research. According to Beyer and Trice (1982), the "affective bonding" that takes place during the research largely determines the attractiveness of its results and generates commitment to utilize their implications. For example, Henshel (1975) suggests that research containing predictions of an appealing future will be utilized and preferred over research that points to a negative or repelling future: "People will work for predicted states they approve of and against those they detest" (p. 103). Similarly, Weiss and Bucavalas (1980) report that results which challenge the status quo are most attractive to high-level executives because they are the persons expected to make new things happen, at least on the level of policy. And, with respect to passion and integrity, Mitroff (1980) urges social scientists to become caring advocates of their ideas, not only to diffuse their theories but also to challenge others to prove them wrong and thus pursue those ideas which have integrity in action.

This section has explored a number of ways in which social theory becomes a powerful resource for change and development in social practice. The argument is simple. Theory is agential in character and has unbounded potential to affect patterns of social action—whether desired or not. As we have seen, theories are not mere explanations of an external world lying "out there" waiting to be objectively recorded. Theories, like powerful ideas, are formative. By establishing perceptual cues and frames, by providing presumptions of logic, by transmitting subtle values, by creating new language, and by extending compelling visions of possibility or constraint—in all these ways social theory becomes a powerful means whereby norms, beliefs, and cultural practices may be altered.

Reawakening the Spirit of Action-Research

The key point is this: Instinctively, intuitively, and tacitly we all know that important ideas can, in a flash, profoundly alter the way we see ourselves, view reality, and conduct our lives. Experience shows that a simple economic forecast, political poll, or technical discovery (like the atomic bomb) can forever change the course of human history. Thus one cannot help but be disturbed and puzzled by the discipline of action-research in its wide-ranging indifference to theory. Not only does it continue to underrate the role of theory as a means for organizational development (Friedlander and Brown, 1974; Bartunek, 1983; Argyris, 1983) but it appears also to have become locked within an assumptive base that systematically distorts our view of organizational reality and inadvertently helps reinforce and perfect the status quo (Brimm, 1972).

Why is there this lack of generative theorizing in action-research? And, more importantly, what can be done to rekindle the spirit, excitement and passion required of a science that wishes to be of vital significance to organizations? Earlier we talked about a philosophy of science congenial to the task. Sociorationalism, it was argued, represents an epistemological point of view conducive to catalytic theorizing. Ironically though, it can be argued that most action researchers *already do* subscribe to this or a similar view of science (Susman and Evered, 1978). Assuming this to be the case, it becomes an even greater puzzle why contemporary action-research continues to disregard theory-building as an integral and necessary component of the craft. In this section we shall broaden our discussion by taking a look at some of the metaphysical assumptions embedded in our conventional definitions of action-research—assumptions that can be shown to govern our thought and work in ways inimical to present interests.

Paradigm 1: Organizing As A Problem to be Solved

The intellectual and spiritual origins of action-research can be traced to Kurt Lewin, a social psychologist of German origin who coined the term *action-research* in 1944. The thrust of Lewin's work centered on the need to bridge the gap between science and the realm of practical affairs. Science, he said, should be used to inform and educate social practice, and subsequent action would then inform science: "We should consider action, research, and training as a triangle that should be kept together" (Lewin, 1948, p. 211). The twofold promise of an action science, according to Lewin, was to simultaneously contribute to the development of scientific knowledge (propositions of an if/then variety) and use such knowledge for bettering the human condition.

The immense influence of Lewin is a complete puzzle if we look only to his writings. The fact of the matter is that Lewin published only 2 papers—a mere 22 pages—concerned directly with the idea of action- earch (Peters and Robinson, 1984). Indeed, it has been argued that his enduring influence is attributable not to these writings but to the sheer force and presence of the man himself. According to biographer Alfred Marrow (1968), Lewin was a passionate and creative thinker, continuously knocking at the door of the unknown, studying "topics that had been believed to be psychologically unapproachable." Lewin's character was marked by a spirit of inquiry that burned incessantly and affected all who came in contact with him, especially his students. The intensity of his presence was fueled further by the belief that inquiry itself could be used to construct a more democratic and dignified future. At least this was his hope and dream, for Lewin had *not* forgotten his experience as a refugee from fascism in the late 1930s. Understanding this background, then, it is clear why he revolted so strongly against a detached ivory-tower view of science, a science that is immersed in trivial matters, tranquilized by its standardized methods, and limited in its field of inquiry. Thus, the picture we have of Lewin shows him to have been a committed social scientist pioneering uncharted territory for the purpose of creating new knowledge about groups and societies that might advance the democratic ideal (see, for example, Lewin, 1952). It was this spirit—a relentless curiosity coupled with a conviction of the need for knowledge-guided societal development—that marked Lewin's creative impact on both his students and the field.

Much of this spirit is now gone from action-research. What is left is a series of assumptions about the world which exhibits little, if any, resemblance to the process of inquiry as Lewin lived it. While many of the words are the same, they have been taken too literally and in their translation over the years have been bloated into a set of metaphysical principles—assumptions about the essence of social existence-that directly undermine the intellectual and speculative spirit. Put bluntly, under current norms, action-research has largely failed as an instrument for advancing social knowledge of consequence and now risks being (mis)understood as little more than a crude empiricism imprisoned in a deficiency mode of thought. A quick sketch of six sets of assumptions embedded in the conventional view of action-research will show exactly what we are talking about while also answering our question about the discipline's lack of contribution to generative theory: *Research equals problem-solving; to do good research is to solve "real problems."* So ingrained is this assumption that it scarcely needs documentation. Virtually every definition found in leading texts and articles equates action research with problem solving—as if "real" problem solving is virtually the essence of the discipline. For example, as French and Bell (1978) define it, "Action-research is both *an approach to problem solving*—a model or paradigm, and *a problem-solving process*—a series of activities and events." (p. 88)[4] Or in terms of the Bradford, Gibb, and Benne (1964) definition, "It is an application of scientific methodology in *the clarification and solution of practical problems*" (p. 33). Similarly, Frohman, Sashkin, and Kavanaugh (1976) state: "Action research describes a particular process model whereby behavioral science knowledge is applied to help a client (usually a group or social system) *solve real problems and not incidentally learn the process involved in problem solving*" (p. 203). Echoing this theme, that research equals problem solving, researchers at the University of Michigan's Institute in Social Research state,

> Three factors need to be taken into account in an organization development [action-research] effort: The behaviors that are problematic, the conditions that create those behaviors, and the interventions or activities that will correct the conditions creating the problems. What is it that people are doing or not doing, that is a problem? Why are they doing or not doing these particular things? Which of a large number of possible interventions or activities would be most likely to solve the problems by focusing on why problems exist? (Hausser, Pecorella and Wissler, 1977, p. 2).

Here it is unmistakably clear that the primary focus of the action-research approach to organizational analysis is the ongoing array of concrete problems an organization faces. Of course, there are a number of differences in the discipline as to the overall definition and meaning of the emerging action-research paradigm. But this basic assumption—that research equals problem solving—is not one of them. In a recent review intended to discover elements of metatheoretical agreement within the discipline, Peters and Robinson (1984) discovered that out of 15 different dimensions of action-research studied, only 2 had unanimous support among leaders in the field. What were these two elements of agreement? Exactly as the definitions above suggest: Social science should be "action oriented" and "problem focused."

Inquiry, in action-research terms, is a matter of following the standardized rules of problem solving; knowledge is the result of good method. "In essence," write Blake and Mouton (1976), "it is a method of empirical data gathering that is

---

[4]Emphasis in this and the following definitions are ours, intended to underscore the points being made. Earlier we noted the importance of language as a subtle cueing device. Keeping this in mind, the reader is asked to pay special attention to the language of problem solving, and perhaps even count the sheer number of times the word problem is used in relation to definitions of action research.

comprised of a set of rather standardized steps: diagnosis, information gathering, feedback, and action planning" (pp. 101–102). By following this ritual list, they contend that virtually any organization can be studied in a manner that will lead to usable knowledge. As Chiles (1983) puts it, "The virtue of the model lies in the sequential process. . . . Any other sequence renders the model meaningless" (p. 318). The basic idea behind the model is that "in management, events proceed as planned unless some force, not provided against by the plan, acts upon events to produce an outcome not contemplated in the plan" (Kepner and Tregoe, 1973, p. 3). Thus, a problem is a deviation from some standard, and without precise diagnosis (step one) any attempt to resolve the problem will likely fail as a result of not penetrating the surface symptoms to discover the true causes. Hence, like a liturgical refrain which is seldom questioned or thought about, Cohen, Fink et al. (1984) tell the new student that *knowledge is the offspring of processing information through a distinct series of problem-solving stages*:

> Action-research begins with an identified problem. Data are then gathered in a way that allows a diagnosis which can produce a tentative solution, which is then implemented with the assumption that it is likely to cause new or unforeseen problems that will, in turn, need to be evaluated, diagnosed, and so forth. *This action-research method assumes a constantly evolving interplay between solutions, results, and new solutions. . . . This model is a general one applicable to solving any kind of problem in an ongoing organization* (pp. 359–360).

Action-research is utilitarian or technical; that is, it should be initiated and designed to meet a need in an area specified by the organization, usually by "top management." The search is controlled by the "felt need" or object of inquiry; everything that is not related to this object should be dismissed as irrelevant. As we are beginning to see, action-research conventionally understood does not really refer to research per se but rather to a highly focused and defined *type* of research called problem solving. Taken almost directly from the medical model, the disease orientation guides the process of inquiry in a highly programmed way. According to Levinson (1972), diagnostic action-research, "like a therapeutic or teaching relationship should be an alliance of both parties to discover and resolve these problems. . . . [The researcher] *should look for experiences which appear stressful to people. What kinds of occurrences disrupt or disorganize people*" (p. 37). Hence in a systematically limiting fashion, the general topic of research is largely prescribed—before inquiry even begins. As we would guess:

> Typical questions in [action-research] data gathering or "problem sensing" would include: *What problems* do you see in your group, including problems between people that are interfering with getting the job done the way you would like to see it done? And *what problems* do you see in the broader organization? Such open-ended questions provide latitude on the part of respondents and encourage a *reporting of problems* as the individual sees them (French, 1969, pp. 183–185).

In problem solving it is assumed that something is broken, fragmented, not whole, and that it needs to be fixed. Thus the function of problem solving is to integrate, stabilize, and help raise to its full potential the workings of the status quo. By definition, a problem implies that one already has knowledge of what "should be"; thus one's *re*search is guided by an instrumental purpose tied to what is already known. In this sense, problem solving tends to be inherently conservative; as a form of research it tends to produce and reproduce a universe of knowledge that remains sealed. As Staw (1984) points out in his review of the field, most organizational research is biased to serve managerial interests rather than exploring broader human and/or social purposes. But even more important, he argues, the field has not even served managerial interests well since research has taken a short-term problem focus rather than having formulated logic's of new forms of organization that do not exist. It is as if the discipline's *concept of social system development* means only clearing up distortions in current functioning (horizontal development) and does not include any conception of a stage-based movement toward an altogether new or transformed reality (vertical development or second-order change).

Action-research should not inquire into phenomena that transcend the competence of human reason. Questions that cannot be answered should not be asked and issues that cannot be acted upon should not be explored (i.e., action-research is not a branch of political philosophy, poetry, or theology). This proposition is a "smuggled-in" corollary to the preceding assumptions. It would appear that once one agrees with the ground rules of a pragmatic problem-solving science, the universe for inquiry is largely predetermined, defined, and delimited in scope. Specifically, what one agrees to a secularized view of a human universe that is predictable, controllable, and rational, one that is sequentially ordered into a series of causes and effects. As both a credit and a weakness, the problem-solving mode narrows our gaze in much the same manner that a blinder over one eye narrows the field of vision and distorts one's perception of depth. As a part of a long-term movement evidenced in social sciences, contemporary action-research embodies the trend toward metaphysical skepticism and denial (Quinney, 1982). That is, it operates out of a sacred void that cuts off virtually any inquiry into the vital forces of life. Indeed, the whole promise of modern science was that it would finally banish illusion, mystery, and uncertainty from the world. An inquiry process of immediate utility (problem solving), therefore, requires an anti-religious, secular spirit that will limit the realm of study to the sphere of the known. And because of the recognition that the formulation of a problem depends largely on one's views of what constitutes a solution, it is not surprising to find that *research on the utilization of research* shows a propensity for social scientists and organizations to agree on studying only those variables that can be manipulated (Beyer and Trice, 1982). As one might imagine, such a view has crippling implications for generative theorizing. For example, as typically practiced, action-research does little in the way of theorizing about or bringing beauty into organizational life. Does this mean that there is no beauty in organizing? Does this mean that the realm of the esthetic has little or nothing to do with organizational dynamics?

The tidy imagery of the problem-solving view is related to what Sigmund Koch (1981) has called, in his presidential address to the APA, the syndrome of "ameaningful thinking." One element of this syndrome is the perpetuation of the scientistic myth which uses the rhetoric of prediction and control to reassure people that their lives are not that complex, their situations not all that uncertain—and that their problems are indeed manageable through causal analysis. In the process, however, science tends to trivialize, and even evade, a whole class of issues that "transcend the competence of human reason" yet are clearly meaningful in the course of human experience. One way in which the field of inquiry is restricted, according to Koch, has to do with one's choice of methodology:

> There are times and circumstances in which able individuals, committed to inquiry, tend almost obsessively to frustrate the objectives of inquiry. It is as if uncertainty, mootness, ambiguity, cognitive infinitude were the most unbearable of the existential anguishes. . . . *Ameaningful* thought or inquiry regards knowledge as the result of "processing" rather than discovery. It presumes that knowledge is an almost automatic result of a gimmickry, an assembly line, a "methology". . . . So strongly does it see knowledge under such aspects that it sometimes seems to suppose the object of inquiry to be an ungainly and annoying irrelevance (1981, p. 259).

To be sure, this is not to argue that all action-research is "ameaningful" or automatically tied to a standardized problem-solving method. Likewise, much of the success achieved by action-research until now may be attributed to its restricted focus on that which is "solvable." However, it is important to recognize that the problem-solving method of organizational inquiry quite systematically paints a picture of organizational life in which a whole series of colors are considered untouchable. In this way the totality of being is obviously obscured, leading to a narrowed conception of human nature and cultural possibility.

Problems are "out there" to be studied and solved. The ideal product of action-research is a mirror-like reflection of the organization's problems and causes. As "objective third party " there is little role for passion and speculation. The action-researcher should be neither a passionate advocate nor an inspired dreamer (utopian thinker). One of the laudable and indeed significant values associated with action-research has been its insistence upon a collaborative form of inquiry. But unfortunately, from a generative-theory perspective, the term *collaboration* has become virtually synonymous with an idealized image of the researcher as a facilitator and mirror, rather than an active and fully engaged social participant. As facilitator of the problem-solving process, the action-researcher has three generally agreed-upon "primary intervention tasks": to help generate valid organizational data; to enable others to make free and informed choices on the basis of the data, and to help the organization generate internal commitment to their choices. Elaborating further, Argyris (1970) states:

> One condition that seems so basic as to be defined as axiomatic is the generation of *valid information*. . . . *Valid information is that which*

describes the factors, plus their interrelationships that create the problem (pp. 16–17).

Furthermore, it is also assumed that for data to be useful there must be a claim to neutrality. The data should represent an accurate reflection of the observed facts. As French and Bell (1978) describe it, it is important for the action-researcher to stress the objective, fact-finding features: "A key value inculcated in organizational members is a belief in the validity, desirability, and usefulness of the data" (p. 79). Then through feedback that "refers to activities and processes that 'reflect' or 'mirror' an objective picture of the real world" (p. 111), the action-researcher facilitates the process of prioritizing problems and helps others make choices for action. And because the overarching objective is to help the organization develop its own internal resources, the action-researcher should not play an active role or take an advocate stance that might in the long run foster an unhealthy dependency. As French and Bell (1978) again explain, an active role "tends to negate a collaborative, developmental approach to improving organizational processes" (p. 203).

As must be evident, every one of these injunctions associated with the problem-solving view of action-research serves directly to diminish the likelihood of imaginative, passionate, creative theory. To the extent that generative theory represents an inspired theoretical articulation of a new and different future, it appears that action-research would have nothing to do with it. According to French and Bell (1978) "Even the presenting of options can be overdone. If the [action-researcher's] ideas become the focal point for prolonged discussion and debate, the consultant has clearly shifted away from the facilitator role" (p. 206).

At issue here is something even more important. The fundamental attitude embodied in the problem-solving view is separationist. It views the world as something external to our consciousness of it, something "out there." As such it tends to identify problems not here but "over there": Problems are not ours, but yours; not a condition common to all, but a condition belonging to this person, their group, or that nation (witness the acid-rain issue). Thus, the action-researcher is content to facilitate *their problem solving* because he or she is not part of that world. To this extent, the problem-solving view dissects reality and parcels it out into fragmented groups, families, tribes, or countries. In both form and substance it denies the wholeness of a dynamic and interconnected social universe. And once the unity of the world is broken, passionless, mindless, mirror-like inquiry comes to make logical sense precisely because the inquirer has no ownership or stake in a world that is not his or hers to begin with.

Organizational life is problematic. Organizing is best understood as a historically situated sequence of problems, causes, and solutions among people, events, and things. Thus, the ultimate aim and product of action-research is the production of institutions that have a high capacity to perceive, formulate, and solve an endless stream of problems.

The way we conceive of the social world is of consequence to the kind of world we discover and even, through our reconstructions, helps to create it. Action-researchers, like scientists in other areas, approach their work from a framework based on taken-for-granted assumptions. To the extent that these assumptions are found useful, and are affirmed by colleagues, they remain unquestioned as a habitual springboard for one's work. In time the conventional view becomes so solidly embedded that it assumes the status of being "real," without alternative (Morgan, 1980; Mennhiem, 1936). As human beings we are constantly in symbolic interaction, attempting to develop conceptions that will allow us to make sense of and give meaning to experience through the use of language, ideas, signs, theories, and names. As many have recently shown, the use of metaphor is a basic mode under which symbolism works and exerts an influence on the development of language, science, and cognitive growth (Morgan, 1980; Ortony, 1979; Black, 1962; Keely, 1980). Metaphor works by asserting that A equals B or is ve   much like B. We use metaphors constantly to open our eyes and sensitize us to phenomenal realities that otherwise might go unnoticed. Pepper (1942) argues that all science proceeds from specifiable "world hypotheses" and behind every world hypothesis rests the boldest of "root metaphors."

Within what we are calling Paradigm I action-research, there lies a guiding metaphor which has a power impact on the theory-building activity of the discipline. When organizations are approached from the deficiency perspective of Paradigm I, all the properties and modes of organizing are scrutinized for their dysfunctional but potentially solvable problems. It is all too clear then that the root metaphor of the conventional view is that *organizing is a problem.* This image focuses the researcher's eye on a visible but narrow realm of reality that resides "out there" and is causally determined, deficient by some preexisting standard—on problems that are probably both understandable and solvable. Through analysis, diagnosis, treatment, and follow-up evaluation the sequential world of organizing can be kept on its steady and productive course. And because social existence is at its base a problem to be solved, real living equals problem solving, and living better is an adaptive learning process whereby we acquire new and more effective means for tackling tough problems. The good life, this image informs, depends on solving problems in such a way that problems of utility are identified and solutions of high quality are found and carried out with full commitment. As one leading theorist describes:

> For many scholars who study organizations and management, the central characteristic of organizations is that they are problem-solving systems whose success is measured by how efficiently they solve problems associated with accomplishing their primary mission and how effectively they respond to emergent problems. Kilmann's approach (1979, pp. 214–215) is representative of this perspective: "One might even define the essence of management as problem defining and problem solving, whether the problems are well-structured, ill-structured, technical, human, or environmental. . . . In this view, the core task of the executive is problem management. Although experience, personality, and specific technical expertise are important, the primary skill of the successful executive is the ability to manage the problem-solving process in such a way that important problems

are identified and solutions of high quality are found and carried out with the full commitment of organizational members (Kolb, 1983, pp. 109–110).

From here it is just a short conceptual jump to the idealized aim of Paradigm 1 research:

Action-research tends to build into the client system an institutionalized pattern for continuously collecting data and examining the system's processes, as well as for the continuous review of *known* problem areas. *Problem solving becomes very much a way of organizational life* (Marguiles and Raia, 1972, p. 29).

I have tried in these few pages to highlight the almost obvious point that the deficiency/problem orientation is pervasive and holds a subtle but powerful grasp on the discipline's imagination and focus. It can be argued that the generative incapacity of contemporary action-research is securely linked with the discipline's guiding metaphor of social-organizational existence. As noted by many scholars, the theoretical output of the discipline is virtually nonexistent, and what theory there is, is largely problem-focused (theories of turnover, intergroup conflict, processes of dehumanization. See Staw, 1984 for an excellent review). Thus, our theories, like windsocks, continue to blow steadily onward in the direction of our conventional gaze. Seeing the world as a problem has become "very much a way of organizational life."

It is our feeling that the discipline has reached a level of fatigue arising from repetitive use of its standardized model. Fatigue, as Whitehead (1929) so aptly surmised, arises from an act of excluding the impulse toward novelty, which is the antithesis of the life of the mind and of speculative reason. To be sure, there can be great adventure in the process of inquiry. Yet not many action-researchers today return from their explorations refreshed and revitalized, like pioneers returning home, with news of lands unknown but most certainly there. Perhaps there is a different root metaphor from which to work.

Proposal for a Second Dimension

Our effort here is but one in a small yet growing attempt to generate new perspectives on the conduct of organizational research, perspectives that can yield the kind of knowledge necessary for both understanding and transforming complex social-organizational systems (Torbert, 1983; Van Maanen et al., 1982; Mitroff and Kilmann, 1978; Smirchich, 1983; Forester, 1983; Argyris, 1970; Friedlander, 1977). It is apparent that among the diverse views currently emerging there is frequently great tension. Often the differences become the battleground for fierce debate about theories of truth, the meaning of "facts," political agendas, and personal assertions of will. But, more fruitfully, what can be seen emerging is a heightened sensitivity to and interdisciplinary recognition of the fact that, based on "the structure of knowledge" (Kolb, 1984), there may be multiple ways of knowing, each of them valid in its own realm when judged according to its own set of essential assumptions and purposes. In this sense there are many different ways of studying the same phenomenon, and the insights generated by one approach are, at best, partial and incomplete. According to Jurgen Habermas (1971) different perspectives can be evaluated only in terms of their specified "human interests," which can broadly be differentiated into the realm of practical rationality and the realm of technical rationality. In more straightforward language Morgan (1983) states:

> The selection of method implies some view of the situation being studied, for any decision on *how* to study a phenomenon carries with it certain assumptions or explicit answers to the question, *"What is being studied?"* Just as we select a tennis racquet rather than a golf club to play tennis because we have a prior conception as to what the game of tennis involves, so too, in relation to the process of social research, we select or favor particular kinds of methodology because we have implicit or explicit conceptions as to what we are trying to do with our research (p. 19).

Thus, in adopting one mode over another the researcher directly influences what he or she will finally discover and accomplish.

It is the contention of this chapter that advances in generative theorizing will come about for action-research when the discipline decides to expand its universe of exploration, seeks to discover new questions, and rekindles a fresh perception of the extra ordinary in everyday organizational life. In this final section we now describe the assumptions and philosophy of an applied administrative science that seeks to embody these suggestions in a form of organization study we call appreciative inquiry. In distinction to conventional action-research, the knowledge-interest of appreciative inquiry lies not so much in problem solving as in social innovation. Appreciative inquiry refers to a research perspective that is uniquely intended for discovering, understanding, and fostering innovations in social-organizational arrangements and processes.[5] Its purpose is to contribute to the generative-theoretical aims of social science and to use such knowledge to promote egalitarian dialogue leading to social-system effectiveness and integrity. Whatever else it may be, social-system effectiveness is defined here quite specifically as a congruence between social-organizational values (the ever-changing non-native set of values, ideas, or interests that system members hold concerning the question, "How should we organize ourselves?") and everyday social-organizational practices (cf. Torbert, 1983). Thus, appreciative inquiry refers to both a search for knowledge and a theory of intentional collective action which are

---

[5]Following Whyte (1982), a social innovation will be defined as: (1) a new element in organizational structure or interorganizational relations (2) innovative sets of procedures, reward systems, or interaction and activity and the relations of human beings to the natural and social environments (3) a new administrative policy in actual use; (4) new role or sets of roles; and (5) new belief systems of ideologies transforming basic modes of relating.

designed to help evolve the normative vision and will of a group, organization, or society as a whole. It is an inquiry process that affirms our symbolic capacities of imagination and mind as well as our social capacity for conscious choice and cultural evolution. As a holistic form of inquiry, it asks a series of questions not found in either a logical-positivist conception of science or a strictly pragmatic, problem-solving mode of action-research. Yet as shown in Figure 3.1, its aims are both scientific (in a sociorationalist sense) and pragmatic (in a social-innovation sense) as well as metaphysical and normative (in the sense of attempting ethically to affirm all that social existence really is and should become). As a way of talking about the framework as it is actually practiced, we shall first examine four guiding principles that have directed our work in the area to date:

PRINCIPLE 1: *Research into the social (innovation) potential of organizational, life should begin with appreciation.* This basic principle assumes that every social system "works" to some degree—that it is not in a complete state of entropy—and that a primary task of research is to discover, describe, and explain those social innovations, however small, which serve to give "life" to the system and activate members' competencies and energies as more fully functioning participants in the formation and transformation of organizational realities. That is, the appreciative approach takes its inspiration from the current state of "what is" and seeks a comprehensive understanding of the factors and forces of organizing (ideological, techno-structural, cultural) that serve to heighten the total potential of an organization in ideal-type human and social terms.

PRINCIPLE 2: *Research into the social potential of organizational life should be applicable.* To be significant in a human sense, an applied science of administration should lead to the generation of theoretical knowledge that can be used, applied, and thereby validated in action. Thus, an applicable inquiry process is neither utopian in the sense of generating knowledge about "no place" (Sargent, 1982) nor should it be confined to academic circles and presented in ways that have little relevance to the everyday language and symbolism of those for whom the findings might be applicable.

PRINCIPLE 3: *Research into the social potential of organizational life should be provocative.* Here it is considered axiomatic that an organization is, in fact, an open-ended indeterminate system capable of (1) becoming more than it is at any given moment, and (2) learning how to actively take part in guiding its own evolution. Hence, appreciative knowledge of what is (in terms of "peak" social innovations in organizing) is suggestive of what *might be* and such knowledge can be used to generate images of realistic developmental opportunities that can be experimented with on a wider scale. In this sense, appreciative inquiry can be both pragmatic and visionary. It becomes provocative to the extent that the abstracted findings of a study take on normative value for members of an organization, and this can happen only through their own critical deliberation and choice ("We feel that this particular

Figure 3.1. Dimensions of Appreciative Inquiry.

finding is [or not] important for us to envision as an ideal to be striving for in practice on a wider scale"). It is in this way then, that appreciative inquiry allows us to put intuitive, visionary logic on a firm empirical footing and to use systematic research to help the organization's members shape the social world according to their own imaginative and moral purposes.

PRINCIPLE 4: *Research into the social potential of organizational life should be collaborative.* This overarching principle points to the assumed existence of an inseparable relationship between the process of inquiry and its content. A collaborative relationship between the researcher and members of an organization is, therefore, deemed essential on the basis of both epistemological (Susman and Evered, 1978) and practical/ethical grounds (Habermas, 1971; Argyris, 1970). Simply put, a unilateral approach to the study of social innovation (bringing something new into the social world) is a direct negation of the phenomenon itself.

The spirit behind each of these four principles of appreciative inquiry is to be found in one of the most ancient archetypes or metaphorical symbols of hope and inspiration that humankind has ever known—the miracle and mystery of being. Throughout history, people have recognized the intimate relationship between being seized by the unfathomable and the process of appreciative knowing or thought (Marcel, 1963; Quinney, 1982; Jung, 1933; Maslow, 1968; Ghandi, 1958). According to Albert Schweitzer (1969), for example, it is recognition of the ultimate mystery that elevates our perception beyond the world of ordinary objects, igniting the life of the mind and a "reverence for life":

In all respects the universe remains mysterious to man. . . . As soon as man does not take his existence for granted, but beholds it as something unfathomably mysterious, thought begins. This phenomenon has been repeated time and time again in the history of the human race. Ethical affirmation of life is the intellectual act by which man ceases simply to live at random. . . . [Such] thought has a dual task to accomplish: to lead us out of a naive and into a profounder affirmation of life and the universe; and to help us progress from ethical impulses to a rational system of ethics (p. 33).

For those of us breastfed by an industrial giant that stripped the world of its wonder and awe, it feels, to put it bluntly, like an irrevelant, absurd, and even distracting interruption to pause, reflect deeply, and then humbly accept the depth of what we can never know—and to consider the ultimate reality of living for which there are no coordinates or certainties, only questions. Medicine cannot tell me, for example, what it means that my newborn son has life and motion and soul, anymore than the modern physicist can tell me what "nothingness" is, which, they say, makes up over 99 percent of the universe. In fact, if there is anything we have learned from a great physicist of our time is that the promise of certainty is a lie (Hiesenberg, 1958), and by living this lie as scientistic doctrine, we short-circuit the gift of complementarity—the capacity for dialectically opposed modes of knowing, which adds richness, depth, and beauty to our lives (Bohr, 1958). Drugged by the products of our industrial machine we lose sight of and connection with the invisible mystery at the heart of creation, an ultimate power beyond rational understanding.

In the same way that birth of a living, breathing, loving, thinking human being is an inexplicable mystery, so too it can be said in no uncertain terms that *organizing is a miracle* of cooperative human interaction, of which there can never be final explanation. In fact, to the extent that organizations are indeed born and re-created through dialogue, they truly are unknowable as long as such creative dialogue remains. At this point in time there simply are no organizational theories that can account for the life-giving essence of cooperative existence, especially if one delves deeply enough. But, somehow we forget all this. We become lulled by our simplistic diagnostic boxes. The dilemma faced by our discipline in terms of its creative contribution to knowledge is summed up perfectly in the title of a well known article by one of the major advocates of action-research. The title by Marv Wiesbord (1976), has proven prophetic: "Organizational diagnosis: six places to look for trouble, with or without a theory." Content to transfer our conceptual curiosity over to "experts" who finally must know, our creative instincts lie pitifully dormant. Instead of explorers we become mechanics.

This, according to Koch (1981), is the source of "ameaningful" thinking. As Kierkegaard (1954) suggests, it is the essence of a certain dull-minded routine called "philistinism:

> Devoid of imagination, as the Philistine always is, he lives in a certain trivial province of experience as to how things go, what is possible. . . . Philistinism tranquilizes itself in the trivial (pp. 174–175).

As we know, a miracle is something that is beyond all possible verification, yet is experienced as real. As a symbol, the word *miracle* represents unification of the sacred and secular into a realm of totality that is at once terrifying and beautiful, inspiring and threatening. Quinney (1982) has suggested with respect to the rejuvenation of   ial theory, that such a unified viewpoint is altogether necessary, that it can have a powerful impact on the discipline precisely because in a world that is at once sacred and secular there is no place, knowledge, or phenomenon that is without mystery. The "miracle" then is pragmatic in its effect when sincerely apprehended by a mind that has chosen not to become "tranquilized in the trivial." In this sense, the metaphor "life is a miracle" is not so much an idea as it is—or can be—a central feature of experience enveloping (1) our perceptual consciousness; (2) our way of relation to others, the world, and our own research; and (3) our way of knowing. Each of these points can be highlighted by a diverse literature.

In terms of the first, scholars have suggested that the power of what we call the miracle lies in its capacity to advance one's perceptual capacity what Maslow (1968) has called a B-cognition or a growth-vs-deficiency orientation, or what Kolb (1984) has termed integrative consciousness. Kolb writes:

> The transcendental quality of integrative consciousness is precisely that, a "climbing out of". . . . This state of consciousness is not reserved for the monastery, but it is a necessary ingredient for creativity in any field. Albert Einstein once said, "The most beautiful and profound emotion one can feel is a sense of the mystical. . . . It is the dower of all true science" (p. 158).

Second, as Gabriel Marcel (1963) explained in his William James lectures at Harvard on *The Mystery of Being*, the central conviction of life as a mystery creates for us a distinctly different relationship to the world than the conviction of life as a problem to be solved:

> A problem is something met which bars my passage. It is before me in its entirety. A mystery on the other hand is something I find *myself* caught up in, and whose essence is therefore not before me in its entirety. It is though in this province the distinction between "in me" and "before me" loses its meaning (p. 80).

Berman's (1981) recent analysis comes to a similar conclusion. The re-enchantment of the world gives rise to a "participatory consciousness" where there is a sense of personal stake, ownership, and partnership with the universe:

> The view of nature which predominated the West down to the eve of the Scientific Revolution was that of an enchanted world. Rocks, trees, rivers, and clouds were all seen as wondrous, alive, and human beings felt at home in this environment. The cosmos, in short, was a place of *belonging*. A member of this cosmos was not an alienated observer of it but a direct

participant in its drama. His personal destiny was bound up with its destiny, and this relationship gave meaning to his life.

Third, as so many artists and poets have shown, there is a relationship between what the Greeks called *thaumazein*—an experience which lies on the borderline between wonderment and admiration—and a type of intuitive apprehension or knowing that we call appreciative. For Keats, the purpose of his work was:

to accept things as I saw them, to enjoy the beauty I perceived for its own sake, without regard to ultimate truth or falsity, and to make a description of it the end and purpose of my appreciations.

Similarly for Shelley:

Poetry thus makes immortal all that is best and most beautiful in the world . . . it exalts the beauty of that which is most beautiful . . . it strips the veil of familiarity from the world, and lays bare the naked and sleeping beauty, which is in the spirit of its forms.

And in strikingly similar words, learning theorist David Kolb (1984) analyzes the structure of the knowing mind and reports:

Finally, appreciation is a process of affirmation. Unlike criticism, which is based on skepticism and doubt (compare Polanyi, 1968, pp. 269ff.), appreciation is based on belief, trust, and conviction. And from this affirmative embrace flows a deeper fullness and richness of experience. This act of affirmation forms the foundation from which vital comprehension can develop. . . . Appreciative apprehension and critical comprehension are thus fundamentally different processes of knowing. Appreciation of immediate experience is an act of attention, valuing, and affirmation, whereas critical comprehension of symbols is based on objectivity (which involves a priori controls of attention, as in double-blind controlled experiments), dispassionate analysis, and skepticism (pp. 104–105).

We have cited these various thinkers in detail for several reasons: first, to underscore the fact that the powerful images of problem and miracle (in)form qualitatively distinct modes of inquiry which then shape our awareness, relations, and knowledge; and second, to highlight the conviction that the renewal of generative theory requires that we enter into the realm of the metaphysical. The chief characteristic of the modern mind has been the banishment of mystery from the world, and along with it an ethical affirmation of life that has served history as a leading source of values, hope, and normative bonding among people. In historical terms, we have steadily forgotten how to dream.

In contrast to a type of research that is lived without a sense of mystery, the appreciative mode awakens the desire to create and discover new social possibilities that can enrich our existence and give it meaning. In this sense, appreciative inquiry seeks an imaginative and fresh perception of organizations as "ordinary magic," as if seen for the first time—or perhaps the last time (Hayward, 1984). The appreciative mode, in exploration of ordinary magic, is an inquiry process that takes nothing for granted, searching to apprehend the basis of organizational life and working to articulate those possibilities giving witness to a better existence.

The metaphysical dimension of appreciative inquiry is important not so much as a way of finding answers but is important insofar as it heightens the living experience of awe and wonder which leads us to the wellspring of new questions—much like a wide-eyed explorer without final destination. Only by raising innovative questions will innovations in theory and practice be found. As far as action-research is concerned, this appears to have been the source of Lewin's original and catalytic genius. We too can re-awaken this spirit. Because the questions we ask largely determine what we find, we should place a premium on that which informs our curiosity and thought. The metaphysical question of what makes social existence possible will never go away. The generative-theoretical question of compelling new possibilities will never go away. The normative question of what kind of social-organizational order is best, most dignified, and just, will never go away, nor will the pragmatic question of how to move closer to the ideal.

In its pragmatic form appreciative inquiry represents a data-based theory building methodology for evolving and putting into practice the collective will of a group or organization. It has one and only one aim—to provide a generative theoretical springboard for normative dialogue that is conducive to self-directed experimentation in social innovation. It must be noted, however, that the conceptual world which appreciative inquiry creates remains—despite its empirical content—an illusion. This is important to recognize because it is precisely because of its visionary content, placed in juxtaposition to grounded examples of the extraordinary, that appreciative inquiry opens the status quo to possible transformations in collective action. It appreciates the best of "what is" to ignite intuition of the possible and then firmly unites the two logically, caringly, and passionately into a theoretical hypothesis of an envisioned future. By raising ever new questions of an appreciative, applicable, and provocative nature, the researcher collaborates in the scientific construction of his or her world.[6]

Conclusion

What we have tried to do with this chapter is present conceptual refiguration of action-research; to present a proposal arguing for an enriched multidimensional

---

[6]For an example of the type of theory generated through appreciative inquiry, see "The Emergence of the Egalitarian Organization" (Srivastva and Cooperrider, 1986).

view of action-research which seeks to be both theoretically generative and progressive in a broad human sense. In short, the argument is a simple one stating that there is a need to re-awaken the imaginative spirit of action-research and that to do this we need a fundamentally different perspective toward our organizational world, one that admits to its uncertainties, ambiguities, mysteries, and unexplicable, miraculous nature. But now we must admit, with a certain sense of limited capability and failure, that the viewpoint articulated here is simply not possible to define and is very difficult to speak of in technological, step-by-step terms. From the perspective of rational thought, the miraculous is impossible. From that of problem solving it is nonsense. And from that of empirical science, it is categorically denied (Reeves, 1984). Just as we cannot prove the proposition that organizing is a problem to be solved, so, too, we cannot prove in any rational, analytical, or empirical way that organizing is a miracle to be embraced. Each stance represents a commitment—a core conviction so to speak—which is given to each of us as a choice. We do, however, think that through discipline and training the appreciative eye can be developed to see the ordinary magic, beauty, and real possibility in organizational life; but we are not sure we can so easily transform our central convictions.

In sum, the position we have been developing here is that for action-research to reach its potential as a vehicle for social innovation, it needs to begin advancing theoretical knowledge of consequence—that good theory may be one of the most powerful means human beings have for producing change in a post-industrial world; that the discipline's steadfast commitment to a problem-solving view of the world is a primary restraint on its imagination, passion, and positive contribution; that appreciative inquiry represents a viable complement to conventional forms of action- research, one uniquely suited for social innovation instead of problem solving; and that through our assumptionsn d choice of method we largely create the world we later discover.

References

Argyris, C. (1973). Action science and intervention. *The Journal of Applied Behavioral Science,* 19, 115–140.

Argyris, C. (1970). *Intervention theory and methods.* Reading, MA: Addison-Wesley.

Argyris, C. and Schon, D. (1978). *Organizational learning: A theory of action perspective.* Reading. MA: Addison-Wesley.

Bartunek, J. (1983). How organization development can develop organizational theory. *Group and Organizational Studies.* 8, 303–318.

Bartunek, J. (1984). Changing interpretive schemes and organizational restructuring: The example of a religious order. *Administrative Science Quarterly,* 27, 355–372.

Bell, D. (1973). *The coming of the Post-Industrial society.* New York: Basic Books.

Beyer, J. (1981). Ideologies, values and decision making in organizations. In P. C. Nystrom and W. H. Starbuck (Eds.), *Handbook of organizational design, Vol. 2.* Oxford University Press.

Beyer, J. and Trice, H. (1982). Utilization process: Conceptual framework and synthesis of findings. *Administrative Science Quarterly*, 22, 591–622.

Blake. R. and Mouton. J. (1976). *Consultation.* Reading, MA: Addison Wesley.

Bohr, N. (1958). *Atomic theory and human knowledge.* New York: John Wiley.

Bradford, L. P., Gibb, J. R., and Benne, K. (1964). *T-group theory and laboratory method.* New York: John Wiley.

Braverman, H. (1974). *Labor and monopoly capital.* New York: Monthly Review Press.

Brimm, M. (1972). When is change not a change? *Journal of Applied Behavioral Science*, 1, 102–107.

Brown, R. H. (1978). *Leadership.* New York: Harper and Row.

Chiles, C. (1983). Comments on "design guidelines for social problem solving interventions." *Journal of Applied Behavioral Science* 19, 189–191.

Clegg, S. and Dunkerley. D. (1980). *Organization, class, and control.* Boston: Routledge and Kegan Paul.

Cohen, A. R., Fink, S. L., Gadon, H., and Willits, R. D. (1984). *Effective behavior in organizations.* Homewood, IL: Irwin.

Cooperrider, D. (I 986). *Appreciative Inquiry: Toward a methodology for understanding and enhancing organizational innovation.* Unpublished Ph.D. dissertation, Case Western Reserve University, Cleveland, OH.

Deal, T. E. and Kennedy, A. A. (1982). *Corporate cultures.* Reading, Mass.: Addison-Wesley.

Dubin, R. (1978). *Theory Building.* New York: The Free Press.

Ellwood, C. (1938). *A history of social philosophy.* New York: Prentice-Hall.

Forester, John (1983). Critical theory and organizational analysis. In G. Morgan (Ed.). *Beyond methods* Beverly Hills, CA: Sage Publications.

French, W. L. (1969). Organization development objectives, assumptions, and strategies. *Management Review*, 12(2), 23–34.

French, W. L. and Bell, C. H. (1978). *Organization development.* New Jersey: Prentice-Hall.

Friedlander, F. (1984). Producing useful knowledge for organizations. *Administrative Science Quarterly*, 29, 646–648.

Friedlander, F. (1977). Alternative methods of inquiry. Presented at APA Convention. San Francisco, Ca.

Friedlander, F. and Brown, L. D. (1974). Organization development, *Annual Review of Psychology*, 25, 313–341.

Frohman, M., Sashkin, M., and Kavanaugh, M. (1976). Action-research as applied to organization development. *Organization and Administrative Sciences*, 1, 129–161.

Geertz, C. (1980). Blurred genres: The refiguration of social thought. *American Scholar*, 49, 165–179.

Gergen, K. (1982). *Toward transformation in social knowledge.* New York: Springer-Verlag.

Gergen, K. (1978). Toward generative theory. *Journal of Personality and Social Psychology*, 36, 1344–1360.

Ghandi, M. (1958). *All men are brothers.* New York: Columbia University Press.

Gorz, A. (1973). Workers' control is more than just that. In Hunnius, Garson. and Case (Eds.), *Workers control.* New York: Vintage Books.

Gould, S. J. (1981). *The mismeasure of man.* New York: Norton and Company.

Gouldner, A. (1970). *The coming crisis of Western sociology.* New York: Basic Books.

Habermas, J. (1971). *Knowledge and human interests.* Boston: Beacon Press.

Haley, J. *Uncommon therapy.* New York: W. W. Norton, 1973.

Hare, P. H. (1976). *Handbook of small group research.* New York: The Free Press.

Harrison, R. (1982). *Leadership and strategy for a new age: Lessons from "conscious evolution. "* Menlo Park, CA: Values and Lifestyles Program.

Hausser, D., Pecorelia, P., and Wissler, A. (1977). *Survey-guided development 11.* LaJolla, Calif.: University Associates.

Hayward, J. (1984). *Perceiving ordinary magic.* Gouldner: New Science Library.

Hiesenberg, W. (I 958). *Physics and philosophy: The revolution in modern science.* London: Allen and Urwig.

Henshel, R. (1975). Effects of disciplinary prestige on predictive accuracy. *Futures*, 7, 92–106.

Hofstede, G. (1980). *Culture's consequences.* Beverly Hills, CA: Sage.

Jung, C. (1933). *Modern man in search of a soul.* New York: Harcourt, Brace and Company.

Keeley, M. (1980). Organizational analogy: Comparison of orgasmic and social contract models, *Administrative Science Quarterly*, 25, 337–362.

Kepner, C. and Trego, B. (1973). *Executive problem analysis and decision making.* Princeton, NJ.

Kierkegaard, S. (1954). *The sickness unto death.* New York: Anchor Books. Translated by Walter Lowrie.

Kilmann, R. (1979). Problem management: A behavioral science approach. In G. Zaltman (Ed.). *Management principles for non-profit agencies and organizations.* New York: American Management Association.

Koch, S. (1981). The nature and limits of psychological knowledge. *American Psychologist*, 36, 257–269.

Kolb, D. A. (1984). *Experiential learning*. Englewood Cliffs, NJ: Prentice-Hall.

Kolb, D. A. (1983). Problem management: Learning from experience. In S. Srivastva (Ed.), *The executive mind*. San Francisco: Jossey-Bass.

Levinson, H. (1972) The clinical psychologist as organizational diagnostician. *Professional Psychology*, 10, 485–502.

Levinson, H. (1972). *Organizational diagnosis*. Cambridge, MA: Harvard University Press.

Lewin, K. (1948). Action research and minority problems. In G. W. Lewin (Ed.), *Resolving social conflicts*. New York: Harper and Row.

Lewin, K. (1951). *Field theory in social science*. New York: Harper and Row.

Lukes, S. (1974). *Power: A radical view*. London: Macmillan.

Mannheim, K. (1936). *Ideology and utopia*. New York: Harcourt, Brace and World.

Marcel, G. (1963). *The existential background of human dignity*. Cambridge: Harvard University Press.

Margulies, N. and Raia, A. P. (1972). *Organization development: Values, process and technology*. New York: McGraw Hill.

Marrow, A. (1968). *The practical theorist*. New York: Basic Books.

Maslow, A. (1968). *Toward a psychology of being*. New York: Van Nostrand Reinhold Co.

McHugh, P. (1970). On the failure of positivism. In J. Douglas (Ed.), *Understanding everyday life*. Chicago: Aldine.

Mitroff, I. (1980). Reality as a scientific strategy: Revising our concepts of science. *Academy of Management Review*, 5, 513–515.

Mitroff, I. and Kilmann, R. (1978). *Methodological approaches to social sciences*. San Francisco: Jossey-Bass.

Morgan, G. (1983). *Beyond method*. Beverly Hills: Sage Publications.

Morgan, G. (1980). Paradigms, metaphors, and puzzle solving in organization theory. *Administrative Science Quarterly*, 24, 605–622.

Ortony, A. (Ed.) (1979). *Metaphor and thought*. Cambridge: Cambridge University Press.

Ouchi, W. G. and Johnson, J. B. (1978). Types of organizational control and their relationship to emotional well-being. *Administrative Science Quarterly*, 23, 293–317.

Pasmore, W., Cooperrider, D., Kaplan, M. and Morris, B. (1983). Introducing managers to performance development. In *The ecology of work*,. Proceedings of the Sixth NTL Ecology of Work Conference, Cleveland, Ohio.

Pasmore, W. and Friedlander, F. (1982). An action-research program for increasing employee involvement in problem solving. *Administrative Science Quarterly*, 27, 343–362.

Pepper, S. C. (1942). *World hypothesis*. Berkeley, CA: University of California Press.

Peters, M. and Robinson, V. (1984). The origins and status of action research. *Journal of Applied Behavioral Science*, 20, 113–124.

Quinney, R. (1982). *Social existence: Metaphysics, Marxism, and the social sciences*. Beverly Hills, CA: Sage Publications.

Rappaport, R. W. (1970). Three dilemmas of action-research. *Human Relations*, 23, 499–513.

Reeves, G. (1984). The idea of mystery in the philosophy of Gabriel Marcel. In J. Schlipp, and L. Hahn, (Eds.), *The philosophy of Gabriel Marcel*. LaSalle, IL: Open Court.

Sargent, L. T. (1982). Authority and utopia: Utopianisms in political thought. *Polity*, 4, 565–584.

Sathe, V. J. (1983). Implications of corporate culture. *Organizational Dynamics*, Autumn, 5–23.

Schein, E. (1983). The role of the founder in creating organizational culture. *Organizational Dynamics*, Summer, 12–28.

Schweitzer, A. (1969). *The teaching of reverence for life*. New York: Holt, Rinehart and Winston.

Small, A. (1905). *General sociology: An exposition of the main development in sociological theory from Spencer to Ratzenhofer*. Chicago: University of Chicago Press.

Smirchich, L. (1983). Studying organizations as cultures. In G. Morgan (Ed.), *Beyond method*. Beverly Hills, CA: Sage Publications.

Sproull, L. S. (1981). Beliefs in organizations. In P. C. Nystrom and W. H. Starbuck (Eds.), *Handbook of organizational design, Vol. 2*. New York: Oxford University Press.

Srivastva, S. (1985). *Executive power*. San Francisco: Jossey-Bass Publishers.

Srivastva, S. (1983). *The executive mind*. San Francisco: Jossey-Bass Publishers.

Srivastva, S. and Cooperrider, D. (1986). The emergence of the egalitarian organization. *Human Relations*, London: Tavistock.

Srivastva, S., Obert, S. and Neilsen, E. (1977). Organizational analysis through group process: A theoretical perspective for organization development. In C. Cooper (Ed.) *Organization development in the U.K. and U.S.A.* New York: The Macmillan Press.

Staw, B. (1984). Organizational behavior: A review and reformulation of the field's outcome variables. *Annual Review of Psychology*, 35, 626–666.

Susman, G. and Evered, R. (1978). An assessment of the scientific merits of action-research. *Administrative Science Quarterly*, 23, 582–603.

Thelen, H. (1954). *Dynamics of groups at work*. Chicago University of Chicago Press.

Torbert, W. (1983). Initiating collaborative inquiry. In G. Morgan (Ed.). *Beyond method*. Beverly Hills, CA: Sage Publications.

Van Maanen, J., Dabbs, J. M., and Faulkner, R. R. (I 982). *Varieties of qualitative research*. Beverly Hills, Calif.: Sage Publications.

Watzlawick, P., Weakland, J., and Fish, R. (1974). *Change: Principles of problem formation and problem resolution*. New York: Horton.

Weick, K. E. (1983). Managerial thought in the context of action. In S. Srivastva (Ed.), *The executive mind*. San Francisco: Jossey-Bass.

Wiesbord, M. (1976). Organization diagnosis: Six places to look for trouble with or without a theory. *Group and Organization Studies*, 1, 430–447.

Weiss, C. H. and Bucuvalas, M. (1980). The challenge of social research to decision making. In C. H. Weiss (Ed.), *Using social research in public policy making*. Lexington, MA: Lexington Books.

Whitehead, A. N. (1929). *The function of reason*. Boston: Beacon Press.

Whyte, W. F. (1982). Social inventions for solving human problems. *American Sociological Review*, 47, 1–13.

Chapter 4

INTERNATIONAL AND INTELLECTUAL ROOTS OF APPRECIATIVE INQUIRY

Kenneth L. Murrell, Ph.D.

University of West Florida

Abstract

The following paper presents a background study of the emergence of the concept known in the U.S. as Appreciative Inquiry. Special attention is given to historical roots as experienced by this author in both the intellectual contributions of Sir Geoffrey Vickers and in the application of a parallel process to AI practiced by development professionals in the Middle-east and Africa over 20 years ago. Their approach, developed by the Coverdale group of the U.K., was based on finding successful practices and documenting those interventions, which worked in assisting rural development projects and particularly small village development. Also discussed will be the set of core assumptions implicit in this emerging theory of AI and a sampling of cases where the theory is being tested and developed. The author concludes by presenting his perspective on the nature of the philosophy inherent in AI and a plea to keep the spirit of dialogue open to many different views as more people begin to experiment and enjoy learning how to effectively build more successful practices with AI.

Murrell, K.L. (1998, Winter) *Organization Development Journal*, 6 (4), 13-17.

Introduction

Intellectual Roots of AI

The work of Sir Geoffrey Vickers, who could be compared to the current English writer Charles Handy, started publishing his work in the late 50's and early 60's in the U.K. and then in the U.S. As a new O.D. professional in the early 70's I was particularly taken by two of Vicker's more influential, though not widely known books. In his *Art of Judgement* and *Freedom in a Rocking Boat: Changing Values in an Unstable Society* the effect on me and many others at that time was a completely new understanding of the concept of appreciation. Vicker's notion of appreciation was that "the appreciated world is selected by our interests; for only some interest would lead U.S. to notice any of its constituents." What I heard him saying clearly was that there is only the appreciated world because that is what we choose to pay attention to and so if a better world was desired then we should start to pay special attention to the elements of our world which are already better. Focus on what is right and not just what is lacking was the message. As an ex-60's protestor and also a Vietnam veteran this concept and its timely appearance not only made sense to me it also gave me some glimmer of hope in a historical period where hope was not very fashionable.

While being highly influenced by Vicker's notion that appreciation represented a deep and penetrating understanding as well as a focus on what one wanted to make of their world I was at the same time beginning to read an emerging literature best represented by the very popular work *The Social Construction of Reality* by Berger and Luckman. This new philosophy of science, so well articulated by Thomas Kuhn's notion of scientific paradigms as an example, was stating it clearly that one could have some considerable influence over the nature of reality one was experiencing and if that were possible then why should we not go about choosing to see as well as creating more humane and satisfying worlds for ourselves. Fortunately for me it was only a few years later that I was off living in Cairo, Egypt and given a chance to see how these theories could be put to use.

As I left the American corporate world with a set of incredible, rich, positive and many negative experiences, I chose to take my O.D. knowledge and values where I thought they might do some good. At this point I was greatly disappointed that a country like the U.S. with all of its resources and knowledge did not appear to be interested in social or organizational change as much as seeking the individual security that self-serving greed was promising. My experience with mainstream corporate O.D. while working internally for a large U.S. multinational was a mix of the greatest use and misuse of O.D. I thought I might ever see. Little did I then know that this paradox was to be quite prevalent wherever I went. So after becoming what

I felt was marginalized, even in my own culture, the opportunity for a new frontier was the most exciting call I could have hoped for.

Cross-Cultural Practices

In being given an opportunity to reconstruct my own world as an expatriate in a very foreign environment and living alone without the luxury of any social or material familiarity from my home culture I had to try and do O.D. in ways I had never been prepared for. This placed a special pressure on me to not just practice what I had been trained to do but far more importantly to learn many things new. I was keenly aware that trying to lead others in adopting American or Western practices was a most limiting trap. Even though in many ways that was the expectation and what nearly every one of my many American educated Egyptian colleagues were attempting, I knew this would not work. What I came to later discover was the futility of the notion that as an O.D. professional I would be of assistance in helping others solve their problems. This was to also be a great learning experience for me as I saw and experienced the routines and rituals of problem solving based interventions crash and burn all around. Actually the crashing and burning was usually timed to coincide with the takeoff departure of the jets flying the horde of what I labeled the tourist or carpetbagger consultants back to the west. For someone living in the local culture, these were most impressionable experiences. To this day, I have a critical reaction when I hear about my O.D. colleagues off flying around the world to do well with their O.D. bag of tricks.

After now working and traveling in over 60 countries, I am most critical of myself and have been very sensitive to how little I can do if I don't learn to appreciate the local situation and partner with someone from the country. To gain this knowledge it would help to require all O.D. professionals to spend at least three to five years living totally outside the culture they were raised in.

What I was to learn in Egypt in the late 70's far exceeded what little I can imagine I was able to leave behind. In particular I was fortunate to have been asked to work with a group of consultants and local managers developing what was to be my introduction to "appreciative inquiry." The group worked under the auspices of the Coverdale organization and as far as I knew it was a U.K.-based development program. I later discovered a book about the Coverdale organization by Max Taylor (1979), but my learning came from being directly involved with a team of their consultants on several different activities in and around Cairo and East Africa. The Coverdale approach was built around the ideas that it would be far more effective if before anything else it were possible to discover and disseminate all that could be found out about what they labeled successful practices. What this looked like was a series of interviews and cases being prepared that fully described the organizational successes and the special achievements to be found in how the village or the particular development project was managing to make life better or more meaningful. Building on success rather than being obsessed with what went wrong was the central focus of the theories of Ralph Coverdale and his organization as I experienced them in Africa and Egypt in the late 70's.

This quick encounter with such a radically different approach in a startling way set me up to completely rethink how I had been taught O.D. should work. It brought me to an awareness that my cultural sensitivities about not wanting to take American management to others was right and that I needed to look deeply, i.e., fully appreciate, what the local situation offered. What a location for learning this. Here I sat in the virtual birthplace of civilization and with so much history surrounding me that when I traveled to Europe I always teased my friends about coming to the new world to visit the barbarians.

What could I learn when I started to look for successes in the local situation? It did not take long to see another side of not just Cairo but in particular the small villages I traveled in throughout East Africa. This new appreciation gave me a way of seeing what had been achieved and what was possible rather than only the problems that a scarcity and deficit perception points out. To this day that simple experience of looking first for success and then sharing with others what works has been one of the most important lessons in my life.

After about four years back in the U.S., I had the good fortune of hearing David Cooperrider explain to an audience of fellow university professors his work on something he and others were calling "appreciative inquiry." As a serendipitous event I was struck with how similar were his conclusions and his abundant passion for a new way of being with my own excitement and certainty about this more appreciative way of doing O.D. I may have had a chance then to tell Dave a bit about my experiences but in the rush of the conference we went separate ways. After a few more years our paths started crossing on a more regular basis and I have tried hard to keep up with his work and writings and value very much his friendship and empathy. The AI literature is growing and the passion of this hope-filled theory is expanding. As appreciative inquiry and those involved are seeking life-affirming alternatives they are creating new appreciated worlds.

Core Assumptions

The set of core assumptions that I believe are shared between many of U.S. who have been thinking and working in an appreciative frame are most important to articulate and discuss. Each of U.S. comes at this field a little differently and in that diversity there can be potential for either strengthening or in confusing the practitioner. We need to keep this dilemma uppermost in our minds along with a sense of humility about the idea of nothing really being new but all human thought is a synthetic process of many millions of minds.

The most central orientation that I believe exists in AI is in its dependence on a life-affirming position as opposed to a problem focused one. In this simple statement comes the spirit and soul of the AI activity. In this attention to the creative process, as opposed to the curative, lies the foundation of hope. Problem solving methodologies have swamped our discipline as they have almost all of the professions, at least in most of the industrialized world. The attention given to deficit and scarcity thinking is one of the most common patterns associated with organizational malaise and alienation. It is something we can change.

Next as a core assumption is the principle of reality being a social construction as opposed to an external "objective" and empirically verifiable reality. What this means is that we as humans in relationships with others engage in a sense making and language creating process that then shapes and labels what it is that we call "real". In doing this we jointly agree on what the world not only appears to be by our focus and attention but that we institutionalize its existence based on our unique shared assumptions and create if you will our paradigm or view of reality. This creation of a collective cosmology that helps U.S. to communicate and interact is full of choices about what we focus on and care about. It is not so simple that we can create just anything we want but the power of our collective will and vision will highly shape what we choose to call real. In dealing with the natural world we obviously have some significant limits to what we can create given the tangible physical realities that we can confirm to exist through our senses but our choice of names and values attached to these stimuli are very much influenced by U.S.. In Meg Wheatley's newest book *A Simpler Way*, she effectively argues for an understanding of the universe not as a machine but as an order seeking and self organizing and more organic phenomenon. In this way if we see the world as she paints it, it will be more likely we can go about organizing our lives and work around more harmonious and humane relationships and not the control and dominance models based on a world of conflict where only the fittest survive.

Cooperation and natural organizing based on activity centered in freedom to act rather than in control or constraints of action will allow U.S. to create new forms of organization only limited by what we can dream or discover through trial and adaptation. As Geoff Bellman presents in his writings to be published late in 1996 we each lay down a "signature path" that reflects how we have chosen to live on this planet and with others. Based on our actions, beliefs and relationships we again can see how we, particularly O.D. professionals in a society, help shape and form reality by constructing our individual and joint paths or life practices. This social construction perspective is what gives hope to the AI process in that we are able to influence how our world might exist. What we pay attention to or the paths we set out, create realities and construct the "appreciated worlds" via Vickers and the better worlds those of U.S. using AI would like to see or can imagine possible.

A corollary to the social construction principle is the idea that we also go about creating language and meaning by how we choose to look at and label things. In the words of Suresh Srivistava, David Cooperrider's senior colleague at

Case Western Reserve University, we can either choose to see a half- full or a half-empty glass of life. If our worldview is grounded in deficit thinking or the half-empty notion of reality then we will be prone to act as if this were true and to then actually help create that assumption not only in ourselves but also in others. This occurs also in the language we then use to define our reality and if it is deficit based, the language becomes one of deficit or problem-oriented, and our words chosen continue to focus our attention on what is wrong, who is at fault and the nature of our problems. This language system and its attention to the scarcity of positive or healthy expressions then continues the half empty assumption and we get fixated relying on the language best geared to defining or describing what is lacking or wrong. Social bonding in a culture of angst is particularly susceptible to this lowest common denominator of complaint and creates a world of cynicism and despair. But there is still the chance to look for the positive, and not in some naive or Pollyanna-ish fashion, rather in the hope of creating better conditions by seeing what is possible rather than what is not. This more positive view is often over-whelmed by how much we talk about and have expressions for the negatives in our world. In this deficit-based problem-oriented language system we reinforce the construction of a reality based in the half-empty metaphor. Cynicism flourishes where the common social glue is formed around finding what is wrong. Even when we set out to slay the dragons, problems to be killed, we end up at best where we started. Building positive futures on the bodies of dead problems fails to excite the same creative energies as inventing new ways of being, built on values in the culture we still cherish.

To galvanize and energize group or organizational effort it appears a vision of what is possible often has more power than simply the avoidance of pain or fighting for my share of a very limited set of resources. To pay attention, and to even celebrate what is working and what is successful takes a considerable amount of rethinking for some people locked into negative scenarios. Yet when we want to create hope and build exciting visions of what is possible it is much more helpful to work from a positive potential than be locked into deficit categorizations and evalu-ations of what is wrong.

Again this is not a naive or happy face philosophy as much as it is a recogni-tion of what forces and what type of realities will help move people and organiza-tions towards taking positive action and to encourage the creation of more life affirming systems. Human systems that are built from hope rather than despair. Cynicism is not so easily overcome by focusing on such a positive potential but the goal is to at least balance the cynical reaction with one more grounded in the assumption of self and organizational empowerment. The acceptance of the victim role and the defense mechanism of becoming cynical are not proven as very useful strategies for organization development. Even more risky is taking on O.D. as some holy war and to see others as enemies where opposing viewpoints seductively lock U.S. into mortal combat.

In an active stance of passive resistance to cynical and negative defense reactions there are recommended actions that are grounded in the above core AI assumptions. There are also creative strategies and responses for building commitment around more positive strategies. The essential belief in doing AI, in my experience, is still grounded in two traditional assumptions of O.D. The first is in trusting the process and the second is in accepting the people as they are. When either of these cannot be done it is less likely an AI or an O.D. process will go far.

In AI, it is trusting that in all human organizations and societies there is much that is good, but that this good is often overlooked. Helping to find and to define what is good is one core assumption of AI. Second is to accept the client system or community and the people involved as fully human and not to go about trying to counter the cynical or the negative by directly attacking their views. To accept their belief in their reality is often necessary before they can grant you the right to yours. Even more important is to give them the opportunity to fully experience the other more positive realities in their life by giving them the credit and recognition that can be honestly attached to their own successes and accomplishments. The other option is to help them to search for and examine what are the unique characteristics of the successful practices of other systems like their own. Help them go out and find what works and ask them to help bring those practices back to their own organization or community. And in celebration of these life-affirming realities much good can be created.

What all of this requires is the development of human relationships built around what works and what can be discovered to be working in similar situations. Seeding the search process with team building and relationship building activities will help the process discover the life affirming nature of positive human relationships. Success will help build or create more success but again this is not a simplistic or naive faith. This requires some very dedicated action to find and then to help create more positive scenarios. In short a lot of support for all those involved in this process is required. The consultant or the facilitator is guided by his or her own philosophy of AI and only when that faith is strong with the requisite support systems in place is there a good chance for success. Another old adage of O.D. may well apply here in that only the consultant who is grounded and supported is likely to help a client system move beyond their current state.

This brings out the final core assumption in my set of AI assumptions. Only a healthy and spiritually grounded consultant should be trying to help create a process like this one, which takes tremendous faith and patience. The client system deserves the best and so does the consultant or leader who is willing to be fully engaged in living this philosophy. That means a healthy and balanced perspective on the nature of this work is required along with a well-developed sense of humor and ability to appreciate humility in both self and others. Physical health is also a necessity and it should go without saying. Unfortunately all of U.S. have likely experienced the loss of a friend or colleague who has not been taking appropriate care of him or herself. In the past we have lost many in the O.D. profession too early because there personal health was secondary to what could be described as a nearly compulsive if not obsessive need to do O.D. work. In balance there is health and the maintenance of that requires considerable support. The loss of those who do not take care of themselves are the saddest losses. At the same time we should learn to appreciate and celebrate those that do take good care of themselves and recognize them for the long-term contribution that they often reflect.

A Sampling of AI Oriented Cases

In addition to the briefly mentioned work of the Coverdale group, there were many other development projects in Africa worth mentioning and today with the Global Excellence in Management program lead by David Cooperrider and Jane Watkins there are many more strong and active examples of AI thinking emerging. My experience with an appreciative frame in both Egypt and Sudan centered around mobilizing local groups and villages to document and then share the successful practices each location had developed over the years. In some cases these were mechanical and technical improvements, for example in irrigation or harvesting methods, much like our own Department of Agriculture had been helping to disseminate through its extension model used all over the world. In addition social and organizational successful practices became the subject of story and case description and encouraged to be shared in all kinds of forms and forums. Another group of development experts using a similar practice of sharing successes was the Institute of Cultural Affairs which is the subject itself of a AI case just published in the *O.D. Practitioner* by Tojo Thatchenkery. Back in the 70's the ICA had projects in nearly every time zone around the world and though their formal process was not then defined as an appreciative model it contained some early features, I was particularly impressed with its work with song and celebration.

My own O.D. work in the non-industrial world while living in it was increasingly based on looking for local strengths and significant successes. From this my O.D. work evolved in many different forms. A few years later I found myself working for the UN Development Program in Gambia, Somalia, and Ethiopia. In each case I took what I considered a combination of process consulting based models and a highly appreciative stance to conduct a series of interventions focused on helping to develop the capacity of local management development institutes. In each case a partnership team was developed with local involvement whose purpose was to evaluate and recommend what the UNDP and the host country could do to strengthen the capacity and sustainability of their development activities. In each case the focus of attention was placed on the unique strengths and successes already experienced in order to build toward an even stronger future state. Many times this caught several stakeholders off guard since the traditional approach had been much more aimed at finding problems and evaluating individuals. Both aims of the work were accomplished but the evaluative steps were redefined as preliminary findings where the local staff was given a chance to immediately design improved measures to respond to their unmet challenges. In this way the critical elements of the report were formed as catalysts for change proposals for how to design better future states. Considerable attention was given to the successful practices and given the nearly impossible conditions many of these projects were formed under these successes were quite significant. We encouraged the public display of the lessons learned and in few cases helped to write up for publication the sharing of these lessons. In all countries the local staff was treated with respect and attention flourished on all their good work wherever it could be found. Having lived in these environments myself, as had usually the other team members, it was easier to recognize the hurdles placed on these projects and very important to offer encouragement and affirmation.

Critical issues were also normally raised, but the difference in response to these were quite amazing. The energy to correct deficiencies and improve methods came from a team based appreciative stance. All of those involved had experienced outside evaluation tensions before and had witnessed how often this produced nothing more than denial or defensiveness. In each of the cases using a more appreciative stance it was apparent the local group after the evaluation still had the desire as well as the capacity to improve and to continually commit to the projects they had created. Being treated in a more affirming style than was often provided left behind in each case a level of hope not often experienced in these type missions for the United Nations.

Using this same style, I was able over the last three years to work with several different hospitals and health care systems that have been experiencing nearly as much stress and turmoil as my African managers had to deal with. In each case the approach used was to design an intervention based on my principles of empowerment and the appreciative stance of AI. In the most dramatic case, a 500-bed hospital facing severe competition I was asked to serve as the sole external consultant to what was labeled then, at the height of the reengineering frenzy, a re-engineering project. Quickly the executive level sponsor group, agreed to put the emphasis not on downsizing but on restructuring the whole hospital operating process. We set out to do this with 100% staff direction and drive and no outside experts were invited in to design the restructuring for the managers. Three large teams of managers were assigned to carefully review each operation of the hospital from patient input, treatment and output oriented functions rather than from the traditional flow of separate activities designed around particular specialties. Over the next four months everything possible was done to help the teams carefully consider all the strengths and capabilities currently existing and to then design a new future state of operating at a much-improved level. The appreciative side of this activity was built on a commitment to the people in the organization and an agreement by senior management to provide all the help and assistance needed by the design teams to do their work. All through this process the issue of what was working well was blended in with bench marking across the country with other systems' examples of successful practices. This was not carried out as a problem to be fixed but as a way to reinvent health care delivery in a rapidly changing environment. The dedication and skill of the 40-60 managers devoted to the design effort was greatly appreciated by the hospital community. The impact of the redesign was minimal on staffing levels as compared to many so-called re-engineering projects driven by outside consultants.

One of the most useful elements of the whole process was in confirming to the managerial staff that they could indeed determine more of their own fate than a group of outside consultants. An initial phase of a AI intervention was also recently conducted by one of my senior graduate students in our O.D. and Leadership Program. The project was sponsored by our Provost at the University of West Florida and directed by me with the assistance of written materials from David Cooperrider and John Carter who were both willing to share their AI papers with me. The O.D. student was John Forlini who is also a senior manager with Foxborough Company a leading instrument control firm. As a part of his practicum John spent three months in setting up and conducting initial interviews with a cross-section of faculty and administrators to help discover and share the spirit and commitment inherent in their dedication to higher education. Our university, like all of those in the 90's, has been experiencing a continuing series of budget cuts and declining faculty morale. John's intervention based on AI principles was aimed at finding out what was strong and right at the University rather than what was typically being identified as more doom and gloom. His report to senior administrators was soon being circulated as the Forlini Report and billed as the only useful examination of the current crisis situation. The report received much attention and raised expectations for follow-up and more complete AI activity that at this time is still being desired. In order to move this more positive intervention forward a lead facilitator is being sought who can gain trust from a system that is used to seeing itself being abused and neglected. The AI tone of John's feedback of why people still do care about the University centered around the issue of service. Service was identified as the source of the original calling faculty and administrators both felt. The service ethic helped explain their reasons for doing their daily jobs in increasingly difficult times. The process started a series of conversations about what was important in the work of a university instead of only what were the major problems with the current lack of support. This helped shift the issue back to a discussion of quality concerns that had often been left out of the moaning and groaning about external funding or mandates. A different appreciated world was beginning to be formed and this had a hand in shifting the policy discussion beyond complaining about or defending budgetary constraints. Service as a core value helped to better focus not only on quality concerns but also recognition of the unique strengths of the institution in its dedication to teaching and to students.

In all cases where I have seen an AI approach offered there is evidence that it does help reframe the discussion from an "ain't it awful" to a more broadly based analysis and appreciation of what might be done better. Critical to this is an appreciation shown to what is working, or the half-full glass metaphor. Difficult as this can be, it is essentially a result of the questions asked or the issues raised. If the intervention is designed to look for strengths in a system, they will be found. If a problem oriented method surfaces all that is wrong then that becomes the center of attention. Given our fast paced and complex world we seem at any moment to be about creating a new world order or bringing forth a fresh new paradigm. This energy of creation and the potentialities for a new century and a new millennium best define the times we are given to work in. For anyone in O.D. there could be no better time to be alive. All of the doors opening and creativity awakening offer so much in the way of hope and new opportunities. From these few first-hand experiences I am convinced these are the times for O.D. to reinvent itself I also hope that this responsibility to recreate O.D. will be taken seriously by our culture and all of its institutions, even those now halfway around the world but who are more closely linked than ever before. I am committing myself to work on this agenda of a reinventing of O.D. and believe AI has a significant role to play in that process.

The Emergent Platform for a New O.D.

Appreciative Inquiry represents much of the philosophical revisioning of O.D. In its more positive and life affirming aspects it is the needed transition agent to help move O.D. back to the cutting edge field that it was nearly 50 years ago. As discussed earlier many of the core values are very consistent and in fact come out of O.D. practice and theory developed over the last half-century. The next century offers even more.

The challenges of post-war America and Europe were very much the focus of attention of our founders of what was to evolve into O.D. Today we can see an equally challenging landscape but this one stretches across all the time zones and is formed in both the northern and southern hemispheres. Even more importantly it is a challenge facing all of humanity directly no matter what socioeconomic class or country they live in.

The creation of a new and hopefully better civil society is how some try to explain the challenge. I prefer to think of it as creating a third global sector of organizations and communities consciously aware that their responsibilities are to help create a more livable and moral planet for our children and grandchildren. The reason I prefer to see the creation of a third way is not just because of the discounting of government and business that continues to occur but more because I firmly believe a third model will offer to the other two more dominant sectors something of value as each one of them is forced to change. These forced changes are driven by several major structural shifts that are occurring in economics and politics and a rapidly building period of destabilization in many of our institutions. In addition, assumptions about how the world works and other basic philosophical beliefs are

also undergoing major changes. This in itself is not as much a driver as is the
emerging and I predict greatly expanding spirit of human creativity. Given what is
occurring in the arena of information movement the next most likely watershed
event will be the development of more creative alternatives than have ever existed
before. Humankind will move towards the reinventing of itself and its institutions
as the need presents itself.

Without a doubt the need is there! To respond to that need we must first
recognize that our existing institutions, both government and business, are found
wanting by the public. Also there is a growing awareness of the limits of technological fixes, as is most obvious in medicine with AIDS and cancer, and that spreading social problems and fears of crime on the street call into question our capacity
to fix our world. Improvements are now seen to be dependent on completely new
thinking and the kind of creative social change not given consideration since the
days of the last major period of destabilization, the 60's. What will hopefully be
different in this period of continual upheaval is that instead of trashing our institutions out of fear and anger we may create social and organizational change built on
a more affirming and appreciative platform. These changes can be designed with
greater degrees of participation and inclusivity. As with the AI and many new O.D.
approaches like Future Search these participative and inclusive designs are very
open systems based. The experimentation and creativity of these approaches are
the most exciting elements of these designs for many of U.S. but the more impressive side may be in the size of the groups or organizations that are able to participate. Given where the telecommunication revolution seems to be taking U.S. there
may be no limits to what we can do to bring people together to create the better
worlds that we can imagine and then begin to implement. This is what gives me
hope.

As a foundation, or infrastructure as I am writing about it in a new book, there
are five major platforms of knowledge that are required if we are to together recreate
our world. I have called these the core components and they represent what I feel
we need to learn and discover together in order to prepare ourselves for the challenging responsibilities facing U.S.. Spirit, community, work, wisdom and transformation are the five and each is worthy of a life long dedication to better
understanding. I am giving myself another 20 years to pursue each of these five
areas in both the depth and with the practice in applying that might help move the
field of O.D. forward. The common linkage throughout this set of core issues is the
role of appreciation, meant both as a full and deep understanding as well as an
acceptance of other thoughts and successes. These successful experiences if used
well can guide more enlightened action. The linking value of AI is also to be built in
with the action component of trusting the process. That is of letting the systems
wanting to change guide and direct that process rather than the outside expert or
facilitator. In this the role of an AI/O.D. professional is going to often be more
educator than consultant. This goes back to the earlier assumption that anyone
wanting to help lead an AI process needs to be very informed on the core assumptions and the philosophy that this requires one to accept, understand and live by.

Concluding Points

What I have tried to offer in this article is a way of looking at the work of Appreciative Inquiry as a lifelong commitment to helping in the process of recreating our world one day at a time. By looking at the international and global challenges facing U.S. it is important to recognize how much a part of that larger world we are already living in. Also there are very few things that one can consider so uniquely new that there is not a broader history we can find and learn from. In AI this is particularly true. Historically there have been many advocates of a more life affirming approach and philosophy than any one of U.S. might be aware. Our task is to find out what they have been able to achieve from this outlook and to help develop today's theory and practice even further.

As a final example of the power of AI, I would like to offer one more case of when I have witnessed what happens when both a problem oriented and an appreciative approach are used in the same system. For nearly ten years now I have been experimenting with teaching about organizations and O.D. from the perspective of first having the students or training participants create a simulated organization. In the many different forms I use in this work the common design is what I have come to call a "live case study" where the 12-200 individuals in the room go about creating a multi-leveled and multi-department organization that must produce a real product in order to economically survive. So far in the over fifty cases I have facilitated no organization has ever been built with either the intention of failing or with the avowed goal of liberating the human spirit. Each organization has simply been an extension of the individual participant's assumptions about what an organization is expected to be. In 1995, the third year doing this with the Pepperdine M.S.O.D. group, under the sponsorship of Joanne Preston, I changed my debriefing pattern to incorporate a test if you will of AI theory. After the students had spent a normally frustrating two to three hours of trying to get a simple three-level organization to operate we began a debrief by randomly asking every other participant to form an inner circle, which then numbered about 15, and to answer the traditional questions that any good consultant might ask about the organization they had just created. I asked them to simply share their experiences.

With no more lead-in than that, the conversation quickly turned to all that was wrong with the organization they had jointly just created. The normal problem oriented critique then followed with particular attention to how poor the communications were and how confused everything appeared. Not being sure this pattern would emerge since the group had just spent two days with David Cooperrider teaching them about AI I was not prepared to see how quickly people seemed able to go to a problem oriented discourse. I then at the end of this debriefing session asked how many of them would want to work in the company that they had just created. I don't recall a single positive response to the question.

To better test what might happen if I started the debrief itself with just a simple change in questioning, I asked the rest of the class to switch chairs with the first half of randomly chosen students and to also spend about 30-40 minutes in a debrief of the simulation.

This time my lead question was to tell U.S. about all the positive attributes of the organization they had just created and to comment on the unique strengths observed. With only this question set up to lead the discussion the mood shifted dramatically when the positives that were experienced were focused on. The appreciative comments were forthcoming even though we were essentially discussing the same simulated organization. At the end of this session I asked how many would like to work again in this organization they had just created and near unanimous support was offered to going to work in the organization they had just described after focusing on what was positive in their experience.

The lesson might appear simple and this one test of a single organizational simulation is not going to convince anyone that has not had a similar experience. But given a few more times to test the theory it is very apparent to me people strongly prefer to be a part of an organization they can identify positive experiences with. Asking anyone what is wrong where they work is going to produce a lot of data. I might even be willing to label this the Dilbert Effect in that we can all come out with the negative and inane examples of how the organizations we work in are in trouble. The amazing thing about the Dilbert Principle is that even the senior executives can laugh about all the dumb things that everyone else is doing in their organization. Maybe even a few are laughing at themselves but the common theme is that there are really a lot of very stupid people and programs out there in our organizations.

The real question then left to U.S. is to then develop a way to go to the aid of organizations and the people in them and help them identify the strengths and capabilities of their human systems and their human creativity and spirit. I love a joke as much as anyone but when our organized human activities become identified as only problems I greatly fear that the energy and creativity to change them may be easily siphoned off by a cynical defense reaction at the very time we need all the help we can get. My fear is that we may be not only convinced of our own impotence in changing our organization but in the need for some external force or great charismatic hero to step in and save U.S. all. Historically it is obvious where this could take U.S.. Given the increasing potential for tremendous social upheaval in our world this fear of an emerging demagogue is a realistic one.

The more hopeful scenario we can create is that we can learn to use the strengths of an AI and O.D. approach and a set of values consistent with these. Maybe then we can create the more empowered third sector and a healthier civil society we all seem to long for. From this can emerge even more experimentation in developing community and liberating structures of work that help bring back the hope and positive expectations that have been part of earlier periods of renaissance and renewal. It is too easy to forget how many times the human spirit has been challenged and nearly broken only to emerge once again. Perhaps our successes in ending the state of cold war that has existed for most of U.S. throughout our lives and the miracles of South Africa and other numerous cases of success have not been looked into carefully enough to pull out more lessons for today's challenges.

As the old wise one said, is the glass half-full or half-empty, and for the rest of U.S. which is the glass we want to look through. Given that what you see is often what you get we do have some rather significant choices to make. The even more critical nature of those choices concerns the many generations that will follow U.S.. How will we go about imagining and acting on the world that we want to leave behind. As the Native Americans remind U.S., give thought to the next seven generations, they will inherit much more than our material possessions. The spirit of hope and appreciation we leave behind may be the greater gift in that a culture grounded in that set of values may more likely survive the seven generations and prosper in ways we as a culture are struggling to discover.

References

Bellman, Geoffrey (1996). *Your Signature Path: Gaining New Perspectives on Life and Work*. San Francisco: Berrett-Koehler.

Berger, Peter & Luckmann, Thomas (1966). *The Social Construction of Reality*. Garden City, NY: Doubleday.

Murrell, Kenneth L. (1997). Emergent theories of leadership for the next century: towards relational concepts. *Organization Development Journal*. Volume 15, no. 3, pages 35-42.

Taylor, Max (1979). *Coverdale on Management*. London: Heinemann.

Thatchenkery, Tojo J. (1996). Affirmation as facilitation: a postmodernist paradigm in change management. *O.D. Practitioner*. Vol. 28 nos. 1 & 2. Pages 12-22.

Torbert, Wm. R. (1991). *The Power Of Balance: Transforming Self, Society, and Scientific Inquiry*. Newbury Park: Sage.

Vickers, Sir Geoffrey (1965). *The Art of Judgement*. New York: Basic Books.

Vickers, Sir Geoffrey (1970). *Freedom in a Rocking Boat*. Middlesex, England: Penquin Press.

Wheatley, Margaret (1997). *A Simpler Way*. San Francisco: Berrett-Koehler.

Chapter 5

FIVE THEORIES OF CHANGE EMBEDDED IN APPRECIATIVE INQUIRY

Gervase R. Bushe Ph.D.
Simon Fraser University

In this paper I will describe five different ways of thinking about how an appreciative inquiry can create change in social systems. Appreciative inquiry is a form of action research that attempts to create new theories/ideas/images that aid in the developmental change of a system (Cooperrider and Srivastva, 1987). The key data collection innovation of appreciative inquiry is the collection of people's stories of something at its best. If we are interested in team development, we collect stories of people's best team experiences. If we are interested in the development of an organization we ask about their peak experience in that organization. If enhanced leadership is our goal, we collect stories of leadership at its best. These stories are collectively discussed in order to create new, generative ideas or images that aid in developmental change of the collectivity discussing them.

I am concerned that as appreciative inquiry becomes "fashionable" two undesirable things are happening. One is that any inquiry that focuses on the "positive" in some way gets called appreciative inquiry (AI). I have already come across a consulting firm that asked people to rate how good the organization was on a number of items on a 5-point scale and called this appreciative inquiry. The result will be that the unique power of this idea gets corrupted and lost and appreciative inquiry becomes just another discarded innovation on the junk heap of "failed" management effectiveness strategies, like QWL, TQM, BPR, etc. Anyone involved in any of these processes knows they all contained excellent ideas and useful techniques but "failed" because of consultants calling whatever they did by the currently fashionable acronym who sold these to managers who didn't know the difference.

A second concern is that some practitioners, especially graduate students, can develop a zealous attention to "appreciation" without any theoretical rhyme or

Appeared in R. Engdahl (ed.) (1998) *Proceedings of the 18th World Organization Development Congress.* Wilmington, NC: Cameron School of Business, UNCW, pp. 101–109.

reason to their practice. Promoting appreciation where there has been little can, of itself, generate a wave of energy and enthusiasm but that will go away just as quickly as the next challenge or tragedy to a social system rears its head.

In this paper I want to appreciate appreciative inquiry as, itself, a generative metaphor that has led me to new ideas and images of how to change social systems. I do this also to caution against the indiscriminant application of appreciative inquiry, calling for a disciplined and reasoned approach to its use. I believe that AI can be very helpful in the right time and the right place. We need, however, to develop a model of where and when that is. Some people seem to believe that use of appreciative inquiry is more an ideological than practical question, and that its use will always have a positive effect. I strongly question that. From a purely practical standpoint I think researchers and consultants will find that systems full of deeply held and unexpressed resentments will not tolerate an appreciative inquiry until there has been some expression and forgiving of those resentments. From a theoretical perspective there is the question of what happens to negative images and affect if they are "repressed" from collective discussion by a zealous focus on the "positive". Experience from psychoanalysis, sociology and medicine suggest repression usually results in some nasty side effects.

Secondly, we need to embrace different ways of inquiring appreciatively but to do so, we need theory that tells us what ways will work—how and why. In this paper, I offer a way to begin thinking about both questions, especially the latter. I will first review two key theories of change contained in the writings of Cooperrider: the social construction of reality and the "heliotropic hypothesis". Then I will present three ideas that I have stumbled across in my use of AI: the organization's "inner dialogue", resolving paradoxical dilemmas, and appreciative process. Each directs us to different ways of thinking about and implementing an appreciative inquiry when our purpose is developmental change.

Socially Constructing Reality

Those familiar with AI know that the dominant theoretical rational for AI is post modernist European philosophy (for an excellent summary related to this theory of change see Barrett, Thomas and Hocevar, 1995). From this point of view there is nothing inherently real or true about any social form. All social organization is an arbitrary, social construction. Our ability to create new and better organizations is limited only by our imagination and collective will. Furthermore, language and words are the basic building blocks of social reality. Rather than seeing language as a passive purveyor of meaning between people, post modernists see language as an active agent in the creation of meaning. As we talk to each other, we are constructing the world we see and think about, and as we change how we talk we are changing that world. From this perspective, theory, especially theory that is encoded in popular words or images, is a powerful force in shaping social organization because we "see what we believe". Creating new and better theories/ideas/images is, therefore, a powerful way of changing organizations. Appreciative inquiry seeks these new images in and among people's best intentions and noblest aspirations, attempting a collective envisioning of what the group could be at its very best.

From the practical standpoint the problem is how do we get people to dream alternative futures together, to envision new patterns of social organization that are better than what they currently have or may ever have individually experienced? My own experience as an OD consultant is that it is very difficult to get a group of people who work together to talk about things they might hope for but have never seen. This is especially true in business organizations which tend to have a culture that values "hard headedness" and devalues "fanciful thinking". It is scary to verbalize those basic human desires for community, love, fealty, making a contribution in an organization where that is not the norm. To talk about "how things could be" when no one has ever actually seen them that way is to open oneself up to ridicule and embarrassment. Indeed, if there is a lot of repressed yearning in the system, anyone who names what is yearned for is sure to be ridiculed and shamed as a defense against experiencing that yearning. About the best one can expect is that people will talk about things they have experienced elsewhere, or read about, since they can defend themselves against ridicule by pointing to places where those noble aspirations and intentions are being lived.

I have found that an appreciative inquiry, where people listen to each other's stories about micro moments in organizational life where the best in us is touched, can create a unique climate for collective dreaming where the forces of ridicule and repression are momentarily suspended. There is something about telling one's story of "peak" organizational experiences, and listening to others, that can make a group ready to be open about deeply held desires and yearnings. I am sure that there are other factors, beside the AI technique, that are necessary to make this happen (e.g., quality of leadership) but the technique is astounding in the speed with which it can create such a climate in the right place at the right time. Into this climate, then, a different kind of conversation can take place and from that, a different social reality can evolve.

One more point about the social construction of reality. From this point of view means create ends and this is especially true about our means of inquiry. How we go about studying something will impact what we "see" and in some cases, will even create what we then "discover". At the core of appreciative inquiry is "inquiring with the heart". What that means is difficult to describe on paper, a lot easier to teach in practice. For myself it means that before I ask a question or make a statement I locate my consciousness in my heart region and notice how my thoughts and questions are shaped and let those be what I say. In my personal and professional life this has had a consistent, profound, healing effect on my interactions with others. I think it was Jung who said that inquiry with the head only can never heal as the head is concerned with analysis which only serves to cut things up and examine them in parts. The heart, however, is concerned with bringing things together and wholeness and it is from here that inquiry can be healing. Can analytical forms of action research, which cut up an organization or group for analysis, attending to all the "problems" and "deficiencies" (based on the theory of the researcher/consultant) ever hope to really heal a system; to make old wounds go away and add health and vitality to the relationships in that system? I no longer think so. Can appreciative inquiry? If it is carried out with an open heart, I think it can.

More could be said about the social construction of reality theory of change embedded in AI but let me turn to implications of this theory for OD practice. First, it means that the way the inquiry is carried out is very important. Techniques which help to open the hearts of those engaged in the inquiry should aid it. For example, Cooperrider (1996) has talked about the heightened quality of interview data that come from having children interview adults and I think some of this impact can be explained by the heart opening potential of that. Secondly, this means that the key to creating change in the organization is creating new theories/ideas/images that enter the everyday language of system members. Therefore, both the process of creative ideation and the process of importation of that creativity into popular usage are critical for change. Once we collect the stories, then what? From this perspective the hard work of change begins. I do not think nearly enough about these two processes has been written about.

The Heliotropic Hypothesis

In an intriguing paper Cooperrider (1990) presented his "heliotropic hypothesis" which is that social systems evolve toward the most positive images they hold of themselves. These images are not necessarily conscious in that they may not be discussible by the members of that social system, but nevertheless he argues that such images exist and the more they "affirm" the group the more firmly they hold the group to a pattern of being prescribed by the theory/idea/image the group has of itself at its very best. When these images are out of step with the requirements the social system faces the group will experience itself as dysfunctional and rational attempts to fix itself will not work until the underlying "affirmative image" of the group is changed. Appreciative inquiry, therefore, attempts to create a new and better affirmative image for the social system, one better aligned with the organization's critical contingencies.

Surprisingly, there have been no published attempts to assess the validity of this hypothesis and I will not attempt to argue for or against it here. But it is an important theory of change embedded in AI and as such, has important implications for OD practice. From this point of view the quality of the output of the AI, the affirming image, is all important for its change potential. How this affirming image is constructed needs to be thought about carefully. Does it have to be a managed process or can we trust that the process of AI will itself unfreeze the system so that a better affirmative image will naturally form? If managed, who needs to be involved in generating the image? How do we know when we have a good enough new image? How can we know which images will "stick" while others fall quickly into disuse? These are the sorts of questions that the AI practitioner, operating under this theory of change, ought to have answers to.

The Organization's Inner Dialogue

Now we turn to 3 theories of change that have been evoked for me by AI. The first I call changing the organization's inner dialogue and it comes from the observation that if you think of organizations using the metaphor of human consciousness, with many different voices saying things within one's mind, there are layers of awareness in the organization, just as there are in the human mind, of what is being said. In the human mind we have the most conscious layer, which tends to be a rational layer, of things we are aware we are saying to ourselves. The organizational analog for this are the things that are said between people in "official" meetings of the organization—things that are said out loud so that everyone present can hear. These are events like committee meetings, departmental meetings, workshops and offsite retreats, strategic planning sessions and the like. This I call the conscious, rational part of the organizational mind. What is said here is "discussible" by all employees who are in attendance and in that sense the organization as an entity is consciously aware of it.

Between and around events, however, are things people talk about in smaller groups or in confidential conversations. Often these entail interpretations and judgements about the events that these people would not verbalize in an "official forum of organizational business", like a meeting. As such, the organization as an entity is only partially aware and to the extent that these perceptions, interpretations and judgements are not discussible in any official forum of organizational business, they are out of awareness. They are like the "inner dialogue" of the human mind that operates at a subconscious level. In individuals these are the day dreams that we quickly forget or may not even notice that we are having, the patterns of thinking and judgement that operate just out of awareness but powerfully effect our conscious, "rational" thoughts. Psychologist call these scripts or schemas and some therapies, like neuro-linguistic programming and rational-emotive therapy, operate mainly at this level of consciousness.

I want to suggest 3 things that can form the basis of using AI as a change strategy:

1. Organizations have an inner dialogue made up of the things people say to each other in small confidential groups that are undiscussible in official forums of organizational business.

2. This inner dialogue is a powerful stabilizing force in social systems that accounts for the failure to follow through on rationally arrived at decisions. It is here where people's real thoughts and feelings about what is discussed in official forums are revealed and communicated.

3. This inner dialogue is mainly carried through the stories people tell themselves and each other to justify their interpretation of events and decisions. The change theory is: If you change the stories you change the inner dialogue. Nothing the "rational mind" decides it wants will actually happen if the "inner dialogue" is resistant to it.

When people talk in the hallways and over coffee it is often stories of past events that they use to justify the interpretations and judgements of current events. These stories get passed on and embellished with time and their historical veracity is irrelevant to the impact they have on how people make sense of organizational events. From this point of view AI can change an organization if it changes the stories that circulate in the organization's inner dialogue. Let me give an example.

One organization I work with has a strong and deep (but changing) inner dialogue about the lack of "real leadership" in the organization. Of course this is not discussed in official forums. Just the opposite. Those in authority are praised and accolades given for their leadership prowess. But in the inner dialogue, just the opposite happens. Authorities are described as gutless wonders who have no integrity, blow with whatever wind is strongest and can only be relied on to act politically in their best interest. Little wonder then, that almost none of the "soft" organizational strategies agreed upon during a major strategic planning exercise had been implemented three years later. In an appreciative inquiry into leadership, people in this organization interviewed their executives about the greatest acts of leadership they had seen in the organization as well as what they would considered their own peak leadership experiences.

The interviewees were stunned by the stories their leaders told – almost always stories about great personal integrity and courage where someone took the "right" stand even though it was politically unpopular or highly risky. Stories about events from the past that involved these leaders were radically changed as new appreciations about the motives and meanings behind their actions evolved. As these stories changed, greatly different interpretations of the current actions of leaders began to emerge in the parts of the organization that had been involved in the appreciative inquiry. Leaders were now being supported by the inner dialogue where in the past they were resisted, and some really different organizational strategies were implemented in the "soft" side of the business.

From this theoretical point of view, the key to OD practice is the stories and the way in which these are communicated to others in the organization. Those most impacted by the new stories are those who get to hear them, first hand, from those who tell them. Finding ways to help make that happen are clearly important. The use of interview protocols where people simply capture a few key images or "quoatable quotes" does not make sense from the inner dialogue view of change. Rather, what is required are richly woven short stories, written in the first person. The interviewer's job is not to simply transcribe what the interviewee said, like a journalist, but to use the craft of the literary writer to make a document full of vignettes that will invite and delight those who read them. As well, it is critical that the data not be anonymous, as in typical action research feedback reports, but directly attributed to whomever the story came from. Following on from the logic of the inner dialogue view, it might even be better to skip the writing all together and help people really hear each other's stories. Some possibilities are using edited videotapes of people telling their stories and bringing large numbers of people together where individuals take turns at a microphone telling their stories. From the inner dialogue view of change, what is critical to creating change is not the generation of new images/theories but the telling and retelling of stories that create new and more efficacious meanings that support organizational evolution.

Resolving Paradoxical Dilemmas

Another way in which I have seen AI lead to developmental change is in offering images that resolve paradoxical dilemmas for groups (Bushe 1998). All groups, especially those in organizations, face paradoxical requirements where they are asked to simultaneously do mutually incompatible things. In one study I was able, in about 2 hours, to help project managers in an MIS organization list 28 paradoxical requirements they experience in their organizational life. These are things like organizational injunctions to "staff up projects to ensure the best people are doing the work" and "staff up projects to ensure developmental opportunities for staff"; "always meet deadlines" and "never give customers defective work"; and so on. For the most part managers find ways to work around such paradoxical dilemmas and they get the work done in spite of them. But as Smith and Berg (1987) point out, groups can become stuck in a paradox where the nature of the paradoxical dilemma facing the group is unconscious or undiscussible. In such a case, a group will look and feel "stuck", constantly repeating failing patterns, finding itself with the same issues over and over that never seem to get resolved, all the while losing energy and motivation to continue operating as a group.

An AI with a team can evoke stories and images that aid the team in moving through the paradox it is stuck in. Let me give an example. An "empowered work team" of analysts was stuck over what Smith and Berg (1987) call the paradox of authority. The issue was that people were not willing to authorize others to act on the group's behalf but at the same time some wanted authority to act on the group's behalf in dealing with others in and outside the organization. The group had not discussed the problem this way. Rather, a sense was developing that "this empowered work team stuff just doesn't work" as the group became paralyzed by the inability of members to take action without having to convene a meeting of the group to get sanction. This was experienced by all as very frustrating.

As a team building intervention each member described to the whole team the best team he or she had ever been a member of (Bushe and Coetzer, 1995). One member told the story of working on a charity fund-raising drive with people who had been loaned, full time for 3 months, from their respective companies. Each person had pursued independent, creative initiatives in raising funds while at the same time fully supporting the initiatives of others. There was a program of activities to be done that had built up over the years and was fully documented for them. Over and above that, individuals pursued the group's core mission however they thought best.

The team reacted a little differently to this story than it had to others. Members were quieter and more withdrawn. It then dawned on me that this story offered a way out of the authority paradox (which, at the time, was one of a number of alternative explanations I had for their stuckness). I asked how the group was able to let others have free reign without fearing someone, due to inexperience or eagerness, would get them into a bind? He said "we decided we had no way of knowing if we could trust each other so we figured we had more to lose by not trusting than by trusting". At this another member piped in "so trust costs less".

The image of "trust costs less" blended this groups bottom-line business identity with the essential element for the resolution of the paradox. Because it was such a novel combination of those words, it opened up new gateways to emotional issues in this group. They were able to explore what the price of distrust was. Some were angry about how much other's distrust had cost them. People were able to admit that they hadn't felt trusted, hadn't been trusting others and that they believed trust would cost less. From there it was easy to decide on the "core program" and general objectives for individual initiatives.

It is probably true that all sizes of social systems can become stuck in an undiscussible paradoxical dilemma. One way out, and perhaps the only way out, is the development of new images that jostle conventional thinking and offer new ways of acting. Take for example the impact the image "sustainable development" had on what, to that point, seemed the intractable opposition of the business community and environmentalists. From this point of view, then, the change potential of AI is in it's capacity to offer such images. The implications for OD practice lead to very different implementation scenarios. For instance, we would want to have some kind of diagnosis, or set of hypothesis, about the kinds of paradoxical dilemmas facing the system before we begin the inquiry so that we can be sensitive to possible ways out presented in the stories. We would be most concerned with 'wordsmithing,' the creation of an image that captures people's energy and offers the solution to the dilemma they are caught in. The conduct of an AI from this perspective requires a much greater consultant, manager, or researcher-driven focus than one from any of the other change perspectives where there is a greater emphasis on fostering openness to what emerges from the collective inquiry.

Appreciative Process

While the first four theories I have described relate to AI as an action research process, "appreciative process" (Bushe and Pitman, 1991) is more a change agent technique. I mention it here because the theory of appreciation and its impact on organizations is clearly an important justification for appreciative inquiry (Cooperrider, 1991; Barrett, 1995) and because it has had the greatest personal impact on my consulting practice.

Appreciative process theorizes that you can create change by paying attention to what you want more of rather than paying attention to problems. Cooperrider's (1991) review of the research on sports psychology, the Pygmalion effect and brain functioning supported the ancient wisdom that you get more of whatever you pay attention to. As a change technique, appreciative process involves tracking and fanning. Tracking is a state of mind where one is constantly looking for what one wants more of. It begins with the assumption that whatever one wants more of already exists, even if in small amounts. Fanning is any action that amplifies, encourages, and helps you to get more of whatever you are looking for.

Recently I had a group of Executive-MBA students use appreciative process to create a change in any social system they chose. We were all blown away by the results. For example, one manager's "problem person" became his star employee when he looked for examples of her being a star. Another manager's conflicted and competitive team became a cohesive, cooperative unit when he looked for examples of cohesion and cooperation. Those using it with spouses or children felt that major positive transformations had occurred in their families.

It would be a mistake to say these are only examples of behavioral modification—of reinforcing desired behaviors. While there is some of this, the most critical part of appreciative process required for it to work is a change in the consciousness of the change agent. It begins with an act of belief, often in the face of accumulated evidence to the contrary. It requires a real change of "attitude" for those of us used to being "critical" or providing "corrective feedback". It seems much easier for many of us to know what is missing, what we don't want, what is lacking in others and ourselves All too often the main themes of discussions in organizations are what isn't working, what is wrong, what goals or standards are not being met. What is the impact of that on us? As my EMBA students found out, it seems to be more difficult and take more effort to notice what isn't missing and get clear about what we really want more of.

While working with a manager who can be bossy, sarcastic, demeaning and nasty, I worked on "seeing" the part of him that is compassionate, wise and wants to be a good leader. The result was that I not only observed much more compassionate and wise behavior, but the part of him that wants to be that way recognized me as an ally and we developed a deep, trusting relationship. I am sure that would never have happened if I had mainly paid attention to the behavior I didn't like. As I was to find out, he was well aware, usually after the fact, of his own meanness. He still acts "poorly", but not as often and as people who work for him come to see him as I do, with not nearly as harmful an impact.

From this point of view, then, appreciative inquiry creates change by focusing attention on where things are working and amplifying them through fanning. Utilizing such a theory, the collection of stories and creation of generative images is not nearly so important, perhaps not even necessary. Instead, what is necessary is a change in the problem oriented, deficiency focused consciousness of those intervening into the system to an appreciative one that believes that there is an abundance of good people, processes, intentions and interactions, just waiting to be seen and fanned.

Summary

In this paper I have reviewed five different theories of change that someone using appreciative inquiry could operate from in an organization development intervention. These are the social construction of reality, heliotropic hypothesis, the organizational inner dialogue, paradoxical dilemmas and appreciative process theories of change. In an earlier paper I argued that the development of AI as an OD intervention would depend on creation of new theory and that good practice would follow (Bushe, 1995). I am even more convinced of it now as I increasingly see evidence of attempts to do appreciative inquiry simply by asking people for "best of" stories with little theoretical or practical consideration of how this will lead to change in the systems being studied. Appreciative inquiry can be a truly revolutionary way in which we study and change social systems. Being someone, however, who believes that balance is where we find the "natural good", I think appreciation needs to be balanced with critical thinking to lead us there.

References

Barrett, F.J. (1995) Creating appreciative learning cultures. *Organizational Dynamics*, Fall 24:2, 36–49.

Barrett, F.J., Thomas, G.F. and Hocevar, S.P. (1995) The central role of discourse in large-scale change: A social construction perspective. *Journal of Applied Behavioral Science*, 31:3, 352–372.

Bushe, G.R. (1998) Appreciative inquiry with teams. *Organization Development Journal*, 16:3, 41–50.

Bushe, G.R. (1995) "Advances in appreciative inquiry as an organization development intervention". *Organization Development Journal*, 13:3, 14–22.

Bushe, G.R. and Coetzer, G. (1995) "Appreciative inquiry as a team development intervention: A controlled experiment". *Journal of Applied Behavioral Science*, 31:1, 13–30.

Bushe, G.R. and Pitman, T. (1991) "Appreciative process: A method for transformational change". *Organization Development Practitioner*, 23:3, 1–4.

Cooperrider, D.L. (1990) Positive image, positive action: The affirmative basis of organizing. In S.Srivastva and D.L. Cooperrider (Eds.), *Appreciative Management and Leadership* (pp. 91–125). San Francisco: Jossey-Bass.

Cooperrider, D. L. (1996). The "child" as agent of inquiry. *Organization Development Practitioner*, 28:1 and 2, 5–11.

Cooperrider, D. L., and Srivastva, S. (1987). Appreciative inquiry in organizational life. In W. Pasmore and R. Woodman (Eds.), *Research In Organization Change and Development* (Vol. 1, pp. 129–169). Greenwich, CT: JAI Press.

Smith, K.K. and Berg, D.N. (1987) *Paradoxes of Group Life*. San Francisco: Jossey-Bass.

Chapter 6

WHAT MATTERS MOST IN APPRECIATIVE INQUIRY: REVIEW AND THEMATIC ASSESSMENT

Therese F. Yaeger
Benedictine University

Peter F. Sorensen, Jr.
Benedictine University

Abstract

This article is a review of more than fifty articles relating to Appreciative Inquiry. Major themes that emerged are identified as contributing to the power of AI, or in other words "what matters most." Here we present each of the themes with illustrations drawn from experiences in a variety of cases and settings. Also included is a review and discussion of articles pertaining to our knowledge of AI through systematic exploration of its impact on performance and emerging trends in the use of AI.

Introduction

This paper focuses on the "state of knowledge" regarding Appreciative Inquiry. While research regarding Appreciative Inquiry is quickly expanding, we present these timely results of our review of more than fifty articles. The results are presented within three major topics all relating to "what matters most" in Appreciative Inquiry. These topics include emerging themes relating to the fundamental principles of AI, and current trends in the application of Appreciative Inquiry regarding its impact on organizational performance. These topics are then followed by a summary of thematic findings on the current state of knowledge regarding what matters most in Appreciative Inquiry.

Major Themes

Ten major themes were identified as a result of this review. Each of the themes is presented here with illustrations. These themes are:

1. The power of the positive question
2. The appreciative inquiry interview
3. Storytelling
4. Future vision/provocative proposition
5. Positive image
6. Collaboration/co-constructing/common ground
7. Anticipatory principle
8. Heliotropic principle
9. Continuity
10. Replacing deficit discourse

Many of the themes are interrelated, however, it is evident that certain themes have become more central to Appreciative Inquiry, at least in terms of the frequency with which they appear in the literature. The themes are generally presented in order of the frequency of their appearance. For example, the positive questions, the appreciative interview and storytelling are all interrelated and frequently mentioned. Continuity and the replacement of deficit language as defined in terms of the concept of hope and future visioning are mentioned less frequently but, nevertheless, represent powerful appreciative concepts and extensions of experiences with AI.

The Power of the Positive Question

The most frequently identified theme, by far, is the power of the positive question. This theme appears in more than 70% of the articles reviewed. The positive question is presented in two modes. One mode of delivery of the positive question is verbally in face-to-face discussion, and the second is delivered as part of the written questionnaire. A number of recent studies have incorporated the positive question as refinements of existing questionnaires. The delivery of the two different forms of the positive question presentation leads to two different processes. The verbal question is, of course, part of an interview process, which leads to a *one-on-one* interpersonal dynamic, while the questionnaire form generates a *group* dynamic in terms of sharing and feedback to a group.

The verbal, positive question is consistently reported to create an immediate and powerful framing effect that is highly and dramatically involving. The question involved is generated by the reflective process set in motion by the question. This process appears most powerful in environments and with individuals that in a way may be described as disproportionately deficit-based. It is almost as if the degree of deficit environment or experience creates a counter-need for increased positive or appreciative experiences. For example, some of the strongest responses to the positive question have been experienced by youth as the interviewers. The following is an illustration of verbal responses to the positive question:

I've never been asked these types of questions by youths in this school. When I do converse with the students it is *usually* for disciplinary reasons (Cooperrider, 1996).

Illustrations of the questionnaire form of the positive question include Rita Williams' example:

Throughout my career here I have had the fortune to work with people who were for me. I've been given every opportunity imaginable. There were times when I was given opportunities that were such a stretch that I didn't even know if I was capable. I have worked for people who could somehow see things in me I couldn't even see in myself. Without that confidence, I don't think my career would have unfolded as it has. (Williams, p. 46).

For more illustrations of questionnaire responses to the positive question, see also Sharkey (1999) and Sorensen, Head, et al. (1999).

The Appreciative Inquiry Interview

The appreciative inquiry interview along with the positive question provides the fundamental vehicle for the AI process. It is the second most frequently mentioned element of AI. As a consequence, a number of interview protocols are available in the literature with examples from the wide range of organizational settings in which AI has been applied, ranging from for-profit corporations (Cooperrider, 1996) to university settings (Head and Young, 1996). Asking the interviewee to "remember a time when" rather than have them answer a limiting question provides powerful journeys as described by Curran and Work (1998):

As we were all familiar with traditional interviewing methods, we knew that for this nontraditional process, it would be essential to free interviewees from a state of mind of "answering" our questions; instead, we would encourage them to tell their own stories. .... The interview structure was meant to serve as a doorway into the person's meaningful recollections, not just to provide a means of gathering focused data.

.... Each of us reported experiencing a deep connection with the interviewees and a profound experience for both parties, as the interviewer followed the journey of the explorer into the possibilities and limitations of the interview.

As a result of provocative interviews, powerful themes often emerge, as demonstrated in the work of Thatchenkery (1996) and Pinto and Curran (1998).

Storytelling

Storytelling is the vehicle that initiates the reflective process which provides a central part of, and critical contribution to, the effectiveness of AI. It is storytelling that personalizes and involves the person in becoming part of the positive history and positive future of the organization to which they belong. Along with the positive question and appreciative interview, storytelling emerges from our review as one of the cornerstone's critical and unique features of AI. Our understanding of storytelling as a vehicle for understanding culture and shaping organizational change is still in its embryonic state, but our review of the AI literature strongly suggests that it is one of the central driving forces in the AI process.

Some of the most dramatic illustrations of storytelling come from community service organizations, for example, the experience described by Holman, Paulson and Nichols (1998) and their work with the St. Joseph Community Health Council in the Hilltop.

The positive voices and experiences the Talkers described stunned professionals who had served this community for years and had never really ventured into it. This neighborhood was characterized by the media as one of the West Coast's most poverty-ridden, dangerous places. Yet, it was full of people who cared about the same things that the professionals did - a nice place to live, a good place to raise their kids, and a community that drew strength from its diversity.

The central role of storytelling at the front end of the appreciative inquiry process is presented by Liz Mellish (1998, 56).

I have found that the time spent storytelling at the front end of the process will be directly reflected in the quality of and commitment to the deliverables at the back end of the process.

The Future Vision/Provocative Propositions

Part of the creation of the future is the design of "provocative propositions." These are statements that bridge "what is" with "what might be." One of the most extensive presentations regarding the provocative propositions can be found in Thatchenkery's work at the Institute of Cultural Affairs (ICA) International in Brussels (1996) and his discussion of the "Appreciative Research Core" which created 18 propositions. The creation of provocative propositions around the core values of the organization as in the case of ICA appears to be a particularly effective way of linking current states to the future. At ICA, for example, propositions were formed around the core values of service/mission and spirituality. The service/mission propositions focused on expanding and broadening the scope of ICA's work; the proposition for spirituality focused on the integration of "life sustaining and community bonding spirit generation practices" into all ICA meetings.

Future Visioning is also described in Browne's Imagine Chicago project where the highlight of the conference turned out to be an exercise in which people were challenged to imagine visions of Chicago's future considered to be ultimately worthy of human commitment, and to identify what would be necessary for those dreams to become reality. (1998, p. 79).

Positive Image

The concept of positive image like so many of the other most frequently identified themes is interrelated to other themes, yet at times, may appear to be an elusive concept. Probably the most concrete illustration of positive images is Bushe's application of AI to teams (1998).

Bush describes AI as a process "that attempts to help groups, organizations and communities create new, generative images for themselves ..." Bushe describes the use of images as leading to developmental changes in the systems in which they are created. His work deals with what he refers to as the "best team" Appreciative Inquiry in which he employs the positive image concept to new and ongoing teams.

['Best Team' Appreciative Inquiry] can help create affirming, generative images that allow for a different discourse, a different set of understandings and opportunities to materialize for a group. In working with teams to develop affirming, generative images, an appreciative inquiry into something other than teams is often appropriate and can have very positive impacts on groups and their members.

For a comprehensive grounding in positive image, see Cooperrider's (1990) *Positive Image, Positive Action.*

Collaboration/Co-Construction/Common Ground

An additional theme that occurs frequently in the literature has to do with sharing — the sharing of peak experiences and personal stories which surfaces what gives life to the organization. The notion of sharing manifests itself in two major ways. First, the idea of bringing people together through sharing in order to move toward a common positive image of the future, surfaces in numerous cases. Madelyn Blair reflects this aspect of creating common ground in the statement of her work at CDI.

They learned that they had remarkably consistent definitions of what energizes them even though they had never talked about this before. They were naming the common ground on which they were standing and working, and were feeling very comfortable. (Blair, 1998, p. 196).

The second major concept of collaboration and co-construction of common ground is in the bridging of groups in conflict. The most dramatic illustration here is United Religions Initiative (Sarah van Gelder, 1998).

The URI gatherings have a tone distinct from that of UN Conferences or many other international gatherings. In order to create the "safe space for spiritual partnership" envisioned by the delegates, organizers drew on a process, known as Appreciative Inquiry, developed by David Cooperrider. This process is designed to help people discover what gives life to their organization and to develop together shared images of future possibilities to be co-created.

An end to violence conducted in the name of religion. It's a radical idea that just might work. Religious leaders from 50 countries are joining in an effort to find out.

The Anticipatory Principle

The anticipatory principle emerges as a theme but with less frequency than other more visible themes. But this principle is one proposition on which appreciative inquiry was founded and has significant implications. The anticipatory principle is described by Whitney when integrating organizational stories with the future.

> ... Stories told about an organization's future are the best determinants of its future... at any point in time the organization's future can be known through the stories told by its stakeholders. In thriving organizations the frequency of positive, hopeful stories is greater than the frequency of negative, cynical stories. What we anticipate is what we enact and give life to as organization reality.

The creation of perceptions of a most positive future – the implementation of the anticipatory principle through the application of an AI intervention with teams – is represented by Head (1999):

> ...The Anticipatory Principle was theorized to be a major foundation for AI ... The results lends support to the theory that AI aids in assisting groups to improve their image of the future and that allows groups to move quickly develop, and perform.

The Heliotropic Hypothesis

The heliotropic hypothesis in a way is the forgotten hypothesis of Appreciative Inquiry. It is the non-existent theme, yet it is powerfully evident in the AI process. It is the hypothesis first presented by David Cooperrider and later identified by Bushe (1996) as the edict that "sound systems evolve toward the most positive images that they hold of themselves."

Our review noted various cases indicating that organization members move more rapidly and effectively in the direction of affirmative imagery (moving toward light) than in the opposite direction of negative imagery. This process of heliotropic propensity, however, was powerfully experienced by Easley (1999) with youth-at-risk (primarily youth gang members) in an appreciative inquiry intervention and search conference at an alternative public school. During the conference dialogue, shifts were observed in the students' abilities to move in the positive direction. Clearly, it started with negative, deficit-based language:

> At the beginning of this intervention, when asked to tell stories about the high points in their lives and talk about their positive attributes, many of the young people stated that they had nothing good to say about themselves. Their behaviors were disrespectful to themselves as well as the individuals around them, yet they wanted to be respected, a theme that dominated the intervention. They talked about how they were behind in their grades, calling themselves "demotes," identifying academic deficiencies and talking about having been sent to an alternative school be-

cause of the behavioral problems they had allegedly demonstrated in their regular schools.

But Appreciative Inquiry suggests that a heliotropic process can and often does awaken the body to its own self-healing powers. By the second day of the conference, with a new vision toward a more promising future, the direction of the students' behavior moved toward a more positive direction:

The behaviors of the students on the second day suggested an internal healing process. Their language changed, also suggesting that they were beginning to understand the power of a different type of language to describe them (Easley, 1999).

Still today, with the use of AI, we are helping gang members seek out the best of "what they are" in order to provide an impetus for their imaging "what might be." (see Easley, et al., 1999).

Continuity

One of appreciative inquiry's most potential applications is in the area of continuity and maintaining what is best in the organization in times when there is heightened potential for descriptive behaviors — periods of transition. "Periods of transition" refers to such situations of changes in leadership, mergers and acquisitions. The potential success with AI to these transitioning periods is due particularly to an increased rate of change among leadership, mergers and acquisitions. For example, the current rate of *unsuccessful* mergers is estimated at seventy percent (Whitney 1998).

Continuity in terms of AI contributing to the change process is described by Whitney and Cooperrider (1998). Recognition that an organization's history can be a powerful source of positive possibilities for the future is central to appreciative inquiry. Successful change initiatives balance inquiry into:

Novelty - new and innovative possibility for organization action;

Continuity - those qualities, processes, or practices that an organization wishes to maintain as it grows in relation to our global well-being; and

Transition - the specific and tangible practices that will change.

For another example of the concept of continuity, see Rainey (1998, 39).

Replacing Deficit Discourse

A central underpinning of AI is the move away from deficit discourse. The dysfunctional role of deficit discourse is a theme that underlies many of the works reviewed. But the work which most specifically deals with that aspect of AI and which extends that dimension of AI is the concept of hope. Ludema's (1996) work refers to *textured vocabularies of hope* and identifies four qualities contributing to the construction of vocabularies of hope; in turn relates each of these four dimensions to dimensions of appreciative inquiry. The four dimensions of hope include: social relationships, the belief that the future can be influenced, maintained by dialogue concerning high human ideals, and the creation of positive affect and action. Here AI is described as contributing to hope through the constructionist and collaborative principles, the anticipatory and provocative principles, the poetic and the positive principles, and the simultaneous and pragmatic principles.

Current Trends with the Application of Appreciative Inquiry

One of the major trends in appreciative inquiry has been the coupling of AI with other approaches to Organization Development. The three most frequently cited approaches include: the use of large group methods; survey feedback and instrumentation; and team building developments.

Large group methods

Recently the most dominant trend in AI is the expanding role of large group methods. Here AI joins with a stream of work undertaken by Bunker and Albin, Weisbord, and Axelrod. The clearest illustration of the coupling of AI with large group methodology is in the Appreciative Inquiry Summit.

Among the most exciting applications of appreciative inquiry is the appreciative inquiry (AI) summit. An AI summit differs from other large-scale meeting processes in that the process is fully affirmative. It focuses on discovering and developing the organization's positive change core and converting it into strategic business processes such as marketing, customer service, human resources development, and new-product development. It launches the whole organization into new directions (Whitney and Cooperrider 1998).

The AI Summit is described as having been applied with groups ranging from 50 to 1800 people.

Survey Feedback and Instrumentation

A second trend in combining appreciative inquiry with organization development approaches is the integration of survey feedback and instrumentation. Here the major effort has been in the application of AI methods - primarily the positive question. Most of the work to date deals with the use of the Organization Culture Inventory (OCI), as a measure of twelve culture styles - culture styles associated with organization performance (Cooke and Lafferty 1989).

This work has taken on three shapes. First, the reframing of the OCI question in terms of peak experiences, when the organization was most alive, using responses to peak experiences for defining the culture and creating feedback and challenges around the positive qualities of the organization. Following the survey feedback method, these responses are used to assist the systematic building of these qualities for the future. Some of the advantages of this approach, which have been expressed, include the description of organization culture and visions of the organization using a concrete model of organization culture grounded in the empirical literature concerning organization performance.

Second, it builds on one of the most powerful and well-developed change techniques in the OD field. Historically, survey feedback along with action research, was one of organization development's five original roots. It is a process of collecting data from an organization through the use of questionnaires, and then using the collected data to develop change interventions with which to improve an organization. Coupling appreciative inquiry with survey feedback eliminates the problem-solving modes of questionnaires and refocuses the energy of the organization on more positive images of the future.

Third, initial attempts at identifying organization culture as defined by national cultural values suggests that AI may transcend national cultural boundaries, may represent a common human experience, and may have the potential for organizational change which is universal and not limited by national cultural values. (For preliminary findings on AI and national culture values, see Sorensen, Head, et al., 1996.)

Other questions and opportunities raised by the application of AI to culture relate to AI as a way of surfacing latent positive cultures. Discussions that organization culture cannot be changed have been raised; this may however, be the case that because organization culture is a complex phenomenon comprised of both dysfunctional and functional attributes which shift around a sustaining core over time, that AI is a way of *resurfacing positive attributes* that have become dormant. (Sorensen, et al. 1999).

Another aspect of the latent culture phenomenon is the question of under what condition do the positive cultural attributes emerge. One study suggested that the more positive cultural attributes emerge under conditions of crisis (Sharkey, 1999). This is consistent with the literature, which argues that crisis creates collaboration, mobilizes positive energy and focuses energy (Head, Sorensen, et al, 1997). It is also consistent with the conflict management literature, which indicates the one way of reducing conflict, and increasing collaboration is through the identification of a common ground.

Team Building

Numerous cases regarding team-building improvements were cited. While appreciative inquiry often compels an individual to rethink their personal efforts, teams and groups were consistently the object of most documented studies. For effective team and group appreciative inquiry cases, see Barrett, et al. (1995) Bushe (1998), and Hammond and Royal (1998).

Coinciding with team building is the effectiveness of the team facilitator. Reflecting on the skills of a facilitator, Mellish reflects on how the appreciative process involves the team facilitator's true commitment to people and process in change and this commitment can be shared and can deliver outcomes to clients [teams/groups], which exceed traditional planning and evaluations methods. Here Liz Mellish (1998) reflects on her experiences with appreciative inquiry:

"... A perceptive and anticipatory knowledge of the contextual issues faced by the client so as to be able to usefully direct energies toward an outcome within which all parties can see themselves operating productively."

Acute Listening: I am experiencing the development of an «appreciative ear». Listening for how people create possibilities, listening for their stories and examples of their best experiences and ideas in organizations...

Positive Care, where the best facilitators acknowledge the context of their life experience, their assumptions and commitment to assisting the client achieve the best possible outcome from this process.

Insatiable Curiosity in that the facilitator needs to demonstrate a genuine interest, a wonder if you will, in the day-to-day proceedings of organizational life.

Spontaneously reframing questions, "While the positive thrust of inquiry... appears straightforward ...

holding on to the belief that the process is meaningful, worthwhile and productive involves the facilitator in multiple spontaneous reframing, inputting and provocative inquiry processes.

Thematic Findings: What Matters Most About Appreciative Inquiry

Appreciative Inquiry, not unlike organization development, continues to grow in popularity and practice. Both AI and OD are practiced in turbulent environments where constant change compels us to seek a better environment for human interaction. Although our research on AI is limited to hardly a decade of practice, we know even less regarding AI as an OD approach, or even the sustainability of planned change in general.

So with this review, we are reminded that appreciative inquiry still exists in its nascent stage. Anecdotal data, however, is overwhelmingly positive. As a result of these numerous publications, presentations, and discussions, we have concluded that, based on this review, that Appreciative Inquiry "matters," that it has become one of the fastest-growing approaches in the field of OD, and that further review and assessment should continue in order to strengthen and encourage its development. Further, four noteworthy findings have surfaced through this assessment.

1. AI is strongly supported by the existing and developing body of organization development and change literature pertaining to organizational performance. When people are asked to identify peak organizational experiences and to relate positive images, they inevitably express these experiences in terms of organizational characteristics which are consistent with positive organizational climates, cultures and performance based on the organizational literature of the past sixty years.

2. AI is clearly related to positive organizational cultures.

3. AI improves team performance.

4. AI may transcend national cultural boundaries and be grounded in and reflective of a universal human experience.

References

Barrett, F.J., Thomas, G.F., Hocevar, S.P. (1995). "The central role of discourse in large-scale change: A social construction perspective." *Journal of Applied Behavioral Science,* 31:3.

Blair, M., (1998). "Lessons from Using Appreciative Inquiry in a Planning Exercise." In Hammond, S. and Royal, C. (Eds.) *Lessons from the Field: Applying Appreciative Inquiry*. TX: Practical Press Inc.

Browne, B. "Imagine Chicago: A study of intergenerational Appreciative Inquiry." In Hammond, S. and Royal, C. (Eds.) *Lessons from the Field: Applying Appreciative Inquiry.* TX: Practical Press Inc.

Bushe, G., (1998). "Appreciative Inquiry with Teams." *OD Journal, Volume 16, No. 3, Fall 1998.*

Bushe, G. (1995). "Advances in AI as an Organization Development Intervention." *OD Journal, Vol. 13, No. 3, Fall 1995.*

Cooke, R., and Lafferty, J., (1989). *Organization Culture Inventory,* Plymouth, MI: Human Synergistics, Inc.

Cooperrider, D., (1996). "The Child as Agent of Inquiry." *OD Practitioner,* Vol. 28, Nos. 1 and 2, 1996.

Cooperrider, D., (1996). "Resources for Getting AI Started: An Example OD Proposal." *OD Practitioner,* Vol. 28, Nos. 1 and 2, 1996.

Cooperrider, D.L. (1990) "Positive image, positive action: the affirming basis of organizing." In S. Srivastva & D. L. Cooperrider (eds.), *Appreciative Management and Leadership.* San Francisco: Jossey-Bass.

Curran, M., Work, G. (1998). "Creating Opportunities for Learning: A graduate class experiences AI in order to learn more about it." In Hammond, S. and Royal, C. (Eds.) *Lessons from the Field: Applying Appreciative Inquiry.* TX: Practical Press Inc.

Easley, C. A. (1999). *The Role of Appreciative Inquiry in the fight to save our Youth.* Ph.D. Dissertation. Benedictine University, Lisle, IL.

Easley, C., Yaeger, T., and Sorensen, P. (Jan 1999). Saving Tomorrow's Workforce. *Training Today.*

Hammond, S. and Royal, C. (Eds.) *Lessons from the Field: Applying Appreciative Inquiry.* TX: Practical Press Inc.

Head, R. (1999). "Appreciative Inquiry as a Team Development Intervention for Newly formed Heterogeneous Groups," presented at the International Association of Management.

Head, R., Young, M. (1996) "Initiating Culture Change In Higher Education Through AI." OD Journal, No. 2, Summer 1998.

Head, T., Sorensen, P., Preston, J., Yaeger, T. (1999). "Is Appreciative Inquiry OD's Philosopher's Stone?" In Cooperrider, D., Sorensen, P., Whitney, D., Yaeger, T. (Eds.) *Appreciative Inquiry: Rethinking Human Organization Toward a Positive Theory of Change.* Champaign: Stipes Publishing.

Holman, P, Paulson, A., Nichols, L. (1998). "Creating a Healthy Hilltop Community: Coordinating hospital planning with the needs of a community." In Hammond, S. and Royal, C. (Eds.) *Lessons from the Field: Applying Appreciative Inquiry.* TX: Practical Press Inc.

Jones, D., (1998). "A Field Experiment in Appreciative Inquiry." *OD Journal, No. 4, Winter 1998.*

Ludema, J. (1999). "From Deficit Discourse to Vocabularies of Hope: The Power of Appreciation." In Cooperrider, D., Sorensen, P., Whitney, D., Yaeger, T. (Eds.) *Appreciative Inquiry: Rethinking Human Organization Toward a Positive Theory of Change.* Champaign: Stipes Publishing.

Mellish, L. (1998). "Strategic Planning: Appreciative Inquiry in a large-scale change at an Australian University." In Hammond, S. and Royal, C. (Eds.) *Lessons from the Field: Applying Appreciative Inquiry.* TX: Practical Press Inc.

Pinto, M., and Curran, M. (1998). "The Laguna Beach Education Foundation, Schoolpower." In Hammond, S. and Royal, C. (Eds.) *Lessons from the Field: Applying Appreciative Inquiry.* TX: Practical Press Inc.

Rainey, M. (1996). "An Appreciative Inquiry into the Factors of Culture Continuity During Leadership Transition: A Case of LeadShare, Canada. *OD Practitioner,* Vol. 28, Nos. 1 and 2, 1996.

Sharkey, L. (1999) "Changing organizational culture through leadership development: A case in leadership transformation." *OD Journal, No. 3, Fall 1999.*

Sorensen, P., Head, T., Gironda, L., Larsen, H. (1996). "Global Organization Development: Lessons from Scandinavia." *OD Journal, No. 4, Winter 1996.*

Sorensen, P., Head, R., Sharkey, L., Spartz, D. (1999). "Appreciative Inquiry Meets the Logical Positivist." In Cooperrider, D., Sorensen, P., Whitney, D., Yaeger, T. (Eds.) *Appreciative Inquiry: Rethinking Human Organization Toward a Positive Theory of Change.* Champaign: Stipes Publishing.

Thatchenkery, T. J. "Affirmation as Facilitation: A Postmodernist Paradigm in Change Management." *OD Practitioner,* Vol. 28, Nos. 1 and 2, 1996.

Van Gelder, S. "Making Peace Between Religions." *Yes! A Journal of Positive Futures.* Fall, 1998.

Watkins, J., Cooperrider, D., (1996) "Organizational Inquiry Model for Global Social Change Organizations." *OD Journal, Vol. 14, No. 4, Winter.*

Whitney, D. (1996). Postmodern Principles and Practices for Large Scale Organization Change and Global Cooperation." *OD Journal, Vol. 14, No. 4, Winter.*

Whitney, D. and Cooperrider, D. (1998). "The Appreciative Inquiry Summit: Overview and Applications" *Employment Relations Today,* Summer, pp. 17-28.

Williams, R. (1996) "Survey Guided AI: A Case Study". *OD Practitioner,* Vol. 28, Nos. 1 and 2, 1996.

PART II

Case Stories, Resources for
Appreciative Inquiry Practice
and Empirical Testing

This second section, *Case Stories, Resources for Appreciative Inquiry Practice and Empirical Testing*, consists of 15 articles relating to the application of AI. The initial article by Barrett and Cooperrider has a special place in the literature of AI. It received a Best Paper Award in 1988 from the Academy of Management and tells the story of the transformation of the Medic Inn through the concept of the generative metaphor.

In Chapter 8 Gervase Bushe presents a second award-winning paper, "Advances in Appreciative Inquiry as an Organization Development Intervention" which won the Best of the OD Journal in the 20th Century Award in 1995 from the OD Institute. In the article Bushe helps define the parameters for legitimate AI practices and discusses the application of AI to teams.

In Chapter 9, Cooperrider discusses the Imagine Chicago project — the prototype for a number of community applications of AI that were to follow. The specific process and resources needed for starting an AI project are the topic of Chapter 10. The story of LeadShare is presented by Mary Ann Rainey in Chapter 11. LeadShare is the story of the first field application of Appreciative Inquiry. It is the story of how LeadShare, a partnership of nearly 350 accountants and management consultants applied AI in the identification of "life giving forces" through AI interviews for the purpose of maintaining and enhancing the positive core culture through a major event in management succession.

"Survey Guided Appreciative Inquiry: A Case Study", Chapter 12, by Rita Williams presents an illustration of the integration of AI with a classic OD intervention – survey feedback. It is the story of a major AI application to an $11 billion regional commercial bank in the US.

In Chapter 13, Whitney and Trosten-Bloom introduce the concept of the "six freedoms" in relation to the 4-D cycle. These six freedoms include: the freedom to be known in relationship, the freedom to be heard, the freedom to dream in community, the freedom to choose to contribute, the freedom to act with support, and the freedom to be positive. It is based on the application of AI at Hunter Douglas Window Fashions Division, the largest and most successful division of Hunter Douglas International.

Next, Head and Young present a case in Chapter 14 based on a culture change initiative in a private university. The article presents the process used, outcomes and learnings. The following chapter by Easley, Yaeger and Sorensen present a special and unique application of AI, its application to Chicago street gangs.

The international application of AI is presented in Chapter 16. Here Barros and Cooperrider present the use of the AI Summit at Nutrimental in Brazil. The case is of particular interest in that it takes place within a country where the national cultural values are described as being in contrast with the core values of Organization Development. In "Appreciative Inquiry with Teams", Chapter 17, Bushe describes four different ways to use Appreciative Inquiry in team building.

In Chapter 18, Mohr, Smith and Watkins present the application of AI to program evaluation or "embedded evaluation" of a Discovery Simulation developed by SmithKline Beecham designed to help scientific leaders and key contributors work effectively with the new drug discovery process. In "Appreciative Inquiry as a team development interventions for newly formed heterogeneous groups." Chapter 19, by Robert Head reports on the results of a field experiment designed to examine the effect of AI on the speed of development, quality of output and group expectations pertaining to future interactions and performance.

In Chapter 20, David Jones reports on the results of a field experiment designed to assess the effect of AI on management retention in 94 restaurants of a national Fortune 500 restaurant chain. Results reports a $100,000 savings in terms of reduction and an impressive $1 million projected savings related to the AI intervention.

Chapters 19 and 20 are award-winning papers both dedicated to the reporting of major field experiments evaluating the results of AI interventions in comparison to results from traditional OD interventions and control groups. Robert Head won the Best Paper Award in 1999 from the International Management Association while David Jones won the Best Paper Award in 1998 from the OD Institute.

The last chapter in this section, Chapter 21, reports on and summarizes the results of AI when integrated with the traditional OD technique of team development and survey feedback. The chapter reviews the results of five projects all of which report findings that indicate the enhancement of traditional OD interventions when combined with Appreciative Inquiry.

Chapter 7

Generative Metaphor Intervention: A New Approach for Working with Systems Divided by Conflict and Caught in Defensive Perception

Frank J. Barrett
Post Naval Graduate School

David L. Cooperrider
Case Western Reserve University

Abstract

This article proposes that one way to help a group liberate itself from dysfunctional conflict and defensive routine is through the introduction of generative metaphor. By intervening as a tacit, indirect level of awareness, group members are able to generate fresh perceptions of one another, thereby allowing for the revitalization of the social bond and a heightened collective will to act. After exploring insights into the recent literature on social cognition and selective perception, a case is presented in which generative metaphor was successfully used to help a dysfunctional group build (1) liberated aspirations and the development of hope, (2) decreased interpersonal conflict, (3) strategic consensus around a positive vision for the future, (4) renewed collective will to act, and (5)

Barrett, F.J. and Cooperrider, D.L. Generative Metaphor Intervention: A New Approach to Intergroup Conflict. *Journal of Applied Behavioral Science*, Vol. 26, No. 2 (1990), pp. 219-240.

*egalitarian language reflecting a new sense of unity and mutuality in the joint
creation of the group's future. Stages of the generative metaphor intervention are
discussed, and propositions are developed concerning those factors that will
likely enhance the generative potential of metaphor as an agent for a group
development and organizational change.*

Introduction

Under conditions of intergroup and interpersonal defensiveness, how can an
organization engage in dialogue seeking to create a common vision, a positive
image of a collectively desired future? This dilemma, which raises many core questions about the dynamics of social cognition, stereotyping, and the mechanisms of
awareness, has been faced by many managers and organization development (OD)
consultants who have worked with groups paralyzed by anxiety, defensiveness,
and negative attributions. Too often we have failed to understand the nature of
human cognition that leads to the formation of negative stereotypes and self-
perpetuating attributions. Our efforts to transform defensive routines, when attempted at all, have conventionally been problem focused. However, direct efforts
to solve such problems often heighten the very problems they attempt to solve:
When attempts are made to make people conscious of their negative attributions
toward others and of their defensive attributions in relationships, they all too frequently respond by becoming more defensive. How is it even possible then to
foster dialogue among competing members of an organization whose impressions
and judgments of one another have been well ingrained? We proposed in this
paper that (1) working at a tacit, indirect level of awareness through constructing a
generative metaphor that deliberately fosters formation of new impressions and
judgments allows new meanings to be given birth, and (2) building an appreciative
context rather than a problem-solving context helps generate the positive affect
required for building social solidarity and a renewed capacity to collectively imagine a new and better future.

This article is divided into four sections. First, we explore insights from the
recent literature on social cognition and selective perception. Second, we introduce
the concept of generative metaphor and argue that such metaphor invites new
openings for fresh perception, especially when a deliberately supportive or appreciative environment of inquiry is constructed. Third, we illustrate the use of generative metaphor in a case study on intervention method. Finally, we conclude with
a set of propositions about how active yet indirect inquiry into a related domain can
liberate a group in ways that more conventional OD problem-solving methods
could not begin to effect.

Social Cognition and Selective Perception

Social cognitive psychologists have provided dramatic evidence in the last decade regarding how the availability of information in the memory affects human judgments and the fundamental cognitive processes involved in the acquisition, retention, retrieval, and use of information about others (Hill, Lewicki, Czyzewska, & Boss, 1989). They have shown how people do not easily change their interpersonal theories, assumptions, expectations, and impressions, even when evidence contradicts them (Cantor & Mischel, 1977; Higgins & McCann, 1984; Hill et al., 1989).

Once judgments and theories about others have been formed, those judgments have a tendency to persevere even in the face of totally discrediting information, especially if one is engaged in forming a causal explanation to account for the impression or theory one has formed (Anderson, Lepper, & Ross, 1980). The simple process of explaining why one has a certain theory about some one may in fact have the unintended consequences of strengthening the impression and making it more resistant to change, even if the information upon which it is based, is completely discredited. For example, imagine a situation in which a traditional teambuilding intervention is being done with a group of managers who are divided by competition, jealousy, and "turfism". A direct intervention, as advocated by many conflict resolution theories, would call for managers to articulate why they see one another as troublesome or problematic. Following the perseverance effect in social cognition theory, once one puts forth a causal explanation for one's belief, the belief is actually strengthened. Therefore, if one were to say one sees a co-worker as crabby and unapproachable because the co-worker is selfish, moody, and insecure, the chances would be greater that, merely because one formed and articulated this causal explanation, one's belief about the co-worker would be stronger. One becomes even more convinced that the co-worker is selfish, moody, and insecure.

What happens when people perform behaviors contrary to the stereotype we have formed? When people do perceive behavior in one another that is inconsistent with the original schemas, they may notice the inconsistency, but it often tends not to alter the original impression. One study (O'Sullivan & Durso, 1984) showed that evidence that disconfirms an impression is noticed and remembered, but the original impression itself is not altered. When subjects were shown information that was atypical of a previously forward stereotype, it actually facilitated their recall of the original stereotype. Seeing a core incongruency may require more information processing, but actually facilitates recall of the original impressions. So, for example, imagine again that one has a well-formed image of one's co-worker as selfish, moody, and insecure. Even if the co-worker were to engage in action contrary to this image (e.g., the co-worker offers to take one out to lunch, or makes a large contribution to charity), one would process this atypical information, but the original stereotype would likely remain – and in all probability the negative image would paradoxically be strengthened. One would tend to explain the core incongruency in terms of the stereotype (recall that the act of putting forth an explanation will strengthen the original schema). So, to continue, one might then say to oneself, "He (or she) is only taking me to lunch because he (or she) wants something" or "He (or she) is contributing to charity because of feeling guilty about being so self-oriented." Thus, if we were to appreciate the nature of this dynamic when applied to traditional OD, we would see that many of our activities, such as diagnostic action research or encouraging direct and candid "confrontation meetings" among different groups, may unintentionally reinforce those very dynamics they seek to amend.

Nobody has synthesized the processes of selective perception better than Goleman (1985), who argues that (1) the mind often protects itself against anxiety by dimming awareness, (2) this cognitive process creates a blind spot, a zone of blocked attention and self-deception, and (3) such blind spots occur at every level of system, from individuals to groups, to organizations and to societies. When people are threatened with anxiety, there is a strong human tendency to deny parts of the world. When, for example, one feels threatened and begins to prepare oneself for a stressful event, one tends to bias many pieces of information as confirming the appraisal of threat (Beck, 1967). The active denial of the world to allay the threat of anxiety takes many forms, including avoided associations, numbness, flattened response, dimming of attention, constricted thought, memory failure, disavowal, and blocking through fantasy (Horowitz, 1983).

Similarly, it appears that one's present affective state of mood largely determines what one is able to perceive, learn about, or recall from memory. According to the work of Alice Isen and her colleagues, mood, cognition, and action form an inseparable triad and tend to create feedback loops of amplifying intensity. Studies have demonstrated, for example, that people who are "primed" into a negative mood state are able to recall significantly fewer pleasant memories of their past than are people in a positive mood state (Isen, Shalker, Clark, & Karp, 1978). Likewise, it has been shown that a negative mood state cues a person to think about negative things (Rosenhan, Salovey, & Hargis, 1981) and increases a person's capacity for perceiving mood congruence or negative things in self and others (Bower, 1981; Isen & Shalker, 1982).

Hence, what we see from this important research is the natural human tendency to form judgments and notice traits in others based on previously formed categories or on current mood states. Further, these categories and mood states are often primed and made ready to guide perception through social interaction. This process of cognitive cueing, which is part of the natural process of enculturation or socialization, often remains outside of a person's or group's awareness. Further, once impressions and judgments are formed, as in the halo effect or Pygmalion dynamic in the classroom (see Jussim, 1986, for a review), they tend to persevere. Furthermore, when the context is marked by feelings of fear, threat anxiety, and protectiveness, the dynamics of perception become even more entrenched (Goleman, 1985). Under conditions of fear and anxiety, individuals and groups will dim awareness and deny what is going on in the world. Hence, people often guard against seeing the very things that might allay their fears. To understand this paradox is to understand one of the central challenges of working with systems divided by conflict and caught in defensive perception.

Generative Metaphor For Opening Perception

With all these forces acting to constrict awareness and attention in ways that people seem ill-prepared to control, under what conditions can their well-ingrained interpersonal perceptions be expanded? If attention is prefocused under conditions of anxiety, and if people have formed judgments of one another that persist in spite of inconsistent behavior and discrediting information, what process can be engaged to enhance and enrich interpersonal perception? How, as OD practitioners, can we intervene to help groups out of self-perpetuating defensive strategies without the direct and often reinforcing confrontation of these defensive routines?

To answer these questions, we discuss the concept of generative metaphor (Schon, 1979; Srivastva & Barrett, 1988) as a way of supporting the cultivation of fresh perceptions and the acquisition of new schemas of others. But first, it is important to discuss a number of important properties or principles of metaphor.

Principles of Metaphor

1. Metaphor is an invitation to see the world anew. Metaphor presents a way of seeing something as if it were something else. Metaphor transfers meaning from one domain into another and thereby enriches and enhances both domains. Metaphor acts as a way of organizing perceptions and provides a framework for selecting and naming characteristics of an object of experience by asserting similarity with a different, seemingly unrelated object or experience. The subsidiary subject of the metaphor organizes perceptions of selecting and emphasizing certain details and suggesting implications that may not have been seen. For example, in the metaphor "man is a wolf," the ravaging, predatory nature of man is given focus; whereas the metaphor "man is a flower" focuses more on the delicate, beautiful nature of human beings blooming to fruition, going through season-like changes. Metaphors are, therefore, filters that screen some details and emphasize others. In short, they "organize our view of the world" (Black, 1962). Further, metaphor acts as a subtle transaction between contexts, as an entire set of characteristics can almost spontaneously be transformed from one set to another to create new contextual meaning. For example, in the metaphor "man is a wolf", my picture of man acquires more colorful detail: I now see him hairy and on all fours, saliva dripping from this mouth, with piercing and ferocious eyes and long fangs awaiting his prey. Also, in the interaction between domains, the wolf begins to take on human qualities: I see the wolf as purposeful and intent, having feelings and thoughts.

Because metaphor can instantaneously fuse two separate realms of experience, it is transformative. As Robert Nisbett suggests, metaphor is powerful because of its capacity of semantic and cognitive reconstruction:

Metaphor is, at its simplest, a way of proceeding from the known to the unknown. It is a way of cognition in which the identifying qualities of one thing are transferred in an instantaneous, almost unconscious flash of insight to some other thing that is by remoteness or complexity unknown to us. The test of essential metaphor...is not any rule of grammatical form, but rather the quality of semantic transformation that is brought about. (Nisbett & Ross, 1985, p. 4)

The potential for semantic transformation is what makes artists, poets, leaders and scientist alike so attuned to the power of metaphor, and aware of its potential for directing perception enriching awareness, and transforming the world. Good metaphors provoke new thought, excite us with novel perspectives, vibrate with multivocal meanings, and enable people to see the world with fresh perceptions not possible in any other way.

2.   Metaphor facilitates the learning of new knowledge. Petrie (1979) proposes that in confronting radically new knowledge, metaphor can be useful. As anomaly is created, an experience is apprehended that is outside one's present frame. It is through immersion in the experience, active thought experimentation, testing, and correction that expansion of cognitive frames begins to occur. Thus, for the young science student who is cognitively blocked in trying to grasp the structure of the atom, the metaphor "the atom is a solar system" could indeed be useful. The student might begin to "see" neutrons and electrons revolving around the gravitational center. He or she might then engage in such active thought experimentation long enough to allow a new understanding of the atom to emerge.

3.   Metaphor provides a steering function for future actions and perceptions. Social order and social structure are not preordained, but are achieved through members' construction of reality. Social action achieves form through the metaphor in actor's heads (Turner, 1974). As Pepper (1942) pointed out, "root metaphors" provide the social group with a whole set of categories through which the social group interprets the world. For example, in the 17th century the universe was seen as a machine, which effected not only the activities of physical science, but whole fields of moral philosophy and human psychology. In the 19th century, for example, Marxist theory operated according to an embryonic metaphor. Social orders were seen as proceeding from the "womb" of preceding others, with transformation periods likened to the "birth" of a new order. The state of capitalism was seen as carrying the "seeds" of its own destruction. These metaphors spawn categories and terms that drive people to initiate actions congruent with the metaphors informing their beliefs. One example of how a group's or society's root metaphors can provide a steering function for future action is that of the United States' involvement in the Vietnam War: it can be argued that its involvement was connected to the cognitive categories that emerged from one root metaphor – the domino theory. Once the U.S. began to see Communism taking over countries, causing them to topple one after another, policy makers were left with little choice but to stop this "evil" momentum.

4. Metaphor invites active experimentation in areas of rigidity and helps people overcome self-defeating defenses. Milton Erikson's work in psychotherapy provides perhaps the best example of this principle (see Haley, 1973). Erikson's approach is to circumvent the patient's areas of resistance and to work with the neurosis indirectly and metaphorically. Learning becomes transferred to the area of difficulty and "suddenly" the patient is able to change previously rigid perceptions and behavior. Erikson discusses, for example, the case of a couple having sexual difficulties. Rather than confront this delicate area directly where patients resist revealing their insecurities, he begins to work at the metaphorical level. He proposed that the couple enjoy a long, leisurely meal, taking time to enjoy the succulence and sweetness of the food rather than rush through to satisfaction. Together they discuss their eating habits: the man's tendency to rush to the main course of meat and potatoes; the woman's preference for leisurely enjoyment of the appetizer, the atmosphere, the pre-meal activities, and the preparation. Erikson then deliberately instructs the couple to engage in another meal and this time to prolong each course and attend to their positive sensations. Such experimentation beings to have an effect on their sexual relationship: Learning is subtlety transferred to the area of difficulty and the couple begins to change their behavior. Defensive routines are not confronted head on; they are circumscribed. Problems are not identified, discussed, analyzed, or even challenged. In fact, Erikson is careful to avoid such discussion because the couple, as he explains, are least in need of further "education" into the unfortunate mess their lives are in. They already know about it. Thus, it is active experimentation and involvement in the metaphorical domain that helps the couple overcome resistances in the area of rigidity. Imagine, for example, what would happen if Erikson used a direct problem-solving approach with the troubled couple. Supposed he were to sit down and face the man and say, "So what seems to be the problem you are having in bed with your wife? We must discover the cause of this dysfunction because it appears you're not making her happy." Such an approach would challenge the man's self-esteem and in all likelihood would trigger defensiveness, insecurity, embarrassment, and painful self-consciousness. Under such conditions of threat, it is unlikely that either person would be open to learning or rational behavior change. Rather each person would begin to look for reasons and excuses to explain her or his behavior. Perhaps each would even begin to blame the other and possible experience a worsening of the sexual relationship.

Generative metaphor, then, is an invitation to see anew, to facilitate the learning of new knowledge, to create new scenarios of future action, and to overcome areas of rigidity. There is a subtle, indirect component to generative metaphor. As Nisbett noted, fresh insights are transferred instantaneously, almost unconsciously, bringing about semantic and perceptual changes. In Milton Erikson's clinical practice, areas of resistance are bypassed (in a sense "fooled") only to become the object of sudden transformation.

A Case Study: The Medic Inn

The Medic Inn is a 380-room hotel facility with two dining rooms, a bar, several meetings rooms, and a large ballroom. It is owned and operated by the Midwest Clinic Foundation (MCF), a large tertiary care center with a 1000-bed hospital. The Medic Inn was privately owned and operated by a hotel chain until it was purchased by MCF in 1981 to offer lodging and food to patients and their families. MCF recently expanded and built a new, large clinic facility on the east side of the hotel, and with the expansion the hotel was also renovated: A large, elegant lobby was built, the dining room was renovated, and the top floors were converted into elegant, high-priced rooms especially designed to serve foreign dignitaries.

While changes were made in the physical facilities, MCF retained the managers of the hotel to operate it. As one MCF administrator put it: "We're not in the hotel business and we really know nothing about running one, so we decided to keep the people who were on board." We were hired in 1984 originally to do a benefit, compensation, and job audit through the Human Resources Division of MCF. As an entry intervention, however, we proposed to do an employee attitude survey. We met with the four top managers of the Medic Inn, and they belatedly agreed to our proposal to conduct a survey of all 260 employees.

The managers of MCF were suspicious of us from the beginning. It soon became clear that their suspicion and distrust extended to the Medic Square Hotel Company, the for-profit group of administrators set up by MCF. In conversation with the general manager, it became apparent that he was afraid of losing his job. We conducted an employee attitude survey and continued to work with the group in team-building sessions and facilitating various task force meetings. What became increasingly clear after almost 14 months of working with the group was that the management group was divided by interpersonal and interdepartmental conflicts and had a history of little cooperation. The four top managers were aware that the administrators of MCF wanted the Medic Inn to become a four-star facility, a designation granted to high-quality hotel and restaurant service facilities. Since the Medic Inn had a long way to go to achieve this status, this goal added pressure to the group. It is difficult in a short case description to give a flavor of the degree of interdepartmental conflict, but we cite a few examples to help clarify the climate.

Among the top four managers, consisting of the general manager, the manager of food and beverage, the rooms manager, and the accountancy manager, there was a history of backbiting and what they referred to as "sandbagging" one another. When the four held their weekly planning meetings, the meetings were laborious, and they had a difficult time arriving at a decision. Below is one example of the kind of exchange that occurred between them. This dialogue comes from a meeting that occurred approximately two months before the intervention we describe in this article.

John: (general manager): What's changed since we started these regular meetings?

Tim: (manager of food and beverage): Nothing.

Fred: (manager of accountancy): I agree. All we do is bicker.

Long pause.

Rick: (manager of rooms): There's more separation between the Food and Beverage Department and the Rooms Department than ever before.

Long silence.

Tim: A year ago we agreed to move toward a four-star status. We've taken care of some of the physical things and it looks nice, but we haven't taken care of the people things. We still don't have a common goal. And before we even try to talk about a common goal, I want to hear a personal commitment from people. I don't feel it, I don't see it. Sometimes I hear people say it. But I wonder how deep people's commitments are to this. I don't know where Rick is.

Rick: Could we keep this discussion on a business level and keep personal relationships out of it?

Tim: The way some of the departments have been run, I'm not sure everybody even wants to be part of this team.

In private conversations, the four managers were even more candid about their frustration with one another and their hostility. One said of the other: "Tim thinks he's better than everybody else. He blasts and sandbags people behind their backs."

Among the next level of managers, 13 middle managers who reported directly to the four top managers, interdepartmental conflict was also evident. This is how some members described the group.

The people are confrontive and insecure. It seems like people are involved in too many power plays instead of just working together. Ron (a food service manager) and Fredricka (a rooms manager) can't even talk to each other. They're supposed to work together to plan the new construction on the 17th floor dining room, and every time they try to discuss something they end up yelling at each other. I think they actually try and make each other look bad.

I think people are jealous of each other here. It seems like food and beverage managers get raises all the time. They get taken care of. We (room managers) are ignored when it comes to raises and promotions.

Members were defensive, and some felt that their efforts to help and cooperate were treated with suspicion and interpreted as intrusions. This frequently led to the withdrawal of energy.

The other day I told Fredricka about the party of 30 we are catering a week from Thursday. I tried to talk to her very carefully and gently. I asked her if there's anything we could do to help. She bit my head off again just like I knew she would. She goes, "Nobody ever tells us anything. You think I don't know how to do my job here or what?" Stuff like that. It makes me want to just avoid her.

The interpersonal tension and competition that existed became an obstacle to people's capacity to generate a vision and strategic plan for the future of the Medic Inn and what needed to happen to make it a four-star hotel. Most members found it difficult to generate ideas and struggled with a pessimistic response and deficiency orientation.

When managers met to discuss the future plan for the Medic Inn, there was little sense of hope or belief in their own efficacy to create the future. Many members generated passive, cynical accounts, often belying a fear that MCF would withdraw support for any strategy they enacted. As one manager put it:

MCF has not given us a vision. I don't trust the plan they talk about. They keep calling to get new numbers. That shows how insecure it is. It's a game they keep rewriting…It will just be a cost decision and they will keep spending it (money) until someday they'll say, "This has gotten out of hand," and I'll be gone.

Members continued to generate scripts of impending doom. During planning sessions, accounts of fear and debilitating thoughts emerged. These versions of constraint and doom operated like depressive cognition (Beck, 1967) and fostered withdrawal from action and responsibility.

Fred: They've given us a blank check.

Karl: We get money way too easy. No one rejects anything we ask for. Doesn't that bother anybody? Am I the only one who's bothered by it?

Rick: I agree. I'm just waiting for the hammer to fall…I'm afraid they're going to wake up and discover this thing can't work like this. There is no way. They're going to pull the plug on us.

The group needed to engage in dialogue in order to develop consensus about goals and a vision of what is possible in building a four-star excellent organization. And yet there was an inherent dilemma: How could a group of people divided by competition and turfism engage in dialogue with one another? Further, how could a group with depressed aspirations talk about how it could become a four-star hotel? When they looked at themselves and at one another, they saw only deficiency and unmet expectations. It was as if the worse was always expected, and had just not happened yet.

As consultants, we were faced with a dilemma: The traditional problem-solving approach to HR/OD would call for us to analyze the dilemmas in the group, feed back the problem themes, and ask the group members to face the issues, and generate solutions.

So ingrained is the problem-solving mentality that most OD consultants and action-researchers scarcely are able to envision alternatives. As Cooperrider and Srivastva (1987) have shown, the language of the field continues to be guided by a deficiency model of the world. It is as if the field itself revolved around a root metaphor that says "organizing is a problem to be solved" and therefore OD equals problem solving; to do good action research is to solve "real problems."

So ingrained is the assumption that it scarcely needs documentation. Virtually every definition of OD, especially as it relates to action research, equates the discipline with problem solving, as if problem solving were its very essence. The language of "problem" is pervasive. For example, as French and Bell (1978) define it, "action-research is both an approach to problem solving – a model or paradigm, and a problem solving process - a series of activities and events" (p. 88). In terms of the Bradford, Gibb, and Benne (1964) definition, "It is an application of scientific methodology in the clarification and solution of practice problems" (p. 33). Similarly, Frohman, Sashkin, and Kavanaugh (1976) state that the discipline's essence is "a particular process model whereby behavioral science knowledge is applied to help a client (usually a group or socials system) solve real problems and not incidentally learn the process involved in problem solving" (p. 203). Echoing this theme, researchers at the University of Michigan's Institute in Social Research state,

> ... three factors need to be taken into account in an organization development (action-research) effort: The behaviors that are problematic, the conditions that create those behaviors, and the interventions or activities that will correct the conditions creating the problems. What is it that people are doing or not doing, that is a problem? Why are they doing or not doing these particular things? Which of a large number of possible interventions or activities would be most likely to solve the problems by focusing on why problems exist? (Hausser, Pecorella, & Wissler, 1977, p. 2)

When organizations are approached from the conventional deficiency perspective of the discipline, all properties and modes of organizing are scrutinized for their dysfunctional but potentially solvable problems. According to Levinson (1972), therefore, organizational analysis is done to "discover and resolve these problems... The consultant should look for experience(s), which appear stressful to people. What kinds of occurrences disrupt or disorganize people" (p. 37). Similarly, French (1969) advises that the OD practitioner look for problems:

Typical questions in data gathering or "problem sensing" would include: what problems do you see in your group, including problems between people that are interfering with getting the job done the way you would like to see it done? And what problems do you see in the broader organization? Such open-ended questions provide latitude on the part of respondents and encourage a reporting of problems as the individual sees them. (pp. 183-185)

To repeat, as consultants to the hotel we were faced with a dilemma: Traditional problem-solving approaches to HR/OD would have called for us to (1) identify the key problems of the group – the "felt needs" – (2) analyze the cases of the problems, (3) feed back the problem themes, and (4) ask the group members to candidly face up to their issues and generate collaborative action plans. We decided that it would be counterproductive to do this. Members already knew about the tensions in the group. They already had multiple logics and compelling theories to explain and justify the current state. In fact, it occurred to us that the last thing the group needed at this point was further education – a more sophisticated education – on the dilemmas and seriousness of their plight. To face these issues and to develop elaborate analyses of the causes did not seem to be productive, and in fact might well have only heightened awareness of the tensions, constrained possible new perceptions of one another, and depressed aspirations even further. As in the myth of the two-headed hydra, we were beginning to believe that any one problem directly eliminated would be quickly replaced by two more. Our task was to break out of the current frame altogether.

Rather than ask the group members to directly face their tension, to become introspective, and to look at themselves and at their own problems, we proposed that they become active inquirers, focusing on a domain outside their own.

In the rest of the section we outline exactly what we did by discussing the four stages in what we now call the Generative Metaphor Intervention Process (GMIP), including (1) journey into metaphor, (2) poeticizing the world, (3) possibility expansion, and (4) return to the original domain.

Step 1: Journey into Metaphor

In an effort to enable the group to break through its ingrained schemas, interpersonal stereotypes, static perceptions, and dimmed awareness to protect against intrusions of anxiety, we proposed a generative metaphor for the organization: That is, we constructed a situation in which the system could creatively focus attention on another domain, in this case that of another organization.

Our choice of metaphor (another organization) was guided by two considerations. First, it was felt that, by definition, the metaphor needed to be related to, but sufficiently different from, the Medic Inn itself. To develop a transaction across contexts, we needed a refocusing of the group's attention on something new and potentially evocative. Second, there was the challenge of stimulating interest:

What was it that would capture the group's excitement on a broad and collective level?

The solution was to find an organization in the same service industry, but one whose mission, market niche, and level of performance departed dramatically from those of the Medic Inn. Significant as well, it was felt that the journey into metaphor should in fact be a journey. The task was to cultivate a sense of adventure to help shift the group's frame of reference away from historical reality and into the realm of anticipatory reality. The idea was to use the journey into metaphor as a way of refocusing attention not only onto another physical domain but onto another temporal domain as well – in this case, away from the strictures of the past toward the unbridled opportunities of the future. Eden (1988) has written extensively on the importance of building hope and a positive anticipatory reality in organizational change, as part of the self-fulfilling prophecy phenomenon. Following Petrie's (1979) theory of learning through metaphor, an anomaly must be introduced that stimulates active thought experimentation and subsequent expansion of cognitive frames.

The introduction of anomaly began with a prescription to the top three levels of management. We proposed (1) an immediate elimination of the many interpersonal problem-solving meetings that were taking place, and (2) the creation of a representative task force to plan a collective journey to Chicago's famous Tremont Hotel, one of the finest four-star hotel properties in the country. At the same time we acknowledged the many interpersonal and intergroup difficulties throughout the Medic Inn but suggested these be "put on hold" – that time would probably have to take care of things. We argued that, at this point, the group did not need to solve all its problems. It needed first to experience becoming a "learning system," free from the day-to-day task of running the hotel. From that point on, we resisted all attempts on the part of the Medic Inn managers to draw us into a problem-solving mode. We deliberately guided conversations away from the areas of most difficulty and consciously began stimulating and nurturing conversations that resonated with a sense of excitement, adventure, and positive anticipation about the journey to come.

Step 2: Poeticizing the World

Arrangements were made with the Tremont Hotel. The visit with 30 managers from the Medic Inn would take place not immediately, but in five months. We reasoned that the sheer anticipation of the trip, and the idea of a significant adventure together would prove to be as important as the journey itself. Having placed a sense of collective positive anticipation at the foreground of the group's consciousness, we wanted to keep it alive as long as possible. As it turned out, this element – the creation of a positive anticipatory ethos – became a powerful effective force in the building of social solidarity. We reasoned that it would be out of such strength – this new sense of connection that the Medic Inn would later be able to grow beyond its current deficiencies and difficulties.

The design of the journey into metaphor called for a five-day visit. The first day was to include a brief site visit of the Tremont Hotel and then an eight-hour workshop on a unique method of organizational analysis call appreciative inquiry (discussed further below). Day two was to feature an organization-wide analysis of the Tremont conducted by the 30 Medic Inn managers themselves as field researchers. Their task, put briefly, was to the enter the field setting to make as many observations and conduct as many interviews of Tremont staff as possible in an eight-hour day. As explorers, their focus was to be selective. Their task was to cognitively bracket all seeming imperfections and deficiencies at the Tremont to discover those that exhibited fundamental strength and value in terms of the system's people, its management process, its culture, and methods of organization. Deliberately appreciative in nature, the inquiry into the new domain was to revolve around a number of core questions.

1. What were the peak moments in the life of the hotel – the times when people felt most alive, most energized, most committed, and most fulfilled in their involvement?

2. What was it that Tremont's staff members value most about themselves, their tasks, and the organization as a whole?

3. Where excellence had been manifested what were the organizational factors (structures, leadership approaches, systems, values, etc.) that most fostered realization of excellence?

4. What were the most significant embryonic possibilities, perhaps latent within the system, that signified realistic possibilities for an even better organization?

The overarching aim of the organizational analysis workshop was to reawaken the Medic Inn management team's "appreciative eye." Building on the philosophy of appreciative organizational inquiry (as outlined in Cooperrider & Srivastva, 1987), we emphasized learning how to perceive organizations as creative constructions, as entities that are alive, vital, and dynamically emergent. More than a method or technique, the appreciative mode of inquiry was presented as a way of living with, being with and participating in the life of a human system in a way that draws one to inquire beyond superficial appearances to the deeper life-generating essentials and potentials of organizational existence. The appreciative eye, we proposed, is what allows one to value that which has fundamental value; it allows one to see what Bruner speaks of as the "immensity of the commonplace" or, in Joyce's reverent phrase, "the epiphanies of the ordinary" (in Bruner, 1986).

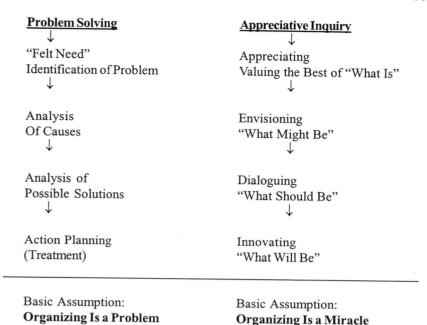

Problem Solving	**Appreciative Inquiry**
↓	↓
"Felt Need"	Appreciating
Identification of Problem	Valuing the Best of "What Is"
↓	↓
Analysis	Envisioning
Of Causes	"What Might Be"
↓	↓
Analysis of	Dialoguing
Possible Solutions	"What Should Be"
↓	↓
Action Planning	Innovating
(Treatment)	"What Will Be"

Basic Assumption:	Basic Assumption:
Organizing Is a Problem	**Organizing Is a Miracle**
To Be Solved	**To Be Embraced**

Figure 1. Training Notes on Appreciative Inquiry

During the training we contrasted the conventional problem-solving model with the stages of appreciative inquiry (see Figure 1) and did some skill-building role plays to prepare the group for appreciative interviewing. Most important, a context was formed through philosophical discussion of appreciation as a way of knowing and relating to the world. The diverse quotations reproduced below (as quoted in Cooperrider & Srivastva, 1987) begin to give a flavor of the sprit we were working to cultivate.

(Appreciation) thus makes immortal all that is best and most beautiful in the world...it exalts the beauty of that which is most beautiful...It strips the veil of familiarity from the world, and lays bare and naked its sleeping beauty, which is in the spirit of its forms.

—Shelley

As soon as man does not take his existence for granted, but beholds it as something unfathomably mysterious, thought begins... Ethical affirmation of life is the intellectual act by which man ceases simply to live at random.

—Schweitzer

The most beautiful and profound emotion one can feel is a sense of the mystical...It is the power of all true science.

—Einstein

If I were to wish for anything, I should not wish for wealth and power, but for the passionate sense of the potential, for the eye which, ever young and ardent, sees the possible. Pleasure disappoints, possibility never. And what wine is so foaming, what so fragrant, what so intoxicating, as possibility!

—Kierkegaard

Generative metaphor, we argue, enables groups to overcome defenses and liberate energy. In part, such liberation is achieved by cutting through constrictions of habit and cultural automaticity in perception. Generative metaphor is, therefore, poetic in nature. It is an instrument for seeing the world in new ways and in new combinations – it opens our lines to an expanded range of possible worlds. The poet's function, argued Aristotle, is to describe not the thing that has happened, but the kinds of things that might happen (i.e., what is possible). The poetic process helps us appreciate the fact that many futures are possible and that human realities are both discovered and created. As Bruner (1986) has elaborated, the function of the poetic is to open us to the hypothetical, to the range of meanings that are possible. He uses the term "to subjunctivize" to describe the linguistic process that renders the world less fixed, less banal, and therefore more susceptible to re-creation. And this is what is meant when we refer to phase two as the phase of poeticizing the world. Through appreciative inquiry, we hoped to stimulate within the Medic Inn group as a whole an artistic vision capable of seeing and creating possible worlds.

One final comment is important. As participants began to experiment with the appreciative mode, we observed a relaxation of tensions, a new climate of lightness and freedom, playfulness and laughter, and a shift from the language of problem solving to the language of learning (e.g., "I wonder...what I'll discover about the Tremont's front desk operation"). Part of the relaxation of tensions was due to all the participants' attention being turned away from themselves as a group. The new common gaze was at the Tremont. At no time did we suggest to the Medic Inn managers that they might begin to look at themselves appreciatively. The entire emphasis was on bringing attention to another domain.

Step 3: Co-creation of Possibility

The next day began with immersion in the experience. It was a day of data collection, active experimentation, and attention to the details in the metaphor domain. Again, the purpose of this approach was (a) to help the Medic Inn group become a learning system – to help them learn about themselves – but (b) in a subtle, indirect way by immersing themselves in the life and detail of another system by using an appreciative mode of inquiry.

Arrangements were made for the Tremont staff to meet with members of the Medic Inn staff. The Medic Inn group conducted interviews   h their counterparts as well as with members from other departments. So, for example, the Medic Inn banquets manager interviewed not only the Tremont banquets manager, but also the rooms manager. They not only interviewed staff members, but because they stayed at the Tremont as guests, they were instructed to note in their journals as many other features as possible. They collected numerous details, for example, on how service was delivered, how their beds were made, how the washrooms were cleaned, how food was delivered, and how employees talked to one another and to guests. In addition to noticing physical layouts, they collected data on how employee meetings were run, who attended and what issues were discussed, and how training programs were conducted.

The following day of data analysis was designed for dialogue and reflection on the experience in the related domain. After dividing the Medic Inn managers into mixed subgroups, we asked for reports on every discovery. Indeed, the managers were keen observers. The groups generated list upon list of a myriad of factors that were found to be associated with organizational excellence. And the data were inspiring. Said one manager, "I can't believe the things that housekeeping does. What they do in terms of employee recognition and involvement is so simple – but it works. Their room exhibitions are something any hotel could begin immediately, at no cost!"

Just as an artist intent upon expressing the positive values of a landscape would select the values the artist appreciates and would express these and not the indifferent features, the managers of the Medic Inn were beginning to give full voice to their own highest aspirations and values. During the "report-outs," it was not uncommon for people to "wander beyond" their data. Extrapolating from the best of "what was," the Medic Inn managers began to envision "what might be." For five and one-half hours the group discussed its most interesting and exciting discoveries. The energy level was high. Communications were flowing. Then the group members were given one more important task: They were to take the best of what they could find at the Tremont and use that to create a visionary portrait – a genetic blueprint – of the ideal "four-star" hotel operation. This portrait was to be shared the next day with all the Tremont staff in the form of a feedback meeting. It was to be given to the Tremont as "a gift."

The key point is that the Medic Inn managers were not merely articulating their findings. They, in concert with one another, were creating new values and new possible ways of seeing organizational life through the act of valuing. As Nietzsche one remarked, "Valuing is creating: hear it, ye creating ones! Valuation is itself the treasure and jewel of valued things" (quoted in Cooperrider, 1990).

Equally important, the attention was again focused on another domain. Among other things, this encouraged greater creativity in the envisioning process. Because it was not "their vision" for their hotel, the group members were freed from their habitual cynicism, doubt, and obstacle identification. Nascent ideas were given a chance. People experienced being listened to and heard. The group had become an aesthetic forum for sharing and crafting new meaning. It had become a safe place, even if only indirectly, for people to share their aspirations, dreams, and images of possibility.

What became increasingly clear as the members were engaged in this exercise was that given this task, they were able to make private aspirations public ones. There were few obstacles due to defensiveness or negative attributions toward one another, ostensibly because the subject matter related to something other than themselves. In the meantime, they were becoming less strange to one another and less constricted in their exchanges. Indeed, people were beginning to experience more connection than disconnection, more consensus then dissensus, and more things to value about one another than to devalue.

In one unexpected transaction, for example, the two managers who were most at odds agreed publicly to "bury the hatchet." They literally had not spoken to each other in over six months.

The group applauded as the feud was put to rest with an open hug. One of the two broke out in uncontrollable laughter, exclaiming that he couldn't believe he agreed with almost everything the other person said.

On the last day, we suggested that the group members direct their attention to their own organization, and envision and imagine what activities and plans they could engage in to begin to achieve excellence. Again, we were surprised at the unexpectedly high level of energy and the number of creative ideas that people generated. Unlike the group process exhibited before the Chicago retreat, this one left us feeling as if we were observing a totally different collectivity. Members were able to wish, to imagine possibilities for themselves. Whereas before they saw only deficiency in one another, they now talked about one another's potential as we led them through a role-negotiation activity. For example, the dining room manager, who had frequently been at odds with the housekeeper, sent the following message at the end of the workshop: "I never realized how much we take your work for granted. You have a tough thankless job…and by the way, you're a nice person." Through renewed interpersonal ties such as these, discourse took on a whole new rational tone and substance. Broad consensus was reached on five primary dimensions of what should constitute a four-star hotel. At the end of the retreat, after discussing details of uniforms, behavioral norms, and policies, the group formulated for the first time a mission statement for the Medic Inn. Aspirations were liberated and a whole new sense of hope was stimulated. As one participant summed up, "The decisions and strategies agreed to here will completely change our future."

In the rest of this article we look more closely at the consequences of the generative metaphor intervention by looking at specific changes in the discourse of the groups in the months immediately following the Tremont retreat.

Consequences of the
Generative Metaphor Intervention

Following Heidegger (19)   , knowledge emerges within a horizon of possible meanings created and delimited by the given culture. It is this social horizon of cultural meaning that generates tacit knowledge structures known as schemas. The group, in a sense, is held together by a collective image or script that antici- pates possible action. (Boulding, 1966; Cooperrider, 1990; Polak, 1973).

Prior to the Chicago retreat, this management group subscribed to a deficiency script for possible action. They did not imagine that it was possible to plan a positive future for themselves as a group. The horizon of meaning marked by this script triggered the negative images and schemas that managers held of one an- other.

As a result of the generative metaphor intervention, a number of consequences can be discerned.

1.   Liberation of aspirations and expressions of preference for the future.

One consequence of the generative metaphor intervention was that altered the collective horizon of possible meanings, expanding members' beliefs about the kind of actions possible in creating the future of the hotel. As Whitehead wrote, "Human civilization is driven forward by notions too general for its existing lan- guage" (Whitehead, 1955). Ricouer (1974) and others have noted that when hu- mans begin to dimly perceive new notions, expressions are often metaphoric. Following Turner (1974), metaphor or collective imagery precedes the calculus for action. Following the Tremont experience, members began to put forth new notions of possible action in **tentative, metaphorical language.** At the first planning meet- ing following the retreat, members began to discuss what the Medic Inn should "look like". They began to propose what the bell stand and front desk should "look like." An entire list of renovations and alterations was proposed by the group making comparisons to the Tremont. There emerged a "four-star" language to reflect images of uniforms, behavioral norms, policies, and procedures. Members from different departments who previously could barely speak to on another began to develop a common language as details for physical revisions and personnel moves were discussed.

Once this common language grounded the group, there were expressions of hope and liberated aspirations. Members began to make reference to possible futures and abandoned the previous script of cycles of vengeance that had locked them into referring to past behavior. Members began to subjunctivize the world (Bruner, 1986), and to express preferences and wishes for the hotel's future.

For example, the following statements were taken from transcriptions of the first planned meeting after the Chicago retreat.

"You know, I'd **like to see** more energy from the employees..."

"What got me really was the coffee club they started (at the Tremont) and I wondered, why wouldn't we do something like that **if we could...**"

"We could meet monthly **if we decide** and..."

Such subjunctivized talk represents a liberation from old static structures. For this group, it can easily be argued that discourse of this kind marked the beginning of its empowerment to create/recreate the sociocultural world in alignment with its values. But first, something else needed to be addressed.

2.   A reinterpretation of the past in terms of ideological .
conflicts rather than in terms of interpersonal tension or personal
deficiency.

As Ricouer (1974) noted, when new insight emerges, it is accompanied by a crucial reinterpretation of the past. It was not by chance, therefore, that members began to reframe the conflict-ridden past as a symptom of a "divided house," that lacked a common vision (even the choice of language "divided house," presupposes that members have developed an image of what a "united house" looks like). Reframing the past in these terms triggered a process whereby members began to attribute causality for interpersonal tension to a larger social-ideological framework. Conflicts among individuals could no longer be seen as a resulting from personality deficiencies that reside **inside** of members. Rather, they had come to be seen as manifestations of an ideological split between departments and department managers. A forthcoming example illustrates this point.

3.   Members began to imagine that future planning for the
hotel should be a collective endeavor rather than something "top
managers" do.

It became legitimate for members to confront and hold one another to the commitments made by the "Chicago Group." Whereas previously frequent references were made to those "know–nothings on top who have their heads the sand," there emerged a new script for who could legitimately enter the dialogue/planning sessions. A new language emerged that remained active for years after the intervention (see Barrett, 1990). Members continue to use the term Chicago Group, conjuring up reminders of the commitments made and the possible actions proposed by different departments. Not only was it deemed legitimate for the 16 managers to engage in the planning process, but it became legitimate for a middle manager to confront one of the top managers in the name of the Chicago Group.

When members exhibited what was considered dysfunctional or unsupportive behavior, they were often challenged. After two monthly meetings, one of the members was dissatisfied with a top manager's directions and addressed him: "I don't know how we're supposed to do that. What about Chicago? Have we forgotten about Chicago?"

Six months after the Chicago retreat, an interpersonal conflict between two managers from different departments surfaced in regard to how a customer complaint had been handled. The issue was discussed at a meeting of the Chicago Group, and as the conversation progressed it became clear that other such recent incidents reflected a difference in ideological interpretations. As the group began to discuss the troublesome area, they began to discover that the two manager's differences were emerging from the different ideological signals they were receiving from their top managers. Finally, one member addressed the group:

> It's becoming clear that Kelly thinks what he's doing is right and Felicia thinks that what she is doing is right. And they're not getting this out of thin air. It must be a difference between you two guys (she points to Tim and Rick, the heads of food and beverage and rooms departments, respectfully). You guys need to get your heads together.

The top management team was appalled, and after a short discussion in private agreed that negotiation was needed and planned an off-site retreat for the next month. When the time came for them to address the issue at the retreat, there was a new urgency in their voices. As Tim put it:

> The Chicago group noticed something and they're right, we're marching to two different drummers. We have to straighten it out. We owe it to them, actually. We'll look like fools if we don't.

To cite another incident, eight months after the retreat, Tim, the food and beverage director, was overheard making a statement criticizing the service delivery in the Rooms Department. That afternoon at the regular staff meeting, Jean, the front desk manager, confronted the group:

> I overheard a remark today made by one of the food and beverage managers that somehow the Rooms Department is holding this hotel back. Excuse me, but I thought we went to Chicago just to stop this kind of thing – to be a team. If someone has a complaint about how we are doing, he should bring it up in the open.

On the surface, this incident looks like a return to the old divisiveness and turfism. But upon closer inspection, we can see some key developmental differences.

(A) Members now have a shared script for what it means to talk openly to one another to explicitly challenge one another's tacit assumptions. Prior to the Chicago retreat, there was no script to imagine what a conversation called "confronting the departmental spilt" or "challenging a top director" might sound like.

(B) Members now have a denotative language ("Chicago," "the Chicago Group," "team") that carries rich connotations. When one member says, "What about Chicago?" there are a whole series of reverberations of meaning triggered for each member, tied to a previously unimagined picture of a team working toward a four-star rating.

(C) Previously disjointed members were able to jointly create scripts for possible action. They were now able to put forth possibilities that were not contingent upon eliminating competing interpretations. Whereas previously subgroups would bond by creating negative attributions of outgroup members or other subgroups, members could now bond around possible common futures. People previously seen as incompatible had become imagined as belonging in the same room.

4.   Reframing the purpose of the hotel. Following Habermas (1981), critical consciousness emerges through interaction and dialogue.

Eventually through continual dialogue, the group's critical reasoning began to take shape. For approximately 10 months the group continued to meet around strategic plans and to propose unique social and physical changes at the Medic Inn. The data collected from the Tremont continued to act as a subtle conduit to trigger ideas and necessary actions. Members, however, began to debate about the appropriateness of instituting some of the Tremont features at the Medic Inn. The Tremont, after all, was a luxury hotel designed to serve downtown business guests. The Medic Inn was built to serve the medical needs of patients and guests at MCF.

A whole series of questions were raised around certain details that pushed members to reflect on the unique purpose of their hotel, and on such issues as the need for a swimming pool, the need for a valet parking service, the appropriateness of 24-hour room service, and the appropriateness of building a first-class restaurant that might exclude middle-class guests.

Each of these ideas was debated, and some were approved while others were discarded as "inappropriate for a hotel that was built to support a medical facility." As difference emerged, members began to **differentiate** between the Tremont and the Medic Inn and to propose a unique purpose for the Medic Inn. Finally members came to the conclusion that the traditional market-driven thinking that drives the Tremont and other hotels did not apply to the Medic Inn. As one manager put it,

Let's face it. We're unique. We can't think like the Tremont. We're not here to make a profit from business guests. According to strict-profit sense, they shouldn't even give money to build anything in this hotel. But we're beginning to realize, **we're not in the hotel business**. This isn't a regular hotel. We're here to serve the Medic Foundation and the participants.

Eventually fewer and fewer references were made to the programs at the Tremont Hotel as members began to create a unique sense of identity for the Medic. Inn. The imaginative expansion that began in Chicago continued beyond even the consultants' expectations. To cite just one example, the group instituted a program in which employees elected their peers to sit as a "jury" and hear appeals and grievances employees had about their bosses. Employees who felt they had been unfairly treated could argue their cases before this jury, which had the power to overturn any previous decisions. The mere proposal of such an option would have been inconceivable to the cognitive ecology of the group prior to the retreat.

Conclusion and Discussion

In an environment in which managers feel a sense of insecurity and competition, they are likely to have developed schemas that include negative attributions of one another, category traits that frame one another in a negative light. We know from social-psychological research that these schemas and theories that explain others' behavior are not easily changed, even when evidence contradicts the traits we have attributed and even when we notice a behavior inconsistent with those traits. In fact, some research suggests that once we assign a trait to another, our noticing inconsistent behavior actually strengthens and reaffirms the original trait to another, our noticing inconsistent behavior actually strengthens and reaffirms the original traits we have assigned. Furthermore, cognitive psychology research has shown that when we are under stress — for example, when we fear being verbally attacked by another or fear losing status or a job – we assume a protective stance. In such a state, we often feel cognitive intrusions of the imagined stressor event, anticipating the negative event as part of our defensive posture. As we guard against these intrusions and the symbolic reenactment of the stressor event, we pay a price: dimmed awareness and preselected attention. We choose to notice certain stimuli and disregard others. Given an environment of insecurity (such as the one described briefly in this case), we can begin to appreciate the intrapsychic forces that would encourage one to relegate another into a restricted frame, thereby placing the self at a safe distance. We can begin to appreciate how attention becomes almost prefocused, how a competitive environment would encourage negative attributions toward others, and how positive gestures, when attempted, may not get noticed. Given these dynamics, we put forth the following propositions.

    1.   To enhance genuine dialogue toward building innovative and creative ideas for the future of the organization, an environment must be created that supports the possibility of cognitive reappraisal and new schema development by

members. This should be a deliberately supportive environment that encourages members to direct attention away from familiar stimuli and habits that would cue familiar schemas.

2.   Generative metaphor is an invitation to see the world anew and can be used as an intervention into intergroup and interpersonal conflict. The generative metaphor is a vehicle whereby learning is "suddenly" transferred from one area of strength to an area of difficulty, enabling problems to be   lved" without direct engagement with the problems.

3.   Metaphor is generative to the extent to which it serves to break the hammerlock of the status quo, serves to reorganize perceptual processes and in-grained schemas, helps provide positive and compelling new images of possibility, and serves as a bridge for nondefensive learning among contexts.

4.   For groups and other larger collectivities, the generative potential of meta-phor depends not only on its content, but also on the processes of inquiry and interaction that are engendered. Processes of co-appreciative inquiry will heighten the generative potential of metaphorical intervention. Co-appreciative processes of inquiry will heighten the generative potential of metaphor because of the following.

(A) Appreciation is a poetic process that fosters a fresh perception of ordinary life. Unlike the evaluating stance of problem solving, which is based on the as-sumption of deficiency, appreciation refers to an affirmative valuing of experience based on belief, trust, and conviction (c.f. Cooperrider, 1990; Cooperrider & Srivastva, 1987; Kolb, 1984).

(B) Co-appreciative inquiry processes create a learning environment that fos-ters empathy, hope, excitement, and social bonding among people around desired values.

(C) The appreciative mode engenders a creative stance toward life by drawing people to inquire beyond superficial appearances into the life-enhancing proper-ties of organizational existence. Through affirmation of the best of "what is", the appreciative mode ignites envisioning into "what might be". Co-appreciation in-spires the collective imagination and thereby opens the status quo to the joint creation of new possible worlds.

5.   By regaining a sense of unity and participation in the joint creation of reality in a related but distinct domain, groups will be able to grow beyond their historical difficulties through an almost unconscious learning transaction between contexts. Generative metaphor is frame expanding, facilitates new knowledge, strengthens a group's sense of efficacy, and provides a group with a new, transfer-able ability to manage the subtle dynamics of building relationships and bonding around a common vision.

Our effort discussed in this article is but one in a small yet growing attempt to generate new perspectives on the conduct of organization development based on recent insights into the dynamics of social cognition (e.g., Bartunek, 1984), as well as new understandings concerning the metaphorical basis of organization exist-ence (Morgan, 1986; Weick, 1979). Outside the field of OD practice, metaphor has played an important role in therapeutic and educational encounters (Haley, 1973; Srivastva & Barrett, 1988) and has been shown to be an integral component for the development of culture and community as a whole (Judge, 1990). Although OD practice has paid little attention to the insights in this area, our experiences lead us to believe that excursions into metaphor will open exciting new vistas of research and practice previously unavailable to the field.

Part of the promise lies in the fact that generative metaphor provides a clear option for moving outside a number of the fields' predominant and guiding assumptions. The first, which has been extensively documented, is the assumption that OD's essence is collective problem solving: To do good OD is to solve "real problems" (Cooperrider & Srivastva, 1987). As discussed above, it is as if the field's overarching root metaphor has been that **organizations are problems to be solved** (as contrasted with "creative works of art," for example). Second, as Eric Neilsen (1984) has shown, the vast majority of OD practices are based on the value of direct confrontation or **candidness**:

> Organization Development is the attempt to influence the members of an organization to expand their candidness with each other about their views of the organization and their experience in it, and to take responsibility for their own actions as organizational members. (p. 2)

As a discipline we are in our infancy when comes to intervention theories and practices that (1) operate out of **affirmative** or nondeficiency assumptions about the organizations we work with, and (2) emerge out of respect for the subtle and sophisticated mechanisms of **indirect communication forms**, which are in fact found in highly effective groups and growth promoting relationships. If for no other reason than this, there seems to be ample justification for looking seriously at the case presented in this article. The case, which is offered more as exploratory illustration than proof, will be especially justified if it stimulates reflection on our basic OD assumptions, helps expand our options for action and generates new research into the affirmative and indirect sides of human systems change and development.

There must be caution, however. While we acknowledge the considerable promise of generative metaphor, a number of critical concerts must be explored – in particular, the question of collusion. To what extent could generative metaphor, as a planned intervention, become an unwilling accomplice in the dynamic of group flight (Bion, 1959)?

Is generative metaphor just another form of flight? Does it, because it operates indirectly and outside of explicit awareness also serve to limit individual and group autonomy? Could it be misused as a tool of what Pages (1990) has called the hypermodern era, an Orwellian period whose basic concern is the control and elimination of conflict?

Obviously, these are more than just theoretical questions: They are moral ones. Part of the reason that generative metaphor is, in fact, powerful is that it shapes perceptions, cognitions, and relationships at a preconscious level, much like subliminal communications or even hypnosis. It is clear that we need to exercise a certain caution toward generative metaphor. But more than qualified hope, we need greater understanding: We must learn to distinguish between the creative and destructive uses of generative metaphor if we are to make a genuine contribution.

References

Anderson, C.A., Lepper, M., & Ross, L. (1980). Perseverance of social theories: The role of explanation in persistence of discredited information. *Journal of Personality and Social Psychology*, 39, 1037-1049.

Barrett, F. (1990). *The development of the cognitive organization*. Unpublished doctoral dissertation, Case Western Reserve University, Cleveland, OH.

Bartunek, J. (1984). Changing interpretive schemes and organizational restructuring: The example of a religious order. *Administrative Science Quarterly*, 27, 355-372.

Beck, A. (1967). *Depression: Clinical, experimental, and theoretical aspects*. New York: Harper &Row.

Bion, W. (1959). *Experiences in groups*. New York: Basic Books.

Black, M. (1962). *Models and metaphors*. Ithaca, NY: Cornell University Press.

Boulding, K. (1966). *The image*. Ann Arbor, MI: University of Michigan Press.

Bwer, G. (1981). Mood and memory. *American Psychologist*, 36, 120-148.

Bradford, L.P., Gibb, J.W., & Benne, K. (1964). *T-Group theory and laboratory method*. New York: Wiley.

Bruner, J. (1986). *Actual minds, possible worlds*. Cambridge, MA: Harvard University Press.

Cantor, N., & Mischel, W. (1977). Traits and prototypes: Effects of recognition memory. *Journal of Personality and Social Psychology*, 35, 38-49.

Cooperrider, D.L. (1990). Positive imagery, positive action: The affirmative basis of organizing. In S. Srivastva, D.L. Cooperrider & Associates (Eds.), *Appreciative management and leadership: The power of positive thought and action in organizations*. San Francisco: Jossey Bass.

Cooperrider, D.L., & Srivastva, S. (1987). Appreciative inquiry into organizational life. In W.A. Pasmore & R.W. Woodman (Eds.), *Research in Organizational Change and Development* (Vol. 1, pp. 129-169). Greenwich, CT: JAI Press.

Eden, D. (1988). Creating expectation effects in OD: Applying self-fulfilling prophecy. In W.A. Pasmore & R.W. Woodman (Eds.), *Research in Organizational Change and Development* (Vol. 3, pp. 1-38). Greenwich, CT: JAI Press.

French, W.L. (1969). Organization development objectives, assumptions, and strategies. *California Management Review*, 12 (2), 23-24.

French, W.L., & Bell, C. (1978). *Organizationl development.* Englewood Cliffs, NJ: Prentice Hall.

Frohman, M., Sashkin, M., & Kavanaugh, M. (1976). Action research as applied to organization development. *Organization and Administrative Sciences, I,* 129-161.

Goleman, D., (1985). *Vital lies, simple truths: The psychology of self-deception.* New York: Touchstone Books.

Habermas, J. (1981). *The theory of communicative action.* Boston: Beacon Press.

Haley, J. (1973). *Uncommon therapy.* New York: Touchstone Books.

Hausser, D., Pecorella, P., & Wissler, A. (1977). *Survey guided development II.* La Jolla, CA: University Associates.

Heidegger, M. (1962). *Being and time.* New York: Harper & Row. (Original work published 1927).

Higgins, E.T., & McCann, C.D. (1984). Social encoding and subsequent attitudes, impressions, and memory: Context-driven and motivational aspects of processing. *Journal of Personality and Social Psychology, 47,* 55-70.

Hill, T., Lewicki, P., Czyzewska, M., & Boss, A. (1989). Self-perpetuating development of encoding biases in person perception. *Journal of Personality and Social Psychology, 57,* 373-387.

Horowitz, M. (1983). *Psychological responses to serious life events: The denial of stress.* New York: International Universities Press.

Isen, A., & Shalker, T. (1982). The influence of mood state on evaluation of positive, neutral, and negative stimuli. *Social Psychology Quarterly, 45,* 58-63.

Isen, A., Shalker, T., Clark, M., & Karp, L. (1978). Affect accessibility of material in memory, and behavior: A cognitive loop? *Journal of Personality and Socal Psychology, 36,* 1-12.

Judge, A. (1990). *World governance through metaphor.* Paper presented at the Symposium on Social Innovations in Global Management, Case Western Reserve University, Cleveland, OH.

Jussim, L. (1986). Self-fulling prophesies: A theroetcial and integrative review. *Psychological Review, 93,* 429-445.

Kolb, D. (1984). *Experiential learning.* Englewood Cliffs, NJ: Prentice-Hall.

Levinson, H. (1972). *Organizational diagnosis.* Cambridge, MA: Harvard University Press.

Morgan, G. (1986). *Images of organization.* Newbury Park, CA: Sage.

Nisbett, R., & Ross, L. (1985). *Human inference: Strategies and shortcomings of social judgment.* New York: Prentice-Hall.

O'Sullivan, C.S., & Durso, F.T. (1984). Effect of schema-incongruent information on memory for stereotypical attributes. *Journal of Personality and Social Psychology, 47,* 55-70.

Pages, M. The Illusion and disillusion of appreciative management.(1990). In S. Srivastva, D.L. Cooperrider & Associates (Eds.). *Appreciative management and leadership: The power of positive thought and action in organization.* San Francisco: Jossey Bass.

Polak, F. (1973). *The image of the future.* New York: Elsevier Scientific Publishing Company.

Ricouer, P. (1974). *The conflict of interpretations: Essays in hermeneutics.* Evanston, IL: Northwestern University Press.

Rosenhan, D., Salvoey, P., & Hargis, K. (1981). The joys of helping: Focus of attention mediates the impact of positive affect on altruism. *Journal of Personality and Social Psychology*, 40, 899-905.

Schon, D.A. (1979). Generative metaphor: A perspective on problem-solving in social policy. *Metaphor and Thought.* Cambridge: Cambridge University Press.

Srivastva, S., & Barrett, F.J. (1988). The transforming nature of metaphors in group development: A study in group theory. *Human Relations*, 41, 31-46.

Srull, T.K., & Wyer, R.S. (1980). Category accessibility and social perception: Some implications for the study of person memory and interpersonal judgments. *Journal of Personality and Social Psychology*, 38, 841-856.

Turner, V.W. (1974). *Dramas, fields, and metaphors.* Ithaca, NY: Cornell University Press.

Weick, K.E. (1979). *The social psychology of organizing.* Reading, MA: Addison-Wesley.

Whitehead, A.N. (1955). *Adventures of ideas.* New York: Mentor Books.

Chapter 8

Advances in Appreciative Inquiry as an Organization Development Intervention

Gervase R. Bushe, Ph.D.
Simon Fraser University

Since Cooperrider and Srivastva's (1987) original article on appreciative inquiry there has been a lot of excitement and experimentation with this new form of action research. The technology of appreciative inquiry as a social research method and as an organization development (OD) intervention are evolving differently. Here I will mainly focus on it as an OD intervention. Currently there is no universally accepted method for doing an appreciative inquiry and it is premature to offer a "recipe" for how to do it. There is, however, a fairly well accepted set of parameters for distinguishing between what is and is not a legitimate appreciative inquiry. In this paper I will describe the basics of this technique and report on some innovations I and colleagues have experimented with to extend the appreciative approach. First, however, an introduction to the theory behind the technique.

What is Appreciative Inquiry?

Appreciative inquiry (Cooperrider and Srivastva, 1987), a theory of organizing and method for changing social systems, is one of the more significant innovations in action research in the past decade. Those who created action research in the 1950s were concerned with creating a research method that would lead to practical results as well as the development of new social theory. It was hoped that action research would be an important tool in social change. A key emphasis of action researchers has been on involving their "subjects" as co-researchers. Action research was and still is a cornerstone of organization development practice.

OD Journal, Vol. 13, No. 3, pp. 14-22. Fall 1995.

While always controversial as a scientific method of inquiry, action research has recently come under criticism as a method of organizational change and as a process for developing new theory. In their seminal paper Cooperrider and Srivastva criticize the lack of useful theory generated by traditional action research studies and contend that both the method of action research and implicit theory of social organization are to blame. The problem is that most action research projects use logical positivistic assumptions (Sussman and Evered, 1978), which treats social and psychological reality as something fundamentally stable, enduring, and "out there". Appreciative inquiry, however, is a product of the socio-rationalist paradigm (Gergen, 1982, 1990) which treats social and psychological reality as a product of the moment, open to continuous reconstruction. Cooperrider and Srivastva argue that there is nothing inherently real about any particular social form, notranscultural, everlasting, valid principles of social organization to be uncovered. While logical positivism assumes that social phenomena are sufficiently enduring, stable and replicable to allow for generalizations, socio-rationalism contends that social order is fundamentally unstable. "Social phenomena are guided by cognitive heuristics, limited only by the human imagination: the social order is a subject matter capable of infinite variation through the linkage of ideas and action". (Cooperrider and Srivastva, 1987, p. 139). Socio-rationalists argue that the theories we hold, our beliefs about social systems, have a powerful effect on the nature of social "reality". Not only do we see what we believe, but the very act of believing it creates it. From this point of view, the creation of new and evocative theories of groups, organizations, and societies, are a powerful way to aid in their change and development.

Like most post-modernists, Cooperrider and Srivastva argue that logical positivistic assumptions trap us in a rear-view world and methods based on these assumptions tend to (re) create the social realities they purport to be studying. Further, they argue that action researchers tend to assume that their purpose is to solve a problem. Groups and organizations are treated not only as if they have problems, but as if they are problems to be "solved". Cooperrider and Srivastva contend that this "problem-oriented" view of organizing and inquiry reduces the possibility of generating new theory, and new images of social reality, that might help us transcend current social forms. What if, instead of seeing organizations as problems to be solved, we saw them as miracles to be appreciated? How would our methods of inquiry and our theories of organizing be different?

Appreciative inquiry "refers to both a search for knowledge and a theory of intentional collective action which are designed to help evolve the normative vision and will of a group, organization, or society as a whole" (Cooperrider and Srivastva, 1987, p.159). Cooperrider makes the theory of change embedded in appreciative inquiry explicit in a later paper on the affirmative basis of organizing (Cooperrider, 1990). In this paper Cooperrider proffers the "heliotropic hypothesis"—that social forms evolve toward the "light"; that is, toward images that are affirming and life giving. In essence his argument is that all groups, organizations, communities or societies have images of themselves that underlay self-organizing processes and that social systems have a natural tendency to evolve toward the most positive images held by their members. Conscious evolution of positive imagery, therefore, is a viable option for changing the social system as a whole.

One of the ironies Cooperrider helps us to see is that the greatest obstacle to the well-being of an ailing group is the affirmative projection that currently guides the group. To affirm means to 'hold firm' and it "is precisely the strength of affirmation, the degree of belief or faith invested, that allows the image to carry out its heliotropic task" (Cooperrider, 1990, p. 120). When groups find that attempts to fix problems create more problems, or the same problems never go away, it is a clear signal of the inadequacy of the group's current affirmative projection. Groups, therefore, do not need to be fixed; they need to be affirmed and "every new affirmative projection of the future is a consequence of an appreciative understanding of the past or present" (p. 120).

Appreciative inquiry, as a method of changing social systems, is an attempt to generate a collective image of a new and better future by exploring the best of what is and has been. These new images, or "theories", create a pull effect that generates evolution in social forms. The four principles Cooperrider and Srivastva (1987, p. 160) articulate for an action research that can create new and better images are that research should begin with appreciation, should be applicable, should be provocative, and should be collaborative. The basic process of appreciative inquiry is to begin with a grounded observation of the "best of what is", then through vision and logic collaboratively articulate "what might be", ensuring the consent of those in the system to "what should be" and collectively experimenting with "what can be". One significant published research study that used an appreciative inquiry methodology looked at the processes of organizing that are used by international non-governmental organizations (Johnson and Cooperrider, 1991).

Appreciative Inquiry as a Method of Change

An appreciative inquiry intervention can be thought of as consisting of these three parts:

Discovering the best of . . . Appreciative interventions begin with a search for the best examples of organizing and organization within the experience of organizational members.

Understanding what creates the best of . . . The inquiry seeks to create insight into the forces that lead to superior performance, as defined by organizational members. What is it about the people, the organization, and the context that creates peak experiences at work?

Amplifying the people and processes who best exemplify the best of . . . Through the process of the inquiry itself, the elements that contribute to superior performance are reinforced and amplified.

The emphasis in my approach is on designing inquiry methods that amplify the values the system is seeking to actualize during the all phases of the inquiry process. I believe this is one key feature that distinguishes appreciative inquiry from other interventions. How to actually do that in practice is not so easy but as the pace of environmental change accelerates, we must find more rapid change processes for organizational renewal. The great promise of appreciative inquiry is that it will generate self-sustaining momentum within an organization toward actualizing the values that lead to superior performance.

The original form of appreciative inquiry developed by David Cooperrider involved a bottom-up interview process where almost all organizational members were interviewed to uncover the "life-giving forces" in the organization. People were asked to recall times they felt "most alive, most vital, most energized at work" and were then questioned about those incidents. The interview data were then treated much the same as any qualitative data set; through content analysis the consultants looked for what people in the organization valued and what conditions led to superior performance.

This analysis was fed back into a large planning group which was charged with developing "provocative propositions". Provocative propositions were statements of organizational aspiration and intent, based on the analysis of the organization at it's very best. These propositions were then validated by organizational members along two dimensions: (1) how much does this statement capture our values? and (2) how much are we like this? Nothing more was done with the data, analysis or propositions. John Carter of the Gestalt Institute of Cleveland, one of the early implementors of this approach, counsels against using the propositions as a set of standards or goals to then begin problem-solving around (Carter, 1989). Using the gestalt therapy notion of figure-ground, John argues that most inquiry methods make something figural, focusing attention.

Appreciative inquiry, he claims, creates ground. By coming to agreement on a set of provocative propositions, people have a compelling vision of the organization at its best and this in itself motivates new behaviors. People will take initiative and act differently without an action plan because the provocative propositions align organizational vision with employee's internal sense of what is important.

As a planned change technique, this approach lacked focus and didn't do as good a job of amplification as many of us would like. I continue to experiment with new techniques for generating discovery, understanding, and amplification. Here is a brief rundown on my current thinking.

Discovering

The initial appreciative inquiries attempted to study organizations as a whole. More recent interventions have begun to limit themselves to a few issues. This appears to make the process more manageable and understandable to others. Now, unless we are trying to help a company develop a future vision for the entire organization, appreciative inquiries focus on strategic human resource issues like empowerment, teamwork, leadership, customer service. Appreciative inquiry may have applications for other, non-HR issues but I don't know of anyone who has tried it (e.g., how to best organize an information system). One of the more interesting recent applications has been with gender issues in organizations. Marjorie Schiller of Quincy, Massachusetts has been working with corporations that found that traditional approaches to dealing with sexual harassment in the workplace (e.g., hire a harassment coordinator, gather survey data, do a lot of training) only resulted in more reported sexual harassment! Using an appreciative inquiry approach, teams of men and women are studying what co-gender work experiences are like at their very best and this seems to be having remarkable results.

After a couple of failures I learned that doing an "appreciative interview" is not as easy as it looks.

Simply talking about one's "peak" experience can easily degenerate into social banter and cliché-ridden interaction. The hallmark of successful appreciative interviews seems to be that the interviewee has at least one new insight into what made it a peak experience. I have noticed a bundle of behaviors that seem to distinguish those who are good and poor at appreciative interviewing (Bushe 1997). The key seems to be suspending one's own assumptions and not being content with superficial explanations given by others; to question the obvious and to do this in more of a conversational, self-disclosing kind of way than is normally taught in interviewing courses. There seem to be real limits to who can do this well and I have not been able to train people quickly (1 day) to be able to attend to others appreciatively. It appears that one of the early assumptions, that we could teach organizational members to run the data collection process by themselves, does not work as well as we'd hoped. People who have the basic ability to listen to others "generously", however, can be taught appreciative inquiry in about a day and a half. I have found the best results from teaming insiders with outsiders and doing paired interviews. David Cooperrider has noticed that using younger insiders to interview organizational elders results in a very special energy and the quality of images and data seems better.

I've come to the conclusion that getting the stories that people have about the topic is what is most important. Researchers and other linear thinkers have a tendency to want to generate abstract lists and propositional statements out of the interviews and this needs to be curtailed during the interview process or the same old lists and propositions get recycled. Fresh images and insight come from exploring the real stories people have about themselves and others at their best.

We've also found that people love to be interviewed appreciatively. Recently a team I was leading completed a series of appreciative interviews about leadership with the senior executives of a major telecommunications company. As you can imagine, many were loath to give up any time in their busy schedules to be interviewed. We asked for an hour. Most interviews actually lasted two and a half hours, with the executives canceling their appointments and just wanting talk on and on.

Understanding

It has been necessary to find ways of making the data useful for group interpretation. Large data sets on organizational peak experiences required more time and effort than busy managers could afford. We've experimented with structuring the data collection and reporting to reduce the ambiguity of the data and make it easier for large groups to work with. The main innovation has been the inquiry matrix (Bushe and Pitman, 1991). Prior to data collection, senior managers decide what elements of organizing they want to amplify in their organization (e.g., teamwork, quality, leadership), and an organizational model that they feel best captures the major categories of organizing (e.g., technology, structure, rewards, etc.). A matrix is then created of elements by categories. For example, there would be a cell for teamwork and technology, teamwork and structure, quality and technology, quality and structure, and so on. The data collection effort focuses on each of the cells. More importantly, the matrix focuses the analysis of the data and the generation of provocative propositions.

I have found that the quality of new understandings and insights created during an appreciative inquiry is strongly effected by the quality of stories and insights generated during the interviews.

Unless new understandings arise during the initial appreciative interviews, later analyses may simply recreate the initial mental models people come to the analysis with. Without important new insights, the process loses energy fast and leads to cliched propositions. Appreciative inquiry really challenges those doing the analysis to leave their preconceptions behind and approach the data with "the eyes of a child".

Write-ups of the interviews are very important. I've found that detailed recounts of the stories and most interesting quotes are what is needed and that these are best written in the first person. The output of appreciative interviews are a series of stories and quotes written in the language of those who told them.

What is normally the "data analysis" stage of action research needs to be done totally differently in an appreciative inquiry. I no longer call it "analysis". I haven't found a great term for it yet but I've used 'proalysis' and 'synergalysis'. At this point in an appreciative inquiry I want to get as many people as possible reading the most important interviews and stories in order to stimulate their thinking about the appreciative topic. Then I try to orchestrate one or more meetings where organizational members and consultants try to go beyond what they were told by the interviewees to craft propositional statements about the appreciative topic that will capture people's energy and excitement. We're not trying to extract themes from the data or categorize responses and add them up. We're trying to generate new theory that will have high face value to members of the organization. What makes this legitimate research, I believe, is that we go back to those we interviewed with these propositions and ask them if we have captured the spirit, if not the letter, of the meaning of the interviews. If they say yes, then I believe we have generated new theory based on something more real than simply imagination and good intentions.

Amplification

I believe that as a social intervention device, the quality of the dialogue generated is much more important than the "validity" of the synergalysis of the data. Studying the best of what is creates excitement and energy and this is a key part of the amplification process. I and others have been trying to find ways to further amplify what is exciting and energizing for people and effective for their organizations.

The number of people involved in all phases of the appreciative inquiry has obvious implications for this. I would like to experiment with getting very large numbers of people into something the size of a hockey arena to do consensual creation and validation of provocative propositions but to date have not found a client system willing to do this.

Once a set of propositions have been developed, they can be "tested" through a survey in the organization. The survey can ask to what extent they believe the proposition to be an important component of the topic under study and to what extent they believe the organization exemplifies the proposition. Simply filling out such a survey can do a lot toward spreading the ideas throughout the organization. Then communicating the results of the survey showing the strength of consensus about the importance of each proposition gives organizational members license to do more of it in their everyday work.

One major innovation has been to create thematic feed-back documents that identify who is giving the "quote" and the context the quote was given in. Instead of lists of anonymous quotes to illustrate themes found in conventional feedback reports, people get to read what their fellow employees are saying about their best experiences. You can imagine how much more dialogue and energy this creates.

Tom Pitman of Grand Rapids, Michigan and Geoff Hulin of Santa Cruz, California have experimented with video-taping the interviews and editing them into short, focused pieces on different themes. As a feedback device, videotape clips have proved to generate a great deal more energy and shared imagery than written reports. Again, the goal here is to create appreciative dialogues about the issues under study that result in new affirming images. The opportunities here continue to increase as new applications that marry video and computer technologies proliferate.

Where to next

We may find that the notion of "appreciative process" (Bushe and Pitman, 1991) as a consulting and change strategy has a larger and more lasting impact than large scale appreciative inquiries. My personal consulting style has undergone a radical transformation in the past 6 years as I have struggled to adopt an appreciative stance in my work. Now I pay attention to what is working well, the qualities of leadership or group process that I want to see more of, and try to amplify them when I see them. This is in direct contrast to my training where I learned to see what was missing and point that out. In the past I focused on understanding the failures and pathologies of leadership and organization. I thought that awareness was the first step in development and so I felt it was my job as an OD consultant to make people aware of just how bad things really were. Now I am focusing on helping people become aware of how good things are, on the genius in themselves and others, on the knowledge and abilities they already have, on examples of the future in the present. From this stance I am finding that change happens more easily, people don't get as bogged down in uncertainty or despair and energy runs more freely.

The appreciative lens has opened up a new vista for viewing and understanding the process of change in human systems. For example, I developed a form of appreciative inquiry for team building, experimentally tested it, and found it significantly improved a team's process and performance (Bushe and Coetzer, 1995). The method, as used in the experiments, goes as follows:

First, group members are asked to recall the best team experience they have ever been a part of. Even for those who have had few experiences of working with others in groups, there is a 'best' experience. Each group member is asked, in turn, to describe the experience while the rest of the group is encouraged to be curious and engage in dialogue with the focal person.

The facilitator encourages members to set aside their clichés and preconceptions, get firmly grounded in their memory of the actual experience, and fully explore what about themselves, the situation, the task, and others made this a "peak" experience. Once all members have exhausted their exploration, the facilitator asks the group, on the basis of what they have just discussed, to list and develop a consensus on the attributes of highly effective groups.

The intervention concludes with the facilitator inviting members to publicly acknowledge anything they have seen others in the group do that has helped the group be more like any of the listed attributes

This research has stimulated new group theory and new change theory. Graeme Coetzer, at Simon Fraser University, and I are working on a theory of "group image" that may offer insights into how groups function and dysfunction. I believe that the most important next steps for appreciative inquiry will be theoretical breakthroughs in understanding leadership, facilitation, and change processes in social systems. After this will come new techniques.

References

Bushe, G.R. (1997) *Attending to Others: Interviewing Appreciatively*. Vancouver, BC: Discovery and Design Inc.

Bushe, G.R. and Coetzer, G. (1995) Appreciative inquiry as a team development intervention: A controlled experiment. *Journal of Applied Behavioral Science*, 31:1, 19–31.

Bushe, G.R. and Pitman, T. (1991) "Appreciative process: A method for transformational change". *OD Practitioner*, September, 1–4.

Carter, J. (1989) Talk given at the Social Innovations Global Management conference, Weatherhead School of Management, Case Western Reserve University, Cleveland Ohio November 13–17.

Cooperrider, D.L. (1990) Positive image, positive action: The affirmative basis of organizing. In S.Srivastva and D.L. Cooperrider (Eds.), *Appreciative Management and Leadership* (pp.91–125). San Francisco: Jossey-Bass.

Cooperrider, D.L. and Srivastva, S. (1987) "Appreciative inquiry in organizational life". In R. Woodman and W. Pasmore (eds.) *Research in Organizational Change and Development: Volume 1* (pp.129–169). Greenwich, CT: JAI Press,

Gergen, K. (1982) *Toward Transformation in Social Knowledge*. New York: Spring-Verlag.

Gergen, K. (1990) Affect and organization in postmodern society. In S. Srivastva and D.L. Cooperrider.

Cooperrider (eds.), *Appreciative Management and Leadership* (pp.153–174). San Francisco, Jossey-Bass.

Johnson, P.C. and Cooperrider, D.L. (1991) Finding a path with heart: Global social change organizations and their challenge for the field of organization development. In R. Woodman and W.Pasmore (eds.) *Research in Organizational Change and Development: Volume 5* (pp.223–284). Greenwich CT: JAI Press.

Sussman, G.I and Evered, R.D. (1978) An assessment of the scientific merits of action research. *Administrative Science Quarterly*, 23, 582–603.

Chapter 9

THE "CHILD" AS AGENT OF INQUIRY

David L. Cooperrider
Case Western University

The sense of wonder, that is our sixth sense. And it is the natural.
—D. H. Lawrence

What is the role of wonder in OD? What creates a sense of wonder as we inquire into organizational life, and what spoils it? What are the varieties of wonder? What is the connection of wonder to knowledge? To the imagination? To the flowering of relationships? What happens to the storyteller, for example, when the room is filled by people sitting forward, listening, even smiling, with a sense of wonder? Why is uninhibited wonder something we generally restrict to children? If doing good inquiry is at the heart of OD, why then so little talk of things like awe, curiosity, veneration, surprise, delight, amazement, and wonder—in short, everything that serves to infuse what OD has traditionally referred to as the "spirit of inquiry".

Presented here is a thesis, a proposition, regarding the future of OD. It is a stand which I take with some hesitation, even with some tentativeness. It is a proposition I will illustrate with an "N" of one, hardly a proof. But it has, I think, some wisdom in it; one might even argue the idea was modeled in the lives of early pioneers like Kurt Lewin, Mary Parker Follett, Herb Shepard and others. The thesis emerges from years of experimenting with what my colleagues and I have termed "Appreciative Inquiry". It goes something like this: We have reached *the end of problem solving* as a mode of inquiry capable of inspiring, mobilizing, and sustaining human system change, and the future of OD belongs to methods that affirm, compel, and accelerate anticipatory learning involving larger and larger levels of collectivity. The new methods will be distinguished by the art and the science of asking powerful, positive questions (soon there will be an "encyclopedia of questions" that brings together classic formulations like Maslow's interview protocols on peak human experience and Vereena Kast's exceptional studies of joy, inspiration, and hope). The new methods will view realities as socially constructed and will therefore become more radically relational, widening the circles of dialogue to groups of 100s, 1000s, and perhaps more—with cyberspace relationships into the mil-

OD Practitioner, Vol. 28, Nos. 1 and 2, 1996, pp. 5-11.

lions. The arduous task of intervention will give way to the speed of imagination and innovation; and instead of negative, criticism, and spiraling diagnosis, there will be discovery, dream, and design. Social construction will mean constructive constructing. And the metaphor speaking best to our primary task and role—"the child as the agent of inquiry"—is one where wonder, learning, and the dialogical imagination will be modus operandi.

Let's Illustrate: Imagine OD With a Whole City

I want to tell you about a successful businesswoman—a corporate banking executive for 16 years at First Chicago—who one day decided to leave it all to devote her next 10 years to transforming the city's future. Trained in OD, savvy in action–research methodologies, and a visionary in her own right, Bliss Browne asked the question: "What might happen if all of Chicago's citizens were mobilized to give public expression, continuously, to their imagination about a healthy future for the city as a whole, and were invited to claim their role in bringing that vision to life?" Could it be, she paused, "we human beings create our own realities through imagination and conversational processes, and *the creation of positive images on a collective basis in our three million person city might well be the most prolific activity* that individuals and organizations can engage in if their aim is to help bring to fruition a positive and humanly significant future?

Preposterous? "Perhaps", commented a Chicago Tribune journalist: "But Browne is the sort who thinks big and takes unorthodox action. . . . She's used to challenges. Browne was in the first class of 125 women who graduated from Yale University in 1971, and she was among the first women ordained into the priesthood of the Episcopal Church in 1977 (and then her career as corporate executive).[1]

It began, then, with a conference where community and business leaders met to discuss how imagination, economics, and faith could make the city a better place. But there were major concerns: surveys for example, showing 85% of Americans losing faith in both the future of our cities as well as the institutions that govern them, images of cities as hellholes (just look at the demonized picture of urban America in our movies and the nightly news); and the malaise of our young where the negative images have been correlated with apathy, cynicism, fear, discrimination and other damaging behavior. Ways are needed, agreed the participants, to rebuild essential connections, to renew hope, to reinvigorate human creativity and leadership at all levels. "How one conceives of the city shapes how one lives in the city," argued Browne. Even more, "Cities echo creation. They are a living symbol of our ability to imagine and create, to turn our visions into tangible products. They are an inventory of the possible, and incarnation of human capacity and diversity. Cities concentrate forces of darkness and light, and hold the world in miniature."

IMAGINE CHICAGO, now four years old, located at 35 E. Wacker Drive, was born out of that and subsequent meetings. IMAGINE CHICAGO is a catalyst for civic innovation, working to bring people who live and work in Chicago to the realization that they are the owners and creators of Chicago's future.[2] The MacArthur Foundation funded the first several years' pilot. And when theories and practices of change were sought out, Appreciative Inquiry (AI) was selected as the approach most likely to help serve as "a catalyst for civic innovation".[3]

The outcomes have been dramatic. The "pilot" included more than 800 individuals in more than 40 neighborhoods with involvement of more than 100 community organizations and schools. For example, IMAGINE CHICAGO, in collaboration with Barbara Radner, Director of The Center for Urban Education at DePaul University, developed a citizenship curriculum now being used by 4000 Chicago public school students (more on these exciting results later). Though only a young organization, IMAGINE CHICAGO has already attracted broad recognition: a national award in 1995 from Eureka Communities in Washington D.C. for its "exemplary work on behalf of children and their families"; citation by the Mayor's Youth Development Task Force in 1994, and perhaps the most profound recognition, that of being emulated. . . . There is now an IMAGINE DALLAS organization, as well as plans in other cities and in other parts of the world, namely an initiative called IMAGINE AFRICA.

A Most Extraordinary Learning

One of the important logistical questions for IMAGINE CHICAGO had to do with scale: How to create an appreciative "action research" cycle with such a large system. When I first met with the design team they asked about "mass mobilization" methods for each of the phases (see Figure 1) in appreciative inquiry. Discovery, Dream, Design and Destiny.[4]

There was talk, very early on, of wanting to conduct appreciative interviews with one million people—at least one interview for every household in the city. Now it appears, as the whole thing is blossoming, that many more than that will happen as new requests, programs, opportunities, and technologies are multiplying. But more important than scale was the other key question: *Who* should do the interviews? Should data collection be done by professors? OD consultants? Doctoral students from University of Chicago?

This is where the remarkable learning happened. It is one that continues to leave me breathless. The pilot's very best interviews—resulting in the most inspiring stories, the most passion filled data, the most textured and well illustrated examples, the most daring images of possibility—were all conducted by *children* of Chicago. The most powerful interviews were when children of all races and cultures did interviews with the city's "elders"—priests, CEOs, school principles, parents, entertainers, artists, activists, mystics, scientists. It was the *intergenerational dynamic of the dia-*

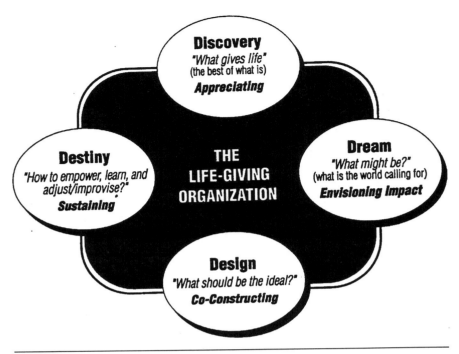

Figure 1.1. Appreciative Inquiry 4 "D" Cycle.

logue that made the data collection stage soar. One is reminded of Margaret Mead's hypothesis that the best societal learning has always occurred when three generations come together in contexts of discovery and valuing—the child, the elder, and the middle adult. Let's look further.[5]

Appreciation and Wonder

An observer described the chemistry in the interviews as "magical". One 72-year-old respondent said at the conclusion of his interview: "I really thank you for this conversation. You got all of me. That hasn't happened too often in my life. You forced me to share my visions, and crystallize them into clear images. This has given me tremendous hope. Now that I can articulate clearly, I know they are do-able."

In the classic interview, for example, a 13-year-old requests a time to meet with his principal. As interviewer he raises many questions: "As you reflect on your career, can you tell me the story of a highpoint, a time you felt most alive, most impactful, most successful in terms of contribution to this school and community?" The principle scratches her head even starts a bit slowly, but soon is in full voice. The youngster, listening to the drama, gets so excited with the story of courage and conviction that he cannot sit quiet. He interrupts the flow and blurts out—"so what was it about you that made it a high point . . . what are your best qualities . . . can you tell me what you value most about yourself?" A little later the topic switches to more volatile topics, like race relations. Again the positive query: "Thinking about your school's contributions to building higher quality multiracial and/or multicultural relationships, what have you done in this area that has made the biggest difference? What one thing are you most proud about?" The stories are told, one after the other. The interview lasts an hour longer than planned.

Later, an evaluation team follows up with the school principle to get feedback on the dynamic of the interview. Typical comments included:

- "I've never been asked these types of questions by youths in this school. When I do converse with the students it is *usually* for disciplinary reasons."

- "That night, after the interview, I laid wide awake. I could not sleep. I kept replaying the conversation. I got back in touch with a lot of things important to me.

- "You know, during that interview I really felt like I was on the pulpit. I got animated. I was literally looking into the face of the future, exploring the essential elements of the good society. This conversation *mattered*.

Barbara Radner's studies are now showing that when the appreciative civic inquiry methods are brought into the curriculum (in 13 Chicago Public Schools) children's achievement in all areas including math, reading, writing, etc., rises significantly in comparison to controls. In doing the interviews, children are hearing stories they would never hear on the news, on TV, or even in the more common cynical discourse of society at large. They are developing their own images of possibility and hearing experiences where change has happened for the better. One young person, Willie J. Hempel, was so excited and moved by his experiences he started volunteering his time to IMAGINE CHICAGO every day after school: "It was during my interview with Ed Brennen, CEO of Sears, that my dreams and hopes were ignited. You find you have so much in common in terms of hopes for our city. And you find out people like Ed really care, not just about money but social justice causes, about me as a young person and about our future . . . my ideas about people like Ed and the politicians I interviewed all changed, and so has my life. That is why I want to volunteer my time now; it is all about making change happen." *Where appreciation is alive and generations are re-connected through inquiry, hope grows and community expands.*[6]

Today, IMAGINE CHICAGO is taking the lessons of its pilot into five major project initiatives: The Urban Imagination Network, City Dialogues, Creating Chicago: A Citizens Guide, City Connections, Citizen Leaders, and Sacred Places. In all of these, the spirit—if not the actual process—of the intergenerational inquiry and change methodology will guide the way.

Dag Hammarskjold once said, "but we die on the day when our lives cease to be illuminated by the steady radiance, renewed daily, of a wonder, the source of which is beyond all reason." The *child as the agent of inquiry* is something I think all of us in OD need to reclaim and aspire to: openness, availability, epistemological humility, the ability to admire, to be surprised, to be inspired, to inquire into our valued and possible worlds, to wonder. In my own work in OD I have found that it does not help, in the long run, to begin my inquiries from the standpoint of the world as a problem to be solved. I am more effective, quite simply, as long as I can retain the spirit of inquiry of the everlasting beginner. The only thing I do that I think makes the difference is to craft, in better and more catalytic ways, the *unconditional positive question*.[7]

Unfortunately, and this is true of myself, it is not often that I begin a new OD inquiry feeling a profound state of wonder; what William James so aptly called the state of "ontological wonder". For me, the doorway into wonder is more matter-of-fact. Pragmatically, it is not so much a process of *trying* romantically to go back to the state of being a child; nor is it the same path as taken by the person in spiritual retreat. It begins in ordinary circumstances of discovery, conversation, and the deepening relationship all endowed by the positive question. *Inquiry itself creates wonder. When I'm really in a mode of inquiry, appreciable worlds are discovered everywhere. The feeling of wonder is the outcome. Of course it also cycles back. A good positive question, like Karl Weick's notion of "small wins", can change the world.*

IMAGINE CHICAGO, as a nascent example of one, is hardly enough to say that it provides answers for the future of OD. But there are clues, insists Browne: "My job, our job, is to be a home to the mysteries of city and its future . . . it is not about having answers." Albert Einstein put the option best, "There are only two ways to live your life. One is as though nothing is a miracle. The other is as though everything is a miracle."

References

[1]*Chicago Tribune*, "Imagine Shaping a Better Chicago" by Terry Wilson, section 2, page 2. Tuesday, June 13, 1995.

[2]Browne, Bliss, "Imagine Chicago: Executive Summary", 1996 (for more information call 312-444-9913).

[3]Cooperrider D.L. and Srivasta, S. "Appreciative Inquiry Into Organizational Life" in Pasmore and Woodman (eds.) *Research in Organization Change and Development*, Vol. 1, pp. 129–169.

[4]Cooperrider, D. et. al. *Appreciative Inquiry Manual*. Unpublished Notes. Case Western Reserve University, 1996.

[5]Barrett, Frank "Creating Appreciative Learning Cultures", Vol. 24, *Organizational Dynamics*, Sept. 1995, pp. 36.

[6]Ludema, James. *Narrative Inquiry*, Unpublished Ph.D. Dissertation, Department of Organizational Behavior, Case Western Reserve University, Cleveland, Ohio, 1996.

[7]Wilmot, Timothy, *Inquiry, Hope and Change.* Unpublished Ph.D. Dissertation, Department of Organizational Behavior, Case Western Reserve University, Cleveland, Ohio, 1996.

Chapter 10

Resources for Getting Appreciative Inquiry Started: An Example OD Proposal

David L. Cooperrider
Case Western Reserve University

Over the past several years people have been asking more and more for practical tools that will help them transform their OD consulting practice away from the diagnostic problem solving approaches toward more appreciative inquiry methods. One of the most common requests (when I do workshops on Appreciative Inquiry) is for examples of proposals—proposals that set the stage for OD contracting. This article presents a "composite picture" of several actual proposals that have led to major OD work. The "AMX" proposal represents the best of several projects that combine Appreciative Inquiry and Future Search. The corporate names used in this composite proposal are fictitious.

What I like most about the "whole system" change process spelled out here is that it completely lets go of problem solving. In my view, the problem-solving paradigm, while once incredibly effective, is simply out of sync with the realities of today's virtual worlds. Problem solving is painfully slow (always asking people to look backwards historically to yesterday's causes); it rarely results in new vision (by definition we say something is a problem because we already implicitly assume some idea, so we are not searching to create new knowledge of better ideals, we are searching how to close gaps), and, in human terms, problem solving approaches are notorious for generating defensiveness (it is not my problem but yours).

Organizations are centers of human relatedness, first and foremost, and relationships thrive where there is an appreciative eye—when people see the best in one another, when they can share their dreams and ultimate concerns in affirming ways, and when they are connected in full voice to create not just new worlds but better worlds. Douglas McGregor was convinced of the power of positive assumptions about human beings. The AMX proposal is an example of an OD proposal that, in practical ways, mobilizes the appreciative process to the fullest extent I know how. The proposal was written the week Congress passed legislation that

OD Practitioner, Vol. 28, Nos. 1 and 2, 1996, pp. 23-33.

would deregulate the telecommunications industry, changing the rules that guided the industry for over 60 years. AMX, one of the organizational giants, was literally in chaos with thousands being laid off. Facing the largest whole system transformation in their corporate history, the CEO asked, "How can we connect everyone to the adventure of creating the new century telecommunication organization?"

The AMX Connects! Proposal

Accelerating Organizational Learning For Winning the New Century

Background. During the past several years, AMX has positioned itself to take advantage of what may prove to be the greatest single business opportunity in history: the creation and management of the Information Superhighway. Part of this positioning has been the clear articulation of the new strategic "ABC" vision and reaffirmation of the goal of being the most customer responsive business in the industry. Along with the vision has come action. There are literally hundreds of successful new initiatives—reengineering, product innovations, new alliances, public relations campaigns, employee empowerment strategies, etc.—all combining to give birth to the new AMX. The entire system is in the thick of fundamental organizational transformation, and exists in a world where the economic, technological, and regulatory foundations of the business have radically changed. It simply is not the same business it used to be.

Important questions, therefore, are many: How can leaders accelerate positive transformation where the process of corporate change is revolutionary in result and evolutionary in execution? How can people reduce the time lag between exciting organizational innovations (initiatives, large and small, that illustrate what the new century AMX organization can and should look like) and organizational storytelling, sharing, advocacy, and mass learning from those innovations? How will employees sustain, over a period of years, corporate confidence and faith in

---

[1]According to recent surveys by Yankelovich, 85% of Americans have lost confidence in the future. People report little confidence that current institutions and leaders will do the job. They see the gap between promised rhetoric about a better future and the continued breakdown, in the present, of many systems. Likewise the negative discourse and storytelling which dominates the media, politics, and the popular culture at large, is associated with increased levels of apathy among young and old, cynicism, fear, discrimination, and other damaging behavior. What is happening throughout society obviously has a spillover effect in our corporations. Especially during times of major transition, ways are needed to rebuild essential connections, to renew hope, and to reinvigorate human creativity and leadership at all levels.

AMX's abilities to make fundamental change even in the midst of inevitable set-backs? How can AMX complement its problem-solving culture with an apprecia-tive mindset that selectively sees, studies, and learns from every positive new development? Can AMX develop and reclaim an oral tradition of storytelling that connects people across corporate generations and that propels the speed and spread of good news? How can AMX leaders decisively connect people through-out the system to the Future Search, and engage everyone in a "can do" way as social architects of the new century organization—a transformed organizational entity that lives its vision in all its structures, systems, strategies, management behaviors, job designs, partnerships everything that the company does.'

Purpose

•   The mission of AMX Connects! is to accelerate positive whole system trans-formation by actively connecting people to the "ABC" vision through the practice of Appreciative Inquiry.

Objectives

•   To bring the "ABC" vision alive for 67,000 people at AMX by engaging a critical mass of people in an Appreciative Inquiry into the most positive and compelling organizational innovations, practices, and traditions that (1) best illustrate the translation of the "ABC" vision into transformational action and (2) provide an anticipatory glimpse into the kind of organization AMX should and might become in the new century.

•   To deliver tangible follow-up to the 1995 Leadership Workshop (which builds on the momentum of the Aspen, Colorado success where 140 regional and corporate executives were introduced to the theory of Appreciative Inquiry), and tie together executive education with real-time organization transforma-tion. By co-leading the Appreciative Inquiry/Future Search process at the regional and corporate levels, the "action learning" design will contribute as much to leadership development as it does to organization development.

•   To augment AMX's problem solving culture with an appreciative mind set that provides a paradigm shift in ways of looking at managerial analysis of all kinds—e.g., new options for approaching organization analysis, customer fo-cus groups, strategic planning methods, reengineering studies, employee sur-veys, performance appraisal processes, public affairs methodologies, diversity initiatives, benchmarking approaches, merger integration methods, and many others.

•   To build an affirmative atmosphere of hope and confidence necessary to sus-tain, over the next several years, the largest whole-system transformation in the company's history.

• To discover and pioneer connections between Appreciative Inquiry/Future Search Conference methodologies (often involving hundreds of people inter-actively) and the voice, video, and data capabilities of AMX's advanced tele-conferencing technologies. The potential for building connection and commitment to the future directions of the company are enormous: corporate visioning, advocacy, and good news telling will not be isolated to a few tech-nical gurus, senior visionaries, or communication messengers, but will engage potentially thousands. When it comes to bringing vision alive, process is just as important as product. People want to be listened to and to be heard. The large group conference methodologies discussed below are truly impressive in their ability to cultivate the thrill of being a valued member in the creation of new and exciting futures.

Leadership

• AMX Connects! will be led by President Sheldon Abrahms; Susan Taft, Vice President Public Affairs; John Williams, Vice President of Organization Develop-ment, and the 140 individuals involved with the recent Leadership Conference. David L. Cooperrider and Associates from Case Western Reserve University's Weatherhead School of Management will provide outside guidance.

Timing

• The appreciative organizational inquiry and learning process will be formally inaugurated in 1996 with a workshop on Appreciative Inquiry. Participants will be the leadership group of 140 through 1996 and 1997. Appreciative Inquiry will be introduced and Future Search Conferences completed in every region of Operations. Results from each of these will form the basis of a synthesizing corporate-wide Future Search in the spring of 1998 and will culminate with a future report—images of The New Century AMX Organization—to be issued by the "think tank" group of 140.

---

[2]For an overview of the social constructionist theory behind the approach, see Cooperrider D.L. and Srivastva S. "Appreciative Inquiry Into Organizational Life" in Pasmore and Woodman (eds.) *Research in Organization Development and Change*, JAI Press, 1987. Also for more on the scientific studies of human behavior that provides a deeper logic for the appreciative approach, see Cooperrider D. "Positive Image, Positive Action: The Affirma-tive Basis of Organization" in Srivastva and Cooperrider's *Appreciative Leadership and Management: The Power of Positive Thought in Organizations*. Jossey Bass Publishers, 1990.

The ABCs of Appreciative Inquiry

In a typical Appreciative Inquiry, the process will lead up to a major Future Search Conference, two or three days in length, where a whole organization or representatives of the whole (anywhere from 100 to 1,000 people) will come together to both construct images of the system's most desired future and to formulate creative strategies to bring that future about. Often, an organizational model like the 7-S framework will serve as a template for building "possibility propositions" in each of the key organizational design areas—for example, what will the ideal organizational structures or systems look like in the future (the conference organizers will specify how far into the future to think . . . usually 3–5 years out). The stages for bringing the whole thing off productively typically follow the ABC sequence:

A. Appreciative understanding of your organization (from the past to present);

B. Benchmarked understanding of other organizations (exemplary models to learn from); and

C. Creative construction of the future (sometimes called the Future Search Conference).

One possible design would be to launch, in each of the regions, a broad-based set of Appreciative Inquiry interviews leading to a regional Future Search conference. The design of the interviews would stress storytelling and study into the "ABC" vision in action—examples of being "the easiest company to do business with"; times when people feel truly "empowered", examples of new forms of "servant leadership"; illustrations of how AMX is "winning in the new world"; etc. All of these interviews would be done face-to-face by AMX managers and employees within the region. All the best quotes, stories, and illustrations would be compiled into a regional report and used to inspire a regionally based Future Search Conference into "AMX In the New Century: Images of Organizational Possibility". At the Future Search Conference, with 100 to 2,000 people, participants meet for two or three days to design the organization's most desired future and formulate creative strategies to bring that future about. The key product is a planning document made

---

[3]See Wilmot, Tim (1995) "The Global Excellence in Management Program: A Two Year Evaluation of 25 Organizations Using Appreciative Inquiry" Case Western Reserve University For detailed analysis of large group methods and outcomes—from Ford Motor Company, First Nationwide Bank, SAS, Mariott, and Borning—see Jacobs, R. (1994) *Real Time Strategic Change: How to Involve an Entire Organization In Fast and Far Reaching Change*, San Francisco: Berrett Koehler Publishers. For ten case studies of the Future Search methods see Weisbord, M. (1992) *Discovering Common Ground: How Future Search Methods Bring People Together To Achieve Breakthrough Innovation, Empowerment, Shared Vision, and Collaborative Action*, San Francisco: Berrett-Koehler.

up of "possibility propositions" describing the collective hopes and dreams people feel inspired to bring about. In the search conference mode, people learn to think of the future as a condition that can be impacted and created intentionally out of values, visions, and what's technically and socially feasible. Such purposeful planning greatly increases the probability of making the desired future come alive. What is unique about the Future Search Conference method as described here is (1) its Appreciative Inquiry Foundation (often experienced as a liberating personal paradigm shift for people); and (2) the broad base of authentic participation that is demanded.

We live in a world of relentless economic change, based on 21st century technologies. Now we struggle to discover management methods equal to the complexity. The power of Appreciative Inquiry and the whole system focus of Future Search combine, our experience shows, to both accelerate and sustain change. Transformation happens faster, at lower cost, and with more inspired collective follow-up than older, more piecemeal or fragmented approaches. Studies show that one well facilitated Future Search with "everybody"—a metaphor for a broad cross-section of stakeholders—will produce more whole systems learning, empowerment, and feelings of connection around business vision than hundreds of fragmenting small group meetings.

The Future Search Conferences, held in each of the regions, would then be capped off with a corporate-wide Future Search of the top 140, the leadership group and key stakeholders representing the whole. If held concurrently in each of the ten regions, the potential for linking up via teleconference for positive story-telling across regions might add a creative and powerful integrative dimension. Literally thousands could be involved in real-time inquiry and transformational planning around the "ABC" vision. Each Future Search would involve something like the following:

1. A conference coordinating committee at the regional level of 4–6 people would meet to plan dates, time, location, meals, group meeting tasks, and who should attend. The goal is to get "the whole system" in the room, or at least strong representation of all those that have a clear stake in the future of the organization. Often then, this includes people "outside" of the organization like customers, community members, partner organizations, etc. The ground rule is that whomever comes to the Future Search must be there for the whole meeting and has the opportunity for full voice in the deliberations.

2. Participants (from 100 to 1000 people) sit in groups of eight to ten, with flip chart paper or a chalkboard available. Depending on the focus and assigned tasks, groupings may vary during the conference. All output from small group discussion is recorded, all ideas are valid, and agreement is not required to get ideas recorded.

3. The conference has four or five segments, each lasting up to a half day Each segment requires that people (a) look at or build a data base, (b) interpret it together, (c) draw conclusions for action.

4. The first major activity focuses on macro-trends likely to affect the organiza-
    tion in the future. Each group is asked to make notes on significant events,
    changes, and trends they see merging by looking at each of the past three
    decades from three perspectives: significant changes and events that hap-
    pened at the world, personal, and institutional /industry levels over each of the
    past three decades. Each table reports to the total group, and a facilitator notes
    trends. The total conference then interprets the most positive macro-trends—
    those trends that indicate opportunities for building a better organization,
    society, or industry. Even the macro trends that appear negative or threatening
    often generate creative thinking on hidden opportunities or possibilities for
    creating the future people want.

5. The second major activity focuses on the appreciative analysis of the organi-
    zation. Each group has a copy of the Appreciative Inquiry report that was
    compiled earlier, with quotes, stories, and comments from all the appreciative
    interviews. Three questions are then posed to each group:

    (a) What are the most outstanding, moments/stories from this organization's
        past that make you most proud to be a member of this organization?

    (b) What are the things that give life to the organization when it is most alive,
        most effective, most in tune with the over-arching vision, etc. (make a list
        of up to ten factors)? and

    (c) Continuity: What should we try to preserve about our organization—
        values, traditions, best practices—even as we change into the future?
        Again, consensus is not needed as the results are displayed and dis-
        cussed by the whole conference.

6. The third major activity focuses on the benchmark understanding of the best
    practices of other organizations. Each group is given the report from benchmarking
    studies and is asked to make a list of the most interesting or novel things being
    done in other organizations. The list should include things that are interesting,
    novel, or even controversial and provocative. The list is not an endorsement of
    any of the practices—it is simply a compilation of interesting or new ideas and
    practices. There is to be no discussion of whether or not to adopt the practices in
    the present organization. If benchmark studies have not been done as part of the
    pre-conference Appreciative Inquiry process then group members should gener-
    ate the list from things they have seen in other organizations have heard or read
    about. Reports are made to the whole conference and people are asked to com-
    ment on the most interesting or novel ideas.

7. The fourth major activity focuses on the future, especially the creative con-
    struction. New groups are formed and are given a half day to develop a draft of
    a preferred, possible future. The focus is on translating the business vision
    into inspired organizational vision. The focus is on the organizational dimen-
    sions of the future. Using a model like the 7-S model or a homegrown model of

organizational design elements, groups develop a set of "possibility propositions" of the ideal or preferred future organization (3–5 years into the future).

8. The fifth major activity focuses on the next action steps. Groups are then asked
    to reflect on what has surfaced and, depending on the nature of the groupings,
    to make three lists of suggested action steps: commitments they want to make
    as individuals to move the vision forward; action steps their region, and work
    unit, might take; and things the organization as a whole might do. Action
    proposals are shared in a total group session and a steering committee is
    formed to discuss proposals for the total organization, prioritize themes, and
    prepare a report to be presented at the capstone Future Search.

Whole System Involvement

In a comprehensive study of successful habits of visionary companies, Stanford
University researchers Jerry Porras and James Collins put it simply:

It's become fashionable in recent decades for companies to spend countless
hours and sums of money drafting elegant vision statements, values statements,
purpose statements, aspiration statements, mission statements, purpose statements,
objective statements, and so on. Such pronouncements are all fine and good—indeed,
they can be quite useful—but they are not the essence of a visionary company. Just
because a company has a "vision statement" (or something like it) in no way guaran-
tees that it will become a visionary company! If you walk away from this book thinking
that the most essential step in building a visionary company is to write such a statement, then you will have missed the whole point. A statement might be a good first
step, but it is only a first step. (Taken from *Built to Last*, 1994.)

Translating core vision into everything the company does requires ways of
connecting everyone—evoking ownership, commitment, understanding, involvement, and confidence in the vision's promise. This proposal provides a doable way
to proceed: it is logistically possible and financially feasible to design a process
where all of operations (67,000 people) are involved. Everyone, at a minimum, would
be a participant in the Appreciative Inquiry as an interviewer, interviewee, or both.
And up to 10,000 would participate in at least three other engaging activities of
learning and doing: workshops on Appreciative Inquiry (one day long); conducting the interviews (doing 5–10 interviews); and one or more Future Search Conferences (three days in length). The working assumption, at the regional level, is that
approximately 1,000 people would participate in a day long introduction to Appreciative Inquiry. They would subsequently be charged with completing 5–10 interviews apiece, and then would serve as delegates to the regional Future Search
Conference.

Measuring for Results

AMX Connects! will measure its results by asking how each step, and the whole process, achieves discrete, agreed upon objectives. This is a demanding approach that will force everyone involved to focus on how the method of Appreciative Inquiry actually affects the way people think, communicate, and act in relation to the process of whole system transformation. Some of the areas of expected impact include:

- Reduction in the time lag between organization innovations (innovations that are consistent with the "ABC" vision) and their spread throughout the corporation.

- The strengthening of a "can do" climate of hope and confidence in the corporation's ability to manage the transition and realize its transformational goals.

- Significant increase in the corporation's positive internal dialogue about the future (e.g., less cynical and deficit oriented discourse, less fear; less negativity; more vocabularies of positive possibility; more rapid spread of good news developments).

- Development of a more appreciative leadership mindset and culture which provides managers with new options for dealing with corporate and customer surveys, re-engineering, strategic planning analysis, team-building, merger integration, performance appraisal and others.

- Significant increase in the feeling of connection to the corporation's "ABC" vision at all levels and regions of AMX Operations.

Sustainability

The telecommunications industry is going through a profound change that involves reassessment of economic foundations, technological infrastructures, organizational forms and processes, and managerial mindsets. The whole-system transformation being called for is both comprehensive in scope and fundamental in nature. There are a number of things, therefore, that must not be overlooked. First, we must not overlook the reality of people's resistance to such profound change—to even thinking about it—since it involves challenge to the inner assumptions which have become an inherent part of the culture and individual ways of constructing the "way things ought to be". Nor should we fail to note that the coming changes will bring about a great deal of fear and uncertainty; in fact, keeping down the fear is probably the greatest challenge of all, since only with low levels of fear can people see clearly and take the right actions. But perhaps most important is the need to address questions of sustainability. What will make the appreciative inquiry/future search methodologies as outlined earlier more than just a one-time high? What will be done to sustain learnings at regional, corporate, and individual levels? Our own evaluations of Appreciative Inquiry and the evaluation studies of large group Future Search Conferences suggest the following five strategies for long term sustainability.

1. Skillbuilding: The Process of Organizational Transformation is a School for Leadership Development. In many respects, there is really no such thing as organizational transformation, there is only individual transformation. Because of this, especially with the leadership group of 140, every major session will involve both organizational analysis and personal planning as well as skillbuilding modules around all the phases of appreciative inquiry and the methods of facilitating interactive, large group meetings. In GE's recent whole system "Workout Program", for example, it was found that the most important outcome of the initial large group Workouts was managerial skill development—the Workout conference methodologies have become a way of life for almost two-thirds of the work units. Of course, Chairman and CEO John F. Welch played a major role in making the new participatory methods a priority. He was notorious in his surprise appearances at local Workout sessions and was consistent in his message: "building a revitalized 'human engine' to animate GE's formidable 'business engine'."

2. Extending Appreciative Inquiry Into Change Efforts Where There Will Be High Value-Added. Already there are plans being made by various AMX staff to use the appreciative methodologies to re-think and revitalize organization development practices like corporate surveys, customer focus groups, public affairs projects, etc. These efforts at extending Appreciative Inquiry should be made more systematic and priority driven. Our suggestions is that we should prioritize no more than five major extensions of Appreciative Inquiry—for example AIs contributions to merger integration methods, organizational surveys, process re-engineering, and diversity initiatives. Each of these efforts should be carefully documented and written up later in the form of a practitioner manual (e.g., a merger integration manual, or a customer focus group manual). Appreciative Inquiry involves a paradigm shift that will vitally transform, for example, how mergers or diversity initiatives are approached. The key, early on, is to prioritize several areas where there will be a high value added contribution and, in those areas, take the appreciative approach to the hilt.

3. Customized Regional Follow-up Consultation. In preparation for the Future Search Conferences, and in response to needed follow-up at the regional level, there will be a consultant/facilitator team made up of internal AMX professionals (e.g., OD, HR, PA) and a specialist from Cooperrider and Associates. This consultant team will commit, up front, to ten days of consulting follow-up at the regional level to tailor-make a response to the initiatives generated at the Future Search Conferences. By definition, the customized response is un-

known at this time, but our experience shows that the commitment to ten days of follow-up consultation is the single most important thing that can be done to ensure sustainability. In a recent study of Appreciative Inquiry with 25 organizations, it has been found that ninety percent of the organizations are continuing with the appreciative methodologies, some two years after the start (see Wilmot, 1995). An essential attribute of the sustainability was that in each case, all ten days of promised follow-up consultations were in fact used. Likewise, the follow-up was completely at the initiative and request of the organizations themselves. Each organization had to "apply" in writing for the follow-up: what were the goals, what kind of support did they need (e.g., facilitation, training, outside evaluation, retreat design, organization analysis, one-one personal counseling). The lesson is simple: we must plan for sustainability from the beginning, and the commitment to the customized follow-up opportunity is critical.

4. Advanced "Internal Consultant" Learning Partnership. Each year, there will be two special sessions among all internal AMX change agents that are involved with Appreciative Inquiry and the Future Search Conferences. The learning partnership will deal with advanced theoretical and practice issues, and will use clinical/field-based modes of learning. The purpose will be to build internal skills and competencies, to build a support network among AMX units and regions, and to make good use of the program's evaluation studies for advanced professional development.

5. Appreciative Inquiry "On-line". Already there have been discussions with specialists at AMX about how to accelerate the spread of innovations and good news storytelling by adding an Appreciative Inquiry protocol to the new AMX on-line suggestion program. An analogy here is useful: an ongoing Appreciative Inquiry will be to the "whole system transformation" what time-lapse photography is to the visible blossoming of an otherwise imperceptible flower. Putting Appreciative Inquiry on-line is a very exciting venture that has yet to be done anywhere. There is no question the time is ripe for this to happen; and it makes sense that it would be inaugurated at AMX, where leadership in the positive human impact of advanced technology lies at the forefront of the corporate mission. One way to introduce the on-line approach would be to conceive of the 67,000 interviews as mini-training sessions in Appreciative Inquiry After each interview, people would be given a short booklet with simple instructions on how to use the internal on-line "web page". Stories and new images would be made available on a continuous basis. An award could even be established for the stories that best anticipate and give a glimpse of the new AMX, living its vision today. The implications of Appreciative Inquiry on-line are far reaching and exciting indeed. We are infants when it comes to our understanding of the power of this kind of non-hierarchical information sharing and whole system dialogue. The results could be revolutionary.

In the course of developing the ideas described above, it has become clear that people at AMX have this hope that there's a little window of opportunity for really responding to a radically changed business environment. That window of opportunity, and the current season of hope being expressed, is going to last about as long as Sheldon Abrahms, in the early days of his new presidency, uses this occasion to boldly enroll everyone in the positive transformation. To make it all work we (as an internal/external team) will not only need to work collaboratively, responsively, and flexibly as a "learning organization," but we also will need to be united around a shared revolutionary intent.

Conclusion

The relational, large group, participatory methods outlined here fly in the face of old hierarchical, piecemeal problem-analytic approaches to change. Likewise the appreciative paradigm, for many, is culturally at odds with the popular negativism and professional vocabularies of deficit that permeate our corporations and society at large. Most important, however, there are people, many people throughout AMX, that feel the time has come to make the "positive revolution" happen. These are the individuals that are just waiting to step forward and lead. The constructive, creative, and indispensable voices of the new AMX already exist. But their critical mass has yet to be legitimized. AMX Connects! is about mass mobilization; it is about the systematic creation of an organization that is in full voice. It is about transformation of the corporation's internal dialogue. It is about creating, over the next several years of discovery and transition, a center stage for the positive revolutionaries.

Chapter 11

An Appreciative Inquiry into the Factors of Culture Continuity During Leadership Transitions: A Case Study of LeadShare, Canada

Mary Ann Rainey
ComEd

LeadShare (LS), a partnership of nearly 350 accountants and management consultants in Canada, embodies a unique blend of tradition and innovation which has proved successful, often placing it at the forefront of change. LeadShare's inception dates back to the mid-nineteenth century, close to the time Canada became a country. Within the past 25 years, LeadShare has expanded its spectrum of client services and reshaped itself for double-digit growth, currently ranking among the top accounting firms in Canada.

Human Resources is a critical function at LeadShare. The firm values human capital and recognizes the need to hire the right people to produce and deliver quality products and services. Today, individuals recruited by LS have far more complex qualifications because competition for competent people is intense. The need for professional development is just as urgent.

More than ever, LS people have to be futurists. The firm must be capable of looking ahead, discerning what is on the horizon, and preparing for it. The goals LS has for itself are the same as those of its clients: do the best today and anticipate and be poised to do even better tomorrow As a partnership of shared management, preparation for tomorrow is a collective effort.

OD Practitioner, Vol. 28, Nos. 1 and 2, 1996, pp. 34-41.

Roundtable

In anticipation of transitions in two key executive positions within the span of three years, the organization set in place a succession plan to ensure minimum disruption and to prepare for leadership entering the next millennium.

LeadShare launched the "Roundtable" initiative; Roundtable to suggest leadership without hierarchy, shared resources, and cross-functional networks. The objective of Roundtable is to enlighten the next generation of leaders about the firm's history and tradition and their ingredients of success. A desired outcome for Roundtable participants is to develop a group of agents of culture who sustain the firm's traditions, practices, and behaviors while multiplying the factors of success.

Using current values, assumptions, and motivations as stepping stones to new ones requires knowledge of what the current ones are. Unfortunately, cultural assumptions are usually taken for granted and therefore difficult to see (Schein, 1985). LeadShare realizes that it must find ways to articulate the implicit aspects of its culture if it expects to grow in new directions. A move in that direction is to provide a venue for partners to talk about their experiences and views about what is different, special, and valuable about the firm. Freud (1921) spoke of five "principle conditions" for raising collective life to a higher order: (1) some degree of continuity; (2) some definite idea; (3) interaction among the group; (4) traditions, customs, and habits; and (5) definite structure. These principles serve as a useful preamble to the methodology that guided Roundtable. That methodology is Appreciative Inquiry.

Appreciative Inquiry

Appreciation is a *selective perceptual process* which apprehends "what is" rather than "what isn't." It represents a capacity to be selectively attentive to the lasting, essential, or enlivening qualities of a living human system. Appreciative management, as a process of valuing, consists of a rigorous ability to disassociate all seeming imperfections from that which has fundamental value (Cooperrider 88, p. 4).

According to the theory's creators, David Cooperrider and Suresh Srivastva, in its most basic meaning, Appreciative Inquiry is a form of organizational study that selectively seeks to locate, highlight, and illuminate the "life-giving" forces of a firm's existence (1987).

There are two essential questions behind any appreciative study:

1.   What makes organizing possible; and
2.   What are the possibilities of newer and more effective forms of organizing.

Four basic principles guide Appreciative Inquiry:

1. Exploring the life-giving forces of the firm should be *appreciative* in nature. The appreciative approach looks for what "works"; those peak aspects that serve to activate partners' energies and competencies.

2. Exploring the life-giving forces of the firm should be *applicable*. It should lead to knowledge that can be validated and used productively

3. Exploring the life-giving forces of the firm should be *provocative*. Appreciative knowledge is, by nature, suggestive of what might be. Looking at the best of "what is" kindles the thought of "what might be"; it also challenges the firm to become the best of "what is possible".

4. Exploring the life-giving forces of the firm should be *collaborative*. It should foster healthy dialogue about the way things were, the way things are, and the way things can be.

Several dimensions of the AI process contribute to its uniqueness as a tool for succession planning (see Table 1). Foremost is the shift from the traditional "great man" approach to succession to one that emphasizes collectivity and collaboration. Harlow Cohen argues that managerial high performance is a function of collective effort (Cohen, 1986). Cohen believes that managerial work is characterized by (1) high dependence on others; (2) continuous ongoing activities with no defined beginning or end; and (3) a preponderance of time spent in face-to-face interaction. Collaboration is defined in terms of consciousness, choice, caring, and commitment. Collaboration operates within a relational system characterized as a just system based on fairness, mutuality and responsibility (Appley and Winder, 1977).

The primary objective of AI in the Roundtable program is to assist LeadShare in envisioning a collectively desired future, and then collaboratively carrying forth that vision in ways which successfully translate intention into reality and belief, and then into practice.

The Roundtable was a component in a major organization development intervention that spanned two decades at LeadShare. Roundtable itself was a multiyear intervention with core activities occurring during a six-month period (see Table 2). Work included development of the AI interview protocol, data collection, thematic analysis of data, data feedback, and identification of future direction.

Collection of Data

Over 700 pages of data were collected throughout an 18-month period using common social science methods which included:

1. **Interviews.**   The 40 partners who were selected to participate in Roundtable conducted open-ended formal interviews with the entire population of partners

Table 1. Comparison of Traditional Approaches to Succession and AI

	Conventional	Appreciative Inquiry
Unit of analysis	Primacy on individual	Primacy on group
Type of analysis	Problem and organization diagnosis	Embraces a solution
Source of vision current	New leader, the 'Messiah'	Three generations of leaders
Pre-succession succession	Psychological trauma disruption	Valuing, visioning, dialogue creating the vision
Post-succession	Alienation	Culture continuity

in the firm. Each interview lasted about two hours and covered questions about their experience in the firm and six topic areas; (1) partnership; (2) determination to be winners; (3) diversity; (4) Consensus decision making; (5) possibilities/positive thinking; and (6) conditions for people to excel. The topics and interview questionnaire were created by external consultants in collaboration with members of the organization's Management Committee. Roundtable participants were instructed by video on how to conduct an Appreciative Inquiry.

2. **Historical Documents.**   Reports, articles, speeches, newsletters, unpublished papers, and memoranda were reviewed and content analyzed.

3. **Observations.**   Office visits, committee meetings, and retreats were attended which provided a firsthand experiential basis for understanding the culture of the firm.

4. **Survey.**   In a second phase of the research, a survey was conducted at the Annual Meeting of the partners to provide convergent validity to the interview data. Developed by the 40 Roundtable participants, the survey summarized the six topic areas based on the "7 S framework" (see Peters and Waterman, Jr., 1982). The partners gave two ratings on a 7-point Likert scale: (1) the extent to which they felt the survey statement represented an important "ideal" to continue to be pursued by the firm, and (2) the extent to which the survey statement was reflected in practice.

Analysis of Data

For purposes of reliability and objectivity, the raw data was analyzed by two independent researchers in addition to the author. Word counts and interpretations were consistent among the three. The qualitative data and results from the survey provided a set of descriptive themes. From these themes emerged a preliminary description of a set of characteristics around the concept of "culture continuity".

Table 2.   Roundtable/AI Design

May	• Data collected to identify affirmative topics to be explored • Affirmative topics identified • Affirmative topics discussed with Management Committee and modified
June	• Questionnaire developed
June/July	• Roundtable participants conduct interviews
July	• Interview data summarized
August	• Roundtable participants and staff receive samples of data from interviews
September	• Roundtable participants and staff receive summarized version of interview data • Roundtable session: Retreat at Mt. St. Marie, Ontario • Roundtable session focused on: 1. Reaffirming the affirmative topic choices and creating a common base of data for all participants 2. Stating provocative propositions about the life-giving properties in the firm 3. Consesus validation of propositions using force-field analysis and debate 4. Identifying the next steps for experimenting with provocative propositions
October	• Administration of Consensus Validation Survey at Annual Partners' Meeting

The following are the major themes of our analysis:

1. **The Feeling of Unity.**   This refers to general solidarity. Unity is exemplified through shared decision making, partner support, working and playing together, the annual meeting, other meetings and anniversary celebrations.

2. **Respected, Responsible, Inspirational Leadership.**   Partners focused on "success generating success" and confidence in the courageous and responsible leadership of the firm. Service to the client is not sacrificed through the commitment to success, growth, and profitability. Automatic committee rotations increase understanding and appreciation of various factors in the firm and provide continuity. Communication and participation before action and major changes build consensus and strengthen the feeling of "partnership". Deliberation guards against hasty decision making and the potential loss of things absolutely critical to the success of the firm.

3. **Justice and Equality.**   The consensus building process, the "one partner, one vote" decision making structure, the development and partnership system. The financial and remuneration structure, the commitment to diversity and autonomy, and the partner exit counseling program breed an environment based on fairness, choice, appreciation, openness, and care.

4. **People Development and Professional Competence.**   Constant learning and the development of partners are priorities. Partners should not only be

competent in their respective skill areas, but they must also have the ability to attract and retain top quality people and instill in them personal pride.

Major Themes with Selected Data

The following are the major theme areas with selected representative data. These examples are provided to build some sense of clarity around the thematic framework.

1. The Feeling of Unity
    *   LeadShare does a very good job of making all the offices feel that they are a part of the whole. There is an ongoing feeling of unity among the partners, most likely from day-to-day experience. The partnership seems to work well. When you come away from the annual partners' meetings, you walk with a spring in your step.
    *   Different specialties are encouraged to combine forces. Also, there is the "one firm" attitude, which fosters cooperation. Different groups are combined with a unified top management team and national profit sharing, which allows the success to be shared.
    *   The managing partner's monthly memos are very important. It is clearly evident that he puts a lot of thought and time into them and through them the feeling of one firm is created. The feeling that we as a firm and as individual partners are very valuable, i.e., the feeling of "wholeness" comes through.
2. Respected, Responsible, Inspirational Leadership
    *   The leadership does not dictate. It sacrifices quick decisions for gathering a majority view. This is the way it should be.
    *   Through the whole process of choosing our leaders, we provide for continuity within the firm for building consensus.
    *   Communication is the key word. It's letting partners know what the issues are prior to final decisions and obtaining feedback and input from them. Obviously, where partnership is so large, it may be difficult to do this on all issues, but we have found it beneficial at annual partners' meetings to have breakout groups where partners are able to have input on things of national concern.
    *   No matter how small your office is or how far away you may be from the center of Canada, you still have very good feeling that you are making a contribution. Someone is listening to what you are saying. Your input counts.

Justice and Equality

- At LeadShare, it's equality: it's one pot, one partner, one vote.

- There is a great sense of pride among partners that LeadShare, against heavy odds, turned a challenging region into a success story. The managing partner spared no expense for translations and set an example by learning French.

- I've been involved in two or three instances where we have counseled partners out—it's a difficult process; and without a doubt, the firm has been fair with these, maybe more than anyone else would have been.

- We started out being autonomous, and organized into a national firm later. Our roots through the merged units are to be autonomous, so we centralized. The main thrust was to keep the autonomy of the local offices.

- Merger issues with [a particular firm] where certain outstanding merger issues were settled through cooperation in a manner that was most fair.

- When the firm lost a lawsuit, the manner in which the partners rallied around the individual partner involved was quite impressive.

People Development and Professional Competence

- In recognition that we are in a knowledge business, our leaders direct and the partners accept responsibility for significant self development—including personal, professional and people management skills.

- We feel that management of continuity is prepared well in advance so that when a change does occur, it is not disruptive. The confidence is in younger partners. There are efforts to develop the management potential of younger partners.

- The Roundtable. It's an interesting process in worrying about continuity from one leadership to the next. This process involves a number of perspectives from different partners as well as getting in touch with our strengths so that we don't move too quickly to change things that are absolutely critical to our success.

The Factors of Culture Continuity

Following are eleven propositions that emerged when the thematic framework was taken to a higher level.

1. Commitment to the concepts of "partnership" through communication, consensus building, "one partner, one vote," face-to-face interaction, partner development and evaluation, profit sharing, and confidentiality of unit allocation, all which supports a feeling of fairness and trust.

2. The firm continues to provide high quality, personalized, prompt, and diversified services as well as offering clients the best value for their money

3. The vision of the firm is communicated through everyday behavior and performance.

4. The concept of shared ownership demands that each partner be responsible for the future of the firm.

5. The concept of leadership goes beyond professional services and management processes—it includes the ability to inspire and nurture talent and innovation.

6. People at all levels are developing professional and client service skills. These skills include technical competence in their respective disciplines and a knowledge of current technology.

7. The firm attracts, recruits, and retains the best people across disciplines to develop as professionals.

8. The partnership attracts, develops, and retains people who are intelligent, hard working, energetic, possess good interpersonal skills, and have the courage to change barriers into opportunities.

9. The firm aggressively pursues specialty mergers, acquisitions of service firms and hires recognized experts to expand the diversity of services, skills and people, all to expand the firm's base.

10. The basic strategy for obtaining profitable growth in both the domestic and international environments is through harnessing positive and innovative thinking and using the most current technological and communications capabilities available.

11. Each partner is responsible for leaving a legacy in terms of building firm assets, which includes people, clients, and services.

Conclusion

To the extent that organizations want to maintain internal effectiveness and external adaptability, they need to know what their fundamental values are so they can build a template by which to juxtapose people. Appreciative Inquiry is one technique that can highlight values and help build consensus around what is important to individuals in a firm. AI can help an organization know where it is and where it wants to go, by defining criteria and identifying people who can get them where they need to go.

Appreciative Inquiry highlights the values individuals stand for and allows for rearticulation and reprioritization of those values. In this context, it is a process in pattern enhancement. Values are not simply rearticulated through AI, they are rearticulated more profoundly. Appreciative Inquiry is designed to elicit the ideals of the organization and to give substance to those ideas through a concrete interactive process. It also is designed to make sure people see the connections between their values and the system's.

Beyond this, we found that Appreciative Inquiry builds culture. By taping both common ground and shared values, AI mobilizes the maximum amount of commitment and increases members' confidence in what it is doing. It helps individuals clarify what it is they want to do and promote solidarity that represents a key source of rejuvenation as hard work depletes people's energies.

We also found that Appreciative Inquiry permits adaptation to the environment. In a professional organization, where the likelihood is high that new employees will bring with them the latest techniques, expertise, and knowledge necessary for keeping pace with emerging environmental demands, AI is likely to lead to the cementing of values that are indeed adaptive. If recruitment and development is from good schools and brings individuals with good sensors, and the system allows for learning and adaptation, then sharing values will be a growth process for the organization.

On the other hand, in those organizations displaying low recruitment and turnover, AI may prompt inbreeding and reinforce values that are behind the times, and therefore, threatening to organizational survival. Organizational culture may be very satisfactory for its members but not very adaptive to its environment. Consequently, Appreciative Inquiry could reinforce old, outdated systems values, thereby cementing blindness to the environment.

When AI is used as a succession technique, there is always the threat of demotivating persons not identified as fast trackers. There also is the very legitimate question of: *Are those who are identified as leaders of the future really managers or are they heretics?* To the extent that the system reflects the ideals of the membership, the organization may be down the path of its greatest ignorance. Other approaches to the succession process that introduced actors who backed the prevailing values may represent better guards or protection against this drawback.

Finally, it's clear that Appreciative Inquiry provides many contributions to collective and collaborative efforts and may be most ideal in those settings. It also appears that Appreciative Inquiry may be better suited to environments where fundamental changes have a low probability of occurrence because as much effort is required to maintain specialized cultures as is required to create them. Who should know that better than the partners of LeadShare, Canada.

References

Appley, D.G., and Winder, A.E. (1977). "An Evolving Definition of Collaboration and Some Implications for the World of Work." *Journal of Applied Behavioral Science*, 13, 297–91.

Cohen, Harow (1986). The Social Construction of Managerial High Performance. Unpublished Ph.D. dissertation; Case Western Reserve University, Cleveland, OH.

Cooperrider, D. (1986). "Appreciative Inquiry: Toward a Methodology for Understanding and Enhancing Organizational Innovation. Unpublished Ph.D. dissertation; Case Western Reserve University; Cleveland, OH.

Cooperrider, D. (1987). "Appreciative Inquiry in Organizational Life." *Research in Organizational Change and Development*, Vol. 1, 129–69. JAI Press.

Freud, S. (1921). *Group Psychology and the Analysis of the Ego.* 1922, London: Hogarth Press. Complete works, Vol. 18.

Gephart, Jr., R.P (1978). "Status Degradation and Organizational Succession. An Ethnomethodological Approach." *Administrative Science Quarterly*, 23, 553–581.

Gerth, H., and Mills, C. (1946). From Max Weber: *Essays in Sociology.* New York: Oxford University Press.

Gorden, G.E., and Rosen, N. (1981). "Critical Factors in Leadership Succession." *Organizational Behavior and Human Performance*, (27), 227–254.

Grusky, 0. (1963). "Managerial Succession and Organizational Effectiveness." *American Journal of Sociology*, 69, 21–31.

Jacobs, B. (1986). "Heir conditioning." *Public Relations Journal*, (3), 24–28.

Lieberson, S. and O'Connor, J.F (1972). "Leadership and Organizational Performance: A Study of Large Corporations." *American Sociological Review*, 37, 117–130.

Pfeffer, J. (1977) "The Ambiguity of Leadership." *Academy of Management Journal*, 2, 104–112.

Schein, E. (1985) *Organizational Culture and Leadership.* San Francisco: Jossey-Bass.

Schwartz, H. and Davis, S. (1980). "Corporate Culture and Business Strategy." *Harvard Business Review.*

Smith, J. E., Carson, K. P and Alexander, R.A. (1984). "Leadership: It Can Make a Difference." *Academy of Management Journal,* (27, 765–776).

Weick, K. (1979) *The Social Psychology of Organizing.* New York: Random House.

Chapter 12

Survey Guided Appreciative Inquiry: A Case Study

Rita F. Williams

The purpose of this article is to explore Appreciative Inquiry (AI) as a powerful example of one of the most often used Organizational Development (OD) methods, survey guided development. To date, survey guided development has been wedded almost exclusively to a problem-solving view of OD. However, Wendell French and Cecil H. Bell, Jr., in *Organizational Development* (1995) describe second generation OD methods which include nontraditional interventions.

The context for the application of OD approaches has changed to a more turbulent environment. While there is still a major reliance on OD basics, considerable attention is being given to new concepts, interventions, and areas of application. Second generation OD includes interest in organizational transformation, organizational culture, the learning organization, teams and their various configurations, total quality management, visioning, and the whole system in the room."

This article proposes a radical rethinking of the survey-guided method from the perspective of AI. Appreciative Inquiry is a form of organizational analysis first developed by Dr. David Cooperrider of Case Western Reserve University. The purpose of survey guided AI is to invite whole system exploration into an organization's highest human values. Instead of problem diagnosis, there is inquiry into hopes, dreams and visions. Instead of the survey itself being a "mirror of what is" it is an intervention into what "might be." (see Table 1).

Background

The Appreciative Inquiry process was successfully used as an intervention in an organization that was in a serious crisis. It served as a catalyst for change and as a vehicle for focusing an entire organization on a collective vision of the future. The site was an $11 billion regional commercial banking institution located in the Midwest which will be referred to as First Peoples Bank (FPB). The organization evolved from a rich history that consistently reflected dedication to serving its customers

OD Practitioner, Vol. 28, Nos. 1 and 2, 1996.

218

Williams

Table 1. Notes on Appreciative Inquiry

Problem Solving	Appreciative Inquiry
"Felt need" Analysis of Causes	Appreciating valuing the best of "What is"
Analysis of causes	Envisioning "What might be"
Analysis of Possible solution	Dialoguing "What will be"
Action Planning (Treatment)	Envisioning "What will be"

and their communities. The company's roots go back to 1893, when the bank was founded. In the decades that followed, the company established its strength in the industry through financial stability, asset growth, and product development. It was one of the few institutions to guarantee funds to its customers following the stock market crash of 1929 and to remain open throughout the Great Depression. Key highlights include:

- **1950s.** the branch-banking network grew
- **1960s.** the addition of a new building, and new automation for operations
- **1970s.** among the first banks in the Midwest to introduce automated teller equipment and cards; the company name changed reflecting a constantly broadening position
- **1980s.** gained a presence in 11 states with significant operations in Ohio, Indiana, Michigan and Texas

After deregulation went into effect in the late 1980s, the banking industry became unstable. Crisis and change had become a way of life as acquisitions, mergers, and problems with foreign loan portfolios created an unstable environment. In the late 1980s, FPB was beginning to feel the strain. An organization that had previously set an aggressive course for the future with confidence and without hesitation, suddenly had an air of uncertainty about its future business strategies. The leaders feared that the wrong decision would have long-term negative consequences. In the early 1990s the organization began to experience even more difficulty. Some of the Strategic Business Units (SBUs) at FPB were very profitable while others lost money and became a drain on profits. There was a hostile takeover attempt, major loss in profits for the year, all occurring within two consecutive years of record earnings. Loan losses from a risky foreign loan portfolio were balanced by drastic cost cutting measures including a corporate-wide downsizing, which involved laying off over 850 of FPB's 8,000 employees.

As Vice President of the organization, I was the project manager on the cost-cutting program. The project deliverables involved the development and implementation of a detailed plan for downsizing, including a resource guide and training method for the management team. Aggressive employee relation plans and programs were needed to stabilize the organization. Outplacement assistance was put in place for laid off staff along with comprehensive communication strategies to keep everyone informed. Uncertainty surrounding the downsizing created concern about retaining the high quality staff needed to move the organization forward.

Because managers were affected by the downsizing, a vision and statement of values was created by the organization's leaders and reviewed with each staff member. A more sincere effort was deemed necessary by managers because of the seriousness of the situation. There was a growing consensus about the need for a powerful intervention which would identify the organization's values and commit the staff to a vision of the future.

The process of Appreciative Inquiry (AI) could help in the identification of a common vision and values. However, there was concern that most of the previous AI applications had included healthy and/or growth oriented organizations. There were many unanswered questions about the potential impact of engaging an organization that was experiencing difficulty in the AI process.

The corporate human resources communication plan called for an aggressive employee relations campaign. The major focus of the campaign was on the construction of a common vision of the future around which employees and managers could align their efforts. It was critical that the vision statement be based on the values and ideals contributed by staff and that an opportunity for employees be available at all levels to develop an agreement and buy-in to this vision. Despite the risk, it appeared that Appreciative Inquiry was the best tool for accomplishing this goal. In the initial stages of this intervention, it was difficult to predict how far the process would go. The typical AI process included five phases (see Table 2). At FPB, a pilot was developed that involved one-on-one interviews with 250 randomly selected employees.

Table 2. Key Phases of the Process

An Overview	
Phase 1	Affirmation topic choice (Definition)
Phase 2	Inquiry into the "life-giving properties" (Data collection and discovery)
Phase 3	Articulation of possibility propositions (Visioning the Ideal—dreaming)
Phase 4	Consensual validation/agreement (Design through dialogue)
Phase 5	Co-construction of the preferred future (Destination)

Appreciative Inquiry Intervention

Phase 1: Affirmative Topic Choice

An interview protocol was created by using primarily open-ended questions which were designed to help people identify the best of "what is" and to allow the topics to emerge. Unlike traditional surveys that focus on participants' opinions, AI focused on the participants' experiences and observations and promoted storytelling of positive and significant events during their careers. An example of an interview protocol is shown in Table 3.

Phase 2: Inquiry Into 'Life-Giving Properties'

The data collection and discovery phase was handled by 20 of FPB's senior human resources staff who, altogether, interviewed 250 bank employees. Each interview was designed to inquire into the life giving properties of the organization as perceived by these employees. The interviewees represented a cross section of staff across the corporation at all levels in the organization. The HR interviewers received training on theory, practice, and application of AI through workshops and practice sessions. The 250 interviews took approximately three weeks to complete. Overall responses were extremely positive, and they generated powerful stories and examples of situations when the organization was functioning at its best:

- "We have a billing clerk that has taken ownership of her job. She says, "We can make it better if we do things differently." She is not afraid to initiate. And she gets recognized. She is a change agent. To be an owner is to be in the business of making continuous improvements.

Table 3. Sample Interview Protocol

1. What attracted you to FPB?
   - What were your initial excitements and impressions when you joined the company?
2. Without being humble, what do you valuemost about yourself, the organization, your work?
   - What is the single most important thing the company has contributed to your life?
3. Looking at your entire experience, can you recall a time when you felt most alive, most involved or most excited about working at FPB?
   - What made it an exciting experience?
   - Who were the most significant others?
   - Why were they significant?

- "Throughout my career here I have had the fortune to work with people who were for me. I've been given every opportunity imaginable. There were times when I was given opportunities that were such a stretch that I didn't even know if I was capable. I have worked for people who could somehow see things in me I couldn't even see in myself. Without that confidence, I don't think my career would have unfolded as it has."

Comments from employees interviewed about the AI process included:

- "We need to do this throughout the organization."

- "This is the Perfect time for us to be working towards generating a common focus."

- "I feel better just being interviewed. The questions were hard, but they made me think, and showed me why I stay here and why I want to be a part of FPB's future."

Phase 3: Articulation of Possibility Propositions/ Emerging Themes

The collected data was analyzed and summarized into a report that identified ten emerging values. The values were fashioned from the interviewee's actual experience and reflected the culture of FPB as they understood it from an appreciation of its proven strengths. They also represented a bold extension of those strengths— a focused vision to which people said they aspire as an organization.

The major themes were stated as provocative propositions which bridged the best of "what is" with the understanding of "what might be". They were provocative because they stretched the realm of the status quo, and helped suggest a course of action for the future. Because of this, the values reported were stated in the present tense, not because they had been totally attained, but because people were saying this was their present "ideal" based on experiences when the organization was at its best. In the report, each proposition was supported by actual employee quotes that detailed specific events and/or experiences (Table 4 briefly describes the ten themes).

A summary of the report was reviewed with FPB?s CEO and President. They were surprised by the depth and breadth of the employees? responses. One commented that it was exciting to know that among tellers, clerks and managers there were common values and collective commitment to the future.

The information was so compelling that they felt the entire executive management team should review it. A two-day off-site planning conference was held to present the findings and to develop a plan to move the process forward.

Table 4.   Core Values Emerging Themes

We value people
The company flourishes because each individual is valued as a precious resource.

Responsive performance
FBP is a corporation made up of people who take pride in their work, and who consider responsive performance as modus operandi.

Service and caring
"To serve others"—our unifying purpose. We provide excellent and innovative products that add value and exceed the expectations of those we serve.

Unifying structures
The formal structure is clearly understood but not constraining. FPB supports the use of networks, project teams, and task forces to manage issues that cross formal boundaries.

Honesty
Integrity is expected. It is a way of life. And it begins and ends with example, not procolomations.

Ownership
Employees act as Owners. Owners do things that hired hands will not see.

Being a significant corporation—rock solid
FPB's rock solid stability is a core value that gives life to the organization. People stay because of the stability. customers stay because FPB has been steady. Steady, Sturdy and Stable.

Community
FPB's image in the community is precious. The involvement and commitment has been consistent. It is one of the most important legacies we have inherited.

Being in full voice
When FPB is in full voice, three things occur: (1) new ideas are given full consideration; (2) information is openly shared; and (3) participation in decision making is pushed to the lowest possible level.

Servant leadership
Leadership at FPB is a process of serving others. It involves seeing potential in people in ways that they cannot even see themselves. It involves removing obstacles, coordinating, educating, listening, and coaching.

Phase 4: Consensual Validation Agreement

The senior management team decided that all employees in the organization should participate in the process and have an opportunity to give their input. The call for action included a plan to administer a written survey to all 8,000 employees over a 30-day period. Unlike traditional "off the shelf documents" this survey was internally developed, reflecting the emerging themes identified in the pilot and exploring values, ideals and practices of the organization. The questionnaires allowed all employees to: (1) have a voice in identifying what is important to the company and to them as individuals; (2) evaluate how well they practice those ideals today; and (3) indicate how much they have experienced their values in their career.

Employees were asked to think about times when they were really excited about FPB, where they thought it was going, what it was doing and what they were doing at the time that made it exciting (see Table 5). This vitality was the life and

Table 5. Examples of consensus validation survey

Employee survey—confidential
Building on our proven strengths

Instructions: What follows is a series of statements about the way our organization should work, works, or has worked. For each statement, consider these three ratings:

- Important to me as an IDEAL. How important, on a sacle of 1 to 7, do you think the statement should be an ideal for FPB to pursue?
- Practied NOW in the Present. Using the scale of 1 to 7, how well do you think FPB lives the statement today?
- To what extent have you EXPERIENCED THIS IN YOUR CAREER AT FPB? Again using the scale.

1. FPB has been recognized as progressive—even ahead of its times—in the treatment of people.

• Important to me as an ideal	1	2	3	4	5	6	7
• Practiced now	1	2	3	4	5	6	7
• Experienced in my career	1	2	3	4	5	6	7

2. We have high expectations of ourselves. We deliver the best.

• Important to me as an ideal	1	2	3	4	5	6	7
• Practiced now	1	2	3	4	5	6	7
• Experienced in my career	1	2	3	4	5	6	7

3. Employees at all levels are aware of our customers' needs and are committed to responding with first-class service. We put ourselves in our customers' shoes and remember that—from the phone calls we answer to the paperwork we process—the way we do our jobs and work together significantly affects our customers' lives.

• Important to me as an ideal	1	2	3	4	5	6	7
• Practiced now	1	2	3	4	5	6	7
• Experienced in my career	1	2	3	4	5	6	7

4. FPB has a reputation as being a rock solid, secure and prestigious financial institution. FPB maintains its reputation through good business decisions and sound business practices.

• Important to me as an ideal	1	2	3	4	5	6	7
• Practiced now	1	2	3	4	5	6	7
• Experienced in my career	1	2	3	4	5	6	7

5. We recognize the value of each employee's contribution and eliminate the obstacles to get the job done.

• Important to me as an ideal	1	2	3	4	5	6	7
• Practiced now	1	2	3	4	5	6	7
• Experienced in my career	1	2	3	4	5	6	7

strength of the organization; it was the proven strengths that they would build upon. That inspection was important to all.

The data was collected so that a statistical analysis could be performed to review it for the organization as a whole and by SBU. The following coding system aided in the development of reports, feedback and action planning:

- Exempt or Non-exempt Status
- Years of Service
- Location (City and State)
- Strategic Business Unit (SBU)

The fixed response questionnaire made it easy to conduct a quantitative analysis in a short period of time. In addition to the fixed responses, the survey included a section with blank space that asked for additional comments and posed the following open-ended question: If you could develop or transform FPB in any way what would you do to heighten its vitality and overall health?

The data collection phase of the process was conducted in orientation meetings with employees in each SBU, kicked off by the senior executive. A videotape, featuring a message from the Chairman and President, described the goals of the project, and the steps of the "Call for Action" initiative. Participation was voluntary and each employee was encouraged to give his/her input.

Approximately 6,500 of the 8,000 employees participated in the survey This was an exceptional response. Even more surprising was the response to the open-ended questions that asked for their ideas and comments. Of the 6,500 surveys, 4,000 contained extensive responses. Many wrote suggestions and comments, some as long as two and three pages. It seemed that a safety valve had been opened to release constructive energy and thoughtful responses creating a collective hope and vision for the future. A team of HR professionals analyzed the data and prepared detailed reports for the entire organization and SBU.

The data was fed to the management team and employees through meetings across the organization. Of the ten themes included in the survey, the following topics emerged as values and strengths:

- Rock Solid Business Practices
- Exceptional Customer Service
- Honesty

In the thematic analysis of the open-ended comments at the end of the survey the value of teamwork emerged as a strength.

Phase 5: Construction of the Preferred Future

Team leaders were trained to facilitate brainstorming sessions with focus groups of employees throughout the organization. The goal of these sessions was to identify ways to build on the identified strengths and to take action in their work group to improve productivity and performance. These brainstorming sessions provided an opportunity for ongoing dialogue, action and commitment to change. A workbook was developed so that the data was uniformly collected and reported to Corporate Human Resources. Opportunities identified included both organizational and SBU specific initiatives. (See Table 6 for using the theme exceptional customer service.)

Impact of AI Process on FPB

The AI process powerfully impacted the nature of the conversations in the organization, causing a fundamental shift in the daily dialogue. Employees began to view problems as opportunities and the optimism inherent in the conversations led to feelings of empowerment; employees were ready to take action in the face of possibility rather than staying frozen in the face of problems and circumstances.

The exceptional response of the staff reinforced the fact that an intervention like AI can breathe life, strength and a proactive response to a crisis. A consensus and shared vision allowed the organization's leaders to move forward aggressively to stabilize the situation. Within one year of the AI interviews, the organization merged with another bank forming a large national holding company. It appeared that understanding its strengths made it easier for the organizations to honor those things that should be preserved. Part of the merger negotiation included selling a group of branch offices to another bank. The management of the new bank com-

---

Table 6. Putting our valued commitments to work

Discussion workbook for focus groups

Customer service
FPB provides first-class customer service.
    We go the extram mile to provide excellent service
    We provide caring, responsive service
    We exceed customer expectations
    We have high expectations of ourselves
    We work together
    We deliver the best

Team discussion
A. What we do best and should keep doing.
    What do we have in place that shows great customer service? ("Customers"
        can be fellow employees, too.) Why does it work well?
B. What we should begin or start doing.
    What new things should we introduce to improve customer service?
C. What we should change or stop doing.
    What are we currently doing that we should question, change, or stop doing?

mented on the positive and productive outlook of the FPB staff. They felt that their attitudes made the transition easy and that they were more receptive than their own staff members. The FPB case is a true example of the positive impact AI can have in the most negative situations.

Conclusion

The AI process in FPB served both as a catalyst and invitation. This was an invitation to participate in an organization-wide process where everyone at each location had the opportunity to think strategically and imaginatively about the future of the organization. As a catalyst, the report provided inspiring snapshots of the future. The information revealed the many strengths of the organization when it was working at its best. There, it must be acknowledged, is an undeniably positive quality about AI. Some of this stems from the nature of the questions that are asked and the responses that are collected. Equally important, much of this quality comes from tapping into the real sense of optimism people feel about the company and its prospects for the future.

In retrospect, several distinguishing features make this case unique. First, the AI intervention was spontaneously initiated by the HR department without the customary rigmarole of top management clearances. The self-sustaining enthusiasm of the employees generated a momentum of its own resulting in over 8,000 employees being surveyed in thirty days.

Second, the AI process collapsed the customary distinctions between leader and follower or between manager and employee by providing everyone in the organization with a meaningful sense of engagement in the organizational renewal process during a prior acute crisis.

Third, the case is an eloquent testimony to the power of AI as a transformative force; the survey questions generated powerful stories that unleashed the collective imagination of the workforce generating boundless optimism that stabilized the situation. AI, in the ultimate analysis, provided a powerful paradigm shift that led employees to view their current situation through a completely interpretive lens wherein problems were viewed as possibilities and the best of "what is" stimulated imagination of "what can be". It provided a new mode of consciousness akin to what Einstein alluded to when he said, "No problem can be solved from the same level of consciousness that created it."

Chapter 13

THE LIBERATION OF POWER: EXPLORING HOW APPRECIATIVE INQUIRY "POWERS UP THE PEOPLE"

Diana Whitney, Ph.D.
The Taos Institute
Amanda Trosten-Bloom
The Taos Institute

Introduction

Over the past 5 years, we and others around the globe (Khalsa and Kaczmarski, 1996; Ludema, 1997; Bushe, 1998) have discovered a way of working that consistently and dramatically liberates peoples' sense of individual and collective power. The liberation of that power, along with peoples' willingness to exercise it on behalf of their organizations, adds "value" to the organizations and businesses in question. That philosophy, practice, and way of working is called Appreciative Inquiry.

In case after case, using Appreciative Inquiry as a process for strategic organizational change, we have seen remarkable transformations in the way people work together and in the results they achieve. We have participated in the drama of personal transformation as people have discovered who they are at their best. We have seen high performance in the face of positive possibility – rather than crisis. And we have heard stories, over and over again, about the positive impact of Appreciative Inquiry on people's *personal*, as well as professional, lives.

Having been repeatedly surprised and delighted, as we've watched the enthusiasm with which people have engaged themselves with their organizations' change initiatives, we have begun to ask ourselves what's happening. Why is it that people get so excited and want to participate with Appreciative Inquiry? Why is it that participation so readily leads to innovation, productivity, employee satisfaction and profitability? What is it that creates such possibilities for personal transformation and for people to discover and be their best at work? What are the conditions that foster cooperation throughout a whole system of highly diverse groups of people? In short, the central question of our reflection, and the question addressed in this paper is, *What is it about Appreciative Inquiry that "powers up the people?"*

The "Power-full" Organization

Think with us for a moment about the questions: What is the *value* of a human being? And, what is it that organizations value about human beings?

Beyond the *inherent* worth and value that every human being on the planet holds, organizations' answers to these questions can and do vary widely. Now, as we've taken our first steps into the 21st century, corporations around the globe "value" human beings' at anything from a few cents per hour (or the equivalent thereof) to millions of dollars per year - depending on their answers to such questions as: Who *are* the people? What *unique skills or background* do they bring to the picture? How capable are they of making independent decisions? Of *actively influencing* their work environment and the world around them? In short, what value can they *add* to the organization or business?

Now, let's restate the question. What is the value of a *"powerful"* human being? A person who knows that *the world is subject to human influence*? Who knows that she *personally* has the power to change the world? Who chooses to *exercise* that power for the good of the whole? Who encourages and grooms the people around him to *join* him in exercising that power? Who invites others into cooperation to discover, dream and design the future?

"Ah," we hear you say, "now *that* is a different question!" That kind of person is "valued" much more highly, in organizations today, than the person who simply "shows up and does what she's told." *That* kind of person is "worth" a great deal more, in organizational and business terms.

When the individual and collective power of human beings is unleashed, organizations become "power-full."

A power-full organization is one in which people care about and work towards being the *best they can possibly be* - personally, as well as organizationally. It is a place where people seek to work by what we might call "spiritual ideals" – peace, harmony, justice, love, joy, wisdom and integrity. It is a place in which people take responsibility for dreaming and for acting upon their dreams.

A power-full organization is one in which power – the capacity to create, innovate, and to influence change – is an *unlimited* (vs. "zero-sum") relational capacity and experience. It is shared freely; and in the process of being shared it grows. People exercise power in ways that are inclusive . . . that nurture and expand the people around them.

Imagine an organization in which people are motivated, energized, and committed to being the best. Imagine the possibilities for innovation and excellence.

Imagine the impact that such an organization might have on its industry . . . on the world.

This article draws upon our work with just such an organization: Hunter Douglas Window Fashions Division in Broomfield, CO. This thousand-person manufacturing company - the largest and most successful Division of Hunter Douglas International - innovates, manufactures, and fabricates high-end window covering products.

In the spring of 1997, in response to several years of off-the-chart growth and related changes in structure and leadership, the Division's leadership launched a full-system appreciative inquiry with the intention of:

- Creating a *collective vision* for the future of the organization - one that would engage and excite the entire organization and its stakeholders.
- Re-instilling the *creativity, flexibility, intimacy, and sense of community* that had contributed to the Division's original success.
- Building leadership within the organization (i.e., enhancing the skills of existing leadership, and building the "bench strength" by identifying and training future leaders)
- Transcending the silos that had recently emerged between management and the general work force, and across business units, as well as between operations and "support" functions.

Just one year into its work with Appreciative Inquiry Hunter Douglas reported significant results in productivity, operational improvement, turnover, and employee engagement. Production and productivity improved, particularly in the lower-yield operations. Operations improvement suggestions were up over 100 percent, resulting in hundreds of thousands of dollars in savings through process innovation and operational improvements.

Turnover was the lowest it had been for six years, despite negligible unemployment in the County in which they operate. Participation in tuition assistance was up, especially among hourly employees. In addition, when Dale Carnegie advertised its basic training, six months into the Appreciative Inquiry effort, *22 people* - most of whom were hourly - signed up to participate. (This was up over 100% from the previous year.) The interviewer from Dale Carnegie commented that she had never seen a more positive and enthusiastic group of people before, and inquired about "this [Appreciative Inquiry] program of yours." Six months after initiating Appreciative Inquiry, the Company moved to create a Toastmasters chapter on-site at Hunter Douglas. When sign-up sheets were posted, 48 people volunteered to participate *on their own time.* The majority of these volunteers were production workers from the plant, who had connected the importance of their developing communication skills to their future potential in the organization. Over the coming months, attendance continued at extraordinary rates, and the Company moved to establish a second on-site chapter.

On-site research (Chandler, 1998) quantitatively established positive changes as a result of the Appreciative Inquiry efforts. In particular, Chandler's research indicated that since the implementation of Appreciative Inquiry there were improvements in:

- Employees' understanding of organizational goals.
- Employees' understanding of how their work fit with the organization's goals.
- Employee commitment to the organization's goals.
- Employees' sense of ownership for their work.
- Employees' motivation to be productive, innovative, and creative.

All of these quantitative findings were supported by the qualitative employee comments that were gathered during on-site focus groups.

Perhaps most telling were the results of an unplanned series of "Employee on the Street" interviews which were conducted about nine months into the effort. 75% of the employees who were polled had been only tangentially involved in the Appreciative Inquiry effort. Most of these employees described Hunter Douglas as a kinder, gentler, more open place to work than it had been just nine months before.

What is Appreciative Inquiry?

Appreciative Inquiry ("AI") is an organization development philosophy and methodology that enhances organizations' capacities for positive change and on-going adaptability (Whitney & Schau, 1998). It was developed in the mid 1980's by David Cooperrider, Ph.D. and Suresh Srivastva, Ph.D. of the Weatherhead School of Management at Case Western Reserve University (Cooperrider & Srivastva, 1984). It provides a philosophy and tools for leaders to understand and build upon the *best of what has been and might yet be* within their organizations through inquiry into their *"positive core"* (Cooperrider & Whitney, 1998). An organization's positive core is described as the collective wisdom, knowledge, and capabilities - often undiscussed - of the organization at its best.

Consider the individual words "appreciate" and "inquire." Webster's Dictionary defines the word "appreciate" as follows:

> *1:*   *to value or admire highly;*
> *to judge with heightened understanding;*
> *to recognize with gratitude.*
> *2:*   *to increase in value.*

"To inquire" is defined as meaning:

> *1:*   *to search into.*
> *2:*   *to seek for information by questioning.*

Hence, Appreciative Inquiry guides us to *ask questions with gratitude and a sense of "valuing" . . . in order to increase understanding and enhance value. AI* is *the study of what gives life to a human system, when it is at its best.*
Appreciative Inquiry, as a process, takes place over four phases, which are generally described as the "4-D Process." Based on the assumption that change occurs through thoughtful inquiry into and dialogue about affirmative life-giving forces, the four phases of the process are: Discovery, Dream, Design, and Delivery.

Discovery: Appreciating What Gives Life

The Discovery phase is a quest to identify positive stories and spread them throughout the organization. It brings into focus those things which give life and energy to people, their work, and their organization. It assumes that the life-giving forces are indeed present in every situation, but that our habits of organizing and talking often overlook the positive in favor of analyzing obstacles, resistance, and deficits. The Discovery phase shifts the balance of organizational attention from what *isn't* working to what *is,* and to what *may possibly work* in the future.
Discovery begins with the introduction of Appreciative Inquiry theory and practice to the organization. The purpose of the effort is clarified, and a "core team" is selected to both guide the effort and select topics for the inquiry. Topics are *affirmative*, and are stated in *affirmative language.*
For example, an organization wishing to reduce turnover might study "employee retention." Another wishing to reduce conflict might study "collaboration." In the selection of affirmative topics, organization members are asked to focus on the things they want *more of* in their organization - the things they want to

The *"4-D"* Cycle

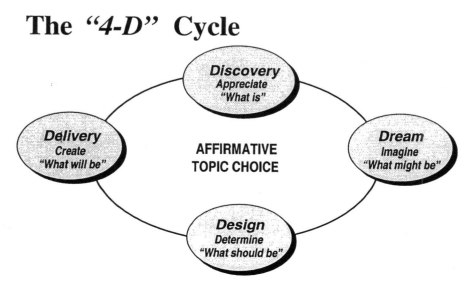

grow. ("What would make this organization *even more* the place you want to work?")

"Appreciative interviews," the core technology of Appreciative Inquiry, are at the heart of the Discovery phase – and are often woven into later phases of the process as well. Generally conducted as a mutual interview among diverse stakeholder groups, they may also be conducted in focus groups. Interview questions are crafted around the affirmative topics, and an interview guide is created, exploring: a) people's beginnings with the organization; b) what they value most about themselves, their work and the organization; c) their appreciative stories related to the topics being studied; and d) their hopes and dreams for the organization and its future. Discovery involves interviewing many - if not all - members of an organization, and often includes interviews with external stakeholders (i.e., customers, suppliers, and community members).

At Hunter Douglas Window Fashions, the Discovery phase engaged the *entire organization* (plus key external stakeholders) in one form or another. A cross-section of the organization (100 people from all functions, business units, shifts, levels, tenure, race, and gender) selected topics for the inquiry and wrote four different interview guides. This same group then initiated interviews with colleagues, customers, suppliers, and stakeholders. Beginning six weeks later, another 200 people joined that first group, to begin both second and third "waves" of interviews.

Over the course of the just six months, 450 employees and 75 stakeholder interviews had been conducted and "synthesized," in preparation for later phases of the process. Interviews were conducted and synthesized with the balance of the work force – another 500 people – over the next six months.

Dream: Imagining What Might Be

The Dream phase is a time for groups of people to engage in thinking big, thinking out of the box, and thinking out of the boundaries of what has been in the past. It is a time for people to describe their wishes and dreams for their work, their working relationships, and their organization.

The activities of this phase often take place in a large group meeting of 50 to over 1000 people. This meeting, known in the field as an Organizational Summit (Whitney & Cooperrider, 1998) encourage participants to consider what their organization (department, business unit, or entire company) is being "called" to do. This connects the work of all members of the organization to a greater purpose and vision.

Working together in small groups of eight, participants share and discuss the data and stories collected in the Discovery phase. Even as these discussions ground them in the most positive aspects of their organization's past, they inspire them to imagine *possibilities* - what *"might be"* for themselves and their organization in relation to the *world.*

Small group conversations have been preceded by one-on-one appreciative interviews, and small groups have been given guidelines for self-management. Participants have been encouraged to "check their titles at the door," and listen for the "lone small voice" - the one with a *different* idea or a *different* way of looking at things. This focus on *relationship and dialogue* builds safety and trust, which in turn inspires lively, enlivening, participative, and highly creative conversations. In fairly short order, divergent groups of people begin to converge towards and focus on the things that bind them together, as opposed the things that pull them apart.

Often, small group conversations are followed by high-energy, creative presentations to the larger group - which in turn inspire even greater ease and creativity. Skits, murals, songs, poems, and commercials are all possible modes of expression for dramatizing the positive possibilities envisioned for the organization and its future.

The Hunter Douglas Dream phase – like its Discovery - has been iterative. The Division's first Organizational Summit – which took place upon completion of the first 500 interviews – very much followed the design described above. Later, Dream activities occurred in conjunction with *whole-system strategic planning* – which was initiated as an annual activity, as a result of the first Organizational Summit.

Design: Determining What Will Be

In the Design phase, organization members and stakeholders (including customers and suppliers) recreate the "social architecture" of the organization, so that *everything* about organizing reflects and is responsive to the organization's most positive past and highest potential.

Whereas the Discovery and Dream phases generate and expand the organization's images of itself, the Design and Delivery phases ask members to *make choices* for the organization. Stakeholders draw on interviews and dreams to select high-impact design elements, and then craft "Provocative Propositions" (or Design Statements) which incorporate the positive core into high-impact processes, systems, and programs.

True to the principles of Appreciative Inquiry, Design Statements are *written in the present tense*. They recreate the organization's image of itself by presenting clear, compelling pictures of how things will be when the organization's positive core is boldly alive in all of its strategies, processes, systems, decisions, and collaborations. In this way, Design Statements redirect daily actions and create future possibilities for the organization and its members.

The Hunter Douglas Design phase has also taken place over many iterations. The seven "Design Statements" created at the first Organizational Summit continue to guide the organization's decisions and actions. Later Design activities included development of Divisional and the Business Unit-level strategies that would bring the company Mission, and Strategic Vision to life.

Delivery / Destiny: Creating What Will Be

Change occurs in *all* phases of an Appreciative Inquiry, as the process provides an open forum for employees to contribute and step forward in the service of the organization. The Delivery process, however, focuses specifically on personal and organizational *commitments* and *"paths forward."*

During Delivery sessions, commitments are made to ensure that the Design Statements are realized. Individuals commit to applications and action plans, small groups work on areas that require collaboration, and teams may be established for new initiatives. Alignment on actions to be taken is high, as a result of the extensive involvement of large numbers of people in the Discovery, Dream and Design phases. The massive number of people engaged in interviews, large group meetings, and critical decision making helps participants get strong sense of what the organization is really about, and of how they can contribute to the future through their personal actions.

At Hunter Douglas, the Delivery phase was initially manifested through "Action Groups" – collections of employees convened around a topic of mutual interest and passion. These teams formulated their own goals and objectives, set their own timelines for completion, and recruited their own "champions" from among the Window Fashions leadership. Participation was about equal between hourly and salaried, production and professional. Through a unique combination of commitment to action and support, they achieved exceptional results over a 1- to 2-year period of time, in areas that were directly tied to the hopes, dreams and aspirations of the organization as a whole.

The 4-D Cycle and the "Six Freedoms"

So what's the relationship between the 4-D Cycle and the liberation of power? Personal and organizational power is liberated – unleashed - when certain essential conditions are present for people within organizations. Our work with the people of Hunter Douglas as well as other organizations suggests to us that there are at least six pre-conditions for the liberation of power. We call these pre-conditions the "Six Freedoms."

The magic of Appreciative Inquiry comes, in part, from the way in which it unleashes *all* of the "Six Freedoms," over the course of just one complete 4-D cycle. Because of this breadth of impact, it has a greater capacity for transforming personal and collective realities than many of the other organizational change processes we've seen to date.

Any *one* of these "Six Freedoms" can significantly affect people's perception of their power within an organizational context. Because individuals learn and are motivated differently; interventions which provide the opportunity for people to experience *multiple freedoms* have the greatest potential to impact the most number of people and ultimately the organization as a whole.

The journey to liberation - from oppression to power - is one of "social emergence." Paulo Freire's work (1970) suggests that the "oppressed" are submerged in reality. They are in a sense "social realists" who believe the world is the way it is and there is nothing they can do about it. They experience and describe themselves without place or power to change things. We have heard this organizational lament all too often, " This is how it has always been around here. It's been this way for the twenty years I have worked here. It is never going to change." These are the voices of the "organizationally oppressed."

It is our experience that the "organizationally oppressed" live and work in all functions, at all levels and in all sectors of organizations. No organizational group, level, or function is always and exclusively more receptive to organizational oppression than another. In some organizations it is the marketing group that doesn't feel heard or able to influence decisions. In others it is manufacturing. In some organizations those at the top express great frustration in not being able to influence the market or shareholders – or to "motivate" employees. In others it is front line employees who experience themselves as invisible and unable to impact the way work (even their own work) gets done. Often, when one group in an organization feels undervalued and unable to influence, so do others.

The first step toward liberation begins when people recognize the world and their organization as open to social change, as created by and through human interaction and creativity. At this stage, people often see and describe positive impact as an attribute of others. *("She is such a great leader. Since she has been here we have made major improvements.")* This other-oriented power is a step toward liberation. It acknowledges the *potential* for social change, while still placing the capacity for influence and change with some "other." Generally, the other is more informed, has more authority, is more experienced or is in someway described as more powerful.

When people realize that they – in relation to others – can and do make a difference, they experience true liberation. Theoretically, we call these people "social constructionists:" people who understand the socially crafted nature of our realities. (Gergen, 1994) Appreciative Inquiry, through the Six Freedoms, creates a relational and narrative rich context which becomes the path on which the journey to liberation takes place. The Six Freedoms are:

1. Freedom to be Known in Relationship
2. Freedom to Be Heard
3. Freedom to Dream in Community
4. Freedom to Choose to Contribute
5. Freedom to Act with Support
6. Freedom to Be Positive

Following is our description of these Six Freedoms, along with examples of ways in which each freedom was experienced and expressed in the words of employees who participated in the Hunter Douglas inquiry. These are voices of the organizationally liberated.

#1: Freedom to be Known in Relationship

"Despite our habit of seeing ourselves as separate, solid 'things,' our minds, our beings are not fixed. We exist in a web of relationships."

Joseph Jaworski
Synchronicity

Human identity is formed and evolves in relationship. "Persons represent the intersection of multiple relationships" (McNamee & Gergen 1999). Our sense of self is a *relational* identity that thrives in communication with others. "Communicative connections to other people are fundamental to the workings of the human mind and self, and to the culture that enriches and sustains our spirits and achievements" (Fogel, 1993). Just as we know and become ourselves in relationship, so do we also contribute to our organizations in relationship. For many people, the quality of their relationships at work is one and the same with the quality of their work life.

All too often in work settings, people are known *in role*, rather than in relationship. They are vice presidents and operators, doctors and nurses, employees and customers – in short, they are perceived as *what they do,* rather than *who they are.* Appreciative Inquiry allows us to know one another *in relationship,* rather than in role. It calls us to know one another not just as unique individuals, but as a part of the *web of relationships* through which "I" exist. The more fully we are known in relationship, the more fully we can come to work and contribute. John Cade, a printer with the Window Fashions Division, reflects on the fundamental human need to be known in this way. "I want to be known, and to 'belong,'" says Cade. "The animal takes care of survival, but the heart – the soul – wants to *belong.*"

Being known in relationship includes knowing one another as *relational beings* – as parents, coaches, artists, bowlers, etc. The more fully I am known in *my relational world,* the more fully I can come to work and contribute.

Appreciative Inquiry breaks the cycle of depersonalization that masks people's sense of "being and belonging." The appreciative interview, which is the core technology of Appreciative Inquiry, is powerfully rooted in the personal and relational. It seeks after and explores in depth people's personal peaks . . . times when they have been most engaged, most alive, and most proud of themselves, their organizations, and their work. It asks them to recall those moments in vivid detail, and to share their experiences with people whom they've heretofore known only "in role" – or not at all. The process affirms people in relation to others, enables new relationships to be formed and enhances respect among people working together on a day to day basis. It gives people the freedom to get to know themselves and others as fundamental to high performance.

Renee Chavez, an inspector with Window Fashions, says, "I did my interviews with people who weren't like me. That helped me meet and get to know people who are very *different* from me: different jobs, different backgrounds, different races."

Cindy Stewart, another printer, describes the interviews as "energizing, every time you do them. It's just a really nice process. They build relationships, give you a chance to connect. They tell people that their ideas are important."

Appreciative Inquiry doesn't *just* build relationships. It also levels the playing field and builds bridges across the artificial boundaries that seem so prevalent in late 20th century organizations. For example, Joe Sherwood, a manufacturing and fabrication process coordinator, says, "In asking the right questions, you bring back enthusiasm and renew relationships. [The interviews] give us an opportunity to go to our bosses and speak up for ourselves." Mark Maier, a machinist, says it even more succinctly: "Appreciative Inquiry blew the communication gap wide open."

Similarly, John Cade comments on the ways in which Appreciative Inquiry in general – and the interviews in particular – help to make other people and their ideas more *accessible*. As he puts it, "Appreciative Inquiry gives us opportunities to *be known* across the boundaries." The "contagious spirit" of the interviews results in a sense of *connection* to others. "As our Appreciative Inquiry effort got fully under way, other people became excited, just like me. I didn't feel alone. For the first time, it was 'me *with* the world. '"

Perhaps the best example of the "Freedom to be Known in Relationship", what Brian Bassett, shipping coordinator, called *"human to human contact"* is the story of Germaine Piper, a third-shift operator who interviewed numerous Vietnamese, Lao, and Cambodian refugees as part of the original Discovery process. When asked what she'd learned from the interviews, she referred to the "heroism" of the people she'd interviewed.

"They left their jobs, their homes, and their families. They lived in and escaped from refugee camps. They traveled to this country under *inhuman* conditions, and finally arrived in the US. And for what? People who had once held professional positions had to take whatever jobs they could get – just because they didn't speak English.

This just isn't right! I've decided that I want to teach them English on my lunch hour. I've decided that if I can teach them English, I might learn some of their language too."

Within a day, Germaine had phoned the Company's Vice President of Human Resources and offered to teach English classes. Ultimately, she ended up coordinating (rather than teaching) a series of English as a Second Language ("ESL") courses that were brought onto the campus from a local community college. (Ironically, the Human Resources Department had been trying for years to get an ESL program off the ground, with no success.) Germaine's dedication and power – liberated through her experience of *getting to know* new people - made an enormous difference in the lives of dozens non-native Hunter Douglas employees. Through the additional support they received, these employees were also "powered up" to contribute to the success of Hunter Douglas its customers.

In today's business world relationships – teams, alliances, partnerships, colleagues - are essential. Work gets done through relationship. "The central economic imperative of the network economy is to amplify relationships" (Kelly, 1998). Through Appreciative Inquiry, the freedom to know and be known in relationship liberates people's energy and ideas. Personal and organizational power emerges when people are known in relationship.

#2: Freedom to be Heard

"I have seen over and over again – all around the world – what happens when people who are not used to being valued feel heard. The experience of being heard allows them to be present and to offer the best of themselves in a way that could not happen otherwise."

The Reverend Canon Charles P. Gibbs
United Religions Initiative

In the process of being heard we become apparent. We go from a voice – the expression of "babbling ideas" – to a being. When another hears us – when they witness and repeat our ideas and stories - we become tangible . . . real . . . significant . . . *somebody.* The sense of not being heard, of having no voice, of not having a say, is the experience of the oppressed – people who feel one down and unable to make a difference. To be heard is to have a recognized and credible voice . . . to be known as a source of creativity, innovation, and influence.

Surprisingly little has been written on the experience of being heard, much more on the act of listening. Listening, as we know it, is a trait or skill of an individual. One can listen without truly hearing – or *knowing* – the other.

Being heard, on the other hand, is relational. To be heard requires another to be listening with sincere curiosity, empathy and compassion, and with an openness to learn. It also requires hearing a *person's story,* as well as his or her words. Appreciative interviews encourage this kind of *relational hearing.* They ask speaker and listener alike to reach beyond the mundane, the theoretical, into personal experience and values. They invite an act of "hearing" that draws out the best of another, encourages the cooperative creation of meaning and identity.

During Appreciative Inquiry, people experience themselves as *being heard* – and as hearing others - in powerful, fulfilling, and energizing new ways. The appreciative interviews *"level the playing field,"* says Brian Bassett. Thus, employees who are traditionally disenfranchised – the "organizationally oppressed" – begin to "show up," think, and imagine in bold and provocative new ways.

But the one-on-one interviews do something equally (if not more) important, to open channels of communication and nurture people's experience of being heard. They unleash a plethora of *stories* – which, through later phases of the process spread and multiple throughout the organization. Ultimately, once the organization has completed its first Design phase, individuals and groups can *recognize* their work, language, insights, and inspiration in the new organization or system. On a practical level, people experience being heard as their ideas and stories are presented, discussed, and put into action.

In 1997, when Hunter Douglas first implemented Appreciative Inquiry as a culture change process, Mark Maier was supervising a group that performed technical maintenance on the company's production machinery. He and his staff felt under-valued, not heard and often ignored – even when it came to maintenance (their expertise). Mark decided to put Appreciative Inquiry to the test. He initiated an inquiry among all of the team's internal customers: engineers, technical support staff, etc. He and his staff collected stories of exceptional support that people had experienced both here and at other companies. He invited people to dream about the service that they'd always wanted, and to describe it in detail. What was the result, when all was said and done? "My people were finally recognized as contributors. (We'd been considered to be the 'black hole' for years!) We *built relationships* with the engineers and the technical support staff. We were *really seen* for the first time ever."

Appreciative Inquiry affords the opportunity to be heard. By setting the stage for the 'Freedom to be Heard" it opens doors for people who feel ignored and without voice to come forward with information, ideas and innovations. It creates a rich context for knowledge creation and exchange.

#3: Freedom to Dream in Community

"It is up to each of us. As we move into the twenty-first century let us align with one another to bring our highest vision into manifestation. We can make personal and collective dreams a living reality. Let us work together. We are the architects of our own destiny."

Rama Vernon
The Fabric of the Future

Visionary leaders have long been recognized assets to their organizations (Kouzes and Posner, 1987). Their capacity to put forth an image, a dream, a sense of possibility that others can rally round has been regarded highly among the traits of transformational leaders (Tichy and Devanna, 1986). But what of the dreams of the people? In today's highly diverse world, neither leadership vision nor shared vision – alone – are enough. (Starhawk, 1999) We need leaders who invite everyone to dream and to realize their dreams. We need organizations to be safe places where people dream and share dreams, in dialogue with one another. We need the "Freedom to Dream in Community."

The images we hold, in our mind's eye and in the stories we tell, directly impact personal and organizational performance, health, and learning (Cooperrider, 1984). Images – be they of a person or an organization – are a kind of *community property*. They are created and maintained in community dialogue, in conversations among members and stakeholders of the community. To enrich an organization's dreaming is to enrich its communally held images and its potential for greater achievement and vitality.

Through one-on-one interviews, story-based synthesis, and collective dreaming processes, Appreciative Inquiry stimulates people's imaginations and opens their dreams up to the whole. This can change people's work and lives, as it did for Brenda Lubben, a ten-year employee of the Company:

"At the end of my interview, I was asked to imagine one thing that would help me do my job even better. I said, 'It would be going to Mexico.' You see, my sample books, the products which I produce, go to one of our fabricators down in Mexico. Can you believe it? *They ended up sending me to Mexico!* The trip made me feel like I really knew my job, like my job was really important to the Company. Just seeing who they were and what they needed gave me better ways to communicate with those folks."

But what is the effect on the *whole*, when these dreams are unleashed? At the second organizational summit, George Sharpe, a business unit vice president , stared at a wall covered with things the organization did exceptionally well. He pondered aloud:

"What does all this say to me, about who we are and what we might become? I have a dream of an organization in which we take this core technology of ours and use it for much more than just window coverings. "

As a result of George's dream – liberated through conversations, stories, and sensory-based imagining – Appreciative Inquiry transformed the strategic direction of the company.

Time after time, Appreciative Inquiry invites people at all levels of the organization into the dreaming process. It creates an impetus for doing things better . . . for *realizing dreams*, be they big or small, personal or organizational. It puts attention on the visionaries, rather than the squeaky wheels – on the path ahead, rather than the problems of the past. And it enables images of hope, potential and being the best to rise, like cream, to the surface of organizational life.

#4: Freedom to Choose to Contribute

"If each of us would ask, "How might I best use my time, energies and talents to serve the larger world?" we would transform this society and transform the planet. It is not for me or anyone else to tell people what to do. It is up to each of us to do those things that we know in our hearts we should do."

Marianne Williamson
The Fabric of the Future

Work can serve to separate us from what matters most to us; or it can serve as the vehicle through which we enact and realize our deepest calling (Fox, 1994). In patriarchal, command and control organizations, some other is said to know what is best for us. A manager, supervisor or employment advisor determines the scope of a job and whether or not we are "suited to it." People are matched to work based on the needs of the organization.

Not so in participatory organizations, where the freedom to choose one's work and learning opportunities is recognized as essential to creativity, cooperation, and well being. When people are matched to work, a job, or a project (or better yet free to *volunteer*) based on their interests and passion, their capacity to learn and to contribute is significantly enhanced. The scope, success and satisfaction of contribution is directly related to the freedom to choose the nature and extent of contribution.

One thing that differentiates Appreciative Inquiry from a number of other organizational change methodologies is that – at its best – people have complete freedom to choose how, when, and to what extent they'll engage in the process. They can and do join *only* when they become curious, stimulated, or inspired by a task, activity, or dream.

Many people choose only to participate in the interviews – and yet even that minimal level of engagement (generally no more than 1 to 2 hours of time) has a liberating effect on those who are involved. Joe Sherwood aptly describes the effect of the interviews alone, "When you see your ideas coming out and coming true, it reinforces your sense of influence. The interviews *opened the door* more than it had been open in the past . . . made it easier for people to simply *talk* to one another and share their feedback, thoughts, and ideas."

Some people get on board later in the process. Kathy Mayfield, for example, didn't have much good to say about the Appreciative Inquiry effort, initially. A printer with several years' tenure, she refused even to be interviewed. But eight months into the process, someone recruited her into an Action Group – formed at the first Summit – that was working on a task that piqued her curiosity and profound interest. Soon she had become one of the strongest supporters of Appreciative Inquiry in the entire organization.

John Cade believes this capacity to choose the nature and extent of one's contribution has a built-in mentoring and developmental quality. "Since some people are more comfortable following than leading," he suggests, "the Appreciative Inquiry process – which is grass-roots and designed to engage people in their own time and way – gives them "a hand to hold" and "helps train people to take responsibility for their own lives."

As is often the case with organizational change, there are some people who are more committed to, enthusiastic about, and engaged in the change effort than others. They become the "informal leaders" of the change effort. And again, because Appreciative Inquiry works to locate and channel people's interests and passions, that kind of involvement is nurtured and supported, rather than contained. Brian Bassett describes the relationship between this kind of engagement and the liberation of power:

> "Because our initial efforts flowed from people's *passions*, people had energy to do the work. This may seem like a no-brainer, but most organizational change efforts give directives, rather than following people's passions.
>
> Once people had success with the work that the really mattered to them – the work that was so important to them that they were willing to change their old habits and *play* – they wanted to act elsewhere . . . to *continue* acting. That's why people at Hunter Douglas kept moving from one [Action Group] to another! It wasn't because they *had* to . . . it was because it felt so good that they didn't want to stop.
>
> I've tasted the fruits of success! I know, deep inside of me, that I have made a difference, and that I'll *continue* to do so."

Not surprisingly, our research suggests that the more engaged people are in the intervention, the greater their experience of personal transformation. Joe Sherwood observes,

> "I've seen a *huge* difference in the people who have really embraced Appreciative Inquiry. Those who were more involved, and more willing to become part of the leadership of the process, seemed to grow the most."

The human gift of free will is exercised in the process of choosing to contribute. "Freedom to Choose to Contribute" brings out the best in people. It leads to learning, a sustained sense of power (the ability to innovate and influence) and an experience of fun at work. When people chose to do a project or piece of work and commit to others to do it, they get very creative and determined about it. They will do whatever it takes and learn whatever is needed to get the job done. And they seem to enjoy both the doing and the results. The "Freedom to Choose" stretches people and their organizations. It invites mutual commitment that is genuine and life giving. In organizations applying Appreciative Inquiry, the workplace is alive with excitement as people creatively contribute to the organization of their dreams.

#5: Freedom to Act with Support

"Leadership is about creating, day by day, a domain in which we and those around us continually deepen our understanding of reality and are able to participate in shaping the future. This, then, is the deeper territory of leadership – collectively 'listening to what is wanting to emerge in the world, and then having the courage to do what is required."

Joseph Jaworski
Synchronicity

To act with support is the quintessential act of positive interdependence. It requires that we understand the dreams of the organization, that we are willing to act in their service, and that we acknowledge the resourcefulness of others. To act with support is to act within a web of relationships. It requires an informed understanding of what the organization wants to become; and an open access to valued resources, capabilities and contributions.

In the first 3 D's, people learn to Discover, Dream, and Design the organization around the things that give life to the system. In the last "D" – Delivery (or Destiny, as it is also known), people are called to *act* on behalf of the things that passionately inspire them . . . the things that they *know* will make a difference in their organization and in the world. They are called to act in the service of the organization, with support from others at *all levels* of the organization.

Much organizational support is limited. To be supported by one part of an organization – one supervisor or one manager – leaves room for doubt, mistrust, and hesitation. Partial support breeds fragmentation. By contrast, when people know that the whole organization is aware of their project and willing to cooperate, they feel safe to experiment, innovate, and learn. In other words, whole-system support stimulates people to take on challenges, and draws them into acts of cooperation that bring forth their best.

Hunter Douglas' Destiny phase was organized in ways that provided both *leadership and organizational* support. Hunter Douglas business unit mangagers supported the Action Groups by consistently offering participants access to information, time, resources, skills training, and professional facilitation. They served as champions for the Action Groups and they served on the Appreciative Inquiry Advisory Team.

When members of the Appreciative Inquiry Advisory Team were asked to describe the support they provided and what they had learned about "leading" an appreciative change effort they commented: "We didn't have to do much [as leaders]. Mainly, we provided guidance and the green light for people. We helped build confidence that people's ideas and plans made sense."

In addition to providing counsel and resources, leadership also supported people's freedom to act by initiating and maintaining a communication network through which the Action Groups' activities and successes were broadcast to the entire organization. The communication network influenced and promoted *organizational support* for the work of the Action Groups. As members of the larger organization recognized and celebrated that their hopes and dreams (which had been expressed through Discovery, Dream, and Design) were taking form and coming to life in the work of the Action Groups, they offered support. Many people joined Action Groups underway and brought with them much needed creative thinking and organizational resources.

Brian Bassett describes the interplay that is suggested between leadership and organizational support, in this Freedom to Act with Support:

"The Action Groups that were formed at the end of the first Hunter Douglas Summit reeducated people about their power and influence in the organization. *We had always had support* to take action on behalf of the organization, but now – suddenly – people were *making resources available* and paying *attention* to what we were doing. They backed us up, and made it possible for us to follow through on – and finally *do* – the things that we knew needed to be done."

Of the initial 14 Action Groups, 11 either met or exceeded their original goals. Freedom to Act with Support resulted in:

- Development of a career pathing and mentoring system
- Establishment of an organization-wide recognition and reward system that was tied to Divisional Values
- Creation of a "virtual" university within the organization
- Initiation of a "new hire orientation" program, through which *every employee* could develop a sense of his or her relationship to the entire business
- Implementation of a high-engagement strategic planning process

But what of the three Action Groups that failed to meet of achieve their goals? Surprisingly, our research shows that this Freedom to Act with Support liberated individual and organizational power *even when the actions "failed."* Tina LaGrange's story powerfully testifies to that effect. She attended the first Summit just a few weeks after she had joined the company. Completely "fresh" to the process, she dove in and began working towards one of her dreams for the company: a cross-training program that would allow people to move from job to job, business unit to business unit. It was an idea that made impeccable sense, given one of the organization's greatest challenges, which was significant, regular, seasonal mandatory overtime.

"I came away from that Summit clear that cross-training was very, very important. I talked to my co-workers, and they all said, 'Yeah, yeah – *they'll* never support this or let it happen. Sure we need it, but it won't go through.'

Well, I joined an Action Group and worked hard. We were given the responsibility and authority to act on our vision. We designed a great program, proposed it to the Advisory Team, and got the go-ahead to test it. Then . . . *nobody signed up!!!*

Once we got over trying to 'drive' it through, we stepped back and thought about it. We realized, finally, that there was a loud, clear message trying to be heard. 'They' weren't the problem – it was the *organization*. The *organization* didn't really have a passion for cross training.

When our cross-training program died, I was disappointed but OK. In the end, the only thing I really accomplished was getting an answer – but that was a *big thing*. It meant that I had the power to *get an answer*."

The capacity to act in the service of the organization is too often limited by the lack of support, perceived or actual. With Appreciative Inquiry, people sense support from one another, from the organization's management and from the whole system. It is exhilarating and highly motivating to act on your own interests and passions while being backed up and supported by people at all levels of the organization. To take initiative is an adventure and a risk for many, to do so with full knowledge and support of colleagues throughout the organization creates a pathway for innovation, learning and self confidence.

#6: The Freedom to be Positive

"Happiness involves skills for everyday living that few people consistently practice. Instead of taking pride in our accomplishments, we tend to be self-critical. Instead of holding positive visions of the future, we run worst case scenarios . . . . Rather than regularly expressing appreciation to those we love, we find fault with them. . . . Genuine pride in a job well done, maintaining hope even during hard times, spontaneously expressing gratitude to someone – these are some of the simple pleasures that can enrich and vitalize our everyday lives, which we just don't enjoy often enough."

Stella Resnick, Ph.D.
The Pleasure Zone

Appreciative Inquiry assumes that every living system has untapped, rich, inspiring accounts of the positive. Link this "positive change core" directly to any change agenda, and changes never thought possible are suddenly and democratically mobilized (Cooperrider & Whitney, 1999).

Renee Chavez describes the effect that this last, seemingly simple Freedom had on her:

"I don't know if it's me or if it's Appreciative Inquiry – but *I like to be positive.* I liked doing the interviews, because I heard more positive things. Because of my involvement with Appreciative Inquiry, I got people thinking more positively. I think that a lot of the improved morale, the communication, the sense of community with the other departments came from Appreciative Inquiry and its positive approach."

Similarly, Tina LaGrange refers to the effect that this Freedom to be Positive had on her and the people around her.

"You know, there were people in the organization who were skeptical about this Appreciative Inquiry stuff. They thought it was just 'pollyannish.' But still they were affected by it. My smiles affected them, even if nothing else did."

What happens to an *organization* when the Freedom to be Positive is unleashed? "You know the old adage, 'Garbage in, garbage out?'" asks Joe Sherwood. "Well, Appreciative Inquiry replaces the 'garbage in' with positive feelings and positive experiences. It creates, instead, a cycle of 'energy in, energy out.' It 'jump starts' organizational change."

How odd to think that people need permission to be positive. And yet so it is today, in organization after organization. In too many organizations communication patterns are "deficit based" focusing attention on problems of the past, in lieu of possibilities for the future. Appreciative Inquiry in its choicefully affirmative stance is a radical departure. Appreciative Inquiry is an invitation to a positive revolution in change.

The "Ripple" Effect

The entire 4-D cycle of Appreciative Inquiry gives people the experience of personal and collective power. It gives them practice in exercising it, and in doing so *responsibly*, for the good of the whole. It breeds *confidence*, as it offers *support and recognition* for successful accomplishments. Having once experienced this liberation of power and the effect it has on the world . . . people are *permanently transformed..*

Liberation of Personal *Power*

Renee Chavez describes the long-term effect that her participation in the Appreciative Inquiry effort had on her self-esteem and sense of personal power. "I think this is a good job, but I *made* it that way. The only person who's going to get me what I want is *me*. Appreciative Inquiry helped me to express myself, and helped me learn to communicate in a better way. It helped me become more of who I've always been."

Likewise, Brian Bassett describes the effect the process had on those whom he observed. "As people tried and got results, they gained confidence. That led to five times as much input, and the desire to *get more involved.*"

Tina LaGrange believes that Appreciative Inquiry had on *permanent effect* on her career at Hunter Douglas:

"Shortly after coming to Hunter Douglas, I applied for a position in the Customer Information Center. I went through the interview process, and was turned down.

So I applied again, and was turned down again.

In the past, I might have stopped after this. I might have felt too discouraged to keep trying. But Appreciative Inquiry told me that I was responsible for doing what I needed to do and getting what I needed to be successful. So I found out what I was missing (which turned out to be technical training), got the training, and reapplied one more time.

This time, I got the job. I had persisted, because Appreciative Inquiry taught me that's how you get things done."

One of the more powerful stories about the long-term effect of Appreciative Inquiry comes from Kathy Mayfield – the "latecomer" to the process.

"[Appreciative Inquiry] created a complete turnaround for me. I'm painfully shy. Before Appreciative Inquiry, I would go down the hall and wouldn't look at anyone. Now I *march!* I talk to everyone – even the 'suits!' Since this change happened, I'm even getting a little better on the 'outside' [i.e., outside of work]. *Now I know I'm somebody.*

You know, I'm luckier than some people. I don't *have* to work. But something happened here that changed the way I saw my work. I realized that I didn't *have* to be here – but that I *wanted* to be here."

These and similar experiences tells us that liberated power breeds the ongoing liberation and expression of power. Power is like the proverbial genie in the bottle:

once liberated, it won't be re-contained. It continues to seek ways of expressing itself, within the organization *and the world.*

Liberation of Others' Power

Within organizations, people begin thinking and acting differently – begin asking questions, thinking for themselves, and engaging people around them in a more positive, more life-affirming way. In the process, they touch the "power" in the people around them. As Dottie Hamilton (stacker) says, "When we use Appreciative Inquiry with others, people feel encouraged to come to us and work with us."

As a result of this *extended liberation of power*, people who weren't involved with the original inquiry begin changing the way that they think and act. Brian Bassett's shipping department is a good example:

"The 'tag line' [for Appreciative Inquiry at Hunter Douglas] was 'All Voices . . . All Opinions . . . All Ideas.' I took that philosophy to heart and created team meetings in the area that I supervise. I would meet with the two most experienced employees in every part of the team every two weeks. We'd talk about different parts of our process, always asking the same two questions: 'How can we do this better?' 'How can we use what we know *works* - as well as what we've *dreamed about and imagined* – to make this the best it can possibly be?'

"Before this, decisions were being made by people who didn't *do* the job . . . people who didn't have much *experience* in the area. Now, I was *asking people* for what they knew. It gave people the leeway and the willingness to speak up. It gave them the confidence to make important changes and decisions related to our work.

"The results were incredible. Overtime dropped. Production increased. Our training process was transformed. You see, by asking for ideas and giving the people the information, skills, and support they to take intelligent action, Hunter Douglas has really saved a lot of money. If you look at and see what someone does well, and provide an environment in which they can build on it, *the things that are wrong get taken care of.*"

As power is liberated throughout the organization, people and cultures are transformed. Renee Chavez says, "The [positive changes in] morale, the communication, the sense of community with the other departments – all of that came from the work with Appreciative Inquiry."

So it's clear that the Appreciative Inquiry – through its Six Freedoms – unleashes personal and collective power within organizations. But what effect does this have on the world as a whole? Organizations have been called the "next frontier" for personal and spiritual transformation. As the place in which people spend most of their waking hours, they are the place that can – and *should* – have the most profound positive effect on how people live their lives in their families, communities, and world.

At Hunter Douglas, participants in the Appreciative Inquiry effort described long-term changes in their family relationships. Dottie Hamilton, for example, says "This works at home with my kids. It helps me get them involved in thinking things through for themselves and getting what they want." Bob Parkins, the Operations Maintenance Coordiantor, says that Appreciative Inquiry has positively affected the way that he relates to his ADHD son. Rinda Becker , an Executive Secretary, says that her use of Appreciative Inquiry on the occasion of her 30th wedding anniversary led to "one of the most insightful and meaningful conversations my husband and I have ever had." If these stories are to be believed, the power that Appreciative Inquiry liberates has the capacity to create transformations way beyond the individuals – even the organizations – that it originally touches.

Our Dream

Earlier in this paper, we described what we called the "power-full" organization. We described such an organization as one in which people care about and work towards being the *best they can possibly be,* personally, as well as organizationally . . . in which power is an *unlimited commodity or experience.*

Over the past several pages, we've talked about and shown how Appreciative Inquiry creates an environment that liberates personal and organizational power. We've illustrated ways in which that liberation unleashes previously unknown capacities for organizational performance. We've shown how liberated people tend to invite and welcome the power of the people around them – both within and outside their organization. We've talked about "power-full" organizations, and the increased "value" that those organizations enjoy.

Here is our dream: *organizations where people seek out and practice opportunities to be their best, and to bring out the best in others.*

Take a few moments now, to imagine an organization in which *everyone's* work life is intellectually, socially, and spiritually challenging and growthful. Imagine that "power-full" organization. Based on the transformations we've witnessed and experienced, we firmly believe that power-full organizations – even a power-full world – are within reach through the philosophy and practice of Appreciative Inquiry.

References

Bushe, G.R. (1995). Advances in Appreciative Inquiry as Organization Development Intervention. *Organization Development Journal, 13 (3), 14 – 22.*

Bushe, G.R. (1998). Appreciative Inquiry with Teams. *Organization Development Journal, 16 (3), 41 - 50.*

Chandler, D. Appreciative Inquiry as a Means of Engaging Employees in the Mission and Strategies of an Organziation. (1998). (Unpublished Masters Thesis, Pepperdine University).

Cooperride, D.L. (1990). Positive Image, Positive Action: The Affirmative Basis of Organizing. In Srivastva, S. & Cooperrider, D.L. ,Editors, (1990). Appreciative Management and Leadership. San Francisco: Jossey – Bass.

Cooperrider, D. L. & Whitney, D. (1999). Appreciative Inquiry. San Francisco: Berrett Koehler.

Fox, M. (1994), The Reinvention of Work. San Francisco: Harper.

Fogel, A. (1993). Developing Through Relationships. Chicago: University of Chicago Press

Freire, P. (1997). Pedagogy of the Heart. New York: Continuum.

Freire, P. (1997). Pedagogy of Hope. New York: Continuum.

Freire, P. (1970). Pedagogy of the Oppressed. New York: Continuum.

Gergen, K.J. (1991). The Saturated Self. New York: Basic Books.

Gergen, K.J. (1994). Realities and Relationships: Soundings in Social Construction. Cambridge, MA: Harvard University Press.

Gergen, K.J. (1999). An Invitation to Social Construction. Thousand Oaks, CA: Sage.

Jaworski, J. (1996). Synchronicity. San Francisco: Berrett-Koehler.

Khalsa, G.S. & Kaczmarski, K. (1996). The United Religions Initiative Summit Conference Summary, June 24 –28, 1996. San Francisco: The United Religions Initative.

Kelly, K (1998). New Rules for the New Economy. New York: Penguin.

Kouzes, J. M. & Posner, B.Z. (1987). The Leadership Challenge. San Francisco: Jossey-Bass.

Ludema, J.D., Wilmot, T.B. & Srivastva, S. (1997). Organizational Hope: Reaffirming the Constructive Task of Social and Organizational Inquiry. *Human Relations, 50 (8), 1015 – 1052.*

McNamee, S. & Gergen K.J., Editors, (1999). Relational Responsibility. Thousand Oaks, CA: Sage.

Resnick, S. (1997). The Pleasure Zone. Berkeley, CA: Conari.

Ryan, M., Editor, (1999). The Fabric of the Future. Berkeley, CA: Conari.

Srivastva, S. & Cooperrider, D.L. ,Editors, (1990). Appreciative Management and Leadership. San Francisco: Jossey – Bass.

Starhawk, "Envisioning the Future," in Ryan, M., Editor, (1999). The Fabric of the Future. Berkeley, CA: Conari.

Tichy, N. M. & Devanna, M. (1986). The Transformational Leader. New York: John Wiley

Whitney, D. & Cooperrider, D. L. (1998). The Appreciative Inquiry Summit: Overview and Applications. *Employment Relations Today* 35, No. 2, 17 - 28.

Whitney, D. & Schau, C. (1998). Appreciative Inquiry: An Innovative Process for Organization Change. *Employment Relations Today* 25, No. 1, 11- 21.

Chapter 14

INITIATING CULTURE CHANGE IN HIGHER EDUCATION THROUGH APPRECIATIVE INQUIRY

Robert L. Head, RODP
Benedictine University
Michele M. Young, Ed.D.
Benedictine University

Abstract

The purpose of this paper is to describe an attempt to initiate culture change in the faculty of Benedictine University utilizing Appreciative Inquiry as the intervention. The traditional academic culture, dating back to the medieval period, is ill-equipped to respond to the public's demand for change and increasing accountability. The fragmentation and alienation which persists in the academy cries for the development of shared purpose and common values if it is to survive. Appreciative Inquiry is designed to articulate and affirm the positive values of an organization. This paper presents a summary of the process utilized, the outcomes of the intervention and the learnings we derived from this experience.

The State of Higher Education

Higher education is in trouble. This sentiment can be heard both without and within the academy today. Whether the focus is the relationship between cost and value, curricular inclusiveness or increasing competition from without, or shrinking resources and balancing priorities from within, change is required and, in fact, long

OD Journal, No. 2, Summer 1998, pp. 65-72.

overdue. The demand for change in higher education has taken many faces, including cost-cutting, outsourcing, business partnerships, faculty retrenchment and curricular redesign, among others.

In 1971, Sanford observed "We find in our institutions of higher learning widespread unhappiness and cynicism." (p. 357). This view was echoed by Jensen (1995) 24 years later when he speaks of the disaffection and cynicism pervasive in our colleges and universities. In a recent research project, Wilger and Massy (1996) interviewed faculty at 20 higher educational institutions. They found the prevailing theme to be one of atomization and fragmentation.

These findings, and others like them, illustrate that the current academic culture is not providing an environment in which faculty can find meaning and fulfillment in their work. The resultant bitterness can sound a death-knell to an organization besieged on all sides.

If the culture of an organization is the sum of the attitudes, beliefs and behaviors of its people, cultural change can only be accomplished by impacting those variables. Cultural assessment and change has long been housed in the discipline of organization development. However, organization development rarely has been utilized in colleges and universities (Boyer and Crockett, 1973).

One possible explanation for this is that the academic culture, with its foundations in rational thought and dialogue, is ill-suited to the feeling and relationship focus of OD. Or, it may be that the autonomy so strongly defended by faculty prevents the collaboration needed to engage in organizational change. A third explanation may be that colleges and universities rarely invest the financial resources necessary to engage in a system-wide OD effort (Bergquist, 1992).

The traditional academic culture is grounded in philosophy, ritual and practice that can be traced back for hundreds of years. In this culture, loyalty to the discipline transcends commitment to the institution. Tradition and custom serve as the bedrock of the professorial identity (Freedman, 1979). Subcultures confuse the issue further, as faculty can be divided by discipline, level of development (Freedman, 1979) and educational philosophy (Bergquist, 1992).

The resistance and complexity generated by these realities requires any OD effort to utilize processes designed to gain the faculty's active support and involvement for experimenting and modeling new behaviors (Boyers, 1973). Since it is anathema to faculty for anything to be imposed from without, the process of change must generate from the voice of the faculty. An OD intervention which seems uniquely designed to fit the academy is Appreciative Inquiry.

Appreciative Inquiry

Appreciative Inquiry (AI), developed by David Cooperrider and Suresh Srivastva, "is a philosophy, it's a methodology for working with organizations, and it's an intervention theory," (Cooperrider, cited in Gotches and Ludema, 1995). The theory of AI is grounded in five principles (Cooperrider, 1994):

1. **Constructionist Principle.** Our capacity for imagination and creation of images of the future allows for human systems (including organizations) to be altered or reconstructed.

2. **Simultaneity Principle.** Seeds of change are planted in the first question asked. Therefore, inquiry and intervention are interrelated and simultaneous.

3. **Poetic Principle.** Organizations are like an open book or poetry. They are open to multiple interpretations and conclusions.

4. **Anticipatory Principle.** An image of the future precedes the actual change.

5. **Positive Principle.** The more positive the question, the more positive the data. The more positive the willingness to participate, the more lasting the change process.

Unlike traditional problem-solving which seeks to identify and analyze problems in systems and relationships, AI seeks to appreciate and dream about their possibilities. Where problem-solving views organizations as a series of problems to be solved, AI looks at organizations as mysteries to be embraced. The Appreciative Inquiry model is constructed in four phases (Cooperrider, 1996):

1. **Discovery.** Determining what it is about an organization that should be appreciated and valued. What gives life to the organization? What in the organization is exceptional?

2. **Destiny.** What we learn in the process of inquiry should lead to sustainable change and growth.

3. **Dream.** Envisioning possibilities for the organization's future. What might be?

4. **Design.** What is the ideal? What is the human potential of organizational life?

Cooperrider (cited in Gotches and Ludema, 1995) states, "AI is a deliberate attempt to look at what gives life to organizations, and use the power of positive questioning to develop a data base out of which we can envision more provocative and positive futures" (p. 7). Barrett (1995) describes the appreciative process as a combination of emotional and cognitive energy which creates a positive image of the future and uncovers the core values of an organization.

There is a growing body of research to indicate that core values lead to organizational effectiveness. Collins (1995) reported on a study of exceptional organizations in the corporate arena. Those firms included Hewlett-Packard, 3M, Disney, Marriott and Motorola, among others. The firms had an average age of nearly 100 years, and combined they outperformed the stock market 15–1 since 1926. The key finding of the research was that these firms, all high-performing organizations, were finding of the research was that these firms, all high-performing organizations, were "guided more by a core ideology—core values and a sense of purpose—than comparison organizations." (p. 84).

Schroeder, Brief and Guzzo (1996) identify two factors that are important in creating sustainable organizational change. The first is changing what members of the organization believe, while the second refers to the degree to which members understand what the organization values. We contend that mutual trust is an outcome of the convergence of these factors. Allowing Benedictine University to identify and commonly agree upon its core values would generate the framework for a shared purpose. This shared commitment will assist the institution in building an environment of trust and fostering constructive responses to change (Policy Perspectives, 1996).

The Change Process

Early in the summer of 1996, key administrators of Benedictine University engaged in a process of updating the 1994 strategic plan which formulated initiatives designed to increase the competitive advantage of the institution. One of these initiatives was related to academic culture. There was tacit agreement that a culture change was integral to any effective improvement in the institution's functioning. Therefore, an initiative related to culture was included in the document. It stated: "Establish a long-term strategy that will address issues that negatively affect morale in an attempt to develop higher levels of trust, cooperation, team-building, and community across the campus."

While no formal assessment of culture had been conducted, substantial anecdotal evidence existed to validate a less than desirable culture and a need for a second-order change. To add validity to these impressions, a content analysis was conducted of the minutes of faculty meetings and memos generated through the previous two years. The results of the content analysis lent support to the initial diagnosis.

Generally, the culture could be characterized as one of fragmentation and mistrust. The lack of trust manifested itself in increasingly intense discussions around governance and participation. Also prevalent was a language of separation and perceived hierarchy between employee groups.

An initial tactical decision was to engage senior members of the faculty who shared in the desire to improve the culture at Benedictine University. The first outcome from this planning group's discourse was to target the fall opening faculty meeting for initiating dialogue around culture. The opening faculty meeting was selected for two important reasons:

1. It brought together all returning and new faculty, who tend to be energized with the prospects of a new year. The hope was to capitalize on the high

TABLE 1. The Benedictine Core Values

Learning Community	A community in which education is the central value where both the sharing and discovery of knowledge are valued and rewarded.
Benedictine Community	A community which shares the values reflected in the "Rule of St. Benedict." A community which seeks to integrate the growth of the mind, body and spirit in every member, while calling each one to discover the presence of God in their own unique life circumstances. A community which strives for openness to the process of change and growth within the context of faithful commitment to the stewardship of God's gifts.
Human Community	A community where diversity is sought and appreciated; where all members of the community are treated fairly in a supportive manner, and provided with the opportunity for meaningful growth and development. A community in which social justice is understood as a driving value which is taught, lived and modeled by members of the community.
Open Community	A community in which differences are dealt with in an open, constructive and appreciative manner free from the fear of retribution; a community which recognizes its relationship to the external community of which it is an integral part; is sensitivie to and appropriately responsive in fulfilling its responsibility to that larger community.
Effective Community	A community in which each member is working toward explicit objectives and valued for their contribution to the mission of the school; a community in which each member internalizes a responsibility for, and is accountable for the most effective use of the organization's resources.
Celebrative Community	A community where the achievements and accomplishments of the members are recognized and celebrated by all; one in which rituals affirming both tradition and change are widely shared.

energy level and positive outlook and to create a collaborative roadmap for change.

2. The meeting had traditionally been used to establish a theme and priorities for the year. Symbolically, it was important that a dialogue on culture occur at this meeting of the full faculty and with visible participation and support of the administration, most notably the president. After considerable discussion, the second outcome of the planning group's efforts was the selection of AI as the

appropriate intervention. The institution had some experience with AI but, to date, had not utilized it to engage the faculty.

The final choice of AI as the appropriate intervention for an academic environment was based on the following:

1. It requires a high level of participation that is not always realized in a traditional problem-solving intervention where there is an exploration of a problem (and, inherently, an identification of cause/blame).

2. It pursues a spirited, intellectual pursuit of an ideal, which is congruent with an academician's pursuit of understanding and truth.

3. Its principles are grounded in the research of Maslow, Lewin, and Gergen (Cooperrider and Srivastva, 1987).

Formatting the Appreciative inquiry intervention was the next task of the planning group. Should we utilize a Search Conference method capturing the energies of the entire faculty simultaneously? Would we have "trained" facilitators interview each faculty member? These are some of the questions with which we wrestled. Given the AI principle of simultaneity, the idea that inquiry and intervention occur together, we chose to have one faculty member interview another. Following the interview, the two individuals would switch roles.

The next task was to develop the AI protocol. A traditional AI model served as the framework covering concepts such as:

•   organization and affiliation

•   organization and personal high points

•   visioning/common purpose

•   collaborative processes/cooperation

•   commitment/empowerment

Another tactical decision was to enlist a senior faculty member, also a member of the planning group, to deliver a brief explanation of AI, the purpose of the inquiry, and specific instructions. This introduction, delivered by a respected natural scientist who had become an enthusiastic supporter of AI's possibilities, was critical to engage the faculty in this intervention.

Of the 86 faculty present, all but one participated in the interview process. Interviews were alive with stories of Benedictine University's strengths which included its students, academic purpose, the diversity and dedication of its people, and the fundamental grounding in the traditions of its Benedictine heritage. For illustration, one comment is included here:

> One of my most satisfying experiences at Benedictine University was working with science faculty from several disciplines to create a successful grant proposal. A novel feature of the proposal was the creation of an interdisciplinary laboratory course intended for all entering science majors. In doing so, faculty members from Biology, Chemistry, and Physics

were able to put aside partisan interests and to transcend the traditional discipline boundaries. The Howard Hughes Medical Institute awarded this proposal $600,000.

The themes and stories that emerged from the interviews were shaped by a volunteer group of faculty into a set of Core Values (Table 1).

Conclusion

Although the adoption of the Benedictine University Core Values, which developed through this intervention and the entire organizational development process, is far from complete, the use of AI in our institution has yielded some promising results. Our assessment of the intervention produced the following learnings:

1. The all but universal (n-1) participation in the intervention lent support to our choice of venue and the content of the protocol.

2. The speed at which we were able to capture data from all faculty proved very economical.

3. The intellectual isolation inherent in the faculty role was bridged by the partnering of faculty and the sharing of values through the interview process.

4. The focus on the positive and the possible produced an upbeat tone rarely found in faculty meetings.

5. The AI intervention produced an environment where cynicism was set aside and faculty were able to transcend the problems and celebrate the strengths of our organization.

6. The themes which were developed from the interview data do reflect a sense of shared values and a commitment to a common purpose among the faculty.

7. The themes developed by the faculty were very similar to those developed in an AI intervention conducted previously with administrators and staff.

In the months that followed the AI intervention, a small group of faculty and administrators (Core Values Group) continued the work begun at the opening faculty meeting. Specific accomplishments of this group include: (1) the development of behavioral definitions for the core values; (2) the creation of a preamble to the core values document; and (3) the development of an implementation plan which will guide the incorporation of the core values into the activities and relationships of all members of the university community.

Of equal importance with the tasks accomplished during this period, the members of the Core Values Group identified several outcomes which were personal in nature. These included areas such as developing a working relationship with extremely committed members of the university community; increasing sensitivity to the environment and culture; identifying the areas of congruency and incongruency between the historical values of the institution and current behaviors; and serving as change agents to help make informed decisions about the future of the organization.

The refinement and adoption of these Benedictine Core Values continues to be a work-in-progress for Benedictine University. However, the successful engagement of the faculty in the AI process and the resultant core values document give evidence of a culture which can once again anticipate a more vibrant future through a shared language of affirmation.

References

Austin, S. (1990). Assessing academic climates and cultures. In W. Tierney (Ed.), *New Direcitons for Institutional Research*, 61–74. San Francisco: Jossey-Bass.

Barrett, F. (1995). Creating appreciative learning cultures. *Organizational Dynamics*. 24, 36–49.

Berquist, W. (1992). *The Four Cultures of the Academy*. San Francisco: Jossey-Bass.

Boyer, R. and Crockett, C. (1973). OD in higher education: Introduction. *Journal of Higher Education*. 44, 339–351.

Collins, J. (1995). Building companies to last. *Inc*. 17, 83–86.

Cooperrider, D. (1994). *A Constructive Approach to Organization Development*. Unpublished manuscript.

Cooperrider, D. (1996). *Appreciative Inquiry Manual*. Unpublished manuscript. Case Western Reserve University.

Cooperrider, D. and Srivastva, S. (1987). Appreciative Inquiry in organizational life. In W. Pasmore and R. Woodman (Eds.) *Research in Organizational Change and Development*. Greenwich, CT: JAI Press.

Freedman, M. (with Brown, W., Ralph, N., Shukraft, R., Bloom, J., and Sanford, N.) (1979). *Academic Culture and Faculty Development*. Berkeley, CA: Montaigne.

Gotches, G. and Ludema, J. (1995). An interview with David Cooperrider on AI and the future of organization development. *OD Journal*, 13, 5–13.

Jensen, E. (1995). The bitter groves of academe. *Change*, Jan-Feb, 8–11.

Sanford, J. (1971). Academic culture and the teacher's development. *Sounding*, Winter, 357–371.

Schneider, B., Brief, A., and Guzzo, R. (1996). Creating a climate and culture for sustainable organizational change. *Organizational Dynamics*, Spring, 7–19.

Shared Purposes. (1996). *Policy Perspectives*. Philadelphia: University of Pennsylvania, Institute for Research on Higher Education.

Wilger, A. and Massy, W. (1993). Prospects for restructuring: A sampling of the faculty climate. *Policy Perspectives*. Philadelphia: University of Pennsylvania, Institute for Research on Higher Education.

Chapter 15

SAVING TOMORROW'S WORKFORCE

Christopher Anne Easley
Benedictine University
Therese Yaeger
Benedictine University
Peter Sorensen
Benedictine University

Fact: The Chicago area is home to one of the largest gang populations in the world.

Question: You might ask: "Why such a topic for a training and development publication?"

Answer: Simply put, today's youth are tomorrow's workforce. For those in the training and development field, social concern for youth as well as adults should be our over-arching responsibility.

Worldwide, young people are dying at record rates from varying forms of violence. Domestically, we are losing far too many to gang violence. Gangs are a major problem in our society, and sociologists, psychologists, and researchers have been studying gang behavior for decades attempting to understand the underlying behavioral patterns that give rise to gang behavior.

Over ten years ago, Johnston and Packard shocked the nation with their "Workforce 2000" demographics (Johnston and Packard, 1986). These changing demographics indicate a significant percentage of youth are affected by gang violence. If we are to maintain and re-populate a viable, thriving work force, corporations cannot stay uninvolved with this gang issue. We are losing our youth, and if they are not physically dying, youth still may be mentally dying.

Current research suggests that our youth can articulate vision; however, many have lost hope in their future. Traditional researchers continue to study youth in gangs as a problem to be solved. In this problem orientation, the researcher develops knowledge by emphasizing a critical approach to social problems believed to arise from the social context (Tenkasi et al., 1994).

Training Today, Jan–Feb, 1999.

Gangs as Organizations

A recent gang report states that many "ethnic" gangs are forming complex organizational structures as they form alliances with other ethnic gangs. Hagedorn examined the structure of "People and Folks," and reported how various gangs have joined together to become "nation" structures. Specifically within the Midwest, the People Nation includes the Vice-Lords, El Rukins and Latin Kings, and the Folks, the Gangster Disciples, and Spanish Cobras (Hagedorn, 1988).

The Department of Justice also published survey results within this report. Of significance were answers to the question: "What do you believe is the biggest contributor to the street gang problem in California?" Respondents cited as issues: poverty; lack of education and job training; breakdown of the family unit; lack of parental control, supervision and family values resulting in the gang family replacing the traditional family; lack of positive role models; lack of community involvement; community apathy; perception that there is a lack of economic opportunity combined with increased economic problems; lack of employment opportunities and adequate jobs to earn a living.

Another question was: "What do you believe will be the most significant trend pertaining to street gangs in California by the year 2000?" The top reply was an increase in the sophistication of the gangs and better organization and structure (Gangs, 2000).

Some researchers are looking at the gang structure from an organizational perspective. Martin Sanchez Jankowski, an associate professor of Sociology at University of California Berkeley, conducted a 10-year study of 37 gangs of varying ethnic backgrounds. The research centered in low income areas, where gangs have been institutionalized for years. The ethnic groups studied included Mexican Americans, African Americans, Salvadorans, Nicaraguans, Puerto Ricans, Dominican Jamaicans, and Irish gangs. Jankowski reported these gangs are an organizational response to inequality and poverty that acts in an entrepreneurial manner (Lockwood, 1993).

While gangs frequently engage in criminal activity, Jankowski reported that crime is not the central issue. Jankowski's study focused on the organizational traits of gangs, which included the nature, dynamics, and impact of the gang's organizational qualities. He reported that one reason that society does not understand the gang phenomenon clearly is that there have not been enough systematic studies undertaken as to how the gang works as an organization (Jankowski, 1991). Sociologists associate the individual gang member with the organization, but do not have much evidence as to what it is about the organization and its macrodynamics that makes the gang member's behavior different from what it would be if he or she were not in an organization (Jankowski, 1991).

Need for Alternative Strategies

Current research on Chicago gangs appears to echo similar data. Youth in gangs are not surrounded by positive images that suggest that they could either control or change their life, their environment, or their future. As researchers and practitioners, we must be careful to avoid posing negative questions to youth involved in gangs, as the very nature of these questions may contribute to the development of gangs.

If we critically examine the research on gangs to date, we understand the need for alternative strategies. Change intervention strategies must be multidimensional, multi-level, qualitative, discontinuous, radical organizational change and includes complete paradigmatic shifts (French and Bell, 1995). Therefore, when examining the gang as an organization, we must give the consideration to gang individuals and attempt to understand gang behavior as a group in the process of interacting. Numerous theories of group development have provided explanations for individual and collective behavior in a group context and group culture. However, few traditional methodologies for group inquiry help us understand the awareness of group members as they are living in the present moment of group life. We must begin to question the assumptions these youth have internalized that drive their behaviors and the behaviors of their gang (Srivastva and Barrett, 1988).

The rise of gangs today suggests that the previous strategies oriented towards changing youth in gangs simply do not work. Organizational development should play a key role in the transformation of youth in gangs. Within the concept of organizational transformation is embedded the need for vision, or the importance of purposes, goals and directions (Golembiewski, 1986). Youth in gangs need a purpose for continuing to live. They also need an alternative vision for using the skills that they possess such as leadership, entrepreneurship, decision making, problem solving, etc.—skills found in corporate board rooms—that Jankowski found in his research. However, if gang youth are continually exposed to interventions that focus on prescriptive, suppressive techniques and emerge from negative deficient orientations, we risk suppressing any anticipatory images they could envision that would suggest moving from their present conditions.

The OD Approach

OD practitioners possess the skills to lead the charge of deactivating gangs—using alternative OD interventions. Within the disciplines of humanistic psychology and OD has emerged the concept of collaborative inquiry (Reason, 1988), which goes past traditional research methodologies that tend to undermine the self-determination and concept of self that "subjects" possess (Heron, 1971, Reason, 1988).

Inquiry into organizational structures studies organizations as evolving, transforming, social constructions, malleable to human choice (Barrett and Srivastva, 1991). Therefore, before attempting to understand the behavior of youth in gangs, we must examine the human choices that individuals in the gang make and the underlying premises for those choices. We must also understand the imagery that drives their choices and the metaphors that they are exposed to.

Currently, research is being conducted using an Appreciative Inquiry (AI) mode of intervention with gangs that approaches "organizing" as a miracle of cooperative human interaction which needs to be affirmed (Cooperrider and Srivastva, 1987; Tenkasi et al., 1994). When using AI with gangs, we seek to locate and highlight the life-giving properties of youth when they function as individuals as well as when they organize. Through affirmation, gang members are most likely to realize what makes them and their ability to work together unique, thus opening possibilities of using gang resources to change the economical and social decay in which they live. Through the use of AI, we are helping gang members seek out the best of "what they are" in order to provide an impetus of their imaging "what might be" (Tenkasi et al., 1994).

Helping Tomorrow's Workforce Today

Most critically, however, youths in gangs must be able to envision a different reality—one that is important to them as individuals and as an organization. With a new year comes a resolution: Let's resolve not to wait until the next millennium to save tomorrow's workforce.

Chris Easley is Director of the DuPage Center for Multiculturalism at Benedictine University where she teaches in the Business Administration and Master's in Management and Organizational Behavior Programs. As a candidate in Benedictine University's doctoral program in Organization Development, her dissertation title is "The Role of Appreciative inquiry in the Fight to Save Our Youth".

References

Barrett, F, and Srivastva, S. (1991). "History as a mode of inquiry in organizational life: A role for human cosmogony", *Human Relations*, vol. 44, pp. 236–244.

Cooperrider, D. and Srivastva, S. (1987). "Appreciative inquiry in organizational life." *Research in Organizational Change and Development*, pp. 140–145.

California Department of Justice. Division of Law Enforcement, Bureau of Investigation (March 1993), *Gangs 2000: A call to action.* The Attorney Generals report on the impact of criminal street gangs on crime and violence in California by the year 2000.

French, W. L. Bell, C. H. *Organization Development,* Englewood Cliffs, NJ: Prentice-Hall, Inc.

Golembiewski, R (1989). *Organization Development, ideas, and issues,* New Brunswick, NJ: Transaction Publishers.

Hagedorn, J., with Macon, P (1988). *People and Folks, Gangs Crime and the Underclass in a Rustbelt City,* Chicago, IL: Lake View Press.

Johnson, W. B. and Packer, A. H. (1987). *Workforce 2000: Work and Workers for the 21st Century.* Indianapolis, IN: Hudson Institute.

Lockwood, A., (1993). The professor of gangs." *Focus in Change,* n 10, p. 10–14.

Reason, Peter (1988). *Human Inquiry in Action, Developments in New Paradigm Research,* Newbury Park, CA: Sage Publications.

Sanchez-Jankowski, M. (1991). *Islands in the Street, Gangs and American Urban Society,* Berkeley: CA. University of California Press.

Srivastva, S., and Barrett, F. (1998). The transforming nature of metaphors in group development: A study in group theory," *Human Relations,* v. 41, Number 1, pp. 31–64.

Tenkasi, R., Thatchenkery, T., Barrett, F. and Manning, M. (1994). "The impact of schemes and inquiry on consultants' constructions of expectations about the client system." *CEO Publications* (G 94-13 (256), 1994) pp. 1–29.

Chapter 16

A Story of Nutrimental in Brazil: How Wholeness, Appreciation, and Inquiry Bring the Best in Human Organization

Ilma O.Barros
Case Western Reserve University
David L. Cooperrider
Case Western Reserve University

What in the world is "wholeness"? Physicist, David Bohm sought to understand wholeness. He wrote: "The English word health is based on the Anglo-Saxon word 'hale', meaning 'whole'; that is: to be healthy is to be whole." And he concluded, "...All of this indicates that man has sensed always that wholeness is an absolute necessity to make life worth living. Yet, over the ages he has generally lived in fragmentation." (Bohm, D. 1980)

What in the world is wholeness? According to Daft and Lengel, integrity is wholeness. They wrote that becoming whole and complete means that the elements of higher self — compassion, honesty, and generosity to others— are developed and expressed. And that being whole requires the subtle and the strong force in one's self to be integrated. Another way to consider wholeness as integrity is to understand wholeness as the capacity to be and to feel connected to a larger whole, to something beyond oneself - a capacity to feel a sense of real accomplishment when one has contributed to the whole.

Wholeness as a desire, wholeness as integrity and yet, we see all around us examples of our propensity to live in fragmentation. Wholeness can then be understood as a complex paradox in human's life. We are all in search for completeness, and therefore we aim to make our organizations, our relationships, our lives, and ourselves whole. Nevertheless, our natural tendency is to divide, fragment and differentiate. This is true in organizational life: fragmented, divided and separated in departments, divisions, and business units. But what happens when there is

Training Today, Jan–Feb, 1999.

innovative strategic planning and decision making that brings the whole organization, the entire system together in the same room? Can this experience bring wholeness? Can this enhance the possibility of integrity and bring out the best of human organizations?

A Story of a System: What is Nutrimental?

Nutrimental Industria e Comercio de Alimentos S.A. is a manufacturer of healthy food products, located in Curitiba, State of Parana, in Brazil. It is a privately held Brazilian corporation, founded in 1968, that produces a wide range of food products targeting several different markets. It employs approximately 700 people and had revenues of US$ 70 million in 1997.

In 1968, when Nutrimental was founded, its purpose was to manufacture bean soup and powder mashed potatoes to supply a public school lunch program from the Brazilian Government. Twenty years later with revenues of US$ 60 million it had a variety of products and a considerable technological, economical, and organizational capacity to not only take the leadership in supplying governmental programs, but also to expand into the consumer market.

In the early 1990's, Nutrimental decided to create a diversification strategy called 'Nova Era' (New Era), that aimed at reducing the dependency from government programs, as well as, enhancing the organizational culture that would be in position to identify, develop and implement the necessary changes for the new Nutrimental.

In 1991, during the implementation of the New Era project, all government programs collapsed with the government canceling orders. From 1992 to 1995 Nutrimental had very limited working capital.

In 1997 the organization decided to face boldly their need to go through a complete transformation. The leadership contacted us at Case Western Reserve University and invited us to work with them as they focused their goals on the development of a workshop that would help the organization regain its confidence and become more competitive. Appreciative Inquiry (A.I.) was the approach selected to help them reach their objective. We worked with them to launch a two-year project that started with an "Appreciative Inquiry Summit" and helped the organization identify its best practices and most important strengths.

Movements Into Wholeness: Whole System Dialogue

Figure 1 is a diagram of an Appreciative Inquiry flow. This cycle is dynamic and can be seen as fast and informal as in a conversation with a friend or colleague. Or it can be seen as formal as an organization-wide analysis involving every stakeholder, including customers, suppliers, partners and the like.

It shows four key stages in AI:

- **Discovery**   mobilizing a system inquiry into the positive change core;
- **Dream**   creating a clear, results-oriented vision from discovered potential and higher purpose;
- **Design**   creating possibility propositions of the ideal organization capable of realizing the new dream; and
- **Destiny**   strengthening the affirmative capability of the whole system to build hope and momentum around a deep purpose and creating processes for learning, adjustment, and improvisation over time.

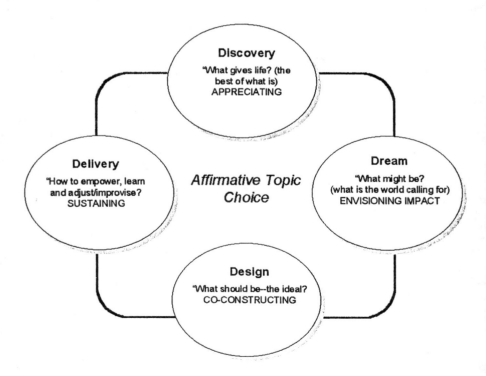

Figure 1. The Appreciative Inquiry "4-D" Cycle

In September 1997 we prepared for the A.I. Summit. The day before the Summit we facilitated a daylong meeting. 180 people attended, including employees, managers, clients and bankers. They were introduced to A.I. and given the opportunity to practice A.I. interviews with each other. The following day we had 700 people in a warehouse inside the main manufacturing plant in dialogue about Nutrimental's past, present and future.

Helping Each Other Into The Power of The Question

After we introduced ourselves and explained why we were there, we invited them to reflect back on positive moments, "We acknowledge that there are good times and not so good moments but we want you to focus on the good for now". They were asked to think about a time when they felt most alive, most effective, and most proud of the organization. We explained that it could be anything: a project they were part of, a relationship with the boss or peers, etc. We encouraged them to take notes about their experiences because later they would have a chance to share their answers with others during the Appreciative Interview process.

The second question we posed had three parts: first think about themselves, second their work and third their organization. We asked them to be bold in their reflection: "What do you value most about yourself, as a human being, a parent, a friend, a colleague? What do you value most about your job, the work you do? What do you value most about your organization?"

The third question was: "Now we want you to use the hat of an anthropologist. Take a helicopter ride, look down to this organization and you will see that it is a living system. What is the core factor that gives life to this organization, a factor without which organizing would not be possible? And the fourth question was: "What are your three wishes for this organization?"

Story Sharing and Deep Listening

Next step was to share their experience with one another. We asked them to find someone, preferably someone they did not know, and share their notes. We encouraged the person who was listening to have the curiosity of a child and to ask as many questions as possible so it would help the other person to remember his/her own experience in more detail. Each person had around 20 minutes to share and then they switched roles.

Making Connections

The entire system did A.I. interviews and after they were done with the interview we asked the pair to find more pairs. They met in small groups to discuss their ideas and share stories as the A.I. cycle continued to unfold. There were 70 small groups with 10 participants in each one. Those who had attended the pre-summit day of A.I. training were asked to join different groups and helped to ensure that the small groups process engaged each other with opportunities for everyone to speak. We gave them one hour to finish this task.

It is in the discovery phase that people start to become aware of their strengths and this is one of the most exciting moments in the Appreciative Inquiry cycle. The opportunity to remember and revive positive aspects of their past merging in everyone's storytelling. Woven into those stories were examples of innovations, courage, effectiveness, and collaboration. Stories full of energy of times that felt "right". These stories filled the room with information and remembrances that gave them the courage to feel responsible for creating the image of the future for their organization. Together in the room they felt both encouraged and the courage to have faith that the changes they would like to see happening were possible. Together they felt that they were capable of making those changes happen.

Whole System Meeting Together Again

After their small group discussions they came back to the large room. We asked them to save the content of their stories for later and to say a few words in relation to how they felt about sharing their experience and listening to other people's experience. [*Depending on the time that you have for the workshop, you may want to ask them to choose one powerful story from their group and ask each group to share with everybody*].

The stories were tremendously powerful. People started to realized that the stories they were telling and listening to were not only bringing a new awareness about their past but were also bringing back the courage, the excitement, the determination, present in the memory of those experiences. We still remember one man who had never spoken before an audience in his whole life. Supported by his group, he stood up and using a microphone told the most amazing stories to 700 people. It was a moment of profound reflection about breaking limits and taking action. This first part of the workshop took the whole morning.

In the afternoon, when they came back from lunch, we asked them: "We want you to think about all the things that, no matter how much Nutrimental changes in the next ten years, you want to maintain"? So we asked them to go back to the same group they were part of in the morning and share their ideas and to take some notes about their discussion.

On the flip chart, they were supposed to make a list of the ten things that they wanted to keep, even with all the changes they wanted to see happening at Nutrimental. They had one hour to finish this task. After they were done they went back to the large group and had their flip chart papers on the wall so others could also see.

The purpose of this question was to help them to identify what they valued most about their organization. Thinking about things they were good at and then thinking about what they wanted to maintain would help them to understand the unique factors (e.g. core processes, values, traditions, relationships, leadership etc.) that made the successful moments possible.

Because we had 70 groups we negotiated with them so half of the groups would present the first task and the other half would present the next one. They agreed and started the 35 groups presentation. While the groups were presenting, the plenary was completely engaged with what was said and after each presentation the next group would start without any disruption to the process.

For the next task we asked them the following question: "In order for Nutrimental to become the ideal organization you imagine, what are the things you think should change?" Again, we asked them to think individually for about 5 minutes and take notes and then go back to their groups. They had 1 hour to finish this task. They should come back with a list of ten things that their group decided should change.

The suggestions were rich and thoughtful. One of the CEOs of Nutrimental, Arthur Leme, passing by the gallery walk said: "*It is interesting that most of the things they are suggesting will directly affect them for the better and several of them I could resolve only by signing a piece of paper. It is also amazing their acknowledgment of some of our practices, I used to think that they had taken for granted, but in fact they are showing how much they have appreciated. That is proof of the importance to open for dialogue*"

The Many Faces of Wholeness

There are many ways in which organizations express the transformations that they are going through. In business terms, results are expressed in a quantitative manner. Figure 2 shows the average return per worker the period between September/96 and April/97 compared to September/97 and April/98.

Figure 2. The Average Return Per Worker

The increase of 22.3% on the average return per worker reflected the dynamic atmosphere of the organization after the A.I. Summit. It also demonstrates the commitment of Nutrimental's personnel to the company's new initiative.

The Spirit of the Whole

Several voluntarily teams were formed with the purpose of implementing the action plans. Many signs and sounds of wholeness emerged throughout the organization. A feeling of connection and a sense of being heard surrounded the whole company. For Joana Lechnicki, machine operator, "*The Appreciative Inquiry gave the employees, including people from the production line, the freedom to know more about Nutrimental. We are all presenting new ideas and collaborating with the company. Before the doors were closed but with the new approach and participation in the process the employees can put their voices on the table and that's why we are all committed and motivated to attain the company's objectives*".

Figure 3 shows an increase of 27% in sales from the period September/96 to April/97 compared to September/97 to April/98. The increase in sales reflects the development of Nutrimental's personnel. After the signs of change in the market place, the team decided to invest in the implementation of the new ideas that came from the Appreciative Inquiry Summit.

Figure 3. The Increase on Sales

Conclusion:

What in the world is wholeness? And how do we move again towards it? It is this kind of intervention, one that liberates human spirits to voice their feelings and thoughts about what really matters for them, that wholeness surfaces. To have the whole system in the same room empowers the human potential and gives wings to everyone's imagination. As a consequence, the sense of recognition that arises makes organizational transformation possible.

The new millennium brings with it a context of globalization and a demand for organization development processes that engage large numbers of people, on line, and in person simultaneously in the co-creation of our shared future. Modern behavioral science, small group theory and systems theory served us well as foundations for organization development principles and practices to date.

We have witnessed the power of this new generation of OD practice that is appreciative in nature, rather than problem oriented. Our experience encourages us to move boldly into whole system process with a radical, participatory view. It invites a cornucopia of diverse voices to be expressed and heard and it will lead to the co-creation of a higher ground for meeting our transformational vision for our organizations and for our world. Seeing the whole again helps us to recommit ourselves to work for a better future for our global village.

Central to this new generation of practice is the Appreciative Inquiry Summit. It is a whole system of positive change process for moving an organization towards its highest potential - the highest ideals imaginable among its members and stakeholders. It is an invitation for participants to discover what gives life - to themselves and to their organization. It is an opportunity for participants to dream of what might be possible if their most cherished values are enacted as organizational realities. And it is a time for the members of an organization to engage with one another in meaningful ways, so that today's interactions, conversations and stories become the seeds of a well-lived destiny.

References:

Bohm, D. (1980). Wholeness and the Implicate Order. Routledge & Kegan Paul: London, Boston and Henly.

Carter, S. L. (1996). Integrity. Basic Books, A Division of HarperCollins Publishers, Inc.

Cooperrider, D. L. (1990). Positive imagery, positive action: The affirmative basis of organizing. In Srivastva, D. L. Cooperrider, & Associates (Eds.), Appreciative Management and Leadership – The Power of Positive Thought and Action in Organizations. San Francisco, CA: Jossey-Bass Management Series.

Cooperrider, D. & Srivastva, S. (1987). Appreciative Inquiry in Organizational Life. In   R. W. Woodman & W. A. Pasmore (eds.) Research in organizational change and development. Vol. 1. Greenwich, CT: JAI Press.

Daft, R. L. & Lengel, R. H. (1998) Fusion Leadership – Unlocking the subtle Forces that Change People and Organizations. San Francisco. Barrett-Koehler Publishers, Inc.

Chapter 17

APPRECIATIVE INQUIRY WITH TEAMS

Gervase R. Bushe Ph.D.
Simon Fraser University

Executive Summary

This article describes the author's thoughts and experiences in trying to help people have conversations that generate new, affirming and generative images. A simple process for running an appreciative inquiry with a team is described. Differences in using appreciative inquiry with new teams and ongoing teams are discussed. Four different ways to use appreciative inquiry in team-building events run by an external facilitator are described. The author goes on to discuss the role of the consultant as wordsmith in an appreciative process with teams.

Introduction

The question I have been thinking about is how do people come to have conversations in groups that generate new, affirming and generative images of the group? By images I mean phrases, metaphors and stories that people invest with shared meanings. By affirming I mean that these images call to the best in us, capturing our heart's yearning and our spirit's intent. By generative I mean images that lead to developmental transitions or that constitute a more developed group identity.

OD Journal, Volume 16, No. 3, Fall 1998, pp. 41-50.

I have been experimenting with a form of appreciative inquiry (Cooperrider and Srivastva, 1987) that I think can help create those kinds of conversations and lead to productive, developmental changes in teams. Appreciative Inquiry is a form of action research that attempts to help groups, organizations and communities create new, generative images for themselves based on an affirmative understanding of their past. Working from a socio-rationalist theory of change, (Barrett, Thomas and Hocevar, 1995, Bushe, 1995, Cooperrider, 1990, Gergen, 1990) these new images are expected to lead to developmental changes in the systems in which they are created. The four principles Cooperrider and Srivastva lay down for appreciative inquiry are that action research should begin with appreciation, should be applicable, should be provocative, and should be collaborative. The basic process of appreciative inquiry is to begin with a grounded observation of the "best of what is", then through vision and logic collaboratively articulate "what might be", ensuring the consent of those in the system to "what should be" and collectively experimenting with "what can be."

In this article I will describe findings from my empirical and clinical (in the sense of Schein, 1987) research in using appreciative inquiry with teams. First I'll describe the "best team" method I have developed and impacts I have observed. I will share my thoughts on the use of appreciative inquiries with teams at different stages of their lifecycle and with some of the different issues they confront. I will look at how the "best team" appreciative inquiry can aid team development even when it doesn't generate new images. I will discuss other appreciative inquiries that can be more useful for team building and other uses for "best team" inquiries in addition to generating affirming images. I conclude by talking about the role of OD consultants in helping teams to craft affirming, generative images.

A "Best Team" Appreciative Inquiry

I developed a form of appreciative inquiry that can be used in small groups. In its simplest form it focuses on developing a shared, generative image of team work and goes like this:

First, group members are asked to recall the best team experience they have ever been a part of. Even for those who have had few experiences of working with others in groups, there is a 'best' experience. Each group member is asked, in turn, to describe the experience while the rest of the group is encouraged to be curious and engage in dialogue with the focal person. The facilitator encourages members to set aside their clichés and preconceptions, get firmly grounded in their memory of the actual experience, and fully explore what about themselves, the situation, the task, and others made this a "peak" experience. Once all members have exhausted their exploration, the facilitator asks the group, on the basis of what they have just discussed, to list and develop a consensus on the attributes of highly effective groups. The intervention concludes with the facilitator inviting members to publicly acknowledge anything they have seen others in the group do that has helped the group be more like any of the listed attributes.

In one business team I worked with one member talked about a group of young men he played pick-up basket ball with and described why they were, in his opinion, such an outstanding "team". He described their shared sense of what they were there to do, lack of rigid roles, easy adaptability to the constraints of any particular situation in the service of their mission. But what most captured the team's imagination was his description of how this group was both competitive and collaborative at the same time. Each person competed with all the rest to play the best ball, to come up with the neatest move and play. Once having executed it, and shown his prowess, he quickly "gave it away" to the other players in the pickup game, showing them how to do it as well. This was a very meaningful image for this group as a key, unspoken, tension was the amount of competitiveness members felt with each other at the same time as they needed to cooperate for the organization's good. "Back alley ball" became an important synthesizing image for this group that resolved the paradox of competitiveness and cooperation.

An appreciative inquiry like the one I described can have a useful impact on a group even if it does not result in any clearly articulated, shared imagery. In an experiment I found that project groups that received this intervention scored significantly higher on task outcomes and group processes than groups that didn't (Bushe and Coetzer, 1995). So there does some to be some benefit to sharing stories and stepping into an appreciative space without requiring highly specialized facilitation.

Sometimes simply creating an appreciative space is all a group needs to produce its own images. But more often than not the process does not simply unfold by itself. It takes some skill on the part of the facilitator to frame, shape and embellish the images group members generate into affirming and generative ones. These skills include a poetic ear, an eye for beauty, a keen sense of what others find inspiring and an open heart that can feel the unconscious yearning in the group.

As a team development intervention, there are times when a more focused inquiry is required than the "best team" inquiry described above. In these cases some subset of teamwork, like leadership or conflict management, is what members need to talk to each other about. So in addition to the skills mentioned above, the facilitator needs to have a good sense of timing and sense of what is called for in the situation.

New Teams

The "best team" appreciative inquiry is particularly appropriate for new teams and may help the team do some important "norming" without having to go through "storming". When teams are first formed, members are trying to establish their personal identities in the group. Much of the "forming and "storming" dynamics come out of the clash of establishing personal identity and the role complementarities these create (Srivastva, Obert and Neilsen, 1977). Role complementarity refers to the fact that for any person to take on a role (e.g., leader) others have to be willing to take on complimentary roles (e.g., followers). Attempts to assert identity in newly formed groups create the unintended effect of forcing others into role compliments, some of which they may not like. This leads to the "storming" phase of group development.

Having the opportunity to tell one's "best team" story provides individuals with an important opportunity to establish their identity in the group. It gives them a chance to tell others, in a somewhat indirect way, what is important to them in relating to other team members, what roles they prefer to occupy, what group characteristics they most value, and so on. This can greatly accelerate the team formation process.

Developing a joint statement of good group qualities makes some norms members want to operate by explicit. Generally, these lists are not much different from the list a group would develop without the first step of telling their stories. These lists, however, have much greater meaning for group members because each point is tied to one or more stories. So much time is spent in organizations writing up lists that I have found listing kinds of activities, by themselves, to have limited value. More often than not the list is soon forgotten. Lists generated after an appreciative inquiry, however, can stick a lot more if the process has real participation from those involved.

If an appreciative inquiry is conducted very close to the beginning of a group's life the last step, appreciating other's contributions, may not be appropriate. That step could be taken later as a way to reinforce the aspirations the group set for itself and provide a cohesion building intervention on its own. If the group has had more than 10 hours of meeting or work time together, however, the last part of the intervention is appropriate.

Sometimes members find it hard to think of anything to appreciate in others, especially right after the question is first asked. This is to be expected as we know that in early group dynamics, members are too focused on themselves to be paying much attention to other people's contributions. When we have finished making the list and I invite people to point out things others have done to help the group be more like the listed attributes, I pause for about 20 seconds and if no one is able to offer anything, I then alter the request. I point out that I am not asking them to describe actions that made the group like the listed attributes, just things that helped the group move in those directions. These could be little things, but small actions can, over time, have large consequences. I then ask them to spend ten minutes alone and think of anything they have personally done to help the group be more like the listed attributes and, if anything comes to mind, to note things others have done as well.

This last step is an important intervention into early group life. It allows for further differentiation of the members. It gives people a chance to describe the intentions behind their past behaviors, increasing the level of disclosure and giving each other more insight into each person on the team. Often, in doing this, people remember things others have done as well and this recognition is important in building group cohesion.

A common experience in newly formed teams is that people are looking for similar things from a good team. This can be a potent learning when one or more of the team members come to the team with a reputation that others are leery of. In one team that used this process, one of the members had a reputation for being cold, uncaring and rigid. At first she refused to take part in telling stories of good teams. After others had completed their stories, however, she said she was now willing to do so and told an extremely touching story of a wonderful team experience early in her career at this organization. By the end of it she (and others) were in tears. The story also described how this team was poorly treated by the organization and helped to explain her fear of getting close to others at work. This event radically altered members' perceptions of this woman, the quality of relationships that developed and the whole development trajectory of this group in very positive ways.

Ongoing Teams

Appreciative inquiry in ongoing teams is both more challenging and has the potential to be a more transformational experience. In newly formed teams a "best team" inquiry is always perceived as useful and appropriate. In teams that have worked together for some time and will continue to work together for the foreseeable future, this is not always the case. If the intervention is not well positioned and/or does not help deal with an important issue members may feel that it is a pollyannish waste of time. Like any action research project, for an appreciative inquiry to be an effective change process key decision makers need to be intimately involved.

I have found some success in using an appreciative inquiry intervention with on-going teams in four different ways, discussed below. Some of these interventions result in the kinds of processes and outcomes called for by Cooperrider's and Srivastva's theory. Others aid groups in different ways.

Team building retreat where the focus is to increase effective relationships

One application of appreciative inquiry with teams is where the team, or team's manager, wants to spend some time building relationships amongst team members. This kind of team building request is often served by having members fill out a personality inventory and then learn about each other's styles and differences.

Appreciative inquiry is a good alternative, especially if the team has already had a personality inventory type of workshop.

In this case, it might be better to have members describe their "best experience in this organization" rather than their best team. This is a judgment call for the facilitator. In either case, the main point is to facilitate a dialogue between individuals and the team where the team gets to understand the interests and aspirations of it's members and where images that have a lot of power for the group are highlighted and played with so that they "stick". I do not recommend members talking about their best team experience in that particular group, however. Times I have done something like that I have found that members will recall a similar experience and after 2 or 3 people have talked about it the process loses steam and members who haven't spoken yet have little to contribute. The likelihood of all having the same "peak experience" probably depends on how long the team has been together.

One of the most powerful examples of this process I am aware of concerned the senior executives of a large utility. This group of eight spent a whole day simply listening to each other's stories about their peak experiences in the organization. Most of them had 30 or more years with the organization. Most of them had spent many years working together. Yet few of them had ever had such an intimate conversation with each other. Even the consultants were amazed at the level of intensity and focus in the group as each member physically went into the centre of the room, told his/her stories, and replied to the questions of their peers.

An inquiry that is appropriate to the issues the group faces

Appreciative inquiry can be a useful intervention when a team finds itself stuck in a rut and needs creative ways out. These can be task related or social process related ruts. When focused on task related issues appreciative inquiry can look a lot like benchmarking (and, unfortunately, poorly organized benchmarking). The difference is that benchmarking is an attempt to discover the best of what is in order to imitate it, while appreciative inquiry is an attempt to uncover the best of our experience in order to develop new shared meanings. It may be that benchmarking is a better process for task issues, especially when they are "closed ended" problems. Appreciative inquiry is, after all, a theory of how to develop social systems, not how to improve efficiency. A lot of things that look like "task issues", however, often have a social process component to them. I am not aware, however, of an example of effectively using appreciative inquiry to get a group out of a task related rut. I have, however, seen "appreciative process" (Bushe and Pitman, 1991) used effectively in this way.

Appreciative process is promoting change by amplifying the best of what is rather than attempting to fix what isn't working. It begins with faith-based positions like you can have more of what ever you want, that there is a genius in everyone, that there is more than enough for everyone. In this case, a consultant, manager or group articulates what it wants more of, looks for any example of it already happening, and tries to increase the magnitude of it happening. Unlike appreciative inquiry, the change does not come from a change in imagery, discourse or meaning but from a change in attention and intention.

Appreciative inquiry is more likely to be useful when the group is in a social process type of rut. This is some pattern of dysfunctional interaction that has been identified and people are willing to put some energy into changing. Using the "best team" inquiry may or may not work well here. To the extent it takes the group away from what it needs to focus on, it will be less than useful and probably resisted. However, it is a good umbrella inquiry in that many different focal issues can be addressed within it. If there is some fear in the group around naming the dysfunctional issue, then "best team" can be a safe way to start broaching the topic. For example, if the relationship with the "boss" is a key issue for team members, but members are afraid to take this up directly, then it can be more safely broached by team members talking about "best team" experiences and the facilitator can ask questions about how the boss acted in each person's best team story. Then when listing the attributes of a good team, the facilitator can pay special attention to characteristics of a good boss of a team. The facilitator can ask the boss about his/her best experience of a boss. Others may be surprised to discover the boss values the same things they do. When it comes time to giving others appreciation the consultant can ask the boss how s/he feels s/he compares to the listed attributes and whether s/he is interested in getting feedback from others. This can be a very gentle and effective setup for a good round of disclosure and feedback.

More often than not, however, the appreciative inquiry will focus on the issue the team is facing. If the team feels there is a general lack of motivation and energy we can inquire into times people have felt most motivated and energized. If there is fear and distrust we can inquire into the biggest experience of trust building people have had. The result of the inquiry will be a new set of ideas and images for how to ameliorate the problem. Often, just the inquiry itself goes some way toward generating the kind of change people are looking for.

For example a senior team in one organization identified a "lack of leadership" amongst middle managers as a key problem. What they were not willing to tell themselves was that they also felt that lack of leadership amongst themselves was a key problem. As part of an intervention into the leadership development process in this company, this group was brought together to have an appreciative inquiry into leadership. They talked about the best examples of leadership within their company that they had witnessed. One key image that emerged for this group was that "great leaders love the people and love the work". As far as anyone could remember, this was the first time that the word "love" had been used at work to describe a manager's job. In fact it was the facilitator who introduced the phrase to summarize a number of stories but people in the group quickly accepted it as descriptive of their experiences. A whole discourse about what it really meant to "love the people" ensued, as well as a discourse about the barriers the organization created to managers "loving" their subordinates. This turned to a deep and intimate conversation about the barriers and fears they experienced in allowing themselves to love their subordinates. This intervention proved to have profound consequences for the entire leadership development process that was subsequently designed. It probably had an impact on these managers as leaders and as a team but I was not able to personally observe the after effects.

Paradoxical intervention into groups stuck in undisclosed resentment

I have had a couple of experiences of consulting to groups where a major theme was undisclosed resentments members had toward each other. They were willing to tell me but were adamant that they were not willing to talk about this at a team building session. In these cases I believed that discussion of the resentments could lead to clearing up misconceptions and fuzzy expectations but I was not allowed to tackle these issues directly. I used to find these assignments very difficult and hadn't had much luck transforming such a group.

The first time I tried AI it was out of frustration and no better ideas to try. The results were a lot better than I expected. At the end of the first day of a two day retreat I led the group in the first two parts of the intervention: telling their stories and listing the attributes. I told them their homework that evening was to think of things that others had done to make the group more like the listed attributes and to come back tomorrow ready to share their appreciation's. The next morning members came into the group with a lot of nervous energy. Then one woman led off by saying that she had not been able to sleep all night because of how angry she was with the group and how little appreciation she was feeling. Others quickly agreed that they had found the exercise difficult for similar reasons. The issues that had been simmering under the surface came boiling up and the group spent the rest of the morning leveling and working through past hurts and resentments. It was a very cathartic session. A great deal of openness was restored. As the session wound down members felt that my intervention had failed and expressed some regret for not having done what I had requested. I thought that was pretty funny and we all had a good laugh as I described my undisclosed frustration of the previous day.

I look at this as a "paradoxical intervention" (Quinn and Cameron, 1988; Watzlawick, Weakland and Fisch, 1974). In this case the intervention does not result in new shared images. Rather it creates a cathartic release by forcing people into a paradoxical tension. By focusing on what they are not feeling (appreciation for each other) the issues that are causing the discordant feelings cannot be contained. This is a powerful intervention and not for the timid. But then so is stepping into the middle of a hostile, frustrated team.

Resolving Group Paradoxes

A perspective on groups that I find useful is that groups get "stuck" because they are enmeshed in a paradoxical dilemma (Smith and Berg, 1987). Paradoxes are endemic to group life and for the most part do not result in stuckness. Rather, they are experienced as "dilemmas" that frame a continuum of choice in decision situations (Billig et al, 1988; Hampden-Turner, 1990). For example, "staff up projects to best utilize the talents of the staff" and "staff up projects to provide staff developmental opportunities" is a common dilemma in project organizations. In most cases such dilemmas are dealt with on a project by project basis, with succeeding decisions balancing off these mutually exclusive values. But when a group becomes stuck, unable to make a decision or take action, it is often because such a paradox is operating at an unconscious level in the group. This does not mean that members are not conscious of it (some probably are) but that the group, for whatever reason, is not able to talk to itself about it.

The first example I gave in this paper described such a situation. The group's ability to develop further as a team was stuck because of the competition-cooperation paradox and the appreciative inquiry led to a new image the resolved the paradox for the group. This can be one of the most transformative results of an appreciative inquiry—the development of images that resolve underlying paradoxes for a group. If the facilitator is aware of the nature of the group's unresolved paradox then s/he can be paying particular attention to stories and images that have the potential to help the group find a way out. Let me give another example.

An "empowered work team" of analysts was stuck over what Smith and Berg (1987) call the paradox of authority. The issue was that people were not willing to authorize others to act on the group's behalf but at the same time some wanted authority to act on the group's behalf in dealing with others in and outside the organization. The group had not conceptualized the problem in this way. Rather, the group became paralyzed by the inability of members to take action without having to convene a meeting of the group to get sanction. This was experienced by all as very frustrating and a sense was developing that "this empowered work team stuff just won't work". During an appreciative inquiry into best team experiences one member told the story of working on a charity fund-raising drive with people who had been loaned, full time for 3 months, from their respective companies. Each person had pursued independent, creative initiatives in raising funds while at the same time fully supporting the initiatives of others. There was a program of activities to be done that had built up over the years and was fully documented for them. Over and above that, individuals pursued the group's core mission however they thought best.

The team I was working with reacted a little differently to this story than it had to others. Members were quieter and more withdrawn. It then dawned on me that this story offered a way out of the authority paradox (which, at the time, was one of a number of alternative explanations I had for their stuckness). I asked how the group was able to let others have free reign without fearing someone, due to inexperience or eagerness, would get them into a bind? He said "we decided we had no way of knowing if we could trust each other so we figured we had more to lose by not trusting than by trusting". At this another member piped in "so trust costs less".

The image of "trust costs less" blended this groups bottom-line business identity with the essential element for the resolution of the paradox. Because it was such a novel combination of those words, it opened up new gateways to emotional issues in this group. They were able to explore what the "price of distrust" was. Some were angry about how much other's distrust had cost them. People were able to admit that they hadn't felt trusted, hadn't been trusting others and that they believed trust would cost less. From there it was easy to decide on the "core program" and general objectives for individual initiatives.

This seems to be a common quality of generative images: they jostle conventional thinking by jostling up word combinations. In doing so they offer opportunities to find synthetic resolutions to paradoxical dilemmas. Groups stuck in a paradox may be where appreciative inquiry is the most effective OD tool available.

Culling or Crafting the Images: Beyond Facilitation

In a team building contract there is an expectation that something "significant" will happen in the designated time. In an appreciative inquiry, that presumably means generating new, affirmative images. In this last section I want to take up an issue with the method itself, applied to teams by a hired consultant.

In an appreciative inquiry it is usually one person who comes up with the image that the group then adopts. I suppose consulting practice might vary along a continuum from those who feel their job is mainly to cull images from the offerings of members to those who believe their job is to help craft the images. In practice I find myself working at highlighting the maps of those members who seem to have the most complex, developed, affirming and generative maps of groups. If they are not able to, I will try to frame, shape and embellish their stories into phrases members use to talk to each other in new ways. I'm not saying this is the "right" way to do appreciative inquiry—its just what I notice myself doing when I have been hired to do team-building and I am trying to help people have conversations that generate new, affirming, generative images. I think the power of appreciative inquiry as a change method relies on someone who can wordsmith these experiences and stories into pithy statements (provocative propositions). If a member of the group can provide that, great. If not, I try my best. It may be that part of the role of the consultant in an appreciative inquiry is "wordsmith".

I find myself paying attention to what most moves me in what others are saying, notice what moves others, and then work at helping people articulate it in "sticky language". That requires using moist, juicy poetic language, not dry, technical or precise language. It is not often that I stumble across a new idea or image of group health and vitality but people often find my ideas and images different from theirs. Am I putting words into their mouths or am I helping them to frame and embellish what is tacit in their stories? I suppose I'm doing both. Is that how appreciative inquiry works with a one consultant organization development intervention? I think so.

Conclusion

A simple process based on the principles of appreciative inquiry that I've referred to as the "best team" inquiry has been experimentally shown to effect groups positively. In this article I've tried to look at why. I tried to show how it helps members of new teams establish personal identity and differentiate themselves. New teams can also benefit from this way of generating "group guidelines" and appreciative recognition can help to build group cohesion. Ongoing teams can benefit from a "best team" inquiry in several ways. It can help to create a safe gateway into difficult issues for a group. When lack of appreciation is the issue, It can create so much tension in members that they deal up their resentments and expectations. It can aid the development of shared mental maps of group success. It can help create affirming, generative images that allow for a different discourse, a different set of understandings and opportunities to materialize for a group. This can be therapeutic for a group stuck in a paradox. In working with teams to develop affirming, generative images, an appreciative inquiry into something other than teams is often appropriate and can have very positive impacts on groups and their members. As a change process appreciative inquiry is a powerful "pull" strategy and can sometimes transform a relationship or a group.

References

Barrett, F.J., Thomas, G.F. and Hocevar, S.P. (1995) "The central role of discourse in large-scale change: A social construction perspective". *Journal of Applied Behavioral Science*, 31:3, 352–372.

Billig, M., Condor, S., Edwards, D., Gane, M., Middleton, D. and Radley, A. (1988) *Ideological Dilemmas: A Social Psychology of Everyday Thinking*. London, UK: Sage.

Bushe, G.R. (1995) "Appreciative Inquiry as an Organization Development Intervention". *Organization Development Journal*, 13:3, 14–22.

Bushe, G.R. and Coetzer, G. (1995) "Appreciative inquiry as a team development intervention: A controlled experiment". *Journal of Applied Behavioral Science*, 31:1, 13–30.

Bushe, G.R. and Pitman, T. (1991) Appreciative process: A method for transformational change. *OD Practitioner*, 23(3), 1–4.

Cooperrider, D.L. (1990) Positive image, positive action: The affirmative basis of organizing. In S.Srivastva and D.L. Cooperrider (Eds.), *Appreciative Management and Leadership* (pp. 91–125). San Francisco: Jossey-Bass.

Cooperrider, D.L. and Srivastva, S. (1987) "Appreciative inquiry in organizational life". In R. Woodman and W. Pasmore (eds.) *Research in Organizational Change and Development: Volume 1* (pp. 129–169). Greenwich, CT: JAI Press.

Gergen, K. (1990) Affect and organization in postmodern society. In S. Srivastva and D.L. Cooperrider (eds.), *Appreciative Management and Leadership* (pp. 153–174). San Francisco, Jossey-Bass.

Hampden-Turner, C. (1990) *Charting the Corporate Mind*. New York: Free Press.

Quinn, R.E. and Cameron, K.S. (Eds.) (1988) *Paradox and Transformation*. Cambridge, MA: Ballinger.

Schein, E.H. (1987) *The Clinical Perspective in Field Work*. Newbury Park, CA: Sage.

Smith, K.K. and Berg, D.N. (1987) *Paradoxes of Group Life*. San Francisco: Jossey-Bass.

Srivastva, S., Obert, S.L. and Neilsen, E.H. (1977) Organizational analysis through group processes: A theoretical perspective for organization development. In C.Cooper (Ed.), *Organizational Development in the U.K. and the U.S.A.* (pp. 83–111). New York: Macmillan.

Watzlawick, P., Weakland, J. and Fisch, R. (1974) *Change*. New York: Norton.

Chapter 18

APPRECIATIVE INQUIRY AND LEARNING ASSESSMENT:
An Embedded Evaluation Process in a Transnational Pharmaceutical Company

Bernard J Mohr
Synapse Group, Inc.
Elizabeth Smith
Professional Consultant
Jane M Watkins
Watkins & Kelly

This paper tells the story of a collaboration between SmithKline Beecham and The Synapse Group. Inc. – how we came to work together on a ground breaking project for both parties; how the project unfolded; and, the outcomes and learning both parties achieved from the experience. It concludes with an Epilogue that sets the story in the context of Appreciative Inquiry and the emerging paradigm.

Prologue

During 1998, the Research and Development division of SmithKline Beecham Pharmaceuticals undertook an evaluation of a major and innovative simulation- based training programme, the SB Discovery Simulation.

This training programme had been designed to help scientific leaders and key contributors work effectively within the new drug discovery research paradigm.

Mohr, B.J., Smith, E., & Watkins, J.M. (2000) Appreciative inquiry and learning assessment. *OD Practitioner: Journal of the Organization Development Network, 32* (1), pp. 36-52.

Over the course of three intensive days, participants worked in research teams utilising a dynamic computer model of the drug discovery process. The aim was to create a realistic learning environment in which a drug company attempts to maximise its portfolio of research efforts over a ten-year period.

At the time of this evaluation process, 480 people from SmithKline Beecham in the US and the UK had attended the programme - a critical mass of the original target population. End of course evaluations were conducted for each programme. The data collected was largely favourable, with participants reporting an increase in knowledge and understanding in a number of areas. Suggestions for improvements were acted upon wherever appropriate, so that the programme was continuously refined during the roll-out.

The Organisation Development (OD) group, who had led the design and delivery of the Discovery Simulation in conjunction with senior Discovery research scientists, were satisfied up to a point that the simulation now worked well and consistently elicited positive responses from those who attended. However, they had made a major investment in this programme, and decided it was important to conduct an in-depth evaluation study to ascertain whether it had made a significant and lasting impact on the organisation. If such an impact could be demonstrated, they also wished to determine how to further capitalise on this investment.

To find an outside evaluator, SmithKline Beecham put out an invitation to tender (a process referred to in the US as an RFP or Request for Proposal) to several consulting groups which they knew would offer different approaches, but still with the expectation that they would conduct a reasonably traditional evaluation process where the consultants interview people in the company, compile the data and give the client a report of their findings. The usual report includes the strengths and weaknesses of the simulation and its outcomes, and recommendations from the consultants for next steps.

One of the companies that received the invitation to tender was The Synapse Group, Inc., a consulting firm based in Portland, Maine. The Synapse consultants responded with a proposal that turned traditional evaluation thinking on its head. The proposal suggested the use of Appreciative Inquiry to conduct a "valuation process," sometimes called "Embedded Evaluation". They believed that this approach could give SB information about the strengths of the programme in ways that would create positive forward momentum - by taking the best of what had happened and using it to create a collective image of a desired future as a basis for moving the programme in the direction of its best practices.

One Story – Two Voices

Stories contain a richness and depth of experience not typically found in more traditional reviews of past work. Because of this richness, and because stories are so central to the practice of Appreciative Inquiry, we have chosen to tell the story of this project in two voices as a way of sharing our memories with you. The consultant (**Synapse**) and the client (**SB**) initially wrote their separate stories without reference to each other. The following story has been created by interweaving pieces from these two original narratives.

Getting Started

SB: *Our story, as the client, begins in June 1997, while we were still in the midst of delivering the Discovery Simulation. We knew we wanted to conduct an in-depth evaluation study and ideally we wanted to have it completed by the end of the year to enable us to make timely decisions about any re-development and re-launch of the programme in 1998. A team of three of us who had been closely involved with the design and delivery of the programme formed a committee to produce an invitation to tender for the evaluation project, to interview a short list of consultants, and then to select and oversee the work of the chosen consultant.*

The invitation to tender described the following aims of the evaluation study:
- (i) to assess whether the learning reported at the end of the programme had translated into changes of behaviour and improved performance back in the workplace;
- (ii) to reinforce the learnings from the programme;
- (iii) to gain insights into the most effective use of simulation technology in order to apply best practice to the design and development of future programmes;
- (iv) to collect data that would help to inform decisions about further applications of the existing Discovery Simulation, and potential follow-up activities.

Synapse: As the consultant our story begins in July of 1997 with a phone call from a colleague who was thinking outside the box. His call caught me doing some catch-up reading in the makeshift office on the second floor of our summer house. It was great to hear his voice, until he told me the purpose of his call. "Would you be interested in responding to an RFP [Request for Proposal] for an evaluation study?" he asked.

Perhaps it was the hamburger I was still digesting but the two terms "RFP" and "Evaluation Study" gave me indigestion . While I have always found great value in jointly crafting a customised journey of learning and change with a client, the term "RFP" can all too often mean participating in a sham process designed to satisfy internal bidding regulations while all along the client has already determined who the best person is for the job. Worse yet, my experience to date with "Evaluation Studies" is best captured by a person being evaluated who said, "Look, for the last year, we have been putting our blood and guts into creating a success here – and now you come along with a mandate from upper management to tell them if what we are doing is any good? And you want our participation? Give me a break!"

So, it was with some considerable reluctance that I told my colleague, "Sure, have them send me the RFP". I was almost ready to say goodbye, when he added "Actually, I was wondering whether you might do this as an appreciative process?" This took me by surprise! How, I asked myself, could the positive perspective of Appreciative Inquiry (AI) be applied to a fundamentally critical review process and still produce "valid" results?

My practice had for the last several years been moving away from deficit based situation analyses, towards a focus on innovation through understanding and expanding that which is working well in a system. But, I obviously hadn't yet shifted my own paradigm sufficiently to imagine the possibility of an evaluation which didn't emphasise primarily the gaps or, as we euphemistically call them, the "opportunities for improvement". And so began an incredible journey which would stretch the practice boundaries of the emerging field of Appreciative Inquiry and involve us with a willing client to explore somewhat uncharted seas. Thank goodness for colleagues who can see possibilities!

SB: As we completed the invitation to tender we realised that we were asking a lot of one consultant and indeed from a single approach to evaluation. We had a broad range of objectives, and good reasons for wanting to accomplish all of them in this study! We thought we might ultimately have to compromise on some, but we weren't ready to do so just yet and wanted to get a range of views on how much could be accomplished.

For this reason we cast a wide net in sending out the invitation to tender, deliberately selecting consultants from both the UK and the US who represented a range of contrasting approaches. The consultants we contacted included the Synapse Group, whom one of our selection team knew professionally, and had already established that they might have an interest in tendering.

Synapse: *By the time the RFP arrived in late August, the then head of the SB Pharmaceuticals R&D OD group had participated in our firm's annual summer gathering in Maine. At that meeting we had described some of the theory and research underlying Appreciative Inquiry to him and we had got to know a bit about the organisation (SB) that was to become our client. The RFP described, in traditional but extremely clear and competent form, the company's wish to evaluate the success of their computerised simulation based workshop for senior scientists. But this RFP was different in other ways. The RFP had a clarity of focus and tone of openness to innovation that was exhilarating. Clearly someone had given a lot of thought to this document! My attitude towards the whole project shifted upwards significantly.*

Intrigued with the possibility of conducting an evaluation from an appreciative perspective I also knew that what we might propose to the client not only ran counter to prevailing assumptions about good evaluation, but to my knowledge had not been done quite this way before. In fact I was worried that even the language of "appreciation" would set off warning bells in a client who was focused on "evaluation". I realised I needed help with shifting from a traditional approach to evaluation to one guided by the philosophy and principles of AI.

Fortunately, Jane Watkins, a Synapse consulting associate and a partner in our NTL sponsored workshops on AI, had recently done developmental work at Cambridge in something she called "Embedded Evaluation." I called her, explained the situation and invited her to join me in a preliminary client teleconference, with the goal being to see if the client might be interested in a "Valuation" process rather than an "Evaluation" process. To our surprise and great delight, in this very first contact with the client project team, they indicated both understanding of the drawbacks of traditional evaluation while expressing enthusiasm for an Appreciative "Embedded Evaluation" approach. The sun seemed to shine more brightly and my heart beat faster. We were starting to roll.

The clients had expressed their interest and openness, although they hadn't yet made any commitments . The ball was back in our court. We had to move from the conceptual to the practical stage. The client needed a proposal, and they needed it yesterday of course! Over the next 8 months we were to revise the original proposal three more times - in a continuing journey of partnership with our clients and a commitment to ongoing adjustment in a process which would increasingly become a forward focused intervention in its own right, rather than the backward look of a typical evaluation study. Our first proposal had six phases as shown below:

PHASE 1: INFORMATION AND PLANNING

A. Consultants familiarise themselves with the company and the discovery Simulation programme through written data and some key informational interviews.

B. With SB OD, jointly identify a project reference group that will be our primary planning and guidance team

C. Meet with project reference group for briefing to:
   - familiarise reference group with Appreciative Inquiry (including review of related scientific research, underlying theory , an experiential activity plus Question and Answer);
   - clarify project goals, roles, approach and key assumptions;
   - describe draft work plan and identify any obstacles or changes required.

D. Present a work plan (revised as needed from the above information) to our reference group for the go-ahead.

PHASE 2: SELECT AND TRAIN SB "INTERVIEWERS"
A. Select SB "interviewers"
B. Train SB "interviewers"
C. Create interview protocol customised to SB Discovery Simulation
D. Complete stakeholder scan and assign interview responsibilities

PHASE 3: CONDUCT INTERVIEWS/COLLECT DATA
A. SB "interviewers" conduct 8-10 interviews per person

PHASE 4: PRELIMINARY DATA ANALYSIS
A. Compile data from interviews
B. Identify themes

PHASE 5: IDENTIFY MAJOR LEARNINGS AND PRELIMINARY RECOMMENDATIONS
A. Identify the programmes strengths, suggest areas to redesign, and develop tentative next steps
B. Brief reference group on findings and validate preliminary recommendations for applicability in SB culture

PHASE 6: FINALIZE RECOMMENDATIONS AND PROPOSE NEXT STEPS
A. Define suggested next action steps (based on reference group validation of data and preliminary recommendations.)
B. Prepare final report and present to client

SB: The initial contacts we had with the Synapse Group both intrigued and puzzled us! The Appreciative Inquiry and associated Embedded Evaluation approach was new to us all, and the detailed theoretical background provided in the RFP response was a lot to take in. However, as a group of OD and learning specialists we were enthusiastic about finding out more and potentially adding a new "tool" to our "kit bag". We also felt that in Appreciative Inquiry we might have found an approach that was broad enough to address most, if not all, of our objectives – something that was going to prove to be more than just an evaluation of the programme.

In our ensuing discussions with the consultants we began to grasp the essence of what AI is all about. The idea of looking for what is exceptional in something and seeking to do more of that rather than looking for what is wrong and fixing it ran completely counter to our classic views of evaluation – but perhaps that was the appeal, since we had already done plenty of the latter as we evolved the programme! We felt that this approach would be particularly useful in helping us to tease out the key positive elements of the simulation experience – ensuring we captured this learning for future simulation programmes in SB. It also seemed to offer a way of reinforcing and building on the learning and experience people had taken from the workshop.

We had two major concerns with the approach. The first was that we were working with a group of Discovery Research scientists, whose training, ways of thinking and approach to their work are exceedingly analytical and critical, which to our thinking at that time seemed antithetical to the AI approach. We were concerned that they might feel we were avoiding looking at the negative, simply seeking positive reinforcement and generally being too subjective and not rigorous enough in our approach. The second was that the proposal called for all the alumni of the Discovery Simulation (around 480) to be part of the study, participating both as interviewers as well as interviewees. This was potentially a major organisational intervention which we did not feel could be supported at that time, and we also did not feel able to ask for any individual Discovery scientist to give more than an hour apiece to the study.

In discussion with the consultants we were able to address the second concern by scaling down the approach. Instead of having Simulation alumni conduct the interviews we agreed to assemble an evaluation team comprising the two consultants, the three members of the SB evaluation selection committee, two other SB representatives from HR and OD respectively and a former Discovery Directory who had been acting as consultant to and faculty on the programme. Between us we would interview approximately 20% of the programme participants. Thus instead of completely "outsourcing" the effort to the consultants, as we had originally intended, we made ourselves part of it (and in doing so committed a much greater amount of our time and effort), but we stopped short of increasing the resource required of the Discovery group.

We continued to grapple with the first concern. As we deepened our understanding of AI in relation to the scientific approach we came to realise the two approaches are not the antithesis of each other, since appreciating what is good does not preclude applying constructive and rigorous critique. We also came to understand how we could use interview questions about wishes for the future to surface the criticisms, but in a way that immediately turned them into recommendations that moved things forward. Nevertheless, we felt that the AI approach was likely to encounter some resistance in what was essentially a problem-solving culture – but we decided to take the risk and go with it!

Synapse: *Within a month after the first proposal and following several more trans-atlantic telephone calls, we had collaboratively determined the changes that would be needed in our original proposal. A couple of weeks later we had begun work. The major adaptations we made to our first proposal from our perspective included: (i) deciding to proceed without a steering committee (called project reference group in the first proposal), (ii) using the external consultants as inter-viewers in addition to using the internal project team in that role and iii) scaling the number of interviews back to about 100 from the original proposal of doing all 480 participants that had completed the training programme.*

Where we had assumed the need for a steering committee composed of senior managers who would be "barrier busters" and "champions" for this project, our clients explained that this was a role better filled by their simulation "design team" – the people who had developed the content for the computerised simulation, the impact of which we were to evaluate. Although we had proposed to limit our role to the development and support of the internal SB team of scientist interviewers, our clients explained that the time of their scientists was too scarce and asked us to bolster the SB interviewer team by conducting some of the interviews ourselves. Frankly, this was a hard pill for us to swallow. Even though it meant more billable time for us as consultants (always nice), it went against our core beliefs that processes such as this are much more effective when implemented by the client system. The clients however were persuasive, and firm! We agreed to participate in the interviews – and as it turned out, we were absolutely delighted with that decision.

Scaling back from a plan to interview all 480 scientists who had participated in the simulation to a decision to interview about 100 people was also a problem-atic choice in our view. From an AI perspective, the likelihood of change in the client system is directly correlated with the number of people directly engaged in appreciative interviews. Naturally we wanted to interview 100% of the target population in order to maximise the impact for the client system. But, we soon realised that this would be biting off more than the client system could chew for the moment.

SB: A final change from the client's perspective was realising that we had to accept that this approach was going to take longer than we had originally scheduled for the project. We pushed our deadline back by 3 months to allow ourselves enough time for our preparation as AI interviewers and to partner in development of the customised protocol.

Phase 1: Information and Planning

SB: The compromise project plan then unfolded. We began by providing the consultants with as much information as possible about the Discovery Simulation, and they were each able to spend some time observing part of a programme.

Our first steps also included informing the Discovery Simulation Design Team of the approach we would be taking. This was a team of senior scientists who had designed the Discovery Simulation and acted as faculty throughout the roll-out of the programme. Their main interest was in finding out the impact of the Simulation experience back in the workplace and to gather information to support and inform a second phase roll-out. They broadly supported the approach and were very interested in seeing the results, but were not ready or able to participate in the interviewing team. However, they did agree to have the interview protocol tested on them before it went out to the wider audience, which was a very valuable step in our preparation for the study. (This data was included in our overall data set, which initially seemed strange to us, as it seemed to run counter to "pure evaluation" methodology. We came to understand that in this approach, all data can be considered and contributes to the richness of the whole).

Phase II: Select And Train Interviewers From Client System

Synapse: *By mid – December we had jointly identified the small team of SB people (our "core group") who would join us in creating the customised protocol, conducting the interviews, analysing the data and writing the final report. The group was drawn from both sides of the Atlantic since the interviewee group itself was transnational.*

SB: The next step was for the SB team to deepen its understanding of the approach. We agreed to accomplish this in two workshops, one for the US-based team and one for the UK-based team, where the consultants would share with us more of the theoretical background to AI and their experience of its application, and give us an opportunity to explore it further, both through discussion and practical exercises.

Face to face time is always at a premium and its use has to be maximised at SB! Therefore we also built time into these same workshops to draft and pilot the interview protocol which would be used in the evaluation study. The goals for the first two day "AI Orientation Workshop" with the UK members of our core group were agreed to as follows:

By the end of this workshop, to have:

1. Clarified the difference between the AI/Embedded Evaluation approach and traditional evaluation approaches.
   • Introduce Appreciative Inquiry
   • Discuss the shifting paradigm
   • Examine the theory of change that underlies this approach
   • Explore Appreciative Inquiry principles and practices

2. Agreed on desired outcomes and critical success factors for this evaluation process - and how we will get there.
   • Discuss the desired outcomes and critical success factors
   • Discuss the major phases of the AI/ Embedded Evaluation approach

3. Jointly developed a customised draft interview protocol for gathering data using this approach - and have practised it.
   • Agree importance of how we capture data and what data to record
   • Create a draft customised interview protocol
   • Practise AI interviewing skills

4. Jointly created a plan for collecting and analysing the evaluation data.
   • Identify Stakeholders
   • Agree key steps in data collection
   • Decide how the data will be collected, organised and compiled

5. Agreed on next steps (actions, responsibilities and dates) for all of us.

Drafting the protocol was an interesting experience for us because our previous training and inclination kept taking us back to more classic evaluation questions that were at odds with the appreciative approach. We were constantly struggling to remain within the new mindset. We also wanted to add more and more questions to ensure that we got at everything we were looking for in the evaluation study objectives – with the danger that the interview protocol would become unwieldy.

Testing the protocol was even more interesting and challenging. Introducing the interview methodology and then keeping up the AI perspective throughout the interview was something we found needed practice. Dealing appropriately with negatives without seeming to avoid the issue, and drawing out stories from people whose memories of the Simulation were several months old, were two particular challenges. However, the experience was also more rewarding than we expected. We found that mostly the test interviewees responded well to the approach (even though they commented that it was different from what they were used to), and were able to describe vivid pictures and examples. It was also enjoyable to be "allowed" to some extent to participate in the dialogue with them, rather than take the usual more aloof interviewer's stance! Finally, it was interesting to note that the questions that yielded the richest and most useful data tended to be adaptations of the generic AI questions rather than the more specific ones we had added! By this stage we were getting really enthusiastic about the use of this approach.

Synapse: *The workshop was successful. Our participants (the UK SB interview team whom we called our 'core group') walked away with an enthusiasm and understanding of what we were trying to accomplish that both astonished and excited us.*

Now we needed to prepare for the second workshop in the USA – which meant some homework for the Synapse consulting team.

We needed to (i)refine a bit more the protocol that had been developed and piloted in the last few days (ii) create the detailed summary sheets to be used at the end of each interview. Additionally our clients (the workshop participants) asked us to (iii) modify the upcoming US orientation workshop with more time being devoted to discussion of the emerging paradigm and its connection to AI theory, as well as (iv) including more time to practise the interviews using the customised protocol.

By mid January we had conducted the second version of the orientation workshop (this time in the US) and the interviewees had been contacted and scheduled. With some slight modifications to the protocol and the supporting documentation, we were ready to start the Inquiry process.

The protocol we developed is shown below:

INTERVIEW PROTOCOL
FOR SB DISCOVERY SIMULATION

1. Before we get to the questions about the Discovery Simulation, I'd like to know a bit about your experience here at **SmithKline Beecham** and I'd like to do it in the style of Appreciative Inquiry. Could you tell me a **story** about a time at SB when you felt particularly **excited, creative, productive?** What happened? Who was involved? What part did you play?

2. Now I'd like to ask you about your **participation in the Discovery Simulation.** Can you tell me a **story** about a **high point** when you felt excited and engaged in the course of participating in the **Discovery Simulation?** Looking back at

that experience, what made it exciting? Who was involved?
Describe the event in detail. Are there other high points?
Probe: What did you learn that you valued?

3. One of the purposes of the Discovery Simulation is to provide
    opportunities for you to learn about both the Discovery
    process and about your style of working with a team. The
    desired outcome is for you to feel that the things you experi-
    enced during the workshop are useful in your work in the
    organisation and in your life in general.

3a. In that context, can you tell me some examples (stories) of ways
    that the **things you experienced** during the Simulation work-
    shop have had a **positive impact on your work and/or the
    quality of your life at work**? Tell me a **story** about that. What
    happened? Can you tell me another story (example)?

3b. As you look at this list, are there any stories that come to mind
    on any of these areas?
    • Your leadership style and skills
    • Planning/strategy of your existing research effort
    • Your interaction with other departments
    • Willingness to take risk
    • Managing in the context of the discovery portfolio
    • Your membership on a project team
    • Your ability to champion your research effort
    • Ability to manage projects
    • Making termination, go/no go phase change decisions

3c. If you had **three wishes for how we leverage our investment
    in the Discovery Simulation** program, what would they be?
    (Future simulations? Things that would be helpful to you on
    your job in the future? Ideas for further use of this simulation?
    Etc.?)

4a. Now, I'd like to ask you a few questions about the Discovery
    organisation itself:
    What is it that <u>you</u> value most about the Discovery
    organisation?

4b. In your opinion, what is the **core value** (driving force; essence;
    underlying principle; life giving force) of the **Discovery
    organisation?** What is it that, if it did not exist, would make the
    Discovery organisation totally different from how it is now?

4c. The future of organisations is greatly impacted by the images
we hold. Our images are often expressed in our desires and
hopes for the future. In that context:
If you had **three wishes for the future of the Discovery
organisation**, what would they be?

Phase III: Conduct Interviews (Collect Data)

SB: Over a six week period we conducted one-to-one interviews each lasting approximately an hour with a representative sample of Discovery Simulation participants in both the US and UK. The final data set represented information collected from 109 interviews, including those conducted during the testing phase.

We continued to develop our AI interviewing skills on the job as we carried out the interviews, sharing tips and experiences with each other as we went along. Our experience in the piloting turned out to be true of our experience in the full-scale interviewing phase – by and large the scientists interviewed were quickly engaged in the interview approach and were able to draw out rich stories of their experiences on the Discovery Simulation, of its application back on the job, and their general experience of working in the Discovery Organisation. In this process their memories and learnings were reinforced. The interviews also yielded many creative insights and ideas for the future. Overall the experience was positive and energising for both interviewers and interviewees.

Synapse: *Many of the interviewees commented on the unanticipated positiveness of the interview experience. Most of the interviews ran beyond the allotted time. Less than 2% of the interviewee population reported any negative experience of the interviews. As each interview was completed our core group members sat down and filled in the interview summary sheet shown below; the sheets were then e-mailed to the consultants.*

Interview Summary Sheet - SB Discovery Simulation Evaluation
Interviewee name: Department:
Years experience in SB :   Current roles in SB:
Past Roles in SB: Date/Location of Simulation Attended:
Was person a "DMC" or "Team Member" or "other"
(specify) in simulation:
Interview Location (US/UK ?)
Interviewer Name: Date of this interview:

1. Stories	a. What was the most compelling story (or stories) that came out of this interview <u>that describe the experience of the workshop</u>? b. What was the most compelling story (or stories) <u>that describe how the</u> <u>learnings are being applied?</u>
2. Learnings	What were other learnings/applications reported in this interview?
3. Wishes	a. What were the three wishes for the Discovery Simulation? b. What were the three wishes for the Discovery Organisation?
4. Values	a. What did the individual value in the Discovery Organisation? b. What was the core value for the Discovery Organisation?
5. Quotes	What were the most quotable quotes that came out of the interview? What questions do these relate to?
6. Implications	What did you learn through this interview that will make a difference in how you/SB plans and manages other training designs?
7. Other	a. Other interesting things you heard in this interview. Anything else you want to say?

Synapse: *Now came the part that we were to love the least – collating the data electronically. As the summaries (containing wonderful stories and quotes) from each interview arrived by e-mail, the two Synapse consultants assembled them in several files – one file contained all the summary sheet data from all the interviews, the other file contained all the responses assembled by question. Although editing was limited to deletion of repeated words and spelling correction, this process seemed to take forever. The hours became days and the days became nights as we decoded e-mail attachments and moved the data into the correct files. Finally, we had it all in a highly readable format.*

Phase IV: Preliminary Data Analysis and Phase V: Identify Major Learnings And Preliminary Recommendations

SB: The next step was to process the data, pull out the themes, and take a first pass at drafting the evaluation report. The consultants had recommended that we take two two-day workshops to do this, but as we are always trying to do more with less, we had decided we would do it in one!

Synapse: *With some anxiety about compressing 4 days of work into two, we designed the next workshop which we had titled the "report writing" workshop.*

This time the whole core group, all the members from both sides of the Atlantic, convened in the UK offices. By now we had developed, with the client, a draft Table of Contents for the final report – shown below:

DRAFT TABLE OF CONTENTS

I.   INTRODUCTION and EXECUTIVE SUMMARY
A. Introduction To This Report
B. Executive Summary Of Findings–What The Data Says About:
    i. When the Transfer of Learnings is at its best....
    ii, When the Discovery Simulation is at its Best....
    iii. When the Discovery Organisation is at its best.....
C. Executive Summary Of Conclusions— Ideas About What Could Be
D. Executive Summary of Recommendations

II.   THE DISCOVERY SIMULATION
A. Background, Purpose, Goals, Implementation

III.   THE EVALUATION PROCESS
A. Embedded Evaluation: Description and Rationale for a
    Different Evaluation Philosophy
B. What we did, when, with whom and why

IV.   FINDINGS - What The Data Says About When Things Are At
Their Best And Wishes For Change
A. Introduction to this Chapter
B. The Transfer of Learnings - themes and supporting data
C. The Use of Simulation Technology in the Discovery Organisation -
    themes and supporting data
D. The Discovery Organisation - themes and supporting data
V.   CONCLUSIONS - Ideas About What Could Be
A. Introduction to this Chapter
B. Provocative Propositions for The Transfer Of Simulation
    Learnings To The Workplace
C. Provocative Propositions for The Discovery Simulation
D. Provocative Propositions for The Discovery Organisation
VI.   IMPLICATIONS/RECOMMENDATIONS FROM THE DATA
A. Introduction to this Chapter
B. For The Use Of The Current Simulation
C. For The Use Of Simulations As A Training Technology
D. For The Discovery Division *(Including Possible Future Uses Of AI)*

Along with this draft Table of Contents, the inputs to the report writing workshop were the Interview Summary Sheets (as they had been emailed to us), the aggre-

gated data collated by question, and each team member's own individual interview notes.

Using these inputs, we worked as a team to pull together all data necessary to outline the findings and conclusions chapters of the final report, which included our provocative propositions – statements of the image for the future of the enterprise. Additionally, we wanted to get agreement on how data would actually be used, and ideas for formatting of the data into various reports. With this in mind, we worked for two days following the agenda shown below.

DAY ONE	DAY TWO
• Goals and agenda	• Review/modify provocative propositions
• Debrief of our interviewing experiences	• For each PP, identify themes within the PP and for each theme, list illustrative supporting data i.e. - quotes/stories
• Review of what the final report will contain (i.e. -suggested Table of Contents)	• Data check - have we missed anything important
• Each person shares what stood out for them from their own interview data	• For each PP, develop "implications and recommendations"
• Read the data (each of us reads a new set of 11 summary sheets and scans the aggregated/ collated data file)	• Agree on how data will be used and ideas for fromatting the data formatting of the data
• Pull out themes re: - the Discovery Organisation - the Discovery Simulation and learnings from it - the transfer of learnings	• Agree on next steps
• Write initial draft of Provocative Propositions (PP's) "When things are at their best" - in the Discovery Organisation - in the Discovery Simulation - in the transfer of learnings	• Debrief our workshop and closure

SB: The quantity of data was somewhat daunting but the consultants structured the workshop into phases that helped us to work through it. I was still concerned that we were not doing it full justice, but with hindsight I think we did pull out the majority of the most important themes and examples. We sorted the findings under the topic headings "The Transfer of Learnings", "The Use of Simulation Technology" and "The Discovery Organisation". Under each topic we identified a number of key themes which we articulated in a short paragraph, and we assembled a quantity of supporting examples under each theme.

We also spent time working on a Provocative Proposition for each topic. Despite our ever deepening understanding of AI, we had difficulty with the concept of Provocative Propositions, and struggled with how they were going to be useful to us! One insight that helped in mapping this across to SB culture and methodology was to make links with our classic SB problem solving approach of *Current Situation, Future Desired Target* and *Proposals*. Provocative Propositions are akin to Targets, although much more powerful, visionary and evocative in their language. We did succeed in drafting three powerful propositions which were not much altered after the workshop.

Synapse: *These were long days and we knew by the end of the first day that we should have done this in two workshops. The amount of emotional energy that was in the data was simply too much to process in one cut at it. But we made great headway and by end of the second day we had done enough so that the consultants along with a subset of the core group were able to generate a draft report for review by the whole core group via a lengthy teleconference.*

SB: One area that I felt we had not fully addressed in the workshop was the wishes data. Although we had incorporated this into the Provocative Propositions and it had been in our general thinking as we developed the themes, we had not systematically categorised the data, and we knew this would be important in our presentation to the heads of the Discovery organisation. We had still to develop the recommendations, and had just the beginnings of the draft report. We had indeed needed the second two-day workshop!

Therefore, to supplement the workshop, a couple of weeks later we held an extended team teleconference to do some more work with the wishes and the recommendations, and this took us another big step further.

The teleconference itself was designed to take into account that participants were in five different locations – in Portland, Maine, Washington DC, suburban Philadelphia, and in Redhill and Harlow, England. We used part of our time for whole group discussions and part of the time for geographically based "breakout tasks" – during which the line was kept open.

Synapse: *This worked like a charm. People reported enjoying the opportunity to work in small groups and have some whole group discussions at the same time – all without leaving their home offices.*

Phase VI: Finalise Recommendations And Write The Report

SB: Over the next few weeks we continued to work with the data in ones and twos off-line, with periodic input and review by the rest of the group via e-mail and telephone – refining the themes, choosing the best stories and examples, process- ing the wishes data and the interviewers' reflections and ensuring all was incorpo- rated. We also worked up some initial recommendations for next steps. The con- sultants took the first pass at a working draft of the evaluation report and then passed it to us in SB for modification and final production in an appropriate format.

We identified a number of audiences which needed different types of data, and we developed individual versions of the report for each audience, somewhat in paral- lel. This was our time to struggle. The process of producing these final reports felt onerous and time-consuming and hard to bring to closure. The consultants as- sured us that the AI process was intended to be iterative, that it should build and grow and continue to involve more and more people and that it was therefore in the nature of AI that there wasn't really an "end point". However, we agreed that for the purposes of the evaluation study we needed to have certain milestones which marked the closure of the study itself and the final detailed report was one of these.

The Discovery Simulation Design Team was our first audience. Drawing on the detailed data and the topics and themes generated from the two-day workshop, we drafted a summary report which we shared with the team in an extended teleconfer- ence. They broadly accepted the findings, although the style of the report caused them to check with us that we had fully represented the more critical comments. They then moved on to help us prioritise and refine the recommendations.

The second audience was the Discovery leadership group, represented by commit- tees based in the US and the UK. For this group we pulled the key points from the report into a presentation, including a few representative quotes from the more vivid stories collected. The committees were very open to the findings presented. As the key decision making group, they provided further input to our recommenda- tions, and then gave their enthusiastic support to the next phase.

For the most senior leadership group in Discovery we produced a very short high level briefing document, but this barely needed to be used, since they were already fully in tune with the feelings and decisions of the two committees.

The reports described above included both the simulation specific data and the more general organisational data, but the recommendations concentrated on the simulation side, since this was the brief of the evaluation study. However, we felt that the organisational data was worthy of separate consideration by the Discovery leaders and therefore we created a separate report that drew out just the organisational data with some commentary, but stopped short of making actual recommendations since this was outside our remit. This report was presented to the senior Discovery leaders only.

Finally, we had committed to report back to all participants in the evaluation study. This process was delayed until all recommendations had firmed up and the next stage was fully agreed and underway, so that we had something substantive to report in terms of outcomes. The participant report comprised a version of the original summary report plus an update on next steps.

When the detailed report was eventually completed its primary function had evolved to serving as a reference and source document for the evaluation study.

The various shorter reports and extracts took on the format and feel of traditional SB documents, but I believe that the flavour of the AI approach still came through - particularly in the richness of the summary findings and recommendations.

Outcomes of the Evaluation Study

From SB's perspective there have been positive outcomes of the evaluation study at a number of levels. Firstly, the AI approach did indeed enable us to address all of our key objectives as follows:

1. We were able to assess and demonstrate the degree and nature of the impact of the Discovery Simulation on people's experience and behaviour back in the workplace, in a vivid and powerful way, as illustrated by the following sample quotes:

"I have noticed greater participation in ongoing studies by some of my people. One person came to me and said, 'How or where can I apply my technology to make a greater impact on the organisation?' She has since been talking to many more people than she did before."

"Understanding the wider context has given me a different perspective on termination decisions. I realise now that for the greater good it may be right for me to propose terminating my work, even though it is in an early phase. Before I would never have done so."

"My awareness of the overall process has given me a better feeling of what others contribute and this makes me feel better about my own contribution, how I am a worthwhile member because I have a better sense of the community."

"It was a bit like doing rehearsals. Now I have greater confidence in what I'm doing. I feel assurance about my own decisions. Now I ask more confidently in real life."

"The simulation has brought about a closer integration between Clinical Pharmacology and Discovery. Several Clinical Pharmacologists have attended, and they now come along to [a particular management meeting], and listen to and participate in discussions about Discovery. Now we have input on a whole lot of things we never had before."

2. For the people who participated in the study it provided a means of reinforcing and building on the learning they had achieved as a result of the simulation – so in a very real way it provided a follow-up to the workshop for this group.

3. We gathered valuable information regarding what makes simulations effective and engaging as a learning methodology, which will be harnessed in the design and delivery of future simulations within SB.

4. We gathered a mass of convincing and enthusiastic support for continuing with the use of simulations in general, and the further development and delivery of the Discovery Simulation in particular. We also gained key insights into how to modify the programme both to increase its effectiveness and make it accessible to a wider audience.

We were able to use our findings and recommendations to dialogue with the Discovery leadership regarding the relative benefits of investing in programmes like these (versus straight scientific training and individual skills development). As a result we have top level support and commitment to go ahead with the re-design, development and delivery of the Discovery Simulation in a variety of new formats. Indeed, this is already underway and will form a significant part of the new R&D business process curriculum over the next 2-3 years.

In addition we collected powerful organisational data, which is available to the Discovery organisation as a potential platform for significant further change. However, perhaps most importantly we have found out that people fundamentally like working within the Discovery organisation, and maybe we can find ways to better tap in to this huge source of potential energy.

We have also discovered that this approach is not only acceptable to, but in most cases positively welcomed by Discovery scientists, contrary to our original misgivings! We succeeded perhaps because of the pragmatic and cultural adjustments we made along the way, but this means that we can consider further organisational interventions utilising the AI approach. We can carry forward the type of modifications we made, or maybe we can take a few more risks next time.

For ourselves we have learnt a new methodology that we have found is applicable to a variety of projects and activities at work, and we have begun tentatively to try out the concepts in other arenas, such as developing competency profiles and teambuilding.

We have also challenged our thinking in relation to how learning becomes embedded in an organisation. In future learning interventions we would like to explore the contextual issues further, and consider how to make the environment more conducive to transferring and supporting learning back on the job.

Finally, on a personal basis we have found an approach that may help us to turn around our thinking patterns and move forward in a new way.

Learnings and Reaffirmations From This Case

Some months after the final report had been distributed and when its recommendations were well underway to being implemented, the external consultants (Bernard Mohr and Jane Watkins) sat down with the SB Project Manager (Elizabeth Smith) for the purpose of asking "in retrospect, what did we learn from this work together?" As we discussed what we had learned we realised that what was a reaffirmation of an existing belief for one of us was might be a new learning for another. For ease of reporting, we show both the reaffirmation and the learning in a combined list below.

AI does work for evaluation purposes, particularly at level 3 of the Kirkpatrick model* (i.e. identifying behavioural changes) and also works as an organisational intervention. The biggest question we had when starting this project was whether Appreciative Inquiry would allow us to answer, to the clients' satisfaction, the fundamental organisational concerns of " how well is this Simulation going and is it a good investment for the corporation?" In the foregoing Outcomes section of this paper, we indicate that not only were these traditional evaluation questions effectively met with this approach but the corporation benefited from both the learning reinforcement that occurred and the richness of data which would not have been captured in a normal evaluation process. We believe this is due not only to the flexible nature of the AI approach but also is an outcome of the joint partnership style of working between consultants and clients – a style of working that is part and parcel of good Appreciative Inquiry. We also learned that things which from a traditional evaluation process might be considered impure, (e.g.- the use of leading questions; the use of data from the pilot; the use of people who have a vested interest in the outcome as interviewers/data collectors) are not only OK but are actually helpful within an Embedded Evaluation/AI process.

Joint partnership between consultant and client generates a synergy not present when the consultants and clients relate to each other in a more traditional manner (e.g. the consultant as expert or vendor). Since a fundamental premise of Appreciative inquiry is that we construct our reality in every interaction and conversation, the roles and expectations we agree to as clients and consultants are extremely important to the outcomes we then produce. By agreeing to avoid the more traditional consulting roles of either vendor/trainer or expert data gatherer and analyst, the clients and consultant were freed up to work collaboratively and adaptively. The consultants were able to participate as interviewers which allowed them to contribute more to the data compilation activities. Both the consultants' experience of the AI interviews and the client/project teams' experience was so positive that the energy both parties received from the experience made working together even easier, enabling the consultants to become more part of the team with the clients, and being seen as having similar stake in the learning and outcomes. This in turn made much more possible the ongoing adaptation of the theory and process to the local conditions, which we see as key to enabling innovative applications of Appreciative Inquiry.

When consultants share the theory and research base of AI with the client system, the joint partnership between them is further enabled. Making assumptions about what clients will or will not be comfortable with can lead to unnecessary constraints on the project. Consultants, imagining their clients to be extremely task focussed (as we did), may bring a limiting assumption about how much their clients want to know about the conceptual underpinnings of the approach that is being used. This can create an insidious dependency on their clients' part, which is in direct opposition to the goal of joint partnership. Although it may be an artefact of working in a culture where intellectual understanding is highly valued, the external consultants were surprised by the clients' request for more in-depth knowledge about AI. When the consultants responded positively to this, the clients were further enabled as full partners. With greater knowledge of the principles and less conceptual dependence on the consultants, the clients could contribute creative ideas about how to overcome organisational constraints.

"Consultant, innovate thyself." Before the client can receive innovative assistance, innovation must be present in the worldview of the consultant. Consultants often focus on the need for opening up the thinking patterns of their clients without considering the same need on their part. As mentioned in our story, had it not been for a colleague's "out-of-the box" thinking about the possibility of applying Appreciative Inquiry to an evaluation project, we might never have had this wonderful experience! We again learned that innovations, to anyone's thinking, (in this case the consultants thinking), are likely to come from an outside source, from someone not wearing the existing blinders of the moment.

The "four generic" AI questions (i.e. peak experience, personal values, core life-giving factor and wishes for the future) were the ones that produced the richest data, and it takes time to digest all that data. Although we incorporated into the final protocol all of the traditional evaluation questions from the original RFP, the client consistently experienced the responses to the four (slightly modified) generic AI questions to be the most valuable in terms of the overall goals of the evaluation. The richness of the data gained from the four generic questions allows many more questions to be answered than might be answerable with a more traditional quantitative model of evaluation. We do, however, want to point out that since the data generated are in a qualitative/narrative form, the amount of time to digest the volume of data is significant.

The organisational data collected was very rich – a bounty that was not fully anticipated at the start of the project. In addition to data focusing on the simulation itself, we accumulated a lot of data about how the back home environment could be modified to more effectively support the back-on-the job application of simulation participants' learning. SB management trusted their internal HR/OD group to conduct this evaluation without a senior level steering committee and that trust was valued by the project team. In retrospect, we realise that by accepting that trust we also accepted the implicit boundary definitions of the project which implicitly limited the outcomes to the goal of identifying improvements in the use of simulation technology at SB. A broader definition at the start might have created pathways for more immediate use of the rich organisation level data that the interviews generated. Ways to make this data useful to the organisation continue to be explored.

As we chatted about our lists we realised once again the power of client/consultant partnership. That which constituted innovation for the consultants was reaffirmation (but not necessarily an innovation) for the client. One case in point was the inclusion of the consultants as part of the interview team. From the consultant perspective this was "innovative" insofar as "normal" AI practice suggests the importance of limiting the active role of the consultant in the interviewing/data collection in order to minimise consultant dependency. From the clients perspective their belief in the validity of using external resources for data collection was reaffirmed. Another example was the clients' "learning" that a joint partnership between consultant and client generates a synergy not present when the consultants and clients relate to each other in a more traditional manner (e.g. the consultant as expert or vendor). This was not a new learning for the consultants but a reaffirmation of their deeply held beliefs. As we shared with each other what we had learned, what we saw as innovations and that which we felt was reaffirmed for us, we recognised once more the centrality of our partnership model in allowing the consultant and client to build a common experience, a shared language with which to make decisions and conduct work.

Epilogue

This story so far describes the use of Appreciative Inquiry to evaluate a training programme within SmithKline Beecham. It should be clear from the narrative that there is no set way to "apply" AI as an organisational intervention in the classic Organisation Development (OD) sense. Instead, Appreciative Inquiry is a way of seeing and being in the world. It is based on the belief that we can create what we imagine when we open our minds and our social processes to the widest possible dialogue among the largest number of people who are involved and invested in our enterprise. Appreciative Inquiry applied becomes an empowering and life-affirming way of living in all human systems.

Created by Dr. David Cooperrider and his colleagues at the School of Organisational Behaviour, Case Western Reserve University, Cleveland, Ohio, the appreciative approach to inquiry has become a major innovation in the field of Organisation Development. It has been used to transform a wide range of traditional organisational change processes – strategic planning, team building, restructuring, valuing diversity, almost any and every kind of method for facilitating organisation change.

A basic tenet of AI as a process for organisational change is that the intervention into any human system is fateful and that the system will move in the direction of the first questions that are asked. In other words, if we inquire into what went wrong, the image will be of the organisation as a problem and the energy of the system will go toward trying to fix what is wrong. Alternatively, if the first questions focus the system on its most creative and life-giving moments, the system will look toward its successes and create images of a positive future congruent with the positive energy that is generated.

The underlying assumption of Appreciative Inquiry is that "organisations are solutions to be embraced." As human systems designed to be creative and innovative, organisations, in the view of AI, are full of solutions. It is their diversity, multiplicity and forward movement that need to be highlighted and built upon.

As a way of being in the world, Appreciative Inquiry is grounded in Social Constructionist thought, a worldview that asserts that we use language and knowledge to create the world as we know and understand it.

For many centuries we have believed that the world was knowable and predictable. We thought that we could believe only what we could see or prove in some objective fashion. We embraced the proof methods of pure science as though they applied to human behaviour, which led us to think of our social organisations as machines. If we embrace the Social Constructionist view of the world, we begin to understand that language is not a way to understand the world; it is the power of language and the relational use of it that actually creates the world. In other words, we see what we believe. To understand how and why AI works, one must understand and embrace these beliefs about how the world works.

This shift in how we understand the world leads us to an entirely new way of thinking about our social organisations. We begin to see that our organisations are not predictable machines, but rather human constructions that are moulded and changed by the images that human beings have of them.

In its practice, Appreciative Inquiry is the art of discovering and valuing those factors that give life to an organisation or community or group. In its most practical construction, Appreciative Inquiry is a form of organisational study that selectively seeks to locate, highlight and illuminate the life-giving forces of the organisation. When we inquire into the things in our organisations that are life giving, we begin to understand that we can choose to focus on those qualities. Through asking others to join in our inquiry, we can have a considerable impact on the image of our organisation and, ultimately, on the way it functions.

And so it was with the "valuation" process of the Discovery Simulation training programme within SmithKline Beecham. The focus was on what worked well; what had positive impact on the participants; what positive impact carried into the organisation. Not only did the data reflect a generative and creative picture of the Simulation itself, it also told a powerful story of the pride, loyalty and commitment that the people of SmithKline Beecham feel for their company.

Chapter 19

APPRECIATIVE INQUIRY AS A TEAM-DEVELOPMENT INTERVENTION FOR NEWLY FORMED HETEROGENEOUS GROUPS

Robert L. Head, Ph.D.
Benedictine University

Abstract

Creating a positive image of the future allows newly formed heterogeneous groups to develop faster and perform at higher levels than heterogeneous groups developing in a traditional manner. The present research was conducted to validate the effectiveness of Appreciative Inquiry (AI) versus traditional team-building or no structured intervention. Eighteen groups of managers, with a total of 124 participants, were created in the United States Postal Service in Milwaukee. The groups were divided between three interventions (AI; team-building; and control) and measured on the basis of development (using the Group Style Instrument, a daily diary, and a single-point questionnaire) and performance (using a group output questionnaire and a daily diary).

The results suggest that groups receiving Appreciative Inquiry develop more team-oriented behaviors, perform at a higher level, and have more positive images of future interactions than groups experiencing either team-building or no structured intervention. The final hypothesis, *that newly formed heterogeneous groups, experiencing Appreciative Inquiry, would have more positive expectations for*

Head, R.L. (2000). Appreciative inquiry as a team development intervention for newly formed heterogeneous groups. *OD Practitioner: Journal of the Organization Development Network*, 32 (1), 59-66 *future interactions and performance,* was designed to test the theory that it is the Anticipatory Principle, a foundation of AI that makes it uniquely appropriate for bridging issues of diversity. Results of data analysis support this hypothesis, as well as the development and performance hypotheses. Finally, a correlation between data collected on images and data collected on performance resulted in a positive linear relationship. Within the overall results, the researcher provided data that AI groups had a more positive image and performed at a higher level than other groups.

Introduction

There are several significant outcomes of the world's transition to a single, global community. Those outcomes include the increase in and sharing of technology, enhancing the speed at which information is transmitted; the internationalization of corporations, implicitly linking the world's economic markets; and the increasing diversity of people in society, calling into question those paradigms predicated on a model of homogeneity.

Each outcome has unique implications and certain common threads. One common thread is that of cycle time or speed. In 1988, U.S. businesses completed 2,300 mergers and acquisitions (Barr, 1996). The number of similar transactions for 1995 totaled 6,700. Mergers and acquisitions for 1996, through only the third quarter, surpassed the number from 1995. From concept to target identification, and from identification to acquisition, corporations are making decisions in time frames of hours and days. The traditional strategic planning and implementation models are ill-equipped to deal with making real-time decisions as are necessary in today's global society. Several multi-national firms, such as Eastman Kodak and IBM, conduct business in more than 50 countries (Adler, 1991). A critical factor of competitive viability is the ability of decision-makers to reach consensus rapidly.

There exists in America an increasing amount of debate on issues related to race, class and gender. For many, there is a strong desire to elevate and even broaden the discussion. Examples of this intensity are found throughout the fabric of our society. Recently, the White House has issued an official apology for the deplorable tactics of research employed in the Tuskegee experiment, acknowledged a problem of sexism in the armed forces, and debated an official apology for the nation's past policy of slavery. But while these significant issues are being discussed, there remain many who would prefer to quiet the debate, believing that more harm than good is generated from acknowledging differences. This polarization of thought can be viewed in the reaction to Supreme Court Justice Thurgood Marshall's 1991 statement that, "I'm not free," (Morrison, 1992, p. 1), and to Olympian Arthur Ashe's statement, "You're not going to believe this, but being Black is the greatest burden I've had to bear" (Ashe and Rampersad, 1993, p. 126). From their statements, it is clear that even success and fame cannot prevent the experience of racial prejudice. Yet there are still those who choose to discount or ignore the feelings of an Ashe or Marshall. In 1991 an executive was quoted in the *Los Angeles Times* as stating, "The rhetoric is so damn hot. A lot of political jockeying is going on, and there's nothing we could say or do that would be in our best interest. So we're remaining mum until the matter is settled" (Morrison, 1992, p. 2).

These examples portray a need for groups to form, develop, and effectively deal with issues of importance to their organizations. In an age that clearly exemplifies the old adage "time is money," the speed at which groups develop can be of strategic advantage to the organization that becomes proficient in the transformation process.

However, there is a growing body of literature suggesting that homogeneous groups develop and perform faster than heterogeneous groups (Watson, Kumar, and Michaelsen, 1993). Previously described is a world that is becoming less independent, and more interdependent. The convergence of cultures, nations, races, and religions creates increasing diversity possibilities. The literature also suggests that heterogeneous groups will develop and perform as well as homogeneous groups, although not as quickly. Supporting this is a review by Bettenhausen (1991) of 250 published studies on small social groups. One of the many findings of his review was that heterogeneity was associated with "lower levels of social integration" (p.363), which is also negatively associated with performance. One emerging concern is that organizations will retain an emphasis on homogeneity in order to benefit from a quicker developmental time frame. The social implications of this in a heterogeneous community are potentially devastating.

Is AI the Answer?

A review of more recent theories of organization development leads to Appreciative Inquiry (AI). Developed by David Cooperrider and Suresh Srivastva, AI is "an approach to organizational analysis and learning that is uniquely intended for discovering, understanding, and fostering innovations in social organizational arrangements and processes" (Cooperrider, 1994, p. 5). Cooperrider (1994) states, "the greatest obstacle in the way of group and organizational well-being is the positive image, the affirmative projection which guides the group" (p. 11).

The purpose of this research is to review the theoretical framework of AI and determine its applicability in the development of heterogeneous groups. The process will include comparing AI and traditional team building as interventions for heterogeneous groups, with the goal of identifying differences in group development and group productivity. The research question generated is, "Can Appreciative Inquiry, as compared to a traditional team-building intervention, or no structured intervention, significantly decrease the time needed for newly created heterogeneous groups to develop and work productively?"

Hypotheses

Hypothesis 1: Newly formed heterogeneous groups, through the experience of AI, will develop faster than newly formed heterogeneous groups experiencing either no structured intervention, or a traditional team-building intervention.

Hypothesis 2: Newly formed heterogeneous groups, through the experience of AI, will perform tasks at a higher quality standard than newly formed heterogeneous groups experiencing either no structured intervention, or a traditional team-building intervention.

Hypothesis 3: Newly formed heterogeneous groups, experiencing AI, will have more positive expectations for future interactions and performance of the group than those experiencing traditional team-building or no structured intervention.

This study extends the research on homogeneous and heterogeneous group development (Watson, Kumar, Michaelsen, 1993) and the use of AI as a team-development intervention (Bushe and Coetzer, 1995). In both cases, development of groups was analyzed. More specifically, this project will investigate the impact of AI on the group development process and performance of newly formed heterogeneous groups. As in the previous studies, this project will review surface-level diversity (sex, race, and organizational level) and not deep-level diversity (thought, job satisfaction, organization commitment, etc.) (Harrison, Price, And Bell, 1998). What distinguishes this project from the previous research is that: 1) it is a field study; 2) it attempts to provide an intervention *prior* to the development of an entrenched problem; 3) it focuses on newly formed heterogeneous groups; 4) it is an study resulting in empirical data following an AI, and 5) it explores the theoretical framework of AI. By doing so, it is hoped that the development process of heterogeneous groups, and the resultant productivity of the groups, will be enhanced. The research will also examine the linkage between the Anticipatory Principle of Appreciative Inquiry and the performance of heterogeneous groups.

Results and Discussion

The setting of the study was the United States Postal Service in Milwaukee, Wisconsin and the sample was drawn from their supervisory and management employees. The population of supervisors and managers in the Milwaukee Processing and Distribution Plant numbers 133 over three work shifts. A total of 124 supervisors agreed to participate.

Hypothesis 1

Hypothesis 1 predicted that newly formed heterogeneous groups, through the experience of Appreciative Inquiry (AI), will develop faster than newly formed heterogeneous groups experiencing either no structured intervention, or a traditional team-building intervention. The 26 statements of the Group Style Instrument (GSI) were analyzed to compare pre-test and post-test responses among the three groups (Control, Team-Building, and AI). Two separate factors of the GSI, team-oriented behaviors and self-oriented behaviors (identified by Watson, Johnson, and Merritt, 1998), were specifically analyzed with the ANOVA (analysis of variance) test. In using ANOVA, the researcher ensured that the groups were randomly selected (following stratification of race, gender, and management classification) from what was assumed to be a normal population. A composite was generated for each factor.

The team-oriented behavior ANOVA yielded the following results: nonsignificant differences for groups, and pre- and post-test responses, with $F(2,32) = .77$, $p > .05$ for groups and $F(1,32) = .40$, $p > .05$ for tests. AI had a higher team-oriented composite on the post-test ($X = 416$), with Team-Building and Control having composites of $X = 386$ and $X = 352$, respectively. The pre-test averages were comparable, with AI having $X = 405$, Team-Building $X = 386$, and Control $X = 404$.

Team -Oriented Composite on GSI: As a Function of Test and Group

The self-oriented behavior ANOVA did produce a significant difference among the groups, with $F(2,32) = 4.10$, $p < .05$. As hypothesized, AI generated the lowest composite mean for self-directed behaviors ($X = 123.83$), in comparison to the Team-Building ($X = 154.75$) and Control ($X = 146.58$) composites. These results were generated through post hoc comparison using Tukey's Honestly Significant

Difference. While the pre-test-post-test responses were not statistically significant, with F (1,32) = 2.46, p>.05, the AI composite showed the largest numeric
change from the pre- to post-test, from an average of 138 on the pre-test to one of
110 on the post-test. Team-Building and Control groups did not display such
radical declines, with Team-Building pre-test X = 158 and post-test X = 151 and for
the Control group X = 151 on pre-test and X = 142 on the post-test.

Self-Oriented Composit on GSU:
As a Function of Test and Group

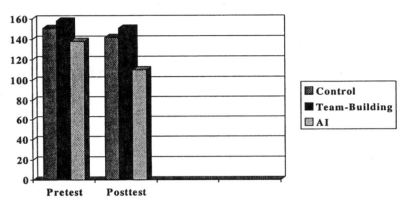

To summarize these ANOVA results, the greatest change on the post-test
measure occurred with the AI group, with the higher scores on team-related statements and lower scores on self-directed statements. This is consistent with hypothesis 1.

Hypothesis 2

Hypothesis 2 predicted that newly formed heterogeneous groups, through the
experience of AI, would perform tasks at a higher quality standard than newly
formed heterogeneous groups experiencing either no structured intervention, or a
traditional team-building intervention. Group performance was evaluated by an
overall grade (i.e., A, B, C, D, or F) that was assigned to each group by executives
of the United States Postal Service. Criteria used in grading included:

• Quality of recommended solution
• Number of perspectives considered
• Number of alternatives generated

·   Recognition of problems that might be encountered with the proposed solu-
     tions and avenues for mitigating the problems

     The overall grades carried a numerical value of $4 = A$, $3 = B$, $2 = C$, $1 = D$, and 0
$= F$. An ANOVA was calculated on those grades and yielded a statistically significant difference, $F(2,50) = 16.21$, $p < .001$. Specifically, the Team-Building and AI
averages were higher than that of the control group, with respective Xs = 3.50 and
3.57 in comparison to 2.33. Team-Building and AI ratings were in the "B" and "A"
range, while the control group ratings ranged from "D" to "B". While the overall
mean scores of AI and Team-Building groups were close (3.57 and 3.50), the AI
group had not only the higher mean, but also the most concentration of As and Bs
at 100% (vs. 83% for Team-Building groups). The Team-Building group, and the
Control group, had at least one grade of C.

Grade Rating for Group Performance

Hypothesis 3

     Hypothesis 3 predicted that newly formed heterogeneous groups experienc-
ing AI would have more positive expectations for future interactions and performance of the group than those experiencing traditional team-building or no
structured intervention. This hypothesis was evaluated by using two different
instruments. The first instrument is a three-question diary that all participants
completed individually following each of the three sessions. The questionnaire
sought the participants':

•   image of what was taking place within their group,

•   view of their group's performance, and

•   view of their group's process.

     For every answer to each question, the researcher and a Registered Organiza-
tion Development Professional independently scored the response as either positive or negative. Though there was almost universal agreement between the

reviewers, some differences existed. In each case, the two reviewers discussed the responses until such time that agreement was reached. Positive and negative comments were totaled and then analyzed via the chi-square test to determine if there were rating differences across the three groups. The chi-square test of independence is appropriate with more than two groups using a nominal level of measurement, and is therefore applicable to this particular course of analysis.

The analysis of group image found a statistically significant difference with $\underline{x}^2$ (2) = 15.04, $\underline{p}$ < .05. AI generated more positive remarks with image than the Control and Team-Building groups, with a total of 100 positives for AI versus 73 for Team-Building and 82 for Control. Another way of stating this is that AI generated fewer negative remarks (18) than the Control (43) and Team-Building (25) groups, as anticipated.

The second question on group performance also yielded statistically significant results with $\underline{x}^2$ (2) = 11.13, $\underline{p}$ < .05. AI once again generated a greater number of positive comments (102) with respect to its overall performance than either the Control (81) or Team-Building (89) groups. Negative remarks were also lower with AI (16) than Control (35) or Team-Building (25).

The final question, dealing with group process, did not produce a statistically significant difference in the comments across the three groups, $\underline{x}^2$ (2) = .42, $\underline{p}$ > .05. All members in the AI, Team-Building, and Control groups rated the process variable very positively, with totals being 103 (AI), 98 (Team-Building), and 91 (Control), in comparison to the overall negative remarks 15 (AI), 18 (Team-Building), and 16 (Control).

The second instrument used to evaluate the third hypothesis was the request for participants to respond to the statement, *I would be willing to work with this group on future projects.* Answers were provided along a 5-point Likert scale, with 1 being 'absolutely yes', 2 'yes', 3 'maybe', 4 'probably not', and 5 'definitely not'. An ANOVA was used to examine whether there were statistically significant differences in how the members of each of the three groups (Control, Team-Building, and AI) expressed a willingness to work on future projects. Post hoc comparison using Tukey's Honestly Significant Difference found a statistically significant difference among the groups, with F (2, 105) = 3.84, $\underline{p}$ < .05, with AI members expressing a higher willingness to work on future projects than the Control group. Respective means were 1.72 and 2.31. AI did not have a significant difference from Team-Building, with results of X =1.72 versus X = 2.02, respectively.

The early position taken by the researcher was that the Anticipatory Principle is the critical foundation that makes Appreciative Inquiry uniquely capable of assisting the development and productivity of newly formed heterogeneous groups. To test this premise, an overall Pearson-product moment correlation was performed. Factors compared were the percentage of positive images obtained for each group at post-intervention times 2 and 3 and the respective performance grade (i.e., 1 = D, 2 = C, 3 = B, 4 = A). The Pearson-product moment correlation was used to determine if a linear relationship existed between group image and group grade. The correlation was statistically significant and highly positive in nature, $\underline{r}$ (34) = .74, $\underline{p}$ < .001. The means and standard deviations for the group image and grade were, respectively, 75.47 percent (18.41) and 2.94 (.98). What is clear is that as the groups' positive image went up, so did their performance grade. Next, a series of Pearson correlations were computed on each of the group's (i.e., Control, Team-Building, and AI) image rating and performance grade. For these correlations, only one yielded a statistically significant, positive correlation, namely the control group's image by grade, $r(10) = .91, p < .01$. The respective means and standard deviations for that group's image and grade were 62.25 percent (19.04) and 2.00 (.85), suggesting that the lower the Control group's image, the lower the overall grade and the higher the image, the higher the performance grade. The Team-Building image by grade was not statistically significant, with $r(10) = .52, p > .05$. The respective means (and standard deviations) for Team-Building image by grade were 75.00 percent (14.48) and 3.33 (.78). Finally, the AI image by grade correlation was not statistically significant, $r(10) = .10, p > .05$. Averages (and standard deviations) for image and grade were 89.17 percent (10.55) and 3.50 (.52).

Conclusion

Previous research has demonstrated that homogeneous groups are quicker to develop and perform than heterogeneous groups (Watson, Kumar, and Michaelsen, 1993). However, research also indicates that heterogeneous groups are more creative and have more perspectives on issues than homogeneous groups (Bushe and Coetzer, 1995; Elsass and Graves, 1997; Harrison, Price, and Bell, 1998; Jackson and Hardiman, 1983; Thomas, 1991; and Watson, Kumar, and Michaelsen, 1993). This study provides evidence that through structured intervention, the performance and process of group development of heterogeneous groups can be enhanced. Specifically, through the application of AI, organizations will not only obtain faster productivity, but will also realize many of the affective benefits of AI.

As Roosevelt Thomas (1991) identified, managing diversity is the best approach to realizing benefits from a workforce that is increasing in diversity. One method of managing diversity is to acknowledge that an active process of assimilation must occur to generate the benefits inherent through diversity.

The results of this study have implications for the way organizations approach the design of training interventions for heterogeneous groups. The importance of assisting group members in creating a positive 'anticipation' of their future is critical to accelerating the development and performance timeline for the group. One reason for the accelerated development time with AI might reside in a model provided by Gervase R. Bushe (1998) that states that a good AI allows the group to move to the norming stage without going through the storming stage. By its very design, traditional team-building includes storming. While team-building is considerably more advantageous than no structured intervention with new groups (as evidenced by the results of this and prior research), the absence of storming makes

AI more advantageous to organizations than team-building for new groups. Adopting AI as the intervention of choice is a sound strategy for organizational workforce development.

The results of this research, while not generalizable, indicate that the development and performance of newly formed heterogeneous groups are enriched through the intervention of Appreciative Inquiry. Specifically, the process solicited more favorable images among the members of AI groups versus the Control and Team-Building groups. AI groups also produced a higher quality work product than the other groups. Finally, AI groups had a more favorable response to the probe on whether they were willing to work together on future projects.

At several points in this research, the Anticipatory Principle was theorized to be the major foundation for AI as it relates to its potential with heterogeneous groups. One could say that the ability to spur group behavior can be enriched by enlarging the shadow of the future. This research linked the images (the shadow of the future) held by each participant in each group following the various interventions, and compares those images to the group's graded performance. As was theorized, there is a positive correlation between image and grade. In comparison to the other groups, AI groups reported both a higher positive image and higher grades. The results lend support to the theory that AI aids in assisting groups to improve their image of the future and that allows groups to more quickly develop and perform.

References

Adler, Nancy J. (1991). *International Dimensions of Organizational Behavior*. Belmont: Wadsworth Publishing.

Ashe, Arthur, and Rampersad, Arnold. (1993). *Days of Grace*. New York: Knopf.

Barr, Stephen. (1996). Meet the New M & A Masters: CFO's Are Taking On The Role Of Investment Banker. *CFO, 12*, 26-34.

Bettenhausen, Kenneth. (1991). Five Years of Groups Research: What We Have Learned and What Needs to be Addressed. *Journal of Management, 17*, 345-381.

Bushe, Gervase. (1998). Appreciative Inquiry with Teams. *Organization Development Journal, 16*, 41-49.

Bushe, Gervase, and Coetzer, Graeme. (1995). Appreciative Inquiry as a Team-Development Intervention: A Controlled Experiment. *Journal of Applied Behavioral Science, 31* (1), 13-30.

Cooperrider, David. (1994). *A Constructive Approach to Organizational Development*. Unpublished manuscript.

Elsass, Priscilla, and Graves, Laura. (1997). "Demographic Diversity in Decision-Making Groups: The Experiences of Women and People of Color". *The Academy of Management Review.* October: 946-973.

Harrison, David; Price, Kenneth, and Bell, Myrtle. (1998). Beyond Relational Demography: Time and the Effects of Surface- and Deep-Level Diversity on Work Group Cohesion. *Academy of Management Review, 41,* 96-107.

Jackson, Bailey, and Hardiman, Rita. (1983). "Racial Identity Development: Implications for Managing the Multiracial Work Force". In *NTL Manager's Handbook.* 107-119. Arlington: NTL Institute.

Morrison, Ann M. (1992). *The New Leaders: Guidelines on Leadership Diversity in America.* San Francisco: Jossey-Bass Publishers.

Thomas, R. Roosevelt. (1991). *Beyond Race and Gender.* New York: AMACOM.

Watson, Warren; Johnson, Lynn, and Merritt, Deanna. (1998). Team Orientation, Self Orientation, and Diversity in Task Groups: Their Connection to Team Performance Over Time. *The Journal of Group & Organization Management, 23, 161-188.*

Watson, Warren; Kumar, Kamalesh, and Michaelsen, Larry. (1993). Cultural Diversity's Impact on Interaction Process and Performance: Comparing Homogeneous and Diverse Task Groups. *Academy of Management Journal, 36,* 590-602.

Chapter 20

A FIELD EXPERIMENT IN
APPRECIATIVE INQUIRY

David A. Jones
Wendy's International

Abstract

Most studies or publications of Appreciative Inquiry focus on the process itself. Although this process emphasis has benefits, relatively little attention, from academicians or practitioners, has been addressed to Appreciative Inquiry use in a specific business setting tracking quantifiable results. In this study, a field experiment utilizing Appreciative Inquiry was conducted within 94 fast-food restaurants of a national Fortune 500 restaurant chain in a major metropolitan area. The purpose of this study was to determine if Appreciative Inquiry could be a useful intervention in enhancing salaried management restaurant level retention. Findings are significantly favorable in that the Appreciative Inquiry test group had 30–32 percent higher retention than the two control groups. Subjects in the Appreciative Inquiry test group expressed a decreased "Inclination to leave" as evidenced by the higher retention rate along with an enhanced appreciation of working within the much-maligned restaurant industry itself. This suggests further field studies using the Appreciative Inquiry methodology in order to expand its use from both an academic and practitioner oriented perspective.

Overview

There are literally thousands of articles and studies focusing on turnover within various organizations and industries. There is also a growing body of literature discussing Appreciative Inquiry. To the best of this author's knowledge, there

---

have not been any studies with quantitative data analysis within the Appreciative Inquiry spectrum.

The closest study was completed by Carter and Johnson (1992), which conducted a study on a Big Eight accounting firm referred to as AK&G. David Cooperrider, founder of Appreciative Inquiry, participated in this study in the role of advisor. Even though this study's methodology was well thought out, planned and executed, it still lacked the presentation of quantifiable results preferred in the business world. The purpose of the following study then was to contribute to the field by attempting to address the central question of application—i.e., can upper management in the hospitality industry use Appreciative Inquiry to increase entry-level management retention?

Understanding Turnover

Employee initiated turnover has been a traditional problem for the hospitality industry. However, the problem has been routinely accepted as bothersome but manageable (Woods and Macaulay, 1989). Woods and Macaulay (1989) stated that employers have not sufficiently examined the problem since the labor pool has always exceeded the number of available jobs.

There are other issues that relate to the routine acceptance of turnover. Senior management has regarded entry-level management employees as temporary employees who would quickly resign when other employment opportunities became available (Powers, 1988). Many entry-level managers take the job as an "interim" position while waiting for an opening in the job or career they really want (Powers, 1988). It is this author's opinion that senior management has subliminally accepted the stereotypical negative image of entry-level hospitality management positions, thereby accepting turnover as a normal cost of doing business. This traditional view of entry-level management turnover has changed in recent years. Three reasons for this change have been a decrease in available employees, increased industry growth and intense competition within the industry (Withiam, 1989).

The Labor Pool

The decrease in the number of available employees partially has been the result of a declining, population growth rate in the United States (Meyers, 1990). The U.S. Department of Commerce has predicted that this trend will continue through the year 2005 (Sack, 1997).

A decrease in the future labor supply will result in the inevitable shortage of workers in many U.S. industries. Withiam (1989) reported that an analyst for the

National Planning Association has predicted that the labor demand in the U.S. service sector will grow at an annual rate of 1.3 percent during the 1990s, while the supply will increase at a rate of only 1.2 percent. The National Restaurant Association has forecast a shortfall of over 1.1 million workers by the year 2000 (Sack, 1997).

Another trend in the U.S. population has had a significant impact on the hospitality industry. The decline in the nation's population growth rate combined with an increase in longevity has greatly changed the demographic composition of the workforce (Ananth and DeMicco, 1991). While the number of individuals between the ages of 16 and 24 has decreased, the number of individuals over the age 55 has increased which is not the targeted age group for hospitality industry management. By the year 2030 the number of adults over the age of 55 has been estimated to be one in three (Ananth and DeMicco, 1991). The department of commerce has predicted that the number of Americans over age 65 will increase from 25 million in 1980 to over 35 million by the year 2000 (Meyers, 1990). The anticipated increase in this older population segment raises the ante for the hospitality industry to rethink its recruiting and hiring strategy. The typical entry-level management recruitment pool currently comes from the ages 18 to 30. Hiring older employees will require rethinking organizational policies concerning education, training, development, compensation, pensions and alternate work programs (Ananth and DeMicco, 1991).

Industry Competititon

Another factor that has changed the hospitality industry's view of management turnover has been intense competition. With increased growth, competition for both market share and human resources has resulted (Lee, 1987: Withiam, 1989). As the availability of employment opportunities increases, employee turnover also has been shown to increase (Huttin, Roznowski and Hachiya, 1985; Mobley, 1982).

Minimizing Employee Shortages

Two main concepts have been proposed as methods to minimize employee shortages in the U.S. hospitality industry. The two approaches consist of (1) a reduction in turnover by increasing employee retention (the focus of this study) and (2) a reduction in the number of required employees through organizational change. The concept of reducing turnover by increasing retention requires senior management to examine current human resource management practices and to make changes in those practices which impact retention (Krone, Tabacchi, and Farber, 1989; Sarabakhsh, Carson, and Lindizren, 1989, Withiam, 1989: Woods and Macaulay, 1989).

This concept has not been unique to the hospitality industry. Woods and Maulay (1989) and Withiam (1989) stated that retention management programs are driven by the following factors: organization culture and structure, recruitment strategy, pay and benefits philosophy, employee support programs and career development systems. They have incorporated these factors into recommendations directed specifically at the hospitality industry.

The second concept of reducing the number of employees through organizational change is a more drastic and long term approach. Advocates of this concept state that emphasis solely on human resource management practices such as recruitment and pay will have a limited affect on the problem (Withiam, 1989). Gregory and Laker (1990) have stated that the hospitality industry has developed a traditional "labor mindset." This mindset has restricted both the industry's definition of the problem and the identification of possible solutions. Overcoming this mindset will require reexamination of the problem using a four part conceptual framework. Parts of this framework include finding alternatives for changing the nature of the following operational variables: the delivery system, the product or service being offered, the production technology and the structure of the service organization (Gregory and Laker, 1990).

Purpose of this Research

The purpose of this study was to determine if Appreciative Inquiry could be a useful intervention in addressing some of these issues by enhancing salaried management restaurant level retention. The methodology will be presented first by discussing the study's value, and moving on to describe the organization, the sample groups, the Appreciative Inquiry process and other instrumentation, data analysis, and results/findings. The contribution to knowledge within this study comes in four forms:

1. Enhanced knowledge of the role of Appreciative Inquiry in entry-level management retention.

2. An Appreciative Inquiry study with specific data analysis.

3. Specific focus on the hospitality industry itself where comprehensive examination is not as prevalent or rigorous.

4. The author has detailed knowledge due to authority position within the study organization that will minimize the acknowledged problem in distinguishing voluntary and involuntary turnover (Mobley, Griffeth, Hand and Meglino, 1979: Muchinsky and Tuttle, 1979; Marsh and Mannari, 1977, Mirvis and Lawler, 1977, Waters, Roach, and Waters, 1976, Hinrichs, 1975; and Letkowitz and Katz, 1969). Only voluntary turnover was considered in this study.

It should be noted that the following Appreciative Inquiry methodology will be (to the best of this author's knowledge), one of only two published detailed articulations on Appreciative Inquiry, and the only one with specific data analysis as it relates to management turnover in the hospitality industry. David Cooperrider has resisted publishing such a "methodology," concerned that it would exacerbate the split between theory and practice if it was applied as an OD technology rather than as a thoughtful inquiry into the nature of organizational life for a particular client (Carter and Johnson, 1992). There is also the risk that in publishing a methodology, it may become reified and cast in stone. The validity of these concerns is shared, although the future value to the research and practitioner communities warrants some form of structure and definition. Therefore, this study is presented as only "one" example of a highly effective intervention and not as the "one" correct way to conduct Appreciative Inquiry, as that would not be congruent with the basic foundation or philosophy of Appreciative Inquiry in the first place.

Methodology

Study Population

For the purposes of this study, the study population included all fast-food restaurant level salaried management personnel within 94 restaurants in a major metropolitan area. This target population was divided into three test groups on a randomized basis. The Appreciative Inquiry test group consisted of 33 locations hereafter referred to as test group #1. Test group #2 consisted of 32 locations that experienced normal "problem-solving" approaches toward retention. Test group #3 consisted of 29 locations that simply went on with business as usual without any interventions targeted at retention. All three test groups were alike in their geographic and demographic composition as a whole. See Table 1 for detailed information on the three test groups.

This study excluded new restaurants opened during the test period of eighteen months to maintain the integrity of the methodology and study results. Specific geographic and demographic data on the test group participants is superfluous as the differences blend together for each of the test groups as a whole.

Instrumentation

The instruments used for this study were a survey, detailed turnover tracking data, an Appreciative Inquiry questionnaire used as a question guide for individual and group interviews, and the Appreciative Inquiry intervention methodology itself.

TABLE 1. Test Group Location / Numerical Specifics

Test Group	# of Locations	Salaried Base #	# / % in City[d]	#/% Suburbs
1(AI)[a]	33	116	12/36%	21/64%
2 (PS)[b]	32	112	13/40%	19/60%
3 (O)[c]	29	102	9/31%	20/69%
Totals	94	330	34/36%	60/64%

[a]Appreciative Inquiry group
[b]Problem Solving group
[c]No Intervention group
[d]# of locations in City or Suburbs

Appreciative Inquiry Intervention Methodology

The primary instrumentation of this study was the Appreciative Inquiry intervention methodology. Appreciative Inquiry is the manipulated independent active variable in this study. The main body of this methodology was emulated from the approach taken by Carter and Johnson (1992) as shown in Table 2.

Early stages were spent resolving issues of design and logistics. The leadership team consisted of the author, six district managers managing restaurants within the test group #1, and six top performing general managers, one from each district.

The culmination of the project was the Appreciative Inquiry test group roundtable meeting. The Project Appreciative Retention Roundtable was a three and one-half day design. The initial challenge was to transform individuals into a community of inquiry with a common purpose and set of data. The Roundtable began in the evening of the first day. We decided to capture the individual experiences in the room during this time. To do so, we facilitated a discussion around four questions:

1. What one word best characterizes your experience of the Appreciative Inquiry group interviews/meetings?

2. What was the most exciting, surprising or humorous thing that occurred during your group interviews/meetings?

3. Based on the meeting, interview and survey data you have, what would be the most important outcome or message for senior management from the roundtable session?

4. What do you believe is the essence or life-giving force of the firm?

The Project Appreciative Retention Roundtable had five objectives as listed below:

1. Reaffirm affirmative topic choices and create a common base of data for all participants.

2. State provocative propositions about the life-giving properties in the firm.

TABLE 2. Stages in Appreciative Inquiry Intervention

1. Initial Appreciative Inquiry rollout and Survey #1
2. Initial meeting with test group #2 and Survey #1 (2 meetings)
3. Initial meeting with test group #3 and Survey #1 (2 meetings)
4. AI group meeting with leadership team.
5. 2nd and 3rd AI rollout and Survey #1 (2 meetings)
6. AI leader meeting on survey review and next steps
7. One AI meeting per month w/Author (15 meetings)
8. Two AI meetings per year w/DMs (18 meetings/6 DMs)
9. AI leadership team meeting-next steps
10. AI Test Group Roundtable Conference and Survey #2
11. Test Group #2 Survey #2 (2 meetings)
12. Test Group #3 Survey #2 (2 meetings)
13. Complete analysis of surveys #1 and #2
14. Project Completion and Communication to all 3 test groups
15. AI leadership team meeting-next steps

3. Consensus validation of propositions using force-field analysis and debate.

4. State realizable provocative propositions.

5. State personal commitments and plan next steps for acting on provocative propositions.

Data Collection and Analysis

Data for this study were collected throughout a two-and-a-half year time period using multiple social science methods including:

I.   Historical Documents. Company documents, published articles, books, and unpublished papers.

2.   Observations. Aside from the meetings scheduled as part of the Appreciative Inquiry intervention, numerous other committee and departmental meetings were attended providing a direct experiential basis for understanding and complementing the survey and Appreciative Inquiry meeting data. Author journal data provided assistance in "weaving" much of the data appropriate for presentation in the results / findings section.

3.   Surveys and Group Discussion of Data. Pre and post surveys were given asking for demographic information along with other questions designed to provide data for retention and turnover analysis. The purpose of the survey was to provide convergent validation around the Appreciative Inquiry intervention. The purpose of administering the surveys in two time periods was to provide a "before and after" picture mainly from the Appreciative Inquiry test group perspective.

4. Turnover Tracking Data. This turnover data tracking tool was implemented one year prior to the study period in order to provide extensive information for analysis purposes. The format of the data allowed the author to minimize the acknowledged problem in distinguishing voluntary and involuntary turnover (Mobley et al., 1979; Muchinsky and Tuttle, 1979; Marsh and Mannari, 1977; Mirvis and Lawler, 1977; Waters, Roach, and Waters, 1976; Hinrichs, 1975; and Letkowitz and Katz, 1969). The cited issues of inaccurate company records, insufficient turnover categories, employees listed as voluntary when they were actually "allowed" to quit, and haphazard record keeping were minimized due to the detail of the turnover tracking data along with the author's ability to ensure detail and accuracy. Only voluntary turnover was considered for this study.

Results and Discussion

In general, the two primary and significant findings of this study were as follows:

1. Management retention at the restaurant level was 32 percent higher in the Appreciative Inquiry test group #1 than test group #3 and 30 percent higher than test group #2.

2. Survey results revealed that the Appreciative Inquiry test group #1 were less inclined to leave the organization than either test groups #2 or #3.

A 32 percent increase in management retention translates to $103,320 savings in hard training dollars alone for the Appreciative Inquiry test group. The following steps below provide the detail for attaining this calculation:

1. The test group consisted of 116 management personnel.

2. 38% pre-test turnover equates to losing 44 people.

3. 26% test-period turnover equates to losing 30 people.

4. This 12% decrease in turnover translates to a 32% improvement.

5. Using an average weekly salary of $615 and a 12 week training period for all management candidates, this translates to $7,380 ($615 × 12) training cost per candidate. Multiply $7,380 by the reduction in turnover (14) and the result is $103,320.

This $103,320 represents only the hard cost of training dollars associated with the replacement of the management people. Lost productivity, recruitment costs, benefits, morale issues, crew turnover caused by management turnover, crew turnover training costs, sales loss due to lost productivity, and legal costs associated with turnover are not included. Using various forms of measuring these losses could easily increase the hard cost tenfold.

Some broader scope and more qualitative results (e.g., Cooperrider, 1996) are presented in summary form below:

The metaphor speaking best to our primary task and role is one where wonder, learning and the dialogical imagination will be modus operandi.

The Future Search conference will produce more whole systems learning, empowerment, and feelings of connection around business vision than hundreds of fragmenting small group meetings.

There is a reduction of time lag between organization innovations and their spread throughout the organization.

The strengthening of a "can do" climate of hope and confidence in the organization's ability to manage the transition and realize its transformational goals.

Significant increase in the organization's positive inner dialogue about the future (e.g., less cynical and deficit oriented discourse; less fear; less negativity; more vocabularies of positive possibility; more rapid spread of good news developments).

Development of a more appreciative leadership mindset and culture which provides managers with new options for dealing with organization and customer surveys, re-engineering, strategic planning analysis, team-building, merger integration, performance appraisal and others.

Significant increase in the feeling of connection to the organization's vision at all levels.

Limitations

Although the findings reported above are meaningful and significant, this study does have some limitations. First, based on these data it is not possible to "prove" that the differences in results should be attributed to the Appreciative Inquiry intervention alone. Regardless of geographic, numerical and demographic similarity within the test groups, the one key factor not analyzed nor taken into account was leadership. The author was more involved with the test group (although limited to the Appreciative Inquiry intervention alone) than the other two which could be considered part of the reason for enhanced retention and financial results.

According to Daft (1995), another limitation is as quoted below quite succinctly:

What works in one setting may not work in another setting. There is not one best way. Contingency theory means, "it depends." For example . . . some organizations may experience a certain environment, use a routine technology, and desire efficiency. In this situation, a mechanistic approach to management that uses bureaucratic control procedures, a functional structure, and formal communication would be appropriate. Likewise, organic, free flowing management processes work best in an uncertain environment with a non-routine technology. The correct management approach is contingent upon the organization's situation.

According to Sorensen, Preston and Head (1997), the above may be minimized when working with Appreciative Inquiry. Appreciative Inquiry has proven successful all over the world, and with types of organizations. Appreciative Inquiry is not a "tool" like team building, grid management, or quality circle—rather it is a innovative approach to change management. Appreciative Inquiry's approach directly attacks one of the few "universal truths" of OD practice—successful OD requires overcoming resistance to change.

Another limitation is the sample size of the test groups in relation to the hospitality industry as a whole along with the geographic restriction of all being located in one major metropolitan area. There are other variables that affect turnover (although most of these were controlled for in the turnover tracking data instrument and subsequent author analysis) that may have not been taken into account.

Directions for Future Research

For the above reasons, further research should be pursued regarding data analysis of the Appreciative Inquiry action research intervention within organizations. There is a growing literature with a qualitative "grounded theory" (Glaser and Strauss, 1967) methodology that is proving the merit and value of Appreciative Inquiry, but inserting some quantitative research into the arena can do nothing but advance this exciting organizational intervention.

The following are specific recommendations for future research:

More multivariate research specific to the fast-food restaurant industry.

More longitudinal studies specific to the fast-food restaurant industry.

A thorough meta-analysis of all major turnover studies within the past ten years.

Clearly, Appreciative Inquiry is a powerful organizational intervention that does not end. It becomes self-sustaining as it creates energy and enthusiasm within the people that it touches.

References

Anath, M., and DeMicco, F.J. (1991). Strategies for Tomorrow's Hospitality Workforce. *FIU Hospitality Review*, 9 (1), 25–37.

Barrett, F.J. (1995). Creating Appreciative Learning Cultures. *Organizational Dynamics*, 24(1), 36–49.

Carter, J.D. and Johnson, P. (1992). *Institutionalizing Change Through Dialogue: The Round Table, An Appreciative Inquiry Organizational Intervention*. John D. Carter and Associates.

Cooperrider, D.L., and Srivastva, S. (1987). An Appreciative Inquiry in Organizational Life. In W. Pasmore and R. Woodman (Eds.), *Research in Organization Chanize and Development* (Vol. 1, pp. 129–169). Greenwich, CT: JAI Press.

Cooperrider, D.L. (1996). Resources for Getting Appreciative Inquiry Started: An Example OD Proposal. *OD Practitioner*, 28, (1 and 2), 23–33.

Daft, R. (1995). Organization Theory and Design, 5th ed., Minneapolis: *Hospitality Research Journal*, 14 (2), West Publishing 155–162.

Glaser, G.G. and Strauss, A.L. (1967). *The Discovery of Grounded Theory: Strategies for Qualitative Research*. Reading, New York: Aldine de Gruyter.

Gregory, S.R., and Laker, D.R. (1990). Changing the "labor mindset" alternative solutions to the labor shortage. *Hospitality Research Journal*, 14 (2), 625–626.

Hinrichs, J.R. (1975). Measurement of Reasons for Resignation of Professionals: Questionnaire versus Company and Consultant Exit Interviews. *Journal of Applied Psychology*, 60, 530–532.

Hutlin, C.L., Roznowski, M., and Hachiya, D. (1 985). Alternative Opportunities and Withdrawal Decisions: Empirical and Theoretical Discrepancies and Integration. *Psychological Bulletin*, 97, 233–259.

Krone, C., Tabacchi, M., and Farber, B. (1989). Manager Burnout. *Cornell Hotel and Restaurant Administration Quarterly*, 30 (3), 58–63.

Lee, D.R. (1987). Why Some Succeed Where Others Fail. *Cornell Hotel and Restaurant Administration Quarterly* 28 (3), 33–37.

Letkowitz, J., and Katz, M.L. (1969). Validity of Exit Interviews. *Personnel Psychology*, 22, 445–447.

Marsh, R., and Mannari, H. (I 977). Organizational Commitment and Turnover: A Predictive Study. *Administrative Science Quarterly*, 22, 57–75.

Meyers, K.W. (1990). The Fast-Food Industry: Company Benefits and Stress.

Mirvis, P.H., and Lawler, E.E., 111. (1977). Measuring the Financial Impact of Employee Attitudes. *Joumal of Applied Psychology*, 62, 1–8.

Mobley, W.H., Griffeth, R.W., Hand, H.H., and Meglino, B.M. (1979). Review and Conceptual Analysis of the Employee Turnover Process. *Psychological Bulletin* 86, 493–522.

Mobley, W.H. (1982). *Employee Turnover: Causes, Consequences, and Control*. Reading, MA: Addison-Wesley.

Muchinsky, P.M., and Tuttle, M.L. (1979). Employee Turnover: An Empirical and Methodological Assessment. *Journal of Vocational Behavior*, 14, 43–77.

Powers, T. (1 988). *Introduction to Management in the Hospital Industry*. New York: John Wiley and Sons.

Sack, K.J. (1997). Industry Surveys: Restaurants. Standard and Poor's.

Sarabakhsh, M., Carson, D., and Lindgren, E. (I 989). The Personal Cost of Hospitality Management. *Cornell Hotel and Restaurant Administration Quarterly* 30 (1), 73–76.

Sorensen, P.F., Preston, P. F., and Head, T. (1997). Is Aprreciative Inquiry OD's Philosopher's Stone? Pre-publication handout.

Waters, L.K., Roach, D., and Waters, C.A. (1976). Estimate of Future Tenure, Satisfaction, and Biographical Variables as Predictors of Termination. *Personnel Psychology*, 29, 57–60.

Withiam, G.W. (I 989). The Labor Shortage Might Not Happen. *Cornell Hotel and Restaurant Administration Quarterly*, 30 (2), 4.

Woods, R.H., and Macaulay, J.F. (I 989). Rx for Turnover: Retention Programs that Work. *Cornell Hotel and Restaurant Administration Quarterly* (1), 79–90.

Chapter 21

APPRECIATIVE INQUIRY MEETS THE LOGICAL POSITIVIST

Peter F. Sorensen, Jr.
Benedictine University
Linda Sharkey
G.E. Capital
Robert Head
Benedictine University
Dale Spartz
Riverside Hospital

This article presents a brief summary and discussion of a series of studies illustrating the contribution of Appreciative Inquiry (AI) to the field of Organization Development (OD). The article discusses the integration of AI with existing mainstream OD interventions and reports the results of empirical studies, testing the effects of AI.

The integration of AI with existing approaches to OD is presented through a discussion of studies dealing with changes in organizational performance, team development, survey feedback and culture change. Team building and survey feedback have historically been core OD interventions. These two approaches are described by Cummings and Worley (1997) as the two earliest interventions in the field and are attributed to the initial work of Kurt Lewin. These approaches continue to be the two most frequently used interventions as cited by Joyce and Kilmann (1991), in their study of more than 300 large-scale change efforts. The central importance of team building and survey feedback is again confirmed by Head, Sorensen, Preston and Yaeger in their article later in this book (see Chapter 15). Their article reports that team building and survey feedback are the first and third most frequently used interventions in international and multinational organizational change projects.

Assessing AI based on empirical studies in the tradition of logical-positivist research methodology may appear to be inconsistent with AI and its social constructionist foundation. However several authors including Robert Golembiewski (1998) and Thomas Head (1997) have argued for the timeliness and appropriateness of such an evaluation. This article takes the position that an assessment based on traditional empirical methods serves to strengthen AI. There has been little such research to date. In fact, Bushe and Coetzer (1995) indicate that no empirical studies existed prior to their work.

Organizational Performance

The first study by David Jones deals with changes in organizational performance and is of special significance in that it represents a particularly rigorous field experiment with more than 90 work units. This study was a recipient of a "Best OD Paper Award" by the OD Institute and is reported more fully in this book (see Chapter 13). In brief, the study dealt with a situation of critical importance to the industry. The field experiment contrasted AI with more traditional human resource approaches to managerial turnover and a control group. The reported quantitative results indicate a clear superiority for AI, with significant organizational improvement. Qualitative findings reinforce the existence of positive change through the identification of such organizational changes as:

- Time reduction in the diffusion of innovations
- Greater confidence in the ability to manage change
- Increases in the organization's positive inner dialogue concerning the future
- Development of more appreciative leadership
- Increased feelings of commitment to the organization's vision

Team Development

Two experimental studies have been reported using Appreciative Inquiry in team development. The first study and probably the first experimental study (Bushe and Coetzer, 1995) reports the results of a controlled laboratory experiment with 96 undergraduate students in an introductory organization development course. The study compares the effects of Appreciative Inquiry on group development with task-oriented team development and lectures on group process. The study supports the effectiveness of Appreciative Inquiry as a team building intervention. The authors suggest that AI may be particularly appropriate for newly formed teams in facilitating team development through the creation of a positive group image. The authors also suggest that AI may be particularly helpful with highly fragmented, fragile groups, or teams in conflict. This observation is consistent with AI applications reported by David Cooperrider and Thomas Head. The application of AI to groups is discussed further in the Bushe article on Appreciative Inquiry and teams, also included in this book (see Chapter 12).

A recent study by Robert Head (1999) of team development incorporating several of the observations addressed by Bushe and Coetzer, is particularly significant in that it directly addresses one of the central principles of Appreciative Inquiry, namely the Anticipatory Principle. The Anticipatory Principle is described as:

> The infinite human resource we have for generating constructive organized change is our collective imagination and discourse about the future. One of the basic theorems of the Anticipatory view of organizational life is that it is the image of the future, which in fact guides what might be called the current behavior of an organism or organization. Much like a movie projector on a screen, human systems are forever projecting ahead of themselves a horizon of expectations (in their talk in the hallways, in the metaphors and language they use) that brings the future powerfully in to the present as a mobilizing agent, to inquire in ways that serve to refashion anticipatory reality—especially the artful creation of positive imagery on a collective basis—may be the most prolific thing any inquiry can do (Srivastva and Barrett, 1990).

The study by Head is also of interest in that it addresses the questions of the effectiveness of AI in facilitating the speed at which teams develop, and the use of the Anticipatory Principle for heterogeneous groups while bridging issues of diversity.

Similar to David Jones, Robert Head employs the methodology of the field experiment. The experiment is comprised of eighteen groups of managers and supervisors, totaling 124 participants from a large governmental agency. The results of the study support AI applications to team development, with the AI groups experiencing more positive group images and higher performance.

Survey Feedback

The final group of studies links Appreciative Inquiry to survey feedback and instrumented or databased change. Each of these studies employed a particular survey instrument, the Organization Culture Inventory (OCI). The OCI defines organization culture in terms of twelve cultural styles resulting in a profile of the organization culture. These twelve styles are clustered into three groupings. These three groupings are: Satisfaction cultures comprised of achievement, self-actualizing, humanistic and helpful styles; People/Security cultures comprised of approval, conventional, dependent, and avoidance; Task/Security cultures comprised of oppositional, power, competitive and perfectionistic styles.

The OCI is based on a number of central and familiar concepts in organizational behavior and organization development. For example, satisfaction styles are associated with Maslow's higher level needs while the two security cultures are associated with Maslow's lower level or security needs. In a similar fashion McGregor's Theory Y assumptions are associated with achievement, self-actualizing, humanistic and helpful styles. These same culture styles share conceptual foundations with such classic OD approaches as Rensis Likert's Systems Three and Four, and Blake and Mouton's Managerial Grid Style 9.9. These Satisfaction styles also appear to be associated with the characteristics of high involvement, high commitment and high performance organizations.

The studies discussed below draw heavily on the Positive Principle of Appreciative Inquiry. The role and meaning of the Positive Principle is defined by Cooperrider:

> Put most simply, it has been our experience that building and sustaining momentum for change requires large amounts of positive affect and social bonding—things like hope, excitement, inspiration, caring, camaraderie, sense of urgent purpose, and sheer joy in creating something meaningful together. What we have found is that the more positive the question we ask in our work the more long lasting and successful this change effort. It does not help, we have found, to begin our inquiries from the standpoint of the world as a problem to be solved. We are more effective the longer we can retain the spirit of inquiry for the ever-lasting beginner. The major thing we do that makes the difference is to craft and seed, in more catalytic ways, the unconditional positive question (Cooperrider, 1990).

The discussion here is based on interventions in five organizations: three private hospitals, a large financial institution and a government agency. In each of these cases participants were asked to respond to the survey instrument in terms of their peak experiences in their organization, the time at which they and the organization were at their best.

The experiences across each of the organizations are highly consistent.

- In each organization, peak experiences were clearly defined in terms of those styles comprised of achievement, self-actualizing, humanistic, and helpful.
- The appreciative patterns were frequently in sharp contrast with perceptions of the existing culture.
- The appreciative patterns were markedly consistent across organizational levels, which was frequently not true for perceptions of the existing culture.
- The appreciative question provided respondents with the opportunity to share common experiences as to when the organization was at its best.
- The AI process clearly facilitated the acceptance of the change process.
- The appreciative question and profile clearly created positive momentum, energy and support for continuing the change process.
- In the cases where the organization's appreciative profile was tracked over time there remained a high degree of consistency between periods.
- Stories relating to peak experiences were consistently about task accomplishment, collaboration, and shared effort.

- The AI experience created the foundation for exploring and developing sustainable positive organization norms.
- The AI experience created a positive image of the possible.

These experiences with AI clearly demonstrate that AI provides an important, perhaps critical, new way of approaching organizational change. It is a change strategy in and of itself, and at the same time, a powerful extension of existing OD technologies. Although AI departs from the problem-solving approach so deeply embedded in OD and management in general it is consistent with much of what we have learned of organizational change from the behavioral sciences over the last 50 years. Nevertheless, there is much that we need to understand. Appreciative Inquiry is very much in its embryonic stage as a comprehensive theory of change. Some of the issues that need to be better understood, for example, include:

What exactly is it about AI, which creates its unique power? and

Under what conditions is it the intervention of choice?

For example, although the Bushe and Coetzer study demonstrates the effective application to teams it was not the most effective intervention under the particular conditions of the study.

Clearly we have a way to go. We need verification provided by experimental studies but probably even more important is the understanding provided by longitudinal studies designed to explore the sustainability of AI-led interventions.

The full appreciation of AI continues to evolve. The need to more fully understand the nature and the role of AI in OD is probably best articulated in an article by Robert Golembiewski appropriately titled *Appreciating Appreciative Inquiry* (1998). The reader is recommended to this article for a comprehensive review, critique and important perspective on AI.

Summary

This article has dealt with the integration and effect of Appreciative Inquiry when combined with two of the foundation and core intervention technologies in OD: team development and survey feedback. Both methods continue to be the most frequently employed methods in the field both nationally and internationally. The article also viewed Appreciative Inquiry from the perspective of the logical positivist and begins to answer the question, "What happens when you test AI using traditional positivist approaches to evaluate its effectiveness?"

Cooperrider describes Appreciative Inquiry as a new paradigm in change management. But it also appears that AI does, in fact, do well by the *old* paradigm of traditional logical-positivist empirical research. Although systematic, empirical testing of AI continues to be limited, the studies that do exist support and strengthen the position of AI. It is our sense that AI has provided new paradigm ways of contributing in a critical manner to two of the most central and historically important approaches in OD as well as to the development of the OD field. AI should continue to be served well by its assessment by more traditional behavioral science methodologies.

References

Bushe G., and Coetzer, G. (1995). Appreciative Inquiry as a team development intervention. *Journal of Applied Behavioral Science*, 31, 13–30.

Cooke, R. and Hartmann, J. (1989). *Interpreting the Culture Styles Measured By the Organizational Culture Inventory: Organizational Culture Inventory Leader's Guide*, Plymouth, Michigan: Human Synergistics, Inc.

Cooke, R. and Lafferty, J. C. (1989). *The Organizational Culture Inventory*, Plymouth Michigan: Human Synergistics, Inc.

Cummings, T. and Worley, C. G. (1993). *Organization Development and Change*, 6th ed., Minneapolis: West Publishing Company.

Golembiewski, R. T. (1998). Appreciating Appreciative Inquiry: Diagnosis and Perspectives on How to Do Better. In R. Woodman and W. B. Pasmore (Eds.) *Research in Organizational Change and Development* (Vol. 11, pp. 1–45).

Head, R. (1999). "Appreciative Inquiry as a Team Development Intervention for Newly formed Heterogeneous Groups," presented at the International Association of Management.

Head, T. C. (1997). Why does appreciative inquiry work? Speculation and a call for empirical study. Working paper. Tennessee State University, Nashville, TN.

Head, T. and Sorensen, P. (1993). Cultural Values and Organization Development. *Leadership and Organization Development Journal*, 11, 3–7.

Joyce, T., and Kilmann, R., (1991). Profiling Large-Scale Change Efforts. *OD Journal*, Vol. 9, No. 2, Summer 1991.

Likert, R. (1962). *New Patterns of Management*, New York: McGraw-Hill

Likert, R. (1967). *The Human Organization*, New York: McGraw-Hill

Sharkey, L. (1999). Changing organizational culture through leadership development: A case in leadership transformation. *OD Journal*, Fall 1999.

Sharkey, L., Sorensen, P., Yaeger, T., "Integrating Traditional and Contemporary Approaches to Change: Culture, Survey Feedback and Appreciative Inquiry." Creating Healthy Organization Cultures Conference, Loyola University, Chicago, IL June 1998.

Sorensen, P., Head, T., Gironda, L., and Larsen, H. (1996). Global Organization Development: Lessons From Scandinavia. *Organization Development Journal.*

Sorensen, P., Head, T., Johnson, K. and Mathys, N. (1991). *International Organization Development*, Champaign, IL: Stipes.

Spartz, D. (1998) Creating Healthy Organization Cultures Conference, Loyola University, Chicago, IL June 1998. "Diagnosing and developing a management culture: A case study in health care"

Srivastva, S., & Barrett, F.J. (1990) Appreciative organizing: Implications for executive functioning. In S. Srivastva, D.L. Cooperrider, & Associates (Eds.), *Appreciative management and leadership*, San Francisco, CA: Jossey-Bass.

PART III

New Horizons

The final section, *New Horizons*, consists of nine chapters dealing with topics which have particular relevance and importance for AI, for the field of OD, and in a way, for humankind as a whole.

The first article reports on a project of particular significance — the United Religions Initiative. The article also presents an interview by Michael Toms with Dee Hock on his concept of the Chaordic Organization.

The next chapter, Chapter 23, raises a fundamental question, one that has critical implications for the potential of AI – does AI transcend national boundaries and national values. The authors draw on their own personal and international research experiences.

In Chapter 24 Thomas Head addresses a central concern in organization development, resistance to change. Head discusses five myths of change and how they relate to AI. Chapter 25 presents the views of Robert Golembiewski, the best-known constructive critic of AI. Golembiewski makes a special and much needed contribution. The perspectives presented include: AI overstates real but qualified differences, lack of linkages to other theory and practice, sparse research literature, lack of a critical imperative, and the need for a situational or contingency approach to AI.

Next in Chapter 26, Diana Whitney describes one of the most effective applications of AI, the AI Summit, which is the integration of AI principles with large group methods. In Chapter 27 Watkins and Cooperrider discuss International Development Organizations, organizations that focus on issues of poverty, oppression, environmental degradation, human rights, and child survival. Here the authors refer to these organizations as Global Social Change Organizations (GSCOs) in relation to the Organizational Inquiry Model and Appreciative Inquiry.

Chapter 28 by Mantel and Ludema extends the discussion of International Development Organization and AI with four diverse case studies from WorldVision's Global Operations. In Chapter 29 James Ludema places AI within the context of hope. Ludema presents the concept that vocabularies of hope serve as a powerful catalyst for positive social and organizational global transformation.

The final chapter by Dawn Dole expands the scope of the book by providing additional sources for the reader's continued journey into Appreciative Inquiry.

Chapter 22

Appreciative Inquiry and the Conscious Evolution of Chaordic Organizations

David Cooperrider, Ph.D.
Case Western Reserve University

I remember the meeting vividly. We were quietly working on an amazing puzzle that was attracting the very best people of any project I've ever worked on. The agenda and puzzling tasks of the committee: to design a worldwide "United Religions" organization that would be a spiritual parallel to the United Nations.

Barbara Marz Hubbard, one of the people at the meeting, excitedly introduced us to Dee Hock, founder and CEO Emeritus of VISA, making a remark that has stayed with me: "Appreciative modes of knowing may be to chaordic, self-organizing systems what deficit or problem-oriented methods of management have been to command-and-control bureaucracy."

At the core of every distinctive form of social organization, says Hubbard, are "memetic codes" that are to social systems what genetic codes are to biological organisms – "the way genes build bodies, memes build cultures, societies, and the noosphere." What we need today, she says, are life-affirming memes or ways of knowing that fosters a positive future." That is what Appreciative Inquiry is centrally about.

Before exploring her thesis in this article, let's first take a more pragmatic look at some "how to" lessons.

Precious little has been written about the practice of lifting up a chaordic alliance. For me, there were many surprises. One of the simpler lessons to state, but one of the deepest in its impact, is: If we want to have dramatic new forms of human organization, we must have equally powerful means to achieve them – means that are congruent with truly radical, self-organizing, chaordic ends.

A version of this work previously appeared in *The Inner Edge*, February/March 2000.

This process, forever poised on the edge of chaos, is not for the weak-hearted. It is exhilarating, messy, relationally uplifting, wonderful, and terrifying. It involves some of the most intense dialogue and listening imaginable. Everyone changes. You see people become better human beings. I wish everyone alive could experience this thrill. But let's go back to the beginning.

A Call from the U.N.

Years before the United Nations' 50th anniversary, the Episcopal Bishop for California, the Rt. Rev. Bishop William Swing, received a call asking his help – or, in essence, to host an event in 1995 to commemorate the signing of the U.N. Charter in 1945 at Grace Cathedral in San Francisco (where the Bishop is located). Bishop Swing was honored to assist.

But as the event grew near, the Bishop felt increasingly troubled. One night he awoke and could not go back to sleep. He had on his mind an observation and a question. The observation: For 50 years through the U.N., our political leaders have demonstrated a moral commitment to at least talk about and struggle for peace. The question: What have world religious leaders done for peace in that same time?

The Bishop did not like the answer. Not only had the world's religions not talked, but religious differences were at the heart of most of the current wars.

That night, Bishop Swing had a vision of a "United Religions Initiative", a project to which he would dedicate the rest of his life – developing a permanent means for all the religions and spiritual movements of the world to come together to promote enduring, daily, interfaith cooperation, thus working to end religiously motivated violence and fostering cultures of peace, justice and healing for the earth. The goal of creating a charter for United Religions was boldly shared at the U.N.'s 50th Anniversary celebration. People cheered, but few believed it possible.

Religions *Together?*

What about the centuries of conflict? How can you build a representative body? What about power and authority? How would the system work? What good is a United Religions charter if nobody embraces it? How – beyond just crafting a charter – can a world-wide commitment be developed? How many years would it take? Can the words "spiritual" and "organization" be united in any meaningful way – or are we likely to be left with yet one more international bureaucracy?

These are some of the hurdles that created unimaginable odds against the idea. But, despite all that, a charter will be signed. The global United Religions (URI) will be born on June 26, 2000. In just four years from the first global summit meeting in 1996, thousands of people have shared their visions and worked together to create the URI. Several million dollars have been raised for URI work taking place on all continents and across nations: People from a variety of religions, spiritual expressions, and indigenous traditions are experiencing unprecedented levels of cooperation vis-à-vis the creation of an organization that is inclusive, non-hierarchical and decentralized – a unique organization composed of self-organizing groups operating locally and connecting globally. By the time the charter is signed, there will be URI organizations (called "cooperation circles") in 30 parts of the world.

URI's ability to work will be due to a few simple concepts: identity (deep purpose and constitutional principles), information (an almost instantaneous spread of innovation and imagination); and relationally empowering inquiry that searches for the best in each other and creates center-to-center unions connecting people deliberately to the positive core of the whole (assets, strengths, aspirations, sacred center, best practices, etc). The result is evolution – a constantly interweaving, but not rigid, process that leads to structure. This is a dynamic connection of circles that are adaptive to endless change, responsive to context, and connected to the infinite capacities of the whole.

What does it take to create such an "entity"? URI suggests these rules:

- There must be an intense commitment to conceptualizing the organization. A team of 10 to 20 people must commit to working together for at least three days every 45 days for the next two years to move through an iterative cycle of articulating purpose, principles, people, concept, and constitution and by-laws. A quicker process is not feasible because so much of what needs to be done is "unlearning" – the inertia of command-and-control practices is unbelievable!

- Also much needed is an interweaving of conversations in and through three modalities: (1) large group (LG) "whole system" planning forums; (2) small group (SG) design team meetings; and (3) building an expanding dialogue (or EC, extended community).

Lifting up a chaordic organization is not so much a matter of just producing a charter as it is of allowing the co-creation of new concepts to occur and a domain-wide commitment to be built. It is not "charter" that concerns us, but "chartering," which reminds us all of the Tao-like relation between content and connectivity.

In this spirit, an annual LG planning conference of 100 to 2,000 people is essential. It builds a tremendous sense of momentum, vision and authorization for the SG design team meetings; the SG meetings subsequently create a depth of content that can be used to ignite conversation with an ever-expanding electronic and face-to-face EC; all three together constantly interweave, and a chaordic structure emerges.

Appreciative Inquiry: A Special Contribution

On May 3, 1996 Bishop Swing asked me, along with a team from the SIGMA Center for Human Cooperation and Global Action at Case Western Reserve University, to guide the four-year process of building a United Religions. The first global summit of religious and spiritual leaders was already scheduled, so we had less than five weeks to prepare the design. The inaugural session would be held at the Fairmont Hotel in the room where the U.N. charter was written. Credit for involving Appreciative Inquiry (AI) belongs to Bishop Swing and Charles Gibbs, who saw AI as an essential methodology.

AI's Positive Foundation

According to AI theory, organizations are, first and foremost, centers of human relatedness: relationships thrive where there is an appreciative eye – when people see the best in one another, when they share their dreams and ultimate concerns in affirming ways, and when they are connected in full voice to create not just new worlds, but better worlds. In practice, appreciate inquiry involves a co-evolutionary search for the best in people, their organizations, and the world around them. It involves systematic discovery of what forces are at work when a system is its most effective, compassionate, and capable in economic, ecological, and human terms.

AI is the art and practice of asking questions to strengthen a system's capacity to apprehend, anticipate, and heighten positive potential. It mobilizes inquiry through crafting an "unconditional positive question," and often involves the exchange of stories among hundreds or sometimes thousands of people. In AI, intervention gives way to imagination and innovation. Instead of negativism, criticism, and spiraling diagnosis, there is discovery, dream and design. AI assumes every living system has untapped rich, inspiring accounts of the positive. Link this "positive change core" directly to any change agenda and changes that seem impossible are suddenly and democratically mobilized.

Shifting Focus to Experience Wholeness

Beyond the shift from a deficit-based theory of change to a life-centric search for the positive core, the other unique factor that makes AI powerful is the experience of wholeness. In the case of the URI, a turning point was when we suggested that participation in the charter writing go beyond the typical religious leaders to involve others with a stake in an effective United Religions: people from the grassroots, youth leaders of NGO's like Save the Children, business leaders, people at the World Bank, and so on. Bringing everyone together, even so-called "outsiders," gives all people a connection to the whole and creates a new human dynamic. Like astronauts who have spoken of experiencing an "instant global consciousness" when they are high above the earth, the experience of bringing the whole system into the room brings higher levels of awareness, compassion, and cooperation.

One of the hardest parts for us, with so many religious leaders present, was the absence of formal speeches. Everyone works together as peers. Everyone comes with opportunity for voice. Our goal is to create a setting nothing short of "full voice." A summit does not work when a leadership group meets separately and seeks out others only to validate a pre-written plan.

To lift up URI, annual global summits have been held since 1996, and regional summits have taken place in South Africa, East Africa, Brazil, Egypt, India, Argentina, Romania, and other countries. The results have often been dramatic. After an AI session at Stanford University, one participant said, "I think everyone left a bit stunned by what a gift the experience had been."

For me, being part of creating this chaordic organization with such moral purpose and positive vision has given me more hope about our world's future than any work I've ever done. It also has left me with a new image of possibility: a metaphor used repeatedly in the dream and design phases was of Indra's net - the cosmic web of interrelatedness extending infinitely in all directions of the universe. Every intersection of the web has a glistening jewel in which all parts of the whole are reflected. Imagine such an organization: composed of reflections that endlessly amplify everyone's strengths, sparkling and glistening. It is an image that is coming alive right now.

The Chaordic Organization:
An Interview with Dee Hock
By Michael Toms

Is the first massive change in organizations in more than 300 years trying to emerge in our lifetime? Dee Hock, the creator of the world's largest organization – VISA, a $1.25 trillion-enterprise – thinks so. People have lost faith in flavor-of-the-month business fads; they no longer believe organizational structures created in the spirit of the old Newtonian mechanistic age can be fixed. The new vision that is emerging looks to biological systems and the universe for lessons on how to self-organize, and to chaos theory for the natural tie between chaos and order. But it's something even more – something so new that Hock invented a term for it: chaord (from chaos and order). Chaordic organizations are arising more frequently – but as archetypes to aid learning, not "models" that can be quickly imprinted on existing organizations, says Hock, the author of the new book *The Birth of the Chaordic Age* (Berrett-Koehler Publishers, 1999). Hock was interviewed exclusively for *The Inner Edge* by Editor Michael Toms of New Dimensions Radio.

The Inner Edge: How is thinking about organizations as "structures" or centers of power turned on its head by chaordic principles?

Hock: The chaordic organization begins with an intensive search for *purpose* – the shared understanding and deep conviction of a community of people. Purpose flows naturally from individuals seeking deeply their reason for coming together. Ask a deceptively simple question: "If there were no constraints whatever, the ideal nature of our organization would..." How you fill in the blank is how you define the organization's true purpose.

After the true purpose is known, the chaordic organization then moves on to a definition of *principles* – the organization's behavioral aspirations, or the way in which the whole and all its parts intend to conduct themselves. Principles are the precepts against which all structures, decisions, actions and results will be judged. They always reflect high moral and ethical values. But they are not prescriptive of behavior, they only describe it. Further, they are not mandatory, rigid rules, and they can never be fully realized. An example is the commandment to "Honor Thy Father and Mother." That's a principle, but it doesn't give instructions on how it is to be accomplished.

From purpose and principles, the chaordic organization flows to *people* and *concept*. People must transcend existing institutional boundaries and practices to get in touch with their deepest feelings. This is what motivates and feeds the chaordic organization. Only after these aspects are addressed does the question of organization and structure emerge as a consideration. Structure is the embodiment of purpose, principles, people and concept. Finally the chaordic organization involves new practices that do not bind participants. Instead of using command-and-control, leaders act as trustees to bring the organization into greater harmony with the human spirit and the natural world.

The Inner Edge: In 1970, VISA was created – perhaps as the world's first "chaordic" organization. What were your thoughts leading up to VISA?

Hock: I was preoccupied with what I saw as a chasm between how institutions profess to function and how they actually do. I think my observations were beginning to germinate even in my youth when I spent so much time in the outdoors. To me, there was a stark contrast between how nature organizes itself and what I saw in organizations.

In the late 1960's when I was the vice president of the National Bank of Commerce in Seattle, I chaired a committee of bank vice presidents looking into the problems plaguing the banking industry. In a pivotal moment, I posed a single question: "If anything in the world were possible, and there were no constraints, what would be the nature — not the structure, but the nature – of an ideal organization whose purpose was to create the world's premier system for the exchange of value?" During our discussions, I wondered if it would be possible to throw away everything we thought we knew about organizational structures and instead try to conceive an organization based on the biological concepts exemplified by nature. If we could do that then, I believed, we could create an organization more in harmony with human spirit and the biosphere. It may be a bit presumptuous, but ours was an effort to rethink or reconceive the very nature of the organization itself.

The Inner Edge: VISA has been a great business success, but has it been a chaordic success?

Hock: The concept of what is chaordic, or a chaordic "success" is still very much evolving. I coined the term "chaordic" to explain that we achieve order out of chaos – the same way the universe works. As complexity theory postulates, everything, even life itself, emerges in a narrow band between chaos and order. In discussions, scientists may fuss over a whole string of adjectives for this concept – auto-catalytic, self-organizing, adaptive, non-linear. I was tired of trying to use 25 different adjectives, so I started exploring my library and lexicons looking for a better word. When I couldn't find one, I decided to invent the word "chaordic" about four or five years ago. I took the first syllable of chaos and the first syllable of order and merged them into a new word, "chaord." VISA fit the concept; it was quasi-governmental, quasi-for-profit, quasi-not-for-profit, quasi-consulting, quasi-franchising, quasi-educational, quasi-social, quasi-commercial, a quasi-political alliance. Paradoxically, it was none of these and all of these. It was chaordic.

I am very proud of VISA and all that it has demonstrated about the power of the chaordic concept of the organization. Even so, VISA is not a model to emulate. It is more like an archetype – something to study, learn from, and improve upon. Although it's difficult to talk about failure, we never got VISA more than a third "right" as an archetype of the chaordic organization.

The Inner Edge: When you speak to audiences about chaordic organizations, how do they respond?

Hock: All types of people seem to grasp what I'm trying to explore. Of course I tell them there is nothing I'm going to say that they don't already know intuitively. The second thing I tell them is that the guru has not arrived. And the third thing is there's no model in the briefcase. The concept of chaordic organizations is about massive cultural and institutional change, in my judgment. If the change that I think we're facing is anywhere near as profound and as quick as I think it's going to be, none of us knows more than 10% to 15% of what we'll need to know. This information is emerging at an extraordinary rate, and there are manifestations everywhere. Chaordic organizations abound: World Weather Watch; the Internet; the Appleseed Foundation; the Society for Organizational Learning; and Alcoholics Anonymous.

As a chaordic organization, the Internet is fundamentally flawed. But VISA was flawed in its own way, too. We only got VISA about a third right.

The Inner Edge: Why is the Internet flawed?

Hock: The Internet has never dealt with the institutionalization of its de-institutionalized structure. It does not have – and never has had – any governance structure that is at all harmonious with or based upon the concepts around which the Internet organized itself. Since it's never dealt with its own institutionalization in a de-institutionalized way, it's subject to its own excesses. It has no immune system to its own excesses, whether it's pornography, or spamming or whatever. It can't control its own diseases.

The Inner Edge: What is your assessment of the world today?

Hock: I think we're on the knife's edge of massive institutional and cultural change. It cannot and will not let the earth go on as it is. I believe there are two forces moving aggressively through the world. One is the centralization of power and wealth, and the old Newtonian command-and-control mechanistic model. The other, which I'll discuss in a moment, is the force of chaos, or the chaordic. First, the force of centralized power and mechanistic models is seen in incredible mergers that were unthinkable a few years ago. It's manifested in the Soviet Union trying to create its empire. It's an old way of thinking, but it's still dominant and powerful. The massive institutional failure we're experiencing is approaching social anarchy. We've got it in many areas of the world already, as well as in significant segments of U.S. society. Institutional failure may get worse, causing the public to demand order in the streets, with more centralization of power occurring, regressing us further to more dictatorial forms of organization than ever before. This time, though, the dictators will be huge multinational corporations acting in concert with nationalist governments.

The second force – the force of chaos or the chaordic – is manifested in the Internet, VISA, the World Weather Watch, in the airline reservations system (that no one owns and controls), and in outsourcing. These are hundreds of manifestations of both forces – huge diametrically opposed movements – and all on a collision course.

The Inner Edge: What then?

Hock: We're not going to be able to stay on the knife's edge. We may not be able to discern the events that will tip us one way or the other. In fact, they may have already happened.

I'm optimistic, however, because we have a great opportunity to move toward chaordic concepts of organization. For the first time in my lifetime, there is a real chance to enhance understanding of organizations and to raise internal consciousness and awareness to move us in a different direction. In my lifetime, we've had the notion that big central governments were going to be the answer. Then, the paragons of virtue were the great hierarchical ITT's, General Motors, etc. Next, we went through a period of public disillusionment in which we question these organizations. However, we continued to believe they were fixable – giving us 20 years of what I call management "nostrums of the month," or fixes. These included quality circles, empowerment, one-minute management, management by objective. There are probably 30 different fixes that became immensely popular and that were massively implemented. But everything got worse, and each idea died.

Now I sense that people are at a stage where they not only have lost confidence in existing forms of organization and leadership, but they no longer believe deep down that they're fixable. Consequently, they are open to exploring entirely new ways of thinking about organizations. If we do this on a broad basis, I believe we'll discover a way of thinking that is compatible with evolution, nature and the earth. Organizations will evolve that are compatible with the human spirit and with the biosphere.

Chapter 23

Is Appreciative Inquiry OD's Philosopher's Stone?

Thomas C. Head
Roosevelt University
Peter F. Sorensen, Jr.
Benedictine University
Joanne C. Preston
Pepperdine University
Therese F. Yaeger
Benedictine University

Can Appreciative Inquiry (AI) be that alchemist's philosopher's stone OD has been searching for? AI, as an approach to organization transformation, has proven its effectiveness in a wide variety of organizations and cultures—from seeking solutions for Romanian orphanages to providing direction to Fortune 500 boardrooms. Regardless of national/corporate culture AI appears to be effective—so is it the "universal" approach to change that we have so long sought for (and taught against)? This paper will present a "stream of thought" which provides an explanation for AI's apparent universal success.

The Journey Begins: True OD Requires An Organization Culture Change

"OD involves both the creation and the subsequent reinforcement of change. It moves beyond the initial attention to implementing a change program to a longer-term concern for stabilizing and institutionalizing new activities within the organization." (Cummings and Worley, 1993, p. 2) It has long been accepted that legitimate OD's "end result" involves a culture change in the client organization. Rensis Likert (1962) supported this notion when he created his "Three-Variable Model" and placed what we now call "organization culture" firmly into the Causal Variable category. In essence, Likert suggests that interventions which fail to effect the causal variables (culture) will only address "intervening level" variables—similar to a physician who only treats a patient's symptoms without eliminating the disease. The patient/client "feels" better but the problem is only masked. The patient is still sick and sooner or later new, and most likely more dangerous, symptoms will emerge.

Lewin's (1952) three-stage change model also supports the belief that "true" OD must involve a change in organization culture. Lewin's first stage, unfreezing, "involves reducing those forces maintaining the organization's behavior . . . sometimes accomplished by introducing information that shows discrepancies between behaviors desired by organizational members and those behaviors they currently exhibit." (Cummings and Worley, 1993, p. 53) Clearly a call for "attacking" the current corporate culture—showing the employees the faults in the present culture and the possibilities of a new culture. This interpretation is further supported by Lewin's final state, refreezing, which "stabilizes the organization at a new state of equilibrium . . . frequently accomplished through the use of supporting mechanisms that reinforce the new organizational state, such as organization culture, norms, policies, and structures." (Cummings and Worley, 1993, p. 53).

In a more contemporary view Tichy (1983) further reinforces cultural change's requirement for "true" change. Organization culture is one of the three "loosely coupled" systems—the others being the technical and political systems. Organization change requires first developing a vision of the organization which involves the three systems being aligned. To achieve this image the three systems must be "uncoupled" and each one, separately, receive intervention. Only after all three systems have been changed can they be "recoupled" to insure continued success.

Implicit in Tichy's model is the understanding that while successful change requires an organization culture modification, that cultural transformation does not have to be "radical", rather it can be incremental in nature (Meyer, Goes, and Brooks, 1992). Possibly Roosevelt Thomas (1990), in his discussion of managing cultural diversity, described the requisite culture change best. Thomas suggests that while sometimes a massive organization culture upheaval is needed, more typically subtle changes are called for. These subtle changes are similar to what a tree surgeon does—trimming a branch here, grafting a part there, and removing (or rerouting) a diseased root, all to reinforce what is "good" about the tree while removing the "bad". Generally employees like the organization's culture—that is often the reason why they remain employees. These people will recognize the need for subtle cultural modifications—retaining the "best" parts, changing the diseased elements, but only removing that which is malignant.

First Bend: Culture Change, Yes, But To What?

It is clear that successful organization interventions require the active alteration of the organization's culture. But a culture change to what? Some theorists have argued for a "universally desirable" culture—typically centering around employee participation. Rensis Likert (1962a, 1967, 1977) is one such individual—making strong arguments for the overwhelming desirability of the "System 4" organization. System 4 is "designed around group methods of decision making and supervision . . . fosters high degrees of member involvement and participation. Work groups are highly involved in setting goals, making decisions, improving methods, and appraising results." (Cummings and Worley, 1993, p. 247)

Blake and Mouton (1975), through their "9,9" (or Team Management) universally desirable Leadership style, also advocate one "all encompassing" organization culture. "9,9" organizations stress "understanding and agreement through involvement—participation—commitment as the key to . . . boss–subordinate (relationships)." (p. 164)

While the notion of a "universally desirable" corporate culture would make everyone's life much simpler the evidence clearly contradicts this belief. Cummings and Worley (1993), in their reviews, note that while Blake and Mouton's "Grid can be successful, but not in all situations." (p. 258), and "although there is evidence to support the effectiveness of system 4 (research and theory) suggests that such success may be limited to certain situations." (p. 251)

The reason for Likert and Blake and Mouton's failures to achieve universal applicability is quite simple. "Despite changes in the environment, organizations are not all alike. A great many problems occur when all organizations are treated as similar, which was the case with both the administrative principles and bureaucratic approaches (Scientific Management and Classical Management Movements) that tried to design all organizations alike." (Daft, 1995, p. 23). The basis for all modern management thought is contingency—the understanding that organizations must be designed for a "goodness-of-fit" with their own unique environment (Pennings, 1992). Daft (1995, pp. 24–25) illustrates the concept quite succinctly:

What works in one setting may not work in another setting. There is not one best way. Contingency theory means, "it depends." For example, some organizations may experience a certain environment, use a routine technology, and desire efficiency. In this situation, a mechanistic approach to management that uses bureaucratic control procedures, a functional structure, and formal communication would be appropriate. Likewise, organic, free-flowing management processes work best in an uncertain environment with a nonroutine technology. The correct management approach is contingent upon the organization's situation.

Clearly there is no "universal" corporate culture. The concept is based upon false assumptions. So, the central question around implementing successful change becomes "Changing the culture, okay, but to what?" Daft has already answered this: the ideal corporate culture is contingent upon the unique influences the client organization faces.

Second Bend: Nation's Culture Influences Organization Culture

The ideal culture for a corporation is dependent upon the organization' s internal and external environments. There is plenty of evidence that supports the belief that the socio-cultural (national cultural values) sector is a major influence on the organization's systems (Daft, 1995). Hofstede (1980) was one of first to empirically study the influence of a nation's culture on management practices. Hofstede found that most countries have a unique combination of four values: masculinity/femininity, uncertainty avoidance, power distance, and individualist/ collectivist. With this evidence Hofstede speculated that management practices developed in one country (based upon its own culture) could not be useful in other countries.

While it is now apparent that Hofstede overstated his case (Sorensen, Head, Johnson and Mathys, 1991), his work has still proved to be an invaluable guide for change theorists. Central for this paper is the work of Jaeger (1986), who reanalyzed Hofstede's data with specific regards to the compatibility of national cultural values with organization development's core values (low uncertainty avoidance, feminine, low power distance, and moderate collectivist). Specifically, Jaeger was able to classify countries as "similar to OD", "somewhat different to OD" (different on 1 or 2 values), and "different to OD" (differing on 3 or all 4 values). Jaeger suggested that the closer a country's culture is to OD's values, the more successful OD interventions would be in that culture. Jaeger (1989) and Head and Sorensen (1993) empirically tested, and confirmed, this hypothesis. A corollary evolved from Jaeger's work—Organization Development interventions can be successful in incompatible cultures—but adjustments are required to achieve a cultural fit. For a detailed example of this corollary, see Head, Sorensen, Larsen and Nielsen (1993), which examines how an intervention (management development) takes on different characteristics in three distinct cultures: Denmark, U.S.A., and the Republic of China.

Recently, this body of research has specifically looked at the relationship between national cultural values and ideal corporate cultures. One example of this research stream is that of Sorensen, Head, Gironda, and Larsen (1996). Utilizing Cooke and Lafferty's (1989) Organization Culture Inventory, Sorensen et al. have been documenting national "ideal" corporate cultures. Before these results are presented, an understanding of the Organization Culture Inventory is needed.

The Organizational Culture Inventory (OCI) is a multi-level diagnostic tool developed by Robert Cooke and Clayton Lafferty. The OCI provides a standardized measure of corporate culture with regards to the behavioral norms and expectations associated with the more abstract aspects of organization culture such as shared values and beliefs. Responses to the OCI have been related to organizational outcomes such as member satisfaction, motivation, teamwork, the quality of products/ services and other criteria of organizational effectiveness such as sales performance. Clearly, the OCI is an appropriate and useful instrument for facilitating culture change programs (Sorensen, Head, Gironda, Larsen, 1996). More importantly for this paper, the OCI has been used and adopted by various national and international organizations and completed by more than 200,000 respondents worldwide. The OCI has been reprinted in French, German and translation keys developed in Spanish and Russian.

The OCI measures an organization's ideal culture with regard to 12 different value styles (Cooke and Hartmann, 1989):

1. Humanistic-Helpful Culture: High priority is placed on constructive interpersonal relationships. Members are expected to be friendly, open and sensitive to their work group and also sharing feelings and thoughts.

2. Affiliative Culture: High priority is placed on constructive interpersonal relationships. Members are expected to be friendly, open, and sensitive to their work group and also sharing feelings and thoughts.

3. Approval Culture: Conflicts are avoided and interpersonal conflicts are pleasant—at least superficially. Members feel like they should agree with, gain the approval of, and be liked by others.

4. Conventional Culture: Conservative, traditional and bureaucratically controlled. Members are expected to conform, follow the rules, make good impressions and always follow policies and practices.

5. Dependent Culture: Hierarchically controlled and non-participative. Centralized decision making leads members to do only as they are told, clear all decisions with superiors, doing what is expected and pleasing those in positions of authority.

6. Avoidance Culture: Fail to reward success but nevertheless punish mistakes. The negative reward system leads members to shift responsibilities to others, avoid any possibility of being blamed, wait for others to act first, and take few chances.

7. Oppositional Culture: Confrontation prevails and negativism is rewarded. Members gain status and influence by being critical and thus reinforced to oppose the ideas of others, make safe decisions, pointing out flaws and are hard to impress.

8. Power Culture: Non-participative organizations structured on the basis of authority inherent in members' positions. Members believe they will be rewarded for taking charge, controlling subordinates while being responsive to demands of superiors.

9. Competitive Culture: Winning is valued and members are rewarded for outperforming one another. Members operate in a win-lose framework and believe they must work against, not with, their peers.

10. Competence/Perfectionist Culture: Perfectionism, persistence and hard work are valued. Members feel they must avoid all mistakes, keep track of everything, work long hours to attain narrowly defined objectives.

11. Achievement Culture: Do things well and value members who accomplish goals. Members set challenging but realistic goals, establish plans to reach them and pursue them with enthusiasm.

12. Self-Actualization Culture: Value creativity, quality over quantity and both task accomplishment and individual growth. Members are encouraged to gain enjoyment from their work, develop themselves and take on interesting activities.

These twelve values are arranged in a "clock" format recording progressive interrelationships and behaviors. The values at the top of the clock (11, 12, 1 and 2) indicate constructive cultures; values towards the bottom of the clock indicate passive, aggressive, and/or defensive cultures. For the sake of comparison the "clock" dimensions are standardized. The further away from the center point, the more prevalent a specific trait is for that organization's culture.

Sorensen et al. (1996), through surveys of fourteen countries' MBA students, have found dramatic differences in OCI profiles based upon the countries' cultural similarity to Organization Development values. Their findings are reported in Figures 1, 2, and 3. Each profile, as expected, is unique, and will be discussed below. One interesting and unexpected finding was that all three groups' profiles did have one similarity. The values of Conventional style (4 o'clock) and Dependent style (5 o'clock) were identified as the least significant in all three groups' profiles. Therefore the discussion of profile differences will focus on the opposite end of the spectrum: those values which are dominant in the profiles.

Figure 1. Organization Culture Inventory Profile for those countries whose culture is very similar to that of Organization Development.

Figure 2. Organization Culture Inventory Profile for those countries whose culture is "somewhat similar" to Organization Development's.

Figure 3. Organization Culture Inventory Profile for those countries whose culture is "very different" from those of Organization Development.

Figure 1 illustrates the ideal corporate culture profile of the three countries (Denmark, Norway, and Sweden) whose values are similar to those of organization development. The two "dominant" cultural values, not surprisingly, reflect the true nature of OD: Self-Actualizing (12 o'clock) and Humanistic-Helpful (1 o'clock). Figure 2 illustrates the ideal corporate culture profile made up of respondents from seven countries falling into Jaeger's "somewhat different from OD" category: Austria, Canada, Finland, France, Germany, Great Britain, and the United States. One distinguishing element of this profile is the lack of a clearly dominant set of values. While Achievement (11 o'clock) and humanistic (1 o'clock) values are dominant, they are not "overwhelmingly" so. Self-Actualizing (12 o'clock), Affiliative (2 o'clock), and Oppositional (7 o'clock) are all very close to having the same level of significance in these countries. Figure 3 illustrates the ideal corporate culture profile for the 4 countries whose values are "very different" from those of organization development (Belgium, Brazil, Chile, and Italy). Not unexpectedly, these countries' profiles indicate a set of dominant values, which are polar opposite of organization development's. Oppositional style values (7 o'clock) and Power style (8 o'clock) dominate in this profile.

While the "somewhat different" countries' profile muddies the interpretation, if one compares the profiles of "similar" and "different" countries, a clear conclusion arises. It does appear that countries with different value sets do indeed have different "ideal" corporate cultures. Countries whose values are similar to OD's will desire organization cultures dominated by "Top Of The Clock" values, while countries whose values are very different to OD's will prefer cultures which stress "Bottom Of The Clock" beliefs. Therefore, looking back to the earlier question, "Change—but to what," there is now an answer—successful change will reflect movement in organizational values towards the organization's "ideal". This "ideal" will be greatly influenced by the country's cultural values in which the organization is located. Therefore, with condolences to Likert and Blake and Mouton, for some countries the OD consultant's task is to change an organizations culture to emphasize oppositional and power values—exactly opposite of what these theorists suggest.

Third Bend: No Universal End Result. But What About Tools?

Clearly, there is no universal set of values, no universal culture, no universal end result—each consulting situation requires a culture change custom tailored for its own unique set of requirements. Most interesting is the fact that often times these culture changes, being brought about through organization development, will take the shape of OD's antithesis. One would think that OD tools could not function correctly to bring about such a "negative (from their design)" result. However, there is plenty of evidence showing that OD does work in countries with "very different" cultures (see for example Boss and Variono's description of OD in Italy (1987); Fuch's (1987) discussion of OD practices in Chile).

The next question, logically, becomes: "If there is no universal 'end result' for OD, is there a set of tools, or a tool, which can facilitate the culture change process regardless of what form that change will take? Head and Sorensen (1993) and Jaeger (1989), present two studies, which indirectly tests this hypothesis. Combined, they examined the use, and usefulness, of 15 different OD interventions, in 12 different countries. The combined results are found in Table 1. There were no "universally" used, or effective, tools. Team Building came the closest to universality, being used and effective in 8 countries (66%). MBO was the only other intervention used in more than 50% of the countries (7), but it was only reported effective in 33% (4) of the countries.

It is also important to remember, as mentioned earlier, that even those interventions which are utilized in a wide variety of countries will undoubtedly be adjusted in order to match the country's cultural values (Head, Sorensen, Larsen, and Nielsen, 1993). Such adjustments are required to avoid falling victim to the false assumptions often found in international/multinational organization development (Johnson, Head and Sorensen, 1989). Of specific interest here is the *Unity of Practice Assumption* (p. 310).

Organization Development techniques are clearly defined, as labeled. If there are subtle gradations and shadings from one application to another, and shifts in definition when the application takes place, then a central anchor point is lost in the understanding and evaluation of Organization Development techniques. In particular, adjustments which may take place in another culture, and which may be critical for the understanding of the adaptation of Organization Development to that culture, may go unrecognized and unmeasured.

Table 1. OD Interventions Reported Use and Effectiveness in 12 Different Coutries

Intervention	Number of Countries Reporting Use	Number of Countries Effective Reporting Effective
Team building	8	8
Management by objectives	7	4
Survey feedback	6	6
Quality of work life	5	2
Transaction analysis	5	2
Process consultation	5	4
Job design	4	4
Career development	4	1
Role Negotiation	4	0
Confrontation	3	3
Physical settings	3	0
Organization mirror	2	0
Force field analysis	2	2
3rd party consultation	2	2
Collateral organization	1	1

Fourth Bend: Okay, But What About A Different Kind of Tool?

Apparently there are no universal OD interventions which can facilitate organization culture change to a desired end result. Or is there? Recently, a new technique has been developed by David Cooperrider and associates known as Appreciative Inquiry (AI). AI has proven successful all over the world, and with all different types of organizations.

Appreciative Inquiry's (Srivastva and Cooperrider, 1990) approach to organization development is rooted in discovering the positive forces that give meaning to an organization, focusing upon what is right, not wrong. Attention is focused on remembering peak experiences when situations were positive and working well, and allowing those positive experiences to guide the change process. This contrasts with the problem solving approach which first identifies the problems and what is wrong with the organization. Appreciative Inquiry, by focusing on what is working right and how the challenges that the organization is facing can be addressed, creates a positive atmosphere for change and avoids the resistance and loss of hope for a better future encountered through the more traditional approaches.

Appreciative Inquiry assumes that the change process is guided by the first questions we ask of the participants. If negative questions begin the process, this will set a negative climate—if positive questions are asked, this will help the process move in a positive direction.

Typically, the first step in Appreciative Inquiry involves an interviewing process centering upon four key questions:

1. Describe a peak experience or high point
2. Describe things valued most about (a) yourself, (b) nature of one's work, (c) the organization
3. Describe Core Factor that gives "life" to the organization
4. Describe three wishes to heighten vitality and health of the organization.

These four questions guide the change process in a positive direction. From the interviews, common topics or themes typically emerge, i.e., quality, commitment, customer service. These topics are explored in detail, focusing on when the organization has experienced them at their best, not worst.

The four basic principles of Appreciative Inquiry (Cooperrider, 1990) are:

1. Inquiry into "the art of the possible", the appreciative approach gets inspiration from "what is" and aims at valuing, learning and understanding.
2. What's possible should be applicable, what is discovered in an organization should generate knowledge that can be used, applied and validated.
3. What's possible should be provocative, an organization should be open-ended, learning how to take part in its own evolution.
4. Human potential of organizational life should be collaborative.

This is very different from the assumption that "organizations are problems to be solved." This problem solving approach is one that is familiar and on which most interventions are based. Problem solving includes:

1. Identifying key problems (what is wrong?)
2. Analyzing key causes (whose fault is it?)
3. Analyzing solutions (what must be changed to correct it?)
4. Developing an action plan (what is politically feasible?)

Contrast these with AI's four steps:

1. Discovery and valuing
2. Envisioning
3. Dialogue
4. Co-construction of the future.

Journey's End: Why Appreciative Inquiry

Why might appreciative inquiry prove to be Organization Development's "philosopher's stone", turning every consulting project into golden success? AI is not a "tool" like team building, grid management, or quality circles, rather it is an innovative approach to change management. AI's approach directly attacks one of the few "universal truths" of OD practice—successful OD requires overcoming resistance to change.

Table 2 illustrates exactly how AI resolves the primary causes for employees to resist change. Aside from just removing change resistance, AI also accomplishes two other principle goals of OD consultants—regardless of what culture they operate in: acquiring employee ownership into the program, and maximizing employee input into the design of the new system.

Conclusion

We will take a somewhat different approach to this paper's conclusion. Rather than simply restate what has been written, we believe that an example of AI's universal potential will best support our thesis.

The client was a two-hospital "chain". Significant and constant conflict had ground the organization's progress to a halt. The bickering also began to be known in the community, negatively impacting the organization's image. The conflict was not centered around the differences between the two hospitals. Rather, as many

Table 2. How Appreciative Inquiry Undermines Resistance to Change

Reason for Employee Resistance	How Does AI Reduce Resistance
Fear of the unknown—we know what we have, but we don't know what change will bring.	AI works from the known—the organization is trying to "recapture" the already experienced peaks.
Change can cause the employee to question his/her self-image—"Can I do the new task?"	AI begins with what employees like most about the existing system—making the peak experiences the norm. The implication is that at the same time non peak experiences will be adjusted/removed.
The employees feel imposed upon—they have to do all the work for the change, but only the "organization" will reap the benefits.	AI clearly puts the "gain" into personal terms. The process focuses on how to permit each employee tonstantly experience the personal satisfaction that occurred during the "peak experiences".
The employees feel imposed upon—they have to do all the work for the change, but only the "organization" will reap the benefits.	AI clearly puts the "gain" into personal terms. The process focuses on how to permit each employee tonstantly experience the personal satisfaction that occurred during the "peak experiences".
The employees view this change process as another "fad"—"why adopt anything new when management is going to forget it in a coupld of weeks anyway?"	AI does not appear to be a revolutionary concept. Its goal can be seen as making "what is going on now" better. It is logical, and fits into the current paradigms—managers are always trying to get the current system to be more effective and efficient.

experienced in working with hospitals can identify with, the conflict centered upon the differences between the medical and administrative staffs.

The consultant was called in to help the organization find a resolution to the conflict at the executive level. While the tensions were felt throughout the hospitals it appeared that the source was at the management level. For the most part the two sets of combatants only interacted regularly at the executive level; lower level participants merely adopted the attitudes of their managers; thus spreading the problem throughout the organization.

The executive team had already tried everything, working with a wide variety of consultants to resolve the problems—nothing seemed to work. Why? It quickly became obvious that the organization was suffering from a split personality: there were two sets of very different corporate cultures. Simulations of the two OCI profiles can be found in Figures 4 and 5.

Faced with a situation where none of the "usual" tools would work, the "new" consultant turned to appreciative inquiry (he had just been exposed to it and AI intrigued him—enough to try it on his own without any formal training). Appreciative

Figure 4. Organizational Culture Inventory Profile for the Hospital's Administrative staff.

Figure 5. Organizational Culture Inventory Profile for the Hospital's medical staff.

Inquiry seems to have worked—at least this is what the client reports about a year after the initial session (the consultant had several "sessions" over 6 months). The executive team has broken out of the "grid lock" and has worked well together—even initiating several projects that had been placed on "political" hold.

Appreciative Inquiry was immediately accepted by the team—it literally caught them unaware. The team was prepared for another "problem solving" session and were startled when asked to recall those times when things had worked well. Of course there were the initial comments which had to be dismissed, such as "things have never worked well", and "peak experiences—it's whenever the (other side's) members were absent." When pressed to come up with a few specific examples the group responded. Possibly the biggest break came when both "sides" identified several of the same experiences. This permitted specific analysis, perfect for both groups, with regards to why things worked well in these cases.

The end result of the sessions was to create a "rules of the road" set of behaviors and attitudes which would govern the inter "side" of interactions. These rules (named this way because many of the participants had a common interest in motorcycles, unknown to all before the sessions) were positive in nature—not a list of "thou shall nots". Some examples were "We will truly investigate a situation from several perspectives before suggesting possible solutions;" "While we might disagree with each other's ideas—we all have similar motives;" "Conflict can be our best resource—differences can lead to improvements;" and "Consensus does not have to mean unanimity".

What really happened? It was clear to everyone that the two "ideal cultures" could not be melded into one common—the differences were more related to the parties' professional values than anything else. So the organization has begun to create a "third" culture—specifically aimed at the executive team when they are interacting (as opposed to performing their individual tasks). This third culture was a direct result of tapping into the common peak experiences—when the group did function well. No one had to compromise their personal values and beliefs, or change what they "wanted"—only what they did in the old status quo situation. They were not trying to invent something new, only recapture what they had lost.

Appreciative Inquiry has proven successful in a wide variety of national and corporate cultures—even those with split personalities. Why? We argue, hopefully successfully, that a major reason is that it overcomes the universal problem—resistance to change. Are there other reasons? Possibly so. We encourage you to join us and explore the possibilities together.

References

R. Blake and J. Mouton, 1975, "An Overview Of The Grid", *Training and Development Journal.*

R. W. Boss, M. V. Variono, 1987, "Organization Development In Italy," *Group and Organization Studies*, 12, 245–256.

R.A. Cooke, J. Hartmann, 1989, *Interpreting the Culture Styles Measured By The Organizational Culture Inventory: Organizational Culture Inventory Leader's Guide*, Plymouth, Michigan: Human Synergistics, Inc.

R.A. Cooke, J. C. Lafferty, 1989, *The Organizational Culture Inventory*, Plymouth, Michigan: Human Synergistics, Inc.

D. Cooperrider, *Appreciative Inquiry, A Constructive Approach to Organization Development*. Cleveland: Case Western Reserve University.

T. G. Cummings and C.G. Worley, 1993, *Organization Development and Change*, *5th ed.*, Minneapolis: West Publishing Company.

R. Daft, 1995, *Organization Theory and Design, 5th ed.*, Minneapolis: West Publishing.

C. Fuchs, 1987, "Organizational Development Under Political, Economic and Natural Crisis," *Organization Development Journal*, 5, 37–45.

T. Head and P. Sorensen, 1993, "Cultural Values And Organizational Development," *Leadership And Organization Development Journal*, 11, 3–7.

G. Hofstede, 1980, *Culture's Consequences: International Differences in Work-Related Values*, London: Sage.

A. Jaeger, 1986, "Organization Development and National Culture: Where's the Fit?" *Academy of Management Review*, 11, 178–190.

A. Jaeger, 1989, "Organization Development Methods in Practice: A 5-Country Examination," in *Advances In International Comparative Management*, 4, 113–130, Greenwich, CT: JAI Press.

K. R. Johnson, T. Head, and P. Sorensen, 1989, "Cross-Cultural Organization Development: Suggestions for Paradigm Development", *Academy of Management Best Paper Proceedings*.

K. Lewin, 1951, *Field Theory In Social Science*, New York: Harper and Row.

R. Likert, 1962, "New Patterns in Sales Management," in *Changing Perspectives In Marketing Management*, ed. M.R. Warshaw, Ann Arbor: University of Michigan Bureau of Research.

R. Likert, 1962a, *New Patterns of Management*, New York: McGraw-Hill.

R. Likert, 1967, *The Human Organization*, New York: McGraw-Hill.

R. Likert, 1977, "Management Styles and The Human Component," *Management Review*.

A. Meyer, J. Goes, G. Brooks, 1992, "Organizations in Disequilibrium: Environmental Jolts and Industry Revolutions," in G. Huber and W. Glick, eds., *Organizational Change and Redesign*, New York: Oxford University Press.

J. M. Pennings, 1992, "Structural Contingency Theory: A Reappraisal," *Research in Organizational Behavior*, 14, pp. 267–309.

P. Sorensen, T. Head, L. Gironda, H. Larsen, 1996, "Global Organization Development: Lessons From Scandinavia," *Organization Development Journal*, in print.

P. Sorensen, T. Head, K. Johnson, and N. Mathys (1991), *International Organization Development*, Champaign, IL: Stipes.

Srivastva, S., and Cooperrider, D., 1990. *Appreciative Management and Leadership*. San Francisco: Jossey-Bass.

R.R. Thomas, 1990, *Beyond Race and Gender*, New York: AMACOM.

N. Tichy, 1983, *Managing Strategic Change: Technical, Political, and Cultural Dynamics*, New York: John Wiley.

Chapter 24

Appreciative Inquiry: Debunking The Mythology Behind Resistance To Change

Thomas C. Head, Ph.D.
Roosevelt University

Appreciative Inquiry, as a method for introducing and facilitating organizational change, has proven itself a successful and robust methodology. In many ways Appreciative Inquiry might be considered Organization Development's Aspirin. It works for almost everyone and for almost any problem, but no one knows exactly why. One possible explanation, explored here, is that Appreciative Inquiry is successful because it almost entirely eliminates resistance to change.

Every OD consultant knows that change resistance often is the most significant barrier to a successful intervention. A recent study by Hammer and Associates estimates that 67 percent of all organization re-engineering interventions fail, and that sixty percent of all these failures are directly attributable to employees resisting the intervention (Moomaugh, 1999). Resistance to change surfaces as the primary cause for failure in resolving international conflicts, inner city gang rivalries, Total Quality Management programs, as well as standard OD interventions ranging from Goal Setting to the Learning Organization.

The key to understanding resistance to change, and also why Appreciative Inquiry reduces it to a manageable level, lies with the fact that resistance is typically caused by the change process (the how) instead of the intervention itself (the what). Defending this proposition relies on three arguments. First is logic. What sane individual would resist job enrichment or improvements in the quality of work life? It is not logical to fight an intervention that will increase one's self worth,

---

Head, T.C. (2000). Appreciative inquiry: Debunking the mythology behind resistance to change. *OD Practitioner: Journal of the Organization Development Network, 32* (1), 27-35.

satisfaction, and self image (granted, while also improving organizational performance). Second is research. Thomas Packard (1995), in reviewing social service sector TQM projects, concludes that the interventions will work, but *only* if the project is implemented correctly. The Hammer and Associates re-engineering study (Moomaugh, 1999) linked such change process issues as lack of executive consensus, lack of senior-executive champion, unrealistic expectations, and late staff involvement with resistance to change as the root of failure. The final argument relies on examining the typical suggestions for managing resistance to change: employee participation in diagnosis and design, managerial empathy, total and honest communications, and rewarding employee efforts. None of these techniques are directly related to an actual intervention, rather they all focus on how the intervention is planned and implemented.

If process flaws cause resistance to change, managing the resistance requires adapting the process instead of the intervention. Many incorrectly view Appreciative Inquiry as an intervention. Appreciative Inquiry, in itself, is not an intervention. Rather, it is an innovative process for organizational assessment and intervention design.

The mechanics and theory of Appreciative Inquiry are discussed, in detail, elsewhere in this journal (for an in depth discussion, refer to Cooperrider, Sorensen, Whitney and Yaeger, 2000). Briefly, Appreciative Inquiry is a process for diagnosing an organization's need for change, but one that focuses on the positive elements of the organization. Appreciative Inquiry requires organizational members to identify those "peak" times when everything operated perfectly. Next, the participants establish what factors were behind these peak experiences. Finally, it is an easy step (at least conceptually) to establish interventions that will make the peak experience factors the norm, rather than the exception.

Appreciative Inquiry appears, and actually is, quite simple (again, at least conceptually). Without a doubt simplicity is one key to it's remarkable success. Just as important for its success is how the Appreciative Inquiry process assists change agents in managing resistance to change. This assistance is two dimensional. First, appreciative inquiry debunks the mythology surrounding change resistance. Second, appreciative inquiry removes, or at least reduces, many of the underlying causes of resistance to change.

Appreciative Inquiry And The Myths of Resistance To Change

Everyone recognizes the significant role employee resistance plays in the change process. However, for some reason this recognition has not led to equally significant research efforts, and therefore understanding. Few Organization Development books devote more than a few pages to managing resistance. Its importance, coupled with the lack of knowledge, has led to many myths surrounding resistance to change. Designing and implementing interventions based upon these myths at best might lead to minor inconveniences, but at worst will surely derail the entire change program. Appreciative Inquiry, by its nature, permits the change agent to see the truth behind the myths.

Myth 1: Resistance is always "bad"

Psychologists often say that fear typically is not harmful to an individual. In fact fear can lead to some positive outcomes. Fear often builds character and, more importantly, stops an individual from performing stupid and dangerous acts. While fear might contribute to change resistance, resistance and fear are not the same constructs. However, what is true for fear is also fear for resistance to change.

Most consultants, and clients, perceive resistance to change as an evil dragon that must be vanquished before attaining the goal. There is no question that managing resistance to change is essential for a project's success, but the same is true of all aspects of the change process. Resistance to change is not "bad," nor is it "good," it simply "is," and if managed correctly will prevent an organization from doing something "stupid." Resistance can serve as a signal that there is disagreement about how to proceed, and that the organization should "look before it leaps."

Resistance to change may also significantly improve an intervention's quality if managed correctly. Change resistance doesn't develop from nothing - there are concrete reasons behind employees' resistance. Identifying these reasons provides a wealth of information for improving an intervention and its implementation. If there are aspects of the change which are not understood by the employees clearly additional information is required. But why do the people require information? Was the change not originally described with sufficient information quantity and quality? Was the description believed? Was there an explanation at all? The change agent must seek, rather than avoid, the answers to these questions. Granted, the answers may point out previous shortcomings, but they will also provide clear directions for smoother implementation. Resisting change also develops from concerns about the intervention's details. These concerns, from individuals with an intimate knowledge of the current situation, need to be examined instead of dismissed. If the concerns are unfounded providing more information is all that is needed. If the concerns are valid incorporating them, through collaboration, into the intervention's design shall only improve the intervention's quality.

To properly manage this particular myth requires creating an environment where resistance to change is not perceived as an "evil" by those designing and implementing the change. The environment must encourage all members to honestly and openly contribute input (both facts and opinions). Appreciative Inquiry is an excellent methodology for creating such a positive change environment. Because people offer their comments from a position of what is "right," "good," and "desirable" in the organization, instead of "wrong," "bad," "ineffective," no one is reluctant to contribute. Of equal importance, when focusing on the positive, is that no one seeks to attach blame. Putting it succinctly, no employee has ever been executed for being the bearer of good news - and the employees are comfortable in this role.

Myth 2: There will always be resistance to change

As with many myths, there is some truth behind the belief that no matter what is being attempted the change agent will meet with resistance. Walk into a crowded room and offer everyone twenty five dollars with no "catches." Inevitably many will ask questions, others will be suspicious, and a few will refuse to take the money (author's note - this is all supposition, I've never actually tried this experiment, but have always wanted to).

The moral of the experiment is that no matter how attractive the change some employees will be suspicious enough that they put up some resistance. One must remember, however, that most people took the money, just as most employees will embrace the change after their questions have been answered.

The danger in this myth lies not with "will" there be resistance, rather with how significant is the resistance. If the change agent and client assume that the inevitable resistance will be significant (as they often do) they will integrate this assumption into the intervention's design and communication. In essence, by anticipating significant resistance, the change agent establishes a self-fulfilling prophesy. Employees perceiving this negative assumption buried within the communications will naturally seek to establish the "truth." After all, if everything is as "they" (the management) say, why do "they" think "we" (the employees) will be reluctant to accept the change?

It is safe to assume that no matter how attractive the change some resistance is to be expected. The change agent must find a way to ascertain where resistance will arise, its roots, and its severity, all without planting, or reinforcing, the idea in the employees' heads. Appreciative Inquiry provides an excellent method for accomplishing these tasks. First, as will be discussed later in detail, Appreciative Inquiry naturally eliminates many of the standard reasons behind change resistance. Appreciative Inquiry operates under the assumption that resistance actually will not occur, for who would resist replicating a peak experience? Therefore, if any self fulfilling prophesy develops, it will be to inhibit, instead of facilitate, resistance to change. Appreciative Inquiry could actually push the organization too far. The extreme positive environment arising from the technique might convince employees that their concerns are groundless or absurd, thus robbing the change agent from valuable diagnostic information.

Myth 3: With resistance it's all or nothing.

Change is all or nothing. Change is win-lose. Change is war. This is often how managers view resistance to change. The employees are either "for us or against us." Change resistance typically does not occur as either black or white, rather there are numerous shades of gray.

Most employees are reasonable, sane, and somewhat rational. When faced with an understandable need for change, and an intervention that makes sense, people will accept the process. Refer back to the fictional experiment. When offered money with no "catches" it is normal to expect people with questions - either spoken or unspoken. Either way, once the questions are reasonably answered, most individuals will accept the offer. Granted, their acceptance will range from wild enthusiasm to moderate suspicion, but they *will* take the money.

When confronted with change, it is natural that employees will have questions. These questions are not meant as signs of hostile resistance. The employees are simply gathering information with which to form an opinion. The way a manager, or change agent, responds will significantly impact subsequent opinions. So, how do many managers react to employee questions? First, they might feel challenged or threatened, in which case their response might be "I think it is a good idea, and that's why we're going to do it." Managers might also be surprised, or baffled, by the questions and respond by simply repeating themselves assuming the simply weren't hear correctly the first time. Finally, the managers could fail to understand the significance of the question, or simply be unprepared to answer, and respond with all the clarity of a politician running for office. In all of these cases the result is the same, the employees' questions remain unanswered and the subsequent frustration can easily lead to resistance escalation.

Managers and change agents need to perceive questions as simply employees seeking information - there are no deep hidden meanings that threaten success.. Employees need answers to their questions - both those asked and unasked. Appreciative Inquiry's positive approach to introducing change creates an environment where data and ideas are freely exchanged in order to discover all the possibilities instead of the problems. Information answers the questions, often before they are verbalized, and therefore resistance is minimized. If anything, the probing created by the tentative resistance to change will enrich the discussion surrounding the intervention thereby leading to creative dialogues, and therefore a much improved version of the proposed change process.

Myth 4: Resistance to change is a group level construct.

An interesting phenomenon often occurs sometime early in the change implementation process. Managers, when thinking of change, switch from first person singular to third person plural. Managers begin with "I think this project is a good idea" but end with "They (employees) will fight it." This perspective may lead managers to an entire set of faulty decisions, for they are working under a false assumption. Managers believe that resistance to change is a group level construct when it actually occurs at the individual level. Resistance to change, like motivation and satisfaction, takes place in the human mind, and therefore managing it must also take place within (and not between) the employee.

Groups cannot be resistant to change. Granted, every single group member might resist the change, but each individual will resist it for his/her own personal reasons. If each individual has his/her own reason for resistance, group level solutions will always prove inadequate. In using a group level approach to managing resistance the best a change agent can hope for is to placate a majority (you can't please all the people all the time). The worst case is that no one will be satisfied by the perceived half-hearted attempt and alienated by the attempt ("Don't 'they' get it?," "Didn't 'they' listen to me?").

Resistance occurs within the individual, and therefore any attempt to bring the resistance out in the open and work with it must also be focused within the individual. What is needed is a technique where each person's concerns and ideas are included into the planning process. Appreciative Inquiry, again, is an excellent method to accomplish this task. Just as everyone's reasons for resistance will be unique, everyone's peak experience (or at least the reasons for identifying that peak experience) will be unique. Appreciative Inquiry encourages everyone to contribute their own peak experiences, and the reasons behind them. Consequently, all employees are heard and (more importantly) understood, thereby permitting the maximum integration of individual ideas into the final solution. Resistance to change becomes a tool for improving the intervention rather than an obstacle to overcome.

Myth 5: You must "buy" the employees' commitment

It is often said that immediately upon hearing the organization is going to change three questions pop into all employees' minds. These three questions, in order, are: 1) Why?, 2) How will this effect me?, and 3) What's in it for me? Managers, having experienced many changes themselves, are well aware (even if it is at the subconscious level) that each subordinate is thinking these questions. Herein lies the root of the myth that if you want employees to commit themselves to the change you will have to "buy" it through pay raises or similar concessions, and this purchase will be expensive.

Obviously, this myth is pure Theory X, which is interesting in itself because almost all contemporary interventions utilize Theory Y for a base. Gary Yukl (1983), in his classic work on power, points out typically one cannot "buy" (reward power) commitment. The most likely outcome with reward power is simple compliance - employees will go along with the change, but without real motivation. Another possible outcome from attempting to "buy" employee acceptance is increased resistance to the change. First, offering incentives to accept changes can easily appear as bribery. Most employees do not like to think they can be "bought," particularly at the level many managers offer. Once again, managers also run the risk of creating a self-fulfilling prophesy. If the change is so desirable, why must management buy labor's commitment? For example, one hospital offered its nurses a five cents an hour pay increase for accepting a major change in scheduling policy. The nurses' response was anger, suspicion, and open resistance. The nurses, who quite possibly would have agreed to the change with no additional compensation, were insulted that management felt they could "buy" loyalty for an additional two dollars a week. The nurses also engaged in heavy speculation about "what was really going to happen." The hospital abandoned the change.

When discussing any organizational change managers must be prepared to supply the answers for the three questions (Why? How will it effect me? What's in it for me?). If management and changes agents do not have the answers, possibly they haven't thought the change out in sufficient detail. Either the leaders need to slow down and develop the answers, or they need a process for employees to quickly obtain their own answers. This myth about buying commitment obviously comes from the final question. The question isn't, by definition, based on greed - it's a natural result of the motivation process. Management is asking employees to change behaviors and improve the organization, effort to performance in expectancy theory terms, and they want to know that the performance is linked to outcomes, and that the outcomes are desirable. Management also forgets that often the strongest outcomes are intrinsic (pride, growth opportunities, achievement, enjoyment) rather than extrinsic (pay, benefits).

Appreciative Inquiry overcomes both managerial shortcomings. Employees immediately answer their own questions. By emphasizing the desire to recreate the peak experiences the "why" is obvious - the organization wants to get to where everything works at the optimum level. Employees, knowing what the peak experience involved, also know how it effected them. Finally, the reward lies in the simple fact that if successful, the change will lead to dramatic increases in employee satisfaction and morale.

Appreciative Inquiry And The Reasons Behind Resistance To Change

Head, Sorensen, Preston, and Yaeger (2000) first presented the idea that Appreciative Inquiry's success is due primarily to the fact that it naturally removes most of the major reasons why employees resist change. Without doubt, there are reasons for employee resistance to change not covered here, and it is probable that Appreciative Inquiry does not address all the reasons, but it is clear that the technique does significantly remove many of the major sources of resistance.

One of the primary driving forces behind employee resistance is the uncertainty and ambiguity that change creates, in other words, the fear of the unknown. Using Appreciative Inquiry's process working through the employees' past peak experiences, there is no unknown. The employees are actually the source of all information, and this data is used to recreate, and possibly improve upon, what has already been experienced.

Often, resistance to change is simply based upon the fact that employees like the old system. They are comfortable with what, and how, they operate, and have been for many years. Even people who don't like everything about the old ways must have some things they find enjoyable or else they would have left. The employee likes what he/she has now and might even acknowledge the possibility of enjoying the new system even more. At the same time there is an equal probability of disliking the new order. Many people are risk takers, but few are willing to gamble on something as important as job satisfaction. Appreciative Inquiry begins the change process with what employees like most about the existing system, making the peak experiences the norm. There is no risk involved in the change because the employee is certain she/he will like the new system. Many will not even perceive the change as a new system, rather it is simply recapturing the best of the current system and removing any difficulties.

Another primary reason behind resistance is that change often causes the employee to question her/his self-image, forcing the question "Can I do the new task?" Those of us who grew up before the personal computer era witnessed the significant panic and subsequent resistance that ensued among clerical staff as these mysterious boxes out of science fiction were placed on every secretary's desk. Because Appreciative Inquiry builds upon what the employee has experienced there is no self doubt. The employee is certain they can do "it" because they have already successfully done "it." In fact, because the new system most likely will focus upon those elements which employees feel are their strong points, they will view themselves as more competent for the new system than they were in the old.

Often in change efforts employees resist because they feel imposed upon. Labor does all the work in implementing the change, management gets all the credit, and only the "organization" (stockholders) reap the benefits. Appreciative Inquiry clearly provides a personal "gain" for all employees. Each individual sees how their efforts will be rewarded through increases in job satisfaction and an "ideal" working environment.

Most diagnostic approaches create an environment of blame. When a consultant begins the change process by listing all the organization's problems, no matter how positive she/he tries to be, everyone in the process will seek either to establish who's responsible, or to avoid taking responsibility. This negativity can even carry on into the change process. People will be reluctant to take responsibility for activities to avoid the blame if the change fails. Groups will fall into the paralysis by analysis trap for the same reason. Consequently, the change is doomed to failure. However, when the consultant uses Appreciative Inquiry, becoming the focus of attribution is a source of pride. Few, except for modesty, would be reluctant to admit their role in establishing a peak experience. Individuals and groups are excited to assume responsibility in creating a system they know will not fail.

A final source for resistance to change is simply that the employees view the intervention as just another "fad." A common question, often verbalized, is "Why adopt anything new when management is only going to forget it in a couple of weeks anyway?" Most changes are, by definition, revolutionary in nature. Interventions are planned and deliberate attempts at throwing out the old and taking on the new. It is also a fact of life that most interventions never succeed in establishing the new order. Management and labor lose interest, either because the results are too slow in coming or because they were not as significant as hoped for. Either way the organization quickly shops around for the next sure-fire solution. Employees quickly realize that it is easier to resist any change rather than bounce around from one new process to another. Appreciative Inquiry is not a "revolutionary" change process. The goal is simply to take the current system to it's greatest known potential. There will be few, if any, artificially high expectations, and implementation should be comparatively rapid. The changes Appreciative Inquiry brings are logical and fit into the current organizational paradigm.

Conclusion

Beckhard and Harris (1987) suggest a formula that predicts the degree of resistance an intervention will encounter. The equation focuses on three primary factors: level of dissatisfaction with the status quo, desirability of proposed change, and the practicality of the change. Another variable, the cost of changing, is also included into the equation. Beckhard's equation lends further support to the belief that Appreciative Inquiry works, at least in part, because it permits the change agent to easily manage resistance to change.

Establishing employees' peak experiences as the organizational norm should make the change highly desirable for most, if not all, employees. Because the process is recreating what has already been accomplished few will doubt its practicality. Finally, no matter how dissatisfied, or satisfied, people are with the status quo they should all see that the change process will simply emphasize what is currently the system's best while eliminating what is worst. Therefore, according to Beckhard's model, the only real threat for developing significant resistance lies with the intervention's cost.

Cost will always be a concern, especially when dealing with managerial resistance to change. However, assuming that a cost affective intervention is possible, Appreciative Inquiry will remove the base causes for resisting change. The technique also naturally debunks the common held myths surrounding resistance to change. Appreciative Inquiry provides the consultant with a process for facilitating change that properly manages change resistance. Overcoming the resistance barrier does not guarantee a successful change, but clearly it is a major part of the battle.

Appreciative Inquiry is a highly useful tool for Organization Development change agents. For many, this knowledge is enough. But think of how much more useful the technique would be if we understood how and why it worked. To answer these questions will require significant research effort. Such research projects must begin with speculation. The belief that Appreciative Inquiry is successful because it naturally reduces resistance to change is speculation (based on logic). Organization Development, as a field, must take the next step and empirically test this, and other, dimensions of Appreciative Inquiry.

References

Beckhard, R., & Harris (1987). *Organizational Transitions: Managing Complex Change (2nd ed.)*, Reading, MA: Addison Wesley

Cooperrider, D., Sorensen, P., Whitney, D., & Yaeger, T. (2000) *Appreciative Inquiry*, Champaign, IL: Stipes Publishing.

Head, T., Sorensen, P., Yaeger, T., and Preston, J. (2000). Is Appreciative Inquiry OD's Philosopher's Stone? in *Appreciative Inquiry*, D. Cooperrider, P. Sorensen, D. Whitney, & T. Yaeger, (Eds.), Champaign, IL: Stipes Publishing.

Moomaugh, R. & Associates (1995). *Re-Engineering: Why It So Often Fails*, Valley Center, CA: Organizational Universe Systems.

Packard, T. (1995). TQM and Organizational Change and Development, in *Total Quality Management in the Social Services: Theory and Practice*, B. Gummer & P. McCallon (Eds.), Albany, NY: Rockefeller College Press.

Yukl, G. & Taber, T (1983). The Effective Use of Managerial Power, *Personnel*.

Chapter 25

THREE PERSPECTIVES ON APPRECIATIVE INQUIRY

Dr. Robert T. Golembiewski
University of Georgia

This essay explores a paradox. Appreciative Inquiry (henceforth AI) has been the prominent new approach to planned change for at least the last decade, but one of the most telling things that may be said about AI is that it has received little of what may be called "really appreciative inquiry." Hammond (1995, 1996), a friendly observer, conveys the total sense of it in his whimsically but accurately titled *The Thin Book of Appreciative Inquiry*. This shortfall would be remedied by such add-on features to a clearly attractive AI core:

*   subjecting attractive notions to situational analysis – of which conditions contribute to success, or failure, in what proportions

*   comprehensive and comparative testing, both internally and relationally, to estimate the efficacy of versions of the target treatment – to estimate the "within" efficacy of versions of the basic treatment, as well as to estimate the "between" efficacy of the target treatment as contrasted with alternative treatments.

Why this situation exists no doubt always will be elusive, but some useful progress can be made in describing major facets of this focal paradox. Here, three related perspectives on AI get attention:

*   AI as a conceptual and operational island;
*   AI as discouraging inquiry;
*   AI and two fundamental concerns

Golembiewski, B. (2000). Three perspectives on appreciative inquiry. *OD Practitioner: Journal of the Organizational Development Network, 32* (1), 53-58.

AI As Island

Perhaps basically, AI afficionados portray it as a kind of island, both conceptually as well as in its broad theoretical framework. Not only is AI newly with us, that is to say, but many supporters see it as sui generis. In Kuhnian terms, AI gets portrayed as paradigmatic in two senses: as post-paradigmatic successor to all earlier approaches to change; and as the neo-paradigm to replace all deficiency approaches.

If at the risk of being too broad, but only at a small risk (Golembiewski, 1998a), most proponents differentiate AI from most or all other approaches to planned change. For example, those supplanted approaches feature problem-solving, and to AIers that is a fundamental shortfall. That is, we are told, problem-solving is inherently deficiency-oriented, encourages the locating and placing of blame, and (in the consequent bargain) tends to induce resistance as well as to create additional problems while always failing fundamentally.

For good or ill, in addition, this basic AI position is seldom qualified. Far more rather than less, consequently, the basic AI position is apt to be exaggerated and that may be costly. Let three points illustrate the broader argument which has been made elsewhere in detail (Golembiewski, 1998a).

1. AI Overstates Real but Qualified Differences.

Certainly, AI stands by itself in its degree of unqualified emphasis on the "positive" in change. Just as certainly, however, AI overstates the degree of the differences between it and other approaches to change.

Let a few illustrations do the job of highlighting the overstatement in the typical AI rejection of all problem-solving approaches as negative and deficiency-oriented. Thus, every survey/feedback design in which I have been associated was problem-solving but also was built around some version of a balance: what are the positive things in this organization?; and what things need remedial attention, and in what order? Relatedly, the basic contracting mode in OD implies a similar balancing:

- What things can be continued, pretty much as is?
- What things must be started in this organization?
- What things should be stopped?

This diagnosis then becomes the basis for bargains and exchanges. The prototypic question is: What degree of beginning Act A by some people will be required to arrange for stopping Act B by others?

In the vast majority of planned change designs, "balance" similarly dominates, which raises questions about AI's basic claim. It is not clear what AI's usual insistence on singularity implies for both theory and practice, but those issues definitely will not be solved by setting up conceptual strawmen to be gravely demolished. Moreover, the basic AI charge is bold in two senses. AI in effect finesses the substantial success rates of conventional balanced designs, now apparently well-established by the early work of Golembiewski and his associates (1981) and Nicholas (1982), as well as by the 20-plus independent surveys of evaluative studies of OD efficacy that have accumulated since then (Golembiewski, 1998b). Moreover, AI offers no similar tests of its own efficacy.

2. Lack of Linkages to Other Theory and Practice.

Relatedly, and with possible costs, AI does not get either linked with other relevant theory and practice, or have such linkage explicitly rejected for specified reasons.

Some may consider this only your author's problem, but let me suggest why the concern is more than self-referential. Consider the well-established treatment progression in third-party consultation or peacemaking (e.g., Walton, 1969). He advises an initial emphasis on differentiation – to explore and provide context for the issues-in-contention. Then comes integration, building on but beyond the products of the first phase to manage conflict, or even resolve it.

Now AI's resolution-by-definition seems clear enough: such a sequencing is deficiency-oriented, and hence not ideal or perhaps even effective. But this easy rationale surely needs elaboration, even if correct. Are Walton and those of like mind simply wrong? And what to make of the substantial practice and research that Walton describes as useful? Or is AI better for some type-cases, and Walton's approach always suspect or perhaps useful in specified other type-cases?

Even more troublesome to me are AI's unexplored interface with Gerry Harvey's (1988) "going to Abilene." How would AI deal with associated phenomena? I do not know; and AI does not appear at all concerned, even though the tsunami of attention to Abilene over the years encourages attention, even requires it.

My best guess? AI could only worsen such a condition, and for two reasons. Even raising the possibility of Abilene seems out-of-bounds for AI; and, moreover, successfully diagnosing Abilene would presumably be a "negative." Hence, AI probably would not help isolate Abilene dynamics. Indeed, AI might make matters worse by reinforcing the fear of loss of an attractive membership on which Harvey's type of Abilene rests.

The significance of such lacks of linkage do not inspire confidence, even though no one can predict the incidence of Abilene. My own practice suggests Abilene is much more frequent in government than business, but no reliable estimates of incidence exist.

Now this simplifies the issues about Abilene in major ways, and the concern about testing the failure to test for linkage increases as a consequent. In reality,

Abilene is only one version of several other types of "crises of agreement." To variable but noteworthy degrees, each conceptual sub-type marches to its own drummer (e.g., Golembiewski, 1990, pp. 133-143). Worst still, this feature of AI seems inherent, or at least deep in the vitals of current AI formulations. Commonly, AI discourages analysis. Indeed, on apparent principle, some prominent AIers assign a very low priority to diagnosis or analysis, and some even seem to disparage them (e.g., Cooperrider, 1997).

AI As Discouraging Inquiry

It is curious to even write the title above, but AI has at least a curious approach to "inquiry.' Indeed, perhaps better said — and even at the risk of a charge of preciosity, AIers have a basic predisposition to fail to appreciate inquiry. Two selected points illustrate this basic contributor to the paradox which this essay highlights.

1. Sparse Research Literature.

Revealingly, from my point of view, AI has not inspired much of a research literature in its nearly two decades of prominence. Applications there have been, and beaucoup; but the existing descriptive literature numbers only a few contributions, and those are far-between.

In sum, a comprehensive review of AI (Golembiewski, 1998a) required two conclusions: the research cupboard was substantially bare; and the results of that slim literature are mixed, despite the boosterish tune of the general AI commentary and anecdotal literature, which are both widely available.

This position, in my mind, requires few qualifications, at least through the date of my comprehensive search of the AI literature and practice (Golembiewski, 1998a). There, energetic search yielded so little that the key issue was not the evaluation of research. Rather, the question became: what factors contribute to the rarity and far-betweenness of research about approach that is so positively recommended, by so many, with so few qualifications?

I can only speculate about a working answer. Paramountly, perhaps, the term "appreciative inquiry" may be curiously disarming for people like myself who are intrigued by AI but remain external to it. The external "constructive critic" – which is my view of myself with respect to AI – may be cautious about unfairly applying to AI conventional criteria of reliability and validity. I found myself being unusually tentative, not wishing to be what AI proscribes – that is, deficiency-oriented, judgmental, unresponsive to the highest aspirations in the human species, and critical of the inevitable bobbles along the way. I finally convinced myself that really caring about AI required subjecting its literature to conventional scrutiny.

For those inside the AI tent, I am obviously less qualified to comment. But if one really believes that developing the truly appreciative question is where it's really at, as prominent AIers note, the intricacies of "rigorous research" may seem quite unattractive, if not repulsive. Relatedly, AI idealogs often have announced a commitment to "social constructionism," in most forms of which my sense of "rigorous research" is seen by others as the imposition of a one-time-elite not aware enough to recognize its self-servingness, and too self-referential to realize that its time of hegemony has not only passed but that is its conventions have become seriously limiting.

In the time since I completed my 1998 survey, to be as inclusive as possible, I have become aware of AI research in the pipeline. Some of this work has been completed, especially in dissertations coming out of the OD doctoral program at Benedictine University. Indeed, I have been privileged to see some of this work in various stages of development (e.g., Robinson-Easley, 1999; Jones, 1999). So far, the work available to me requires no modification of the position based on my earlier and full search of AI theory and practice.

2. Lack of A "Critical Imperative."

Relatedly, the AI approach does not provide a clear let alone honored role for what I would consider constructive criticism. Indeed, only a small handful of citations fit this category, with Head (1997), Bushe and Coetzer (1995), and Golembiewski (1998a, 1999) being both representative as well as conveniently available. This aversion seems to characterize both people outside as well as inside the AI tent. Outsiders like myself may be inhibited about raining on someone else's parade, and the very positive character of general AI commentary also may inhibit the blight of the critical impulse, which obviously does not fit AI logic.

Perhaps best said, my personal view of knowledge development features support and opposition – not on the model of the barbarians at the gates, slashing at defenders, but certainly extending to a robust acerbity under provocation. Positively put, I have in mind the institutional efforts of Lee Bradford in the early days of "the laboratory approach" to seek involvement of a broadening range of interests and viewpoints, based (I always believed) on the possibility of learning from them about how to improve or about the need for fundamental revision of the core mission. Of course, Lee was mindful that converts also could result from the process.

Also in OD, major attention and honor went to people – Jerry Harvey and Marv Weisbord come to mind first – who functioned in the role of constructive critic, and typically in the mainstream media like the *OD Practitioner*.

In extreme form, such a role has been institutionalized in formal organizations as a counterbalance of conventional self-interests. These roles include: the ombudsman role in government; some consumer affairs offices in business; and the "devil's advocacy" role in some delicate activities of the Roman Catholic Church.

I see no such initiatives in AI; although I have recommended such a role for AI efforts. Indeed, I cannot easily imagine such approaches in AI, given personal experiences. Consider that even the modest balance in this symposium was achieved only by an offer to this author to contribute a piece within a week at the end of the manuscript preparation period.

Two Fundamental Concerns

Basically, this writer has two concerns related to normative issues: Why AI?; and AI under which conditions?

1. Why AI?

In a few words, what values define the appropriate zone for AI applications, and especially as if they are potent and "work." To illustrate the arena of concern, to what degree are AI appliers responsible for "downstream consequences" in those cases in which "upstream" applications do not direct attention to "negative" or problematic concerns? Consider only two type-conditions with such normative implications:

- a board of directors is to exercise its legal and professional obligation to review the activities of an executive group
- many orphans are available for adoption after experiencing extended periods of being warehoused under need-depriving conditions, with some resistances existing among local health professionals as well as adopters.

Is AI appropriate under the two conditions, given that the focus on "appreciation" might create a euphoria that does not recognize let alone encourage a balance of positive and negative features. For example, some probability exists that a focus on both "positive" and "negative" features could be useful or even necessary in both of the two situations above. That is:

- the executive group might be involved in well-camouflaged conflicts of interest; and
- some substantial proportion of the orphans, because of their harsh childhood treatments, might be expected to experience major developmental problems post-adoption.

Now, AI as I understand it, would neither encourage nor test for such a positive/negative balance. Basic AI questions for inquiry, that is to say, might well have a biasing effect on resulting decision-making:

- What are the best conditions that describe the association between a board and its executives?

- How would an adopted child add to the full experience of a married couple with no children, or without enough children as the couple sees it? And in what ways would adoptions ease the lives of the children and also of local healthcare and political authorities?

2. When AI?

Relatedly but with a more-decidedly operational emphasis, your writer is convinced that AI has some useful applications, but too little clarity exists about when, where, and how. The AI literature does not seem much concerned about the second query, however.

The details are beyond the present scope, but let us grant (for example) that AI seems to have much to recommend it as a generic icebreaker. Thus, relevant designs get people thinking about attractive and positive things; with the dual probable consequences of engaging energies as will of reducing resistance. Great!

We can and should go further concerning AI applicability. Thus, Bushe and Coetzer (1995) usefully detail five situations of common applicability, if limited. Elsewhere, also, your writer attempts to generalize across a broader range of applications (Golembiewski, 1999), and distinguishes four classes of AI applications.

References

Bushe, G. R., & Coetzer, (1995). "Appreciative Inquiry As A Team Development Intervention," *Journal of Applied Behavioral Science, 31*, 13-30.

Cooperrider, D. L. (1997). "The Child As The Agent of Inquiry," *OD Practitioner,* 28, 5-11.

Golembiewski, R. T. (1999). "Fine-Tuning Appreciative Inquiry," *Organization DevelopmentJournal, 17*, 21-28.

Golembiewski, R. T. (1998a). "Appreciating Appreciative Inquiry." Pp. 1-46, in R. Woodman and W. Pasmore, editors, *Research in Organization Development and Change*. Greenwich, CT.: JAI Press.

Golembiewski, R. T. (1998b). "Dealing with Doubt and Cynicism About Organization Change, the Old-Fashioned Way: Empirical Data About Success Rates in OD and QWL." Pp. 17-35, in M. A. Rahim, R. T. Golembiewski, and C. Lundberg, editors, *Current Topics in Management*. Greenwich, CT.: JAI Press, Inc.

Golembiewski, R. T. (1990). *Ironies in Organizational Development*. New Brunswick, N. J.: Transaction Publishers.

Golembiewski, R. T., Proehl, C. W., Jr., and Sink, D. (1981). "Success of OD Applications in the Public Sector," *Public Administration Review*, 41, 679-682.

Hammond, S. A. (1995, 1996). *The Thin Book of Appreciative Inquiry*. International Society for Performance Improvement.

Harvey, G. (1988). "The Abilene Paradox," *Organizational Dynamics, 17*, 17-34.

Head, T. C. (1997). "Why Does Appreciative Inquiry Work?: Speculation and A Call for Empirical Research." Working paper, Tennessee State University, Nashville, TN.

Jones, D. A. (1999). "A Field Experiment in Appreciative Inquiry." Working paper. Benedictine University, Lisle, IL.

Robinson-Easley, C. (1999). *The Role of Appreciative Inquiry in the Fight to Save Our Youth*. Unpublished doctoral dissertation, Benedictine University, Lisle, IL.

Walton, R. E. (1969). *Third-Party Consultation*. Reading, MA.: Addison-Wesley.

Chapter 26

Postmodern Principles and Practices for Large Scale Organization Change and Global Cooperation

Diana Whitney, Ph.D.
The Taos Institute

Globalization as Opportunity and Imperative

As the new millennium dawns in time as it has already in consciousness, possibilities for global cooperation emerge in ways never before imagined. Religious leaders around the globe are coming together to discuss the conditions of the world and how they and their religions can contribute to peace. Business, government and NGO leaders from opposite sides of the globe are meeting to share best practices for organizing and for creating global cooperation and social justice. People who may never meet in person are becoming friends and doing business via the Internet. And hundreds of people who care about the environment and culture of mountain regions around the world are meeting, in person and via the Internet, to envision possibilities, to share stories and to bridge resources.

The development of communication technology creates both possibilities and expectations. With the ability to communicate simultaneously around the globe comes a demand to do so.

Colleagues around the world no longer receive a summary of the meeting two days later; now they participate via teleconferencing, video conferencing or online networking. Global simultaneity is fast becoming the way of doing business.

With the ability to share information without imitation comes the expectation that needed information be available anytime of the day or night, anywhere in the world. Information is no longer a limit to cooperation. It is possible and expected that wherever we are in the world we have the same information in front of us as we meet and do business. Information accessibility, availability and equity are givens in the emerging business environment.

OD Journal, Vol. 14, No. 4, Winter 1996.

With the ability to organize large groups of people communicating online about areas of common interest comes the expectation to do so as a matter of practice. Intranets are now as important a business process as typing was two decades ago. Ongoing conferences and dialogues are commonplace on company Intranets as well as on the Internet. In the past few months I have participated in: an ongoing dialogue among academic colleagues around the world about dialogue, an ongoing conference as a member of The Mountain Forum, an ongoing meeting of founders of The Taos Institute and an ongoing meeting of the planning group for an Appreciative Inquiry Organization Summit. Each of these conversations among numbers of people ranging from 8 to 800 is ongoing. As an interested party I can participate as I like based upon whatever criteria I bring to the use of my online time and the management of relationships and responsibilities in multiple, diverse domains. Connections and conversations are there waiting to be engaged and supplemented. Large group conversations, online and face to face, are becoming primary means of organizing for global cooperation and impact.

The Unfolding Context for Life and Word in the New Millennium

As communication technology spreads around the world from urban center to rural village, from educational center to local craft cooperative, from Fortune 50 company to customers around the globe, we are discovering the essential relatedness of all members of our global village. The greater our exposure to the diversity of humankind; the stronger the realization that we are all related—different and related. What happens in one part of the globe effects the life of the whole. Communication technology enables this to be known and experienced.

The awareness of relatedness is unfolding in the physical sciences as well as the social sciences. In *Wholeness and the implicate Order*, David Bohm, a quantum physicist, outlines a general theory of the universe in which he suggests that everything is connected to everything else. The notion on essential relatedness goes beyond human relations to a connectedness of all life and consciousness.

As new communication practices emerge they create the metaframe within which life at work and at home exist. With information readily available, a premium is placed on processes of interpretation and meaning making. As larger and larger groups of people become engaged in information sharing there is created a demand for processes which engage larger and larger numbers of people in interpretation and meaning making. Sense making in organizations moves from the arenas of interpersonal and small group communication into the arena of public conversation. Organizing becomes a process of simultaneously, online or in person, engaging large numbers of people in inquiry and conversation about their collective possibilities.

And so human life in the new millennium organization is emerging as a technology assisted highly relational and interpretively rich flow of large-scale public conversations.

Modern Models and Methods of Organization Development

Methods of organizing to accomplish results in business, government, social service, education as well as religion in the past sixty plus years have been based on the physical and behavioral sciences of the early 1900s. The science of the modern era, like its organizational counterparts was organized around notions of relational objectivity, mechanistic efficiency and never ending progress.

The dominant metaphor for industrial age organizations was the machine. Efficiency of human effort was the means of achieving better productivity and hence greater profitability. Theories of Scientific Materialism led to time and motion studies aimed at describing human effort in machine like terms. Organizational Improvement rested on the ability to figure human action as coordinated with machine action; and to determine the most efficient patterns of action. Human behavior was studied as a means of improving industrial efficiency.

In response to this overly mechanized approach, organizational consultants and scholars began to put their views of "human" into human behavior. The T-Group evolved and The National Training Laboratory emerged as vehicles to help managers become aware of feelings. The dominant notions were that better people make better organizations; and that better people are those who are in touch with their feelings and can be appropriately sensitive to the feelings of others including co-workers. Human behavior was studied as a means of improving individual effectiveness and hence organizational effectiveness. As the behavioral sciences focused attention on individual development and psychology so too did organization behavior focus on the individual as the center of causality and change.

Organizational behavior, while individual centered, was conceptualized as operating on three levels—the individual, the group and the organizational. The study of group processes led to principles of organizing based on the process of group development and the experience of people in groups. Form, storm, norm and perform became code words for the story of how groups develop; and for the personal and interpersonal dramas of group work. People in groups were described as having varying needs for inclusion, affection and control. A group's effectiveness and hence organizational effectiveness was said to result from awareness of and attention to these varying needs. Other theories went beyond the notions of individuals in groups to a concern for group process itself. As group effectiveness became a focus for organization development group theories posited group goals, roles, responsibilities, leadership, relationships and helpful mechanisms as central to success.

Whatever the view of group behavior, there was one common thread — the potential for improvement through intervention by an objective external other—an organization development consultant. Processes for team building based on small group theories emerged as means of hastening business start-ups, product development and manufacturing efficiency. The total quality movement continues to build upon the focus on group effectiveness as a means to organizational effectiveness.

At the macro level theories of Action Research were being developed and enacted by organization consultants as agents of change. Organization Development was defined by French and Bell as,

> a planned, systematic process in which applied behavioral science principles and practices are introduced into an ongoing organization toward the goals of effecting organization improvement, greater organization competence, and greater organization effectiveness.

Action Research developed as a means of ensuring that change was data based and participatory. Data was important as the basis of good knowledge and good-decision making. Data in a modern scientific sense was objective and untainted by subjective views. There was an operational belief that information; meaning and the people involved and affected could be separated. Group theory began to suggest a crack in their belief as it showed that participation led to greater commitment and greater productivity. The degree and nature of participation influenced the meaningfulness of a given organizational effort. Organization development as a field became an advocate for participation in the workplace.

Action Research processes generally engaged organization members in some variation of four basic stages:

1. Data Collection
2. Feedback and Planning
3. Implementation
4. Monitoring and Revising

Action Research processes were based on the assumption that an objective outside party—consultants—could through interviews, interactions and observations develop an objective picture of the organization. It was thought that such an objective picture, when reflected back to organization members, might help them think about their organization in new and enhancing ways. Following a feedback session plans for change were created that generally initiated activities "top down". Change management was a leadership task to be driven from the top of the organization. In too many cases top management was a leadership task to be driven from the top of the organization. In too many cases top management became the drivers without asking themselves what they believed or without holding themselves accountable for demonstrable change. In other and generally more successful cases, the idea that change starts at the top meant that senior management engaged themselves in processes of learning and development.

Action Research while a process applicable to small group change, became the vehicle for total system change. The dominant metaphor for the organization shifted from machine to system. Organization theorists began writing about organizations as open systems (Katz and Kahn, 1966).

The challenge for the field of organization development became the question of how to effect change in organizations as large systems. Adding knowledge of the behavioral sciences, small group theory and cybernetic systems theory to practical wisdom based on years of experience in organization development have caused the bar to be raised in the field of organization development. Among them, Marvin Weisbord, Kathleen Dannemiller and Harrison Owen who with colleagues have pioneered large scale change in organizations.

Each of these theories of human behavior has left their mark on organizational life in the 1990s. Organization development has a rich past of theory and practice. The challenge we face as practitioners today is the development of theory and practice suited to the new millennium, and to organizing on a global scale. As with all successful social change, we must evolve our work by honoring the past, by recalling the best of what was, and by creating a context for a future richly woven with the successes of our past. We must do this while at the same time envisioning possibilities beyond what has been, and future scanning for the emerging edges of innovation and social transformation. On the horizon of theories of social change are notions of postmodern social science. I believe they hold potential for furthering the practice of organization development to the level of global cooperation.

Postmodern Principles for Organizing in the new Millennium

What we need in particular are not more effective procedures for the general will to have its way, but a real conversation. We must talk in the public forum about the things that finally matter and about common measures that will give these things a secure and prominent place in our midst.
—Albert Borgmann, Crossing the Postmodern Divide.

Much is being written about postmodernism and organizing (Bergquist, 1993; Borgman, 1992; Hassard and Parker, 1993). New ways of thinking about organizations and new theories and methods of management and leadership are emerging (Boje and Dennehy, 1993). They are growing out of postmodern principles in the social sciences and are now fertile ground for social innovation in the fields of organization development and global organizing. The following summary of an affirmative post-modem social science is quoted from Pauline Marie Rosenau's *Post-Modernism and The Social Sciences*. It is offered as one writer's overview of postmodernism and ought not be read as an inclusive or comprehensive description. Following each of her points I suggest implication for the field of organization development and especially for the arena of large-scale change and global cooperation.

1. "Yet, one thing seems clear, postmodernism in all of its forms, shakes us loose of our preconceptions, our 'normal' way of doing social science. It asks some of the most potent questions we are capable of phrasing."

This suggests that a postmodern organization development would emphasize the practice of inquiry and questioning. We would seek to understand the way inquiry operates as a means of social creation. And we would develop the theory and practice of inquiry as an organizing process. Data would be valued as a position in a story, an understanding determined by a relational rich context, rather than as a relational objective bit of information. Inquiry would be valued and enacted as a process of social meaning making rather than a process of data collection.

2. For these post-modernists the pursuit of knowledge results in a sense of wonder and amazement (Murphy, 1988). It is an encounter with the unexpected, a 'voyage into the unforeseen' (Graff, 1979).

The postmodern organizational consultant would see organizations as David Cooperrider suggests, as mysteries to be unfolded, rather than as problems to be solved. We would use wonder and delight as criteria for meaningfulness rather than the modern sentiments of concern and worry. Organization development would be propelled by a sincere sense of wonder and curiosity so great that it cannot be ignored, rather than by the all too familiar stories about problems of doomsday proportion.

Organization development consultants would engage with clients to learn and to explore possibilities for a better future, rather than to plan and to ensure predetermined results. Organization development consultants would become partners in the co-creation and conscious evolution of shared organizational destiny. Excitement, enthusiasm, wonder, and amazement would be signs of organizational success.

Notions of leadership shift dramatically from the leader as authority or one responsible for vision, action and organization, to leader who fosters public conversations among multiple stakeholders. Leadership becomes a process of ensuring relational meaning making, of ensuring that multiple, diverse voices are heard, of creating and holding space for stories to be shared and meaning to be made among globally disparate and diverse people.

Leadership must also be the process by which the voices of all of our relatives are honored, given space and heard. Leadership must learn to invite, create and celebrate organizations of full voice.

3.   "The post-modern social science is process oriented. It leaves room for a socially sensitive, active human being, groping for a new postmodern politics, religion and life in general: New Age, New Wave, new post-modern social movements."

And we are groping for new postmodern forms of organizing—the network organization, the virtual organization, the eco-conscious organization, the agile organization. For the past decade we have been talking about the reinvention for the corporation (Nasbitt), the reinvention of government (Gore) and the reinvention of work (Fox). A postmodern organization development must help business, government, religious and social leaders not only to reinvent but also to create forms of organizing for the new millennium. We must attend to organizing via processes of social interaction through which personal and collective identities, meaning and destiny emerges. These processes are uniquely conversational at the interpersonal, small group and large-scale levels of change.

Organization development in the new millennium must focus on the processes for the mass mobilization of inquiry, dialogue and public conversation both on line and face to face. Postmodern organizations may be no more than ongoing conversations among interested parties. The notions of organizations as structures—buildings, organization charts, hierarchies, standard policies and procedures are giving way to notions of organizing as conferences—temporary, as well as ongoing, conversations among diverse people with common interests and dreams for the future.

4.   "The affirmative (Postmodernists, would retain history as a form of story telling, as a local narrative without privilege. . . . There could be as many different and conflicting histories as there are consumers of the historical text."

As we collectively tell stories of our past and interpret them through the values of today, we not only make history meaningful but we also provide continuity to life. A postmodern organization development would honor story telling as a means of conveying values and giving life to the people, culture and organization. History would be treated as a potential source of positive images for the future, rather than as a singular story of how it was in the good old days.

No particular history or story would be considered more significant than another would. Emphasis would be placed on the process of story telling. As people tell the stories of their work lives they place themselves in a relational web of values and meaning. Story telling is a way of giving voice to one's identity and of taking one's place in the organizational world of work. Employees throughout the world are asking to have a say and to be heard. A postmodern organization development would ensure opportunities for public story telling as a process for large-scale change.

The deconstruction and reconstruction of history can be both a healing process and a vehicle for positive change. For example, for women who have heard few if any stories about women in power as business leaders, philosophers, goddesses or military leaders the realm of possibilities for the construction of their identities is limited. Recognizing the potential of history as a source of meaning for the future, feminists have actively engaged in processes to reconstruct history as herstory. To include stories of women in leadership in all of life, including business, government and religion, and to talk about what happened that allowed women to be written out of history liberates the feminine potential for all people.

5. "Post-modernists reject modern views of linear time and predictable space. . . . Without modern time and space, absence and presence become arbitrary, causality an impossibility, and reality an invention."

Organization development in the new millennium will recognize not only the impossibility but also the futility of seeking causality. As a field of practice it will turn toward the discourse of creation as a means of organizing, and away from the discourse of causality. In doing so practitioners will seek processes for helping people to understand work life as a social invention. We will need to become facile at helping people see how we socially construct our worlds, and how we might reconstruct them to better suit our values and the demand of a new age. Reality as an invention suggests that we view organizations, business endeavors and work itself as social inventions. An emerging postmodern metaphor for organizations is as social inventions rather than as machines, or as systems.

6. "The affirmatives' post-modern social science is likely to be influenced by their substantive focus on the margins. . . . Their goal is to speak for those who have never been the subject (active, human), but who are rather so often assumed to be objects (observed, studied). They would include new voices and new forms of local narrative."

In every conversation, culture or organization there are voices on the margins. Generally they hold great promise for innovation and for change in the culture or organization upon whose edges they depend for their definition as marginal. There are, however, some voices missing or marginalized from the powerful discourse that gives design and meaning to our lives as global citizens. The voices of women, children, people of color, the environment, and indigenous people are some of the voices that have not had space or attention in the modem scientific era. A postmodern organization development would discover ways for marginalized voices to become active and equal in the creation of our collective future.

We must learn to delight in and learn from the stories of people which give meaning to their local identities as plumbers, mothers, doctors, union members, managers, Americans, Africans or Mexicans; while at the same time fostering the creation of meta-narratives that give meaning to life as global citizens. There is a need for processes of global cooperation that give meaning to local determination and action within the context of global citizenship.

7. "New post-modern political movements are on the agenda of at least some affirmatives, as are broader and more authentic forms of participation and democracy."

A postmodern organization development would be radically participatory, not for the purpose of commitment and ownership, but rather for the purpose of co-creation and evolution. Acknowledging our essential relatedness, we would seek to engage everyone who is interested in processes of organization development. To act in ways that knowingly influence us all without involving the multitudes becomes an act of "old paradigmitis".

We must seek to further participatory democracy through all means possible, online and face to face. John Nasbitt's 1982 megatrend is unfolding as we continue to balance high tech-high touch. Large-scale processes, public conversations and global cooperation become essential vehicles for broader participation.

8. "Others need a post-modern social science that emphasizes emotion, personal fulfillment, even faith, spirituality, and the irrational."

Organization development has emerged as a field of study and practice through which views of human and organizational effectiveness are developed and realized in the workplace. Postmodern discourse about human and organizational effectiveness flows with notions of spirituality, consciousness and evolution. Current best sellers about management and organization counsel us to reinvent work so that life and livelihood flow from the same source of spirit (Fox, 1994), to reawaken spirit at work (Hawley, 1993) and to see leadership as art (DePree, 1989).

Postmodern organization development practices must find ways to surface hope among people, hope that the future of their dreams may indeed be realized. We must draw upon sources of wisdom, vision and inspiration that have for centuries been considered the realism of spirituality and faith. Elsewhere I have written of spirituality as a postmodern organizing principle.

Organizing effort that give attention to the virtues and values we hold in highest regard will lead the way into the 21st century. In keeping with a postmodern social science I leave the above text to the reader for interpretation and application. For each of us these ideas afford different insights, learning and action possibilities. It is in conversation that we might make sense together of these words and in doing so give life to collective possibilities that could not exist separate from our relatedness and interactions.

Lessons from the Past Twenty Years

In the past twenty years working as an organization development consultant I have experienced the emergence of several processes for large scale organizing. I have even been privileged to contribute to the invention of some. It seems to me that these processes have been In the process of emergence, a sort of social coming forth, that has them arriving into prominence just-in-time. What follows is a brief review of three of the most commonly deployed large scale processes—Open Space, Future Search and Real Time Strategic Change. My intent is to highlight what each offers from a post-modern framework.

Open Space Technology is said to have been created by Harrison Owen when he recognized that conference attendees seemed to be more energized and excited by coffee break conversations than by the "formal" conference presentations and discussions. It places value on space as a relational context defined by time, place and listeners willing to witness others telling their stories. Story telling is part of the Open Space vocabulary and process. Each meeting no matter what the specific organizational setting begins with a telling of the story of Open Space—how it came into being, which was involved and how it has served over time.

Open Space works on the energy and commitment of choice. A topic is selected for the meeting by its hosts. Attendance and participation are voluntary. Even the nature of participation is a choice that must be made by participating. Open Space is guided by three rules and one law. The Three Rules of Open Space are:

1. Whoever shows up are the right people.
2. What ever happens is the only thing that could happen.
3. When it is over it is over.

Open Space provides the invitation for people to meet with others based on a shared interest, and to interact with one another in whatever ways are most meaningful to them until they determine to move on.

The Open Space Law of Two Feet tells participants to do what they want to do, and to go where they are interested, contributing and/or learning. As Harrison Owen says, "If you are not where you want to be, use the law of two feet and get up and go somewhere else". The law of two feet sets a community norm of coming and going without worry about disrupting someone else's conversational reality. It also ensures that what interests people is what gets attention. In this way it is a forum for the enactment of what is most meaningful to people involved.

Process is central to organizing using Open Space. Ways of becoming speaker and listener are redefined in terms of self-interest and mastery. There are no formal rules defined by Open Space Technology. Whoever gathers as participants do so with equal opportunity to speak and be heard. The potential for full voice exists in Open Space. Participants do, however, bring relational patterns from other contexts to Open Space. In this way Open Space becomes a microcosm for the larger organization and/or society in which participants reside. Open Space can only be as open and full voiced as the participants, in relation to one another are able to create.

While a forum for public conversation, Open Space places a premium on individual responsibility and self-mastery. Individuals propose sessions and make choices about participation. Diversity and the expression of multiplicity may emerge but are not defined into the process. No voice is purposefully excluded, nor are otherwise marginalized voices purposefully included. To this extent Open Space is a mirror of current organizational values and patterns of expression. It is not, in my experience, a technology for the collective deconstruction and reconstruction of patterns of organizing. Because of its voluntary nature it does not ensure that all stakeholders participate in conversations about their collective future.

As a large-scale process, Open Space has been successfully applied to foster discussion and planning about a wide range of topics, in a wide range of settings. As an organizing device it has been used to organize meetings and conferences ranging in size from 30 to 300. A more detailed description of Open Space and its applications can be found in Harrison Owen's book, *Open Space Technology*. As a form of organizing large-scale public conversations and contributing to global cooperation, Open Space is abundant with postmodern possibilities.

Real Time Strategic Change is defined by Robert Jacobs as, "the simultaneous planning and implementing of individual, group, and organization-wide changes." It is further described as, "an informed, participative process resulting in new ways of doing business that position an entire organization for success, now and in the future." The following description relies upon quotations from Real Time Strategic Change by Robert Jacobs. The process itself draws extensively upon the work of Kathleen Dannemiller, herself a brilliant social innovator.

Real Time Strategic Change (RTSC) involves a critical mass of people, generally from the same organization, in the process of change. Participants are invited based on criteria established to ensure that the "right number and type of people" are involved. This guideline allows for the inclusion of all recognized stakeholders. A premium is placed on real time as a process for "working through the real issues with the real people affected by them, and getting real results." What people and how many of them constitute critical mass are a question to be answered with each RTSC event.

RTSC is indeed a conversational process; participation is invited and occurs as those attending engage in structured dialogues. During RTSC people are identified by their organizational roles and positions. Participants are pre-assigned to max-mix groups of 8–12 people.

Participation in max-mix groups encourages people to listen to multiple and diverse voices during their discussions. Max-mix, by design, brings people from cross functions, cross business units and cross-levels in the organization into contact and communication with one another.

Group discussions are guided by specific questions. Group tasks are clearly defined in terms of questions for discussion. A common set of questions deployed following a presentation includes:

1. What did you hear?
2. What are your reactions?
3. What questions for understanding do you have?
4. For whom?

The overall RTSC process aims to influence: "Who is involved in developing broad views (meta-narratives) of the organization? What perspectives (voices) are included? And, how do these views (stories) become the basis of information used to support people in making change?" I have added postmortem textual terms in parenthesis.

RTSC is an inherently cooperative process aimed at creating common understanding within the organization. individual voices are expressed within each group and merge to become the group voice. Individual voices are channeled toward common ground through a structured process. Max-mix groups invite diverse voices to be expressed and also limited as they merge into one group voice.

Application of small group theory in a large-scale context has contributed to the success of RTSC. It uses the best of what we know about small group process and inter-group effectiveness to address the need for greater participation in discussions of strategic importance to an organization. It leverages the advantages of simultaneity and critical mass to achieve greater participation and greater speed in the process.

Designed upon principles of systems theory, RTSC is information oriented. It operates on the basis that informed are better able to make change. A wide variety of information is shared and discussed during RTSC events including leadership's vision for the organization, the customers' perspective, and the views of competition, government and other stakeholders. Throughout the process emphasis is placed upon understanding rather than upon invention or co-creation. Experts speak and small groups discuss what they heard. Questions for understanding are aimed at adoption, or at best adaptation of ideas rather than co-creation.

One interactive process called "valentines" invites cross functional groups to give each other feedback on performance. Based on small group methods and the assumption that feedback leads to change this process again is information centered rather than meaning centered. Functional groups are expected to receive and act on feedback from other groups in their organization without opportunity for collaborative interpretation and meaning making.

RTSC engages large numbers of people, 50–5000, from the same organization in a large-scale process using principles and practices of small group theory. There is much to be learned from RTSC about how to attend small group process in the course of building an organization-wide context rich with strategic information.

"Future Search" was the phrase first used by Marvin Weisbord in his 1987 book, *Productive Workplaces*. Future Search, the process, has evolved through the work of many organizational scholars and practitioners over the past two decades, including Ronald Lippitt, Eva Schindler-Rainman, Eric Trist, Fred and Merrelyn Emery. Future Search, the practice, is delightfully described and illustrated by Marvin Weisbord and Sandra Janoff in *Future Search: An Action Guide to Finding Common Ground in Organizations and Communities*. The following quotes are theirs. "A Future Search is a large group planning meeting that brings a 'whole system' into the room to work on a task focused agenda." It is based on the notion that common ground binds an organization or community. As a result, the Future Search process is designed to assist the search for and creation of common ground.

There is an explicit emphasis on shared vision as a guide for responsible individual and collective action, as the recommended uses of Future Search highlight:

1. "Future Search processes lead stakeholders to create a shared future vision for their organization or community."

2 "Future Search meetings enable all stakeholders to discover shared intentions and take responsibility for their own plans."

3. "These events can help people implement a shared vision that already exists."

The principle of 'global exploration before local action' serves to guide the design of Future Search meetings. The past is explored through wall charting and story telling about memorable personal, global and local events that occurred during the organization's past 30 years. The public and collective remembering of the past serves to invite voices that may have been silenced during the actual events of the past. It serves as a process for the deconstruction of commonly held relational realities. And it creates an open space for the creation of a shared future.

Future Search seeks to manage two essential and at times opposing forces: the desire for common ground and the expression of multiple and diverse voices. There is a recognition built into the design that validating every person's reality is essential as a foundation for common ground.

"We wish to validate every person's reality. We believe that there is great value in making psychological boundaries easier to cross—especially the boundary between what's inside our heads and what we say in public."

Future Search might be described as a multilingual process in that it allows for people's varying ways of knowing, learning and expressing themselves to occur and to be valued. The process invites thinking, feeling, reflecting, drawing, mind mapping, time lining, remembering and envisioning. It involves "the whole person" in a task oriented, future focused exploration and creation of the organizations past, present and future.

Underlying the design of Future Search is a strong and abiding democratic ideal. The aim is to get the whole system in the room, to engage all stakeholders in a simultaneous, interactive process and to ensure that those who must take action are involved in its determination. While the preferred number of participants is 64, Future Search methods have been used with smaller groups as well as integrated into processes involving hundreds.

Future Search allows for the remembering and re-interpreting of history and for the co-construction of a shared future vision. It fosters discussion in an open forum, allowing for the expression of multiple voices all aimed toward the organizing principle of common ground. It encourages personal responsibility for ideas and actions in alignment with the collective vision. Based on the commitment to validate every person's reality while aiming for common ground, Future Search illustrates emerging postmodern principles in practice.

The Organization Summit: An Appreciative Inquiry Large Scale Conference

> We have reached the end of problem solving as a mode of inquiry capable of inspiring, mobilizing, and sustaining human system change. The future of Organization Development belongs to methods that affirm, compel, and accelerate anticipatory learning involving larger and larger levels of collectivity.
> —David Cooperrider, *Appreciative Inquiry Workshop Manual.*

Appreciative Inquiry has emerged as a process for social, organizational and global change based on postmodern principles. It is a method that views realities as socially constructed with three bold implications. One, it is radically relational, inviting 100s and 1000s of people into circles of face to face inquiry and dialogue. And, within cyberspace, engaging millions of people in the conversations that shape our global village. Inquiry, based on a sincere desire to learn, guides interactions and invites the process of relational meaning making. Inquiry as a process for learning is simultaneously a process for cooperation, co-creation and change.

Two, Appreciative Inquiry is a dramatically creative process, an ongoing inquiry into of the stories that give meaning to life, work and organizing. It is a process for unfolding history—personal, organizational and global; for deconstructing and reconstructing the past in relation to present and future possibilities; and for discovering those narratives which give life in their expression and continual enactment.

Three, Appreciative Inquiry is decidedly affirmative and constructive in the positive interpretation of the word. It is based on the notion that organizations and communities are "affirmative systems" and according to Srivastva and Cooperrider, "they are guided in their actions by anticipatory 'fore-structurers' of positive knowledge." Organizations are heliotropic, they grow in the direction of the light—the most positive image created and conveyed by their discourse.

The Organization Summit is a large scale event in which organization Co-creators—members, stakeholders and meaning makers (people with the formal and/or informal relational capacity to influence the identity, direction and success of the organizational effort at hand. For example: the media, potential funding sources, students of organization, and leaders from other business or service sectors) engage in an Appreciative Inquiry process.

The Organization Summit engages participants in cycles of discovery, dream, design and destiny rather than diagnosis, problem identification, criticism or gap analysis. Initial Appreciative Interviews along with presentations of anticipatory theory and social construction theory create a shared commitment and curiosity among participants for exploring positive possibilities as a means of learning and organizational development.

The Organization Summit is a mix of dyadic, small group and whole group processes. Based on relational notions of meaning making and social construction theory, interaction among people representing diverse voices is essential. Cross-generational processes have proven most effective in generating stories that enliven leadership as well as hope for the organization's future. The Organization Summit utilizes techniques from other large-scale change processes. From Future Search it borrows the process of creating time lines to tell personal, organizational and global histories. From RTSC it takes ways of orchestrating small group conversations in the context of a large group meeting. It deploys Open Space to foster personal choice and public commitment for unfolding actions.

As the word Summit suggests, The Organizational Summit is a process for moving an organization toward its highest potential—the highest ideals imaginable among its co-creators. It is an invitation for participants to discover what gives life—to themselves, their co-creators and their organization. It is an opportunity for participants to dream of what might be possible if their most cherished values are enacted as organizational realities. It is a rigorous process for participants to design an organization with appreciative competencies. And it is a time to engage with one another in meaningful ways so that today's interactions become the seeds of well lived destiny.

Summary

The new millennium brings with it a context of globalization and a demand for organization development processes that engage large numbers of people, on line and in person, simultaneously in the co-creation of our shared future. Modern behavioral science, small group theory, and systems theory have served us well as foundations for organizational development principles and practices to date. A new generation of organization development practices is being evoked as we enter the twenty-first century. This new generation of practice will be grounded in the postmortem social sciences rather than the physical or mechanical sciences. It will be appreciative in nature, rather than problem oriented. It will be radically participatory as it invites a cornucopia of diverse voices to be expressed and heard in the co-creation of common ground for the future of our global village.

References

Beckhard, R. (1969) *Organizational Development: Strategies and Models*. Reading, MA: Addison-Wesley Publishing Co.

Bergquist, W. (1993) *The Postmodern Organization*. San Francisco, CA: Jossey-Bass.

412 Whitney

Boje, D.M. and Dennehy, R.F. (1993) *Managing In the Postmodern World, 2nd Ed.* Dubuque, IA: Kendall/Hunt Publishing Co.

Borgmann, A. (1992) *Crossing The Postmodern Divide.* Chicago, IL: The University of Chicago Press.

Cartwright, D. and Zander, A. (Eds.) (1953) *Group Dynamics: Research and Theory.* New York, NY: Harper and Row.

DePree, M. (1989) *Leadership is An Art.* New York, NY: Doubleday

Fox, M (1994) *The Reinvention of Work: A New Vision Of Livelihood For our Time.* San Francisco, CA: Harper Collins Publishers.

French, W.L. and Bell, C.H. Jr. (1973) *Organization Development.* Englewood Cliffs, NJ:Prentice-Hall, Inc.

Gergen, K.J. (1991) *The Saturated Self.* Basic Books.

Gergen, K.J. (1994) *Realities and Relationships.* Cambridge, MA: Harvard University Press.

Hassard, J. and Parker, M. (Eds.) (1993) *Postmodernism and Organizations.* London, U.K.: Sage Publications.

Hawley, J.A. (1993) *Reawakening The Spirit In Work.* San Francisco, CA: Berrett-Koehler Publishers, Inc.

Jacobs, R.W. (1994) *Real Time Strategic Change.* San Francisco, CA: Berrett-Koehler Publishers, Inc.

Jaworski, J. (1996) *Synchronicity The Inner Path Of Leadership.* San Francisco, CA: Berrett-Koehler Publishers Inc.

Katz, D and Kahn, R.L. (1966) *The Social Psychology of Organizations.* New York, NY: John Wiley and Sons, Inc.

Naisbitt, J. (1982) *Megatrends: Ten New Directions Transforming Our Lives.* New York, NY:Warner Books, Inc.

Owen, H. (1992) *Open Space Technology.* Potomac, MD: Abbott Publishing.

Rosenau, P.M. (1992) *Postmodernism and the Social Sciences.* Princeton, NJ: Princeton University Press.

Srivastva S. and Cooperrider, D. (1990) *Appreciative Management and Leadership.* San Francisco, CA: Jossey-Bass.

Varney, G.H. (1977) *Organization Development For Managers.* Reading, MA: Addison-Wesley Publishing Co.

Weisbord, M.R. and Janoff, S. (1995) *Future Search.* San Francisco, CA: Berrett-Koehler Publishers, Inc.

Whitney, D. (1994) *Postmodern Challenges To Organization Development.* HRD Global Changes and Strategies for 2000 AD. pp. 617–629. New Delhi, India: Allied Publishers Limited.

Whitney, D. (1995) *Spirituality As An Organizing Principle.* World Business Academy *Perspectives.* Vol. 9, No. 4, pp. 51–62. Berrett-Koehler Publishers, Inc.

Chapter 27

ORGANIZATIONAL INQUIRY MODEL FOR GLOBAL SOCIAL CHANGE ORGANIZATIONS

Jane Magruder Watkins
Watkins & Kelly
David Cooperrider
Case Western Reserve University

> Change is not what it used to be. The status quo will no longer be the best way forward. . . . We are entering an Age of Unreason, when the future, in so many areas, is there to be shaped, by us and for us; a time when the only prediction that will hold true is that no predictions will hold true; a time, therefore, for bold imaginings in private life as well as public, for thinking the unlikely and doing the unreasonable.
> —Charles Handy, *The Age of Unreason*, p.4.

Organizational leaders faced with managing in these turbulent times, are trained and grounded in formerly useful theories, methods and mechanisms that grew out of Taylorism and the movement called scientific management. A product of modernity, the management sciences have employed linear procedures, count and measure methods and the basic assumption that organizations are both rational in their operation and problems to be solved. (Cooperrider, 1987).

Today, sailing into the future full of theories of chaos (Gleik, 1987), complexity (Waldrop, 1992), social construction (Gergen, 1994), and that illusive paradigm called "post-modernism", the question looms large: Are there models of social architecture in existence or being created that will enable the organizations of the future to survive and to thrive? Where do we look for them? How can we recognize them? Are they replicable or must each organization create them anew?

We suggest that the management models for the future are already in existence or are being created daily, particularly by that network of organizations around the globe that are humanitarian in focus, value based and mission driven. David

Watkins, J.M., & Cooperrider, D.L. (1996). Organizational Inquiry Model For Global Social Change Organizations. *Organization Development Journal*, *14*(4), 97-112.

Cooperrider and Bill Pasmore write in the introduction to their article, "The Organizational Dimension of Global Change," in the Journal Human Relations (Cooperrider and Pasmore, 1991, p. 1037):

Today, a vital and pioneering latticework of global social change organizations (GSCO) is spreading across continents, involving people from every nation, in an unprecedented attempt to forge a new vision of the world's cooperative capacity. The people-centered GSCO, we submit, is one of the more important social innovations of the past half-century and is one of the greatest unrecognized resources in the world today.

The first part of this paper briefly traces the history and structure of global social change organizations describing their evolution from aid agencies representing dominant "donor" countries that helped poorer countries in times of disaster, to the emerging global partnership model that is, possibly, the model for all organizations in the global village. The second section suggests conceptualizing GSCOs with "network" structures that consider all major stakeholders as integral parts of the organization requiring internal cooperation at every level. Finally we offer a model for organizational study (called organizational diagnosis in the traditional management methods) that uses the Appreciative Inquiry (Cooperrider, 1987) model to create an in-depth understanding of the organization's strengths as a basis for envisioning the future.

International Development Organizations

Origins

Working in multi-cultural environments, International Development organizations[1] focus on issues of poverty and oppression, environmental degradation, human rights and child survival. They have existed in the West since the first missionaries went into the less "developed" (that is, the less industrialized) continents to bring salvation to the heathen and took with them medical knowledge and a passion for education and clean water.

After World War II, secular organizations emerged based on humanitarian principles. The early post-World War organizations were largely "relief" focused, responding to natural disasters of flood, fire and famine, as well as those tragedies of human making such as war. The concept was that a superior and undeniably richer industrialized world should offer aid and assistance to the less developed nations.

---

[1]International development organizations are known by several names currently used in the field: In the U. S., Private Voluntary Organizations (PVOs); in international nomenclature, Nongovernmental Organizations (NGOs); in Africa, some are called Community Development Organizations (CDOs); and increasingly in countries newly democratizing, as organizations that build civil society. In this paper they will be called International Development Organizations or Agencies. In the inquiry model we use the term Global Social Change Organizations (GCSO) (Cooperrider and Pasmore, 1991).

During the late 1950s, these generally North American and European based aid organizations working in countries in Asia, Africa and Latin America, began to respond to the growing capacity of local people to solve their own problems. The emerging model became known by names such as "technical assistance," and "appropriate technology." During this era the work was being shifted to locally based staffs, but the expatriates were still very much in charge.

It was not until the late 1980s that concepts of equal partnership, shared decision-making, and sustainable development began to replace the donor/donee, helper and helped models for International Development. Today, as governments democratize and civil society grows, thousands of locally controlled organizations have joined the International Development arena.

Emerging Partnerships

In 1984 at Regent's College in London, representatives of Northern and Southern[2] development agencies met to hold a global dialogue that resulted in a special issue of the World Development Journal. The message from the meeting was clear. The South no longer needed Northerners arriving on their shores to "give" them development or even to direct development projects that purported to consult with local people. What the South needed was partnership.

The Northern partners had access to funding and information needed in the South. Help with management practices, particularly as required by large donors, would be useful. And, specifically, the South needed the North to educate their own people and influence their own government's policies on behalf of their Southern partners. The conference participants called for an equal partnership with multiple levels of cooperation. Many Northern agencies took the message to heart and began to expand their own ideas and practices about what cooperation and partnership could mean for their work.

In Dakar, Senegal, January 1990, representatives of international development organization from the United States and Africa met in the second of a series of "North-South" dialogues. For some years the members of InterAction, a consortium of U.S.-based international development agencies, and FAVDO (Federation of African Voluntary Development Organizations), a consortium of African based development field-the challenge of true partnership between Northern and Southern development organizations.

---

[2]In the search for inoffensive nomenclature to distinguish between the wealthier industrialized countries and the variably less wealthy countries of the world, the term "North" is used for the first and "South" for the latter. Various other designations existed over time: rich/poor, 1st world/3rd world; developed/ undeveloped; developed/ less developed, LDCs; etc. For this paper, the terms used are North and South.

No longer could outsiders arrive on foreign shores with ideas about what was needed to improve the quality of life for the poor and oppressed of some underdeveloped nation. The time had come to acknowledge that for any kind of development, human or material, to be implemented successfully, it would have to be the product of the work of the people themselves who would, thereafter, assure its continuation. The old stereotypes no longer held. The issue of sustainability had become a dominant concern of all parties. And imbedded in the concept of sustainability is the necessity for a truly equal partnership.

The dialogues, planned and implemented by the two consortia, brought together leaders from U.S. and African development organizations representing three areas: CEOs, Program Specialists, and Development Education Specialists. By the middle of the second dialogue in Dakar, emotions were running high.

The rhetoric of victim and victimizer, of haves and have nots was hot and heavy. But these people had, over the years, become friends of a sort, or at least cordial colleagues with very similar values and goals. At the height of the fracas in the Program Specialist group, after speeches about equity and exploitation and "We don't need you anyway, just send money," the calm that often follows such a venting of feelings fell on the group. And someone said, "Aren't we really all after the same thing?"

The conversation switched to an examination of shared values and the friendships that had developed through the common struggle. The dialogue turned: "We must think of ourselves as an association of people of good will, without regard to race, gender or national boundaries, who are deeply concerned about the issues of poverty and oppression around the globe."

It was a stunning moment as the group relished the rising of the human spirit embracing the possibility of cooperation and common cause. What better way to keep the poor poor than to have them, and those who strive to work with them, fighting over limited resources and limited power? Only through the magic of human cooperation is there any hope of changing the world order for haves and have nots, privileged and underprivileged, higher and lower dichotomies that themselves serve to dehumanize one half of the partnership. In that dialogue, the true spirit of the movement called "International Development" was articulated and embraced by a significantly influential partnership of development professionals.

This conversation was later recorded in the report, "Toward Partnership in Africa" (page 96):

What becomes clear to participants as this series of consultations ends is that in learning how to be partners, the distinctions of "North" and "South", or "African" and "American" become less important and the values and goals we share come to the fore. Through this process (the consultation), we have built a sense of solidarity, not as Northern PVOs and Southern NGOS, but as a unified group of voluntary development organizations working together to empower the poor and build a better world.

Why did this process work? Much of value has been learned in this process by participants and by their organizations: some specific dos and don'ts involved in effective partnership, and much that is intangible, such as greater understanding of one another's working contexts and outlooks, values and problems, a greater sense of empathy for one another and, perhaps most importantly, a greater sense of solidarity with one another as people engaged in work to empower the poor and oppressed and to build a more just and peaceful world.

In February, 1990, shortly after the Dakar meeting, the first International Conference on Popular Participation in the Recovery and Development Process in Africa gathered representatives from sectors as diverse as governments and grass roots organizations at a conference in Arusha, Tanzania. The preamble to the conference documents referred to the conference as a "rare collaborative effort between African peoples' organizations, the African governments, non-governmental organizations and U.N. agencies in search of a collective understanding of the role of Popular Participation in the development and transformation of the region."

These organizations working across national boundaries in collaboration with people from every social strata in every corner of the globe have discovered the fact that seems absurd in its simplicity: If we want to create a peaceful and generative globe where poverty and oppression are rare and people share in the bounty of the earth, we must do it cooperatively. The more urgent view is that, without such cooperative, our species may simply vanish from an earth rendered uninhabitable by our divisiveness.

Implications for Management

The evolution of relationships between nations and peoples represented by these development agencies is a precursor to the kind of partnerships and relationships that must be practiced by all global organizations. In the 1970s the U.S. Agency for International Development, USAID, commissioned a study carried out by Stark Biddle and thus known as the "Biddle Report," to determine why corporate and philanthropic foundations were reluctant to fund development agencies. The answer reported in the document was that unless these agencies learned to manage themselves more professionally, i.e., more like corporations, there would be no funds forthcoming. The irony today is that corporations are beginning to manage themselves more like these development agencies.

The reason becomes obvious. Development agencies have always had to manage global programs often without adequate communications links, with limited resources and staffs who carry severely heavy workloads, in an unstable and often hazardous environment, operating with multiple cultural norms and behaviors. While their management styles and methods often seemed unorthodox to the business sector, in fact many of them were very well managed for the environment in which they operated.

Today, many corporations are finding themselves working with those same constraints. And they are discovering what development agencies have long known—that scientific management methodologies that need predictability and stable environments simply do not work in the global arena. What, then, will work in this rapidly emerging global village? What organizational arrangements are required? What methodologies are appropriate?

We suggest that the growing practices of partnership, cooperation, and common cause that is becoming the norm in development agencies holds valuable lessons for all organizations in this time of discontinuous chance. Cooperation is a concept that is increasingly being applied to every level of organizing and in every form of organization. From the agricultural cooperative to good team work in a small organization, to visions of the global cooperation of governments, the term has come to symbolize the creative edge in the field of organization development in the 1990s. In a wider context, the proliferation of peace studies and conflict transformation methodologies: the concept of "new games" with their win-win focus; the wealth of new writing on the feminine qualities of cooperation; the Internet; all are phenomena of an increased interest in cooperation as a generative process for human endeavor.

New Approaches

In the late 1970s, in response to the Biddle Report, USAID funded the New TransCentury Foundation with a grant called "Management Development Services" (MDS) that was designed to provide management training and consulting to development agencies who wanted to meet the management criteria stipulated by the philanthropic donor organizations. For 10 years TransCentury, under MDS grant, worked with several hundred U.S.-based development agencies. In several cases the U.S. agencies requested assistance for their overseas staffs.

While the original purpose of the grant was to provide fairly typical management training and assistance to the U.S. agencies, the longevity of the grant made it possible for a great deal of learning to take place on the part of the organizational development professionals providing the training as well as for the agencies themselves. Clearly, the models and methods needed by these agencies were, in many ways, quite different from those used in the business sector. While traditional management and organization theory might inform the process, in the final analysis, a unique process was called for, one suited to the unique environment in which these agencies work. Hierarchy was often dysfunctional. Projects were not finished on time or did not last past the departure of the Northern agency. Western management practices often made no sense in societies that value relationships above task.

The U.S. agencies began to experiment. A major issue became the ability to "walk the talk" While the dialogue about and rhetoric for sharing, cooperation and partnership moved forward in the larger arena, the U.S.-based agencies were struggling with their own hierarchical structures and the largely homogenous nature of their own staffs. In a field where the majority of CEOs are white males and the majority of workers are Caucasian (see Interaction's Grafton Report series), the rhetoric of valuing diversity and embracing partnership across cultures was creating cognitive dissonance. The rhetoric was right but the practice was not aligned with that rhetoric.

InterAction again took the lead. They began to document the makeup of their member agencies and provided workshops at their annual forums as well as dialogue sessions and written materials aimed at helping agencies diversify staff, often to the point of adding people from the overseas partner agencies to U.S. headquarters' staff. The more each staff worked to value diversity in its own ranks and to gain experience working with people from different cultures in their day to day work, the more credibility they had in the field.

Appreciative Inquiry

In the last half of this decade another obvious—though invisible until now—reality dawned on those working with development agencies. The traditional organization development "problem solving" approach, standing alone, seems to have outlived its effectiveness. As both the speed and nature of change are changing[3] many consultants and organizational leaders, even in traditional organizations, are finding that by the time a group identifies the problem, analyzes the causes, formulates the plan of action to correct it and sets about to carry out those actions, the original problem is no longer the problem! This is particularly true in international development where the speed of change is often lightning fast and unpredictable.

New models have begun to emerge to help organizations cope with rapid change and unstable environments. One of the most widespread practices is that of helping organizations to formulate visions and mission statements as a first step in moving their organizations forward. Many in the field, as well as those trying to lead and manage organizations in these turbulent times (Drucker, 1980) are searching for even more creative methods for understanding their organizations, and more innovative, less mechanistic ways to move them forward.

---

[3]George Land and Beth Jarman, in their book Breakpoint and Beyond: Mastering the Future Today comment (pp. 4–5) that, "The surprising fact is that change itself has changed. . . . The old rules mandated changes of degree, not of kind. . . . . These great leaps defy traditional wisdom supporting linear and progressive change. . . . This kind of totally unconventional change process has pushed us to the edge, teetering precariously between two eras. We've reached a Breakpoint!

The pioneering work of David Cooperrider, Suresh Srivastva and their colleagues at Case Western Reserve University has created a methodology called Appreciative Inquiry (Cooperrider and Srivastva, 1987), that has been used successfully as a method of inquiring into the well-being cooperation, a government agency and a large number of non-profit international development organizations. The Appreciative method of studying organizations is particularly appropriate when organizations want to discover more and varied ways to use cooperative processes. Just as diagnosing problems fits neatly into the image of an organization as a machine to be repaired (Marshak), inquiring appreciatively is congruent with a search for cooperative models. It is an ideal approach for understanding how such values drive organizations as international development agencies.

An Experiment

During the past four years, a group of organization development consultants working under another grant from USAID designed and delivered an Institute for PVO-CFO Excellence for the management teams of nearly 30 nonprofit development organizations. These management teams learned how to use an Appreciative Inquiry method for gaining a better understanding of their own organizations and staffs. Outside consultants trained the teams in the use of the approach, but the teams tailored it to their own environments and they, themselves, did the interviewing. The result of this method is a virtual agency-wide conversation about the generative and life-giving aspects of the organization.

Each organization later attended the 5-day Institute with the appreciative stories in hand. The stories and information became the foundation for creating an image of the organization's future. The advantage of the approach is that it combines the best of what is (tradition), with images of the future so that the images and plans are firmly grounded in the best of what is in the organization.

During the Institute, each organization formed the appreciative information into a pattern that gave a picture of their organization's current reality. Traditionally, in the practice of Organization Development, consultants have found it useful to have management teams analyze data using some diagnostic tool that covers all of the relevant aspects of an organization. The Institute consultants experimented with several traditional diagnostic models before it became evident that most such models were created for large profit-making organizations as a way to ferret out problems that needed to be corrected.

Since, as has been noted, most non-profit development agencies are not structured organizationally like large profit-making companies, a different model begins to emerge. The concept of a development agency as a network both internally and externally began to form. What if the internal organization is conceived as a network of major stakeholders, all of whom are decision-makers, resource providers, and, in a very real sense, key players in every aspect of the organization? What might this say about the organization? And what would be the impact of common understanding of the current state of the organization? And what would be the impact of shifting the process from curative (diagnostic) to an ongoing inquiry process that affirms the health of the organization? Could such a model help to create a true "learning organization"? (Senge, 1990).

Furthermore, if these organizations are internal networks, the implications are vast concerning the need for a high level of cooperative behavior inside the organizations as well as with external groups.

This line of thinking led us to create an appreciative approach to understanding (formerly "diagnosing") the organization using the appreciative process for inquiring into the organizations current reality ("collecting data"). While we created this model particularly for the U.S.-based international development agencies participating in the institute, we suggest that it is a model that can be used by that vast array of organizations that make up civic society across the globe.

Organizational Inquiry Model

The Organizational Inquiry Model for Global Social Change Organizations (GSCOs) is a method of inquiring into the health and wellbeing of organizations whose purpose is to improve the quality of life around the globe. Whatever the name, a GSCO is, in general terms, an organization, nonprofit by nature, that has a mission to address such issues as poverty and oppression, human rights, human potential, and environmental concerns of the globe. Because GSCOs are organizations founded on hope and the belief that human beings can work together to improve life on the planet, this Organizational Inquiry Model is designed to inquire into the current reality of an organization and to plan its future by focusing on the successes and the life-giving forces that support the work and the people. Once those forces are located and articulated, the organization can move to affirm, expand and increase those success factors as they imagine the organization's future. This is a departure form the traditional model of organizational diagnosis that searches for the problems and shortcomings of the organization for the purpose of "fixing" it (Marshak, 1993).

This appreciative approach is grounded in the theory of Social Constructionism (Gergen, 1991 and 1994) that holds organizations as social constructions of those who inhabit and "talk" in them. If organizations are imagined and made by human beings, then they can be remade and re-imagined. The constraints of scientific management theory that images organizations as machines are lifted and the possibility of new approaches and configurations emerges. We create what we imagine!

ORGANIZATIONAL INQUIRY MODEL

The terms in rings 2 and 3 of this model are examples only. Each organization needs to fill the 2nd circle with stakeholders that form the leadership of the organization and the 3rd circle with the tasks and processes that are important to their work.

Rationale for this Approach

Global Social Change Organizations (GSCOs) are organized around the principles of service and social transformation. They are committed to creating a world constructed for the common good. Because these organizations are founded on hope and the belief that people can organize themselves to make the world a better place, it would follow that any inquiry into these organizations would seek to find the life-giving forces—those things that the organization does well.

A second factor that mitigates an appreciative analysis has to do with the environment in which these organizations work and the nature of change itself. The ambiguity, sudden shifts and discontinuous change that create the environment in which Global Social Change Organizations work, requires maximum flexibility, a core belief that the work makes a difference and a commitment to ride out the storms. There is rarely time to "fix" problems because of the rapidly changing environment. By focusing on what gives life to their work, these organizations are able to have maximum impact, maintain forward motion and assure an environment that is creative and generative.

4"Breakpoint change abruptly and powerfully breaks the critical links that connect anyone or anything with the past. What we are experiencing today is absolutely unprecedented in all of humanity's recorded history . . . . At Breakpoint, the rule change is so sharp that continuing to use the old rules not only doesn't work, it erects great, sometimes insurmountable barriers to success."

Assumptions of the Organizational Inquiry Model

The Organizational Inquiry Model is built on several assumptions:

The first assumption is that the central organizing principles of Global Social Change Organizations are the clarity about the ultimate IMPACT of the work, the work, the CORE VALUES that are shared, and a common MISSION of a group of people who wish to act in the world from a belief that organizations are instruments for the common human good. These are critical ingredients that provide the foundation for the organization. Without clarity and consensus on these ingredients, no amount of organizational excellence related to task and management will ensure survival. Conversely, organizations with clarity on the IMPACT they want to make, shared understanding of their CORE VALUES and agreement on their MISSION, can survive a great deal of imperfection and ambiguity in their organizational forms. Therefore, the premier task of every GSCO is to carry on a continuous dialogue making meaning of their work. The meaning of these terms as used in the paper are as follows:

Impact: The ultimate goal of our work; the conditions that we plan to change; the reason for our existence as an organization.

Values: The core values that we all share and which form the solid foundation for our work together.

Mission: The work we will do in the world to achieve our ultimate impact.

The second assumption is that Global Social Change Organizations are NETWORKS. In this model, what is usually called the 'organization', that is, the staff that works in the headquarters office and in the field offices, is called the TEAM and is seen as the coordinating body for the NETWORK ORGANIZATION. The organization is envisioned as a network of key stakeholders who gather around the desired IMPACT, VALUES, and MISSION to accomplish tasks that lead to social transformation. The NETWORK ORGANIZATION might include the TEAM; a BOARD; DONORS; PARTNERS; ALLIANCES; and, frequently, VOLUNTEERS. Definitions of these terms are described below. However, each organization will have a unique set of actors in this circle. This model describes one possible configuration.

Organizational Inquiry Model Network

Organization Elements

Team: The core staff of headquarters and field offices that work together collaboratively and whose central task is to provide leadership, coordinate and sustain the work and the relationships of the organization;

Board: Whose task is to set policy, provide guidance and ensure that the organization has the resources it needs to sustain itself;

Donors : Those that supply the resources and whose tasks encompass providing financial resources and programmatic guidance;

Partners: Multiple groups of clients' recipients of services who are responsible for collaborating in all planning and implementation of joint programs;

Volunteers: Groups and individuals who contribute time and skills to the organization;

Alliances: Other institutions entities who join in the work of the organization.

The third assumption is that in addition to the core of the organization and the leadership network, there are key areas for inquiry in the ways the organization organizes its work. Inquiry into these areas enables groups to discover the life-giving forces, success stories and generative spirit of their organizations. In this model, examples for inquiry include: PATHWAY; GOVERNACE; SYSTEMS; STRUCTURE; PEOPLE; PROGRAMS; SUSTAINABILITY; ENVIRONMENT. These terms are defined as:

ORGANIZATIONAL INQUIRY MODEL KEY AREAS OF INQUIRY

Pathway: The guiding principles, strategy, plans and tactics for achieving our mission.

Governance: How we organize, govern and manage ourselves, how we make decisions, how we celebrate our achievements, how our governance process aligns with our values and our theory of development.

Systems: The systems and technologies that we use to manage ourselves, to communicate with each other, and to "conference" with the world.

Structure: The way we organize our work and manage our tasks.

People: The well-being, fair treatment and empowerment of our staff team, partners, board members, alliance, and volunteers; the placement of our people in the right positions to make our work flow smoothly; how we value our diversity and celebrate our differences as organizational assets; how we relate to each other; how our rhetoric about valuing people aligns with our organizational behavior.

Programming: Our development paradigm and the theories that underlie our methods of work; the nature of our work and how it aligns with our vision and values; our programming process.

Sustainability: How we guarantee the people and resources to assure the health and survival of all of our organizational entities; how we steadily increase our capacity; how we function as a lifelong learning organization committed to continuous improvement.

Environment: Our understanding of what 's going on in the world that impacts our work, and, overview of the organizational culture and norms that create our work environment.

How to Use the Organizational Inquiry Model

For each of the elements in (1) the core circle; (2) the NETWORK ORGANIZA-TION circle, and (3) the organization of work circle, you will use the ABCs:

A. Appreciative Understanding of Your Organization;
B. Benchmarked Understanding of Other Organizations;
C. Creation of "Possibility Propositions" To Image Your Organization's Future.

A. Appreciative Understanding Of Your Organization

The process begins with your inquiry into your organization that will provide a clear picture of your organization's strengths, competencies and life-giving forces. Using this approach, you look for those moments when your organization is at its very best. Using an interview process, members of your staff can interview each other in search of organizational excellence. Questions might include:

Think of a time in your work with this organization when you felt excited, joyful and at the peak of your form. Tell a story about that time. Describe what your were doing, what others did and how you felt. Tell the story in a way that creates an image for the interviewer.

Without being humble, talk about the things that you value about yourself; what are the things that you value about your job in this organization; and, what is it that you value about this organization itself, i.e., what, for you, gives life to this organization?

What do you believe are the core values of this organization? That is, what is the key thing without which this organization would not exist?

B. Benchmarked Understanding Of Other Organizations

Once you have initiated the process in your own organization, you may want to seek out and understand the best practices of other organizations. This is best done as a reciprocal process in which you also share your best practices. Such mutual sharing gives both organizations a way to inform their own practices and to adapt and incorporate some ideas that can inspire innovation and improvement.

Often organizations seek out similar groups to "benchmark" but there can be rich learning and exchange between even the most diverse organizations. Negotiations with potential benchmarking partners should include the parameters of the exchange and agreement on questions to be asked. Sample questions include:

What is the most exciting and successful time you have had working with your organization? Please describe for me what made it so exciting. Are there processes from that event time that you have incorporated into your work here? Can you tell me about them?

If you had to say the one best thing your organization does when it is at its most competent, what would that be? Tell me about it. How does it work?

What do you value most about working for this organization?
(These questions are intended to be examples only; you will construct questions appropriate to the study that you want to do.)

C. Creation Of "Possibility Propositions" To Image Your Organization's Future

Once you have gathered information from your own organization and have benchmarked several other organizations, it is time to make sense of that information in search of an image of the current reality that will serve as a spring board to creating an image of your organization's future. This is an exercise that can be carried out at every level of the organization with any mix of staff and stakeholders. The process includes sharing the information and stories gathered from the appreciative inquiry of your own organization and the best practices gathered from other organizations. This sharing is best done as a dialogical process with any written report aimed at capturing the highlights from the stories and sharing the high points of the process itself. A mechanical reporting of facts will not usually lead to exciting "propositions." Once the verbal or written story of the process is finished, the group moves to create the most exciting possible future for the organization that incorporates the best that exists within, plus new and exciting practices discovered from without. Possibility propositions are written as though they are already happening, in the present tense. These become the vision for the organization that guides planning and operations in the future.

This ABC process can be used to study every facet of an organization. This model suggests that a GSCO needs to look, at a minimum, at the two levels described in this model:

The organization itself is conceived of as a network of key stakeholders that make up the decision making and operating body for achieving the mission. The Organizational Inquiry Model suggests in ABC process for each of the 6 elements: Team; Board; Donors; Partners; Volunteer; Alliances (elements should be added or removed according to what is actual in your own organization.)

The second level of inquiry focuses on the various functions and guiding principles of the organization, to include: Impact, Values, Mission, Pathway, Environment, Governance, People, Programming, Systems, Sustainability (Again, you are encouraged to add any other factors that are related to your organization.)

Finally, it is essential that some other interactive process be embedded in the organization as an ongoing dialogue, constantly appreciating, reframeing, and sharing the life of the people and the meaning of the work that make up the GSCO. It is this community meaning-making that creates a flexible, grounded, generative organization. The ABC model can be used as a framework for the ongoing conversations that will create a true learning organization. As the conversation deepens and expands, the framework itself will be changed and embellished as needed to facilitate the learning about the growth and change that are life-giving forces in all organizations.

References

"African charter for popular participation in development and transformation."
(1990) New York: U. N. report on International conference on popular participation in the recovery and development process in Africa.

Biddle, S. (1976). Report on the management practices of U.S. private voluntary organizations. Washington, DC: Study from the Office of Private Voluntary Cooperation (PVC),USAID.

Cooperrider, D. and Pasmore, W.A. (1991). The Organization dimension of global change. *Human Relations.*

Cooperrider, D. and Srivastva, S. (1987). Appreciative inquiry in organizational life. In W. Pasmore and R. Woodman (eds), *Research in organizational change and development, Vol. 1.* Greenwich, CT. JAI Press.

Drabek, A. ed. (1994). World Development.

Drucker,P.F. (1980). *Managing in Turbulent Times.* New York: Harper Collins.

Grafton report. Washington, D.C. InterAction.

Gergen, K.J. (1991) *The saturated self: dilemmas of identity in contemporary life.* New York: Basic Books.

Gergen, K.J. (1994). *Toward transformation in social knowledge.* 2nd edition. New York: Sage Publications.

Gleick, J. (1987). *Chaos: making a new science.* NewYork: Penguin Books.

Handy, C. (1989). *The age of unreason.* London: Arrow Books Limited.

Ingersoll, Phyllis and Jerry. Toward review by Africa: An in-depth review by African and U.S. non-profit development agency staff: Consultation report. Washington, D.C. InterAction and FOVAD.

Land, G. and Jarman, B. (1992) *Breakpoint and beyond: mastering the future today.* New York: Harper Collins Publishers.

Marshak, R. J. (Summer 1993) Managing the metaphors of change. *Organizational Dynamics.*

Senge, P.M. (1990). *The Fifth discipline.* New York: Doubleday.

Waldrop, M.M. (1992). *Complexity: the emerging science at the edge of order and chaos.* New York: Simon and Schuster.

Chapter 28

From Local Conversations to Global Change: Experiencing the Worldwide Web Effect of Appreciative Inquiry

Michael J. Mantel
Benedictine University
James D. Ludema
Benedictine University

Introduction

Most conversations — much like politics and news – are local. Yet in today's global society linked by technological and relational networks, local conversations are rapidly transmitted to new ears and distant lands. As organizational executives and scholars become more aware of the power of language to shape organizational realities (Berger & Luckmann, 1966; Astley, 1985; Gergen, 1994), the importance of how conversations get started, spread, and influence organizational action is increasingly being recognized as crucially important (Hatch, forthcoming). Furthermore, the task of discovering and developing methods of organizational inquiry and change that unleash the power of positive conversation throughout the system is rapidly becoming a core competency for executives and OD professionals. This paper illustrates how appreciative inquiry (AI) has sparked a grass roots revolution of positive conversation and change in global organizations.

Mantel, M.J. & Ludema, J.D. (2000). From local conversations to global change: Experiencing the worldwide web effect of appreciative inquiry. *Organization Development Journal, 18* (12), pp. 42-53.

The illustration begins with World Vision, a large private volunteer organization (PVO) operating relief and development efforts in over 100 countries. Like many PVOs, World Vision's mission is to bring relief to areas with the intense suffering of war, famine, genocide and natural disasters and to develop the capacity of communities interested in extending their reach to sustainable agriculture, health, and education. Success in these environments requires collaboration across dividing lines of culture, geography, religion, sector, and economic status. Consequently, PVOs like World Vision are ideal organizations in which to study innovative approaches to system-wide change in diverse, complex environments. For the practitioner, new modes of organizational change are needed in order to address the growing number of global problems and to race ahead of them to grasp the greater number of positive opportunities. For the scholar, PVOs provide a dynamic laboratory for understanding how positive conversations generate solutions within an environment and spread across diverse environments globally to enact change.

For World Vision, the conversation begun in Romania was heard in Chicago where the discourse was picked up and extended to major cities across the US. Simultaneously it expanded from East Africa to Australia, Canada, West Africa, and other locations around the world. Key staff brought the conversation to their new organizations. Representatives gathered for training. Successes were celebrated and documented, enlarging the webs of dialogue. Each conversation intersected with other conversations, begun at various times, with diverse people both near and far. As each web intersects with the next, the conversation continues to develop. Appreciative inquiry, by creating a worldwide web of positive conversation, is facilitating the spread of a generative organizational change process that is extending across the globe.

Appreciative inquiry (Cooperrider & Srivastva, 1987) is a form of organizational change that is distinguished by its positive assumptions about people, organizations and social relationships. It begins by asking unconditional positive questions that spark positive conversations and action in organizational systems and networks. Elsewhere, we have suggested that it does this in five ways (Ludema, Cooperrider, & Barrett, 2000). First, it breaks the hammerlock of industrial-era hierarchies and bureaucracies by releasing positive conversation within the organization. Second, by inviting participants to inquire deeply into the best and most valued aspects of one another's life and work, AI builds an ever-expanding web of inclusion and positive relationships. Third, as positive vocabularies multiply and people strengthen their ability to put them into practice, AI creates a self-reinforcing learning capacity within an organization. Fourth, by expanding dialogue about positive, innovative possibilities, equalizing relationships, promoting generative learning, and providing broad access to decision-making and organization design, AI creates the conditions necessary for democracy and self-organizing to flourish. Finally, AI provides a powerful reservoir of strengths called the organization's "positive core" (Cooperrider & Whitney, 1999). This positive core, comprised of all the competencies, capacities, achievements, assets, best practices, values, traditions, wisdom, and inspired emotions that lie deep at the heart of the organization, is an organization's most potent renewable source of energy for change.

This paper builds on the above work and demonstrates how AI can be used to enact global change by creating new language that supports positive ways of thinking and doing things. At World Vision, the global changes described are not coming about through executive dictum or decisions made in the boardroom, but through shifting the dominant conversations in the organization about what it could and should be and about how to get there. This story of positive possibility is rapidly becoming an image of the future toward which individual and organizational actions are gravitating. In much the same way that the worldwide web grows horizontally and organically among its users, relational webs supported by the unconditional positive questions of AI allow positive conversations of change to spread and to promote self-organizing throughout World Vision's global organizational system.

We begin this paper by providing a brief introduction to appreciative inquiry as a constructive mode of organizational inquiry and change. We then explore four diverse case studies from World Vision's global operations in which AI was used to create solutions within complex environments and extend learning to new areas through an expanding web of conversation. We conclude by highlighting some of the organizational consequences of AI that account for its power as a democratic and self-generating mode of global organizational change that spreads through positive conversation.

Appreciative Inquiry

AI is a tool for connecting organizations to their positive change core by opening every strength, innovation, achievement, imaginative story, hope, positive tradition, passion, and dream to systematic inquiry (Cooperrider & Whitney, 1999). The positive core becomes visible and active by asking appreciative questions, such as the following:

1. Think of a time in your entire experience with your organization when you have felt most excited, most engaged, and most alive. What were the forces and factors that made it a great experience? What was it about you, others, and your organization that made it a peak experience for you?

2. What do you value most about yourself, your work, and your organization?

3. What is the core factor that "gives life" to your organization?

4. What are the three most important hopes you have to heighten the health and vitality of your organization for the future?

AI then uses the stories generated by these questions to create new, compelling images of the organization and its future.

Appreciative inquiry is based on the premise that human systems grow and construct their future realities in the direction of what they most persistently, actively, and collectively ask questions about. When groups study human problems and conflicts, they often find that both the number and severity of these problems grow. In the same manner, when groups study high human ideals and achievements, peak experiences, best practices, noble accomplishments, these phenomena, too, tend to flourish. In this sense, the way in which an organization attempts to understand itself is fateful. Based on the topics they choose to study and the questions they choose to ask, organizations enact and construct worlds that determine their eventual destiny.

As a method of organization development, AI involves systematic discovery of what gives a system "life" when it is at its best — socially, economically, and environmentally. It involves the art and practice of asking the "unconditional positive question" to strengthen a system's capacity to heighten its positive potential. In AI, intervention gives way to imagination and innovation; instead of negation, criticism, and spiraling diagnosis there is discovery, dream, design and destiny (see Figure I for an illustration of the appreciative inquiry 4-D model).

The purpose of appreciate inquiry is to unleash innovation in the system by connecting organizations to their strengths. The more an organization experiments with crafting and asking the unconditional positive question, the more its conversations tap into its positive core, and the more a positive revolution of change (De Bono, 1992) is unleashed and liberated throughout the system.

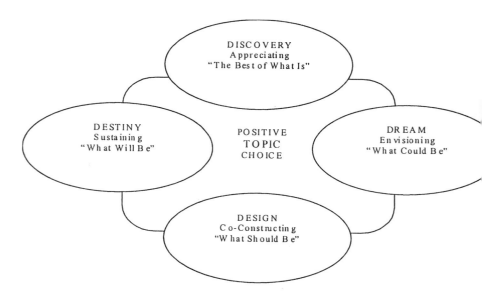

Figure I: Appreciative Inquiry 4-D Model

Creating a Worldwide Web
of Appreciative Inquiry at World Vision

AI was introduced to World Vision in 1990 when the world reacted to news of the medical and institutional crises of Romania's orphans. There was no history from which to learn how to draw together the intellectual, political, logistical and economic resources to respond to these challenges. AI was introduced to create a "knowledge alliance" to address these challenges. Two years later when World Vision began its interventions in the tough inner-city of Chicago, AI was suggested by a member of the Romanian team as a possible approach to discover the assets of the city and to craft a domestic role for this international relief and development agency. The successes of this generative approach in Chicago led members from the Chicago team to bring the methodology to a national discussion on World Vision's organizational approach to collaboration in five major cities in the US. At the same time, it quickly spread from East Africa to Australia, Canada and around the world to additional counties in Africa, Asia, and Latin America and was reinforced through a variety of training opportunities, field research, intervention efforts, publications, and additional organizational change efforts (see Figure II for an illustration of the worldwide web of AI within World Vision). While it is beyond the scope of this paper to describe all of the influences of appreciative inquiry within World Vision, in the next section we highlight four cases in which appreciative inquiry had a significant local impact and then spread horizontally to other locations creating an ever-expanding web of positive conversation worldwide.

Figure II: The Worldwide Web of AI (within World Vision)

The Knowledge Alliance of Romania

Until ABC TV aired a revealing glimpse of Romania's totalitarian system, World Vision's work was primarily medical help, building repairs, and training people through Romanian churches. World Vision was flooded with volunteers, gifts and monetary donations. Scores of relief and development agents had entered the scene; many encountered identical social, economic and political hurdles and found that they were duplicating one another's work. A number of remedies imposed from outside, such as the adoption of orphans by overseas couples, were complicating more than alleviating the chaos. Moreover, there was a growing awareness that, in order to ultimately benefit the Romanian child, the inadequacies of the internal medical and allied health care systems would have to be addressed, particularly in terms of the long-term developmental needs for education and training. These factors made it apparent that the Romanian situation demanded more sophisticated and cooperative strategies.

Throughout early 1990, World Vision shaped and enacted longer-term, collaborative strategies for rehabilitation and sustainable development. World Vision used AI to identify and contact a variety of indigenous and international organizations seeking to have an impact on the orphan situation. A positive interview protocol was created and the participating organizations were invited to inquire into one another's positive change core. Based on the strengths, assets, and resources identified during this discovery process, the organizations worked together to envision and design an approach to the Romanian orphan situation that built on their collective strengths.

A complex global change alliance of over 125 different collaborating organizations (universities, corporations, churches, PVOs, government agencies, and associations) was mobilized resulting in more than $25 million worth of direct aid, supplies, and professional services for the Romanian situation (Bilamoria & Cooperrider, 1991). During the first year alone, up to 40,000 children benefited from training offered to 60 orphanage staff and 250 medical students and academic personnel in partnership with Romanian universities. Additionally, the Romania Knowledge Alliance enabled medical libraries throughout Romania's eight medical schools to be brought up-to-date through advanced CD-ROM and video technologies by providing them with the last 50 years of pediatric information and journals.

An important consequence of World Vision's Romania involvement was realizing the potential of knowledge linkages for bringing into partnership organizations that cross sectors, including volunteer, corporate, government and university interest. One of World Vision's Romanian team brought the appreciative inquiry concepts used in the Romania Knowledge Alliance to an emerging alliance in Chicago.

Vision Chicago

In Chicago, World Vision used AI to form and mobilize a multi-organization alliance called Vision Chicago to address domain-level issues in the city. Focus included housing, economic development, racial reconciliation and education. Vision Chicago has brought together, across traditional boundaries of race, class, culture, sector, and geography a collaborative network of organizations and individuals committed to enhancing the health and vitality of the city.

AI was used to interview a range of people from World Vision, MidAmerica Leadership Foundation (a local PVO based in Chicago) and the Chicago community. Four unconditionally positive questions guided the inquiry:

1. What is it that gives "life" to your community? What do you love most about your community and what has contributed most to its vitality over the years?

2. What are your hopes for your community? What are its positive possibilities and how can they be most powerfully translated into reality?

3. Think of the best, most productive, most energizing partnership in which you've ever been involved. What were the forces and factors that made it possible?

4. What are your highest hopes and deepest aspirations for our partnership as we attempt to have a transformative presence in the City of Chicago?

This inquiry process allowed these organizations to discover in themselves and in each other their positive change core. As people came together across the boundaries of faith, race, class, and sector to share with one another their stories, they began to realize that they share many strengths and assets and hold in common many deeply held values such as a love for their city and a desire to work with each other to strengthen their communities. They also began to realize that their diversity, rather than being a barrier, is a strength that allows them to accomplish much more than any of them could accomplish alone. Through this cross-boundary appreciative inquiry process, slowly the dominant story surrounding Vision Chicago began to shift from one of hopelessness and despair to one of hope and possibility (Ludema 1996).

During its seven years, Vision Chicago has mobilized a network of over 1500 organizations resulting in more than $6 million in direct aid, $13 million in donated products, and 12,000 volunteers to invest in a positive image of the future. In June, 1994 Vision Chicago was recognized by the Council of Foundations as one of eight "Models of Hope" for its pioneering work in rebuilding America's cities and in June, 1999 won the "Best Practices Award" by HUD.

The success of Vision Chicago prompted World Vision United States (WVUS) to create the "Vision Cities Strategy" as its predominant model for action. WVUS researched and applied the concepts discovered in Vision Chicago to additional major cities around the United States.

Vision Cities

The Vision City Strategy represents a shift in WVUS's organizational approach. WVUS is moving away from being strictly a fundraising arm for World Vision International to being a bridging organization that establishes close productive relationships between a wide variety of individuals and organizations committed to social, spiritual, and economic transformation both locally and globally. The model that began in Chicago was applied to several other cities including New York, Los Angeles, Washington DC, Seattle, and Minneapolis/St. Paul. In many of these cities, appreciative inquiry was used to interview a range of stakeholders to identify strengths, assets, resources, hopes, and dreams and to design an inter-organizational architecture to address pressing local issues.

Over the past four years, Vision Cities have mobilized a growing network of over 3,000 organizations resulting in more than $12 million in direct aid and more than $40 million in donated products to address domain-level issues in five major US cities.

While World Vision United States was using appreciative inquiry to develop its operations in the US, World Vision Tanzania was being introduced to this approach by people who had participated in the Romania, Vision Chicago, and Vision Cities initiatives. The appreciative conversation that brought together the knowledge alliance in Romania and collaboration across major cities in the US was spreading at the village level in Tanzania.

World Vision Tanzania

Since 1995 World Vision Tanzania (WVT) has been using appreciative inquiry to build organizational capacity, help form partnerships between organizations, bring multiple organizations together to find common ground, strengthen staff capacity and morale, and empower and finally build community capacity.

In western Tanzania, WVT began the appreciative inquiry discovery process by asking the people of the Kagera Region, "What are you most proud of? What stories concern your most valued traditions? What are your best practices in farming? What made you successful in formal education and schooling? What core factors make life in Kagera possible?" Previously, community conversations had focused primarily on unemployment, AIDS, poverty, etc. But when the people of Kagera began to explore the village's assets — its capacities, the pride of its residents, the cooperative and institutional base of the community — not what might be absent, or problematic, the community's mood changed to one of laughter and celebration as the villagers, one after the other, narrated the good news stories of the proud people of Kagera.

In the Mombo area, WVT's project coordinator used an adaptation of AI to facilitate workshops attended by area leaders focusing on capacity indicators to assess their ability to plan, carry out, and evaluate their self-development. This process involved a relationship-building time when people were encouraged to share their good news stories, their strengths and opportunities, their dreams, and their shared visions. Next, communities determined what capacities were required to achieve their vision. What habits, skills, knowledge, attitudes and values are required in a particular community for it to achieve the vision? Using the plant cycle as a metaphor (planting, germination, growing, fruit/flowering and propagation), communities discussed their level of maturity in selected skills. The communities then developed specific indicators in each category toward the phases or stages of its growth. These indicators help communities monitor and assess progress on a regular basis. Finally, the communities formulated strategies and plans to build capacity to achieve the desired future.

WVT also uses the appreciative inquiry approach in the development of its own staff, its organizational structure, its board of directors, and its approach to local fundraising. Whereas, prior to implementing AI, the majority of WVT staff were high school graduates, now they consistently attract university graduates. Additionally, staff turnover has been reduced from 50% to less than 5%. The geographically-based community development projects are evolving into fully independent community-based organizations. The board of directors has progressed to a higher level of autonomy within the World Vision partnership, and more than $1 million is now being raised locally for operations. In the coming year, they will continue to conduct workshops on appreciative inquiry with their partners in government, the NGO community and with donors (Booy & Ole Sena, 1997).

Insights from the Worldwide Web of Appreciative Inquiry

These cases – Romania, Vision Chicago, Vision Cities, and World Vision Tanzania – are but four of many examples of how positive conversations sparked by appreciative inquiry are spreading democratically and organically around the globe to influence World Vision's programs and organization design. Similar activities are underway in Australia, Canada, West Africa, Asia, and Latin America. And yet, to date, there has been no centralized project, initiative, mandate, or directive to encourage the use of appreciative inquiry. Rather, it has been transferred directly, horizontally, and spontaneously through an ever-expanding web of positive conversation.

This has important implications for organizations that want to disseminate learning and ideas (e.g. mission, vision, values, perspectives, programs, initiatives, and innovations) through large complex systems. In the case of World Vision, what made the rapid spread of appreciative inquiry possible? What enabled it to have an impact on the local level and at the same time spread quickly to other locations on the globe? What allowed it to stay alive even when there was not a corporate strategy to sustain it? What is it about the nature of appreciative inquiry that allows it to extend itself like a web across geography, culture and time to influence change organically? In this final section, we explore four organizational consequences of appreciative inquiry that, based on our learning from the World Vision case and others like it, account for the power of appreciative inquiry as a mode of global organizational change.

#1: AI Brings Out the Best in People and Organizations

As mentioned previously, appreciative inquiry distinguishes itself from other approaches to organization development and change by its positive assumptions about people, organizations, and social relationships. No matter how difficult and desperate the situation may seem, appreciative inquiry affirms that examples of excellence, cooperation, courage, resilience, hope, joy, and inspiration, however small or few they may be, can be found, magnified, and amplified to enhance organizational health and vitality. By asking positive questions, it invites organizational members to discover and build upon their greatest strengths, assets, capacities, and capabilities. This irrepressibly hopeful perspective is compelling and contagious. It touches a deep universal longing to find positive solutions to local and global challenges and provides an almost immediate and primordial sense of satisfaction in the human spirit.

This approach stands in marked contrast to traditional deficit-based methods of organization development that rely on evaluation and diagnosis of problems as their means of learning. Such methodologies hold implicit universal standards of what is right, good, and acceptable and consider everything that does not meet those standards to be a "problem." These deficiency-oriented approaches disregard local differences in culture, practice, and worldview. Consequently, they tend to repel rather than invite organizational interest. Appreciative inquiry, by affirming the deep human qualities that allow individuals and organizations to survive and thrive in their unique location and context and by remaining tenaciously committed to finding positive solutions, attracts organizational attention across cultures. People are drawn to appreciative inquiry because, literally, it brings out the best in them.

#2: AI awakens a set of common higher values.

AI moves beyond bringing out the best in people by focusing people on a set of shared common ideals. It taps into the most noble beliefs and traditions — values such as cooperation, respect, awareness of the divine, living in community, the dignity of work, hospitality, justice, peace, fairness, stewardship of the natural environment — that are common among cultures and gives them life. By searching for, identifying, and articulating the positive core, AI reveals striking similarity of ultimate concerns among people regardless of race, culture, religion or geographical location.

The process of identifying these values begins in the discovery phase when organizational members explore the positive change core in themselves and in others, but it is perhaps most powerfully expressed in the dream stage when participants turn their attention to envisioning their hopes and aspirations for the future. It continues into the design and destiny phases as organizational members invest in the hard yet rewarding work of shaping their organizational architectures to embody these values both as a means and as an end. The discovery of these ideals and the commonalties between cultures has the effect of attracting a wide range of people with diverse perspectives to appreciative inquiry. AI is a radically inclusive approach that draws in a wide range of people and inspires human action in the service of the widest possible good.

#3: AI unleashes freedom and local initiative.

AI allows people to dream and design their organizations and their social reality at the local level. It affirms local culture, tradition, and ways of doing things. This is essential in the context of international organization development where local solutions prove to be most appropriate for local situations and where respect for cultures, differences, and global variety is a required ingredient for change. Furthermore AI, with its focus on strengthening and supporting local decision-making and power, enables sustainable solutions. Within deficit-based approaches, large-scale change in global organizations can be sustained as long as there is a high degree of investment and mobilization emanating from the corporate center. However, when corporate energies wane or attention wanders, local offices begin to focus upon events closer to home and the relevance or engagement of the shared object of attention declines (Zald, 1999).

Through AI, local organizations are able to tap into their own positive core. They discover, identify, and amplify resources that were previously latent or under-expressed. These resources provide a source of remarkable power for people at every level of the system to dream, innovate, and launch new forms of action and organizing. It does not force a single or uniform approach or system on them, and it is not dependent on the corporate center to sustain its energy and impact. Local operations are freed and liberated to innovate, energized by the strengths, assets, and resources they have identified in themselves.

#4: AI Simultaneously Maximizes Process and Results.

Traditional deficit-based approaches to organization development are notorious for generating high levels of resistance to change. As Kanter (1992) points out, this is true for many reasons, not the least of which is a lack of involvement on the part of organizational members. Problems are identified and solutions designed "behind closed doors" and then imposed on the majority of the organization. This approach, of course, violates the age-old OD maxim that "people support what they help to create" (Weisbord & Janoff, 1995). Appreciative inquiry, by putting the locus of inquiry in the hands of the local unit and by inviting an affirmation of the positive change core in each location, shifts power relationships and generates enthusiasm. It does not, however, shirk responsibility or accountability for results. On the contrary, because local organizational members are engaged in the process, they are motivated to invest uncommon energy into envisioning and designing strategies for implementation and action.

In this sense, AI produces cooperation and innovation because it simultaneously addresses strategy, process, and implementation. It affirms that inquiry *is* intervention, that there is a self-reinforcing, synergistic relationship between creating strategy, learning through the process, and producing the results. As people ask themselves unconditional positive questions, they generate new learning about the resources that make their organizing and action possible. They strengthen the relational bonds needed to translate vision into reality and through the process they create new levels of commitment to action. Consequently, process and results are maximized in the same moment, and results are achieved much more quickly.

Conclusion

What we have tried to show in this paper is that by bringing out the best in people, awakening a higher set of common values, unleashing freedom and local initiative, and simultaneously maximizing process and results, AI has the capacity to create a positive conversation that spreads dramatically across a global organization to effect a positive revolution of change.

In our experience, the consequences of AI extend beyond organizational change. AI has the generative power to promote holism and build community at the global level. It is widely recognized that the task of organizational development and international development requires growth at the individual, organizational, and communal levels in order to be successful. Traditional deficit-focused approaches to OD, based in the Newtonian view of science, seek to break organizations and communities into their smallest component parts in order to more effectively observe, analyze and predict them.

The appreciative approach, on the other hand, moves in exactly the opposite direction – integrating the three modes of development. The search for the positive core seeks to identify resources and strengths within the individual, within the organization, within the community, and draws them together into an integrated whole. As a collaborative methodology AI invites organizational members and community members to discover and affirm the best in one another and in their shared traditions and practices. This act strengthens relational bonds and builds community even across boundaries of race, culture, religion, sector, wealth, and geography. Traditional deficit-based approaches to international development leave traditional participants, both *donors* and *beneficiaries,* with a sense of overwhelming need, guilt, and duty, and with an unmet desire for relationship, purpose, vision, and co-creation.

AI approaches enable the donor and the beneficiary to come together in a relationship of mutual appreciation and exchange. By asking each other unconditional positive questions, donors and beneficiaries are able to discover and affirm the good, the true, the better, and the best in each other and in themselves and to join together around a common set of high ideals that meet their shared ultimate concerns. In this sense, AI provides a powerful means for building global community.

References

Astley, G. 1985. *Administrative science as socially constructed truth.* Administrative Science Quarterly, 30, 497-513.

Bilamoria, D., & Cooperrider, D. L. 1991. *The Romanian orphans program: Challenges and responses of the collaborative alliance.* Paper presented at the annual conference of the Association for Research on Non-Profit Organizations and Voluntary Action, Chicago.

Booy, D. & Ole Sena, S. 1999. Capacity building using the Appreciative Inquiry approach. In Myers, B. *Working with the poor.* Monrovia, Ca.: World Vision

Cooperrider, D. L. & Whitney, D. 1999. *Collaborating for change: Appreciative inquiry.* San Francisco: Barrett-Koehler Communications.

Cooperrider, D. L., & Srivastva, S. 1987. Appreciative inquiry in organizational life. In W. A. Pasmore & R. W. Woodman (eds.), *Research in organizational change and development* (Vol. I). Greenwich, CT: JAI Press.

De Bono, E. 1992. *Handbook for the positive revolution*. New York: Penguin Books.

Hatch, M., (forthcoming). *The role of the researcher: An analysis of narrative position in organizational theory*. Journal of Management Inquiry.

Kanter, R. M., Stein, B. A., & Jick, T.D., 1992. *The challenge of organizational change: How companies experience it and leaders guide it*. New York: Harper & Row.

Ludema, J. D. 1996. *Narrative Inquiry: Collective storytelling as a source of hope, knowledge, and action in organizational life*. Unpublished doctoral dissertation. Case Western Reserve University, Cleveland, OH.

Ludema, J. D., Cooperrider, D.L., Barrett, F. J., 2000. Appreciative inquiry: The power of the unconditional positive question. In P. Reason & J. Bradbury, *Handbook of action research*. Thousand Oaks: Sage Publication.

Weisbord, M. R., & Janoff, S., *Future search: An action guide to finding common ground in organizations & communities*. San Francisco: Berett-Koehler Publishers, Inc.

Zald, M. N., 1999. Transnational and international social movements in a globalizing world. In D. Cooperrider & J. Dutton, *Organizational Demensions of Global Change*. Thousand Oaks: Sage Publications.

Chapter 29

FROM DEFICIT DISCOURSE TO VOCABULARIES OF HOPE: THE POWER OF APPRECIATION

James D. Ludema
Benedictine University

Abstract

This chapter proposes that in today's world of high uncertainty and broad cultural and epistemological variety the purpose of social and organizational inquiry ought to be to create textured vocabularies of hope—stories, theories, evidence, and illustrations—that provide organizations and communities with new guiding images of relational possibility. After showing how the critical methods of contemporary organizational science have contributed to a growing cynicism about the future of human institutions by producing vocabularies of deficit, the dynamics of hopeful vocabularies in human systems are explored. A broad review of the literature suggests that vocabularies of hope serve as powerful catalyst for positive social and organizational transformation. They are ignited when organizational members (1) nurture cooperative relationships, (2) exercise a sense of optimism about their capacity to influence the future, and (3) inquire together into their most deeply held values and highest aspirations. Appreciative inquiry is offered as an alternative to critical and problem-focused inquiry methodologies. Eight core principles of appreciative inquiry that support the creation of textured vocabularies of hope are highlighted. The chapter concludes with an invitation to scholars and practitioners to experiment with new modes of appreciative inquiry that generate vocabularies of hope by posing positive questions about the life-giving, life-enhancing aspects of organizations.

Think of the tools in a tool-box: there is a hammer, pliers, a screwdriver, a rule, a glue-pot, glue, nails and screws. The functions of words are as diverse as the functions of these objects.   —Wittgenstein.

We can live three weeks without food, three days without water, and, yes, we can even live three minutes without air, but we cannot live without hope.   —Mumford.

Introduction

It is widely understood that the contemporary world has entered an era in which the complexity and rapidity of social change is virtually unparalleled in human history. The expansion of information technology, the globalization of economic markets, the intermingling of cultures, and the reconfiguration of national and international boundaries are increasing pressures on individuals and organizations to find innovative approaches to addressing their own needs and the needs of society. This shifting global context raises questions of fundamental importance to the social and organizational sciences. Is it possible or even desirable in the current context for social science to play a lead role in building healthy and vibrant social relationships? Can and should social science attempt to remain relevant, or even to become a pioneer of positive possibilities for organizing in the face of such extensive geographical, cultural, and epistemological variety?

Some have grave doubts. Scholars and practitioners from across the social scientific disciplines are becoming increasingly disillusioned with the inability of existing epistemological and methodological alternatives to provide useful insights into human relationships. On the one hand, approaches based in empiricist foundationalism are distrusted for, among other things, resting on shaky theoretical ground and ignoring the impact of context on social phenomena (see e.g., Kuhn, 1970; Feyerabend, 1978; Gergen, 1994a; Denzin and Lincoln, 1995; Argyris, 1973; Bartunek, 1983; Friedlander, 1984). On the other hand, efforts proceeding from the genre of post-empiricist critique are questioned for launching "attacks without alternative" and contributing to a contentious scientific discourse that offers little emancipatory leverage for an increasingly cynical and despairing world (Hazelrigg, 1989, Brown, 1994; Gergen, 1994b; Marcus, 1994).

Thus the questions remain: What should be the role of social and organizational science in the construction of human relationships? How can it recover a central place in making a positive contribution to the enhancement of the human condition? What should be its purposes, commitments, and methods as it attempts to make this contribution in a global context of radical foundationlessness and human plurality?

This paper provides an optimistic response to these questions by proposing that the purpose of social and organizational inquiry ought to be to create textured vocabularies of hope—stories, theories, evidence, and illustrations—that serve as catalysts for positive social and organizational transformation by providing humanity with new guiding images of relational possibility. In much the same way that a hammer, pliers, screwdriver, and rule furnish the tools necessary to build new physical architectures for human inhabitation, textured vocabularies of hope provide the linguistic resources necessary to build new social architectures for transformative human organizing and action.

It is argued that to create powerful vocabularies of hope, two things are needed from organizational scholars and practitioners. First, hopeful research agendas that focus on the life-producing, life-sustaining, life-enhancing aspects of organizations need to be established. Second, constructive methodologies that facilitate the creation of hopeful vocabularies and that themselves become sources of hope by promoting normative dialogue and supporting positive social innovation need to be developed. Appreciative inquiry (Cooperrider and Srivastva, 1987) is highlighted as an approach to social and organizational inquiry that fulfills these purposes. Based on the premises that (1) there is a direct and simultaneous link between our vocabularies of organizing and the ways in which we organize in fact, and that (2) our vocabularies are products of the questions we ask, appreciative inquiry distinguishes itself by posing positive questions that direct our attention to the vital life-giving forces that nourish our best and most valued modes of organizing.

The chapter is divided into four sections. It begins by showing how the critical and problem-focused methods of contemporary social science have contributed to the deconstruction rather than the reconstruction of social relationships by producing vocabularies, not of hope and possibility, but of deficit and deficiency. By so doing, social science has added to a growing cynicism about the future of human institutions and has deepened the despair about its own potential to be a catalyst for positive change. The section ends by suggesting that the time has come to move beyond the limitations of deficit discourse by developing appreciative modes of inquiry that advance vocabularies of human hope.

In section two, the dynamics of hoping in human systems are explored. In order to create methodologies and vocabularies that support human hopefulness, it is essential to understand how hope is generated and sustained in human systems and how it can become a source of social and organizational transformation. A broad review of the literature shows that hope is enkindled in organizations when (1) cooperative relationships are nurtured between organizational members, (2) organizational members have a sense of optimism about their capacity to shape and influence the future, and (3) organizational members inquire together into their deepest values and highest aspirations.

In section three, appreciative inquiry is offered as an alternative to critical and problem-focused inquiry methodologies. It is proposed that the appreciative approach, by intentionally guiding the socially constructive potential of human systems in the direction of their most noble and valued aspirations for the future, generates an ever-expanding selection of textured vocabularies of hope that provide new alternatives for organizing and elevate the human spirit. The process of generating textured vocabularies of hope through appreciative inquiry is illustrated.

The paper concludes with a call to social and organizational science to reaffirm its constructive task by advancing new appreciative epistemologies and methods of inquiry that facilitate the expansion of textured vocabularies of hope. Following Rorty (1980), it is suggested that by advancing vocabularies of hope, social science may, in some small way, reverse the current trends of cultural and organizational cynicism and contribute to a broad and maturing spirit of human hopefulness.

Critical Methods and Vocabularies of Deficit

In the last fifty years, hosts of critical and deconstructive methods for doing social scientific research have emerged (see e.g., Schwandt, 1994; Kincheloe and McLaren, 1994; Olesen, 1994; Stanfield, 1994; and Fiske, 1994). Based on the premise that all claims of truth are arbitrary and should be questioned, these methods provide increasingly sophisticated tools with which to examine, expose, demystify, and debunk existing accounts of reality.

While some scholars celebrate this critical trend because of its emancipatory potential, others see it as a cause for concern. Comparing the methods of post-empiricist critique to those of military combat, Gergen (1994b) writes:

> Critique as a rhetorical move has the effect of demeaning the opposition, generating animosity, atomizing the culture and blocking the way to resolution. . . . [It] carries with it the additional difficulties of favoring the very kinds of totalizing discourses against which it is set, and destroying the grounds of its own rationality (p. 70).

Similarly, for Astley (1985), the arena of management theory has become a "jungle" which is daily becoming "more dense and impenetrable" and is symbolic of "deep fragmentation of the discipline" marked by "intense competing and rival paradigms." For George (1989) the variety of incommensurable perspectives within organizational science has become "a violent babble of competing voices . . . leading nowhere loudly" (p. 269). And for Wollheim (1980) the quicksand of deconstructive reflexivity may lead to complete "immobilization of scholarship."

Of greater concern, however, is the growing awareness that the debilitating effects of critical and deconstructive social science extend well beyond the boundaries of the academic community. Gergen (1994a) argues persuasively that the vocabularies of deficit proffered by much contemporary social science support what he calls broad "cultural enfeeblement" (p. 148). By creating hierarchies of discrimination, eroding naturalized patterns of community, and expanding arenas for self-depreciation, scientific vocabularies of deficit contribute to a pernicious cycle of "progressive [societal] infirmity" (p. 155). To illustrate, the following example (adapted from Gergen, 1994a, pp. 155–161) shows how growth in deficit vocabularies of mental illness have served to compound rather than alleviate individual and societal suffering:

> **First**, based on empiricist presumptions, the disciplines of psychiatry and clinical psychology are formed and begin to create categories of "mental illness."

> **Second**, a collection of mental health professionals emerges and commissions itself with the task and responsibility of diagnosing and curing the multiple forms of mental illness as defined by its members.

Third, mental health professionals translate their clients' problems as presented in everyday language into the alternative language of the profession. Thus, "feeling blue" or "being sad" becomes depression and "getting distracted by everything" or "having a hard time sitting still in school" becomes attention deficit disorder.

Fourth, the mental health profession disseminates its language to the general public through universities, conferences, public policies, books, journals, magazines, newspapers, television, and other electronic media.

Fifth, as vocabularies of mental deficit are disseminated to the culture, they become absorbed into the common language and become encouraged for the construction of everyday reality. In essence, the culture learns how to be mentally ill. Writes Gergen (1994a), "Furnish the population with the hammers of mental deficit, and the world is full of nails" (p. 158).

Sixth, in the final phase of progressive infirmity, vocabularies of deficit are expanded. As people increasingly construct their problems in professional language and seek help, and as professional ranks expand in response to public demands, more resources are available to convert everyday language into a professional language of deficit.

Through this process, deficit vocabularies can come to approximate "small growth industries" (Gergen, 1994a, p. 160) that fuel the progressive enfeeblement of society. See Figure 29.1 for a diagram of this process.

In a similar manner, the vocabularies of human deficit produced by the critical and problem-oriented approaches to social and organizational inquiry diminish the human capacity for positive relational construction by rending and unraveling the intricate social, political, and moral fabrics that make human existence and organizing possible. Writes Gergen (1994b): There is virtually no hypothesis, body of evidence, ideological stance, literary canon, value commitment or logical edifice that cannot be dismantled, demolished or derided with the [arsenal of critical weaponry] at hand" (p. 59). Relying on methodologies that by design are meant to delegitimate and destroy existing organizational understandings, critical and problem-focused methods do little to provide constructive alternative perspectives that point the way to healthier more desired forms of organizing.

In response to the growing body of deficit vocabularies produced by critical and problem-focused methods, a handful of scholars are calling for appreciative approaches to social and organizational science that hold increased potential for revitalizing scholarship and enhancing the human condition. Weick (1982) appeals for an affirmative approach to social science that creates compelling images of human possibility and seeks to discover examples of them in the "real world," even if they are extremely rare. Brown (1994) encourages a "hermeneutic of affirmation" that promotes conversation between scholars and citizens who are committed to "establishing moral authority and inventing positive values as central elements of any polity" (p. 24). Cooperrider and Srivastva (1987), in their original formulation of the now widely applied methodology of appreciative inquiry, call for modes of

1. Scientific disciplines are formed
and begin to create categories of illness (vocabularies of deficit).

2. A collection of professionals
emerges to diagnose and cure the
multiple forms of illness.

3. Everyday language of clients is
translated into deficit vocabularies of
the profession.

4. The profession disseminates its
vocabularies of deficit to the general
public.

5. Vocabularies are absorbed into
common language; the culture learns
how to be ill.

6. Vocabularies of deficit are expanded, becoming "small growth industries" that fuel the enfeeblement of
society.

Figure 29.1. The Link Between Vocabularies of Deficit and the Process of Cultural Enfeeblement.

inquiry that uncover the "ordinary magic, beauty, and real possibility of organizational life" (p. 165) and help scholars and practitioners to "shape the social world
according to their own imaginative and moral purposes" (p. 161). Recognizing the
socially constructive power of social theory to determine the direction and quality
of organizational life, these appeals, each in its own way, urge scholars and practitioners to reverse the debilitating effects of deficit discourse by developing appreciative modes of inquiry that release the empowering potential of vocabularies of
hope. In the final section of this chapter we attempt to show how appreciative
modes of inquiry can contribute to this project, but first, to set the stage for that
discussion, we explore the role that hoping plays in igniting social and organizational transformation.

Vocabularies of Hope as a Source of Social and Organizational Transformation

In this section it is shown that hoping is often described as a holistic, relational way
of knowing that unifies both the tacit and explicit dimensions of experience and
puts them to work in transforming the future. When people inquire into the unexplored reaches of their collective norms, beliefs, and assumptions; values, mores,
and purposes; plans, desires, and wishes; visions, ideals, and dreams, they engage

in the act of hoping by prefiguring a valued and vital future that they hope some day to build, inhabit, and enjoy. These hopeful images of the future, in turn, become powerful catalysts for change and transformation by mobilizing the moral, social, and relational energies needed to translate vision into reality and belief into practice.

This understanding of hope is based on an extensive literature review of the topic from the fields of theology, philosophy, history, political theory, art, music, literature, medicine, psychology, and sociology (see Ludema et al, 1997). While the ways in which hope has been described and understood throughout the ages have varied, many authors suggest that there are four enduring qualities that give hope its power as a source of social and organizational transformation: it is (1) born in relationship, (2) inspired by the conviction that the future is open and can be influenced, (3) sustained by dialogue about high human ideals, and (4) generative of positive affect and action (see Table 29.1 for a summary of these qualities and their relationship to six intellectual traditions of Western thought). The remainder of this section briefly explores each of these qualities.

The Centrality of Relationships

Hope is fundamentally a relational construct. It is engendered in relationship to an "other," whether that other be collective or singular, imagined or real, human or divine. Perhaps the most poignant example of this idea comes from Frankl's (1963) experiences in German concentration camps during World War II. Even in the isolated agony of solitary work duty, Frankl gained hope by imagining himself into a future in which he would be free and reunited with his wife and his most esteemed colleagues at the university. This relational picture of hope stands in marked contrast to much contemporary thought that understands hope as an emotional or cognitive possession of the individual rational agent.

Yet, as Lynch (1965) suggests, hope does not flourish under all relational conditions. It assumes relationships of mutuality in which the value and integrity of all persons is affirmed. Writes Lynch (1965):

I must not be in such a relationship to objects that I vanish out of the picture, I am destroyed. And the reverse is also true: ideally the object in coming to me must find itself. It is the hope for this mutuality that is the secret of all our hopes; it is its absence in substance that makes us hopeless. . . . Hope searches for alternative objects that will not be destructive and that can partake in a relationship of mutuality (pp. 44–45).

Lynch goes on to suggest that this kind of mutuality enlivens hope in the in all relationships, personal or professional: "Hope is the interior sense that there is help on the outside of us . . . when we are especially aware that our purely inward resources are not enough." (p. 40).

TABLE 29.1. Hope's Enduring Qualities as Found in Six Intellectual Traditions of Western Thought.

Intellectual Traditions	Relationality	Future Openness	Ultimacy	Generativity
Greco-Roman		Hope as a source of invention.		Hope spurs creativity and action.
Judeo-Christian	Whether directed at a divine or human other, hope is born when we join with other "efficacious agents."	Hope as a general confidence in God's protection and help.	Love, joy, peace, salvation, redemption, communion with God and others, "the good."	Leads to social involvement.
Enlightenment	Relational hope is a self-fulfilling proposition.	Hope is reasonable when grounded in examples from the past.	Reasonable to hope for the highest good.	Serves as a motive for positive human action.
Phycho-Analytic	Hope is at least partially influenced by past and present others.	Hope is an outgrowth of a pliable vision of wholeness.	Hope as creative urge of Eros.	Hope contributes to social coping, psychosocial development, and individual achievement.
Radical Humanist	Hope as a source of ideological emancipation and authentic consciousness.	Existence is never static; it is always in process of becoming something new, or transcending itself.	Metachronic and transcendent: our most potent hopes offer an image of an ultimate future.	Pursuit of *Ultimum* provides a powerful resource for innovation and action in the present.
Modern (cognitive) Medicine and Psychology	Hope is enlivened in the helping relationship, personal and professional.	Human beings have the capacity to create, evaluate, and alter symbolic constructions.	Hope as a "spiritual" quality; ability to rise above difficult circumstances to renew life.	Hope determines goal-oriented bahavior and is a resource for health and vitality.

In addition to being born in, sustained by, and deepened in relationship, hoping serves as a binding force of community. Kast (1991) shows that hoping allows people to develop a sense of "symbiotic connectedness" with each other. In this symbiosis one feels taken care of, freed from fear of attack, slander and harm, and invested in promoting the health and vitality of others. Similarly, Dauenhauer (1986) suggests that hoping builds community because it encourages exploration of the values and ideals that people share in common. He suggests that when people come together in acts of hoping, they dream and creatively construct the future in ways that reflect their common ideals.

The Importance of Influence-Optimism

Hope springs to life when people understand that the future is fundamentally undetermined and open to human influence. Polak (1973) calls this understanding "influence-optimism." Marcel (1951) describes it as a "fundamental openness," an expectant act of the whole person in which "the soul turns toward a light which it does not yet perceive, a light yet to be born." (p. 31). Moltmann (1991), in a counter-intuitive twist of conventional wisdom, points out that it is only this dynamically open orientation toward the future that can be considered "realistic." Hope recognizes that no matter what current circumstances might be, "everything is still full of possibilities." Writes Moltmann:

Hope and the kind of thinking that goes with it consequently cannot submit to the reproach of being utopian, for they do not strive after things that have 'no place,' but after things that have 'no place as yet' but can acquire one (p. 25).

This influence-optimism has two important implications for organizations. First, adversity need not be accepted as hope's only starting point. As a response to the fundamental openness of the future, hope can thrive under all conditions. Whether in times of difficulty or in times of well-being, hope draws on people's creative resources and allows them to stretch beyond the status quo in search of even more vital possibilities. Second, hope can be understood as a positive orientation toward the future that precedes and anticipates a coherent image of the future. Kast (1991) and Bloch (1986) suggest that, in affirming the "not-yet-seen," hope does not require a clear picture of the future to come alive. On the contrary, hope's positive orientation endures and perseveres even when the future looks bleak or is "still unnamed." As Kast puts it: "By hoping, we walk toward a light that we do not see but sense somewhere in the darkness of the future." (p. 136).

Imagination is portrayed as the engine of hoping: it is the uniquely human function that allows people to participate actively and construct their meaningful realities. For example, describing it as "the gift that envisions what cannot yet be seen," Lynch (1965) gives imagination a central role in fostering a sense of possibility:

TABLE 29.2. Eight Core Principles of Appreciative Inquiry Support the Four Enduring Qualities of Hope.

	The Centrality of Relationships	The Importance of Influence-Optimism	Conversations of Ultimate Concern	The Generativity of Hope
The Constructionist Principle Social knowledge and organizational destiny are tightly intertwined.				
The Collaborative Principle Collaboration opens the way for the social construction of reality and establishes strong relational connections.				
The Anticipatory Principle The image of the future guides the current behavior of any organism or organization.				
The Provocative Principle The most powerful images of the future are those that stretch, challenge or interrupt the status quo.				
The Poetic Principle Organizations are open books. We can study any topic related to human experience.				
The Positive Principle Organizations move in the direction of what they study. The more positive the topics and questions, the more positive the outcomes.				
The Principle of Simultaneity There is a direct and simultaneous link between inquiry and action. Inquiry *is* intervention.				
The Pragmatic Principle The questions we ask set the stage for what we "find" and how we organize.				

> Hope is tied to the life of the imagination—that constantly proposes
> to itself that the boundaries of the possible are wider than they seem. . . . It
> is able to wait, to wait for a moment of vision, which is not yet there. . . . It
> is not overcome by the absoluteness of the present (p. 35).

Hoping, then, involves a continuous inquiry into and affirmation of the best, most positive aspects of people and situations. As Kast (1991) notes, "Hope can be learned first by our being knowingly dissatisfied and rejecting deficiency, and then by our pursuing the daydreams and imaginary worlds that point the way to change" (p. 151).

Conversations of Ultimate Concern

Various authors suggest that not all human vocabularies have an equal capacity to inspire hope. Hope is generated and is sustained when people, facing the mystery of the future, dialogue about their highest human ideals—that which Plato calls the good, the true, and the beautiful; Marcel calls universal values; Bloch calls the absolute, infinite, and unobtainable other; Otto calls the holy; and Fromm calls the transcendent or the spiritual. Tillich's (1957) treatment of "ultimate concern" provides language that illustrates what these authors all seem to be pointing toward. He defines ultimate concerns as those things that sustain and give meaning to life. Tillich writes:

> Man, like every living being, is concerned about many things, above all about those which condition his very existence, such as food and shelter. But man, in contrast to other living beings, has spiritual concerns—cognitive, aesthetic, social, political. Some of them are urgent, often extremely urgent, and each of them as well as the vital concerns can claim ultimacy for human life or the life of a social group (p. 1).

Tillich suggests that dialogue about ultimate concerns generates hope by allowing human beings to transcend the relative and transitory experiences of ordinary life and to build for themselves an existence based on a high moral and spiritual ground.

Marcel (1951) talks in similar terms when he claims that there exists a persistent and inescapable transcendent or noble character to the standards by which human beings govern their collective existence, standards which seem to "belong to a different world, founded on kindness, scruples, sacrifice, a world entirely different from this one" (p. 8). For Marcel, the collective pursuit of these ideals, or what he calls universal values, is the essence of human hoping. Likewise for Bloch (1986) hoping is a continuous movement toward the superlative, the sublime, or in his words, "the best as a totality." The best can have many faces—"Happiness, freedom, non-alienation, the golden age, the land flowing with milk and honey, the

eternal feminine, the trumpet call in Fidelio, and the Christ pattern of the resurrec-
tion day afterwards" (p. 1627)—but it is the condition for hope in any situation.

Frankl (1959) provides a compelling example of how hope grounded in ultimate
concern serves as a powerful life-giving force in human communities. While imprisoned in a concentration camp in Germany, he observed that for many prisoners "there
was a psychological 'giving up,' a loss of faith and belief in the future resulting in
apathy" (p. 64). The hopeless, claimed Frankl, did not long continue to live. However,
even the slightest cause for hope enabled people to persevere even under the sys-
temic horrors and daily executions. Hope was defined by those who survived in the
language of ultimate concerns as a "spiritual freedom, a freedom which cannot be
taken away, a freedom that makes life meaningful and purposeful" (p. 66). Inquiry into
ultimate concerns generates a vocabulary of hope and possibility that serves as a
potent "life-giving" force for transforming social and organizational relationships.
This vocabulary allows people to live beyond current circumstances, transcend the
status quo, and transform present reality into one of greater aliveness by placing it in
the context of broader and deeper possibilities.

The Generativity of Hope

Hoping in an essential ingredient in social and organizational transformation because it spawns generative action. Tillich (1957), in his treatment of ultimate concerns, claims that all products of human creativity, from works of music, literature,
art, and architecture to patterns of social organizing can be seen as symbolic expressions of ultimate concerns. Citing as examples the religious inspiration found
in the art and architecture of pre-modern Christianity and the economic inspiration
found in the works of modern secular culture, Tillich writes: "[Human] spiritual
function, artistic creation, scientific knowledge, ethical formation, and political organization are consciously or unconsciously expressions of an ultimate concern
which gives passion and creative Eros to them" (pp. 107–108).

Similarly Bloch (1986), in his three-volume work The Principle of Hope, asserts
that hope is the source of all human history and culture. To prove his point, Bloch
undertakes a sweeping study of Western culture in which he presents "sketches of
hope" from every conceivable area of human activity. He describes "wishful images in
the mirror," including culturally defined standards of slimness or beauty, the lure of
fairy tales, travel, dance, and comedy, and the wishes for a happy ending that pervade
popular culture; he surveys "outlines of a better world," including social, medical,
technological, architectural, and geographical utopias, as well as "wishful landscapes"
contained in opera, painting, literature, philosophy, and leisure; and finally he sketches
"wishful images of the fulfilled moment," including discussions of the contemplative
life, music, death, and religion (Aronson, 1991).

Throughout his study, Bloch is careful to point out that hope is at work not only in the magnificent works of art and culture of the "masters," but in the dreams, expectations, intentions, wishes, desires, and longings of every member of society. He claims that hope is rigorously existential and can be seen at every moment in our existence: wanting to lose weight, to travel, to be loved and respected, to be successful, to see our children prosper, in paintings, in gardens, in our dreams of being secure and comfortable in old age. According to Bloch, every human creation (idea, relationship, action), which on the surface seems simply to be a mundane response to the vicissitudes of every day life, is in fact a bold proclamation and announcement of a desired future, a living testimony to the generative power of hope.

Hoping becomes a powerful source of social and organizational transformation because it enlivens the human spirit and guides action. Kast suggests that hope leads to joy which in turn transforms people "into persons who are more alive, who are involved, who have energy to act, who believe in change." (p. 108). Similarly, Marcel (1951) draws a connection between hope and what he calls an "ardour for life" (p. 43) that serves as an antidote to despair and stimulates human creativity. Polak (1973) draws the link between hope and action when he claims that human beings exercise influence over the future through the images they project, and in turn these images of desirable future events foster the behavior most likely to bring about their realization. He goes so far as to suggest that the image of the future is the single most important dynamic in the process of cultural evolution:

The rise and fall of images of the future precedes or accompanies the rise and fall of cultures. As long as a society's image is positive and flourishing, the flower of culture is in full bloom. Once the image begins to decay and lose its vitality, however, the culture does not long survive (p. 19).

Polak's conclusion is that for any collectivity its image of the future is not only points the way to the future but also serves as a guiding mechanism that actively promotes certain choices and puts them to work in determining the future (Cooperrider, 1991).

Not all hoping has an equal chance of transforming the future, however. Dauenhauer (1986), Marcel (1951), Moltmann (1991), and Polak (1973) suggest that hoping gains its greatest chances for generativity to the extent that it remains "public property," that is, to the extent that it remains a inclusive act, ever seeking to expand the number of participants and invite open dialogue. Writes Dauenhauer:

Hope promotes the sort of listening or hearing which is not confined merely to having one's own discourse somehow confirmed. It promotes a quest for ever more efficacious and comprehensive discourse . . . [and] works to preserve and expand the number of participants in [this discourse] (p. 99). To this relational formulation Moltmann (1991) adds that hoping, because it is an act of affirming the life and the potential of the other, can never be limited in scope. It must always remain universal in character, committed to inclusiveness and to discovering ultimate concerns that announce "a universal horizon that embraces the whole world" (p. 263).

In sum, the interdisciplinary literature on hope highlights hoping as a primary source of social and organizational transformation. As people come together in relationships of mutuality, affirm a dynamic, open, and evolving future that is "full of possibilities," and collectively dialogue about their highest and most transcendent ideals, they create positive guiding images of the future that provide a compelling logic and source of inspiration for social action (see Table 29.3 for a summary of hope's enduring qualities).

TABLE 29.3. Summary of Hope's Four Enduring Qualities.

Relationship as the Ground of Hope

- Hoping is born and nurtured in a priori relationships of mutual love, care, and support.
- Hoping reaches beyond the self: it prospers when people place themselves in service of the other.
- Hoping is a binding force of community: it provides a sense of symbiotic connectedness with others; promotes feelings of safety and security; and unites people around common values and ideals.

The Contructive Stance of Hope

- Hoping assumes a fundamental openness to the future: it prospers when people recognize the unbounded extent to which relationships and realities are open to creation and reconstruction.
- Hoping precedes and anticipates a coherent image of the future: it comes to life when people assume a posture that is both patient and creative in the face of uncertainty.
- Imagination is the engine of hoping: it allows people to explore the mystery of the future and create promising possibilities for existence.

The moral Dimension of Hope

- Hope is nourished and sustained when people collectively dialogue about their ultimate concerns in a spirit of love and action.
- Hoping is a life-giving act: it renews life by enabling people to place immediate circumstances in the context of broader and deeper possibilities.
- Hoping is a source of Moral Vision: it is a holistic way of knowing that draws on a range of affective, normative, spiritual, and relational resources to spawn moral action.
- Hoping integrates the modes of time: it allows people to draw on the brightest images, ideals, and values of the past to inspire positive possibilities for the future.

The Generativity of Hope

- Hoping is a source of human creativity and culture: everything from works of music, literature, art and architecture to patterns of organizing can be seen as expressions of the hopes of their authors.
- Hoping is a source of positive affect and action: it leads to feelings of joy, well-being, relaxation, and fullness of life and stimulates action by bringing the future into the present as a causal agent.
- Hoping is most generative when it is inclusive; it inspires collective action most powerfully when it remains "public property," invites open dialogue, and seeks to expand its horizon to include all mankind.

Appreciative Inquiry and Vocabularies of Hope

These four qualities of hope—that it is (1) born in relationship, (2) inspired by the conviction that the future is open and can be influenced, (3) sustained by dialogue about high human ideals, and (4) generative of positive affect and action—can be seen at play in the creation of textured vocabularies of hope. In this section we demonstrate how appreciative modes of inquiry, by creating the conditions necessary to nurture these qualities, support the construction of hopeful vocabularies. We begin by demonstrating how textured vocabularies of hope are generated and sustained in society and in organizations. We then explore the ways in which eight core principles of appreciative inquiry support and reinforce the creation of textured vocabularies of hope.

The Structuring of Vocabularies of Hope

As mentioned previously, textured vocabularies of hope can be defined as linguistic constructions that create new images of positive relational possibility, illuminate fresh avenues for moral discourse, and expand the range of practical and theoretical resources available for the construction of healthy social and organizational relationships. In contrast to vocabularies of deficit that erode individual and social well-being, vocabularies of hope serve as linguistic tools that promote the (re)construction of relationships in ways that conform to collective images of the good. The process of social and organizational transformation through vocabularies of hope can be outlined as follows:

First, based on a constructionist epistemology, communities of inquiry and action are formed and begin to explore the most positive, life-giving, life-sustaining aspects of their collective existence. To enrich the range of discourse, communities of inquiry are intentionally designed to include as many relevant voices as possible.

Second, communities of inquiry construct vocabularies of hope by sharing stories, theories, evidence, and illustrations that highlight "best practices" and compelling examples of the forces and factors that give life and sustain their collective existence.

Third, communities of inquiry expand and enrich their vocabularies of hope through processes of normative dialogue and collective visioning.

Fourth, communities of inquiry disseminate their vocabularies of hope through personal relationships, books, journals, magazines, newspapers, universities, conferences, public policies, television, other electronic media.

Fifth, as vocabularies of hope are disseminated to the culture, they become absorbed into the common language and become available for the construction of everyday reality. Best practices and positive examples provide a range of possibilities for societal and organizational innovation. In essence, the culture learns how to be hopeful and inventive.

Sixth, in the final phase of social and organizational transformation, vocabularies of hope are expanded. As people increasingly build their relational vocabularies with "best" examples from the past and "most vital" hopes for the future, more linguistic and normative resources become available to convert dreams into reality and possibilities into practice (see Figure 29.2 for a diagram of this process).

Vocabularies of hope come in all shapes and sizes—theories, ethnographies, case studies, vignettes, empirical data, personal narratives, rhetorical speeches, stories told in the classroom, boardroom, or around the kitchen table. One of the most famous and influential vocabularies of hope in the United States is Martin Luther King Jr.'s speech given at a civil rights march in Washington, August 28, 1963. The speech, and particularly the sentence "I have a dream that my four children will one day live in a nation where they will not be judged by the color of their skin, but by the content of their character," gave voice to the aspirations of an entire nation and has served as a hopeful harbinger of cultural change for more than a generation.

---

6. Vocabularies of hope are expanded and fuel social and organizational (re)construction.

5. Vocabularies of hope are absorbed into common language; organizations and society learn how to be hopeful and to innovate.

4. Communities of inquiry disseminate vocabularies of hope to the general public through multiple channels.

3. Communities of inquiry consensually validate vocabularies of hope through moral dialogue.

2. Communities of inquiry create vocabularies of hope by searching for positive example and "best practices" in society and organizations.

1. Inclusive communities of inquiry are formed and select positive topics for collective inquiry and action.

Figure 29.2. The Link Between Vocabularies of Hope and Social and Organizational (Re)Construction.

On a more scholarly note, the writings of Tavistock Institute founders which brought the principles of social science to bear on the challenges of post World War II reconstruction; McGregor's (1960) Theory X-Theory Y which offered possibilities for a new human-centered form management; Gilligan's (1982) different voice which for the first time highlighted the unique patterns of women's moral development; Kolb's (1984) experiential learning which revealed and affirmed multiple ways of knowing; and Freire's (1994) pedagogy of hope which championed dialogue and advanced the concept of full voice, are but a few of the vocabularies of hope that have emerged in the social and organizational sciences in recent years. Each of these, in its own way, created new images of positive relational possibility, illuminated fresh avenues for moral discourse, and expanded the range of resources available for the construction of enhanced social and organizational relationships.

The Power of Appreciation

Eight core principles of appreciative inquiry support hope's four enduring qualities and make it ideally suited for generating vocabularies of hope (see Cooperrider and Srivastva, 1987 and Cooperrider, 1990). The first two are the constructionist principle and the collaborative principle. According to the constructionist principle, knowledge is a social artifact rather than a product of empirical observation or of individual cognition. It is created by agreement within communities of people. At the same time, knowledge determines action. What a given community of people knows at any particular moment essentially defines for them the options they have available for organizing. In this sense, social knowledge and organizational destiny are tightly intertwined. Consequently, appreciative inquiry affirms that all inquiry into organizational life should be collaborative. A collaborative relationship between participants is essential on the basis of both epistemological and practical grounds. Epistemologically, collaboration opens the way for a truly social construction of reality in which a broad range of participants contribute to the creation of the future. Practically, it facilitates the establishment of strong relational connections.

These two principles support the first enduring quality of hope, that it is born and sustained in relationship. When people come together to inquire into what gives them life, they create positive affect and a strong social bonding which in Kast's terms leads to a strong sense of "Geborgenheit (safety, security, protectedness) upon which all higher feelings—and the energy for action—nourish themselves" (p. 138). It is also in this collaborative act that organizational members literally create new knowledge—new conversations, vocabularies, ways of understanding things—that open up fresh and previously undiscovered alternatives for organizing. Thus the collaborative dimension of appreciative inquiry ignites hope in two ways: it builds strong, supportive relationships between organizational members, and it creates a context, a "holding environment" if you will, in which organizational members can contribute to the social construction of their common future.

The second set of principles that support vocabularies of hope includes the anticipatory principle and the provocative principle. According to the anticipatory principle, it is the image of the future that guides the current behavior of any organism or organization. Just as a flower grows in the direction of the sunlight, so to organizations evolve in the direction of their most compelling images of the future. The anticipatory principle goes on to suggest that because our images of the future are fashioned through discourse (talking to each other), they are indeed open to human influence. In fact, the most important resource we have for generating constructive organizational change may well be our collective capacity to create and exchange shared vocabularies of meaning.

The provocative principle extends this logic into practice by suggesting that the most powerful images of the future are those that stretch, challenge or interrupt the status quo. Such images are rarely strictly rational. As Polak (1973) suggests, it is precisely the picture of a world that is radically different emotionally, aesthetically, spiritually, and relationally that gives images of the future their gripping appeal. By stimulating normative dialogue about how we can and should organize ourselves, these images present provocative new possibilities for social action. In this sense, appreciative inquiry supports the second enduring quality of hope, that it springs to life through imagination in a context of influence-optimism. By affirming that (1) through systematic inquiry and the creation of new textured vocabularies of hope organizational members can shape the social world according to their own moral and imaginative purposes, and (2) the most powerful vocabularies of transformation are those that offer an intuitive, visionary logic for change, appreciative inquiry opens the way for the creative construction of preferred organizational futures.

Third are the poetic principle and the positive principle. According to the poetic principle, organizations are an open book. They can be endless sources of learning, inspiration, and interpretation (like for example, the endless interpretive possibilities in a good piece of poetry or a Biblical text). Thus we can study virtually any topic related to human experience in organizations. We can study alienation or we can study joy; we can study conflict or we can study cooperation; we can study cynicism or we can study hope. According to the positive principle, human beings and organizations move in the direction of what they study. The more positive the topics of inquiry and the more positive the questions asked, the more positive will be the "theories" we come to discover and the vocabularies we come to create. In addition, because of the positive affect and social connection that occurs, the more we inquire into the life-giving aspects of organizational existence, the more effectively momentum for organization change and development will be catalyzed.

These two principles support the third enduring quality of hope, that hope is sustained through dialogue about ultimate concerns. By expanding the universe of our exploration to include the phenomena that claim ultimacy for our collective existence, appreciative inquiry promotes alternative patterns of discourse and generates new bodies of constructive vocabulary that contribute to human hopefulness. Moreover, as the poetic and positive principles would suggest, since the ontological, epistemological, and methodological commitments upon which we base our inquiry will largely determine what we come to discover, know, and contribute to the world of human organizing, the more we inquire into and promote constructive dialogue about our ultimate concerns, the more hopeful will become our theory, the more promising will become its potential for positive action, and the more we will become a source of hope to each other.

The fourth set of principles includes the simultaneous principle and the pragmatic principle. According to the principle of simultaneity, inquiry and change are not truly separate moments but are simultaneous. Inquiry is intervention. Thus the questions we ask as organizational scholars and practitioners set the stage for what we later "find," and what we find becomes the "data" and the "theories" out of which the future is conceived, conversed about, and constructed. According to the pragmatic principle, to be significant in a human sense, organizational inquiry must lead to the generation of knowledge that can be used, applied, and validated in action. It needs to be relevant to the everyday experience of organizational members.

These two principles support the fourth enduring quality of hope—its generativity. They suggest that there is an isomorphic relationship between our modes of inquiry and the kind of social realities we help to create. If we, as organizational scholars and practitioners, want our methodologies to support hopeful organizations and produce hopeful social theory, then our methods themselves need to be hope-filled. First, they need to support the kind of human interaction that inspire human hope through relational connection, dialogue about our highest ideals, and co-construction of preferred futures. Second, they need to continuously refocus our attention on the most life-giving, life-enhancing dimensions of our collective existence. As both appreciative inquiry and the construct of organizational hope suggest, such methodologies will generate practical social and organizational theory that expands the range of possibilities for societal and organizational innovation and, in essence, allows our cultures to learn to be hopeful and inventive.

Conclusion

The language of hope in human systems has important implications for our continuing task as social and organizational scholars and practitioners. If the premise that hope is a primary source of positive knowledge and action in organizational life is accepted, and the tenets of social constructionism—that knowledge is a social artifact, that language is the means by which knowledge is developed, that there is an inextricable link between language, knowledge, and action—are embraced, then it can be concluded that the creation of textured vocabularies of hope may well be the most powerful tool available to us if our aim is to generate constructive organizational understandings that open new possibilities for human organizing and action.

Yet, the structuring of vocabularies of hope is less a technique than it is a commitment. As Rorty (1980) points out in his comparison of Dewey and Foucault, the methodological approach that we adopt is in no way forced upon us by the "nature of things;" it is simply a matter of choice, tone, or moral outlook. Dewey contributed to the growth of human hope by promoting inquiry into high human ideals—notions of truth, rationality, progress, freedom, and democracy. He affirmed the human will to truth, not as the urge to dominate but as the urge to create, an urge to enhance the human condition. By so doing, Dewey made a simple methodological choice to pursue a constructive option that, according to Rorty, eventually filled his theory with an "unjustifiable hope, and an ungroundable but vital sense of human solidarity" (p. 208).

It is to this kind of commitment that we are invited as social and organizational practitioners by appreciative modes of inquiry. Deep and appreciative exploration into ultimate concerns has the capacity to inspire hope precisely because it compels us to transcend the ego, to put ourselves in service of a cause that is beyond us yet that we make our own, and to move toward "the best as a totality." Much needed is further experimentation with new modes of appreciative inquiry based on a theory of hope with a specific agenda of ultimate concerns. We may find that the more we inquire appreciatively into life's fundamental and ultimate concerns, the more our instrumental, transitory, and provisional issues (which at times seem so focal) will take care of themselves because of the human hope and solidarity that has been enlivened. We will most certainly find, as this chapter would suggest, that the very act of appreciation will itself contribute to transforming our organizations into places of genuine human hopefulness.

References

Argyris, C. Action science and intervention. *The Journal of Applied Behavioral Science*, 1973, 19, 115–140.

Argyris, C., and Schon, D. *Theory in practice: Increasing professional effectiveness*. San Francisco: Jossey-Bass, 1974.

Aronson, R. The principle of hope by Ernst Bloch. *Review Essays*, 1991, 46, 220–232.

Astley, G. Administrative science as socially constructed truth. *Administrative Sciences Quarterly*, 1985, 30, 497–513.

Bartunek, J. How organization development can develop organization theory. *Group and Organization Studies*, 1983, 8, 303–318.

Bloch, E. *The principle of hope* (translated by N. Plaice, S. Plaice and P. Knight from the German Das prinzip hoffnung). Cambridge, MA: MIT Press, 1986.

Brown, H. B. Reconstructing social theory after the postmodern critique. In H. W. Simons and M. Billig (eds.), *After postmodernism: Reconstructing ideology critique*. London: Sage Publications, 1994.

Cooperridder, D. L., and Srivastva, S. Appreciative inquiry in organizational life. In W. A. Pasmore and R. W. Woodman (eds.), *Research in organizational change and development (Vol. I)*. Greenwich, CT: JAI Press, 1987.

Dauenhauer, B. P. *The politics of hope*. New York: Routledge and Kegan Paul, 1986.

Denzin, N. K. and Lincoln, Y. S. *Handbook of qualitative research*. Thousand Oaks: Sage Publications, 1994.

Fals-Borda, O., and Rahman, M. A. (eds.) *Action and knowledge: Breaking the monopoly with participatory action research*. New York: Intermediate Technology/Apex, 1991.

Feyerabend, P. K. *Science in a free society*. London: Thetford Press, 1978.

Fiske, J. Audiencing: cultural practice and cultural studies. In *Handbook of qualitative research*, N. K. Denzin and Y. S. Lincoln (eds.). Thousand Oaks, CA: Sage Publications, 1994.

Frankl, V. E. *From death camp to existentialism*. Boston: Beacon, 1959.

Frankl, V. E. *Man's search for meaning*. New York: Washington Square, 1963.

Freire, P. *Pedagogy of the oppressed*. New York: Continuum, 1984.

Freire, P. *Pedagogy of hope: Reliving pedagogy of the oppressed* (translated by R. R. Barr). New York: Continuum, 1994.

Friedlander, F. Producing useful knowledge for organizations. *Administrative Science Quarterly*, 1984, 29, 646–648.

George, J. International Relations and the Search for Thinking Space, *International Studies Quarterly*, 33, 179–269.

Gergen, K. J. *Toward transformation in social knowledge*. New York: Springer-Verlag, 1982.

Gergen, K. J. *Realities and relationships: Soundings in social construction*. Cambridge: Harvard University Press, 1994.

Gergen, K. J. The limits of pure critique. In H. W. Simons and M. Billig (eds.), *After postmodernism: Reconstructing ideology critique*. London: Sage Publications, 1994.

Gilligan, C. *In a different voice: Psychological theory and women's development*. Cambridge: Harvard University Press, 1982.

Hazelrigg, H. *Claims of knowledge: On the labor of making found worlds*. Tallahassee: The Florida State University Press, 1989.

Heron, J. *Experience and method: An inquiry into the concept of experiential research.* Surrey UK: University of Surrey, Human Potential Research Project, 1971.

Kast, V. *Joy, inspiration and hope* (translated by D. Whitcher). College Station, TX: Texas AandM University Press, 1991.

Kilmann, R., Thomas, K., Slevin, D., Nath, R., and Jerrell, L. (eds.) *Producing useful knowledge for organizations.* New York: Praeger, 1983.

Kincheloe, J. L. and Mclaren, P. L. Rethinking critical theory and qualitative research. In *Handbook of qualitative research,* N. K. Denzin and Y. S. Lincoln (eds.). Thousand Oaks, CA: Sage Publications, 1994.

Kolb, D. A. *Experiential learning: Experience as the source of learning and development.* Englewood Cliffs: Prentice-Hall, 1984.

Kuhn, T. S., *The structure of scientific revolutions, 2nd rev. ed.* Chicago: University of Chicago Press, 1970).

Ludema, J. D., Wilmot, T. B., and Srivastva, S. Organizational hope: Reaffirming the constructive task of social and organizational inquiry, *Human Relations,* 50(8), 1997.

Lynch, W. F. *Images of hope.* Notre Dame: Notre Dame Press, 1965.

Marcel, G. *Homo viator* (translated by Emma Craufurd). Chicago: Henry Regnery, 1951.

Marcus, G. E. What comes (just) after "post"? The case of ethnography. In N. K. Denzin and Y. S. Lincoln (eds.), *Handbook of qualitative research.* Thousand Oaks: Sage Publications, 1994.

Mcgregor, D. *The human side of enterprise.* New York: McGraw-Hill, 1960.

Moltmann, J. *Theology of hope* (translated by J. W. Leitch from the German Theologie der hoffnung). New York: Harper Collins, 1991.

Morgan, G. *Images of Organizations.* Newbury Park: Sage Publications, 1986.

Morgan, G. *Imaginization.* Newbury Park: Sage Publications, 1993.

Olesen, V. Feminisms and Models of Qualitative Research. In *Handbook of qualitative research,* N. K. Denzin and Y. S. Lincoln (eds.). Thousand Oaks, CA: Sage Publications, 1994.

Polak, F. *The image of the future* (translated and abridged by E. Boulding from the Dutch Die toekomst is verleden tijd). San Francisco: Jossey-Bass, 1973.

Reason, P. (ed.) *Human inquiry in action.* London: Sage, 1988.

Reason, P., and Heron, J. Research with people: The paradigm of cooperative experiential inquiry. *Person Centered Review,* 1986, 1, 456–475.

Reason, P., and Rowan, J. (eds.) *Human inquiry: a sourcebook of a new paradigm research.* Chichester, UK: Wiley, 1981.

Rorty, R. *Consequences of pragmatism.* Minneapolis: University of Minnesota Press, 1980.

Schon, D. A. *The reflective practitioner: How professionals think in action.* New York: Basic Books, 1983.

Srivastva, S., and Barrett, F. J. The transforming nature of metaphors in group development: A study in group theory. *Human Relations,* 41, 31–63, 1988.

Srivastva, S., Cooperrider, D. L., and Associates. *Appreciative management and leadership: The power of positive thought and action in organizations.* San Francisco: Jossey-Bass Pubs., 1990.

Stanfield, J. H. II. Ethnic modeling in qualitative research. In *Handbook of qualitative research,* N. K. Denzin and Y. S. Lincoln (eds.). Thousand Oaks, CA: Sage Publications, 1994.

Schwandt, T. A. Constructivist, interpretivist approaches to human inquiry. In *Handbook of qualitative research,* N. K. Denzin and Y. S. Lincoln (eds.). Thousand Oaks, CA: Sage Publications, 1994.

Tandon, R. Participatory research and social transformation. *Convergence,* 21, 5–15, 1989.

Taylor, C. Interpretation and the sciences of man. In P. Rabinow and W. M. Sullivan (eds.), *Interpretive social science: A second look.* Berkeley: University of California Press, 1987.

Torbert, W. R. Why educational research has been so uneducational: The case for a new model of social science based on collaborative inquiry. In P. Reason and J. Rowan (eds.), *Human inquiry: A sourcebook of new paradigm research.* Chichester, UK: Wiley, 1981.

Torbert, W. R. Teaching action inquiry. *Collaborative Inquiry,* 5, 1991.

Tillich, P. *Dynamics of faith.* New York: Harper and Row, 1957.

Whyte, W. F. (ed.) *Participatory action research.* Newbury Park, CA: Sage, 1991.

Weick, K. E. Affirmation as inquiry. *Small Group Behavior,* 1982, 13, 441–450.

Wittgenstein, L. *Philosophical investigations* (translated by G. Anscombe). New York: Macmillan, 1963.

Wollheim, R. *Art and its objects* (second edition). Cambridge, MA: Cambridge University Press, 1980.

Chapter 30

APPRECIATIVE INQUIRY RESOURCE LIST

Dawn Cooperrider Dole

The following list of AI resources is an ongoing project. Please write to coopdole@modex.com to add a current citation. Thank you.

Barrett, F. & Peterson, R. (2000). Appreciative Learning Cultures: Developing Competencies for Global Organizing. Journal of Applied Behavioral Science, vol. 31(3), pp. 353-372. contact: 1-805-499-0721

Barrett, F. J. (1998). Creativity and Improvisation in Jazz and Organizations: Implications for Organizational Learning. Organization Science, *9(5),* 605-622. contact: 1-800-343-0062

Barrett, F. J. (1995). Creating Appreciative Learning Cultures. Organizational Dynamics, *24*(1), 36-49. contact: 1-800-262-9699

Barrett, F. J., & Cooperrider, D. L. (1990). Generative Metaphor Intervention: A New Approach to Inter-group Conflict. Journal of Applied Behavioral Science, *26*(2), 223-244. contact: 1-805-499-0721

Barros, I., & Cooperrider, D. (2000). How wholeness, appreciation and inquiry bring out the best in human organization. Organization Development Journal, vol. 18, no. 2, pp. 22-29.

Bowling, C., Ludema, J., & Wyss, E. (1997). *Vision Twin Cities Appreciative Inquiry Report* . Cleveland, Ohio: Case Western Reserve University, Department of Organizational Behavior.   contact: 1-216-368-2055 or 1-216-368-2215

Bunker, B. B. (1990). Appreciating Diversity and Modifying Organizational Cultures: Men and Women at Work. In Srivastva, S., & Cooperrider, D. L. (Eds.). (1999). *Appreciative management and leadership: The power of positive thought and action in organization* (Revised Edition ed.). Euclid, Ohio: Williams Custom Publishing. contact: 1-800-537-7054.)

Bushe, G. R. (reprinted 1999). Advances in appreciative inquiry as an organization development intervention. Organization Development Journal, 17(2).

Bushe, G. R. (1998). Appreciative inquiry with teams. Organization Development Journal, 16(3), 41-50. Bushe, G. R. (1995). Advances in Appreciative Inquiry as an Organization Development Intervention. Organization Development Journal, 13(3), 14-22.

Bushe, G. R., & Coetzer, G. (1995). Appreciative Inquiry as a Team Development Intervention: A Controlled Experiment. Journal of Applied Behavioral Science, 31(1), 13-30. contact: 1-805-499-0721

Bushe, G. R., & Pitman, T. (1991). Appreciative Process: A Method for Transformational Change. Organization Development Practitioner, 23(3), 1-4. contact: 1-201-763-7337

Chaffee, P. (1997 Fall). Ring of Breath Around the World: A Report of the United Religions Initiative Global Conference. United Religions, A Journal of the United Religions Initiative(4). contact: 1-415-561-2300

Chaffee, P. (1997). Unafraid of the Light: Appreciative Inquiry and Faith Communities (Unpublished Manuscript). Interfaith Center at the Presidio: San Francisco, CA. contact: 1-415-775-4635 or email: PJChaffee@aol.com

Chin, A. (1998). Future Visions. Journal of Organization and Change Management, (Spring).

Cooperrider, D. L. (1986). Appreciative Inquiry: Toward a Methodology for Understanding and Enhancing Organizational Innovation. Unpublished Doctoral Dissertation, Case Western Reserve University, Cleveland, Ohio. contact: 1-216-368-2055 or 1-216-368-2215

Cooperrider, D. L. (1990). Positive Image, Positive Action: The Affirmative Basis of Organizing. In Srivastva, S., & Cooperrider, D. L. (Eds.). (1999). Appreciative management and leadership: The power of positive thought and action in organization (Revised Edition ed.). Euclid, Ohio: Williams Custom Publishing. contact: 1-800-537-7054.

Cooperrider, D. L. (1995). Introduction to Appreciative Inquiry. In W. French & C. Bell (Eds.), Organization Development (5th ed.,): Prentice Hall. contact: 1-800-643-5506

Cooperrider, D. L. (1996). The "Child" As Agent of Inquiry. Organization Development Practitioner, 28(1 & 2), 5-11. contact: 1-201-763-7337

Cooperrider, D. L. (1996). Resources for Getting Appreciative Inquiry Started: An Example OD Proposal. Organization Development Practitioner, 28(1 & 2), 23-33. contact: 1-201-763-7337

Cooperrider, D. (2000) The surprise of friendship at the carter center. Organization Development Practitioner, vol. 32, no. 2, pp.46-49. email: membership@ODNetwork.org or call 1-973-763-7337.

Cooperrider, D. (2000) Appreciative inquiry and the conscious evolution of charodic organizations. Inner Edge, vol. 3, no.1, pp.12 - 15.

Cooperrider, D. (2000). Appreciative Inquiry in Action. Global Social Innovations, Journal of the GEM Initiative, vol. 1, issue 3, Winter.

Cooperrider, D. (2001). *AI: The beginnings :Toward a methodology for understanding and enhancing organizational innovation, (This is Cooperrider's original dissertation from 1985 revised; w/forward entries by Gergen and Srivastva) Lakeshore Publishing, Cleveland, Ohio. contact: rogerw@lakeshorepublishers.com or see: www.lakeshorepublishers.com

Cooperrider, D. L., Barrett, F., & Srivastva, S. (1995). Social Construction and Appreciative Inquiry: A Journey in Organizational Theory. In D. Hosking, P. Dachler, & K. Gergen (Eds.), *Management and Organization: Relational Alternatives to Individualism* (pp. 157-200). Aldershot, UK: Avebury Press.

Cooperrider, D. L., & Bilimoria, D. (1993). The Challenge of Global Change for Strategic Management: Opportunities for Chartering a New Course. Advances in Strategic Management, *9*, 99-141.

Cooperrider, D. L., & Dutton, J. (Eds.). (1998). *No Limits to Cooperation: The Organization Dimensions of Global Change.* Newbury Park, CA: Sage Publications. contact: 1-805-499-9774 or email: order@sagepub.com

Cooperrider, D., Kaplin, A., & Kaplin, B. (2001). An encyclopedia of positive questions. Lakeshore Publishers, Cleveland, Ohio. Contact: rogerw@lakeshorepublishers.com or see: www.lakeshorepublishers.com

Cooperrider, D. L., & Khalsa, G. (1997). The Organization Dimensions of Global Environmental Change. Journal of Organization and Environment, *10*(4), 331-341.

Cooperrider, D. L., & Pasmore, W. A. (1991). The Organization Dimension of Global Change. Human Relations, *44*(8), 763-787.

Cooperrider, D. L., & Srivastva, S. (1987). Appreciative Inquiry In Organizational Life. In W. Pasmore & R. Woodman (Eds.), *Research In Organization Change and Development* (Vol. 1, pp. 129-169). Greenwich, CT: JAI Press. contact: 1-203-323-9600 ext. 3003

Cooperrider, D. L., & Srivastva, S. (1998). An Invitation to Organizational Wisdom and Executive Courage. In S. Srivastva & D. L. Cooperrider (Eds.), *Organizational Wisdom and Executive Courage* (1st ed., pp. 1-22). San Francisco, CA: The New Lexington Press. contact: 1-800-462-4620

Cooperrider, D. L., & Thachenkery, T. (1995). Building The Global Civic Culture: Making Our Lives Count. In P. Sorensen, T. Head, N. Mathys, J. Preston, & D. Cooperrider (Eds.), *Global and International Organization Development* (pp. 282-306). Champaign, IL: Stipes Publishing L.L.C. contact: 1-217-356-8391

Cooperrider, D. L. et. al. (1996). Appreciative Inquiry Manual . Cleveland, Ohio: Unpublished notes. Case Western Reserve University, Department of Organizational Behavior.   contact: 1-216-368-2055 or 1-216-369-2215

Cooperrider, D.L., & Sorensen Jr., P.F., & Whitney, D., & Yaegar, T. (Eds). (2000). Appreciative Inquiry: Rethinking Human Organization Toward a Positive Theory of Change. Champaign, IL: Stipes Publishing. contact: 1-217-356-8391

Cooperrider, D., Whitney, D., (2001). Appreciative Inquiry Handbook: A constructive approach to organization development and change. Lakeshore Publishers, Cleveland, Ohio. contact: rogerw@lakeshorepublishers.com or see: www.lakeshorepublishers.com

Cooperrider, D.L., & Whitney, D. (2000). A positive revolution in change. In Handbook of Organizational Behavior (second edition), Golembiewski (Ed.) Marcel Decker, Inc. New York.

Cooperrider, D.L., & Whitney, D. (1999). Appreciative Inquiry. San Francisco, CA: Berrett-Koehler   Communications. contact: 1-800-929-2929

Cooperrider, D. L., & Whitney, D. (1999). Appreciative inquiry: A positive revolution in change. In P. Holman & T. Devane (Eds.), The change handbook: Group methods for shaping the future (pp. 245-261). San Francisco: Berrett-Koehler Publishers, Inc.

Cooperrider, D. L., & Whitney, D. (1996). Appreciative inquiry: A workshop [A set of eight audio-tapes presented by The Taos Institute]. Boulder, CO: Perpetual Motion Unlimited. contact: 1-303-444-3158

Cooperrider, D. L., & Whitney, D. (1998). When stories have wings: How "relational responsibility" opens new options for action. In S. McNamee & K. Gergen (Eds.), Relational responsibility . Thousand Oaks, CA: Sage Publications. contact: 1-805-499-9774

Cummings, T. G. (1990). The Role of Executive Appreciation in Creating Transorganizational Alliances. In Srivastva, S., & Cooperrider, D. L. (Eds.). (1999). *Appreciative management and leadership: The power of positive thought and action in organization* (Revised Edition ed.). Euclid, Ohio: Williams Custom Publishing. contact: 1-800-537-7054.

Curran, M. (1991). Appreciative Inquiry: A Third Wave Approach to OD. Vision/ Action, December, 12-14.

Davis, K., (2001). Appreciative Inquiry Reveals Community Hopes. Assets Magazine, Winter 2001. Published by Search Institute. see: www.search-institute.org

Elliott, C. (1999). Locating the Energy for Change: An Introduction to Appreciative Inquiry. University of Cambridge Publishers.

Frost, P. J., & Egri, C. P. (1990). Appreciating Executive Action. Srivastva, S., & Cooperrider, D. L. (Eds.). (1999). *Appreciative management and leadership: The power of positive thought and action in organization* (Revised Edition ed.). Euclid, Ohio: Williams Custom Publishing. contact: 1-800-537-7054.

Fry, R., Barrett, F., Seiling, J., & Whitney, D, (2001). Appreciative Inquiry and Organizational Transformation: Reports from the Field. Quorum Publishers, Westport, CT.

Fuller, C., Griffin, T., Ludema, J., (2000) Appreciative Future Search: Involving the Whole system in Positive Organization Change. Organization Development Journal, vol. 18, issue: 2, pages: 29-41

Gergen, K. J. (1990). Affect and Organization in Postmodern Society. In Srivastva, S., & Cooperrider, D. L. (Eds.). (1999). *Appreciative management and leadership: The power of positive thought and action in organization* (Revised Edition ed.). Euclid, Ohio: Williams Custom Publishing. contact: 1-800-537-7054.

Gibbs, C., & Ackerly, S. (June 1997). *United Religions Initiative Global Summit Summary Report.* Paper presented at the United Religions Initiative Global Summit Summary Report, San Francisco, CA. Contact: 1-415-561-2300

Golembiewski, B. (2000). Three perspectives on appreciative inquiry. OD Practitioner: Journal of the Organization Development Network, 32(1), 53-58.

Golembiewski, R. T. (1998). Appreciating appreciative inquiry: Diagnosis and perspectives on how to do better. In W. Pasmore & R. Woodman (Eds.), Research in organizational change and development (Vol. 11, pp. 1-45). Greenwich, CT: JAI Press.

Golembiewski, R. T. (July 1997). *Appreciating Appreciative Inquiry.* Paper presented at the Annual Meeting of the International Conference on Organization Development, Colima, Mexico.

Gotches, G., & Ludema, J. (1995). Appreciative inquiry and the future of OD. Organization Development Journal, 13(3), 5.

GTE. (1997). GTE Asks Employees To Start a Grassroots Movement To Make GTE Unbeatable in the Marketplace. *GTE Together, Published by GTE Corporation, Dallas, TX,* 15-19.

Hammond, S. (1998). What is appreciative inquiry? The Inner Edge, 1(2), 26-27.

Hammond, S. (1996). *The Thin Book of Appreciative Inquiry.* Plano, TX: Thin Book Publishing. contact: 1-888-316-9544

Hammond, S., & Royal, C. (Eds.). (1998). *Lessons From the Field: Applying Appreciative Inquiry.* Plano, TX: Published by Practical Press, Inc. and Distributed by the Thin Book Publishing Company. contact: 1-888-316-9544

Harman, W. W. (1990). Shifting Context for Executive Behavior: Signs of Change and Revaluation. In Srivastva, S., & Cooperrider, D. L. (Eds.). (1999). *Appreciative management and leadership: The power of positive thought and action in organization* (Revised Edition ed.). Euclid, Ohio: Williams Custom Publishing. contact: 1-800-537-7054.

Head, R. L. (2000). Appreciative inquiry as a team-development intervention for newly formed heterogeneous groups. OD Practitioner: Journal of the Organization Development Network, 32 (1), 59-66.

Head, R. L., & Young, M. M. (1998). Initiating culture change in higher education through appreciative inquiry. Organization Development Journal, 16(2), 65.

Head, T. C. (2000). Appreciative inquiry: Debunking the mythology behind resistance to change. OD Practitioner: Journal of the Organization Development Network, 32(1), 27-35.

Head, T., & Sorensen, P. (2000). Is appreciative inquiry the philosopher's stone? In D. L. Cooperrider, P. F. Sorensen, D. Whitney, & T. F. Yaeger (Eds.), Appreciative inquiry: Rethinking human organization toward a positive theory of change: Stipes Publishing L.L.C.

Hopper, V. (1991). An Appreciative Study of Highest Human Values in a Major Health Care Organization. Unpublished Doctoral Dissertation, Case Western Reserve University, Cleveland, Ohio. contact: 1-216-368-2055

Hubbard, B. M. (1998). Conscious Evolution: Awakening the Power of Our Social Potential. Novato, CA: New World Library (See chp. 11 on AI). contact: 1-415-884-2100

Johnson, P. (1992). Organizing For Global Social Change. Unpublished Doctoral Dissertation, Case Western Reserve University, Cleveland, Ohio.

Johnson, P. C., & Cooperrider, D. L. (1991). Finding A Path With Heart: Global Social Change Organizations and Their Challenge for the Field of Organization Development. In R. Woodman & W. Pasmore (Eds.), Research in Organizational Change and Development (Vol. 5, pp. 223-284). Greenwich, CT: JAI Press. contact: 1-203-323-9600 ext. 3003

Johnson, S., & Ludema, J. (Eds.). (1997). Partnering To Build And Measure Organizational Capacity: Lessons From NGOs Around The World. Grand Rapids, MI: Christian Reformed World Relief Committee.

Johnson, S. P. (1998). Straight to the Heart: Cleveland Leaders Shaping the Next Millenium. Unpublished Doctoral Dissertation, Case Western Reserve University, Cleveland, Ohio.

Jones, D. A. (1998). A field experiment in appreciative inquiry. Organization development journal, 16(4).

Kaczmarski, K., & Cooperrider, D. L. (1997). Constructionist Leadership in the Global Relational Age. Journal of Organization and Environment, 10(3), 234-258.

Kaczmarski, K., & Cooperrider, D. L. (1998). The Birth of a Worldwide Alliance: The Story of the Mountain Forum. In D. L. Cooperrider & J. Dutton (Eds.), No Limits to Cooperation: The Organization Dimensions of Global Change . Thousand Oaks, CA: Sage Publications. contact: 1-805-499-9774

Khalsa, G. S., & Kaczmarski, K. M. (1997 Summer). Chartering and Appreciative Future Search. Global Social Innovations, Journal of the GEM Initiative, Case Western Reserve University, 1(2), 45-52. contact: 1-202-822-6188 or email: gem@vita.org

Khalsa, G. S., & Kaczmarski, K. M. (June 1996). The United Religions Initiative Summit Conference Summary. Paper presented at The United Religions Initiative Summit Conference Summary, San Francisco, CA. contact: 1-415-561-2300

Liebler, C. J. (1997 Summer). Getting Comfortable With Appreciative Inquiry: Questions and Answers. *Global Social Innovations, Journal of the GEM Initiative, Case Western Reserve University, 1*(2), 30-40. contact: 1-202-822-6188 or email: gem@vita.org

Liebling, A., Price, D., & Elliott, C. (1999). Appreciative inquiry and relationships in prison. Violence & Abuse Abstracts, 5(4).

Livingston, J. (1999). An appreciative inquiry interview with Robert Golembiewski: The human and organizational dimensions of global change. Organization Development Journal, 1(17), 109.

Lord, J. G. (1995). *The Philanthropic Quest: A Generative Approach for Professionals Engaged in the Development Process.* Cleveland, Ohio: Philanthropic Quest International. contact: 1-216-831-3727 or email: Lord@Lord.org or www.appreciative-inquiry.org

Lord, J. G. (1998). *The Practice of the Quest: Evolving a New Paradigm for Philanthropy and Social Innovation - A Casebook for Advancement Professionals Grounded in the Quest.* Cleveland, Ohio: Philanthropic Quest International. contact: see Lord above

Ludema, J. D. (2000). Appreciative future search. OD Practitioner: Journal of the Organization Development Network.

Ludema, J. D. (2000). Power of the unconditional positive question, *Handbook of action research.* Pages: 189-199. Sage Publications Ltd London, England

Ludema, J. D. (2000). World wide ripple effect. OD Practitioner: Journal of the Organization Development Network.

Ludema, J. D. (2000). From deficit discourse to vocabularies of hope: The power of appreciation. In: *Appreciative inquiry: Rethinking human organization toward a positive theory of change.* Editors: Cooperrider, D. L.; Sorensen, P. F.; Whitney, D.; Yaeger, T. F., Pages: 265-287Stipes Publishing L.L.C., Champaign, IL.

Ludema, J. (1993). Vision Chicago: A Framework For Appreciative Evaluation . Cleveland, Ohio: Case Western Reserve University, Department of Organizational Behavior.

Ludema, J. (1994). Vision Cities As Partnerships That Build Community: An Appreciative Inquiry Into Vision Chicago. Cleveland, Ohio: Case Western Reserve University, Department Of Organizational Behavior.

Ludema, J. (1996). *Narrative Inquiry.* Unpublished Doctoral Dissertation, Case Western Reserve University, Cleveland, Ohio.

Ludema, J., Wilmot, T., & Srivastva, S. (1997). Organizational Hope: Reaffirming the Constructive Task of Social and Organizational Inquiry. Human Relations, 50(8), 1015-1052.

Ludema, J., Cooperrider, D. & Barrett, F. (2001). Appreciative inquiry: The power of the unconditional positive question. In *Handbook of Action Research.* (Reason and Bradbury, Eds.) Sage Publications: London, pp. 189-200.

Mann, A. J. (2000) Variations on a theme: The flexibility of the 4-D model. Global Social Innovations, Journal of the GEM Initiative vol. 1, issue: 3, pages: 12-15, winter issue.

Mann, A. J. (1997 Summer). An Appreciative Inquiry Model for Building Partnerships. Global Social Innovations, Journal of the GEM Initiative, Case Western Reserve University, 1(2), 41-44. contact: 1-202-822-6188 or email: gem@vita.org

Mantel, M. J., & Ludema, J. D. (2000). From local conversations to global change: Experiencing the worldwide web effect of appreciative inquiry. Organization Development Journal, 18(Part 2), 12. pgs. 42-53.

Mohr, B. (2001). Appreciative Inquiry: Igniting Transformative Action. The Systems Thinker, vol: 12 issue: 1, pgs: 1-6, Feb.

Mohr, B. and Watkins, J. (2001) Appreciative inquiry: change at the speed of imagination. Jossey-Bass.

Mohr, B. J., Smith, E., & Watkins, J. M. (2000). Appreciative inquiry and learning assessment. OD Practitioner: Journal of the Organization Development Network, 32(1), 36-52.

Muscat, M. (1998). Imagine Chicago: Dreams and visions for a 'second city' of the future. The Inner Edge, 1(2), 23-24.

Odell, M. (2000). An Appreciative Inquiry conversation guide: Creating a small forum in which leaders of the world religions can gather in mutual respect and dialogue. Global Social Innovations, Journal of the GEM Initiative vol: 1, issue: 3, pages: 23-26, winter.

Olson, E. E.; Eoyang, G. H. (2001). Facilitating organization change; Lessons from complexity science. Jossey-Bass/Pfeiffer, San Francisco, CA.

Pages, M. (1990). The Illusion and Disillusion of Appreciative Managment. In Srivastva, S., & Cooperrider, D. L. (Eds.). (1999). Appreciative management and leadership: The power of positive thought and action in organization (Revised Edition ed.). Euclid, Ohio: Williams Custom Publishing. contact: 1-800-537-7054.

Pepitone, J. S. (1995). Future Training: A Roadmap for Restructuring the Training Function. Dallas, TX: Addvantage Learning Press (See ch. 4 on AI).

Quinn, R. E., (2000). Appreciative inquiry as a method of support. In: Change the world, pgs: 219-223, 245. Jossey-Bass, Inc., San Francisco, CA.

Raimy, E. (1998). Precious Moments. Human Resource Executive, 12(11). 1 and 26-29. contact: 1-215-784-0910.

Rainey, M. A. (1996). An Appreciative Inquiry Into the Factors of Culture Continuity During Leadership Transition. Organization Development Practitioner, 28(1&2), 34-41.

Robinson-Easley, C. A. (1998). The Role of Appreciative Inquiry In The Fight To Save Our Youth. Unpublished Doctoral Dissertation, Benedictine University, Naperville, IL. contact: 1-630-829-6207

Royal, C. (1997). *The Fractal Initiative: Appreciative Inquiry and Rethinking Social Identities.* Unpublished Doctoral Dissertation, Fielding Institute. Santa Barbara, CA. Contact: 1-805-687-1099

Royal, C. (1994) *The NTL Diversity Study, The Use of Appreciative Inquiry to Discover Best Experiences Around Diversity in a Professional OD Organization.* NTL Institute for Applied Behavioral Science, Alexandra, VA. Contact: 1-800-777-5227

Royal, C. (1996) *Appreciative Inquiry.* Occasional Paper for The MacArthur Foundation. contact: 1-312-726-8000

Royal, C. (1996) *Appreciative Inquiry, Community Development and Sustainability.* Occasional paper for the MacArthur Foundation. contact: 1-312-726-8000

Ryan, F. J., Soven, M., Smither, J., & Sullivan, W. M. (1999). Appreciative inquiry: Using personal narratives for initiating school reform. The Clearing House, 72(3), 164.

Salter, C. (2000). We're trying to change world history. Fast Company. Issue 40, p. 230. contact: www.fastcompany.com/online/40/wf_swing.html

Sena, S. O., & Booy, D. (1997 Summer). Appreciative Inquiry Approach to Community Development: The World Vision Tanzania Experience. *Global Social Innovations, Journal of the GEM Initiative, Case Western Reserve University, 1*(2), 7-12. contact: 1-202-822-6188 or email: gem@vita.org

Schiller, M.; Holland, B.; Riley, D. (2001). Appreciative Leadership. Taos Institute Press. contact: mrsentp@worldnet.att.net

Schiller, M. (1998). A dialogue about leadership & appreciative inquiry. Organization Development Journal, 16(4), 79.

Sorensen, P. F., as Guest Editor. OD Practitioner: Journal of the Organization Development Network, 28, Nos. 1 and 2, (1996). email: membership@ODNetwork.org or call 1-973-763-7337.

Sorensen, P. F., Yaeger, T. F., & Nicoll, D. (2000). Appreciative inquiry 2000: Fad or important new focus for OD? OD Practitioner: Journal of the Organization Development Network, 32(1), 3-5. email: membership@ODNetwork.org or call 1-973-763-7337.

Sorensen, P. F., & Yaeger, T. F. (1997). Exploring organizational possibilities: Appreciative inquiry. Training Today, 7-8.

Sorensen, P. F., & Yaeger, T. F. (1998). A universal approach to change: Appreciative inquiry. Training Today, 7-8.

Srivastva, S., & Barrett, F. J. (1990). Appreciative Organizing: Implications for Executive Functioning. In S. Srivastva, D. L. Cooperrider, & Associates (Eds.), *Appreciative Management and Leadership : The Power of Positive Thought and Action in Organizations* (1st ed., pp. 381-400). San Francisco, CA: Jossey-Bass Inc.

Srivastva, S., & Cooperrider, D. L. (Eds.). (1999). *Appreciative management and leadership: The power of positive thought and action in organization* (Revised Edition ed.). Euclid, Ohio: Williams Custom Publishing. contact: 1-800-537-7054.

Srivastva, S., & Cooperrider, D. L. (Eds.). (1998). *Organizational Wisdom and Executive Courage*, (1st ed.). San Francisco, CA: The New Lexington Press. contact: 1-800-462-4620

Srivastva, S., Cooperrider, D. L., & Associates (Eds.). (1990). *Appreciative Management and Leadership: The Power of Positive Thought and Action in Organizations* (1st ed.). San Francisco, CA: Jossey-Bass Inc. (out of print) See: Srivastva 1999.

Stavros, J. M. (1998). *Capacity Building: An Appreciative Approach, A Relational Process of Building Your Organization's Future.* Unpublished Doctoral Dissertation, Case Western Reserve University, Cleveland, Ohio. contact: 1-248-360-6613 or 1-216-368-2205

Thachenkery, T. J. (1996). Affirmation as Facilitation: A Postmodernist Paradigm in Change Management. Organization Development Practitioner, *28*(1), 12-22. Contact: 1-201-763-7337

Watkins, J. M., & Cooperrider, D. (2000). Appreciative inquiry: A transformative paradigm. OD Practitioner: Journal of the Organization Development Network, 32(1), 6-12.

Watkins, J. M., & Cooperrider, D. L. (1996). Organizational Inquiry Model For Global Social Change Organizations. Organization Development Journal, *14*(4), 97-112.

Watkins, J. M., & Mohr, B. (2001). Appreciative inquiry: Change at the speed of imagination. San Francisco, CA: Jossey-Bass/Pfeiffer.

Webb, L. D. (1999). Appreciative inquiry as a way to jump start change. At Work: Creating a More Enlightened World of Business & Work, 8(2).

Whalley, C. (1998). Using appreciative inquiry to overcome post OFSTED syndrome. Management in education, 12(3), 6.

White, T. W. (1996). Working In Interesting Times. *Vital Speeches Of The Day, LXII*(15), 472-474.

Whitney, D. (1998). An appreciative inquiry approach to organization change. Career Development International, UK, Special Edition.

Whitney, D. (1998). Let's change the subject and change our organization: An appreciative inquiry approach to organization change. Career Development International, Special Edition, 314-319.

Whitney, D. (1998 Spring). Appreciative Inquiry: An Innovative Process for Organization Change. Employment Relations Today.

Whitney, D. (1998 Summer). The Appreciative Inquiry Summit: Overview and Applications. Employment Relations Today.

Whitney, D., & Cooperrider, D. L. (1998). The appreciative inquiry summit: Overview and applications. Employment Relations Today, 17-28.

Whitney, D., & Cooperrider, D., (2000). Collaborating for Change: The Conference Model. Berret-Koehler, San Francisco, CA. contact: 415-288-0260

Whitney, D. & Cooperrider, D.L. (2000). Appreciative inquiry: A transformative paradigm. Journal of the Organization Development Practitioner, vol. 32. no. 2, pp. 6-13. email: membership@ODNetwork.org or call 1-973-763-7337.

Whitney, D. & Cooperrider, D.L. (2000). Exploring appreciative inquiry. Perspectives: Journal of the World Business Academy, vol. 19, June, pp. 48-68.

Whitney, D., & Cooperrider, D. L. (2000). The appreciative inquiry summit: An emerging methodology for whole system positive change. OD Practitioner: Journal of the Organization Development Network, 32(2), 13-26. email: membership@ODNetwork.org or call 1-973-763-7337.

Whitney, D., & Schau, C. (1998). Appreciative Inquiry: An innovation process for organization change. Employment Relations Today, 11-21.

Whitney, D., & Shau, C. (1998). Appreciative inquiry: An innovative process for organization change. Employment Relations Today

Whitney, D. & Trosten-Bloom, A. (2001). A journey towards positive change. Lakeshore Publishers, Cleveland, Ohio. contact: 1-800-537-7054 or email: rogerw@lakeshorepublishers.com

Williams, R. F. (1996). Survey Guided Appreciative Inquiry: A Case Study. Organization Development Practitioner, 28(1&2), 43-51.   email: membership@ODNetwork.org or call 1-973-763-7337.

Wilmot, T., & Ludema, J. (1995). Odyssey Into Organizational Hope. In D. Marcic (Ed.), Organizational Behavior Experiences and Cases (3rd ed.,). New York: West Publishing Company. contact: 1-718-858-7549

Wilmot, T. B. (1996 Summer). Inquiry & Innovation in the Private Voluntary Sector. Global Social Innovations, Journal of the GEM Initiative,   Case Western Reserve University, 1(1), 5-12. contact: 1-202-822-6188 or email: gem@vita.org

Wishart, C. G. (1998). Toward a Language of Human Abundance: The Holistic Human Logic of Sustainable Development. Unpublished Doctoral Dissertation, Case Western Reserve University, Cleveland, Ohio. contact: 1-216-368-2055 or 1-216-368-2215

Woodman, R. W., & Pasmore, W. A. (Eds.). (1998). Research in organizational change and development: An annual series featuring advances in theory, methodology and research (Vol. 11). Stamford, CT: JAI Press.

Yaeger, T., Sorensen, P., "What Matters Most in Appreciative Inquiry: Review and Thematic Assessment." In Cooperrider, D., Sorensen, P., Whitney, D., and Yaeger, T. (1999) *Appreciative Inquiry: Rethinking Human Organization Toward a Positive Theory of Change*, Champaign: Stipes Publishing.

Yaeger, T. (1999). Responses from Russia: An appreciative inquiry interview with Konstantin Korotov, RODP. Organization Development Journal, 17(3) pgs: 85-9.

Yballe, L. & O'Connor, D. (2000) *Appreciative Pedagogy: Constructing Positive Models for Learning.* Journal of Management Education .vol: 24, issue: 4, pages: 474-483 contact: 315-445-4790

Zemke, Ron, (2000). David Cooperrider: Man on a mission. Training , vol: 37, issue: 11, pgs: 52-53, Nov.

Zemke, R. (1999). Don't fix that company! «Appreciative inquiry» is a new approach to organizational development that focuses on what works rather than what doesn't. It just might change the way you think about your job. Training, 36(6), 8.

The inter-religious friendship group: A visible force for peace. (2000). Weatherhead: The Magazine of the Weatherhead School of Management, Winter, 18-19.

For more information on Appreciative Inquiry see the following websites:

http://www.appreciative-inquiry.org

www.taosinstitute.org

www.thinbook.com

To subscribe to a quarterly electronic newsletter dedicated to Appreciative Inquiry contact: www.aradford.co.uk/AInewsletter.htm . To subscribe, go to 'subscribe' in the Welcome letter on: www.aradford.co.uk and pay for your subscription using a credit card.

Conversations in Social Construction: A Video Series See:
www.masterswork.com or call: 1-800-476-1619.

To order **an audiotape series on Appreciative Inquiry** call:
Perpetual Motion Unlimited at 303-444-3158.